Macroeconomic Policies and Poverty Reduction

Macroeconomic Policies and Poverty Reduction goes beyond the traditional literature on poverty, dealing with this critical topic in a technically sophisticated, yet accessible, manner.

Recognizing that economic growth is crucial for poverty reduction, this book nevertheless emphasizes the importance of particular country circumstances in mediating the relationship between growth and poverty reduction. The innovative essays use country case studies to analyze how the political economy of budgetary decisions, financial reforms, and trade liberalization, and periods of crises affect inequality and poverty. Fresh perspective on the international context is offered through studies of odious debt as an additional rationale for debt relief and uncoordinated and volatile aid flows. Contributors include Anne Krueger, Nicholas Stern, Orazio Attanasio, François Bourguignon, Ravi Kanbur, Michael Kremer, Martin Ravallion, and Robert Townsend.

Ashoka Mody and Catherine Pattillo are at the International Monetary Fund.

Routledge Studies in the Modern World Economy

Macroeconomic Policies and Poverty Reduction

Edited by
Ashoka Mody and
Catherine Pattillo

Routledge
Taylor & Francis Group

LONDON AND NEW YORK

First published 2006 by Routledge

Published 2017 by Routledge
2 Park Square, Milton Park, Abingdon, Oxon OX14 4RN
711 Third Avenue, New York, NY 10017, USA

Routledge is an imprint of the Taylor & Francis Group, an informa business

Copyright © 2006 International Monetary Fund

Typeset in Times New Roman by
Newgen Imaging Systems (P) Ltd, Chennai, India

British Library Cataloguing in Publication Data
A catalogue record for this book is available
from the British Library

Library of Congress Cataloging in Publication Data
A catalog record for this book has been requested

ISBN 13: 978-0-415-70071-9 (hbk)
ISBN 13: 978-0-415-64982-7 (pbk)

Contents

viii *Contents*

Figures

x *Figures*

Boxes

Tables

Contributors

Orazio Attanasio is Professor of Economics at University College London and a Research Fellow at the Institute for Fiscal Studies. He has earlier taught at Stanford University and the University of Chicago, and has been an advisor to the World Bank and the Inter-American Development Bank. He is currently an Associate Editor of the *Journal of the European Economic Association*, and has previously been the Managing Editor of the *Review of Economic Studies*.

Emanuele Baldacci is currently the Senior Researcher in the Italian Statistical Agency (Istat). He has been an Economist in the International Monetary Fund's Fiscal Affairs Department and a Senior Economist for Social Protection in the Latin America and Caribbean Region of the World Bank. He has also been a consultant for the Fund and the Bank on fiscal policy, expenditure policy, and social protection.

Andrew Berg is Chief of the Developing Issues Division of the IMF's Department of Policy Development and Review. Prior to that he spent several years in the IMF Research Department. He has a PhD in Economics from MIT and an undergraduate degree from Harvard. He has also worked at the US Treasury, including as Chief Economist of the Mexican Task Force in 1995–96 and Deputy Assistant Secretary for East Asia and Latin America in 2000–01. As an associate of Jeffrey Sachs, he advised the Polish Government during 1989–91. He has published articles in a variety of professional journals on, *inter alia*, the economics of transition, dollarization, and the use of early warning systems for predicting currency crises.

François Bourguignon is the Chief Economist and Senior Vice-President of the World Bank. He has served as an advisor to many developing countries, the OECD, the United Nations, and the European Commission. He has been Professor of Economics at the Ecole des Hautes Etudes en Sciences Sociales in Paris and has held academic positions with the University of Chile, Santiago, and the University of Toronto. Bourguignon has authored and edited several books as well as numerous articles in leading international journals in Economics.

Aleš Bulíř is currently a Senior Economist in the IMF's Policy Development and Review Department. Bulíř has graduate degrees in Economics and Statistics from the LSE and Prague School of Economics. Prior to joining the Fund he was a Reader in Economic and Finance and Advisor to the Czech National Bank, positions that he resumed during his sabbatical in 2002–03. He has published articles in professional journals on, *inter alia*, exchange rates in transition economies, volatility of aid, and the economics of planning.

Paul Cashin is currently Deputy Division Chief in the IMF's Western Hemisphere Department. During 1998–2003 he worked in the IMF's Research Department where he undertook research on current account sustainability, exchange rates in developing countries, commodity prices and terms of trade volatility, and economic growth. Prior to joining the Fund in 1998, he was Assistant Professor at the University of Melbourne and Senior Research Economist at the Ministry of Agriculture, Australia. He received a PhD in economics from Yale University in 1993 and holds a graduate degree in agricultural economics from the University of Melbourne.

Stefan Dercon is the Professor of Development Economics of the University of Oxford. His main interests are the economics of risk, poverty, and vulnerability.

Elizabeth Frankenberg is Assistant Professor of Sociology and Director of the Training in International Population Sciences Program at the University of California, Los Angeles. She was awarded the Dorothy Swaine Thomas prize by the Population Association of America (PAA) and on the PAA Board of Directors. Her research focuses on the relationships between health, family, and community. She has led two waves of the Indonesia Family Life Survey and is leading the Study of the Tsunami Aftermath and Recovery in Sumatra, Indonesia.

Xavier Giné is an Economist in the Finance Team of the Development Research Group. Prior to joining the Bank he was a Postdoctoral Fellow and Lecturer at the Economic Growth Center at Yale University. He holds an MA and a PhD in Economics from the University of Chicago.

Pinelopi K. Goldberg is Professor of Economics at Yale University. She received a Diploma in Economics from the University of Freiburg, Germany, in 1986, and a PhD in Economics from Stanford University in 1992. She specializes in the areas of International Trade, Industrial Organization, and Applied Microeconomics. She is Research Associate at the National Bureau of Economic Research, Fellow of the Econometric Society, and Research Associate at the Center for Japan–US Business and Economic Studies.

Gabriela Inchauste is an Economist in the International Monetary Fund. She works at the IMF's Institute. Earlier, she was with the Fiscal Affairs Department where she analyzed expenditure policy issues and participated in several IMF technical assistance and negotiating missions. Ms Inchauste holds a PhD from the University of Texas at Austin.

Seema Jayachandran is an Assistant Professor of Economics at the University of California, Los Angeles and an affiliate of the Bureau for Research and Economic Analysis of Development. She is also currently a Robert Wood Johnson Scholar at the University of California, Berkeley. Her research is on labor, health, and political economy issues in developing countries. She holds a PhD from Harvard University, master's degree from the University of Oxford, and a bachelor's degree from MIT.

Ravi Kanbur is T.H. Lee Professor of World Affairs, International Professor of Applied Economics and Management, and Professor of Economics at Cornell University, USA. Ravi Kanbur's main areas of interest are public economics and development economics. He has published widely in those areas.

Michael Kremer is the Gates Professor of Developing Societies in the Department of Economics at Harvard University and Senior Fellow at the Brookings Institution. He is a Fellow of the American Academy of Arts and Sciences and a recipient of a MacArthur Fellowship and a Presidential Faculty Fellowship. Kremer's recent research examines education and health in developing countries, immigration, and globalization. He and Rachel Glennerster have recently published *Strong Medicine: Creating Incentives for Pharmaceutical Research on Neglected Diseases*. His articles have been published in journals including the *American Economic Review, Econometrica,* and the *Quarterly Journal of Economics*. Kremer previously served as a teacher in Kenya. He founded and was the first executive director of WorldTeach, a non-profit organization which places more than two hundred volunteer teachers annually in developing countries (1986–89).

Anne Krueger has been the first Deputy Managing Director of the International Monetary Fund since September 1, 2001. Before coming to the Fund, Ms Krueger was the Herald L. and Caroline L. Retch Professor in Humanities and Sciences in the Department of Economics at Stanford University. She was also the founding Director of Stanford's Center for Research on Economic Development and Policy Reform; and a Senior Fellow of the Hoover Institution. Ms Krueger had previously taught at the University of Minnesota and Duke University and, from 1982 to 1986, was the World Bank's Vice President for Economics and Research. She received her undergraduate degree from Oberlin College and her PhD in Economics from the University of Wisconsin.

Timothy Lane is currently Assistant Director in the IMF's Policy Development and Review Department. During 1998–2004, he was responsible for work on various analytical and policy issues mainly related to IMF-supported programs, including the experience with capital account crises, IMF conditionality, the framework for assessing debt sustainability, and the macroeconomic implications of foreign aid. He has also worked in the European and Research Departments. Prior to joining the IMF in 1988, he was an Assistant Professor in Economics at Michigan State University. He received a PhD in Economics

xviii   *Contributors*

from the University of Western Ontario. He spent the 2004–05 academic year at the University of Oxford as Oliver Smithies Visiting Fellow of Balliol College and an academic visitor in the Department of Economics.

Paolo Mauro is Chief of the Strategic Issues Division in the IMF's Research Department. He obtained a PhD in Economics from Harvard University.

Luiz de Mello is Senior Economist at the Economics Department of the OECD.

Ashoka Mody is currently an Assistant Director in the European Department at the International Monetary Fund where he has been since 2001. Earlier he was for several years with the World Bank where his last assignment was to manage the writing and production of annual publication *Global Development Finance*. He has worked at AT&T's Bell Laboratories, and has been a Visiting Professor at the University of Pennsylvania's Wharton School.

Catherine Pattillo is a Senior Economist in the IMF African Department. Previously in the IMF Research Department, she has written on areas including currency crises, debt, growth, investment, monetary unions, terms of trade, African macroeconomic issues and firm behavior in Africa. Before joining the Fund, she was an Economics Fellow at the Oxford University. She holds a PhD from the Yale University and a BA from the Harvard University.

Nina Pavcnik received her BA in Economics from Yale University in 1994, and her PhD in Economics from Princeton University in 1999. She is an Associate Professor in the Department of Economics at Dartmouth College, a faculty research fellow at the National Bureau of Economic Research, and a research affiliate at the Centre for Economic Policy Research. Her recent research has examined the impact of trade policy on labor markets and child labor in developing countries.

Luiz A. Pereira da Silva is the Secretary of State, International Affairs at the Ministry of Finance in Brazil. Prior to this appointment, he was Lead Economist and Special Adviser to the Chief Economist and Senior Vice-President of the World Bank. He has also held other positions in France, Japan, and South Africa. His areas of work include macro-economic modeling of financial crises and poverty. He has authored and edited several scholarly articles and books. He holds a PhD in Economics from the University of Paris I (Sorbonne).

Martin Ravallion is Senior Advisor in the Development Research Group of the World Bank. He has advised numerous governments and international agencies on poverty reduction, and has written extensively on this and other subjects in Economics, including two books and over 150 papers in scholarly journals and edited volumes. He serves on the editorial boards of ten Economics journals and is a Senior Fellow of the Bureau for Research in Economic Analysis of Development.

Ratna Sahay, a national of India, is an Assistant Director in the Western Hemisphere Department. She heads the regional surviellance mission to the six ECCU Fund member countries. Ms Sahay holds a BA in Economics from Miranda House, Delhi University, an MA in Business Economics from Delhi University, and a PhD in Economics from New York University. Ms Sahay's IMF career includes: Advisor to Stanley Fischer, First Deputy Managing Director, IMF; Advisor to Michael Mussa, Economic Counselor and Director of Research Department and Chief of the Macroeconomic Studies Division of the Research Department. She has also worked as desk economist for developing and transition countries in the Asian and European Departments. Prior to joining the Fund, Ms Sahay taught at New York University, New York, and Delhi University, India. Ms Sahay has written and published widely on capital flows, dollarization, inflation stabilization, foreign aid, foreign direct investment, financial markets and crises, debt and fiscal issues, international trade, privatization, poverty and macroeconomic policies, and economic growth. She has served as co-editor of *IMF Staff Papers* and Chair of the *Working Group on Fund Research* at the IMF.

James P. Smith holds the RAND Chair in Labor Markets and Demographic Studies and was the Director of RAND's Labor and Population Studies Program from 1977 to 1994. He has led numerous projects, including studies of immigration, the economics of aging, black–white wages and employment, the effects of economic development on labor markets, wealth accumulation and savings behavior, and the interrelation of health and economic status among the elderly. He has twice received the National Institutes of Health MERIT Award, the most distinguished honor NIH grants to a researcher.

Nicholas Stern is Adviser to the UK Government on the Economics of Climate Change and Development, reporting to the Prime Minister. He is the Head of the Stern Review on the Economics of Climate Change. He is also the Head of the Government Economic Service. He has been the Second Permanent Secretary to Her Majesty's Treasury from 2003–05, and from 2004–05 he has been the Director of Policy and Research for the Prime Minister's Commission for Africa. He is currently Visiting Professor of Economics, London School of Economics and Political Science, and Visiting Fellow of Nuffield College, Oxford.

Duncan Thomas is Professor of Economics and Director of the California Center for Population Research at the University of California, Los Angeles. His research focuses on the health and well-being of low-income populations with particular emphasis on intra-family dynamics. He co-directed two waves of the Indonesia Family Life Survey and is leading the Work and Iron Status Evaluation, a randomized treatment-control intervention study in Indonesia. He is on the Board of Directors of the Population Association of America as well as the Bureau of Research on the Economic Analysis of Development. He is co-editor of the *Journal of Human Resources*.

Robert M. Townsend is the Charles E. Merriam Distinguished Service Professor in Economics and the College at University of Chicago. He was awarded the Econometric Society's Frisch Medal in 1998 for his paper "Risk and Insurance in Village India." He is also active as an advisor and consultant for international institutions and government agencies including the World Bank, the International Monetary Fund, the Inter-American Development Bank, and the Federal Reserve Bank of Chicago. He is a member of the American Academy of Arts and Sciences, and this year was honored as the keynote speaker for the prestigious Simon Kuznets Memorial Lecture Series at Yale University.

Matti Tuomala is Professor of Economics at University of Tampere, Finland. Matti Tuomala's main areas of interest are public economics and inequality. He has published widely in those areas.

Part I

Issues in macroeconomics and poverty

Can public policies lower poverty?

An overview

Ashoka Mody and Catherine Pattillo*

The global incidence of extreme poverty – the percentage of the world population with incomes less than $1 a day – and the absolute numbers of poor people have been falling since 1981. The first target of the Millennium Development Goals – to halve, between 1990 and 2015, the proportion of people in extreme poverty – is likely to be met at the global level (World Bank, 2004). The data underlying these trends remain controversial. Bhalla (2002) argues that the extent of global poverty reduction has been greater than these figures indicate, while Deaton (2002) has emphasized inconsistencies in reported poverty trends.

Although the global incidence of poverty is declining, progress has been uneven across countries (Figure 0.1) and some of the most challenging problems lie ahead. At one extreme, East Asian economies have been extremely successful in tackling poverty as past decades have produced spectacular growth that has increased opportunities for fruitful employment. Projections suggest a continuation of these trends. In contrast, in Sub-Saharan Africa, the incidence of poverty and, especially, the number of poor people has been rising. In 2015, nearly half the African population is expected to have incomes below the poverty line. South Asian trends have been favorable to poverty reduction, but the size of the numbers in poverty will remain large for several years (Figure 0.2).

At an April 2001 workshop, Stanley Fischer, then the Fund's First Deputy Managing Director, highlighted why the International Monetary Fund (IMF) needed to extend its analytical capabilities beyond its traditional focus on macro-economic stabilization to include an assessment of the effects of IMF-supported programs on the incidence of poverty. The IMF, he noted, lends to many countries where poverty is an overriding problem, and its policy advice (e.g. on fiscal spending, taxation, and inflation) affects poor people in special ways. Moreover, policies will not be politically sustainable unless they lead to equitable outcomes. And beyond such pragmatism, he argued, lies a moral obligation for the IMF to address the sources and consequences of poverty.[1]

The chapters in this book take seriously Fischer's challenge and consider how economic policies, crises, and income distribution interact with each other and with economic growth to deliver poverty outcomes. Recognizing the generally accepted proposition that economic growth is crucial for poverty reduction, this book nevertheless emphasizes the importance of particular country circumstances

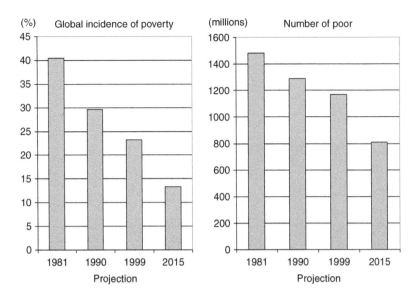

Figure 0.1 Global poverty ($1 a day poverty line).

Sources: http://www.developmentgoals.org/Poverty.htm#percapita for 1990, 1999, and 2015 values.
http://www.worldbank.org/research/povmonitor/ for 1981 values.

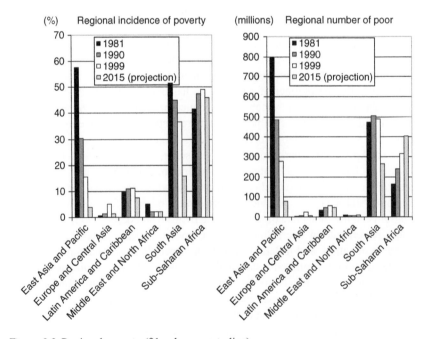

Figure 0.2 Regional poverty ($1 a day poverty line).

Sources: http://www.developmentgoals.org/Poverty.htm#percapita for 1990, 1999, and 2015 values
and http://www.worldbank.org/research/povmonitor/ for 1981 values.

in mediating the relationship between growth and poverty reduction and hence presents several country studies focusing on policy measures for, and the political economy of, poverty alleviation. This line of research is of relatively recent origin, reflecting a view that specific country circumstances matter in the determination of poverty outcomes. As such, many of the essays use micro data and innovative techniques to analyze how fiscal policies, structural policies such as financial reforms and trade liberalization, and large shocks and policy responses affect inequality and poverty.

Many of the chapters in the book were first presented at an IMF conference in March 2002 and have been subsequently revised and updated. We have been fortunate also in adding other ongoing research to this collection. Three overarching policy lessons emerge from this analysis. First, fiscal policies are potentially valuable for reducing poverty but are subject to important political economy forces that limit their usefulness. Second, structural policies, relating, for example, to financial sector and trade liberalization, not only unleash long-term growth but also are likely to increase inequalities, implying somewhat reduced effectiveness in lowering poverty. Third, crises that originate in natural disasters are particularly harmful to the poor in low-income countries; in contrast, recovery from financial crises in middle-income countries is easier and hence the impact on the poor is less severe.

The current consensus and the open questions

In principle, poverty reduction occurs through two channels: first, growth raises average incomes and, hence, reduces poverty; second, poverty is reduced even more when the rise in incomes especially benefits the poor. Reflecting a widely held consensus, Kraay (2003) finds that in the medium-to-long run, much of the variation in poverty trends can be attributed to growth in country average incomes. However, he finds that changes in income distribution are also empirically important in determining poverty reduction.

The perspective that growth in average incomes is the most important channel for poverty reduction is supported by two of this book's chapters in Part I. These chapters suggest, as do other studies based on cross-country growth regressions, that country policies do not impact poverty trends over and above their effect through growth.[2] Sahay *et al.* (Chapter 1) ask whether, given the rate of per capita GDP growth, economic policies account for improvements in the human development index, which is highly correlated with poverty. They document the stylized fact that none of the policy or institutional variables considered has a significant and robust association that has either pro-poor or anti-poor implications. Berg and Krueger (Chapter 3) find persuasive the evidence that trade openness is an important determinant of growth. However, they conclude that trade openness does not have systematic effects on poverty beyond its effect on growth.

Ravallion (2004) stresses, however, that focusing on average effects based on cross-country regressions masks the wide variation across countries in the impact of a given growth rate on poverty. Averages across countries, he argues (p. 15), "can be quite uninformative about how best to achieve pro-poor growth in specific countries." Going beyond the cross-country averages, the initial level of inequality and changes in inequality over time are the main proximate causes of the differing rates of poverty reduction at given rates of growth.[3] Ravallion finds, for example, that poverty responds only slowly to growth in high inequality countries.[4]

To inform policy, it therefore becomes important to understand the dimensions of inequality that matter, including, for example, access to both private (human and physical) capital and public goods. However, Kraay (2003) finds that cross-country evidence is particularly uninformative in pointing to the determinants of changes in income distribution. Thus, while cross-country evidence provides some guidance on measures that spur growth, the policy analyst faces a greater challenge in proposing measures to influence distribution. Kraay (2003) is led to suggest the need for more micro-level and case study research. Similarly, Ravallion (2004) calls for more country-level studies on the underlying determinants of changes in inequality and the specific factors influencing the growth elasticity of poverty.

The chapters in this book address this common call from different perspectives for country-level studies of the determinants of changes in inequality. However, to set the stage and provide a link to the cross-country literature, Part I has three chapters: a summary of the literature on macroeconomic policies and poverty; a survey on the important topic of trade and poverty; and an overview of state-of-the-art methodologies for analyzing public policies, shocks, and poverty. The chapters in Parts II and III, then, analyze the poverty implications of fiscal policy (changes in the progressivity of taxation or large spending cuts) as well as structural policies such as financial liberalization and trade reform. Part IV focuses on the impact of large shocks or crises on both income distribution and average consumption growth that underlies poverty measures. The rest of this overview chapter clarifies the channels through which fiscal and structural policies influence poverty, highlights briefly the international policy dimensions raised in two of the chapters, and concludes by suggesting the policy directions that emerge from the chapters in this book.

Public policies: channels of impact on poverty

What are the channels through which public policies and shocks affect income distribution and poverty? Fiscal policy – changes in the tax structure; changes in spending, transfers, or subsidies; increases in prices of publicly provided services; or reductions in public sector employment or real wages – can have both direct and indirect effect on income distribution (Agénor, 2002). Spending changes, for example, could reduce the consumption of the poor or their purchasing power, but the ultimate effect depends on the extent to which social expenditure disproportionately benefits poor or rich households. The indirect effects of fiscal policy operating through changes in aggregate demand are not clear-cut: mechanisms operate both to reduce aggregate demand and, hence, worsen poverty in the short run, though long-run effects may be more beneficial if, for example, inflationary pressures are contained.

As financial liberalization, growth, and inequality evolve over time, the implications for poverty reduction are complex. Financial liberalization may benefit the poor by allowing greater access to credit and improving risk sharing. Improved access to credit could allow poor households to better smooth consumption in bad times, invest in riskier but more productive technologies, and invest more in education. However, financial liberalization could worsen inequality. The ability to earn higher interest rates on savings tends to benefit the wealthy most. And the availability of credit to finance investment could assist potential low-wealth entrepreneurs who are not from the poorest strata of society. In such a setting, growth accompanying financial liberalization may have limited poverty reduction effects.

The links between trade liberalization and income distribution and poverty are similarly complex. Trade liberalization lowers import prices for poor consumers and producers, and increases export prices for poor producers. In capital-scare developing countries, trade liberalization may be expected to increase the relative wage of low-skilled workers. Liberalization of agricultural markets could increase income for poor rural households (chapter 2, Winters, 2000). Another channel of influence is the effect on government revenue from trade taxes, and thus the government's ability to fund social programs for the poor (Bannister and Thugge, 2000). Trade liberalization could also worsen income distribution, however, by encouraging the adoption of skill-biased technical change that benefits better-off workers (Chapter 9).

Financial crises also clearly have large, economy-wide effects. The slowdown in economic activity could lead to real wage declines and job losses in both the formal and informal sectors. The informal sector could be particularly hard hit if displaced formal sector workers move into informal jobs, lower overall demand reduces demand for informal sector services, and the currency depreciation lowers earnings of non-traded sectors (Bourguignon and Morrison, 1992; Lustig and Walton, 1998). Higher import prices, particularly for imported food, following the currency depreciation could also hurt net food consumers (Sahn *et al.*, 1997). Governments often respond to crises with fiscal retrenchment, and the spending cuts could lower social expenditures, while removal of food subsidies could exacerbate any fall in the income of the poor (World Bank, 2000). For all of the above channels however, the ultimate effect on income distribution will depend on patterns of consumption, employment, and public spending incidence of different income groups.

Crises, or large negative shocks more generally, may be of special concern if they have asymmetric effects – that is, if large contractions worsen poverty significantly but the subsequent expansion does not undo the damage. In such circumstances, crises will have persistent effects, where short-lived shocks plunge households into poverty from which they are unable to recover as the economy improves. Cross-country studies have not found support for asymmetric effects of large negative growth shocks on the share of income that goes to the poorest quintile or poverty (Ravallion, 2001; Dollar and Kraay, 2002). However, it has been argued that if poor families are forced to take children out of school in response to large adverse shocks, and they do not return to school during the recovery, economic downturns may have irreversible impacts on the human capital of the poor (Lustig, 2000). Similarly, lower investments in nutrition and health could hinder families' ability to escape from poverty. Empirically, the potential of crises and shocks to lead to persistent poverty traps is an important open question (Fallon and Lucas, 2002). Existing evidence is mixed: Loshkin and Ravallion (2001) do not find support for a shock-induced poverty trap; while the evidence in Alderman *et al.* (2001) and Hoddinott and Kinsey (2001) is consistent with permanent impacts of shocks such as these of droughts, through health and education outcomes. In this volume, Chapter 12 finds persistent effects of the 1980s famine and rainfall shocks on rural household consumption growth in Ethiopia.

It is clear that each of the various policies and shocks operates through complicated channels, with both direct and induced economy-wide effects that have an impact on the distribution of income and poverty. Additionally, in the real world, of course, governments change more than one policy at a time. The interactions between these different forces operating on poverty trends present challenges to policy makers who wish to deal with them in an integrated manner. Bourguignon *et al.*'s chapter (Chapter 2) reviews tools and methods currently available to address this challenge, and points to areas needing improvement. Their preferred methodology is a three-layer approach: a top layer of macro modeling tools for analyzing the impact of shocks and policies on macroeconomic aggregates; an intermediate layer with tools that disaggregate these predictions into various sectors and factors of production, and a bottom layer consisting of a micro-simulation model that uses household data to analyze the distributional consequences of changes in prices, factor rewards, and employment levels. The authors point out the practical flexibility of such an approach: since many different types of models could be employed in each layer, they could be developed in different institutions or government ministries and "hooked together."

International context

Most of the chapters in this book present country-level analysis of the links between public policies and income distribution and poverty. In addition, two chapters deal with important international issues that developed countries have debated in the global effort to reduce poverty: external debt relief and aid. In the second half of the 1990s, high external indebtedness of poor countries has received increased attention from policy makers and public opinion around the world as one of the main factors contributing to limit poverty reduction. International financial institutions as well as bilateral creditors have responded by implementing the Heavily Indebted Poor Countries (HIPC) Initiative, which provides debt relief to countries pursuing IMF and World Bank reform programs.[5] In 1999, the Initiative was strengthened by making social policy reform – including higher spending on social sector programs like basic education and health – more centrally linked to the debt relief. Chapter 4's premise, an additional rationale for debt relief, is that some debts were illegitimate in the first place. Kremer and Jayachandran argue that sovereign debt incurred without the consent of the people and to benefit the elite should be considered odious and successor governments should not be responsible for repayment. They suggest that empowering an independent institution to assess whether regimes are legitimate could be a policy that would curtail odious debt. The chapter, however, highlights the difficulties in assessing legitimacy of governments through several country examples, including those in the context of external debt in post-war Iraq.

A watershed event in the fight against global poverty was the Millennium Declaration – signed by 189 countries in September 2000 – leading to adoption of the Millennium Development Goals (MDGs) which set specific targets for eradicating poverty and other sources of human deprivation. The Monterrey Consensus (2002) has stressed mutual responsibilities in the quest for the MDGs – calling on developing countries to improve policies and governance, and developed countries to allow more access to their markets and provide more and better aid. The findings in Chapter 5 of this book suggest that there is much scope for improved coordination and management of aid. Bulíř and Lane conclude that aid shortfalls are not wholly predictable: aid flows are more volatile and less reliable than other sources of revenue, particularly for countries heavily dependent on aid. They show that aid-receiving governments' ability to plan poverty-reducing spending is also made more difficult as actual aid disbursements fall short of donors' planned commitments.

Policy messages

The chapters in this volume have implications for public policies to address deteriorations in inequality and responses to crises and shocks, essential to speed up the process of poverty reduction that accompanies economic growth. Three policy messages can be distilled, corresponding to the parts on public finances, finance and trade, and crises and shocks.

- *Fiscal policy tools can be used to reduce inequality and provide social safety nets, but are subject to domestic political economy pressures.*

In Chapter 6, Ravallion asks who is protected when crises or reforms result in large budget cuts. He shows that the answer is theoretically ambiguous, depending on how the wealthy value spending on the poor, versus a "power effect," gauging the strength of political power to protect pro-poor sending. Drawing on micro-based empirical studies of social programs in India, Bangladesh, and Argentina, Ravallion finds that spending on the *non-poor* is protected from budget cuts; targeting tends to worsen during fiscal contractions. While the results strengthen the case for efforts to protect pro-poor spending at times of aggregate fiscal adjustment, they also show the political difficulties of doing so, leading Ravallion to discuss the policy implications for design of effective safety net policies.

Kanbur and Tuomala (Chapter 7) seek to explain the spectacular increases in inequality in the transitional economies of Central and Eastern Europe. They use an optimal income tax model to show that privatizations and decreases in the public provision of public goods could explain increasing pre-tax inequality in transition economies in the 1990s. The increase in pre-tax inequality induces a response of greater progressivity. However, the governments also became less averse to inequality (reflecting social and political changes) and non-tax revenue decreased with the shrinking of the state enterprise sector, tending to counteract increased progressivity and resulting in increased post-tax inequality.

- *Financial liberalization and trade reform open up growth opportunities, but may also widen inequalities in the short run.*

In Chapter 8, Giné and Townsend find that Thailand's financial liberalization during 1976–96 strongly contributed to high growth rates, but was also associated with increasing inequalities. The financial liberalization brought welfare gains and losses of quite sizable magnitudes to different groups. The primary winners were talented potential entrepreneurs who were able to invest in businesses when access to credit opened up. However, the liberalization also induced greater demand by entrepreneurs for workers, higher wages, and therefore lower profits for existing business people.

Attanasio *et al.* (Chapter 9) note that the evidence suggests that trade liberalization in Colombia during the 1980s and 1990s has led to increased efficiency and growth. They find, however, that the reforms were also associated with greater wage inequality and an increase in the relative wages of skilled workers. Tariff reductions contributed to each of the operative channels: increasing returns to college education (driven by skill-biased technological change in response to increased foreign competition), lower industry premiums for sectors with higher shares of unskilled workers, and a shift of the labor force toward the informal sector. The authors note, however, that trade liberalization explains only a small share of the worsening wage inequality in Colombia.

- *The effect of crises and large shocks on poverty and income distribution appears to vary between low-income and emerging market economies. In low-income countries, shocks can have direct and persistent effects on the poor, requiring special forms of safety nets. On the other hand, in emerging markets, the evidence is more mixed on the effects of financial crises.*

Baldacci *et al.* (Chapter 10) use both cross-country macro data and micro data from before and after the 1994–95 Mexico crisis to ask how poverty and income distribution is affected by financial crises. The cross-country analysis shows an increase in poverty and worsening of income distribution after crises, transmitted through inflation, unemployment, lower growth, and reduced government spending. The Mexican data also show increases in poverty post crisis, although inequality did not go up, as there was a disproportionate decline in the income of the wealthiest. The authors argue that the provision of targeted safety nets and the protection of social programs from fiscal retrenchment are the important pro-poor policy responses to financial crises.

Using panel data from rural Ethiopia, Dercon (Chapter 11) analyzes the determinants of consumption growth during the 1990s. He finds that rainfall shocks have a substantial impact on consumption that persists for many years. There is also a persistent growth impact from the large-scale famine in the 1980s, helping to explain the diversity of consumption growth across households in the 1990s. These results indicate that there may be a persistent, or even a permanent, effect of uninsured risks on income growth rates, leading to possible poverty traps. Dercon argues that policies providing protection from shocks in the form of *ex ante* insurance and post-shock safety nets could therefore have long-term benefits for consumption growth and poverty reduction.

The 1998 crisis marked a dramatic and unexpected reversal of economic growth in Indonesia – real GDP fell by around 15 percent in 1998. In Chapter 12, Frankenberg *et al.* provide evidence on how households attempt to smooth out the effects of large, unanticipated shocks, and evaluate the consequences of those strategies for welfare indicators. They find tremendous diversity – the crisis was devastating for some households, but brought new opportunities for others. Households reorganized living arrangements, increased labor supply, and deferred expenditure on some goods. Rural households sold gold to smooth consumption, one of the only assets whose value did not decline with the collapse of the rupiah and spiraling inflation. The diversity indicates that targeted safety nets may be complex to structure, but that ongoing longitudinal surveys that can be put into the field very rapidly can assist in public policy design.

Conclusion

Reducing poverty is a key challenge facing the world community. Adoption of the MDGs has focused attention on the reforms needed in country policies and institutions, as well as the support needed from developed countries in order to achieve the goals for poverty reduction and improvements in living standards.

The chapters in this book contribute to understanding the multiple forces that influence changes in poverty, and the diverse and inter-related ways in which public policies and government responses to shocks and crises, can have an impact on the distribution of income and contribute to making economic growth more pro-poor.

There are numerous areas, however, where our understanding of the links between economic policies and poverty outcomes is still quite limited. Chapter 3's methodological overview points out that the profession is still in the early stages of developing methods for analyzing the effect of a number of macroeconomic policies on income distribution and poverty. In particular, further research is needed on the analysis of dynamics in either the very short run such as the impact of crises, or the long run such as the effect of educational policies. Continued research such as that supporting the chapters prepared for this book, using rich micro-level data for country-level studies, can be expected to have substantial returns.

Notes

* The views expressed are those of the authors and should not be viewed as representing those of the IMF.
1 Workshop and Panel on Macroeconomic Policies and Poverty Reduction, April 12–13, 2001 (http:/www.imf.org/external/np/res/seminars/2001/poverty/indebt.htm), IMF Washington.
2 In contrast to this common finding, a recent paper by Ghura *et al.* (2002) found inflation, government size, educational achievement, and financial development to be "super-pro-poor" policies, that is, policies that directly influence the income of the poor after accounting for the effect of growth.
3 There is also a large literature exploring whether more unequal societies grow slower. The evidence is quite inconclusive. Banerjee and Duflo (2003) find that changes in inequality reduce growth, whichever way the changes go. They suggest, however, that it is difficult to interpret these types of evidence causally, given that relationships may not be linear and omitted variable problems abound.
4 From cross-country averages, however, Ravallion (2004) notes that changes in inequality at the country level have little or no correlation with rates of economic growth (Ravallion and Chen, 1997; Ravallion, 2001; Dollar and Kraay, 2002), that is, inequality does not *systematically* worsen with higher growth and thus dampen poverty reduction.
5 As of September 2003, debt reduction packages have been approved for 27 countries providing $51 billion in debt service relief over time (http://www.imf.org/external/np/exr/facts/hipc.htm).

References

Agénor, Pierre-Richard. 2002. *Macroeconomic Adjustment and the Poor: Analytical Issues and Cross-Country Evidence* (Washington, DC: World Bank).

Alderman, H., J. Behrman, V. Lavy, and R. Menon. 2001. "Child Health and School Enrollment: A Longitudinal Analysis," *Journal of Human Resources*, 36: 185–205.

Banerjee, Abhijit V., and Esther Duflo. 2003. "Inequality and Growth: What Can the Data Say?" *Journal of Economic Growth*, 8: 267–99.

Bannister, Geoffrey J. and Kamau Thugge. 2001. "International Trade and Poverty Alleviation," IMF Working Paper 01/54 (Washington, DC: International Monetary Fund).

Bhalla, Surjit. 2002. *Imagine There's No Country – Poverty, Inequality and Growth in the Era of Globalization* (Washington, DC: Institute for International Economics).

Bourguignon, François and Christian Morrisson. 1992. *Adjustment and Equity in Developing Countries: A New Approach* (Paris: Organization of Economic Cooperation and Development).

Deaton, Angus. 2002. "Is World Poverty Falling?" *Finance and Development*, 39(2): 4–7.

Dollar, David and Aart Kraay. 2002. "Growth is Good for the Poor," *Journal of Economic Growth*, 7: 195–225.

Fallon, Peter R. and Robert E.B. Lucas. 2002. "The Impact of Financial Crises on Labor Markets, Household Incomes, and Poverty: A Review of Evidence," *World Bank Research Observer*, 17(1) (Spring): 21–45.

Ghura, Dhaneshwar, Carlos A. Leite, and Charalambos Tsangarides. 2002. "Is Growth Enough? Macroeconomic Policy and Poverty Reduction," IMF Working Paper 02/118 (Washington, DC: International Monetary Fund).

Hoddinott, J. and B. Kinsey. 2001. "Child Health in the Time of Drought," *Oxford Bulletin of Economics and Statistics*, 63: 409–36.

Kraay, Aart. 2004. "When Is Growth Pro-Poor? Cross-Country Evidence," World Bank Policy Research Working Paper 3225 (Washington, DC: World Bank).

Lokshin, M. and M. Ravallion. 2000. "Short-lived Shocks with Long-lived Impacts? Household Income Dynamics in a Transition Economy," PRE Working Paper No. 2459 (Washington, DC: World Bank).

Lustig, Nora. 2000. "Crises and the Poor: Socially Responsible Macroeconomics," Working Paper No. POV-108 (Washington, DC: Inter-American Development Bank).

—— and Michael Walton. 1998. "Crises and the Poor: A Template for Action," (unpublished; Washington, DC: World Bank and Inter-American Development Bank).

Moneterrey Consensus. 2002. http://www.un.org/esa/ffd/ffdconf/

Ravallion, Martin. 2001. "Growth, Inequality and Poverty: Looking Beyond Averages," *World Development*, 29(11): 1803–15.

—— 2004. "Pro-Poor Growth: A Primer," World Bank Policy Research Working Paper No. 2342 (Washington, DC: World Bank).

—— and Shaohua Chen. 1997. "What Can New Survey Data Tell us about Recent Changes in Distribution and Poverty?" *Economic Review*, 11(2): 357–82.

Sahn, E. David, Paul A. Dorosh, and Stephen D. Younger. 1997. *Structural Adjustment Reconsidered: Economic Policy and Poverty in Africa* (Cambridge, United Kingdom; and New York: Cambridge University Press).

Winters, Allan L. 2000. "Trade, Trade Policy and Poverty: What are the Links?" CEPR Discussion Paper 2382 (London: C.E.P.R).

World Bank. 2000. *World Development Report 2000/2001: Attacking Poverty* (Washington, DC: World Bank).

World Bank. 2004. *World Development Report: Making Services Work for Poor People* (Washington, DC: World Bank).

1 Macroeconomic policies and poverty reduction

Stylized facts and an overview of research

*Ratna Sahay, Paul Cashin, Paolo Mauro, and
Catherine Pattillo*

This chapter provides a brief and selective overview of research on the links between macroeconomic policies and poverty reduction. Using the Human Development Index as a measure of well-being, the progress made by 100 countries over the 1975–98 period is presented, and its association with macroeconomic factors is explored. Several avenues for future research are also outlined.

1.1 Introduction

While poverty reduction is the key challenge facing the world community, an important debate is taking place on the policies that may help to attain that objective, and on how international financial institutions can contribute toward that goal. This chapter provides a brief and selective review of ongoing research efforts aimed at identifying the policies that can help to reduce poverty. The focus is on issues that relate to the interaction between macroeconomic policies – which are at the core of the International Monetary Fund's (IMF's) mandate – and poverty.

The links between macroeconomic policies and poverty are complex, and the vast literature on poverty does not yet fully specify how one should think about the direct impact of macroeconomic policies on the poor. Likewise, empirical research on these topics remains at a somewhat preliminary stage. Lack of data, particularly in poor countries, often hinders high-quality research. More recently, attempts at cross-country work have been made but are subject to various criticisms, as highlighted in Srinivasan (2000). The only systematic evidence that exists concerns the poverty-reducing effects of economic growth and, to some extent, the beneficial impact of lowering inflation and, not uncontroversially, freeing trade regimes. But in all these areas, the magnitude of the estimated effects on the incidence of poverty has varied widely across countries and across time in the same countries. While poverty reduction has become a new global mantra, the challenge facing the world community looms large, with the specifics of how to spread the fruits of economic progress leaving room for a wide research agenda.

Recognizing the complexity of the relationships and the political economy aspects of reform programs, the world community is redefining the role of the state. The new consensus is that public policy will now be formulated with active participation from different sections of society. Participatory policy making can not only ensure popular support for each country's economic programs, but also can provide a more level playing field for the poorest sections of society, by removing the structural and cultural impediments to pro-poor economic development. According to this new consensus, a one-for-one response from growth to poverty reduction cannot be taken for granted. Rather, appropriate conditions, such as ensuring that exchange rates are not overvalued, easing constraints on domestic credit markets, reducing labor market distortions, building human capital, and increasing access to trade markets, need to be created so that the poor benefit from growth and so that growth rates rise and are sustained.

This chapter is organized as follows. Section 1.2 conducts a survey of the literature on macroeconomic policies, macroeconomic adjustment, and poverty in the run-up to the new emphasis on participatory processes that emerged toward the end of the 1990s. Section 1.3 gives a preliminary look at the data, focusing on a United Nations Development Programme (UNDP)-developed measure of well-being, the Human Development Index (HDI). This section examines changes in the HDI of individual countries between 1975 and 1998, and explores the association between macroeconomic policies and improvements in well-being. Section 1.4 concludes with comments and suggestions for future research.

1.2 Research on macroeconomic policies, macroeconomic adjustment, and poverty

The consequences of macroeconomic policies for the welfare of the poor and on the distribution of income are issues that attract increasing interest from both economists and policy makers. While most analyses of poverty and inequality have been microeconomic in nature, there is an increasing recognition that macroeconomic policies and macroeconomic stabilization programs can have important effects on both the distribution and level of incomes.

The literature on the relationship between macroeconomic policies and poverty is gradually evolving away from an emphasis on the strong link between economic growth and poverty reduction toward an exploration of policies, beyond growth itself, that contribute to both poverty reduction and improvements in the distribution of income. This line of research explores whether macroeconomic imbalances, such as excessive fiscal and balance of payments deficits, large debt and debt servicing costs, and high inflation, have implications for poverty beyond those that they exert on economic growth.

Of interest are the consequences that IMF- and World Bank-supported adjustment programs for income distribution have had on the poor, particularly in the wake of the severe economic crises experienced by many countries in the 1990s. In examining the effects of macroeconomic adjustment on real incomes, the main theoretical model utilized has been the dependent economy model. In addition, several analyses of the actual effects of macroeconomic adjustment programs on income distribution and poverty complement the large literature that examines the relative economic performance of countries undertaking macroeconomic adjustment programs.

Macroeconomic instability (characterized by rising debt-servicing costs, adverse terms of trade shocks, high inflation, and large fiscal and external imbalances) generates an unsustainable excess of aggregate demand over aggregate supply. To restore macroeconomic balance, countries undertake (in conjunction with the IMF and/or the World Bank) macroeconomic adjustment programs. As noted by Lipton and Ravallion (1995), the case for adjustment programs depends on demonstrating that the present social value of the future sequence of consumptions is greater with adjustment than without.

In this context, the workhorse-dependent economy model (which assumes constant terms of trade) is a useful means to highlight the likely effects of structural adjustment on real incomes, particularly the incomes of the poor. In response to excess aggregate demand, restoring internal and external balance means that the price of nontraded goods must decrease relative to that of traded goods (a real devaluation), and domestic absorption needs to fall (typically through lower domestic consumption and net public expenditures). Given that the poor typically possess labor in abundance, and that labor is mobile across the traded and nontraded goods sectors, the Stolper–Samuelson theorem would predict that returns to the abundant factor (labor) will rise. Returns to labor will increase only if the traded goods sector is more labor-intensive than the nontraded goods sector. This seems a plausible assumption for most developing countries which have a comparative advantage in the production of labor-intensive products. Accordingly, the poor should gain as their real wage (in terms of nontraded goods) will rise with structural adjustment, though this may take a long time.

In the short run, however, the impact of the depreciation on the poor may be mixed. The impact effect is to increase the profitability of traded goods production and decrease that of nontraded goods production. This could have adverse distributional effects in some countries. For example, the gains of poor producers in the traded goods sector will be limited if the government does not pass on much of the export price increase to smallholder farmers. The lower profitability of nontraded goods could also worsen poverty, where incomes are already very low for households producing nontraded food crops. Other important caveats to this beneficial effect of adjustment on the poor concern the pattern of fiscal consolidation, particularly if spending cuts target programs that benefit the poor, and the rise in traded goods prices (particularly for food staples) which may adversely affect the urban poor (as net consumers) even as they benefit the rural poor (as net producers). Despite an apparent consensus that the view that structural adjustment (relative to nonadjustment) is uniformly bad for the poor is overdrawn, it is true that the speed of supply-side response to adjustment (as embodied in the dependent economy model) may also have been overestimated for many developing countries.

1.2.1   *Poverty, income inequality, and economic growth*

One possible link between macroeconomic policies and poverty may well be indirect. Good macroeconomic policies are generally considered to lead to higher growth, and higher growth in turn to poverty reduction. Considerable evidence supports the former premise, particularly over the long run – good macroeconomic policies, if sustained, lead to higher growth rates for countries at the same level of economic development. We do not report on this strand of literature here, as it is vast and would detract from the issue at hand.[1]

The theoretical literature on poverty and growth has explored the relationship between relative concepts of poverty (income distribution) and growth. Interestingly, researchers have not yet fully developed a theoretical framework for thinking about the links between absolute poverty levels and income growth.[2] Several empirical studies, however, have been undertaken to understand this link, including country studies and, more recently, cross-country studies. These studies have generally found a strong positive association between income growth and income measures of poverty.[3] An important question is the elasticity of this relationship, or the extent to which the poor benefit from growth. One approach is that of Ravallion and Chen (1997), which uses data from developing and transition countries, where at least two household surveys are available, and finds an elasticity of poverty reduction (proportion of population living on less than 50 percent of the mean) to growth in average consumption of 2.6. Similarly, Roemer and Gugerty (1997) and Dollar and Kraay (2000) use aggregate data and find that a 1 percent rise in per capita income is correlated with a 1 percent increase in the income of the poorest quintile.

However, the estimated relationship between economic growth and poverty reduction varies substantially across studies (Timmer, 1997; Bruno *et al.*, 1998; Hamner and Naschold, 1999). Many of these studies also employ different types of data, methods, and definitions of poverty, income, or consumption growth variables, making comparison difficult. For example, Lipton and Ravallion (1995) reference individual country studies where elasticities of the poverty gap (a measure of poverty intensity) with respect to growth in mean consumption range from 1.5 to 4.1. They note that since poverty headcount (as compared to poverty gap) elasticities tend to be lower, this suggests that the growth-induced benefits of poverty reduction are felt well below the poverty line. Ravallion (1997) also finds higher elasticities for lower poverty lines.[4]

The *World Development Report 2000–01* (World Bank, 2000) points out several qualifications and extensions to the growth–poverty nexus. First, there is large variation in the statistical relationship between national per capita income growth and poverty measures. Given this wide variance in outcomes, many authors point out that the interesting policy question is not the connection of the poor to economic growth on average, but rather the role of policy and economic structure in turning growth into poverty reduction. In other words, both growth and poverty are possibly affected by a third set of factors that we do not yet fully understand.

What explains some of these different cross-country patterns in the relationship between growth and poverty? One important factor is the sectoral pattern of growth, as the poor are typically located in rural areas to a greater extent than in urban areas. There is some evidence from individual country studies that agricultural sector growth has the largest effect on poverty reduction (Datt and Ravallion, 1998, on India; Thorbecke and Jung, 1996, on Indonesia). While Lipton and Ravallion (1995) agree that the balance of evidence supports a correlation between high and growing farm output and falling rural poverty

(Bourguignon *et al.*, 1981), they note that an empirical debate on this issue continues, both for particular and general country cases.

Most recent research has found no systematic global relationship between growth and inequality, either when specifically testing the Kuznets hypothesis (Anand and Kanbur, 1993; Deininger and Squire, 1998; Barro, 2000) or in other analyses (Perotti, 1996; Ravallion and Chen, 1997; Bruno *et al.*, 1998; Li *et al.*, 1998; Kanbur and Lustig, 1999). If the distribution of income does not change during the growth process, the extent of poverty reduction during growth will depend on the extent of initial inequality. A number of studies (Ravallion, 1995, 1997; Timmer, 1997) have shown higher growth elasticities of poverty reduction in countries with lower Gini indices (i.e. a more equitable income distribution). Clearly, the nature of the growth–poverty relationship becomes more complex if inequality changes during the growth process.

While there may be no significant relationship, on average, between income inequality and growth, there appears to be large variation in experience across countries. The same growth rate is associated with very different patterns of inequality change in different countries, which could explain some of the variation in poverty reduction for given growth rates, although this feature has not been systematically explored. Using survey data, Bruno *et al.* (1998) find that rates of poverty reduction respond even more elastically to rates of change in the Gini index than they do to the level of the index, indicating that even modest changes in inequality can lead to sizable changes in the incidence of poverty.

The poor are also hurt by high initial income inequality if countries with a more unequal distribution of income grow more slowly. Deininger and Squire (1998) find a strong negative relationship between initial distribution of real assets (such as land) and long-term growth, and that inequality reduces income growth for the poor but not the rich. Most other studies use data on income inequality, and currently there is no consensus on whether empirically there is a positive or negative link between initial income inequality and growth (Banerjee and Duflo, 1999; Forbes, 2000).

1.2.2   Inflation and the poor

The literature on the relation between inflation and poverty has generally found a significant association between improvements in the well-being of the poor and lower inflation (Easterly and Fischer, 2001). Using panel data on a range of developed and developing countries, Romer and Romer (1998) also find the income share of the poorest quintile to be inversely related to inflation. Bulír (1998) shows that past inflation worsens income inequality. He finds that the effects are nonlinear – reductions in inflation from hyperinflationary levels lower income inequality much more than further reductions to low inflation levels. Earlier research by Cardoso (1992) found that the poor of Latin America were adversely affected by higher inflation, primarily through a decline in real wages (given the rigidity of nominal wages), as their holdings of cash were very small.

1.2.3 Trade liberalization and poverty

While there is extensive research on the impact of trade liberalization on income distribution, the direct links between absolute poverty and trade reform are only beginning to be explored.[5] Winters (2000) sets out an analytical framework for tracing the impact of trade liberalization on individuals and households through changes affecting enterprises (including wages and employment), distribution (price changes and markets), and government (taxes and spending). Viewing trade reform broadly as including any accompanying domestic market liberalization, Winters suggests that the following factors matter: creation or destruction of markets where the poor participate, intrahousehold effects, intensity of factors of production in most affected sectors and their elasticity of supply, the effect on taxes paid by the poor and government revenue, and whether transitional unemployment will be concentrated on the poor. Bannister and Thugge (2001) add that trade liberalization can affect poverty through incentives for investment, innovation, and growth, as well as by influencing the economy's vulnerability to negative external shocks that could affect the poor.

As to empirical work, Winters (2002) summarizes field studies on trade liberalization and poverty in Africa (Zambia and Zimbabwe) and South Asia (Bangladesh and India). The Zambian study found that following domestic deregulation of cash crop purchasing, the poor suffered as functioning markets disappeared and private markets did not develop in some areas, whereas contrasting effects were found for Zimbabwe. In the two South Asian countries, labor market segmentation prevented the benefits of liberalization from spreading widely, and trade liberalization had uneven effects within households. In addition, a study of the first-round effects of trade liberalization in Nicaragua finds that while the fall in the price of agricultural products negatively affects poor producers, it is offset by the income effect of a decline in consumer goods prices (Kruger, 2000).

Another recent strand of research uses computable general equilibrium models to estimate the sectoral price effects of trade liberalization, and traces them to consumption and factor price changes for various types of households. Some preliminary findings are available for South Africa (Devarajan and Van der Mensbrugghe, 2000) and for Indonesia (Friedman, 2000).

1.2.4 Poverty and external debt

Both in the development of, and modifications to, the Heavily Indebted Poor Countries (HIPC) Initiative, much has been written by the IMF, World Bank, and nongovernment organizations on strengthening the link between debt relief and poverty reduction. The focus has been on developing comprehensive poverty-reduction strategies, and in designing adjustment programs to effectively use resources freed up from debt service for the task of poverty reduction. A key point recognized is that the extent to which increased education and health-care spending improves social indicators is dependent on how efficiently the funds are spent and how well they are targeted to the poor (Gupta *et al.*, 1998;

IMF, 2000, Box 4.3). However, an important caveat emerges, that is, to the extent that HIPCs were not servicing some of their debts, debt relief will not provide additional fiscal resources. While lower debt-service payments on existing borrowings should contribute to spending on poverty reduction, new loans and grants are expected to provide the bulk of total resources for that purpose. Despite the importance of the issue, there is still little research on helping policy makers decide how to prioritize the allocation of available resources in accordance with poverty-reduction targets.

There appears to be little work on answering the following questions about the direct relationship between external debt and poverty:

(i) Does high debt increase poverty, and if so, how?
(ii) What is the incidence of poverty in heavily indebted countries – is there a positive correlation between poverty incidence and debt burdens?
(iii) How would an aid allocation geared to meet some poverty-reduction criterion differ from an allocation aimed at achieving debt sustainability?
(iv) Have countries that have improved debt sustainability without debt relief been more successful than other countries at reducing poverty?
(v) What do we know about the relationship between sustainable fiscal deficits, debt sustainability, and poverty?

1.2.5   *Macroeconomic crises and poverty*

World Bank (2000) summarizes country case studies showing that macroeconomic crises tend to be associated with increases in income poverty, and often with increases in inequality (see also Lustig, 1999; Baldacci *et al.*, 2001).[6] An important question raised in this context is whether poverty that arises during the transition would lead to chronic poverty even after the economic crisis has passed. It is argued that since crises are often associated with increases in inequality, such crises reverse previous poverty-reduction gains proportionally more. In contrast, in a cross-country context, Dollar and Kraay (2000) find no difference in the growth–poverty relationship during periods of negative growth (crisis episodes) and periods of positive growth, and so conclude that crises do not affect the income of the poor disproportionately.

Further, there appears to be little or no research so far exploring how or why the extent of worsening poverty differs across crisis-hit countries. Key questions are just beginning to be asked, though not necessarily examined:

(i) Do certain types of macroeconomic policies associated with crises have a more negative impact on the poor than others?
(ii) Do macroeconomic responses that are optimal for the poor differ from responses that are optimal for the economy as a whole?
(iii) What are the most important elements of a pro-poor crisis response?
(iv) What types of safety nets set up before a crisis hits are the most effective in protecting the poor during a crisis? (Ferreira *et al.*, 1999; Lustig, 1999)

1.2.6 IMF programs and poverty

The debate regarding the effects of IMF programs on the welfare of low-income groups has recently been rekindled by the IMF's high-profile involvement in economic crises affecting Brazil, Indonesia, Republic of Korea, Pakistan, and Russia. Programs aimed at restoring internal and external balance through fiscal consolidation, cuts in domestic absorption, and real devaluation are viewed by critics of the IMF as having adverse effects on the poor. Supporters of IMF activities respond that the Fund's programs assist in macroeconomic stabilization and the restoration of international capital flows, which boost both economic growth and the welfare of the poor.

While studies of the macroeconomic effects of IMF programs (on growth, inflation, and the balance of payments, for example) are abundant, studies of the distributional effects of such programs have been rare, with the exception of recent work by Garuda (2000).[7,8] In examining 58 IMF programs over the period 1975–91, he finds evidence of a significant deterioration in the distribution of income (as measured by Gini coefficients) and in the income of the poor (as measured by the income share of the lowest quintile), in the two years following the initiation of an IMF program. This deterioration is most marked in countries with large external imbalances in the preprogram period. However, when preprogram external imbalances are not large, income distribution improves to a greater extent in countries participating in IMF programs than in nonprogram countries.

Of the four main channels by which IMF programs could beneficially affect poverty reduction and the distribution of income – currency devaluation (lowering the price of nontradables relative to tradables), shrinking of fiscal imbalances, increases in growth rates, and decreases in inflation rates – Garuda (2000) finds that real depreciation of the currency is the most plausible mechanism by which IMF programs assist the poor. Easterly (2000) also finds that World Bank and IMF adjustment lending is closely associated with a more depreciated real exchange rate. Real devaluation assists the rural, farm-based poor by raising the domestic-currency value of agricultural goods (the reverse effect would occur for food-consuming urban poor). To the extent that the bulk of poverty is rurally based, and that the labor intensity of production is greater for the tradables sector than for the nontradables sector, then overall poverty can be reduced through the exchange rate channel.

Using data from household consumption surveys for a group of African countries, Demery and Squire (1996) find that those countries that implemented effective World Bank and IMF reform programs have generated declines in overall poverty; those that implemented ineffective reform programs have generated increases in overall poverty. Like Garuda (2000), they find that real exchange rate depreciation is a key component of a successful, poverty-reducing adjustment strategy, through its beneficial effect on export-led economic growth, its changing of the structure of production in favor of labor-intensive agriculture (which employs the majority of the poor), and the reduction of rents earned (through import quotas and exchange controls) by urban households. The important message is that the maintenance of overvalued exchange rates hurts the poor.[9,10]

These results are broadly consistent with analyses conducted by IMF itself as to the consequences for poverty and income inequality of IMF-supported programs. In IMF (1986), the experience of programs in 94 countries in the 1980s indicated that the effect on poverty and income distribution varied with the composition of programs. Poverty-reducing and distribution-improving measures included real devaluation, elimination of exchange controls, expanded access to credit markets, the widening of the tax base to property and income taxes, and the switching of expenditures to basic health care and education. Measures that had the reverse effect included increases in indirect taxes (such as customs duties and value-added taxes), and the erosion of expenditures on social safety nets.

1.3   A preliminary look at the data

Indicators of well-being have improved in the vast majority of countries over the past few decades, though with major variations both within countries and across countries. A well-known composite indicator of well-being is the UNDP's HDI, which UNDP has defined as the arithmetic average of a country's achievements in three basic dimensions of human development.[11] These include longevity (measured by life expectancy at birth), educational attainment (measured by a combination of the adult literacy rate and the enrollment ratio in primary, secondary, and tertiary education), and living standards (measured by GDP per capita in US dollars at purchasing power parity).

The HDI has a number of advantages: it moves beyond per capita income alone as a measure of well-being, it is compiled with uniform data sources and methodology over time and across countries, and it is available for 100 countries on a consistent basis over the period 1975–98.[12] The HDI does not capture income inequality directly. However, *for a given per capita income*, countries where income is distributed more evenly will tend to display greater average longevity and educational attainment, and therefore a higher HDI, because of the obvious limits to longevity and educational attainment faced by individual people.

Both the HDI and per capita income are highly correlated with other widely used measures of poverty such as the Human Poverty Index (HPI) used by UNDP;[13] the share of the population with income less than $1 per day (a World Bank measure); the share of the population that is undernourished (a Food and Agriculture Organization measure); and measures of well-being such as life expectancy, infant mortality, and educational attainment.[14] Figure 1.1 shows the close association among some of these variables. Figure 1.2 reports the association between the HDI and a measure of income distribution – the Gini coefficient.

Table 1.1 provides a complete list of the 174 countries for which 1998 HDI data are available, categorized by regions, and in descending order of their HDI. In general, the African and Asian countries had relatively low HDI, while industrial, transition, and Latin American countries had relatively high HDI. The HDI improved in almost all countries between 1975 and 1998, and, as set out in Figure 1.3, the median value of the HDI in 1998 (0.73) was significantly higher than in 1975 (0.62). At the same time, there was little change in the ranking of

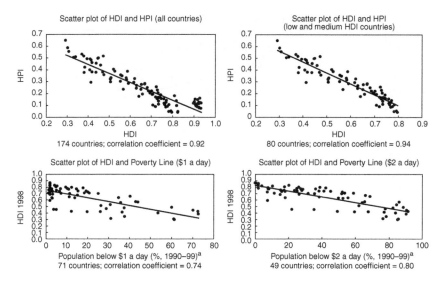

Figure 1.1 HDI, HPI, and Poverty Line: 1998.

Source: UNDP, *Human Development Report* (2000) and World Development Indicators (2000).

Note

a Most recent available observation.

countries by HDI over this period: the cross-country rank correlation between the observations for the HDI in 1975 and in 1998 is 0.98.

Despite the basically unchanged ranking of countries, there is some evidence that low-HDI countries have been "catching up," albeit slowly, with the high-HDI countries. Considering those countries for which HDI data are available for both 1975 and 1998, Table 1.2 shows those countries that commenced in 1975 in groups with relatively low HDI tended to display a greater improvement in HDI (in absolute terms) over the next two decades.[15]

1.3.1 Macroeconomic policies, human development, and income inequality

Poverty in a given country can be reduced by fostering per capita GDP growth,[16] that is, by raising the total resources available to the population, and by increasing the share of those resources going to the poorer segments of that population. A widely held view is that economic growth can be fostered through a set of policies aimed at promoting macroeconomic stability (low and stable inflation, low budget deficits, and sustainable external debt), openness to international trade, education, and the rule of law. A large number of studies based upon cross-country evidence are consistent with that view, although the evidence on whether each individual policy among those listed here raises economic growth is typically not very robust (Levine and Renelt, 1992).[17]

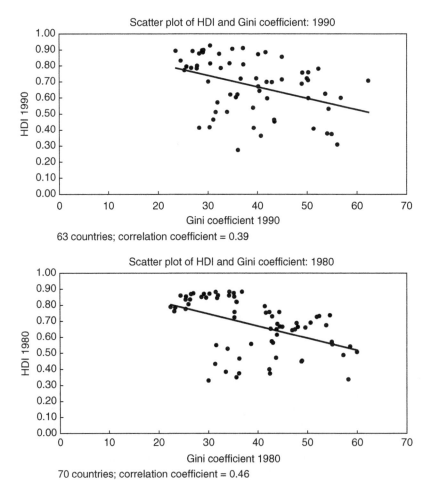

Figure 1.2 HDI and Gini coefficient.

Source: UNDP, *Human Development Report* (2000) and World Development Indicators (2000).

Casual observation is also broadly suggestive of an association between sound macroeconomic policies and rapid improvement in HDI. Table 1.3 shows that, within "low HDI," "medium HDI," and "high HDI" groups of countries, lower inflation, lower variability of inflation, lower external debt, better rule of law, a lower black market premium, and a lower frequency of financial crisis were associated with greater improvement in HDI. At the same time, as in the economic growth literature, it is difficult to show conclusively whether individual policies cause countries to experience more rapid improvements in well-being.

There is also a debate regarding the policies that improve the well-being of the poorer segments of the population for a given growth rate of GDP per capita,[18] and an even more fervent debate about whether certain policies imply a trade-off between increasing total available resources (raising growth rates) and improving their distribution (reducing poverty). In the latter respect, there seems to be broad agreement that policies aimed at improving basic education and health can both raise economic growth and improve distribution, but of course there certainly is no consensus regarding the most effective policies that will raise levels of education and health care.

To examine whether macroeconomic policies have a direct impact on poverty, in a cross-country framework we attempted to estimate the relationship between economic policies and improvements in the HDI (or other indicators of well-being such as life expectancy), for a given rate of growth of GDP per capita. The rationale is that when policies bring about greater improvement in the HDI than would be expected on the basis of the observed rate of economic growth, they are likely to be of particular benefit to the poorer segments of the population. This makes it possible, in principle, to estimate the relationship between economic policies and that component of the improvement in well-being that is unrelated to economic growth.[19]

We examined a large set of potential explanatory variables related to economic policies. The set included many of the variables that previous researchers have used to analyze the determinants of economic growth: inflation and its variance; budget deficits, government spending, and foreign aid as a share of GDP; indicators of openness, such as the ratio of foreign trade to GDP and the black market foreign exchange premium; and indices of the rule of law. It also included others that have received less attention in previous work such as the presence and length of exchange-rate or banking crises, and initial external debt as a share of GDP, see Table 1.3 for a partial list of variables.

When this cross-country regression approach is used, no significant and robust evidence is found that any of these variables are individually associated with

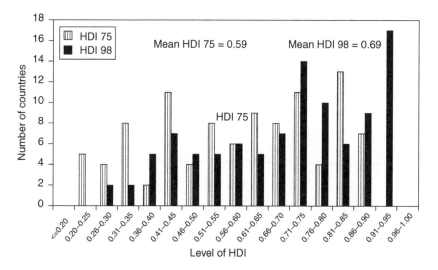

Figure 1.3 Histogram of HDI: 1975 and 1998.

Source: UNDP, *Human Development Report* 2000.

Table 1.1 HDI 1998

HDI			
0.22–0.50	0.51–0.70	0.71–0.80	>0.80
Africa	*Africa*	*Europe/Industrial Countries*	*Europe/Industrial Countries*
Madagascar (0.48)	South Africa (0.7)	Turkey (0.73)	Canada (0.93)
Sudan (0.48)	Cape Verde (0.69)		Norway (0.93)
Togo (0.47)	Algeria (0.68)	*Africa*	United States (0.93)
Mauritania (0.45)	Swaziland (0.66)	Seychelles (0.79)	Australia (0.93)
Djibouti (0.45)	Namibia (0.63)	Mauritius (0.76)	Iceland (0.93)
Nigeria (0.44)	Botswana (0.59)	Tunisia (0.7)	Sweden (0.93)
Congo, Dem. Rep. of the (0.43)	Gabon (0.59)		Belgium (0.92)
Zambia (0.42)	Morocco (0.59)	*Asia*	Netherlands (0.92)
Côte d'Ivoire (0.42)	Lesotho (0.57)	Malaysia (0.77)	Japan (0.92)
Senegal (0.42)	Ghana (0.56)	Fiji (0.77)	United Kingdom (0.92)
Tanzania. U. Rep. of (0.41)	Zimbabwe (0.56)	Thailand (0.74)	Finland (0.92)
Benin (0.41)	Equatorial Guinea (0.55)	Philippines (0.74)	France (0.92)
Uganda (0.41)	São Tomé and Principe (0.55)	Sri Lanka (0.73)	Switzerland (0.92)
Eritrea (0.41)	Cameroon (0.53)	Maldives (0.73)	Germany (0.91)
Angola (0.4)	Comoros (0.51)	Samoa (Western)(0.71)	Denmark (0.91)
Gambia (0.4)	Kenya (0.51)	China (0.71)	Austria (0.91)
Guinea (0.39)	Congo (0.51)		Luxembourg (0.91)
Malawi (0.38)		*Transition Economics*	Ireland (0.91)
Rwanda (0.38)	*Asia*	Croatia (0.79)	Italy (0.9)
Mali (0.38)	Viet Nam (0.67)	Lithuania (0.79)	New Zealand (0.9)
Central African Republic (0.37)	Indonesia (0.67)	Belarus (0.78)	Spain (0.9)
Chad (0.37)	Mongolia (0.63)	Bulgaria (0.77)	Greece (0.88)
Mozambique (0.34)	Vanuatu (0.62)	Russian Federation (0.77)	Portugal (0.86)
Guinea-Bissau (0.33)	Solomon Islands (0.61)	Latvia (0.77)	Cyprus (0.89)
Burundi (0.32)	Myanmar (0.58)	Romania (0.77)	Malta (0.87)
Ethiopia (0.31)	India (0.56)	Macedonia, TFYR (0.76)	
	Papua New Guinea (0.54)	Georgia (0.76)	*Asia*
	Pakistan (0.52)	Kazakhstan (0.75)	Singapore (0.88)
	Cambodia (0.51)	Ukraine (0.74)	Hong Kong, China (SAR) (0.87)
		Azerbaijan (0.72)	
		Armenia (0.72)	
		Albania (0.71)	

Burkina Faso (0.3)
Niger (0.29)
Sierra Leone (0.25)
Asia
Lao People's Dem. Rep. (0.48)
Bhutan (0.48)
Nepal (0.47)
Bangladesh (0.46)
Middle East
Yemen (0.45)
Western Hemisphere
Haiti (0.44)

Transition Economies
Moldova. Rep. of (0.7)
Uzbekistan (0.69)
Tajikistan (0.66)
Middle East
Syrian Arab Republic (0.66)
Egypt (0.62)
Iraq (0.58)
Western Hemisphere
El Salvador (0.7)
Honduras (0.65)
Bolivia (0.64)
Nicaragua (0.63)
Guatemala (0.62)

Kyrgyzstan (0.71)
Turkmenistan (0.7)
Middle East
Libyan Arab Jamahiriya (0.76)
Saudi Arabia (0.75)
Lebanon (0.74)
Oman (0.73)
Jordan (0.72)
Iran, Islamic Rep. of (0.71)
Western Hemisphere
Saint Kitts and Nevis (0.8)
Costa Rica (0.8)
Trinidad and Tobago (0.79)
Dominica (0.79)
Grenada (0.78)
Mexico (0.78)
Cuba (0.78)
Belize (0.78)
Panama (0.78)
Venezuela (0.77)
Suriname (0.77)
Colombia (0.76)
Brazil (0.75)
Saint Vincent and the
   Grenadines (0.74)
Peru (0.74)
Paraguay (0.74)
Jamaica (0.73)
Dominican Republic (0.73)
Saint Lucia (0.73)
Ecuador (0.72)
Guyana (0.71)

Korea, Rep. of (0.85)
Brunei Darussalam (0.85)
Transition Economies
Slovenia (0.86)
Czech Republic (0.84)
Slovakia (0.82)
Hungary (0.82)
Poland (0.81)
Estonia (0.8)
Middle East
Israel (0.88)
Kuwait (0.84)
Bahrain (0.82)
Qatar (0.82)
United Arab
   Emirates (0.81)
Western Hemisphere
Barbados (0.86)
Bahamas (0.84)
Argentina (0.84)
Antigua and
   Barbuda (0.83)
Chile (0.83)
Uruguay (0.82)

Number of countries			
35	38	55	46

Source: UNDP, *Human Development Report* 2000.

pro-poor (or anti-poor) economic growth. Of course, by no means does this constitute proof that these policies do not matter. On the contrary, it suggests that alternative research approaches are needed to find significant and robust evidence of the direction and strength of the effects of these variables on the poor. Other studies have relied on panel regressions which use the information contained in the variation both over time and across countries. These studies have generally also not found significant evidence of links between policy variables and improvements in the relative well-being of the poor, with the possible exception of a significant association with lower inflation (see, for example, Easterly and Fischer, 2001).

1.3.2   Governments' actual behavior

Although simple cross-country regressions do not provide conclusive evidence on the policies that help reduce poverty, it is useful to analyze how governments

Table 1.2 HDI transition matrix[a]

HDI in 1975	Absolute changes in HDI by 1998		
	<0.10	0.10–0.15	0.16–0.20
Low (0–0.5)	Burkina Faso, Burundi, Central African Republic, Dem. Rep. of the Congo, Côte d'Ivoire, Guinea-Bissau, Kenya, Madagascar, Malawi, Niger, Togo, Zambia	Bangladesh, Benin, Botswana, Cameroon, Chad, The Gambia, Ghana, Lesotho, Mali, Mauritania, Nigeria, Papua New Guinea, Senegal, Sudan	Egypt, India, Indonesia, Morocco, Nepal, Pakistan
Medium (0.5–0.7)	Fiji, Guyana, Jamaica, Mexico, Nicaragua, Paraguay, Philippines, South Africa, Zimbabwe	Bolivia, Brazil, Colombia, Dominican Republic, Ecuador, El Salvador, Guatemala, Honduras, Islam Rep. of Iran, Mauritius, Peru, Sri Lanka, Swaziland, Syrian Arab Republic, Thailand, Turkey	Algeria, China, Rep. of Korea, Malaysia, Saudi Arabia, Tunisia
High (0.7–0.8)	Argentina, Costa Rica, Hungary, Panama, Romania, Trinidad and Tobago, United Arab Emirates, Uruguay, Venezuela	Chile, Hong Kong (SAR), Malta	Singapore

Source: UNDP, *Human Development (2000)*.

Note

a Twenty-three industrial countries were excluded from the table because they almost invariably began with very high HDIs in 1975 and tended to have rather small improvements over the following two decades.

Table 1.3 Macroeconomic performance (1975–98)

Rapid change	Average of 1975–98 growth in real GDP per capita[g]	Inflation[h]	Deficit[i] (% of GDP)	Government consumption (% of GDP)[j]	Standard deviation in inflation[k]	Log difference in terms of trade[l]	External debt[m] (% of GDP)	Private capital flow[n] (% of GDP)	Exports and imports (% of GDP)	Openness GDP[po]	Aid[p] (% of GNP)	Rule of law[q]	Black market premium[r]	Percent of years country had crisis[s]
Low HDI														
Slow change in HDI[a]	-0.22	91.50	-4.89	16.17	259.83	-0.33	87.49	2.03	68.21	3.47	13.49	28.80	48.62	44.00
Rapid change in HDI[b]	1.42	13.69	-4.43	12.14	10.81	-0.25	60.74	1.53	47.48	13.07	7.94	34.69	35.35	35.64
Middle HDI														
Slow change in HDI[c]	0.63	151.85	-6.22	13.34	311.63	-0.48	77.18	2.27	66.20	10.73	4.20	40.82	236.99	37.45
Rapid change in HDI[d]	1.85	54.81	-2.56	14.69	179.01	-0.11	45.36	2.92	67.48	28.89	2.56	49.31	103.87	20.24
High HDI														
Slow change in HDI[e]	0.34	82.67	-0.92	13.16	114.53	-0.21	48.77	3.29	63.72	1.66	0.66	59.93	50.98	37.78
Rapid change in HDI[f]	5.34	14.77	1.51	12.04	22.82	-0.51	42.00	6.58	205.77	271.07	0.61	88.64	4.17	7.50

Source: UNDP, *Human Development Report 2000*; World Development Indicators; and International Financial Statistics.

Notes

a Countries in this category include Botswana, Burkina Faso, Burundi, Cameroon, Central African Republic, Congo, Dem. Rep., Côte d'Ivoire, Ghana, Guinea-Bissau, Kenya, Lesotho, Madagascar, Malawi, Mauritania, Niger, Papua New Guinea, Senegal, and Togo.
b Countries include Bangladesh, Benin, Chad, Egypt, Gambia, India, Indonesia, Mali, Morocco, Nepal, Nigeria, Pakistan, and Sudan.
c Countries include Brazil, Colombia, Dominican Republic, Ecuador, El Salvador, Fiji, Guyana, Jamaica, Mauritius, Mexico, Nicaragua, Paraguay, Peru, Philippines, South Africa, Sri Lanka, and Zimbabwe.
d Countries include Algeria, Bolivia, China, Guatemala, Honduras, Iran, Korea, Malaysia, Saudi Arabia, Swaziland, Syrian Arab Republic, Thailand, Tunisia, and Turkey.
e Countries include Argentina, Costa Rica, Hungary, Panama, Romania, Trinidad and Tobago, United Arab Emirates, Uruguay, and Venezuela.
f Countries include Chile, Hong Kong, SAR, Malta, Singapore, and Israel.
g Log difference of real output.
h Percentage change in consumer prices per annum.
i Overall fiscal deficit as a percent of GDP.
j Government consumption spending as a percent of GDP.
k Standard deviation of inflation between 1975 and 1998.
l Log difference in terms of trade between 1975 and 1998.
m External debt as percent of GDP in 1975.
n Private capital flow as a percent of GDP.
o Imports and exports in share of GDP weighted by GDP growth between 1975 and 1998.
p Aid as a percent of GNP.
q Rule of law as defined by Kaufmann *et al* (1999).
r Defined as (parallel exchange rate/official exchange–1)*100.
s Percent of years the country had a financial crisis, during 1970–99.

behave in practice with respect to the policies that are widely believed to help in that regard, especially when they are faced with macroeconomic shocks.

The conventional wisdom is that certain policies, such as fiscal spending on education and health, tend to help the poor.[20] In fact, the international financial institutions have often encouraged countries not to reduce spending on health care and education (at least as a share of total spending, and often also in real per capita terms) at times when fiscal adjustment was needed, and to increase spending on health and education as a share of total spending at times when countries were able to afford increases in overall spending.[21]

This section provides a more detailed, systematic analysis of the composition of large government expenditure cuts (or increases), as an illustration of governments' actual behavior with respect to policies that are believed to affect the poor. Considering 179 countries during 1985–98,[22] there are about 60 (nonoverlapping) instances in which governments cut total spending by more than 5 percentage points over three years. The share of education spending in total spending and the share of health spending in total spending rose in three-quarters of those instances. On average, the share of education spending in total spending increased by 2 percentage points and the share of health-care spending in total spending increased by 1.5 percentage points. (By comparison, the average level of education spending and health spending amounted to 13 and 7 percent, respectively, of total spending during the sample period.) Conversely, the share of education spending in total spending and the share of health spending in total spending declined in about two-thirds of the roughly 30 (nonoverlapping) instances in which governments increased total spending by more than 5 percentage points over three years; in those instances, both education spending and health spending declined, on average, by 1 percentage point of total spending.

These results suggest that spending on health and education is typically more stable than spending on the remaining items in governments' budgets. Therefore, when governments are faced with the need to cut overall spending, the share of education and health spending is far more likely to rise than to decline. In this light, an unchanged share for education and health does not appear to be an especially ambitious target at a time when overall government spending is being cut. Conversely, a decline in the share of education and health spending at a time when overall spending is increasing may partly reflect the more stable nature of these expenditures.

As this simple example illustrates, there seems to be much scope for research on how governments behave in practice with respect to policies that are widely believed to affect the poor, and this line of research may help establish more useful benchmarks in assessing the impact of governments' efforts in reducing poverty.

1.4   Conclusion

On the basis of systematic cross-country studies, the current state of knowledge is that economic growth is associated with improvements in indicators of well-being. However, little has been conclusively proven regarding individual macroeconomic policies that help increase economic growth (given questions about the robustness of many findings), and even less is known about the individual policies that help reduce poverty for a given rate of economic growth. Of course, a wide range of country experiences has made it possible for policy makers to accumulate a certain degree of expertise regarding these issues, the validity of which nevertheless still needs to be confirmed by systematic empirical studies.

This leaves an important and comprehensive research agenda. Further cross-country studies of the types conducted so far appear less likely to yield much value added regarding the effects of macroeconomic policies on poverty. Other issues to be further explored include lags between policy actions and their effects on poverty, and better methods to identify relevant endogenous and exogenous variables. Perhaps the greatest payoff for future research is likely to be obtained through studies based on survey data regarding households or firms for one or a few individual countries, around the time of clearly identifiable macroeconomic shocks. However, while there has been significant progress in recent years, the number of countries for which such reliable surveys are currently available is relatively limited, and continued data collection efforts in this direction may greatly contribute to our knowledge about the links between macroeconomic policies and poverty reduction.

Notes

1 See, for example, Fischer (1993).
2 One mechanism examined in the literature is the relationship between inequality, education, capital markets, and growth (see Banerjee and Newman, 1993; Galor and Zeira, 1993).
3 See Srinivasan (2000) for an assessment of the links between growth, poverty alleviation, and income inequality.
4 There seems to be little systematic work on the differences in the elasticities of the headcount, poverty gap, and squared poverty gap measures with respect to economic growth.
5 Greater trade openness in a number of developing countries has been associated with relative increases in the wages of skilled workers relative to unskilled workers, contrary to what might be expected from the Stolper-Samuelson theory (see, for example, Harrison and Hanson (1999) on Mexico and Beyer *et al.* (1999) on Chile). On trade liberalization and income inequality, see Wood (1997), Morley (1999), and Spilimbergo *et al.* (1999).
6 See Eble and Koeva (2001) for an interesting study of the distributional effects of the Russian crisis.
7 Work by Conway (1994), for example, finds evidence that IMF programs are associated with real depreciation, smaller fiscal imbalances, lower economic growth, and lower public investment. Later work by Dicks-Mireaux *et al.* (2000) finds that IMF lending to low-income countries has raised output growth and improved debt sustainability, yet with no significant effects on inflation. For a more skeptical view, see Przeworski and Vreeland (2000).
8 Earlier work by Pastor (1987) found that the initiation of an IMF program reduced the income share of labor relative to both its preprogram level and in comparison with nonprogram countries. This is indicative of a worsening distribution of income, given that the poor typically possess much labor and little capital.
9 See also the findings of Sahn *et al.* (1996), derived using household survey data on ten African countries during the 1980s. They find that real devaluation, fiscal policy reform, and agricultural market liberalization, which are commonly part of IMF and World Bank adjustment programs, have improved the distribution of income and have not

adversely affected the poor. However, these policies did not result in rapid economic growth, which might have further aided poverty alleviation, due to the poor implementation of adjustment policies.

10 Two points should be noted. First, studies examining reforms and poverty in Africa during the 1980s and early 1990s were limited in scope due to the lack of household survey data. Improvements in data availability for the 1990s are starting to allow more comprehensive analyses (Christiaensen *et al.*, 2000). Second, looking forward, since many African countries have already eliminated large overvaluations of the real exchange rate, it is not clear whether further real depreciation would have a positive impact on their levels of poverty.

11 The HDI ranges between zero (low human development) and one (high human development), and its distribution is non-normal: it is skewed with a relatively long left-sided tail, that is, with the cross-country median HDI exceeding the mean HDI.

12 A potential drawback of the HDI is that it may be positively related to urbanization, as there seems to be an urban bias in the provision of social services. While this is beyond the scope of our study, it may be an interesting avenue for further research.

13 While the HDI measures the overall progress of a country in achieving human development, the HPI focuses on the distribution of that progress. Introduced in the *Human Development Report 1997* (1997), the HPI captures deprivation in three key areas: deprivation in a long and healthy life (as measured by the percentage of people alive today not expected to reach the age 40), deprivation in knowledge (measured by the adult illiteracy rate), and deprivation in economic provisioning (measured by a combination of the percentage of people lacking access to safe water and health services, and the percentage of children under 5 years who are underweight). The HPI is the simple average of these three component indices; see UNDP (2000).

14 The rank correlation (for the 80 developing countries where both indices exist) between the HDI and the HPI for 1998 was extremely high at 0.94.

15 The countries that displayed the greatest improvement in HDI from 1975 to 1998 are from Africa and Asia: Nepal (by 63 percent), Mali (53 percent), Pakistan (48 percent), the Gambia (47 percent), and Chad (45 percent). The countries with the least improvement were Guyana (5 percent), Democratic Republic of the Congo (3 percent), Romania (3 percent), and Zambia (−5 percent).

16 As expected, improvements in HDI are found to be strongly and positively correlated with per capita income growth, though this is largely the result of the inclusion of per capita income as one of the components of the HDI.

17 Robust evidence is obtained when a variable is significant in a battery of regressions that include several combinations of other potential explanatory variables.

18 See Agénor (1999) for cross-country regressions linking macroeconomic variables and poverty rates, while controlling for GDP growth.

19 Therefore, our approach was to regress the improvement in the HDI on initial HDI, per capita GDP growth, and average economic policies during the period, and to repeat the exercise using infant mortality and life expectancy instead of the HDI.

20 See, for example, Gupta *et al.* (1999).

21 While the international institutions have typically encouraged countries to preserve the share of spending on health and education, this has not been a condition for IMF loans. Consistent with this absence of conditionality, the results presented in this chapter are similar if the sample is restricted to those instances involving IMF-supported programs.

22 The data were drawn from the Expenditure Policy Division in the IMF's Fiscal Affairs Department.

References

Agénor, Pierre-Richard. 1999. *Stabilization Policies, Poverty and the Labor Market – Analytical Issues and Empirical Evidence*. Mimeo. Washington, DC: World Bank, September.

Anand, S. and R. Kanbur. 1993. Inequality and Development: A Critique. *Journal of Development Economics*, 41: 19–43.

Baldacci, Emanuele, Luiz de Mello, and Gabriela Inchauste. 2001. Financial Crises, Poverty, and Income Distribution. Paper presented at the IMF Workshop on Macroeconomic Policies and Poverty Reduction. April.

Banerjee, Abhijit and Andrew Newman. 1993. Occupational Choice and the Process of Development. *Journal of Political Economy*, 101: 274–98, April.

—— and Esther Duflo. 1999. *Inequality and Growth: What Can the Data Say?* Mimeo. Cambridge, MA: Massachusetts Institute of Technology.

Bannister, Geoffrey and Kamau Thugge. 2001. International Trade and Poverty Alleviation. IMF Working Paper 01/54, Washington, DC: IMF.

Barro, Robert. 2000. Inequality and Growth in a Panel of Countries. *Journal of Economic Growth*, 5: 5–32, March.

Beyer, Harald, Patricio Rojas, and Rodrigo Vergara. 1999. Trade Liberalization and Wage Inequality. *Journal of Development Economics* 59: 103–23.

Bourguignon, François, Albert R. Berry, and Christian Morrison. 1981. *The World Distribution of Incomes Between 1950 and 1977*. Paris: Ecole Normale Supérieure.

Bruno, Michael, Martin Ravallion, and Lyn Squire. 1998. Equity and Growth in Developing Countries: Old and New Perspectives on the Policy Issues. In *Income Distribution and High-Quality Growth*, edited by Vito Tanzi and Ke-young Chu. Cambridge, MA: Massachusetts Institute of Technology.

Bulír, Alec. 1998 Income Inequality: Does Inflation Matter? IMF Working Paper No. 98/7. Washington, DC: International Monetary Fund.

Cardoso, Eliana. 1992. Inflation and Poverty. NBER Working Paper No. 4006. Cambridge, MA: NBER.

Christiaensen, Luc, Lionel Demery, and Stefano Paternostro. 2000. *Reforms, Recovery and Poverty Reduction in Africa: Messages from the 1990s*. Mimeo. Washington, DC: World Bank, December.

Conway, Patrick. 1994. IMF Lending Programs: Participation and Impact. *Journal of Development Economics* 45: 365–91.

Datt, Gaurav and Martin Ravallion. 1998. Farm Productivity and Rural Poverty in India. *Journal of Development Studies* 34: 62–85. United Kingdom.

Deininger, Klaus and Lyn Squire. 1998. New Ways of Looking at Old Issues: Inequality and Growth. *Journal of Development Economics*, 57: 259–87.

Demery, Lionel and Lyn Squire. 1996. Macroeconomic Adjustment and Poverty in Africa: An Emerging Picture. *World Bank Research Observer* 11 Washington, DC: World Bank.

Devarajan, Shantayanan and Dominique van der Mensbrugghe. 2000. Trade Reform in South Africa: Impacts on Households. Paper presented at the conference on Poverty and the International Economy, sponsored by the World Bank and the Parliamentary Commission on Swedish Policy for Global Development, Stockholm, October.

Dicks-Mireaux, Louis, Mauro Mecagni, and Susan Schadler. 2000. Evaluating the Effect of IMF Lending to Low-Income Countries. *Journal of Development Economics*, 61: 495–526.

Dollar, David and Aart Kraay. 2000. Growth Is Good for the Poor. Working Paper. Washington, DC: World Bank.

Easterly, William. 2000. *The Effects of IMF and World Bank Programs on Poverty*. Mimeo. Washington, DC: World Bank.

—— and Stanley Fischer. 2001. Inflation and the Poor. *Journal of Money, Credit and Banking*, 32: 485–512.

Eble, Stephanie and Petya Koeva. 2001. The Distributional Effects of Macroeconomic Crises: Microeconomic Evidence from Russia. Paper pesented at the IMF Workshop on Macroeconomic Policies and Poverty Reduction. April.

Ferreira, Francisco, Giovanna Prennushi, and Martin Ravallion. 1999. Protecting the Poor from Macroeconomic Shocks: An Agenda for Action in a Crisis and Beyond. Unpublished. Washington, DC: World Bank.

Fischer, Stanley. 1993. Role of Macroeconomic Factors in Growth. *Journal of Monetary Economics*, 32: 485–512.

Forbes, Kristin. 2000. A Reassessment of the Relationship between Inequality and Economic Growth. *American Economic Review*, 90(4): 869–87.

Friedman, Jed. 2000. Differential Impacts of Trade Liberalization on Indonesia's Poor and Non-Poor. Paper presented at the conference on Poverty and the International Economy, sponsored by the World Bank and the Parliamentary Commission on Swedish Policy for Global Development. Stockholm.

Galor, Oded and Joseph Zeira. 1993. Income Distribution and Macroeconomics. *Review of Economic Studies*, 60(January): 35–52.

Garuda, Gopal. 2000. The Distributional Effects of IMF Programs: A Cross-Country Analysis. *World Development*, 28: 1031–51.

Gupta, Sanjeev, Benedict Clements, Calvin McDonald, and Christian Schiller. 1998. *The IMF and the Poor* 52. Pamphlet Series. Washington, DC: International Monetary Fund.

Gupta, Sanjeev, Marijn Verhoeven, and Erwin Tiongson. 1999. Does Higher Government Spending Buy Better Results in Education and Health Care? IMF Working Paper 99/21. Washington, DC: International Monetary Fund.

Hamner, Lucia and Felix Naschold. 2000. Attaining the International Development Targets: Will Growth be Enough, *Development Policy Review*, 18: 11–36.

Harrison, Ann and Gordon Hanson. 1999. Who Gains from Trade Reform? Some Remaining Puzzles. *Journal of Development Economics*, 59: 125–154.

IMF. 1986. *Fund-Supported Programs, Fiscal Policy and Income Distribution*. IMF Occasional Paper 46. Washington, DC: International Monetary Fund.

—— 2000. *World Economic Outlook, May 2000*. Washington, DC: International Monetary Fund.

Kanbur, Ravi and Nora Lustig. 1999. Why is Inequality Back on the Agenda? Annual World Bank Conference on Development Economics. 1999(2000), pp. 285–306. Washington, DC: World Bank.

Kruger, D. 2000. Redistribution Effects of Agricultural Incentives Policies in Nicaragua. background paper for the Nicaragua Poverty Assessment. 2000. College Park, MD: University of Maryland.

Levine, Ross and David Renelt. 1992. Sensitivity Analysis of Cross-Country Growth Regressions. *American Economic Review*, 82: 942–63.

Li, H., L. Squire, and H.F. Zou. 1998. Explaining International Inequality and Intertemporal Variations in Income Inequality. *Economic Journal*, 108: 26–43.

Lipton, Michael and Martin Ravallion. 1995. Poverty and Policy. In *Handbook of Development Economics, Volume II*, edited by J. Behrman and T. N. Srinivasan. Amsterdam: Elsevier Science.

Lustig, Nora. 1999. Crises and the Poor: Socially Responsible Macroeconomics. Paper. Presidential Address. Fourth Annual Meeting of the Latin American and Caribbean Economic Association (LACEA. Santiago, Chile).

Morley, S. 1999. Impact of Reforms on Equity in Latin America. Background Paper for the *World Development Report, 2000/2001*. Washington, DC: World Bank.

Pastor, M. 1987. The Effects of IMF Programs in the Third World: Debate and Evidence from Latin America. *World Development*, 15: 249–62.

Perotti, Roberto 1996. Growth, Income Distribution, and Democracy: What the Data Say? *Journal of Economic Growth*, 1(2): 149–87, June.

Przeworski, Adam and James Raymond Vreeland. 2000. The Effect of IMF Programs on Economic Growth. *Journal of Development Economics*, 62(2): 385–421.

Ravallion, Martin. 1995. Growth and Poverty: Evidence for the Developing World. *Economics Letters*, 48: 411–17. July.

—— 1997. Can High-Inequality Developing Countries Escape Absolute Poverty? *Economics Letters*, 56: 51–7.

—— and Shaohua Chen. 1997. What Can New Survey Data Tell us about Recent Changes in Distribution and Poverty? *Economic Review*, 11(2): 357–82.

Roemer, Michael and Mary Kay Gugerty. 1997. Does Economic Growth Reduce Poverty? Technical Paper. Cambridge, MA: Harvard Institute for International Development.

Romer, Christina D. and David H. Romer. 1998. Monetary Policy and the Well-Being of the Poor. NBER Working Paper 6793. Cambridge, MA: NBER.

Sahn, David, Paul Dorosh, and Stephen Younger. 1996. Exchange Rate, Fiscal and Agricultural Policies in Africa: Does Adjustment Hurt the Poor. *World Development*, 24: 719–47.

Spilimbergo, Antonio, Juan Luis Londoño, and Miguel Székely. 1999. Income Distribution, Factor Endowments, and Trade Openness. *Journal of Development Economics*, 59: 77–101.

Srinivasan, T.N. 2000. *Growth and Poverty Alleviation: Lessons from Development Experience*. Mimeo. New Haven, CT: Yale University.

Thorbecke, Erik and Hong-Sang Jung. 1996. A Multiplier Decomposition Method to Analyze Poverty Alleviation. *Journal of Development Economics*, 48: 279–300.

Timmer, C. Peter. 1997. How Well Do the Poor Connect to the Growth Process? Unpublished. Harvard Institute for International Development.

UNDP United Nations Development Program. 2000. *Human Development Report 2000*, New York: Oxford University Press.

—— 1997. *Human Development Report*. 1997. New York: Oxford University Press.

Winters, Allan L. 2000. Trade, Trade Policy and Poverty: What are the Links? CEPR Discussion Paper 2382 (London: C.E.P.R).

—— 2002. Trade Liberalization and Poverty: What are the Links? *World Economy*, 25(9): 1339–67

Wood, A. 1997. Openness and Wage Inequality in Developing Countries: The Latin American Challenge to East Asian Conventional Wisdom. *The World Bank Economic Review*, 11(1): 33–57.

World Bank. 2000. *World Development Report 2000/1*. Washington, DC: World Bank.

2 Evaluating the poverty impact of economic policies

Some analytical challenges

*François Bourguignon, Luiz A. Pereira da Silva, and Nicholas Stern**

This chapter reports on and synthesizes recent approaches to evaluating the distributional and poverty impact of policy measures and economic shocks. A three-layer methodology is proposed. The bottom layer consists of a micro-simulation module based on household micro data that permits analyzing the distributional incidence of changes in prices, factor, rewards, and possibly employment levels in the labor market. The top layer includes aggregate macro-modeling tools that permit evaluating the impact of exogenous shocks and policies on aggregates such as GDP, the general price level, and the exchange rate. The intermediate layer consists of tools that allow disaggregating the predictions obtained with the top layer into various sectors of activity and various factors of production. These three layers must communicate with each other in a consistent way. Given the challenge in operationalizing this approach, the chapter proposes an eclectic use of tools in each layer to suit the situation at hand.

2.1 Introduction and motivation

Accounting for the effects of economic policy on the distribution of welfare among individuals and households has long been on the agenda of economists. However, doing this satisfactorily has proved difficult. Progress in micro- and macroeconomic analytical techniques and the increasing availability of micro-economic household data are making things easier. At the same time, the ongoing debate on distribution, poverty, and the social effects of globalization has empha-sized the issue as a practical operational objective for national governments, multilateral, and other aid agencies.

Poverty-reduction strategies suggest the need for all economic policy choices to be evaluated *ex ante* and monitored *ex post* for their impact on poverty and dis-tribution.[1] When redistribution and anti-poverty policies consist of cash transfers allocated according to some pre-specified rules, evaluating their impact on the distribution of living standards and poverty might seem straightforward. It seems sufficient to apply the transfer rules to a representative sample of households. This is the essence of "incidence analysis" and micro-simulation techniques used in many countries. In practice, however, things are not so easy. In reality, (a) cash transfers are likely to modify behavior, which in turn can generate economy-wide changes through general equilibrium effects; (b) in most developing countries, transfers are made only indirectly, through public spending or indirect taxation, with allocation rules that are often far from being transparent and may themselves depend on behavior; and (c) the implementation of transfers may be partial or distorted. More fundamentally, poverty-reduction policies are often implemented through both macroeconomic and structural instruments aimed at enhancing economic activity and growth. The actual change in individuals' standard of living generated by these instruments is not easy to work out because of the fundamental difficulty of establishing satisfactory linkages between micro and macro analysis, whether the latter refers to aggregate demand, medium-run growth, or general equilibrium in a somewhat disaggregated framework.

This chapter reviews some of the methods and tools currently available to evaluate the impact of economic policies on poverty reduction and the distribution of living standards, and explores directions for improvement. The discussion refers to ongoing case studies and research where new tools are being tested though the focus is mainly on techniques that are robust and widely (or increasingly) used by academics and policy analysts. In fact, this chapter can be considered as a methodological introduction, or "toolkit" summary of methods for evaluating the distributional and poverty impact of economic policies (see Bourguignon and Pereira da Silva, 2003). The chapter is organized around the common thread of "incidence analysis." But here, incidence analysis is used in a variety of ways, enabling the evaluation of a wide range of policies with a potential impact on poverty. In particular, the chapter covers indirect taxation and subsidies, public spending programs at national and local levels (from *ex ante* and *ex post* points of view), and macroeconomic policies, during periods of either steady growth or crisis. By suggesting that incidence analysis can also be applied to samples of firms, we also touch upon the role of institutions and, more generally, on policies aimed at improving the investment climate.

Indeed, a major and recent advance in approaches to development policies is a systematic focus on how these policies affect poverty and distribution. To be fair, economic development has always been more or less concerned with growth and distribution issues, but not so prominently as today. This new approach can be illustrated in many ways, particularly by the emergence of a set of multiple development goals that explicitly go beyond the narrow focus on aggregate output maximization. For instance the Millennium Development Goals, as addressed in national Poverty Reduction Strategy Papers (PRSPs[2]), are the cornerstone of concessional lending by International Financial Institutions (IFIs) to low-income countries. PRSPs are explicitly geared toward reducing poverty and meeting several social goals rather than only maximizing GDP growth. By definition then, PRSPs require "poverty and distributional analysis" of specified recommended economic policies and strategies. Even though these objectives are usually complements, they may produce trade-offs (e.g. if the pace of growth has some influence on the distribution of economic and social welfare and vice-versa). The demand for this change in focus is urgent, and the need for more distributional analysis comes from practically all quarters: civil society, national governments, nongovernmental organizations (NGOs), bilateral aid agencies, international development agencies, and IFIs.

Practically, most questions being asked fall in the following categories:

1   Changes in size and structure of public spending.
2   Changes in taxation.
3   Structural reforms such as trade policy, privatization, agricultural liberalization, and price decontrol.
4   Changes in the macro framework such as the fiscal, inflation, and exchange rate targets.
5   Exogenous shocks such as trade shocks, capital flows volatility, changes in foreign aid, and foreign payment crises.

These groups of issues are associated with different perspectives on poverty reduction. The first two categories are of a micro-economic nature and call directly for standard incidence analysis of public spending and taxation. The following three questions refer to three kinds of macro policies. The first macro policy is concerned with policy-induced changes in the structure of the economy, either in terms of sectoral activity as with trade or price policies or in terms of firms' ownership (private versus public). The second macro policy has to do with the management of aggregate demand and macro-economic balances. It includes target setting for the main macro instruments as well as the analysis of various types of shocks and the best way to cope with them. The third macro policy is more dynamic and essentially refers to policies aimed at enhancing private investment and growth.

Let us recognize upfront that we are not well equipped to deal with many of the distributional and poverty consequences of the preceding policies. The situation is slightly better for micro-oriented issues – that is, public spending and taxation. There, incidence analysis based on micro-economic data sets is a useful first approach. Several necessary extensions of this technique are presently being investigated and they are reviewed in the first half of this chapter. Things are not as good for macro policies and the second half of the present chapter explores various ways for generalizing micro-based standard incidence analysis to the study of macro policy issues.

In a nutshell, this chapter proposes a three-layer methodology for evaluating the poverty effect of macro-economic policies. The bottom layer consists of a micro-simulation module based on household micro data that permits analyzing the distributional incidence of changes in prices, factor rewards, and possibly employment levels in the labor market. The top layer includes aggregate macro-modeling tools that permit evaluating the impact of exogenous shocks and policies on aggregates like GDP, its components, the general price level, the exchange rate, the rate of interest and the like, either in the short-run or in a long-run growth perspective. The intermediate layer consists of tools that allow disaggregating the predictions obtained with the top layer into various sectors of activity and various factors of production. These three layers should communicate with each other in a consistent way. In view of the analytical difficulty of elaborating the corresponding links, this chapter essentially concentrates on simple mostly sequential top-down integration methods.

2.2 Evaluation of micro-economic policies: incidence analysis of public spending and taxation

2.2.1 *"Standard" micro-economic incidence analysis*

Micro-economic incidence analysis is often used to answer the first question in our list ("What is the poverty-impact of specific changes in the delivery of public services, especially for health and education"). One practical application of this class of analytical techniques is "Benefit Incidence Analysis" (BIA). Pioneering work in developing countries goes back to Meerman (1979) on Malaysia and Selowski (1979) on Colombia. Modern versions of such models include some chapters in van de Walle and Nead (1995), Sahn and Younger (1999) on Africa, Demery (2000), and Younger (2002). The basic idea is to impute as a "benefit accruing" to an individual, a household, or possibly a group of households, the cost of the public provision of a given service on the basis of the consumption or access to those services, as they are observed in conventional or specifically designed household surveys (see Box 2.1).

Box 2.1 Standard BIA (Demery, 2000)

Consider the benefit incidence of public spending on a particular government service – say education. The total incidence of public spending on one group (the poorest income group, the urban population, or the female population) depends on two factors: the use of publicly funded services by that group and the distribution of government spending among various services – benefit incidence will be greater as the government spends more on the services used relatively more by the group. To show this result formally, consider the group-specific benefit incidence of government spending on education:

$$X_j \equiv \sum_{i=1}^{3} E_{ij} \frac{S_i}{E_i} \equiv \sum_{i=1}^{3} \frac{E_{ij}}{E_i} S_i \tag{1}$$

X_j is the value of the total education subsidy imputed to group j. E_{ij} represents the number of school enrollments of group j at education level i, and E_i the total number of enrollments (across all groups) at that level. S_i is government *net* spending on education level i (with fees and other cost recovery netted out), and i (= 1,...,3) denotes the level of education (primary, secondary, and tertiary). Note that S_i/E_i is the unit subsidy of providing a school place at level i. Equation (1) assumes that this subsidy only varies by level of schooling and not across groups. Commonly, government subsidies for services vary significantly by region. Services typically attract higher subsidies in urban than in rural areas. And services are often better financed in the capital city than in other urban areas. These variations in unit subsidies lead to inequalities in the distribution of benefits which should be captured in the analysis. If data permit, benefit incidence involves the estimation of:

$$X_j \equiv \sum_{k=1}^{n} \sum_{i=1}^{3} \frac{E_{ijk}}{E_i} S_{ik} \tag{1a}$$

where the k subscript denotes the region specified in the unit cost estimate, there being n regions distinguished. The *share* of the total education subsidy (S) accruing to the group is given by:

$$x_j \equiv \sum_{k=1}^{n} \sum_{i=1}^{3} \frac{E_{ijk}}{E_i} \left(\frac{S_{ik}}{S}\right) \cong \sum_{k=1}^{n} \sum_{i=1}^{3} e_{ijk} s_{ik} \tag{2}$$

Clearly, this share (and indeed overall inequality in benefit incidence) is determined by two factors: the share of the group in total enrollments at each level of education and in each region (e_{ijk}), and the share of each level of education and region in total education spending (s_{ik}). The e's reflect household enrollment decisions, whereas the s's reflect government spending allocations across regions and levels of schooling. The e and s variables can be defined also for other sectors, so that for health, e_{ij} would represent the share of group j in the total visits to health facility i. And s_i would be the share of total government net spending on health facility i (e.g. primary health clinics).

It is now common to have incidence analysis being conducted at the individual level on the basis of the information available in household surveys. In that case, x_j here would represent the share of individual j in total spending. The concentration curve shown in Figure 2.1 plots the cumulative of x_j against j when all households are ranked by increasing welfare – for example, income per capita. The concentration curve for total spending I – that is, all educational levels in the example here is the sum of the concentration curves for the various individual services – primary, secondary, university.

The BIA involves three steps. First, one has to get estimates of the unit cost of providing a particular service (e.g. education or health). These estimates are usually based on officially reported public spending and the number of users of the service in question. Second, this unit cost is "imputed" as a subsidy to households or individuals which are identified as users of the service, for instance households with children in school, or households whose members visit a health facility, or have access at a reasonably low (or no) cost to facilities such as clinics, family planning, or subsidized piped water. Individuals who use all these subsidized public services are assumed to benefit from an in-kind transfer, even though the actual value they give to this transfer – or their "willingness to pay" for it – may differ among them and may differ from the unit cost faced by service providers. The BIA measures the distribution of this transfer across the population. The third step involves comparing this gain with other dimensions of individual or household welfare, so as to evaluate the redistributive role of the public expenditure under analysis – irrespective of the way it is financed. The most common practice consists of ranking individuals or households by income or expenditure per capita and to examine the share of public expenditures accruing to households below some rank. An example of the resulting "concentration curve" of public education in Indonesia is given in Figure 2.1. Other breakdowns than income are of course worth analyzing.

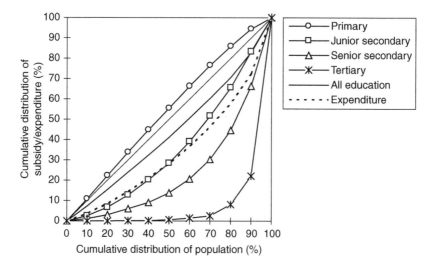

Figure 2.1 Indonesia, benefit incidence of education spending, 1989 (from World Bank (1993) *Indonesia: Public Expenditures, Prices and the Poor*. Volume 1, Country Department III, East Asia and Pacific Region, Sector Report No. 11293-IND, Washington DC (August 31)).

Notes
Benefit incidence results can readily be portrayed in graphic form (Figure 2.1). Tracking the cumulative distribution of total household expenditures against the cumulative population ranked by per capita expenditures gives the expenditure *Lorenz curve*. Such a curve for Indonesia is shown as a dotted line in Figure 2.1. This provides a point of comparison with which to judge the distribution of education spending in Indonesia. The concentration of educational spending by income level is shown in the other curves of Figure 2.1. These graphics convey some important messages. First, compare the concentration curves with the 45° diagonal. If the curve lies above the diagonal, it means that the poorest (say) quintile gains more than 20 percent of the total subsidy (and the richest quintile, less than 20 percent). Such a redistribution is clearly progressive. Second, comparisons may be made with the Lorenz curve (for expenditure or income). Concentration curves lying above the Lorenz curve (and below the 45° diagonal) are progressive relative to income (or expenditure in this case). If beneficiaries were given monetary transfers instead of the in-kind transfer, the distribution of money income would become more equitable. Concentration curves lying below the Lorenz distribution indicate regressive transfers. From Figure 2.1 it is clear that the primary school subsidy was progressive in absolute terms, the concentration curve lying above the diagonal. The senior secondary and tertiary subsidies were regressive (below the Lorenz curve). The overall education subsidy was relatively progressive (lying between the diagonal and the Lorenz curve).

Examining the share of public expenditures or the proportion of people accessing a given service by region or ethnic groups informs on other dimensions of the redistribution taking place through that particular expenditure or service.

In principle, the same kind of imputation methodology at the household level could be used to answer the second question in our list. ("How can the financial and administrative burden of taxation on poor people be reduced?") Knowing how much income a household earns from various sources, or how much it spends on different goods, it would seem easy a priori to compute how much income tax is due – for the richest households, of course – or how much indirect taxes is paid through observed expenditures. In many developed countries, so-called tax-benefit models are actually doing precisely this. They simply apply the official rules for calculating income-related taxes and cash transfers to each household or individuals in a micro data base, thus allowing the evaluation of the "direct" redistributive impact of the tax-benefit system. Such tax-benefit models would probably be useful too in some developing countries where income-related taxes and cash transfers have some importance.[3] In many other countries, however, this represents only a tiny part of the redistribution system, the bulk of taxation being essentially indirect.

In the presence of indirect taxation and tariffs, the simple calculation referred to earlier requires first to figure out the way in which these instruments will modify the prices of the goods consumed by households. Then, observing sufficiently disaggregated budget shares in household budget surveys, it becomes possible to evaluate the distributive impact of indirect taxation. Ahmad and Stern were among the first to run this type of calculation in the case of developing countries and to analyze indirect tax reforms that would contribute to increasing social welfare (see Box 2.2). For a synthesis of their work on India, see Ahmad and Stern (1991).

Box 2.2 Indirect tax incidence analysis (see Ahmad and Stern (1987), in
Newbery and Stern (1987))

In many developing countries, governments have sought to reform their tax system to increase its yield and minimize distortions for producers and consumers. One common move is to shift from direct taxation of imports using tariffs to indirect taxation. Another type of reform consists in replacing a multitude of direct and indirect taxes on consumption by a simple proportional value-added tax (VAT). What would be the effect of these tax reforms on the poor? Ahmad and Stern (1987) use Indian data for the year 1979–80, to analyze the effect of replacing all taxes and subsidies with a proportional VAT. If total indirect taxes represent 8.3 percent of total consumer expenditure, the proportional VAT rate would be 8.3 percent of the tax-inclusive price of all goods. Such a non-marginal reform in prices, however, can be expected to trigger changes – through demand responses – in commodities consumed. But a proportional tax allows one to estimate revenue from total expenditure – assumed unchanged – without any specific assumption on commodities consumed and raises exactly the required revenue. Ahmad and Stern estimate the welfare equivalent variation of expenditures – for each per capita expenditure group, rural, and urban. They find (see the given table) that switching to a VAT would be equivalent to reducing the real expenditures of the poorest rural households by as much as 6.8 percent and increasing those of the richest rural households by more than 3 percent. For urban groups, the poorest are also most affected. There are a number of refinements to the analysis. For example, the treatment of cash-and-kind consumption would lead to a lower estimate of losses for poor rural households, but overall, there would still be losses.

Equivalent variations of expenditures by population group for proportional value added

Group	Percent of the population	Per capita expend. rupees/month (1)	Equivalent variation of expend. (2)	Percent (2)/(1)
Rural				
1	0.28	17.09	−1.142	−0.067
2	0.3	22.63	−1.531	−0.068
3	0.92	27.19	−1.851	−0.068
4	1.68	31.81	−1.674	−0.053
5	2.42	35.14	−1.843	−0.052
6	4.63	42.1	−2.196	−0.052
7	9.34	49.94	−1.002	−0.020
8	15.07	62.07	−1.85	−0.030
9	15.84	78.53	−0.393	−0.005
10	14.6	102.84	−0.247	−0.002
11	7.01	137.93	3.166	0.023
12	3.68	192.92	5.249	0.027
13	0.71	274.69	8.348	0.030
14	0.43	460.15	15.932	0.035
Urban				
1	0.01	13.7	−0.663	−0.048
2	0.03	22.25	−1.094	−0.049
3	0.07	27.51	−0.945	−0.034
4	0.12	31.63	−1.071	−0.034
5	0.3	36.82	−1.229	−0.033
6	0.69	42.36	−0.645	−0.015
7	1.64	50.43	−0.708	−0.014
8	3.45	62.28	−0.8	−0.013
9	4.46	79.08	0.819	0.010
10	5.23	103.5	1.318	0.013
11	3.34	138.84	4.621	0.033
12	2.32	195.1	7.167	0.037
13	0.76	277.15	10.879	0.039
14	0.57	464	19.334	0.042

Source: Ahmad and Stern (1987).

A difficulty that arises when dealing with the incidence of indirect taxation, including tariffs and possibly non-tariff barriers to trade, is how to identify the effect of changing indirect tax rates on the prices faced by households, when they are considered as pure consumers. The calculation is not too difficult in an economy where it can be safely assumed that all firms producing the same goods are subject to the same tax rate and that perfect competition applies. Input–output techniques are available to do this.[4] Things are more complicated when different producers do not face the same rate – as it is the case when comparing formal and informal production units – or when the geographical origin of the goods matter – as with import tariffs. In those cases, complete multi-sector models of the economy must be designed, at a disaggregated macro level, to represent the way in which changes in the indirect tax and tariff system will ultimately result in changes in the consumer prices faced by households. In other words, a "macro" incidence analysis has to be performed prior to the arithmetic standard incidence analysis based on micro-household data. This is particularly true when analyzing the impact of comprehensive tax reforms rather than concentrating on the static incidence of changes in tax rates within a given tax system.

2.2.2   Limitations of the "standard" incidence analysis

The preceding argument suggests that standard BIA cannot really be conducted in isolation from a macro-economic framework when applied to taxation, which somehow seemed to constitute its strength (e.g. as a "stand-alone" analysis). Yet, it has other weaknesses which are not always related to the lack of a macro-economic framework. They are listed later, before we consider ways to overcome them.

A first shortcoming of BIA applied to public expenditures is that it focuses on the "average" (*ex post*) incidence of all expenditures at a given point in time rather than the "marginal (*ex ante*) incidence" of a policy that would consist in increasing expenditures on a service and/or the coverage of that service. In effect, the latter policy option may be of more relevance for policy makers and requires other types of instruments. For example, *ex ante* instruments predicting who will be benefiting from some planned expansion of expenditures on a given service, or *ex post* instruments showing who actually benefited from the expansion that took place. Duclos *et al.* (2001) is right in noting that the "standard" incidence analysis gives information on the marginal incidence only in the case where the expansion of expenditures consists of improving the quality of the service uniformly for all initial users, with absolutely no change in the identity of users. This is, however, a restrictive assumption.

A second serious related drawback is that the standard "average" BIA, and even a marginal incidence analysis that would simply simulate the change in the identity of users, assumes no behavioral response from recipients of subsidies. This shortcoming may also apply to taxation incidence analysis. Two examples will show the nature of the problem. First, say that the government spends more on primary schooling. The standard incidence analysis will say that all users will get more than before. If behavioral response is taken into account, however, one may expect that a better quality of primary education will attract new users, so that the increase in quality will not be as big as if the number of users had remained the same. Behavioral response to changes in the quality and availability of public services is clearly crucial. Second, in the case of a reform of indirect taxation that is reasonably small, it is well known that the change in the welfare of a household may be approximated by the change in the cost of its initial consumption basket arising from induced changes in consumer prices.[5] Actually, households will react to these price changes by moving away from the goods which became relatively more expensive. Knowing this reaction is not necessary for evaluating the welfare gain of the reform, but it is indeed needed to evaluate the change in the public budget or to design reforms which are budget neutral. In those two cases, simply imputing a change of prices to the users of a public service or to the consumers of particular goods is not enough. It is also necessary to know how this change will modify the consumption made of the service or the goods.

Other difficulties in standard incidence analysis, that are often combined with the previous ones, must be noted. For instance, inter-generational aspects of public expenditures aimed at building up human capital are important. In the presence of liquidity constraints and imperfect capital markets, improving the human capital of children through improved schooling or health services cannot be considered as a gain for the parents. Incidence must be evaluated separately for the generation of parents and that of children. In other words, (marginal) incidence analysis needs to be dynamic rather than static. Another (possibly related) difficulty is that traditional incidence analysis uses a single welfare index that is commensurate to income – so that income and the unit cost of schooling, health services, or infrastructure may be conveniently added together and lumped into income redistribution analysis. Instead of this, one might also consider that welfare and poverty are multi-dimensional concepts, so that education, health, or a better quality of life might be valued *per se*, independently of their monetary value.[6]

Some of these difficulties are related again to the absence of a link with a macro-economic framework. First, considering public spending and funding – that is, taxation – independently of each other may often be impossible. For the reason alluded to here in the case of taxation incidence, some kind of macro framework may be needed to understand how tax reforms may translate into changes in consumer prices. But issues go much further than that. A tax or a tariff reform is likely to change, not only consumer, but also producer prices, wages, and profit rates – unless some specific neutrality conditions are met. Therefore, the redistribution that goes through a reform of tariffs and indirect taxation is, under rather general conditions, most likely to go as much through changing the structure of household incomes as through changing the prices they face as consumers. If this is the case, then, clearly redistribution incidence analysis requires a full macro-economic framework that will help figuring out the way in which the structural changes in the economy brought about by an indirect tax or an import tariff reform will map into the household incomes and their distribution. Somehow, standard average or marginal incidence analysis of public expenditures are based upon the assumption that the funding comes from a fully neutral proportional tax on all income sources – or on all uses of income[7] – or from reducing public spending, under the assumption that this reduction too has no effect on the economy. This may not always be satisfactory, unless it is known that taken altogether, the tax system and some components of public spending are not far from this neutrality property.[8]

But of course, one can (and perhaps should) expect sizable macro-economic consequences, not only from tax reforms, but also from some public spending programs. Large public programs in education, health, or infra-structure may affect the equilibrium and the structure of the economy at the time they are undertaken – through increased demand on specific factors or types of labor, also in the future by changing the relative factor endowments of the economy and therefore the distribution of income and poverty. For instance, it seems relevant to ask oneself whether an ambitious schooling program undertaken today might lead after some years to a change in the structure of earnings – unless this program is accompanied by or generates itself changes in labor demand that will preserve the existing earning structure. This kind of concern should in theory be included in incidence analysis, but this requires an interaction with macro-economic modeling. As another example, the incidence of a decision to raise the minimum wage motivated by "redistributive" considerations will not only affect the labor market but may lead to non-neutral fiscal effects through the civil service pension fund.

2.2.3   Recent developments and directions for improvement

The most obvious drawbacks of average incidence analysis of public expenditures, and to a lesser extent taxation, are well understood. Policy makers are aware of the need to adopt a marginal incidence view, that is, to concentrate on the effects of additional expenditures or taxation, and at the same time to take into account behavioral responses to the price or the availability of services and to taxation. Several techniques are being developed to meet their demand. They mostly differ by whether they consider the issue of incidence *ex ante* or *ex post*, that when evaluating a reform before or after it is undertaken.

2.2.4   Ex ante *evaluation of changes in the accessibility of public services and the need for geographical mapping techniques*

Following the simplest approach alluded to here that consists of measuring the incidence of public services by their accessibility in the population, a simple tool would be to combine information in household surveys about actual access to these services and their planned geographic expansion. Ideally, it would then be possible to see how the concentration curve of the access to some specific service could be modified by the geographical expansion of that service, and therefore the pro-poor bias of such a policy.

In practice, this is a difficult task if one has to rely exclusively on household surveys. Their geographical coverage is often limited because of sample size and clustering techniques. In other words, using the tax-benefit models arithmetical framework mentioned earlier to simulate the marginal impact of such policies is likely not to be feasible. Alternatives must be found.

An increasingly used alternative consists in extending the techniques of "poverty mapping" – that is, "census/survey matching" – that allows estimating the mean and the distribution of household characteristics usually not observed in censuses at the level of local communities, provided of course they contain a sufficient population. In other words, the distribution of income and poverty may not be observed in municipalities and rural districts in the census, but it may be inferred from "matching" the census' information with that information in a household survey where income data are observed. Once this is done, it is sufficient to have at one's disposal the map of the accessibility of public services in the country and the way this map is to be modified by policy reform to perform both standard and marginal incidence analysis at the level of the whole country.[9] To some extent this is equivalent to superimposing poverty maps and maps describing the access to education, health facilities, or some specific infrastructure.

Experiences with this type of methodology suggest that one can draw rather accurate maps describing poverty and other socio-economic attributes of the population. These maps may be of considerable value to governments, NGOs, and multilateral institutions interested in strengthening the poverty alleviation impact of their spending, as long, of course, as the same degree of detail may be used in evaluating or designing reforms in the geographical allocation of public spending.

The design of country-wide – or possibly city-wide – poverty maps is now well established and a summary of the methodology can be found in Elbers *et al.* (2001). Superimposing poverty maps and public spending maps – on average or marginal terms – is currently underway. But much remains to be done to encourage further the use of these techniques and to have them applied to all dimensions of public spending – education at various levels, different types of health services, infrastructure, etc. In this respect, it is worth noting that the constraints in building these superimposed maps may not be so much a question of matching censuses with surveys. The difficulty may be to have all the necessary details on the effective geographical allocation of spending – taking into account possible discrepancies between centrally planned and locally effective spending.

2.2.5 Ex ante *marginal incidence analysis and micro-simulation techniques*

That households have access to a particular service does not guarantee that they are using it. The geographical incidence approach described earlier must thus be complemented by some kind of modeling aimed to predict the users of a particular service. In addition, it must be taken into account that changes in public services as well as taxation may modify the behavior of households and therefore their income. Marginal incidence analysis must account for these indirect (behavioral) effects on household welfare.

The "micro-simulation" approach is based on observed household survey data and estimated models of behavioral response (labor supply and occupational choices, production, consumption, schooling demand, demand for health care, etc.). A household income micro-simulation model (HIMS) (Box 2.3) consists essentially of an integrated, econometric model of occupational choice – including schooling as in Gertler and Glewwe (1990) – and income generation for the

Box 2.3 Various levels of HIMS

Consider the elementary income model for a household j given in equation (1):

$$y_j = \left[\sum_i w_{ij} L_{ij} + E_j + R(w_i L_i + E_j; \sum_i S_{i,j}; A_j) \right] \bigg/ P(C_j; p) \qquad (1)$$

where real income y_j is the sum of wage income by household members i supplying L_{ij} unit of labor – which may be zero – at the wage rate w_{ij}, of non-labor income E_j and transfer income $R( )$. The latter depends on gross income, the number of household members attending school $\sum_i S_{i,j}$, and some socio-demographic attributes A_j. Finally $P( )$ is a household-specific consumer price index that depends on the observed budget shares of the household, C_j, and the price vector, p.

First level micro-simulation: pure accounting   At this first level, evaluating changes in welfare (i.e. household income) is assumed equivalent to compute arithmetically how changes in $\Delta R( )$ and Δp – for instance through taxation – affect real income. The change Δ can be interpreted as a change between two intervals of time or a counterfactual. Applications of this first level of analysis concern all types of redistribution analysis with no behavioral response at the agent's level. This is the original framework proposed by Orcutt (1957) and used since then in tax-benefit models in developed countries. The schooling argument in R allows analyzing the incidence of public spending in education for example. But because $S_{i,j}$ is taken as fixed, the incidence analysis with this kind of accounting approach does not capture that part of marginal incidence that is linked to change in schooling.

Second level micro-simulation: structural model of labor supply and partial equilibrium

$$L_{ij} = F(w_{ij}, E_j, P(C_j, p), G_i; R( ); \delta; \omega_{ij}) \qquad (2)$$
$$S_{ij} = K(y_j, G_i; R( ); \phi; \theta_{ij}) \qquad (3)$$

In this second level of analysis, labor supply appears as an explicit function of the wage rate, non-labor income, the household specific CPI, individual and household socio-demographic characteristics, G, and the redistribution system, $R( )$, including the cost of schooling. δ is a set of coefficients to be estimated whereas ω_{ij} is a residual that stands for an individual fixed effect. Schooling is a function of household income y, individual and household socio-demographic characteristics – including school accessibility – G, the redistribution system $R( )$. ϕ is a set of coefficients to be estimated whereas θ_{ij} are residuals. Such a structural model must be estimated on a cross-section of households. It is then possible to simulate directly the impact of taxation, income transfers, or access to school on household welfare, that goes through labor-supply behavioral response and schooling demand.

various individuals belonging to a household, and of taxation incidence à la Ahmad and Stern (1987). The income generation model is based on earning rates – which must be estimated for inactive individuals – and a polytomic occupational model where individuals are allocated to, or choose from inactivity or unemployment, wage work, and self-employment. Schooling may also be part of these choices. An example of this kind of model for simulating schooling related policies is Bourguignon and Pereira da Silva (2003).

The HIMS framework should preferably be used for marginal incidence analysis whenever one assumes that public spending, taxation – or price subsidies – modify significantly the budget constraint faced by households so as to affect their behavior in one dimension or another. For instance, a change in the price of the agricultural crops due to a change in taxation modifies self-employment income and possibly the activity choice of several household members. Better access to schools modifies schooling demand and the total income of the household. Improving local infrastructure may increase the productivity of self-employment, or that of domestic activity thus raising participation in market activities. Changes in the relative prices of consumer and producer goods via taxation or subsidies directly affect not only the real income of the household but also activity choices, if they are strongly income elastic.

The micro-simulation approach resolves many of the problems of the benefit incidence analysis and in particular the lack of behavioral response and the evaluation of policy choices based on averages calculated for large groups of the population. Nevertheless, several questions still arise. How far this approach may go and how comprehensive models may be without becoming unreliable or black boxes? What are the data limitations (e.g. in low-income countries) given the requirements of this approach? What trade-offs are there between simplicity and a fully specified structural model of behavioral response? Are simple scenarios with no behavioral response of any relevance?

In general terms, N_{tq} is the number of households in income fractile q with kids in a given level of school and N_t total school enrollment in year t. Alternatively N_{tq}/N_t may be interpreted as the share of the total schooling cost that is expanded through enrollment on fractile q. In any case, this expression represents the shift in the concentration curves shown in Figure 2.1. It is also possible to define marginal incidence as the share of a given fractile in the total increase in enrollment:

$$(N_{2q} - N_{1q})/(N_2 - N_1)$$

Such a formula is used by Van de Walle and Nead (1995).[10] What is crucial is that there may be a big difference between average incidence at a given point in time – that is, N_1q/N_1 or N_2q/N_2 – and the marginal incidence defined by $(N_2q - N_{1q})/(N_2 - N_1)$.

The marginal incidence formulae allows to evaluate the marginal distributional incidence of programs at the national level under the (implicit) simplifying assumption that welfare gains are essentially proportional to the unit cost of the public service that is evaluated. One may also want to evaluate the marginal incidence of programs with only local coverage, and, more importantly, to assess their effectiveness in both reaching the right people and affecting their behavior and welfare in the appropriate way. While the given marginal incidence formulae allow to handle the targeting part of the evaluation, it will not treat adequately the evaluation of induced changes in the behavior and welfare of program participants. In particular, the assumption of individual welfare gains equal to the average cost of the program seems too strong. Other methods must then be used.

To evaluate the welfare gain due to the program, it seems natural to simply compare the participant's welfare level with the program and that without the program. This is not an easy task, though. The difficulty comes from the fact that while a post-intervention welfare indicator is available, no such indicator is available for the situation without the program. Indeed, by definition, participants are observed only when they benefit from the program but, in general, no data is available on the counter-factual of what would have happened to them in the absence of the program.

Naïve comparisons are still common even though they may be misleading. It is tempting to proxy the "true" effect of the program by contrasting participants versus non-participants or simply by using reflexive comparisons, that is, the same people before and after the program. However, such methods can be very deceptive because of serious "selection" problems. The population of participants is generally not drawn randomly from the whole population, so that one does not know whether the program being evaluated is effective on its own or because it was applied to participants especially receptive to it. Various techniques for *ex post* evaluation of public programs have been designed in recent years to remedy this problem (see Ravallion, 2001a).

In the absence of the proper "randomized" samples, some procedures and tools may be used to fill in the missing observation. These range from, double difference (e.g. collecting baseline data on non-participants and (probable) participants before the program), matching techniques (e.g. match program participants to non-participants from a larger survey on the basis of their *ex ante* probability to participate to the program, and instrumental variables (e.g. use variables that influence participation – but do not affect outcomes given participation – to identify the exogenous variation in outcomes due to the program).

The inherent difficulty in finding an adequate, non-biased "counterfactual" – for example, the baseline effect for participants to a program in the absence of the program that one wants to evaluate – and the difficulties in getting adequate data and survey design for measuring impact are serious obstacles to *ex post* evaluation. Nevertheless, it is of the utmost importance to conduct rigorous, or the best possible, *ex post* evaluation in order to know how the welfare impact of the actual projects of public spending actually compares with what is usually assumed in *ex ante* marginal incidence analysis. Ideally, there should be a constant interaction between *ex ante* and *ex post* analysis. That interaction is presently very far from being systematically conducted because of the small number of *ex post* and *ex ante* evaluations being undertaken[11] for the same or at least comparable types of programs.

Finally, another combination of an *ex ante* with an *ex post* approach can be found in the recent practices that are tracking public expenditures flows through proper surveys. Knowing whether budgeted public spending actually reaches local (geographical) targets seems a crucial first step before assessing whether the "poor" in those local targets are actually reached themselves. In other words, the practice of imputing unit cost of schooling or health services to beneficiaries may be quite misleading if part of these "costs" actually remunerate "intermediaries" between the ministry of finance and local community schools or health centers. A new quantitative approach to conduct a better evaluation of the delivery of public services in that light can be found in Dehn *et al.* (2001).

2.3   Analyzing the distributional and poverty effects of macro policies

The previous sections reviewed a set of policies that could be evaluated using micro-economic techniques. These policies affect poverty essentially through redistribution. By contrast, this section considers policies that affect poverty through growth and changes in the macro-economic structure. In particular, it addresses the policy questions (nos. 3–5) in the introduction: "What is the poverty impact of structural reforms and changes in the macro-economic framework or at the macro-economic level?" This section also addresses the need, stressed earlier, for sometimes linking micro incidence analysis with a macro-economic framework. For example, that should be the case with indirect taxation issues or when the incidence of the program that is analyzed is likely to have sizable macro-economic effect. We start with the current practice in analyzing the relationship between growth and poverty in an aggregate fashion with no concern for individuals and/or households characteristics. Then we move to disaggregated models of various types and the common practice of evaluating impact of programs and policies using the so-called "representative households" to "summarize" the characteristics of groups of individuals and/or households in a given society. Next, we provide examples of the limitations to this approach. Finally we show how these limitations could be overcome by extending the micro-simulation techniques reviewed in the previous sections to deal with the incidence of policies that essentially operate at the most aggregate macro level or at the intermediate sectoral disaggregation level.

2.3.1   Empirical analysis between growth and poverty

If we had a robust and systematic macro relationship between economic growth, poverty, and inequality, things would be easy. Early analysis – see for instance Ahluwalia and Chenery (1974) – look at the effect of growth on poverty as the compounded effect of increasing all incomes in the economy and changing their relative levels at the same time, hoping to find this kind of a systematic relationship. Although empirical evidence (beginning with Kuznets (1955)) seemed initially in favor of this hypothesis, it is now admitted that no such relationship seems to exist. For example, and recently, Dollar and Kraay (2000) suggest that, on average across countries, no simple variable seems able to explain observed changes in the distribution of income over time and during the process of economic development.

They conclude that income inequality – as measured by the ratio of the income of the poorest 20 percent to the mean income – does not show any tendency to be modified with the process of development and the development policy, so that – at least – the income of the poor grows like that of the mean individual in the population. But this analysis might simply be missing important distribution determinants, which cannot be observed on a cross-sectional basis[12] (see in particular Anand and Kanbur (1993) and Deininger and Squire (1998)). So the recent literature has also gone in the opposite direction, searching for empirical evidence in favor of the hypothesis suggested by several theoretical models that inequality in the distribution of economic resources should have a negative impact on growth. Despite initial hopes, evidence appeared weak and little significant as well. See, for instance, Benabou (1996) for a review of the early literature on this issue.

On the poverty front, several recent papers focused on the statistical relationship between economic growth and poverty reduction across countries and time periods. Many of them (Ravallion and Chen, 1997; de Janvry and Sadoulet, 2000; Agénor, 2002) are based on linear regressions where the evolution of some poverty measure between two points of time in a country is explained by the growth of income or GDP per capita and a host of other variables – the main issue being the importance of GDP in determining poverty reduction.[13] The lessons from this cross-sectional aggregate approach are deceptively simple. Of course, GDP growth tends to reduce poverty – with an average elasticity around 2 when poverty is measured by the headcount. However, the very nature of the cross-sectional exercise makes it very hard to draw any conclusion that would be "country-specific." By adopting a cross-sectional regression framework, or by investing too little in functional specification testing, these chapters overlook the point that there is an identity – that can be calculated from the initial distribution of income – relating mean income growth, distributional changes, and changes in poverty.

Ex post, it is always possible to decompose the change in poverty that is due to the uniform growth of income and the change that is due to changes in relative incomes – that is, changes in the distribution. If a household survey is available in the country under analysis, a simple identity relates these various concepts (see Datt and Ravallion, 1993). A spreadsheet software has recently been made available to exploit that identity – see SimSIP-Poverty, Wodon *et al.* (2002). If no household survey is available or if its use is found to be cumbersome, then Bourguignon (2002) proposes an approximation of that identity that seems satisfactory. *Ex ante*, predicting the consequences of a growth policy on poverty can be done with the same technique, at least under the assumption that the policy under scrutiny will be distribution neutral (see Box 2.4). In the following section, we show how to depart from the aggregate approach.

2.3.2   *Macro modeling distribution and poverty with a Representative Household (RH) approach*

The preceding method for evaluating the incidence of growth on poverty could conceptually be generalized to disaggregate representations of growth by sector

Box 2.4 The arithmetic of growth, distribution, and poverty (Bourguignon, 2002)

Ex post the contribution of growth and distributional change to change in poverty between period t and t' may be expressed in the following way – Ravallion and Huppi (1991), Datt and Ravallion (1993), Kakwani (1993) –

$$\Delta H = H_{t'} - H_t = \tilde{F}_{t'}\left(\frac{z}{\bar{y}_{t'}}\right) - \tilde{F}_t\left(\frac{z}{\bar{y}_t}\right) = \left[\tilde{F}_t\left(\frac{z}{\bar{y}_{t'}}\right) - \tilde{F}_t\left(\frac{z}{\bar{y}_t}\right)\right] + \left[\tilde{F}_{t'}\left(\frac{z}{\bar{y}_{t'}}\right) - \tilde{F}_t\left(\frac{z}{\bar{y}_{t'}}\right)\right] \quad (1)$$

where $\tilde{F}()$ is the distribution of "relative income," $z/\bar{y}$ – is the "relative" poverty line that is the poverty line normalized by the mean income and H is the poverty headcount ratio. This simple *identity* consists of adding and subtracting the same term $\tilde{F}_t(z/\bar{y}_{t'})$ in the original definition of the change in poverty. The first expression in square bracket in the RHS of (1) corresponds to the growth effect at "constant relative income distribution," $\tilde{F}_t(X)$, whereas the second square bracket formalizes the distribution effect, that is the change in the relative income distribution, $\tilde{F}_{t'}(X) - \tilde{F}_t(X)$, at the new level of the "relative" poverty line. *Ex post*, observing $\tilde{F}_t(X)$ and $\tilde{F}_{t'}(X)$ is sufficient to perform that decomposition. *Ex ante*, some assumption must be made on $\tilde{F}_{t'}(X)$, the simplest one being that it is identical to $\tilde{F}_t(X)$ – that is, no change in the distribution.

A very simple approximation of (1) may be obtained in the case where the distribution may be assumed to be Lognormal, probably the most common approximation of empirical distributions in the applied literature. It can be shown in that case that the elasticity ε of the poverty headcount (H) with respect to the mean income $\bar{y}$ is given by:

$$\varepsilon = -\frac{\Delta H}{\Delta Log(\bar{y})H_t} = \frac{1}{\sigma}\lambda\left[\frac{Log(z/\bar{y}_t)}{\sigma} + \frac{1}{2}\sigma\right] \quad (2)$$

where $\lambda[\,]$ is the ratio of the density to the cumulative of a standard normal and σ is the standard.

or social groups. It would only be necessary either to observe the growth of specific sectors or to be able to predict them with the appropriate modeling tools. Then, knowing the distribution within these sectors or groups, and their projected size over time, the same identity relationships as shown earlier could be used – as in the Poverty Analysis Macro Simulator model built by Pereira da Silva *et al.* (2002).

Unfortunately, things are not that simple. In particular, the identity described earlier would work as long as there is no movement between the groups or sectors being considered in the analysis, or if those movements were in some sense distribution neutral. This is unlikely, though. For instance, people moving between the formal and informal sectors are not drawn randomly from their sector of origin nor distributed randomly in their sector of destination. In addition, analyzing growth in a disaggregated way may require more sophisticated modeling tools.

Much energy over the last twenty years or so has been dedicated to developing disaggregated models that would permit analyzing simultaneously changes both in the structure of the economy due to some specific growth-enhancing policy and in the distribution of income within the population.

2.3.3   Early "real" models combining sectoral disaggregation and RH groups

Computable General Equilibrium models (or CGEs) probably remain today the first step of any analysis seeking to integrate distribution considerations and economic policy at both the micro and the macro level. Since the pioneer work by Adelman and Robinson (1978) for South Korea and Lysy and Taylor (1980) for Brazil, many CGEs for developing countries combine a highly disaggregated representation of the economy within a consistent macro-economic framework and a description of the distribution of income through a small number of "RHs" meant to represent the main sources of heterogeneity in the whole population with respect to the phenomena or the policies being studied. Models were initially static and rigorously Walrasian. They now often are dynamic – in the sense of a sequence of temporary equilibrium linked by asset accumulation – and often depart from Walrasian assumptions so as to incorporate various macro-economic features or "closures" as well as imperfect competition.

Several "RHs" are necessary to account for heterogeneity among the main sources of household income – or among the changes in income – due to the phenomena or the policies being studied. Despite the need for variety, the number of RH is generally small, however – usually less than 10. The RHs are essentially defined by the combination of the productive factors they own – farmers, rural wage workers, skilled urban workers, unskilled urban workers in the formal sector, etc. Although simple, this disaggregation methodology proved to be very useful and gave many insights into a variety of issues. With time, this approach led to an increasing degree of disaggregation of the production and the demand sides of the economy, in the degree of heterogeneity among agents – by explicitly considering that households within an RH group were heterogeneous but in a "constant" way – in the specification of government transfers and other types of expenditure, and on the structure and the functioning of factor and good markets.

Recent examples of such disaggregated models with a strong focus on income distribution involve Devarajan and Lewis (1991) on Indonesia, Decaluwe *et al.* (1998) on Morocco, etc. It should also be noted that many CGEs are actually used to conduct taxation incidence analysis of the type mentioned earlier.[14] The same models could be extended to provide inputs – that is, the precise consumer price vector – to conduct incidence analysis of taxation at the household level, as seen in the previous section, rather than with RH groups.

Finally, it should be noted that a large number of applications of CGE/RH modeling analyze the distribution effect of trade liberalization – for a recent example see for instance Yao and Liu (2000) and Chen and Ravallion (2002). It is not the purpose of this chapter to summarize this large body of literature.

2.3.4 Macro augmented CGE models with RH groups

Most of the CGEs just referred to are "real" and rely on very simple macro-economic closure rules like savings-determined investment expenditures. Whether static or dynamic, they seem to be more appropriate to address medium-run issues where most markets may be assumed to be in equilibrium and growth is in some sense "balanced." It was soon felt that some extensions were necessary to cover a wider range of policy issues, in particular issues related to the short-run management of the economy. To do so, CGEs have been extended to include money and other financial assets. The "Maquette" designed by Bourguignon *et al.* (1989) for the OECD was the first CGE modeling framework incorporating multi-sectoral disaggregation, income distribution through RHs – and constant heterogeneity within them – macro-economic mechanisms and policy instruments linked to money and various types of financial assets. These developments were particularly interesting to analyze both the macro and the distributional effects of large financial crises and adjustment of stabilization policies.

Since then, improved macro-augmented distributional CGEs have been proposed by a variety of authors in a variety of countries – see for instance Dorosh and Sahn (2000) for applications to African countries. More recently, the "Integrated Model for Macroeconomic Poverty Analysis," or IMMPA, built by Agénor *et al.* (2003) at the World Bank, tries to provide a unifying framework to integrate a financial sector and a broad range of macro-economic closure rules as well as long-run endogenous growth mechanisms within the CGE/RH approach.

Truly dynamic CGEs with inter-temporally optimizing agents endowed with perfect or near-perfect foresight were also developed. They permit a better analysis of transition paths between long-run growth regimes and the effects of policy instruments affecting them. But they were more adapted to intergenerational than more common intra-generational distribution issues. Moreover, only a few applications were made to developing countries.[15]

2.3.5 The approach using disaggregated IS-LM macro-econometric models

While the macro-augmented CGEs examined earlier were capable of analyzing some distributional issues they were unable to account properly for several macro specific phenomena in particular those related to crisis situation where the role of expectations had to be modeled in a more sophisticated way. Another shortcoming of CGEs is that they generally are "calibrated" models relying on a small number of key behavioral parameters the value of which is arbitrarily set – or imported from another country where it has been properly estimated. Other data are simply identified by the assumption that the economy is initially in a state of equilibrium. Progresses in macro-econometric modeling and estimation techniques allow to address many of these macro issues in a more satisfactory way. Unfortunately, these models are not designed specifically to tackle distributional problems. Also, their authors were not concerned primarily by these problems. But the lack of a tradition does not imply that macro-econometric models are incapable *per se* of dealing with distributional problems. There are various ways in which this may be pursued.

The first technique, similar to the CGEs/RH, consisted in a first stage of disaggregating production into various sectors rather than to stay at a fully aggregate level. This approach – which was essentially following the IS-LM tradition – produced a multiplication of increasingly larger sectorally disaggregated macro models in most developed economies (e.g. the Wharton Econometric Forecasting model by L. Klein for the United States, or the "Dynamique Multi Sectoriel" model, DMS, or METRIC for France). Despite their sectoral disaggregation, however, these macro models stayed short of the RH approach, barely touched on distribution issues beyond a breakdown between wages for different labor categories and various types of non-wage income. It would probably have been possible to do better. However, the late 1970s shocks (jumps in oil prices, interest rates, exchange rate volatility between developed countries) seriously weakened the forecasting and analytical power of these models. Their prediction errors undermined their prestige. The Lucas critique sealed their fate.

Since then, the preference is for smaller and more aggregate models – the logical structure of which may be made much more flexible. This suggests a second solution relying on a two-layer approach for taking distributional issues on board. The first layer is a compact, possibly flexible, econometric modeling of all relevant aggregate macro variables (GDP, prices, interest, and exchange rates). The second layer consists of disaggregating employment, production, etc. into a multisector/RH type of framework. The difficulty, of course is to have this second layer made fully consistent with the first one.

One may think of macro-augmented CGE models where some components of the "macro" part would result from econometric estimation. But more integrated approaches are also possible. Early examples of this approach can be found for instance, in a typical IS-LM model for South Africa that was built with the specific purpose to test the effect of macro policies (e.g. the end of Apartheid, growth-enhancing policies, stabilization, etc.) on three specific and distinct groups of the South African population (skilled labor, semi-skilled labor, and unskilled labor). An explicit two-level CES production function was estimated allowing for substitution between these labor categories and capital. The novelty there consisted in relying on the econometric estimation of the behavior of a disaggregated labor market for the three levels of skills in the economy. This was possible ironically because of the data availability in Apartheid South Africa, which was used to classify labor according to racial characteristics (see Fallon and Pereira da Silva, 1994).

Aggregate macro relationships implicit in the preceding approach are of a short-run nature. But they may also want to take into account long-run growth determinants rather than short-run aggregate demand phenomena. The same two-layer approach can be used in this case, too. A recent example of such a structure can be found with the combination of Vector Autoregression (VAR) techniques to project growth with a CGE/RH providing some breakdown of various sources of household income. Recent extensions of the 123 CGE model developed by Devarajan *et al.* (2000) are in this spirit.

2.3.6 Limitations of the RH approach

Although the disaggregation of macro models is an attractive and probably the most obvious way of integrating macro-economic and distributional issues, the RH approach outlined earlier suffers from various limitations.

If mean income differences across a few RH groups explain a substantial part of overall inequality at a point of time, this may not be true at the margin between two points of time, or between a benchmark and a counterfactual simulation. Most decomposition studies of "change" in inequality suggest that changes in the distribution are due to a large extent to changes in the distribution within RH groups. See for instance the pioneer study by Mookherjee and Shorrocks (1983) for the United Kingdom. This is because of the pronounced heterogeneity of several economic phenomena like income shocks among individuals and households belonging to the same RH group, occupational changes, or the fact that two members of a given household may actually belong to groups that are very differently affected by a macro-economic shock or policy. This decomposition of changes in inequality has also been applied to developing countries. Ahuja *et al.* (1997) apply this for Thailand while Ferreira and Litchfield (2001) do it for Brazil. Results are analogous. It follows that the RH approach based on the assumption that relative incomes are constant within household groups may be misleading in several circumstances.

This is especially true when studying poverty. It may be the case that the change – say a fall – in the mean income of an RH, as simulated by the kind of model reviewed in the preceding sections, is relatively limited. Yet, the macro-economic shock under scrutiny can have very heterogeneous effects among households in general or even for those belonging to the same RH. Thus, poverty might be increasing by much more than suggested by the fall in mean income. For instance, some individuals may have lost their jobs in some households, or some households may have more difficulty in diversifying their activity, or their consumption, than others. For these individuals, the relative fall in real income is necessarily larger than for the entire group. If their initial income was low, then poverty may increase by much more than expected under the assumption of distribution neutral shocks – that is, applying the methodology reviewed earlier in Section 2.3.1. By "averaging" the analysis for all households belonging to the same group, the RH approach may thus be driving analysts and policy makers to the wrong conclusions.

In this sense, the appropriate usage of the RH assumption depends on the sources of income of households within each RH group. If there is a great variety of sources of income for the same household, then it is likely that policies that are simulated with the underlying view that they will produce homogeneous results for a group, will lead to weak results.

When using RHs in disaggregated macro models, the challenge is to design a specific breakdown of the household population that guarantees a maximum coverage of possible distribution effects of policy and shocks. However, this objective is likely to lead to a number of RH groups that is much too large for practical purposes. On the other hand, one may also want to follow the fate of individuals rather than households, as it would be the case if the emphasis were put on the effects of macro shocks and policies on women empowerment or any other more specific category of the population. Again this is something that is not possible with the RH approach.

2.3.7   Combining macro modeling and micro-simulation models

The preceding analysis suggests that the most promising direction consists in seeking a true integration between macro models and the observed heterogeneity of households as observed in a household survey. The problem is how to do it. In what follows we explore two possibilities but also stress on some difficulties.

2.3.8   The difficulty of full integration

The first possibility consists in moving from representative to "real" households within the CGE approach. It is theoretically possible. After all, it suffices to replace a small number of RHs by the full sample in the household survey. This, however, requires having at one's disposal the same models at the individual or household level as in CGE/RH models at the RH group level. This could be done by estimating the structural form of micro models of occupational choices, labor supply, and consumption behavior while allowing for appropriate individual fixed effects. This would also generally require assuming that all individuals operate in perfect markets and are unconstrained in their choices. It is likely that advances in computational capability will make it easier to build and estimate this type of model in the future. As of today, despite some significant progress (e.g. Cogneau and Robilliard, forthcoming; Townsend and Gine, forthcoming), most of the work to achieve full integration in these models still needs to be done.[16]

2.3.9   Exploration of the sequential approach (top-down)

A second possibility consists in creating a "link" between macro-economic frameworks and the HIMS described for the *ex ante* marginal incidence analysis of taxation and public spending. The procedure is sequential and starts from the "top" (the macro model) down to the "bottom" (the HIMS). In this approach, the incidence analysis described earlier is done on the basis of changes in consumer/producer prices, wages, and possibly sectoral employment levels that are predicted by some (disaggregated) macroeconomic model.[17] The idea is to use the second level analysis (i.e. reduced form income generation model in Box 2.3

earlier) and to have the changes in prices and in the coefficients of earning, self-employment income, and occupational choice functions and in prices provided by some macro model. The challenge now is to ensure consistency between the micro and macro levels of analysis. Simulating price and wage changes obtained with a macro model into the micro level is not difficult and essentially mirrors the standard incidence analysis. However, simulating changes in occupations – due for instance to the contraction of the formal sector and employment substitution in the informal sector – is more difficult. A method has been developed by Robilliard *et al.* (2001) in a model that simulates the effects of the 1997 crisis in Indonesia (see Box 2.5). Other applications are presently under way for Brazil, Madagascar, and Morocco.

Box 2.5 Linking HIMS and macro modeling: the top-down sequential approach (Robilliard *et al.*, 2001)

(a)   The HIMS framework

A household (real) income generation model is estimated that consists of a set of equations that describe the earnings and the occupational status of its members according to the segment of the labor market where they are operating.

(M)

- Earnings equations by labor market segment.
- Self-employment income function at the household level by type of business.
- Functions that represent the occupational choice (inactive, wage worker, self-employed) of household members by labor market segment (defined by gender, skill, area).
- Idiosyncratic consumer price index.

These equations are estimated econometrically on a sample of observations for some base year. There are all idiosyncratic in the sense that they incorporate fixed individual effects identified by standard regression residuals. A micro-simulation then consists of modifying all or part of these equations. For instance, one may want to analyze the effect on poverty of changing the price of farm products – that is, modifying the corresponding self-employment income function in the appropriate proportion – or wages in a particular labor market segment, or modifying occupational choice behavior in favor of some specific occupation – for example, wage work.

(b)   Linkage with macro models

Suppose that a macro model (CGE, econometric, pure forecasts) may give counterfactual information on the variables that enter the household income model, but at some aggregate level. In other words, the macro model yields information on "linkage variables" like the aggregate level of

---

wages by labor segment, the price of the output of the self-employment sectors, the aggregate level of employment by type of occupation, the structure of consumer prices. *The idea is to modify some parameters in the equations of model (M) so as to make the aggregate results of the micro-simulation consistent with the linkage variables.*

This operation is easy for variables like wage or self-employment income. It is sufficient to multiply the equations by some parameter until the mean wage or self-employment income in the HIMS framework coincides with the value of the linkage variables provided by the macro model. Things are more complicated with occupational choices because the corresponding functions are not linear. Yet, tâtonnement on specific parameters of these functions may be undertaken so as to ensure that the aggregate employment structure resulting from the micro-simulation is consistent with the information provided by the macro model through the linkage variables. No feedback is actually necessary for the idiosyncratic consumer price index.

(c)   Analogy with grossing-up techniques

All these modifications are equivalent to the familiar operation of "grossing up" a household survey so as to make it consistent with data coming from National Accounts on the income side and an employment survey on the occupational side. The only difference is that the latter operation differs from straight re-weighting and is highly (income) selective thanks to the initial econometric modeling of occupational choices.

The top-down sequential approach may be easily combined with standard marginal incidence analysis of changes in public expenditures, taxation, and safety nets that could accompany the macro shocks and policies being studied. It should be noted, however, that it does not allow yet to identify and model the feedback effect of these accompanying measures (e.g. safety nets) back into the macro level.

Interestingly, this approach can work with very different types of macro frameworks. The choice of a macro framework will depend on the specific issue being studied and the availability of modeling tools. The CGE models will of course typically be used to study the effect of "structural reforms" like trade policies or indirect taxation, whereas disaggregated macro-econometric models might be preferred when dealing with aggregate demand issues, as with financial or exchange rate crises. In addition, it is shown later that other tools might be necessary when dealing with long-run growth issues.

The two-layer framework that characterizes the CGE/RH approach described earlier – a flexible aggregate macro model plus a consistent disaggregation into sectors and RHs – to study the distributional impact of macro policies becomes now a three-layer structure. On top, we find a model providing predictions or counterfactuals on standard macro-economic aggregates – GDP, price level, exchange rate, and rate of interest. In the middle lies now a disaggregated multi-sectoral CGE-type of model whose closures should be consistent with the macro results in the upper layer. And at the bottom, we find the HIMS framework with rules that make it consistent with the predictions or counterfactuals provided by the intermediate layer. This three-layer structure results directly from the economic rationale of the phenomenon being studied. One way or another, the analysis of distributional issues must rely on some kind of HIMS framework that sits in our third layer (at the bottom). The (alternative) RH approach would only be applicable to particular cases since it was seen that such an approach could hide important changes in the distribution of living standards or in poverty. Now looking at our other layers, we know that changes in household (real) income are derived, by definition, from changes in relative prices – both on the consumption and the production sides – the structure of wages, and occupational shifts. They may also be due to changes in idiosyncratic income determinants. But it is the first set of changes that our three-layer, micro–macro linkage approach must explain. Clearly this requires some disaggregated (meso) representation of the economy and the labor markets, a role played by the intermediate or second layer of our proposed framework. For several policy issues, and in particular those concerned with structural reforms, this intermediate layer might be sufficient. Finally, many changes at this intermediate layer will be the result of changes in macro policies. Besides, other macro-economic issues may require a well-specified macro model at the top (or first) layer that deals with aggregate demand, the credit market, foreign balance, and the price of domestic and foreign assets.

2.4 Further directions for investigating micro–macro linkages

2.4.1 Introducing dynamics

Much of what is stated about the possible linkage between micro and macro phenomena refers to a static framework. At least, this seems true of the two bottom layers of the three-layer structure just described. Both the intermediate disaggregated multi-sector CGE-like model and the HIMS framework are likely to rely on some kind of medium-run equilibrium assumptions. This is certainly true for the allocation of factors of production across sectors in the intermediate model. But this is also true for occupational choices and earning equations in the HIMS. Even though the usual residuals of econometric estimation might reflect adjustment mechanisms, they are interpreted in the HIMS framework as individual fixed effects and are thus transformed into a permanent component.

Such a static framework may be inappropriate in situations where the upper layer of the structure is meant to describe phenomena where dynamics is important, as for instance in cases of macroeconomic crises. If the upper layer describes the dynamic adjustment of the economy to a new equilibrium, it might be necessary to have this adjustment path reflected both in the intermediate and the micro part of the model. It should be acknowledged that we are not well equipped to deal with this type of issue. Augmented CGE models, meant to handle this kind of situation, are most often based on *ad hoc* assumptions, which may not always be consistent with the modeling choices made in the upper layer. Intertemporal CGE models might be a better tool but they rely on assumptions about the determinants of agents' expectations which might be unrealistic in the short term. It makes these models more appropriate for the analysis of very long-run phenomena. Finally, it is possible to make the micro-simulation of household decisions truly dynamic by representing savings behavior or changes in family composition.[18] But then other particular phenomena remain difficult to model given the available data. How to estimate consumption smoothing or migration behavior without panel data for instance? On the other hand, reconciling this dynamic micro-simulation with the dynamics of both the intermediate CGE-like and the upper layer of the three-layer structure is likely to be difficult.

In view of the difficulty of maintaining the three-layer structure in a truly dynamic framework, it might be held that poverty analysis should rely predominantly on the lower layer of this structure after making it properly dynamic. An approach of this type has been followed by Townsend (Townsend and Ueda, 2001) by simulating the dynamics of income, consumption, and labor supply of cohorts of households facing uncertainty and an imperfect credit market. Several policies of interest may be simulated in such a framework, but they are for the moment limited in scope. Here again, more work is needed to see how far it is possible to go in that direction.

2.4.2   *Introducing long-run growth*

It should also be possible to analyze medium-run growth and the effects of both its pace and its structure on poverty and the distribution of living standards using the three-layer structure discussed in the previous section. However, things are likely to be more difficult when a longer perspective is needed as it would be the case with evaluating the impact of investment of a long maturity on poverty and distribution.

Education and policies fostering human capital accumulation in general provide good examples of that difficulty. The main effect of increasing public spending in these areas today – both in terms of the rate of growth of total income and its distribution – is due to appear in the distant future – say, at least 10–15 years. Therefore, a complete analysis of these policies requires a truly long-run dynamic framework where it should be possible to evaluate the effects of that policy on the distribution today – in particular the negative effect of financing this policy on current income and poverty – as well as on the distribution 10 or 15 years from now. In turn the latter requires projecting how the economy and the whole household population will look like by then, depending on some assumptions about the structure of both economic and demographic growth. Here again, such an analysis may rely on dynamic micro-simulation analysis, although with a longer horizon than in the case considered earlier. Such micro-simulation techniques are available for a constant economic environment. However, linking them satisfactorily with the evolution of the economy and the structure of economic growth requires new efforts.

2.4.3 Firms, institutions, and investment climate

As pointed out earlier, all the progress made, or envisaged, so far with the three-layer framework outlined has consisted of ensuring that adequate, issue-specific, macro-economic frameworks could be adapted to provide a guide for micro-simulations while fully utilizing the heterogeneity found in household surveys. While allowing for a much more detailed representation of occupational choices, income generation, etc., the HIMS (the third layer of our three-layer framework) remains circumscribed to the activity, income, and/or expenditure of households in the economy. In other words, it ultimately deals with private consumption, the labor market and, in some cases, wealth accumulation. Similarly, one may think of applying a similar approach to a population of firms – for example, using industrial survey data instead of household surveys.

Incidence analysis for a sample of firms would consist – in a first level – of measuring the subsidies and taxes on their income (profit) and investment. With simple assumptions about average tax rates, the average incidence analysis conducted for households could be replicated.[19] In addition – but quite distinctly – an analysis of the direct effect of the cost of "corruption" (or "quasi-tax") could be done, when the appropriate data is available, as for instance in the recent micro-economic "investment climate" studies undertaken by the World Bank (see Dollar *et al.*, 2002). Subsequently, one could conceive extending to firms the type of interaction with macro models seen for households. It could be of significant importance to be able to disaggregate the productive sectors of large macro models. In particular, accounting for different investment, borrowing, reactions to macro shocks, or hiring behavior by size of firms within the same sector could permit understanding the interaction between SMEs and larger firms. This could have implications both at the macro-economic level and for distribution (e.g. wage differentiation, profit distribution, exit, and entry of firms).

This type of analysis could also enable one to evaluate more precisely the effect of policies that change the institutional environment that firms face. Based on the incidence analysis of "investment climate" variables on firms' investment, pricing, and hiring behavior that were identified earlier, one could measure first, the different types of effects of the "investment climate" on the level and structure of economic activity and then, the effect of these changes on households.

2.5 Conclusions

This chapter conducts a survey of techniques that are available or under development and aims at evaluating the poverty impact of economic policies. However, the preceding review covers more than what is actually current practice in evaluating the impact on poverty of economic policies. From the caveats and limitations that were mentioned one should not get the impression of a lost cause. There has been progress and there will be progress in determining "what policies are pro-poor?" There are some established consensus on certain aspects of the issue, although there are also counter-intuitive findings. We will conclude by suggesting a few directions for practical implementation. These directions are influenced by two of our "methodological preferences."

The first is the need to shift from average and indirect incidence analysis to marginal incidence analysis in relation to both micro or macro-oriented policies. However, even simple things like marginal incidence analysis for micro-oriented policies, or the growth–poverty calculation are still not systematically in use. A first priority then is to make sure that all available tools are properly and systematically used.

The second is the three-layer structure (i.e. macro, meso-disaggregated, micro) upon which one should build the evaluation of the distributional effects of any kind of macro-oriented policy. Yet, this recommendation for using such a three-layer structure is fully compatible with methodological flexibility at each layer of this structure. The possibility to choose one among various classes of models within each layer was stressed throughout the chapter. In particular, we insisted very much on the possibility of adopting several combinations of models – for example, CGEs and RHs; macro-econometric and micro; CGE and micro – depending on the country, the policy being investigated, and the situation at hand. One interesting related possibility that emerges from this flexibility – *inter alia* for the multilateral institutions and governments – is that a three-layer approach could perhaps allow models built by different ministries or institutions, – or inside a ministry or an institution, different departments or divisions – to be hooked together. This option would only require that any model-builder uses its comparative advantage in one of the layers while ensuring that models are built with the ability to receive inputs from one layer and to transmit other outputs to another layer. For example, the linkage variables between the layers of the framework should be commonly defined by all those modelers participating in the exercise.

The chapter also shows areas where useful tools could be developed and used at a relatively low cost. Pilot studies exist or are nearly complete. It is only a matter of organizing their dissemination. There are promising cases where we have seen the contribution to policy making of geographical mapping, micro-simulation of consumption of public services, indirect taxation/tariffs incidence analysis, etc. We are also making progress in specifying the role of the investment climate using firm surveys.

However, as one should expect in such a comprehensive review, the chapter also reveals several missing tools. We pointed out that the most noticeable hole is the analysis of all issues that are related to dynamics either in the very short run (e.g. the impact of macro-economic crises and their management) or the long run (for instance, the effect of educational expansion). It is necessary to invest in more research in these areas.

Finally, the quality of tools depends on the intensity with which they are used and vice-versa. This is a demand–supply problem. Presently, we probably are far from an efficient equilibrium. While the effort to improve existing tools, develop others, and create the culture of a three-layer approach is considerable, we believe that there is a promising new area of collaboration between different modelers and the ultimate users of these tools.

Notes

* At the time of writing (March 2002), respectively Professor of Economics, DELTA (Paris), Lead Economist, the World Bank, and Chief Economist and Sr Vice-President, Development Economics, the World Bank. We would like to thank – without implicating – Francisco H.G. Ferreira for helpful suggestions. The views expressed here are those of the authors and should not be attributed to the World Bank or any affiliated organization.

1 By *ex ante* evaluation we mean quantitative and qualitative techniques – that can be both micro and macro – to "predict" the likely impact on poverty of a change in policy (e.g. tax, subsidy, trade policy reform, exchange rate regime, etc.) before their implementation. But it is also crucial to evaluate *ex post* the actual impact of policies, the distance from what had been predicted with *ex ante* techniques and actual results of policies; it constitutes the first step to improve the performance of projects and policies (see Ravallion, 2001a).

2 The PRSPs are the new general policy documents elaborated by the governments of developing countries that want to access concessional resources from the IMF and the World Bank. Beginning in 1999–2000, these documents replaced the Policy Framework Papers (or PFPs) written by the staff of the IMF and the World Bank in consultation with national governments.

3 The development of anti-poverty cash-transfer programs like Progresa in Mexico, Bolsa-Escola in Brazil, etc. makes these tax-benefit models very attractive analytical instruments for policy making. On the general issue of the applicability of these models to developing countries, see Atkinson and Bourguignon (1991).

4 See for instance, chapter 11, Newbery and Stern (1987).

5 This is a straight application of the envelope theorem, as illustrated for instance, in Stern (1987) in Newbery and Stern (1987), chapter 3.

6 A logically prior problem is how to value the benefit to recipients. Standard analysis usually imputes cost. But since the amount consumed is not decided by the agent (but by the provider), she is not equating marginal utility to a price, and the value may differ substantially from cost.

7 Like a VAT at a constant rate on all goods and services, including those produced by the informal sector. This tax system is often recommended precisely for its assumed neutrality property.

8 Hence the considerable importance of models of the CGE type used to simulate the effects of tax systems. For an example of such an analysis of the distributional properties of the tax system in developing countries, see Devarajan and Hossain (1998).

9 Assuming of course, that the geographical expansion of a given service does not modify the distribution of the population through migration.

10 See also Duclos *et al.* (2001).

11 For example, it is conceivable that for important programs such as Progresa in Mexico or Bolsa-Escola in Brazil, one compares the expected results of an *ex ante* evaluation done using the techniques mentioned earlier with the data that were available at the time the program was designed and available *ex post* evaluation.

12 On this see Bourguignon (2002).

13 We do not include Dollar and Kraay (2000) here, despite obvious analogies with these papers. By focusing on the relative mean income of the bottom quintile of the distribution,

their paper actually deals with distributional issues or "relative" poverty rather than absolute poverty defined by the number of individuals whose standard of living falls below an arbitrary line.

14 In effect, this may have been one of the first uses of CGEs but this tended to concentrate on developed countries (see, for example, Shoven and Whalley, 1984). For an excellent application of this framework to developing countries, see the model developed by Devarajan and Hossain (1998) for the Philippines.

15 This literature has its origin in the book by Auerbach and Kotlikoff (1987) For applications to developing countries, see Mercenier and de Souza (1994). A related literature (Auerbach *et al.*, 1999) has focused on "inter-generational accounting" and distribution.

16 Of course, there may be intermediate solutions between working with a few representative household groups and with several thousands of "real" households. For instance, one might be satisfied expanding the original RH approach to several hundreds of households defined for instance on the basis of the "clusters" typically found in household survey samples.

17 Instead of relying on the structural HIMS model sketched in Box 2.3, it is possible in some instances to rely on some "reduced form" HIMS model. For an example of these models see Bourguignon *et al.* (2005).

18 On dynamic micro-simulation of household behavior, see Harding (1993).

19 The major caveat to extending the methodologies described earlier in this direction is that the demographics of firms creation and destruction are more complex than that of a population of households.

References

The word processed describes informally reproduced works that may not be commonly available through library systems.

Adelman, Irma and Sherman Robinson. 1978. *Income Distribution Policy: A Computable General Equilibrium Model of South Korea*. Stanford, CA: Stanford University Press.

―― 1988. "Macroeconomic Adjustment and Income Distribution: Alternative Models Applied to Two Economies." *Journal of Development Economics*, 29(1): 23–44.

Agénor, Pierre-Richard. 2002. "Macroeconomic Adjustment and the Poor: Analytical Issues and Cross-Section." Policy Research Working Paper 2788. World Bank, Washington, DC. Processed.

――, Alejandro Izquierdo, and Hippolyte Fofack. 2003. "IMMPA: A Quantitative Macroeconomic Framework for the Analysis of Poverty Reduction Strategies." World Bank Institute, Washington, DC (www.worldbank.org/wbi/macroeconomics/modeling/immpa.htm).

Aghion, Philippe, E. Caroli, and C. Garcia-Penalosa. 1999. "Inequality and Economic Growth: The Perspective of the New Growth Theories." *Journal of Economic Literature*, 37: 1615–60.

Ahluwalia, M. and H. Chenery. 1974. "The Economic Framework." In H. Chenery, M. Ahluwalia, C.L.G. Bell, J.H. Dully, and R. Jolly, eds, *Redistribution with Growth*. New York: Oxford University Press.

Ahmad, E. and N. Stern. 1987. "Alternative Sources of Government Revenue: Illustrations from India, 1979–80." In David Newbery and Nicholas Stern, eds, *The Theory and Practice of Taxation for Developing Countries*. Oxford, UK: Oxford University Press.

―― 1991. *The Theory and Practice of Tax Reform in Developing Countries*, Cambridge, UK: Cambridge University Press.

Ahuja, Vinod, B. Bidani, Francisco H.G. Ferreira, and M. Walton. 1997. *Everyone's Miracle? Revisiting Poverty and Inequality in East Asia*. Washington, DC: World Bank.

Anand, Ritu, and Ravi Kanbur. 1993. "Inequality and Development: A Critique." *Journal of Development Economics*, 41(June):19–43.

Artus, P., M. Deleau, and P. Malgrange. 1986. *Modélisation macroéconomique*. Paris: Economica.

Atkinson, Anthony B. 1981. *Handbook on Income Distribution Data*. World Bank. Economic and Social Data Division, Washington, DC.

—— 1983. *The Theory of Tax Design for Developing Countries*. New York: Social Science Research Council.

—— 1997. "On the Measurement of Poverty." *Econometrica*, 55(4): 749–64.

—— and F. Bourguignon. 1991. "Tax-Benefit Models for Developing Countries: Lessons from Developed Countries." In J. Khalilzadeh-Shirazi and A. Shah, eds, *Tax Policy in Developing Countries*, World Bank Symposium Series. Washington, DC: 216–226.

Auerbach, Alan J. and Laurence J. Kotlikoff. 1987. Dynamic Fiscal Policy. Cambridge, UK: Cambridge University Press.

Auerbach, Alan J., Laurence J. Kotlikoff, and Willi Leibfritz, eds. 1999. *Generational Accounting around the World*. Chicago, IL: University of Chicago Press.

Bagchi, Amaresh and Nicholas Stern. 1994. *Tax Policy and Planning in Developing Countries*. Oxford, UK: Oxord University Press.

Banerjee, Abhijit V. and Andrew F. Newman. 1993. "Occupational Choice in the Process of Development." *Journal of Political Economy*, 101: 274–98.

Benabou, R. 1996. "Inequality and Growth." In *NBER Macroeconomics Annual 1996*. Cambridge, MA: MIT Press.

Bourguignon, F. 2001. "The Distributional Effects of Growth: Micro vs. Macro Approaches." Paper presented at the Prebisch centennial conference, CEPAL, Santiago, July.

—— 2003. "The Growth Elasticity of Poverty Reduction: Explaining Heterogeneity across Countries and Time periods." In T. Eicher and S. Turnovsky, eds, *Inequality and Growth*. Cambridge, MA: MIT Press.

—— and L. Pereira da Silva, eds. 2003. *The Impact of Economic Policies on Poverty and Income Distribution: Evaluation Techniques and Tools*. Washington, DC: Oxford University Press and the World Bank.

——, W. Branson, and J. de Melo. 1989. "Macroeconomic Adjustment and Income Distribution: A Macro-Micro Simulation Model." OECD Technical Paper 1. Organization for Economic Co-operation and Development, Paris.

——, J. de Melo, and C. Morrisson C. 1991. "Poverty and Income Distribution during Adjustment : Issues and Evidence from the OECD Project." *World Development*, 19(1): 1485–508.

——, F. Ferreira, and N. Lustig. 1998. "The Microeconomics of Income Distribution Dynamics in East Asia and Latin America." World Bank Research Proposal 638–18. The World Bank, Washington, DC. Processed.

——, M. Fournier, and M. Gurgand. 2001. "Fast Development with a Stable Income Distribution: Taiwan, 1979–94." *Review of Income and Wealth*, 47(2): 139–63.

——, F. Ferreira, and P. Leite. 2002. "Ex Ante Evaluation of Conditional Cash Transfer Programs: The Case of Bolsa Escola." Policy Research Working Paper 2916. World Bank, Washington, DC.

—— 2003. "Conditional Cash Transfers, Schooling and Child Labor: Micro-Simulating Brazil's Bolsa Escola Program." *World Bank Economic Review*, World Bank. Washington, DC: 17(2): 229–254.

Borguignon, F., M. Fournier, and M. Gurgand. 2005. "Distribution, Development and Education in Taiwan, China." In F. Bourguignon, F. Ferreira and N. Lustig, eds, *The Microeconomics of Income Distribution Dynamics in East Asia and Latin America*: 313–56.

Burgess, Robin, and Nicholas Stern. 1993. "Taxation and Development." *Journal of Economic Literature*, 31(June): 762–830.

Chen, S. and M. Ravallion. 2002. "Household Welfare Impact of China's Accession to the WTO," Chapter 8. *East Asia Integrates: A Trade Policy Agenda for Shared Growth*. World Bank. Washington, DC. 2004.

Chenery, H., M. Ahluwalia, C. Bell, H. Duloy, and R. Jolly. 1974. *Redistribution with Growth*. New York: Oxford University Press for the World Bank.

Cogneau, D. and A.S. Robilliard. Forthcoming. "Poverty Alleviation Policies in Madagascar: A Micro-Simulation Model." In J. Bourguignon and L. Pereira da Silva, eds, *The Impact of Macroeconomic Policies on Poverty and Income Distribution: Macro–Micro Linkage Models*. World Bank and Oxford University Press, New York.

Datt, G. and M. Ravallion. 1992. "Growth and Redistribution Components of Changes in Poverty Measures: A Decomposition with Applications to Brazil and India in the 1980s." *Journal of Development Economics*, (April) 38(2): 275–95.

Decaluwe, Bernard, A. Patry, and L. Savard. 1998. "Quand l'eau n'est plus un don du ciel: Un MEGC applique au Maroc." (When Water Is No Longer a Gift of God: A CGE Applied to Morocco.) *Revue d'Economie du Developpement*, 0(3–4) (December).

Dehn, J., R. Reinikka, and J. Svensson. 2001. *Basic Service Delivery: A Quantitative Survey Approach*. World Bank, Washington, DC. Processed.

Deininger, K. and L. Squire. 1998. "New Ways of Looking at Old Issues: Inequality and Growth." *Journal of Development Economics*, (December) 57(2): 259–87.

de Janvry, A. and E. Sadoulet. 2000. "Growth, Poverty, and Inequality in Latin America: A Causal Analysis, 1970–94." *Review of Income and Wealth*, 46(3): 267–87.

Demery, L. 2000. "Benefit Incidence: A Practitioner's Guide." Poverty and Social Development Group, Africa Region, The World Bank, Washington, DC. Processed.

Demombynes, G., C. Elbers, J. Lanjouw., P. Lanjouw, J. Mistiaen, and B. Özler. 2001. *Producing a Better Geographic Profile of Poverty: Methodology and Evidence from Three Developing Countries*, The World Bank, First Draft Mimeo, 2001.

Devarajan, S. and Hossain, Shaikh I. 1998. "The Combined Incidence of Taxes and Public Expenditures in the Philippines." *World Development*, 26(6): 963–77.

—— and J.D. Lewis. 1991. "Structural Adjustment and Economic Reform in Indonesia: Model-Based Policies vs. Rules of Thumb." In Dwight H. Perkins and Michael Roemer, eds, *Reforming Economic Systems in Developing Countries* (1991): 159–87, Harvard Studies in International Development Cambridge: Harvard Institute for International Development; distributed by Harvard University Press.

——, W. Easterly, D. Go, C. Petersen, L. Pizzati, C. Scott, and L. Serven. 2000. *A Macroeconomic Framework for Poverty Reduction Strategy Papers*, The World Bank, Mimeo.

Dollar, David and Art Kraay. 2000. "Growth Is Good for the Poor." Policy Research Working Paper No. 2587. World Bank, Development Research Group, Washington, DC. Processed.

——, Mengistae, Taye, Hallward-Driemier, Mary, and Iarossi, Giuseppe. 2002. "Competitiveness of Indian Manufacturing: Results from a Firm-Level Survey." Working Paper No. 31797. World Bank, Washington, DC.

Dorosh, Paul A. and David E. Sahn. 2000. "A General Equilibrium Analysis of the Effect of Macroeconomic Adjustment on Poverty in Africa." *Journal of Policy Modeling*, 22(6): 753–76.

Duclos, J.-Y., D. Sahn, and S.D. Younger. 2001. "Robust Multidimensional Poverty Comparisons." Working Paper. Université Raval, Department of Economics.

Elbers, C., J.O. Lanjouw, and Peter Lanjouw. 2001. "Welfare in Villages and Towns: Micro-Level Estimation of Poverty and Inequality." Policy Research Working Paper 2911. World Bank, Development Economics Research Group, Washington, DC. Processed.

Fallon, Peter R. and Luiz A. Pereira da Silva. 1994. "South Africa: Economic Performance and Policies." Southern African Department Discussion Paper No. 7, The World Bank, Washington, DC.

Ferreira, F.H.G. and J.A. Litchfield. 2001. "Education or Inflation? The Micro and Macroeconomics of the Brazilian Income Distribution during 1981–1995," *Cuadernos de Economia*, 38: 209–38.

—— and R. Paes de Barros. 1999. "The Slippery Slope: Explaining the Increase in Extreme Poverty in Urban Brazil, 1976–1996." *Revista de Econometria*, 19(2): 211–96.

Galor, Oded and Joseph Zeira. 1993. "Income Distribution and Macroeconomics." *Review of Economic Studies*, 60: 35–52.

Gertler, Paul and Paul Glewwe. 1990. "The Willingness to Pay for Education in Developing Countries: Evidence from Rural Peru." *Journal of Public Economics*, 42(3): 251–75.

Harding, Ann. 1993. *Lifetime Income Distribution and Redistribution: Applications of a Microsimulation Model*. Amsterdam: North-Holland.

Hentschel, Jesko, Jean Olson Lanjouw, Peter Lanjouw, and Javier Poggi (1998) Combining Census and Survey Data to Study Spatial Dimensions of Poverty: A Case Study of Ecuador, Policy Research Working Paper No. 1928, The World Bank, June 1998.

Kakwani, N. 1993. "Poverty and Economic Growth with Application to Cote d'Ivoire." *Review of Income and Wealth*, 39: 121–39.

Kuznets, Simon. 1955. "Economic Growth and Income Inequality." *American Economic Review*, 45(1): 1–28.

Lysy, Frank and Lance Taylor. 1980. "The General Equilibrium Model of Income Distribution." In L. Taylor, E. Bacha, E. Cardoso, and F. Lysy, eds, *Models of Growth and Distribution for Brazil*. Oxford: Oxford University Press.

Meerman, Jacob. 1979. *Public Expenditure in Malaysia: Who Benefits and Why?* New York: Oxford University Press for the World Bank.

Meier, G.M. and J. Stiglitz. 2001. *Frontiers of Development Economics*. New York: Oxford University Press.

Mercenier, Jean, Sampaio de Souza, and Maria da Conceicao. 1994. "Structural Adjustment and Growth in a Highly Indebted Market Economy: Brazil." In Jean Mercenier and T.N. Srinivasan, eds, *Applied General Equilibrium and Economic Development: Present Achievements and Future Trends*, Ann Arbor: University of Michigan Press. 281–310.

Mookherjee, Dilip, and Anthony F. Shorrocks. 1982. "A Decomposition Analysis of the Trend in U.K. Income Inequality." *Economic Journal*, (December), 92: 886–902.

Newbery, David M.G. and N.H. Stern, eds. 1987. *The Theory of Taxation for Developing Countries*. New York: Oxford University Press.

Pereira da Silva, L., B. Essama-Nssah, and Issouf Samake. 2002. "A Poverty Analysis Macroeconomic Simulator (PAMS): Linking Household Surveys with Macro-Models," Working Paper 2888. World Bank, DEC-PREM (Poverty Reduction and Economic Management Network), Washington, DC. Processed.

Persson, T. and G. Tabellini. 1994. "Is Inequality Harmful for Growth? Theory and Evidence." *American Economic Review*, 94: 600–21.

Ramadas, Krishnan, Dominique van der Mensbrugghe, and Quentin Wodon. 2002. Simsip Poverty: Poverty and Inequality Comparisons using Group Data. World Bank. Washington, DC.

Ravallion, M. 2001a. "Tools for Monitoring Progress and Evaluating Impact." Paper presented at the World Bank–IMF Workshop, July 2001.

—— 2001b. "Growth, Inequality and Poverty: Looking Beyond Averages." Policy Research Working Paper 2558. World Bank Development Research Group, Washington, DC.

—— and S. Chen. 1997. "What Can New Survey Data Tell Us about Recent Changes in Distribution and Poverty?" *World Bank Economic Review*, 11(2): 357–82.

—— and M. Huppi. 1991. "Measuring Changes in Poverty: A Methodological Case Study of Indonesia during an Adjustment Period." *World Bank Economic Review*, 5(1): 57–82.

Robilliard, A.S., F. Bourguignon, and S. Robinson. 2001. *Crisis and Income Distribution, A Micro–Macro Model for Indonesia*, The World Bank, Mimeo.

Sahn, David E. and Stephen D. Younger. 1999. Dominance Testing of Social Sector Expenditures and Taxes in Africa. IMF Working Paper WP/99/172. International Monetary Fund, Fiscal Affairs Department, Washington, DC.

Selowsky, Marcelo. 1979. *Who Benefits from Government Expenditures? A Case Study of Colombia*. New York: Oxford University Press.

Shoven, John B. and John Whalley. 1984. "Applied General Equilibrium Models of Taxation and International Trade: An Introduction and Survey." *Journal of Economic Literature*, 22(3): 1007–51.

Stern, Nicholas. 2002. "Strategy for Development." May 2001 ABCDE Conference Keynote Address. In Boris Pleskovic and Nicholas Stern, eds, *Annual World Bank Conference on Development Economics*, 2001/2002. Washington, DC: The World Bank.

Townsend, Robert M. and Ueda Kenichi. 2001. "Transitional Growth with Increasing Inequality and Financial Deepening." IMF Working Paper WP/01/108. International Monetary Fund, Research Department, Washington, DC.

—— and Gine. Forthcoming. Chapter 8. "Wealth Constrained Occupation Choice and the Impact of Financial Liberalization: Micro Income Distribution and Macro Growth." In J. Bourguignon and L. Pereira da Silva, eds, *The Impact of Macroeconomic Policies on Poverty and Income Distribution: Macro–Micro Linkage Models*. World Bank and Oxford University Press, New York.

UNICEF. 1987. Adjustment with a Human Face. Giovanni Andrea Cornia, Richard Jolly, and Frances Stewart. New York: Oxford University Press.

Van de Walle, Dominique and Kimberly Nead, eds, 1995. *Public Spending and the Poor: Theory and Evidence*. Baltimore, MD: Johns Hopkins University Press.

Yao, Shujie, and Ayiung Liu, 2000. "Policy Analysis in a General Equilibrium Framework." *Journal of Policy Modeling*, 22(5): 589–610.

Younger, Stephen D. 2002. "Public Sector Social Expenditures and Poverty in Peru." *Education and Health Expenditure and Development: The Case of Indonesia and Peru*. 83–147. Development Centre Studies. Paris and Washington, DC: Organisation for Economic Co-operation and Development.

—— 2003. "Benefits on the Margin: Observations on Marginal versus Average Benefit Incidence." *World Bank Economic Review*, 17(1): 89–106.

3 Trade, growth, and poverty

A selective survey

Andrew Berg and Anne Krueger

This survey of the recent literature asks: how important is trade policy for poverty reduction? We consider the effects of openness on poverty in two components: the effect of openness on average income growth, and the effect on distribution for a given growth rate. Evidence from a variety of sources (cross-country and panel growth regressions, industry and firm-level research, and case studies) supports the view that trade openness contributes greatly to growth. Moreover, trade openness does not have systematic effects on the poor beyond its effect on overall growth. Trade policy is only one of many determinants of growth and poverty reduction. Trade openness has important positive spillovers on other aspects of reform, however, so that the correlation of trade with other pro-reform policies speaks to the advantages of making openness a primary part of the reform package.

3.1 Introduction

Twenty years ago a consensus had emerged that trade liberalization strongly promoted growth and poverty reduction. The intervening period has seen a large wave of trade liberalization in the developing world. There has also been a surge of research on openness, growth, and poverty reduction, in part inspired by this experience. In this chapter we survey the recent literature to ask how important trade policy is for poverty reduction. We consider the effects of openness on poverty in two components: the effect of openness on average income growth and the effect on distribution for a given growth rate. We ask two main questions: is trade openness an important determinant of growth and is the growth that is associated with trade liberalization particularly pro- or anti-poor?

We focus on the links between trade and growth because changes in average per capita income are the main determinant of changes in poverty. In the past twenty years, the share of extremely poor people in the world (those living on less than two 1985 dollars per day) has fallen sharply, from 38 percent in 1978 to 19 percent in 1998. Because of population growth, the absolute numbers of poor have declined less, though the reduction in the number of poor from 1.4 billion to 1 billion is probably unprecedented.[1] These changes in poverty are almost entirely attributable to growth itself, not changes in the world income distribution.[2] More generally, there is no systematic relationship between growth and changes in income distribution. Thus, the income of the poor tends to grow proportionally with mean per capita growth.[3]

This suggests that our focus on growth as the core of a poverty-reduction strategy is well-founded. Changes in income distribution could still be important sources of changes in poverty within countries, however, even if they tended to "average out" across countries.[4] Moreover, if faster growth were associated with worsening income distribution, then there would be a limit on how much improvement in poverty we could expect from growth alone. In fact, neither concern turns out to challenge the primacy of growth in driving poverty reduction. The variance in income distribution through time is much smaller than the variance in average per capita income. Moreover, changes in the income distribution and real income per capita through time are weakly, if at all, correlated. These two facts mean that, whatever the causal relationship between growth and changes in income distribution, most variation in income of the poor must be a result of changes in average growth, not changes in income distribution, unless the changes in income distribution are of historically unprecedented magnitudes.[5]

Consider the important example of China. As Quah (2002) shows, no plausible increase in inequality could have swamped the effects of China's rapid per capita growth from 1980 through 1992. Per capita incomes grew by an average of 3.6 percent per annum over that period. During that time, China's Gini coefficient increased from 0.32 to 0.38, a large increase by international standards. Despite the rise in inequality, the number of poor (measured as those living on less than two dollars/day) fell by some 250 million, as rapid income growth swamped the effects of the increase in inequality. Inequality in China would have had to grow more than twice as fast as it did (much faster than observed in any other country during the postwar period) to undo the effects of the rapid income growth.[6]

Even though in general changes in poverty are mostly due to changes in average incomes, it might be that the growth that is due to trade liberalization is different from growth in general. That is, it is possible that trade liberalization generates a sort of growth that is particularly anti- (or pro-) poor. There are strong reasons to suppose that trade liberalization will benefit the poor at least as much as it benefits the average person. If, nonetheless, trade liberalization worsens the income distribution enough, then it is possible that it is not after all good for poverty reduction, despite its positive overall growth effects. This chapter thus also addresses the questions of the relationship between openness and growth and whether trade-related growth or openness has a particular effect on inequality.[7]

In Section 3.2, we discuss some conceptual questions about the relationship between openness and growth. We review the many reasons why openness may contribute to growth, noting, though, that theory is ultimately ambiguous about the relationship. Theoretical developments of the past fifteen years have raised the presumption that openness contributes to growth but also elaborated the alternative "infant industry" view. We then discuss the central question of how to define and measure openness. The various measures of trade liberalization and openness that have been used include measures of policy such as tariff rates and nontariff barrier coverage, on the one hand, and outcome measures such as trade volumes, on the other. We conclude that openness measures are all imperfect, but our preferred measure for many purposes (within the feasible set) is that of Sachs and Warner (1995).

In Section 3.3, we demonstrate two central propositions. First, we show that increases in openness to trade are an important contributor to growth. Second, there is nothing special about trade-led growth that systematically worsens the income distribution and so would undercut openness' powerful positive effect on poverty reduction through faster growth.

In Section 3.4, we return to the question of the nature of openness by discussing its place in the broader set of policy reforms. We emphasize that it is hard to disentangle the effects of openness from those of the broader reform package. We argue, though, that while trade is indeed only part of the package, it is often a key and early instrumental part. Thus, while the association of trade with other positive reforms is an econometric problem, it is a policy opportunity.

3.2   Conceptual issues

3.2.1   *Openness and growth*

In theory, the openness of an economy is the degree to which nationals and foreigners can transact without artificial (i.e. governmentally imposed) costs (including delays and uncertainty) that are not imposed on transactions among domestic citizens. Tariffs and nontariff barriers, domestic content requirements, health and safety requirements (or inspection delays) above and beyond those imposed on the domestic products raise the cost of buying from abroad.[8]

In theory, openness is desirable because relative international prices reflect the international marginal rate of transformation (in a competitive international economy) and should be equated with domestic prices for an efficient allocation of resources.[9] The mechanisms through which an efficient static allocation of resources affects growth are less clear-cut, although a number of channels have been identified. These include the following: (a) an increased efficiency of investment, particularly given the importance of imported capital goods in developing countries, (b) an ability to expand at constant (rather than diminishing) returns for a longer period through access to larger markets (Ventura, 1997), (c) a higher real return to capital in unskilled labor abundant countries that exploit their comparative advantage, (d) the higher rate of domestic saving and/or foreign capital inflow that may be attracted by (a) and/or (b), (e) possible endogenous growth effects arising from more rapid short-term growth in response to trade opening, (f) the discipline imposed on a government to undertake other pro-growth economic policy reforms if there is an open trade regime, (g) the reduction in rent-seeking activities inspired by trade restrictions, (h) the spur to innovation and entrepreneurial activity resulting from competition and access to larger markets, and (i) openness to ideas and innovations generated by openness to trade.

The theory and empirics of long-run economic growth have developed enormously in the past twenty years, so it is natural to place an assessment of the relationship between openness and growth in this framework. The workhorse has been the neoclassical model based on Solow (1956). In this framework, the level of GDP per capita in the steady state will depend on anything that affects the level of productivity, such as distortions that affect the allocation of resources, as well as determinants of the level of the steady-state capital stock, such as the savings rate. The implication for us is that openness, by allowing a more efficient allocation of resources, raises the steady-state level of income and also the growth rate for any country out of equilibrium. In the past twenty years, the main theoretical innovation has been the development of endogenous growth theory. A central theme of endogenous growth theory is that openness may promote long-run growth in a number of ways. Models that emphasize diffusion of technology as the engine of long-run growth can be constructed to predict that countries that are more open will have higher steady-state growth rates (Grossman and Helpman, 1991). Learning by doing is emphasized in Lucas (1988) and Young (1991). Earlier arguments to the effect that opening to trade could allow specialization in industries with scale economies and thereby increase long-run growth are precursors of this sort of argument. (See Bhagwati (1988) and Krueger (1980), for example.)

Should we focus our empirical attention on the relationship between growth and openness or on the relationship between growth and *changes* in openness? For example, if we believe that openness is important for growth, should we be puzzled that China might grow extremely fast while remaining fairly closed, or should we instead focus on the fact that a dramatic increase in the degree of openness has been associated with an increase in the growth rate? Theory makes no clear prediction. In the neoclassical model the most natural formulation is that openness raises the steady-state level of real income. Thus, increases in openness would cause increases in growth rates during convergence to the new higher level. The endogenous growth literature, given its concern to explain country-specific long-run growth rates, would tend to focus on the relationship between growth and openness. However, those endogenous growth models that emphasize how international diffusion of ideas or technology can produce faster growth in developing countries would also imply that changes in openness would lead to increases in growth rates. In practice, we can expect that a variety of processes operate at different times in different countries.[10] Overall, though, our reading is that the most important relationship is between the level of openness and the level of income, or (equivalently) between liberalization and growth.

Despite a consistent emphasis in the literature on how openness can promote growth, theory has always been ambiguous on this point.[11] From a static point of view, the general theory of the second best suggested that in the presence of other distortions, free trade might not be best for growth. The most notable example of such a distortion has always been the infant-industry argument. Despite its focus on learning, openness, and growth, endogenous growth modeling has given some credence to long-run versions of the traditional infant-industry argument. Endogenous growth models can easily imply that a more open country may get "stuck" in industries without learning-by-doing. In this case, closing the economy may help the relatively backward country grow faster. Easterly (2001), for example, emphasizes that models with increasing returns to scale or sufficient externalities can generate a situation in which factors flow from poor to rich areas, so that the poor can get stuck in "growth traps."

Even if growth-inducing channels are dominant, one could challenge their quantitative significance.[12] The importance of openness for growth is therefore an empirical question. One implication is that what we mean by openness, and how we measure deviations from free trade, are key.

3.2.2   Measurement of openness

A range of analytical issues arises in defining and measuring of openness. Since much of the theoretical case for openness as a source of growth is about the costs of market distortions, we should be concerned with policies that distort the market allocation, such as the level and dispersion of tariffs and nontariff barriers (NTBs). Outward orientation does not require the absence of all such distortions; it requires only that the overall system of export subsidies and trade barriers not be biased against exports.[13]

Most empirical analyses of openness look directly at policy measures that restrict trade, such as tariffs, NTBs, and so on. Severe problems arise in the analysis of each of these measures. It is not clear as to how to aggregate across goods to arrive at a meaningful overall measure. A higher tariff (or tariff-equivalent) on commodity A may have lower welfare costs than a lower tariff on commodity B, the same tariff rate may have different effects in different countries, issues arise in comparing different tariff structures regarding the dispersion of tariff rates, and so on. Simple averaging does not capture the relative importance of different categories of goods, while using actual trade weights gives too little weight to high-tariff categories, precisely because the tariff has discouraged trade in that good. Moreover, there is no necessary relationship between official and collected tariff rates.[14] NTBs are extremely hard to quantify, for a variety of reasons.[15] Finally, discriminatory exchange rate policies that offer exporters a more appreciated exchange rate than importers are equivalent to a tariff. This latter policy is easier to measure as the black market or parallel exchange rate premium, though clearly this variable is related not just to trade policy but also to macroeconomic policy more broadly (a point to which we return later).[16]

A variety of measurement problems arise when a country is not wholehearted about its trade liberalization. For example, across-the-board reductions in tariff rates will show up as a reduction in average tariff, but customs officials in reluctant countries frequently respond by reclassifying goods from low- to high-tariff categories, so actual tariffs may remain the same.[17] In addition, there are questions as to how to quantify the uncertainty (regarding, for example, the likelihood of antidumping actions or delays in customs clearance) that can affect openness.

It has been amply documented that countries tend to switch from one form of protection to another, rather than smoothly remove (or increase) protection.[18] Moreover, whether a change in one form of protection has any impact on effective openness depends on whether other forms of protection are binding. For example, a reduction in a tariff rate may not matter if binding NTBs prohibit imports of that good. Thus, in measuring openness it is important to try to control for the possible substitution between various policy measures. Sachs and Warner (1995) attempt to do so by constructing a dummy variable that takes a value of 1 for a country that passes each of five tests of openness: (1) an average tariff rate below 40 percent, (2) NTBs covering less than 40 percent of trade, (3) a black market exchange rate premium below 20 percent on average during the 1970s and 1980s, (4) the absence of a socialist economic system, and (5) the absence of an extractive state monopoly on major exports. In our view, this represents a fairly successful effort to measure the overall importance of trade policy restrictions, though it does not differentiate degrees of restrictiveness of trade regimes. A country barely passing the Sachs–Warner tests would be far from fully open.[19]

The Sachs–Warner measure has been criticized on three main grounds.[20] First, the black market premium measures factors other than trade policy. For example, to the extent that it captures chaotic macroeconomic policy, the Sachs–Warner measure is attributing to openness benefits that should be attributed to macroeconomic stability. We would nonetheless argue that a high premium on the secondary market for foreign exchange acts substantially like a tariff, in that it is likely to drive a wedge between the exchange rate exporters effectively receive (assuming they are supposed to sell their proceeds at the official exchange rate) and the rate paid by importers (who on the margin are likely to pay the parallel rate given the incentives to smuggle). A high black market premium may also reflect chaotic macroeconomic policy in the context of exchange controls. Indeed, Krueger (1978) and many other authors have argued that among the main costs of protection in practice were the associated macroeconomic disequilibria. This represents a much more substantial problem for econometric efforts to distinguish between the influence of macroeconomic stability and openness than it does for policy.

A second criticism is that the marketing board component amounts to a sort of African dummy plus, as it was taken from a World Bank study of African economies undergoing structural adjustment, so that other countries (even other African countries) with powerful export monopolies were excluded. In fact, however, the only countries that are considered closed by this criteria are those in which a mandatory export marketing board controls a large majority of total exports and holds a monopoly position in the sale of foreign exchange for imports, in the process driving a wedge between the rate received by exporters and that paid by importers. Thus, marketing boards in countries such as Canada, Indonesia, and Mauritius do not satisfy these criteria and would not have been classified as closed according to the Sachs–Warner criterion. It is true that most, though by no means all, African countries were rated as closed by this measure. This reflects the facts for Africa, however.[21] More generally, African growth experience is indeed unusual in the postwar era. The fact that coercive and export marketing arrangements are strongly coincident with a regional dummy is suggestive, though of course it hardly captures the richness of the issues with respect to growth in Africa. We place much more weight in what follows on results that are invariant to the inclusion of regional dummies.

Finally, the tariff and quota measures that are subsets of the Sachs–Warner openness variable do not work as well independently as does the aggregated measure. This, however, is consistent with the motivation for such a multivariate indicator in the first place – the frequent substitution of one for the other method of protection.[22]

It is nonetheless clear that these measures of policy are not fully satisfactory. The Sachs–Warner measure as well as others that are available for large cross-country and panel studies simply do not address most of the measurement problems we raised earlier, most notably inadequacies of average tariff rates and NTB coverage ratios. For this reason, a direct measure of openness, exports plus imports as a share of GDP, is sometimes useful. Of course, this measure of openness reflects the level of economic development, geographic factors such as distance from trading partners, and resource endowment, in that countries with unusual resource endowments are likely to trade more. Whether it is still interesting depends on the use to which it is put. For example, empirical results in which endogeneity of this measure of openness is controlled for through the use of exogenous, mostly geographic, determinants of trade are the most useful.

Alcalá and Ciccone (2001) note that this traditional openness measure has a drawback: productivity gains in the traded-goods sector (perhaps due to trade) lead to a rise in the relative price of nontraded services, which may decrease measured openness. Thus, more trade that leads to growth reduces measured openness, biasing downward an estimate of the effects of openness on growth. A solution is to measure what they call "real openness," defined as imports plus exports as a share of GDP in purchasing-power-parity dollars.[23]

Measuring openness as exports and imports as a share of GDP has the feature that it combines the effects of "natural" openness and trade policy. A refinement to measures of effective openness involves adjusting the trade share for nonpolicy determinants of trade shares, such as level of development, distance from potential trading partners, country size, and relative factor endowments. The idea is that the residual from a regression of trade shares on these determinants is a measure of policy openness. Unfortunately, our empirical models of the determinants of trade flows are not sufficiently robust that it is safe to identify the residual with policy, as any specification or other errors in the regression also appear there.[24]

More fundamentally, natural openness as well as policy openness may matter for growth. For example, trade policy openness would be of interest where the concern is the influence of distortions on relative prices and the laissez-faire equilibrium, but natural openness would matter to whether trade causes growth through the sharing of ideas and technology that it implies.

In our survey of empirical work, we necessarily take an eclectic approach to the measurement of openness. Case studies and microeconomic studies often allow for the most detailed and careful measurement of trade barriers. We also consider many analyses that use policy-based measures of openness, particularly that of Sachs and Warner (1995), partly because that is the direction the literature has taken and partly because we consider this to be a broadly sensible, if imperfect, measure. Other simpler policy measures such as average tariffs may be informative in some circumstances. Finally, we pay some attention to studies that use outcome-based measures of openness, such as trade shares in GDP, particularly if care has been taken to control for the endogeneity of openness so measured.

3.2.3 Trends in trade policy

Given the measurement problems, it is perhaps not surprising that it is exceedingly difficult to get systematic measures of the degree of trade liberalization through time and across countries. Dean *et al.* (1994) document the character and extent of liberalization in thirty-two countries in South Asia, Africa, Latin America, and East Asia from 1985 to 1992/93. They examine in some detail a variety of information on average tariffs, coverage of NTBs, and tariff dispersion. They find that trade liberalization has indeed occurred extensively, and sometimes dramatically, though with important regional differences: Latin American countries tended to move the fastest and most comprehensively; most of the South Asian countries made little progress until 1991 outside of reductions in NTBs, while the main source of protection in non-CFA[25] Africa has been and remains lack of foreign exchange, associated black market premium, and extensive exchange controls.[26]

A larger set of countries can be examined, though at a cost in terms of the richness of the openness measures. Tables 3.1, 3.2, and 3.4 present data on maximum and average tariff rates, while Table 3.3 shows some measures of within-country dispersion of tariff rates across goods. Figure 3.1 shows average tariff rates by region. Only a few data points are available for the period prior to 1980. Nonetheless, it is clear that there has been a substantial degree of trade liberalization in recent decades.[27] We now turn to the central question of the chapter, which is what impact trade liberalization has had on the incidence of poverty.

3.3 The relationship between trade and poverty

3.3.1 Trade and growth

The literature on trade and growth is almost as vast as that on growth itself, since openness is a part of much recent theory and most empirical work. Disagreements

Table 3.1 Maximum tariff rates

	1960s maximum tariff rates	*Current maximum tariff rates*
Argentina	521	35
Chile	255	7
Colombia	400	35
Peru	158	20
Singapore	6	0

Source: Choksi *et al.* (1991) for 1960s tariff rates and IMF data for current tariff rates.

Table 3.2 Trends in average tariff rates for developing countries, 1960–2002

Country	Earliest (1960–70)	Earliest (1980–85)	Average (1986–90)	Average (1991–95)	Latest (1996–2002)
Argentina	181	28	25	11	14
Bangladesh		100	93	63	26
Bolivia		12	18	10	9
Brazil		44	42	17	13
Burundi		38	37	7	
Cameroon		28	32	19	18
Chile	83	35	17	11	8
China		50	39	40	14
Colombia	47	61	29	14	12
Costa Rica		21	19	12	7
Côte d'Ivoire		31	26	22	15
Egypt		47	40	33	30
Ghana		43	19	17	16
Guinea		76	10	11	17
India		74	94	54	40
Indonesia	58	29	26	20	7
Israel		8	7	8	8
Jordan		16	16	17	15
Kenya		40	40	30	20
Korea	40	24	18	10	9
Libya		13	23		20
Malawi		22	18	20	16
Malaysia		11	15	14	9
Mexico		27	14	13	17
Morocco		54	23	24	34
Nigeria		33	32	33	25
Pakistan		78	67	57	24
Peru	73	19	41	17	14
Philippines		41	28	23	8
Sierra Leone		26	31	30	16
Singapore	1	0	0	0	0
South Africa		29	15	9	13
Sri Lanka		41	28	24	16
Taiwan, Prov. of China		31	15	11	9
Thailand		32	40	32	17
Tunisia		24	26	28	36
Turkey		40	27	27	14
Uruguay[a]	384	47	30	16	12
Average LDCs	108	36	29	22	16

Source: World Bank data; IMF data; Choksi *et al.* (1991).

Note

a Weighted average tariff rates in 1961. Weights calculated by weighting four-digit ISIC sectors.

and contradictions abound. We can, however, extract several principles that are both plausible and well established. Overall, and perhaps not surprisingly, we find that, while there are deep problems with the measurement of openness, and while establishing causality from openness to growth is difficult, the weight of the

Table 3.3 Standard deviation of tariff rates

	1990–94	1995–98
South Asia		
Bangladesh	114.0	14.6
India	39.4	12.7
Sri Lanka	18.1	15.4
Sub-Saharan Africa		
South Africa	11.3	7.2
Malawi	15.5	11.6
Zimbabwe	6.4	17.8
East Asia and Pacific		
Philippines	28.2	10.2
Thailand	25.0	8.9
Indonesia	16.1	16.6
China	29.9	13.0
Latin America and the Caribbean		
Argentina	5.0	6.9
Brazil	17.3	7.3
Colombia	8.3	6.2
Mexico	4.4	13.5
Middle East and North Africa		
Egypt, Arab Republic of	425.8	28.9
Tunisia	37.4	11.7
Turkey	35.7	5.7

Source: World Bank (2001).

Note
Country observations are for one year in the given time period.

evidence, from a variety of sources, is strong to the effect that openness is an important element explaining growth performance.

3.3.2   *Absolute convergence*

There is some evidence of absolute convergence, at least for sufficiently similar regions within countries and, less clearly, for countries that are integrated through trade. That is, poor countries or regions tend to grow faster than rich regions if they are sufficiently integrated with each other. This suggests that poor countries will grow, and reduce poverty, if they are sufficiently open.

Among regions that are sufficiently open to each other in all senses and with sufficiently similar overall policy environments, poorer ones tend to grow faster than average. Barro and Sala-i-Martin (1995) demonstrate this "absolute convergence" for states of the United States, regions of Europe, and prefectures of Japan over periods of several decades, as well as OECD countries from 1960 through 1985. Over these long and relatively stable periods, poorer regions converged to richer ones at a rate of about 2 percent per year in all three areas. As a result, measures of the variation of intra-regional inequality have fallen steadily.[28]

Table 3.4 Reductions in barriers to trade

Region	Frequency of total core nontariff measures for developing countries, 1989–98	
	1989–94	*1995–98*
East Asia and Pacific (7)	30.1	16.3
Latin America and the Caribbean (13)	18.3	8.0
Middle East and North Africa (4)	43.8	16.6
South Asia (4)	57.0	58.3
Sub-Saharan Africa (12)	26.0	10.4

Source: World Bank (2001).

Notes
Average number of commodities subject to nontariff measures as a percentage of total. Figures in parentheses are the number of countries in each region for which data are available.

Region	Countries imposing restrictions on payments for current account transactions (%)		
	1980	*1991*	*1995*
East Asia and Pacific (9)	33	33	22
South Asia (5)	100	100	40
Middle East and North America (6)	67	67	33
Sub-Saharan Africa (23)	85	83	39
Latin America and the Caribbean (30)	44	60	17
Europe and Central Asia (17)		94	47
Industrialized economies (12)	17	8	0
Total (102)	55	65	27

Source: World Bank (2001).

Note
Figures in parentheses are the number of countries in each regional grouping.

Region	Average black market premium (%)		
	1980–89	*1990–93*	*1994–97*
Total[a]	82.0	78.2	20.3
East Asia and Pacific	3.6	3.6	3.2
Middle East and North Africa	165.6	351.6	46.5
Excluding outliers[b]	7.1	8.8	1.4
Latin America and the Caribbean	48.7	13.1	4.4
South Asia	40.8	45.1	10.1
Sub-Saharan Africa	116.5	28.6	32.2
Excluding Nigeria	112.1	25.8	9.6

Source: World Bank (2001).

Notes
a Sample of 41 developing countries.
b Algeria and the Islamic Republic of Iran.

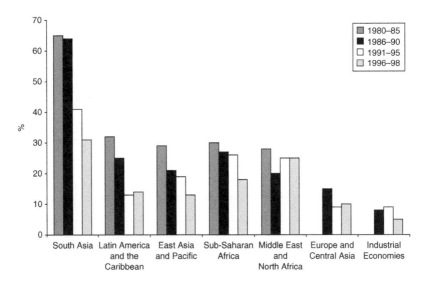

Figure 3.1 Average unweighted tariff rates by region.

Source: World Bank data and World Trade Organization data.

The implication of this result, particularly as extended to countries in the OECD sample, is that poor countries will not just grow but grow relatively fast if they are sufficiently integrated with faster growing countries. Of course, these groups of regions are integrated in many ways other than through trade: they have common laws, factor mobility, no barriers to trade, and common currencies (except for the regions of Europe and the OECD). Thus, this evidence does not speak to whether trade liberalization itself is sufficient to permit poor countries to grow fast. But it does suggest that if a poor region adopts enough common institutions and liberalizes enough (and if its partners liberalize fully as well), then relatively fast growth will ensue.

The OECD countries represent a potentially important exception to the rule that integration must be complete for absolute convergence. How much integration is required? Sachs and Warner (1995) suggest the powerful result that openness to trade, measured as described in Section 3.3.2, is enough. That is, as shown in Figure 3.2, there was absolute convergence among all countries in the world that were open to trade in 1970.

Does this result hold for other measures of trade liberalization and over other time periods? There is some evidence that it does, at least for developed countries. Ben-David (1993) argues that convergence among the main European countries only became marked after 1958, once the trade liberalizations associated with the European Economic Community took place. He also finds that convergence accelerated among various other developed country groups when they executed free trade arrangements. Finally, Ben-David (1996) finds some direct evidence

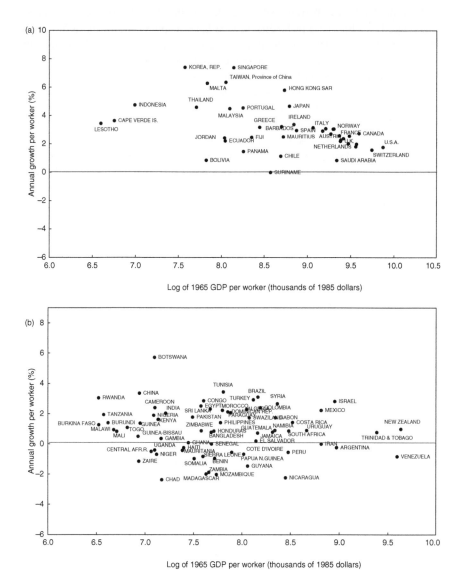

Figure 3.2 Growth per worker and initial GDP per worker, 1965–90: (a) open economies and (b) closed economies.

Source: Sachs and Warner (1995).

that trade is the mediating factor. He groups countries into sets that trade intensively with each other, and then compares them to random groups of countries and finds that the trade-linked countries tend to display absolute convergence, while the random groups do not.

Both the Sachs and Warner (1995) results and the Ben-David results have been challenged. Rodriguez and Rodrik (1999) have disputed the meaningfulness of the Sachs–Warner openness variable; as we discussed earlier, we think the variable is a plausible measure of trade openness. Rodriguez and Rodrik (1999) have also questioned Ben-David's results, among other things pointing out that it is difficult to distinguish the convergence observed among the European countries in the postwar period from the convergence also observed among these countries since 1870 or so (though with the important exception of the interwar period).

What if we compare systematically the change in speed of convergence before and after a group of countries liberalizes trade, with the change in convergence observed over the same time periods for a control group that did not liberalize trade? Slaughter (2001) finds that there is no evidence that the trade liberalizations lead systematically to faster convergence. He does not examine the Sachs–Warner sample, but the point is that perhaps the countries that were open in 1970 were converging even faster in the previous period, when they were closed. Trade openness can be important, as shown by the examples of the OECD countries and the Sachs–Warner results, but it is not necessarily enough. Given the large number of other factors that contribute to growth, we find this result unsurprising. But trade openness is an important piece of the puzzle.

3.3.3   Output and openness: regression evidence

Differences across countries in the level of output per capita are systematically and importantly related to openness. This result seems to hold up even when the endogeneity of openness is taken into account and when controls for other important determinants, such as the quality of institutions and geography, are included.

Empirical work of the past fifteen years has concentrated on cross-country and panel regression analyses. Many papers have concluded that openness to trade is a significant explanatory variable for the level or the growth rate of real GDP per capita.[29]

These results have been challenged on a number of grounds. Most broadly, it is difficult to believe that a simple linear model can capture the deeply complex growth process.[30] Nonetheless, this line of inquiry is worthwhile and has produced, in our view, strong and believable results, despite the difficulties of the enterprise. There is no question that such regression analysis can capture only a small piece of the picture. Nonetheless, the forces that shape the relationship between openness and growth seem so strong that they emerge fairly clearly. Similarly, measurement of all of the variables is difficult, particularly but not only across countries. We have discussed the issue of how to measure openness itself, but similar problems plague the other interesting variables, including real GDP per capita itself. Again, it is remarkable that the results obtain despite the surely pervasive measurement error.

A second deep potential problem relates to the question of causality. It is evident that openness, however measured, may well depend on growth or the level of income. The possible channels are numerous. Wealthier countries can afford better infrastructure for trade, poor countries may need to tax trade relatively heavily, higher incomes may shift preferences in favor of traded goods, and fast growth or high incomes may reduce political pressures for protection. We concentrate on results that are able to disentangle cause from effect through careful use of instrumental variables.

Third, trade policy and outcomes are likely to be highly correlated with other determinants of growth. If these other variables are omitted, trade falsely may take the credit. If they are included, colinearity may make it impossible to tell which really matters. We accept the notion that the links between trade and growth are hard to separate from the policies that typically accompany more open trading regimes, such as more stable macroeconomic policies, more openness to foreign direct investment, more liberalization of domestic markets, less rent seeking, stronger rule of law, and so on. This makes it more difficult to tell whether trade or some other aspect of the "package" is what matters, or indeed whether the different components are too interrelated to assign an independent benefit to one piece. As we will discuss in Section 3.3.4, we view this confluence of policies to be an advantage of open trade policies. Thus we are not troubled by an interpretation of the results that says that more open trade, and the policies that are typically associated, leads to higher incomes.

Rather than review the many studies in this area, we concentrate on two complementary strands. The first looks at the relationship between levels of income and trade openness across countries, using a variety of instruments to control for the possibility of reverse causality from growth to trade and also attempting to test whether the inclusion of other determinants of growth, such as institutional quality and geography, eliminate the relationship between trade and growth. The findings of these studies are that the cross-country variation in the level of GDP per capita and total factor productivity depends on openness, even when openness, measured either as the share of trade in GDP or the policy-based Sachs–Warner measure, is instrumented with plausibly exogenous variables such as distance from trading partners. Another conclusion is that openness is often highly correlated with institutional quality, where institutional quality is defined broadly in terms of the importance of rule of law, the effectiveness of the government, and so on. In an effort to unravel this colinearity of openness and institutional quality across countries, we will turn to a second strand of analysis that examines the relationship between changes in openness and changes in per capita GDP through time.[31]

We focus first on Hall and Jones (1999), who attempt to explain cross-country differences in income per capita. Their basic specification is

$$\log Y/L = \alpha + \beta \tilde{S} + \varepsilon$$

where Y/L is output per worker and $\tilde{S}$ is the (instrumented) value of the "social infrastructure." Social infrastructure is an average of two components. The first is government anti-diversion policies (GADP), as estimated by a private firm, Political Risk Services. This measures law and order, bureaucratic quality, corruption, risk of expropriation, and government repudiation of contracts. The second is the fraction of years during the 1950–94 period that the country was open according to the Sachs–Warner measure of policy openness. These are instrumented with various plausibly exogenous variables that are designed to measure Western European influence: the extent to which Western European languages are spoken, the distance from the equator, and the predicted trade share of an economy, based on a gravity model of international trade that uses only a country's population and geographic characteristics, from Frankel and Romer (1999).

The basic result is that social infrastructure instrumented in this way is highly significant and explains much of the differences across countries in output per worker. (Figure 3.3 shows the impressive strength of the simple relationship between output per worker and social infrastructure.) More importantly for our purposes, the results are similar when using Sachs–Warner openness alone, though apparently it is sufficiently correlated with GADP that disentangling which of the two variables matters most is not possible.

This is a powerful result that addresses many of the toughest specification problems. First, we are comfortable with the association of openness with "social infrastructure" and accept that the two are hard to tell apart, for reasons we have discussed. Second, the instruments are clearly exogenous to income in 1990. Moreover, the ordinary least squares (OLS) estimates of the effect of openness on income are smaller than the instrumental variables (IV) estimates, suggesting any reverse causality from income to openness is dwarfed by errors in the measurement of openness that bias the OLS coefficient down. Third, there is no evidence that the instruments affect income except through their impact on openness.

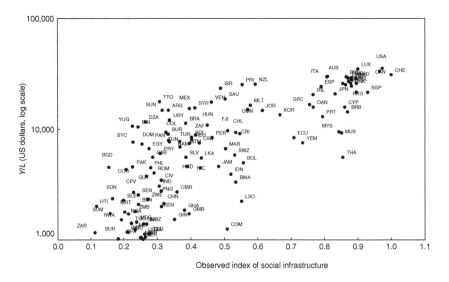

Figure 3.3 Social infrastructure and output per worker.

Source: Hall and Jones (1999).

Suppose, in contrast, that it is not really openness that is the cause of growth; suppose instead that the higher incomes are due to deeper structural and cultural factors that are themselves related to the instruments used in the regression, that is, to distance from partners, language use, and so on. In this case, though, the residuals from the regression of income on trade (instrumented with those structural factors) ought to be correlated with the structural factors themselves. Why? Because the variation of these structural factors not associated with trade openness ought to matter for income. In fact, the residuals are not correlated with the instruments. This allows a rejection of the hypothesis that any of the instruments belong in the income regression. Finally, the result is robust to the inclusion of a variety of other variables on the right-hand side of the income equation, notably distance from the equator, and ethnolinguistic fractionalization.

Similar strong results obtain when openness is measured by trade shares in GDP, rather than the Sachs–Warner policy-based measure, as long as it is also properly instrumented. This result originates in Frankel and Romer (1999) and is expanded in Frankel and Rose (2000). They measure openness as the share of exports plus imports in GDP, and then create a predicted openness measure based on geographic variables such as distance from trading partners, size, having a common border, and being landlocked. This fitted openness measure is not subject to reverse causality from income, but itself is a powerful determinant of the level of real income per capita across countries. As stated, the errors in the income regression are not correlated with the instruments, making it possible to reject the hypothesis that these variables belong in the income regression directly. To control for the possibility that this fitted openness variable is proxying for other factors that may be correlated with the instruments, they include a variety of control variables, including distance from the equator, regional dummies, and a measure of institutional quality. They find that the fitted openness variable largely survives the inclusion of these additional variables.[32]

This general finding is not entirely ironclad. For example, Irwin and Tervio (2000) extend the Frankel–Romer regressions to various time periods in the twentieth century. They find that trade, instrumented by geographic variables, explains income, but that inclusion of a variable measuring distance from the equator greatly attenuates the effect in some samples. Rodrik (2000) also shows that the addition of enough additional variables can make openness insignificant.

A recent refinement to the measure of openness appears to substantially strengthen the robustness of the link between openness, instrumented by geographic variables, and income. As noted earlier, Alcalá and Ciccone (2001) argue that openness should be measured as exports plus imports as a share of GDP in purchasing-power-parity dollars. These authors find that the level of income is strongly related to real openness, when the latter is instrumented with the usual geographic variables. Moreover, this result holds up when a large number of controls are introduced, including institutional quality, expropriation risk, and geographic variables such as distance from the equator, as well as regional dummy variables. These effects are large. Their baseline estimate suggests that an increase in real openness that takes the country from the twentieth percentile to the median value almost triples productivity.[33]

To summarize, the cross-country evidence is strong that openness causes higher incomes. This is true when openness is measured in terms of policy, as in the Sachs–Warner variable, and when it is measured as an outcome in terms of the ratio of exports plus imports to GDP. In the latter case, using purchasing-power parity gross domestic product (PPP GDP) instead of GDP, that is eliminating the effects of cross-country differences in the price of nontraded goods, seems to make the results stronger. This remains true when openness is instrumented using plausible exogenous variables, which themselves appear not to belong in the income regression. Finally, it withstands the introduction of a variety of specifications that add other additional variables, notably controls for geographic factors such as distance from the equator and even regional dummies.

This line of research shows, though, that it is difficult to separate the effects of openness and institutional quality in a satisfactory way. Partly, this reflects the fact that the components of each that can be identified as exogenous (because they are correlated with predetermined instrumental variables such as distance from trading partners and historical determinants of institutional quality) are highly correlated with each other. That is, the variation across countries in the variables and their deep determinants do not allow the identification of separate effects.[34] We therefore turn to a second set of regressions that emphasize differences in openness through time as determinants of changes in growth rates through time, thereby abstracting from slowly changing institutional and geographic issues. Dollar and Kraay (2003) explain growth in the 1990s and 1980s for a set of roughly 100 countries as a function of growth in the previous decade and the change in openness over the decade, plus other controls:

$$Y_{ct} = \beta_0 + \beta_1 Y_{c,t-k} + \beta_2 X_{ct} + \eta_c + \gamma_t + \nu_{ct}$$

and taking first differences,

$$Y_{ct} - Y_{c,t-k} = \beta_1(Y_{c,t-k} - Y_{c,t-2k}) + \beta_2(X_{ct} - X_{c,t-k}) + (\gamma_t - \gamma_{t-k})$$
$$+ (\nu_{ct} - \nu_{c,t-k})$$

where Y_{ct} is the log-level of per capita GDP in country c in time t, k is ten years, X_{ct} is a set of control variables, in particular openness, measured as an average over the decade between $t - k$ and t, η_c is an unobserved country effect that is constant over time, γ_t is an unobserved time-period effect that is common across countries, and ν_{ct} is a serially uncorrelated error. Dollar and Kraay estimate the regression in first differences. Openness is measured as the exports plus imports as a share of GDP.

This approach avoids the difficulty associated with distinguishing the roles of slowly changing geographic, institutional, and cultural factors from openness by looking only at differences through time. In other words, the time invariant country specific term η_c drops out from the estimated equation, so they do not matter for the estimates. This procedure also takes an entirely different approach than the cross-country level regressions to controlling for reverse causality from income to openness, since it permits the use of lagged values of the endogenous predictive variables, openness, and growth, as instruments.[35] While again these instruments pass the appropriate tests of whether they are in fact uncorrelated with the errors in the growth equation, these tests may have low power and the instruments may not be appropriate. We would emphasize, though, that the problems here are entirely different from those associated with the instruments in the cross-country levels approach. Thus, the two sets of results reinforce and complement each other.

The basic result is that changes in trade volumes are highly correlated with changes in growth, with a point estimate suggesting that an increase in the trade share of GDP from 20 to 40 percent over the decade would raise real GDP per capita by 10 percent. This result turns out to be robust to the inclusion of a variety of additional control variables, specifically inflation, government consumption as a share of GDP, and (as measures of time-varying institutional quality) the frequency of revolutions and the amount of contract-intensive money (i.e. M2/GDP).[36]

A further interesting result is foreign direct investment (FDI) as a share of GDP predicts growth in a similar manner to trade openness, and these two variables are too correlated for the data to tell whether each is independently important. While it is unfortunate that the data do not allow us to gauge the relative importance of these two variables, we find it reasonable that the benefits of trade cannot be distinguished from the benefits of openness to FDI. As we discuss in the final section, the fact that trade policy is typically part of a set of reforms, including liberalization to FDI, suggests the importance of trade openness as part of the overall reform package.[37]

We have focused on a small number of regression studies and emphasized how two very different approaches yield a similar result: openness is fairly robustly a cause of growth. Two important caveats are in order. We recognize that there is substantial uncertainty surrounding these estimates. In some specifications openness is not robust, for example, and frequently related variables of interest are too correlated for the data to tell which matters most. As we discussed at the beginning of this section, broad regression exercises of these sorts can only go so far in exploring many of the complexities involved. We thus turn to other sorts of evidence.

3.3.4 *The effects of liberalization on income: case studies*

Case studies have also tended to show benefits from trade liberalization. Clearly, opening to trade does not guarantee faster growth. But one striking conclusion from the last twenty years of experience is that there are no examples of recent take-off countries that have not opened to an important extent as part of the reform process.

An earlier literature convincingly detailed the mechanisms through which import substitution policies worked, or more precisely did not work. Krueger (1978) and Bhagwati (1978) report on studies that measure in detail the degree of effective protection and anti-export bias in nine developing countries. They analyze the phases through which liberalizing countries proceeded during their moves from import substitution toward an outward-oriented trade policy (i.e. one without an anti-export bias). They describe how the distortions from various sorts of protection work their way through the economy in mostly unplanned and undesirable ways. They show how exports and growth responded in those cases where there were substantial trade liberalizations and appropriate accompanying macroeconomic policies.

In more recent years a variety of studies have followed this approach, attempting to define liberalization episodes in a sample of cases and examine the effects of liberalization. The largest study, Choksi *et al.* (1991), analyzes the design, implementation, and outcome of trade liberalizations in each of the 36 episodes in 19 countries between 1946 and 1986. It provides a subjective assessment of the depth of liberalization in each of the episodes. It finds that strong and sustained liberalization episodes result in rapid growth of exports and real GDP.

A variety of other multicountry studies of liberalization episodes give mixed results on effect of liberalization on growth.[38] A central complication is that it is critical not just to label a structural adjustment loan with trade components as liberalization – measuring actual follow-through is critical. Indeed, as demonstrated in Andriamananjara and Nash (1997), most liberalizations are in fact gradual, with different layers of protection being gradually peeled away. Exceptions, such as Chile in the 1970s and Mexico in the 1980s, are rare. Thus, the liberalization event study is difficult to interpret, particularly if actual implementation is not carefully assessed case by case.[39]

What has happened to liberalizers since 1980? There is a relative dearth of systematic case studies completed in the past few years that review the experience of liberalizers in the past ten years or so. Dollar and Kraay (2001) classify countries into globalizers and nonglobalizers based on three criteria: (i) those whose trade as a share of GDP rose most (the top third of the distribution, that is, the top twenty-four countries in their sample) between 1975–79 and 1995–97; (ii) those who have the largest reductions in average tariff over the 1985–89 to 1995–97 period; and (iii) those nine countries that are in both groups.[40] They show that the globalizers enjoyed a substantial increase in growth rates in the 1990s relative to the 1980s (from 1.4 to 3.8 percent growth per year in real per capita GDP growth for the third group), while growth of nonglobalizers went from −0.1 to 0.8 percent.[41]

Sachs and Warner (1995) examine the experience of countries that opened (according to their measure) since 1975, and find higher growth in the two years after liberalization and further out, relative to the years prior to liberalization (even excluding years immediately prior to opening).

Individual case studies inevitably present a varied picture. Country experiences differ radically and trade is only part of the story. Disentangling the various factors is difficult. In our view, though, a common thread across most successful cases of "take-off" is a significant degree of trade liberalization, even if this is not obviously decisive in each case and even if it is not sufficient. (It is less clear that it is not necessary, in that cases of successful and sustained take-off in the postwar years in the absence of trade liberalization are rare to vanishing.)

3.3.5 The channels through which trade affects growth: sectoral and micro studies

Detailed country-specific sectoral studies from the 1970s and 1980s showed substantial costs to inward-oriented policies and failed to find dynamic gains from protection as predicted by infant-industry arguments. More recent microeconomic evidence documents several channels through which openness leads to higher productivity. There is thus ample microeconomic basis for the aggregate relationships discussed earlier. Support for the infant-industry proposition at the sectoral level remains weak.

Perhaps the central finding from the large cross-country studies of trade liberalization in the 1970s and 1980s was the highly distortionary nature of the import substituting regimes being considered; these proved to be much greater than the simple average tariff rates would suggest. These studies emphasized the ways in which inward-oriented trade policies reinforced poor macroeconomic and exchange rate policies. In their careful study of the differences between inward- and outward-oriented regimes in practice, these analyses can be contrasted with many recent discussions of the merits of openness, which are impoverished through a lack of a concrete counterfactual.

Some recent direct evidence that trade promotes productivity growth in developing countries comes from Coe *et al.* (1997) who find that total factor productivity in a panel of seventy-one developing countries is significantly related to the stock of research and development carried out by trading partners. There is clear evidence that trade, particularly the import of machinery and equipment, mediates the diffusion of knowledge: the interaction of trading partner R&D stock with the quantity of machinery and equipment imported from that partner is an important determinant of the size of the productivity effect.

There has been, until recently, little evidence with respect to gains from trade liberalization at the industry and firm level.[42] Bhagwati (1988) argued that there was little direct evidence that export promotion was associated with greater innovation or less x-inefficiency. Recent studies at the firm and industry level have, however, provided support for the idea that trade liberalization has spurred increased productivity, through a variety of mechanisms.[43] Increased import competition lowers margins and increases turnover and innovation. Exit is only the most visible part of the story. For example, Wacziarg (1997) shows that entry rates of new firms into liberalizing sectors were 20 percent higher than in other sectors, in eleven trade liberalization episodes during the 1980s.

While many studies have shown that exporting firms are more productive, causality has been hard to establish, given the plausible hypothesis that increases in productivity (for some other reason) may encourage firms to export.[44] A set of papers has recently examined the relationships between export performance and productivity growth using detailed panels of plant-level data and found, for developed and middle-income countries, that at the plant level, causality seems to run from productivity to exports, not the other way around.[45] That is, export growth follows increases in productivity, but there is little sign that strong export performance implies faster subsequent productivity increases. Thus, if exporting increases productivity, the evidence from richer countries suggests that it does so other than through direct effects on plant-level productivity. Firms in the poorest countries presumably have the most to learn. Thus, it is not surprising to find evidence that firms in such countries achieve more productivity growth after entering export markets. Bigsten *et al.* (2000) find that firms in four African countries do learn from exporting, as well as self-selecting for the export sector, while Kraay (1999) finds learning effects in Chinese enterprises.

Even if exporting firms enjoy unusual productivity increases only prior to entering the export market, causality may still run from the entry into the export market to the productivity increase. Hallward-Driemeier *et al.* (2000), using data from five East Asian countries, find that the productivity gains observed prior to entering into the export market are associated with specific behaviors that suggest directed efforts aimed at penetrating the export market, such as using more foreign technology and imported inputs.

Other studies have looked beyond plant-specific effects of trade in promoting productivity growth. One mechanism that appears important is that exporting plants, which are relatively highly productive, may grow faster than nonexporting plants. Thus, average productivity growth rates are higher as resources shift into the exporting plants. This mechanism appears very important in the United States. According to Bernard and Jensen (1999), from 1983 through 1992, more than 40 percent of total factor productivity growth in the manufacturing sector of the United States resulted from the fact that high-productivity exporting plants grew faster than lower-productivity nonexporting plants. Thus, exporters accounted for much more of the productivity growth in the sample than their share in total employment. It is plausible to expect that of the various channels through which trade could promote productivity growth, those that operate through the diffusion of more advanced technologies from abroad would play the smallest role in the United States. Thus, trade may have more beneficial effects on productivity growth in developing countries than these results suggest.[46]

Trade may also promote productivity growth through its effects on the quality of imported intermediate and capital goods. Many studies show a positive correlation between access to imported inputs and productivity.[47] Demonstration effects across firms and higher competitiveness may also induce innovation and increases in productivity. For example, Clerides *et al.* (1998), who found no within-plant learning from exporting *per se*, found that firms in regions with substantial export activity had lower costs.[48]

Much evidence thus suggests that openness helps productivity growth in manufacturing. This is inconsistent with the infant-industry idea that protection helps support the growth of industry and eventually industrial productivity. Some evidence for learning-by-doing can be found, suggesting some role for protection to enhance productivity growth and allow new industries to eventually become competitive.[49] However, in most cases there is no evidence that protected industries grow faster than others, and even where they do, the costs of protection in terms of higher prices for domestic consumers seem to greatly outweigh any benefits. Krueger and Tuncer (1982) found no evidence that protection abetted productivity growth in a cross-section of Turkish industries.[50] More generally, Bell *et al.* (1984) conclude in their survey that infant firms have experienced relatively slow productivity growth. They believe that underlying this result is the fact that achieving international competitiveness results not just from learning-by-doing, as would be abetted by high levels of protection, but a more active effort. This is consistent with the given results on the positive influence of both import competition and the availability of export markets on productivity growth.

More recent work has continued to deprecate the infant-industry argument. Luzio and Greenstein (1995) study the effect of Brazil's prohibition on micro-computer imports in the 1990s. The domestic industry developed rapidly, but more slowly than international competitors, so the price/performance frontier in Brazil lagged international standards by 3–5 years. The costs to consumers of computers have been as high as high as 20 percent of domestic expenditures on microcomputers.

The given evidence focused on post-Second World War international experience. It has often been claimed that late nineteenth-century tariffs in the United States successfully promoted infant industries, most clearly in the case of the tin-plate industry. In a methodologically careful recent study, Irwin (2000) finds that the tariffs did allow the industry to arise in the United States about a decade earlier than it otherwise would have. Nonetheless, his welfare calculations suggest that the protection did not pass a cost–benefit test. Whatever learning-by-doing was taking place was outweighed by the higher prices paid by domestic users of tin-plate in the United States as a result of the tariff.

More recent evidence on the relationship between protection and productivity growth comes from Jonsson and Subramanian (2001), who look at the relationship between productivity and the decline in protection across industries in South Africa over the 1990s. They find strong effects – a decline in the output price of 10 percent due to tariff reduction results in an increase in the total factor productivity growth rate of 3 percentage points. There is no sign of a larger decline in employment in those industries with the larger decline in tariffs.[51] Support from another direction comes from Dodzin and Vamvakidis (1999) who examine the impact of international trade on industrialization in developing agricultural economies. Those economies that increased their openness (using the Sachs–Warner measure) during 1975–95 experienced an *increase* in their share of industrial production at the expense of agricultural production. Indeed, the least industrialized countries at the time of liberalization tend to experience the most rapid industrialization thereafter.[52]

3.3.6 Trade and poverty

There are strong reasons to suppose that trade liberalization will benefit the poor at least as much as the average person. Trade liberalization tends to reduce monopoly rents and the value of connections to bureaucratic and political power. In developing countries, it may be expected to increase the relative wage of low-skilled workers.[53] Liberalization of agriculture may increase (relatively low) rural incomes. On the other hand, trade liberalization might also worsen the income distribution, for example, by encouraging the adoption of skill-biased technical change in response to increased foreign competition.

If trade liberalization worsens the income distribution enough, particularly by making the poor poorer, then it is possible that it is not after all good for poverty reduction, despite its positive overall growth effects. We have seen that this seems unlikely based on the weak general relationship between growth and inequality. But perhaps trade-based growth is different. We first examine the systematic cross-country evidence then briefly review some of the vast microeconomic literature on the effects of trade liberalization on income distribution. We are not looking here at the question of how trade openness affects income distribution, rather, we want to know how trade openness matters for absolute poverty beyond its effects on growth.[54]

Though the evidence is somewhat mixed, it leans strongly toward the conclusion that there is no systematic relationship between openness and the income of the poorest, beyond the effect of openness on overall growth. Dollar and Kraay (2001) provide the clearest evidence. Using a large panel (137 developing countries from 1950 to 1999), they regress the income share going to the lowest quintile on mean per capita income in their sample. They find that the income of poorest quintile grows one-for-one with average incomes (consistent with the finding we noted in the introduction, that growth does not systematically correlate with changes in the income distribution). They also find that, given growth, openness has a tiny and statistically insignificant effect on income of the poor.[55]

Other studies using panel and cross-section data report similar results: no significant evidence of links between openness and changes in the *relative* well-being of the poor.[56] For example, Cashin *et al.* (2001) analyze a cross-section of countries between 1975 and 1998. They estimate the relationship between economic policies and improvements in a human development index, which is highly correlated with poverty, for a given rate of growth of GDP per capita. They do not find significant and robust evidence that any openness variable (the ratio of foreign trade to GDP or the black market premium) was associated with pro-poor or anti-poor growth.[57]

These statistical analyses with large numbers of countries are in many ways unsatisfactory. The data underlying them are highly problematic, and they attempt to fit different sorts of trade liberalization episodes, in different countries, into a common framework. An alternative approach to looking at how trade liberalization affects the poor is to study in detail individual liberalization episodes. This allows a consideration of the rich variety of mechanisms through which liberalization can affect poverty and of the various ways that specific characteristics of the individuals involved can influence the results. We would like to emphasize, though, one important problem that is more-or-less common to these studies: it is much easier to see what happens to individuals or groups that are directly affected by trade liberalization than it is to observe how the opening plays out throughout the entire economy through time.[58]

On the question of whether the poor benefit more or less than others, no clear pattern emerges from the numerous studies of individual liberalization episodes.[59] This is not surprising, as any particular liberalization will change relative prices and incentives throughout the economy. A few generalizations can nonetheless be extracted from these studies. Poor consumers tend to benefit from trade liberalization as do other consumers. Liberalization of agricultural trade typically has the strongest effects on the poor, since in most countries most poor are engaged in small-scale agriculture. In general, trade protection usually induces an anti-agricultural bias, so liberalization should help; the poorest among small farmers may, though, be relatively ill placed to benefit.

3.4   Trade and the broader policy environment

We have examined a large amount of evidence about the effect of openness on growth and poverty. Much of this evidence is vulnerable to the criticism that the effect of openness has not been isolated from the effects of many other reforms that were often implemented at the same time. In the case studies and before–after comparisons, for example, effects of liberalization of trade are hard to disentangle from the effects of macroeconomic stabilization, internal price liberalization, changes in the foreign exchange system and the exchange rate, liberalization of the capital account, the introduction or elimination of social safety net programs, and a host of other measures.

This correlation of openness with other elements of reform is indeed a difficult econometric problem. We do not consider it to be a problem from the point of view of the design of reform programs, however. First, trade is a particularly important component of reform. Second, trade openness has important positive spillovers on other aspects of reform so that, on the whole, the correlation of trade with other pro-reform policies speaks to the advantages of making openness a primary part of the reform package. Finally, there is little evidence that there are other reforms that must precede an effective trade reform, though there are many reforms that are complementary.

Insofar as the data do speak, they tend to single out trade openness as a particularly important reform. The various policy variables hypothesized to promote growth are in many cases highly correlated. But as Sala-i-Martin (1997) has shown, among the variables more robustly related to growth are the Sachs–Warner openness measure and the black market exchange rate premium. According to Easterly and Levine (2001), openness (measured as the ratio of trade to GDP) and the black market premium are highly significant in a regression including several other policy variables.

It is indeed true that reforms tend to come in packages of various sorts. Thus, this is a problem for identifying the effects of different sorts of reforms. It is not, however, a policy problem. On the contrary, in our view trade reforms are a central aspect of the overall reform package. If trade openness is associated with lower inflation, for example, then it makes it more difficult to say which is the key factor in a regression or case study, but it makes it easier to recommend trade openness.

In interpreting the role of trade reform as distinct from other aspects of policy, it is important to distinguish between preconditions, desirable complements, and beneficial reform "spillovers." In our view, there are few true preconditions, that is, reforms in the absence of which trade openness is a poor idea. Openness seems to promote growth in the poorest countries as well as in others. Ades and Glaeser (1999) find that, among relatively closed economies, the poorest in 1960 also grew the slowest between 1960 and 1985, but that low initial income is *not* correlated with slower subsequent growth in open economies. They argue that in closed economies low initial income reduces potential benefits from scale economies, but that trade openness, by allowing access to broader markets, overcomes this problem. More broadly, there is little evidence of a "growth trap" in the sense of a situation in which countries become too poor to take off. For example, Jones (1997) notes that, of the 18 poorest countries in 1965 in his sample of 121, 4 grew at least one point faster than the United States over the 1960–88, while 11 grew about as fast as the United States. Parente and Prescott (2000) point out that all the growth miracles of the twentieth century occurred in countries starting far behind the richest. Ng and Yeats (1996) argue that protectionist trade policies and related macroeconomic distortions played a key role in Africa's relative marginalization in world trade between the 1950s and 1990s, not external protection in OECD markets or an unfortunate specialization in exporting goods of declining world importance, though the latter also played a role.

Many factors can make trade reform more or less successful. For example, a more egalitarian initial income distribution implies that a given amount of (distribution-neutral) growth has a larger impact on the poverty rate, all else held equal.[60] There is also evidence that certain factors such as higher rates of education permit the poor to benefit more fully from growth.[61] Of course, these are not arguments against trade reform but rather for pursuing these complementary reforms as well. Some measures may be co-requisites of trade liberalization, at least in the sense that in their absence, the trade liberalization policy may not endure. As Choksi *et al.* (1991) argue based on case studies, for example, trade liberalizations in the presence of chaotic macroeconomic environments and overvalued exchange rates are likely to be reversed.[62]

The most important set of relationships, in our view, has to do with positive spillovers from trade reform. In many cases and in many ways, trade liberalization is itself a precondition or a complement to other sorts of reforms and thus facilitates their success. The fact that trade reform often happens as a package, from this point of view, is a strength of trade reforms, even if it is an econometric challenge.

There are a variety of reasons why trade openness might promote other sorts of reforms. Openness provides powerful channels for feedback on the effect of various policies on productivity and growth. For example, competition with foreign firms can expose inefficient industrial policies. Trade raises visibility of failure in other areas. Trade raises the marginal product of other reforms, in that better infrastructure, telephones, roads, and ports translate into better performance of the export sector and, less visibly, this raises productivity for domestic goods as well. Trade liberalization may change the political reform dynamic by creating constituencies for further reform.[63]

Two areas in which trade interacts with the capital account deserve special attention. First, the evidence is clear that FDI has important benefits for growth, and hence for poverty, in developing countries. As has been recognized for some time, allowing FDI behind important trade barriers can lead to large and stubborn distortions. Moreover, openness to FDI is highly correlated with openness to trade. Thus, an open trading regime is an important counterpart to allowing in substantial and productive FDI.[64]

Second, the large crises observed in several emerging markets in the past decade have given new force to an old sequencing argument – that trade liberalization should precede capital account liberalization more broadly. There is mixed evidence that the income distribution systematically worsens during crises, but of course the poorest are likely to be least able to adjust to declines in income.[65] Trade shocks and openness have not, in general, been important causes of recent exchange rate crises.[66] On the other hand, growth following crises and sharp contractions in the current account deficit are stronger in more open economies, presumably because the exchange rate depreciation associated with the crises leads to a stronger export response in more open economies. Thus, trade openness is increasingly important in a world that is growing otherwise more integrated.[67]

It is sometimes argued that an absence of adequate prior institutional reform may limit the gains from openness. Dani Rodrik, for example, has argued that the efforts spent implementing trade reform would be better spent on other sorts of reform, primarily institutional.[68] It should be clear that, in our view, the positive spillovers from openness to other reforms are more than powerful enough to overcome this sort of effect. Successful institutional reform is likely to be a powerful complement to trade liberalization, but there is little or no evidence to suggest that waiting on such institutional reform is a good idea. On the contrary, there is strong evidence that openness may encourage institutional reform and in particular reduce corruption, as argued in Krueger (1974). Ades and Di Tella (1999) find that corruption is higher in countries where domestic firms are sheltered from foreign competition by natural or policy-induced barriers to trade, and that the size of this effect is large: almost a third of the corruption gap between Italy and Austria can be explained by Italy's lower exposure to foreign competition.[69]

3.5 Conclusion

We have surveyed the literature and extracted three main propositions about trade policy and poverty: (1) poverty reduction is mainly about growth in average per capita income, (2) trade openness is an important determinant of growth, and (3) the growth that is associated with trade liberalization is as pro-poor as growth in general.

On the first proposition, there is ample evidence that the main cause of changes in absolute poverty is changes in average per capita income. Long-run trends reinforce the point that the relationship between poverty and openness is dominated

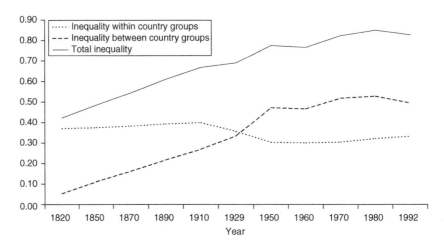

Figure 3.4 World income inequality.

Source: Bourguignon and Morrisson (2002), mean logarithmic deviation from table 3.2.

by growth. First, within-country inequality has been relatively stable and not a source of much of the change in overall global inequality. Thus, any globalization-induced changes in within-country inequality are a small part of the story. Bourguignon and Morrisson (2002) chart global individual inequality between 1820 and 1992 and divide it into between-country and within-country components (shown in Figure 3.4). Most of the story of world income distribution is the rise in between-country inequality until about 1950 and perhaps the slight decline since 1980. Sala-i-Martin (2002) concentrates on the more recent period and finds that overall global inequality has been falling since 1980, thanks to between-country convergence.

By concluding that openness tends to increase growth, we suggest that if poor countries opened more, poverty would fall. Both Bourguignon and Morrisson (2002) and O'Rourke (2001) in their surveys of historical trends in globalization and inequality conclude that globalization has been, broadly speaking, a force for between-country convergence among participating countries. Until the third quarter of the twentieth century, though, other factors such as unequal spread of the Industrial Revolution and nonparticipation by some countries in the world economy overwhelmed this effect.

With respect to the second proposition, the evidence that trade openness is an important determinant of growth is varied. First, we know that countries and regions that are sufficiently similar along a broad number of dimensions, such as states in the United States, regions of Europe, or even countries of the OECD, tend to converge to similar levels of income. It is plausible that trade openness is an important part of this convergence process and hence part of bringing poverty rates down in poorer countries. Of course, many other factors are potentially at play in this convergence process.

Cross-country and panel regressions allow us to examine the separate roles of some of these factors. In cross-country regressions of the level of income on various determinants, openness seems to be the most important policy variable, despite the measurement problems. The toughest question is how to disentangle the effects of openness from those of the good institutional environment that usually accompanies openness. A quick perusal of the variables considered in measuring good institutions makes it clear why these must be important in the development process: voice and accountability, lack of political instability and violence, effective government, manageable regulatory burden, rule of law, and absence of corruption. Trade can only be an aspect of the development process, and these institutions are also clearly central. We argue, though, that openness is in many ways a contributor to a strong institutional environment. More broadly, the fact that openness is highly correlated with quality of institutions across countries should give long pause to anyone contemplating the adoption of what amounts to a novel (or tested and failed) development strategy that does not involve openness to trade.

The regression evidence on determinants of changes in income within countries through time allows us to distinguish between the effects of institutional variables and trade openness, for the simple reason that institutional variables do not vary much through time, so that it is unlikely that changes in trade openness can be confused with their effects. These regressions also show a central role for increases in openness in promoting growth.

We would not find these regression results particularly convincing if there were not a substantial quantity of case study and industry and firm-level research documenting the various ways in which openness contributes to export, productivity, and ultimately income growth. Perhaps the central finding from the large multi-country studies of trade liberalization in the 1970s and 1980s was the highly distortionary nature of the import-substituting regimes prior to liberalization. Somewhat more recently, others have followed this approach, attempting to define liberalization episodes in a sample of cases and examine the effects and also finding that strong and sustained liberalization episodes result in rapid growth of exports and real GDP. Recent studies at the firm and industry level have delineated some of the ways that trade liberalization and the resulting increase in import competition works to increase productivity, and have shown that an emphasis on exports helps as well. Consistent with the evidence on the benefits of trade for productivity growth, the infant-industry argument has consistently failed to find empirical support.

Our third main proposition is that trade openness, conditional on growth, does not have systematic effects on the poor. The aggregate evidence shows that the income of the poorest tends to grow one-for-one with average income. Of course, in some countries and in some periods the poor do better than average, and sometimes they do worse. But openness does not help explain which of these outcomes occurs. The micro evidence from a large number of individual liberalization episodes also shows that there is no systematic relationship between trade liberalization and income distribution. Thus, trade openness has contributed to growth that has resulted in an unprecedented decline in absolute poverty over the past twenty years. Changes in income distribution within countries have, on the other hand, contributed little to net changes in poverty incidence. (This is true also over longer periods.) Indeed, the change in income distribution in the last fifteen or so years has been slightly pro-poor.

Much of the evidence that openness promotes growth and poverty reduction is vulnerable to the criticism that the effects of openness have not been isolated from those of other reforms undertaken prior to or with trade liberalization. This is an econometric but not a policy problem, however. Openness has important positive spillovers on other aspects of reform, so the correlation of trade with other pro-reform policies speaks to the advantages of making openness a primary part of the reform package. Moreover, there is little evidence that other reforms must precede an effective trade reform, though there are many that are complementary.[70]

Openness is not a "magic bullet," however. Trade policy is only one of many determinants of growth. Thus, it should not come as a surprise that even though trade is an important determinant of growth, and there has been substantial trade liberalization in the last twenty years, growth in the 1980s and 1990s has been disappointing, resulting in a correspondingly modest (if unprecedented) decline in poverty.[71] This should not distract us from the importance of trade liberalization in developing countries, however. Trade can only be an aspect of the development process. However, the breadth of evidence on openness, growth, and poverty reduction, and the strength of the association between openness and other important determinants of high per capita income such as the quality of institutions, should give long pause to anyone contemplating the adoption of a novel (or tested and failed) development strategy that does not center around openness to trade.

In this chapter, we have emphasized the importance of the policies of developing countries themselves in generating growth. Industrial countries have also maintained market access barriers and agricultural policies that penalize typical developing country products, and their removal would help reduce poverty and guarantee greater benefits from developing country trade liberalization.[72] Nonetheless, it is a deep mistake to consider trade opening and tariff reductions to be a game in which only bilaterally negotiated liberalizations are advantageous.

Notes

1   These numbers are from Sala-i-Martin (2002), who measures poverty rates based on income for developing and developed countries. Chen and Ravallion (2001) find similar trends though higher poverty rates. They define poverty in terms of consumption and consider only developing countries. The focus on consumption is a priori attractive but only makes a substantial difference only if it is assumed that the extreme poor save a significant share of their income.
2   Changes in the world distribution of income during the 1987 through 1998 period have been slightly pro-poor (Chen and Ravallion, 2001).
3   See, for example, Roemer and Gugerty (1997), Dollar and Kraay (2001), and Deininger and Squire (1998). Ghura *et al.* (2002) find in large panel of countries that

the elasticity of income of the poor with respect to average income at 0.94 is close to (though significantly different from) 1.

4 Ravallion (2001).

5 Quah (2002) emphasizes this point.

6 In India, also, a huge (in terms of headcount) reduction in poverty has taken place. Measurement of poverty in India has been subject to substantial dispute, but a careful analysis in Deaton and Drèze (2002) suggests that poverty fell dramatically, from 35 percent in 1987/88 to 29 percent in 1993/94 and 23 percent in 1999/2000. The fall would have been to 21 percent had growth in the 1990s been exactly income neutral. Meanwhile there are also many cases of growth with improvements in the income distribution.

7 Note that we are concerned here with the incidence of absolute poverty, not relative poverty. We discuss income distribution because the information on whether openness has particular implications for poverty *beyond its effects on the growth rate* is largely contained in the literature on openness and income distribution.

8 Transport costs are not artificial – except in cases where high-cost domestic shipping is protected, since they reflect real resource costs.

9 A rigorous statement of the optimality of free trade requires a number of additional assumptions, such as an absence of (or tax compensation for) externalities and other market imperfections, well-functioning competitive domestic factor markets, and no monopoly power in trade. But even if these assumptions were fully met, the issues of measurement that we address in the next section would still arise.

10 Pritchett (2000) points out the need for an eclectic set of models.

11 Indeed, to the extent that many analysts have a tendency to move from the proposition that something is true in a given model to the view that this is somehow evidence for its truth, theory has gotten in the way of an analysis of trade policies. See Krueger (1997) and Srinivasan (2001).

12 The same, of course, applies to the empirical importance of infant industry considerations.

13 A uniformity of incentives, including a low variance of import and export tariffs and subsidies across products, is also important, however. See Krueger (1995) for a discussion of the relationship between free trade, outward orientation, and laissez-faire policies.

14 Pritchett and Sethi (1994) find almost no relationship between official rates and collection rates for a given item in three developing countries.

15 Anderson and Neary (1996) introduce an index number designed to measure the overall restrictiveness of a system of trade protection. Unfortunately, its implementation is sensitive to assumptions regarding the structure of NTBs that are difficult to justify empirically.

16 Edwards (1998) and Barro and Lee (1994) demonstrate the use of the black market exchange rate premium as a measure of distortion and lack of trade openness.

17 See Berg *et al.* (1997) for an example.

18 Dean *et al.* (1994), discussed later in the chapter, document this nicely for a large number of countries.

19 The Sachs–Warner measure may suffer from being a product of its times, in that many protectionist countries have turned to different mechanisms than those emphasized in this measure, such as phytosanitary, sanitary, and technical standards that serve protectionist purposes. Moreover, many countries engage in contingent protection, in which there is a threat to impose large tariffs in the event of major import penetration. The share of imports covered at any point in time is small, but the deterrent effect on imports may be large.

20 See Rodriguez and Rodrik (1999) and Harrison and Hanson (1999). Sachs and Warner (2001), upon which we draw here, provide a spirited defense of their measure. See also Orsmond (1992) on black market exchange rates.

21 Bates (1981) discusses the harmful implications of extractive marketing boards at great length.

22 Thus, the conclusion in Pritchett (1996) that various measures of trade policy, such as tariffs and NTB coverage rates, are not correlated is not surprising. His result that outcome-based measures and each of the various policy measures are not correlated is more surprising, though it may reflect a negative correlation among the various measures as well as other measurement problems. Wang (2001) finds that bilateral trade in different categories of goods is highly dependent on the bilateral tariffs on those goods. He shows that where the policy is well measured, the results can be clear. Moreover, Alcalá and Ciccone (2001) show that the Sachs–Warner measures, as well as some of its components, predict their measure of "real openness."

23 Dollar and Kraay (2002) also measure openness as exports plus imports as a share of PPP GDP. Of course, PPP measures are also highly imperfect. Moreover, as Rodrik *et al.* (2002) point out, "real openness" as defined above may introduce a bias opposite to that it attempts to correct, in that any improvements in productivity of traded good production may result in higher measured "real openness."

24 Wolf (1994), Leamer (1988), and Spilimbergo *et al.* (1999) attempt to measure openness as a residual.

25 The "Communauté Financière Africaine" (CFA) is a group of countries in West and Central Africa that use the same currency, the CFA franc.

26 Sharer *et al.* (1998) collect detailed information on NTBs and tariffs for six countries in the 1990s. They combine the results on NTBs and tariffs into one signal measure. This measure is available since 1997 for a large number of countries.

27 Krueger (1995) discusses trends in trade policy in the postwar period. See World Bank (2001) and Martin (2001) for data on trade barriers since 1980.

28 The fall over time in the standard deviation of incomes across countries is "sigma convergence." For the world as a whole, there has not been absolute convergence if countries are the basic unit of analysis. For individuals, there has been convergence in recent decades; the difference between the two results is due to the relatively rapid growth of India and China.

29 A few selected examples are Alcalá and Ciccone (2001), Dollar (1992), Edwards (1998), Harrison (1996), Barro and Lee (1994), Lee (1993), Easterly and Levine (2001), Dollar and Kraay (2001, 2002), Irwin and Tervio (2000), Islam (1995), Sala-i-Martin (1997), Hall and Jones (1999), Frankel and Rose (2000), Frankel and Romer (1999), Greenaway *et al.* (1998) Surveys of the growth literature are numerous; we have drawn on Edwards (1993), Durlauf and Quah (1999), Klenow and Rodriguez-Clare (1997), Barro and Sala-i-Martin (1995), and Easterly (2001).

30 Srinivasan (2001).

31 Dollar and Kraay (2002) take this approach. Two highly influential papers in the neoclassical tradition, Mankiw *et al.* (1992) and Young (1995) emphasized factor accumulation as the source of growth. These papers shed little light on the role of openness, however. Mankiw *et al.* argue that most (in fact about three-quarters) of the variation in levels of output per capita can be explained by variations in the (exogenous) rate of savings and population growth. Young demonstrates that most of the growth in the four Asian tigers during the post-1960 period can be attributed to (exogenous) accumulation of capital, especially human capital. We, in contrast, wonder about the role of openness in permitting such high savings rates over a long period to be used productively and about the relationship between openness and incentives to invest. In our examination of the empirical evidence below, thus, we concentrate on papers that attempt to explain these factors in terms of policy as well as other determinants such as institutions and geography. See Durlauf and Quah (1999) and Klenow and Rodriguez-Clare (1997) for related comments.

32 Jones in a personal communication reports that the explanatory power of the social infrastructure variable remains strong with the inclusion of a regional dummy variable for Africa, which itself is marginally significant and negative.

33 Dollar and Kraay (2002) also find that using PPP GDP in the denominator yields a more robust determinant of income. As discussed in note 23, Rodrik *et al.* (2002) note that this way of measuring openness creates its own distortions.

34 A debate about whether it is possible to distinguish between institutions, openness, and geography has continued in several very recent papers. Easterly and Levine (2003) report, in regressions similar to Hall and Jones (1999), that institutions trump openness when both are instrumented. In a similar framework, Rodrik *et al.* (2002) report that institutions trump openness and geography. On the other hand, Dollar and Kraay (2002) show that when both institutions and openness are instrumented, it is difficult to distinguish the two effects. It would seem that whether it is possible to distinguish these effects depends on exactly which specification and sample are used.

35 Specifically, $Y_{c,t-3k}$ is an instrument for the first term, while $X_{c,t-k}$ is an appropriate instrument for the change in the second term. The required identifying assumptions are that openness may be correlated with contemporaneous or lagged shocks to GDP growth but not with *future* shocks to the growth rate, and that the shocks to GDP per capita V_{ct} are serially correlated. See the original paper or Caselli *et al.* (1996) for details.

36 Dollar and Kraay (2002) find that changes in a variety of other measures of institutional quality also do not affect growth.

37 Easterly and Levine (2001) apply a similar technique to a panel of seventy-three countries over the 1960–95 period, using non-overlapping five-year periods rather than decades. Their key result is that two measures of openness, trade shares and the black market premium, are both significantly related to growth in a panel of countries, even when controlling for endogeneity, permanent country-specific effects, and a variety of other possible determinants of growth.

38 Greenaway *et al.* (1998) and Harrigan and Mosley (1991) review this literature.

39 Greenaway *et al.* (1998) find in a broad panel with annual data that liberalization episodes do indeed lead to growth, though there is some evidence of a "*j*-curve" effect with an initial negative effect.

40 These nine are Argentina, Bangladesh, Brazil, China, Colombia, India, Nicaragua, Thailand, and Uruguay. The different base year for tariffs is mandated by lack of prior data. Rodrik (2000) criticizes this procedure on various grounds, including the different base years. He finds the results sensitive to details of how the two groups are formulated.

41 This result is true for simple and population averages and if globalizers are defined only in terms of changes in trade shares. For the second group of globalizers, based on changes in tariffs, the nonglobalizers and globalizers have similar increases in growth rates from the 1980s to the 1990s.

42 Rent-seeking behavior (Krueger, 1974) has also been hard to quantify.

43 This section draws heavily on Hallward-Driemeier (2001).

44 Roberts and Tybout (1997) develop and test a model in which sunk costs of entry into exporting imply that only relatively productive firms will find it worthwhile to export. They find that causality goes from productivity to exporting, not the other way around.

45 Clerides *et al.* (1998) look at Mexico, Colombia, and Morocco, and Bernard and Jensen (1999) at the United States, with similar results.

46 However, Isgut (2001) finds strikingly similar results for Colombian firms. Hallward-Driemeier (2001) argues that this is a consistent finding in studies that compare firms before and after liberalization episodes.

47 Hallward-Driemeier (2001) discusses some of them briefly.

48 Many studies have shown important demonstration or proximity effects for foreign multinational corporations on productivity of nearby exporting domestic firms (see Aitken *et al.* (1997) for Mexico and Haddad and Harrison (1993) for Morocco). More generally, there is strong evidence of the productivity-enhancing effect of foreign direct investment at the plant level. In Section 3.5 we touch on the relationship between FDI and trade openness.

49 Of course, even in this case, subsidies would be preferred to protection.

50 This result has been criticized by Harrison (1994) who noted that in some specifications there is actually a positive relationship between the degree of protection of the industry and productivity growth. As noted in Krueger and Tuncer (1994), however, the underlying point remains. While the evidence on productivity differentials is mixed and depends somewhat on the specification used, in no case can the size of a productivity growth differential in favor of the protected industry begin to justify the level of protection afforded that industry, in present value terms.

51 Jonsson in personal communication argues that reverse causality from productivity growth to tariff reductions is implausible. His discussions with policy makers suggested that they did not know which industries had higher productivity or a fortiori were likely to have higher productivity growth. Tariffs tended to be cut in sectors with high initial tariffs; political factors were also important. See also Choudhri and Hakura (2000) who find across countries that increased import competition enhances overall productivity growth.

52 In their survey, Bell *et al.* (1994) also find little evidence supportive of infant industry protection.

53 Evidence on this latter question is mixed.

54 A good recent survey is found in Bannister and Thugge (2001).

55 This result is robust to the inclusion of regional dummy variables and decade dummy variables. It also holds for relatively poor countries only, and whether the income of the poor is regressed on growth using ordinary least squares, or whether, given the possibility of reverse causality from income distribution to growth, growth is instrumented. The result on the irrelevance of openness to distribution holds whether openness is measured in terms of trade volumes, trade volumes purged of the effects of geography as a measure of policy, or the Sachs–Warner variable.

56 That is, these studies have not found links between openness and the well-being of the poor beyond those associated with higher average per capita income growth. See for example Edwards (1997), Roemer and Gugerty (1997), and Ghura *et al.* (2002).

57 Lundberg and Squire (2003), in contrast, find in a panel of countries that the Gini coefficient for income inequality is significantly and positively related to instrumented Sachs–Warner openness. In separate regressions by income group, Sachs–Warner openness is negatively correlated with growth among the poorest 40 percent, but strongly and positively correlated with growth among the middle 60 percent and wealthiest 40 percent (these are overlapping samples). One reason these authors get a different result than Dollar and Kraay (2001) and others in the literature may be that they have a much smaller sample, a result of their effort to include many more explanatory variables in the regression, variables that are only available for a subset of the countries analyzed in Dollar and Kraay (2001).

58 For example, we noted earlier that exports seem to promote productivity growth not through what they do to individual plants but through how they allow the exporting plants to grow faster, drawing resources from other less productive sectors.

59 This paragraph and the next draw heavily on McCulloch *et al.* (2001).

60 This comes from the interaction between the shape of the income distribution and the effect of an equiproportional increase in income for everyone.

61 Ravallion and Datt (2001) make this argument in looking at the effects of growth on poverty across regions of India.

62 Bannister and Thugge (2001) emphasize the value of making reforms as broad as possible, sequencing and phasing them to allow for adjustment, and implementing social safety nets and other reforms that facilitate adjustment to the new trade policy. Poulton *et al.* (1999) emphasize the value of targeted welfare interventions to ensure that the poorest rural households benefit from trade liberalization. Sharer *et al.* (1998) put more weight on the need to consider fiscal implications when designing trade liberalization programs.

63 Krueger (1980) makes this argument and provides various examples.

64 See for example Michaely (1986), Edwards (1986), and Choksi *et al.* (1991).

65 Lustig (2000) finds strong and durable negative effects of crises on the poor. de Janvry and Sadoulet (2000) find that recessions have strong negative effects on inequality in Latin America. Over a broader sample, Baldacci *et al.* (2002) and Dollar and Kraay (2001), looking systematically across episodes, find little evidence of a consistent relationship between economic downturns or crises and income distribution.

66 The important emerging market crises of the 1990s, for example, were not in general associated with terms of trade shocks. See Kaminsky and Reinhart (1999) and Berg *et al.* (1999).

67 Gupta *et al.* (2000) and Milesi-Ferretti and Razin (1998). Easterly *et al.* (2000) find broadly supportive results in their large panel. In their sample of sixty developing countries, trade openness does not increase the probability of economic downturns. They also find that openness has mixed effects on the volatility of output. Openness causes higher growth, which itself lowers the volatility of growth, though there is also a direct positive effect of openness on volatility.

68 See for example Rodrik (2001).

69 Ades and Di Tella (1999) measure outward orientation in two ways: trade distance (that is, the distance from major trading partners) and import penetration (imports as a share of GDP). They instrument with country size and population to control for the endogeneity of this measure. The difference in outwardness between Italy and Austria is due to the second of these two measures. See also Gatti (1999). Wei (2000) regresses trade intensity on natural determinants such as distance from trading partners, and argues that it is the component of openness that is correlated with these natural factors that explains corruption across countries, not the residual, which might be associated with policy. Rodrik *et al.* (2002) also find that trade openness has a positive influence on the quality of institutions.

70 India's experience over the last twenty or so years illustrates many of the important points in our argument (see Krueger, 2002). As noted in note 6, India has benefited from rapid increases in average income and a large reduction in poverty since 1987. Meanwhile, it began some modest reforms, including trade opening, at about the same time, with a substantial deepening of reform in the early 1990s. India's example is a reminder of the importance of concentrating on the relationship between openness and the level of income: some reforms, including trade liberalization, made a large difference to a very poor country, but India remains poor and relatively closed. Moreover, a variety of institutional and economic reforms in addition to further openness are needed to sustain progress. But the centrality of trade opening in the progress achieved to date cannot be doubted.

71 Easterly (2001) finds that good policy continued to matter for growth in the 1980s and 1990s, but overall disappointing performance was mostly due to negative shocks, particularly declines in developed country growth rates and increases in US interest rates.

72 On this topic, see IMF Staff (2002).

References

Ades, Alberto F. and Edward L. Glaeser. 1999. "Evidence on Growth, Increasing Returns, and the Extent of the Market," *Quarterly Journal of Economics*, 114(August): 1025–45.

—— and Rafael Di Tella. 1999. "Rents, Competition, and Corruption," *American Economic Review*, 89(September): 982–93.

Aitken, Brian, Gordon H. Hanson, and Ann E. Harrison. 1997. "Spillovers, Foreign Investment, and Export Behavior," *Journal of International Economics*, 43(August): 103–32.

Alcalá, Francisco and Antonio Ciccone. 2001. "Trade and Productivity," CEPR Discussion Paper No. 3095 (London: Centre for Economic Policy Research).

Anderson, James E. and J. Peter Neary. 1996. "A New Approach to Evaluating Trade Policy," *Review of Economic Studies*, 63(January): 107–25.

Andriamananjara, Shuby and John D. Nash. 1997. *Have Trade Policy Reforms Led to Greater Openness in Developing Countries? Evidence from Readily Available Trade Data* (Washington, DC: World Bank).

Baldacci, Emanuele, Luiz de Mello, and Gabriela Inchauste. 2002. "Financial Crises, Poverty, and Income Distribution," IMF Working Paper 02/04 (Washington, DC: International Monetary Fund).

Bannister, Geoffrey J. and Kamau Thugge. 2001. "International Trade and Poverty Alleviation," IMF Working Paper 01/54 (Washington, DC: International Monetary Fund).

Barro, Robert J. and Jong-Wha Lee. 1994. "Sources of Economic Growth," *Carnegie-Rochester Conference Series on Public Policy*, 40(June): 1–46.

—— and Xavier Sala-i-Martin. 1995. *Economic Growth* (New York, London, and Montreal: McGraw-Hill).

Bates, Robert H. 1981. *Markets and States in Tropical Africa: The Political Basis of Agricultural Policies* (Berkeley, CA: University of California Press).

Bell, Martin, Bruce Ross-Larson, and Larry Westphal. 1994. "Assessing the Performance of Infant Industries," *Journal of Development Economics*, 16(September–October): 101–28.

Ben-David, Dan. 1993. "Equalizing Exchange: Trade Liberalization and Income Convergence," *Quarterly Journal of Economics*, 108(August): 653–79.

——1996. "Trade and Convergence among Countries," *Journal of International Economics*, 40(May): 279–98.

Berg, Andrew, Eduardo Borensztein, Catherine Pattillo, and Gian Maria Milesi-Ferretti. 1999. *Anticipating Balance of Payments Crises: The Role of Early Warning Systems*, IMF Occasional Paper No. 186 (Washington, DC: International Monetary Fund).

Berg, Elliot, Tom Lenaghan, Daouda Diop, Mamadou Mbengue, and Abdoulaye Ndiaye. 1997. "Sustaining Private Sector Development in Senegal: Strategic Considerations," CAER II Discussion Paper 9 (Cambridge, MA: Harvard Institute for International Development).

Bernard, Andrew B. and J. Bradford Jensen. 1999. "Exceptional Exporter Performance: Cause, Effect, or Both?," *Journal of International Economics*, 47(February): 1–25.

Bhagwati, Jagdish N. 1978. *Anatomy and Consequences of Exchange Control Regimes* (Cambridge, MA: Ballinger Publisher Co.).

——1988. "Export-Promoting Trade Strategy: Issues and Evidence," *World Bank Research Observer*, 3(January): 27–57.

Bigsten, Arne, Paul Collier, P. Dercon, M. Fafchamps, B. Gauthier, B. Gunning, J. Gunning, R. Oostendorp, Catherine Pattillo, M. Soderbom, F. Teal, and A. Zeufack. 2000. "Exports and Firm-Level Efficiency in African Manufacturing," Centre for the Study of African Economies Working Paper No. 2000/16 (Oxford: University of Oxford).

Bourguignon, Francois and Christian Morrisson. 2002. "Inequality among World Citizens: 1820–1992," *American Economic Review*, 92(4): 272–44.

Caselli, Francesco, Gerardo Esquivel, and Fernando Lefort. 1996. "Reopening the Convergence Debate: A New Look at Cross-Country Growth Empirics," *Journal of Economic Growth*, 1(September): 363–89.

Cashin, Paul, Ratna Sahay, Catherine Pattillo, and Paolo Mauro. 2001. "Macroeconomic Policies and Poverty Reduction: Stylized Facts and an Overview of Research," IMF Working Paper 01/135 (Washington, DC: International Monetary Fund).

Chen, Shaohua and Martin Ravallion. 2001. "How Did the World's Poorest Fare in the 1990s?," *Review of Income and Wealth*, 47(September): 283–300.

Choksi, Armeane M., Papageorgiou, Demetris, and Michael Michaely. 1991. *Liberalizing Foreign Trade Volume 7 Lessons of Experience in the Developing World* (Cambridge, MA and Oxford: Blackwell).

Choudhri, Ehsan U. and Dalia S. Hakura. 2000. "International Trade and Productivity Growth: Exploring the Sectoral Effects for Developing Countries," *IMF Staff Papers*, 47: 30–53.

Clerides, Sofronis K., Saul Lach, and James R. Tybout. 1998. "Is Learning by Exporting Important? Micro-Dynamic Evidence from Colombia, Mexico, and Morocco," *Quarterly Journal of Economics*, 113(August): 903–47.

Coe, David T., Elhanan Helpman, and Alexander W. Hoffmaister. 1997. "North–South R&D Spillovers," *Economic Journal*, 107(January): 134–49.

Dean, Judith M., Seema Desai, and James Riedel. 1994. "Trade Policy Reform in Developing Countries since 1985: A Review of the Evidence," Discussion Papers, No. 267 (Washington, DC: World Bank).

Deaton, Angus and Jean Dreze. 2002. "Poverty and Inequality in India: A Reexamination," Research Program in Development Studies Working Paper Number 215 (Princeton, NJ: Princeton University).

Deininger, Klaus and Lyn Squire. 1998. "New Ways of Looking at Old Issues: Inequality and Growth," *Journal of Development Economics*, 57(December): 259–87.

de Janvry, Alain and Elisabeth Sadoulet. 2000. "Growth, Poverty, and Inequality in Latin America: A Causal Analysis. 1970–94," *Review of Income and Wealth*, 46(September): 267–87.

Dodzin, Sergei and Athanasios Vamvakidis. 1999. "Trade and Industrialization in Developing Agricultural Economies," IMF Working Paper 99/145 (Washington, DC: International Monetary Fund).

Dollar, David. 1992. "Outward-Oriented Developing Economies Really Do Grow More Rapidly: Evidence from 95 Ldcs. 1976–1985," *Economic Development and Cultural Change*, 40(April): 523–44.

—— and Aart Kraay. 2002. "Growth Is Good for the Poor," *Journal of Economic Growth*, 7(3): 195–225.

—— 2003. "Institutions, Trade, and Growth," *Journal of Monetary Economics*, 50(1): 133–65.

—— 2004. "Trade, Growth and Poverty," *Economic Journal: The Journal of the Royal Economic Society*, 114(493): F22–F49.

Durlauf, Steven N. and Danny T. Quah. 1999. "The New Empirics of Economic Growth," in *Handbook of Macroeconomics*, ed. by John B. Taylor and Michael Woodford (Amsterdam, New York, and Oxford: Elsevier Science North-Holland).

Easterly, William. 2001. "The Lost Decades: Developing Countries' Stagnation in Spite of Policy Reform 1980–1998," *Journal of Economic Growth*, 6(June): 135–57.

—— and Ross Levine. 2001. "It's Not Factor Accumulation: Stylized Facts and Growth Models," *World Bank Economic Review*, 15: 177–219.

Easterly, William Russell. 2001. *The Elusive Quest for Growth* (Cambridge, MA: MIT Press).

—— and Ross Levine. 2003. "Tropics, Germs, and Crops: How Endowments Influence Economic Development," *Journal of Monetary Economics*, 50(1): 3–39.

——, Roumeen Islam, and Joseph Stiglitz. 2001. "Shaken and Stirred: Explaining Growth Volatility," in *Annual World Bank Conference on Development Economics*, ed. by Boris Pleskovic and Nick Stern (Washington: World Bank).

108 *Andrew Berg and Anne Krueger*

Edwards, Sebastian. 1986. "The Order of Liberalization of the Current and Capital Accounts," in *Economic Liberalization in Developing Countries*, ed. by Armeane M. Choksi and Demetris Papageorgiou (New York: Blackwell).

—— 1993. "Openness, Trade Liberalization, and Growth in Developing Countries," *Journal of Economic Literature*, 31(September): 1358–93.

—— 1997. "Trade Policy, Growth, and Income Distribution," *American Economic Review*, 87(May): 205–10.

—— 1998. "Openness, Productivity and Growth: What Do We Really Know?," *Economic Journal*, 108(March): 383–98.

Frankel, Jeffrey A. and David Romer. 1999. "Does Trade Cause Growth?," *American Economic Review*, 89(June): 379–99.

—— and Andrew K. Rose. 2000. "Estimating the Effect of Currency Unions on Trade and Output," NBER Working Paper 7857 (Cambridge, MA: National Bureau of Economic Research).

Gatti, Roberta. 2004. "Explaining Corruption: Are Open Economies Less Corrupt?" *Journal of International Development*, 16(6): 851–61.

Ghura, Dhaneshwar, Carlos A. Leite, and Charalambos Tsangarides. 2002. "Is Growth Enough? Macroeconomic Policy and Poverty Reduction," IMF Working Paper 02/118 (Washington, DC: International Monetary Fund).

Greenaway, David, Wyn Morgan, and Peter W. Wright. 1998. "Trade Reform, Adjustment and Growth: What Does the Evidence Tell Us?," *Economic Journal*, 108(September): 1547–61.

Grossman, Gene M. and Elhanan Helpman. 1991. *Innovation and Growth in the Global Economy* (Cambridge, MA and London: MIT Press).

Gupta, Poonam, Deepak Mishra, and Ratna Sahay. 2003. "Output Response To Currency Crises", Working Paper 03/230 (Washington: International Monetary Fund).

Haddad, Mona and Ann Harrison. 1993. "Are There Positive Spillovers from Direct Foreign Investment? Evidence from Panel Data for Morocco," *Journal of Development Economics*, 42(October): 51–74.

Hall, Robert E. and Charles I. Jones. 1999. "Why Do Some Countries Produce So Much More Output Per Worker Than Others?" *Quarterly Journal of Economics*, 114(February): 83–116.

Hallward-Driemeier, Mary. 2001. "Openness, Firms, and Competition" (unpublished; Washington, DC: World Bank).

Hallward-Driemeier, Mary, Sokoloff, and Iarossi. 2002. "Exports and Manufacturing Productivity in East Asia: A Comparative Analysis With Firm-Level Data" (National Bureau of Economic Research Working Paper Series (US), No. 8894: 1–63, April 2002).

Harrigan, Jane and Paul Mosley. 1991. "Evaluating the Impact of World Bank Structural Adjustment Lending: 1980–87," *Journal of Development Studies*, 27(April): 63–94.

Harrison, Ann. 1994. "An Empirical Test of the Infant Industry Argument: Comment," *American Economic Review*, 84(September): 1090–95.

—— 1996. "Openness and Growth: A Time-Series, Cross-Country Analysis for Developing Countries," *Journal of Development Economics*, 48(March): 419–47.

—— and Gordon Hanson. 1999. "Who Gains from Trade Reform? Some Remaining Puzzles," *Journal of Development Economics*, 59(June): 125–54.

International Monetary Fund. 2002. "Improving Market Access: Toward Greater Coherence between Aid and Trade," Issues Brief, available at http://www.imf.org/external/np/exr/ib/2002/032102.htm

Irwin, Douglas. 2000. "Did Late Nineteenth Century U.S. Tariffs Promote Infant Industries? Evidence from the Tinplate Industry," *Journal of Economic History*, 60(June): 335–60.

—— and Mark Terviö. 2000. "Does Trade Raise Income? Evidence from the Twentieth Century," NBER Working Paper 7747 (Cambridge, MA: National Bureau of Economic Research).

Isgut, Alberto E. 2001. "What's Different About Exporters? Evidence from Colombian Manufacturing," *Journal of Development Studies*, 37(June): 57–82.

Islam, Nazrul. 1995. "Growth Empirics: A Panel Data Approach," *Quarterly Journal of Economics*, 110(November): 1127–70.

Jones, Charles I. 1997. "On the Evolution of the World Income Distribution," *Journal of Economic Perspectives*, 11(Summer): 19–36.

Jonsson, Gunnar and Arvind Subramanian. 2001. "Dynamic Gains from Trade: Evidence from South Africa," *IMF Staff Papers*, 48(1): 197–224.

Kaminsky, Graciela L. and Carmen M. Reinhart. 1999. "The Twin Crises: The Causes of Banking and Balance-of-Payments Problems," *American Economic Review*, 89(June): 473–500.

Klenow, Peter J. and Andres Rodriguez-Clare. 1997. "Economic Growth: A Review Essay," *Journal of Monetary Economics*, 40(December): 597–617.

Kraay, Aart. 1999. "Exportations Et Performances Economiques: Etude D'un Panel D'entreprises Chinoises (Exports and Economic Performance: Evidence from a Panel of Chinese Enterprises with English Summary)," *Revue d'Economie du Developpement*, 7(June): 183–207.

Krueger, Anne O. 1974. "The Political Economy of the Rent-Seeking Society," *American Economic Review*, 64(June): 291–303.

—— 1978. *Liberalization Attempts and Consequences: Foreign Trade Regimes and Economic Development* (Cambridge, MA: Ballinger Publisher Co.).

—— 1980. "Trade Policy as an Input to Development," *American Economic Review*, 70(May): 288–92.

—— 1995. "Policy Lessons from Development Experience since the Second World War," in *Handbook of Development Economics*, ed. by Jere Behrman and T.N. Srinivasan (Amsterdam, New York, and Oxford: Elsevier Science North-Holland).

—— 1997. "Trade Policy and Economic Development: How We Learn," *American Economic Review*, 87(March): 1–22.

—— 2002. *Economic Policy Reforms and the Indian Economy* (Chicago, IL and London: University of Chicago Press).

—— and Baran Tuncer. 1982. "An Empirical Test of the Infant Industry Argument," *American Economic Review*, 72(December): 1142–52.

—— 1994. "An Empirical Test of the Infant Industry Argument: Reply," *American Economic Review*, 84(September): 1096.

Leamer, Edward E. 1988. "Measures of Openness." in *Trade Policy Issues and Empirical Analysis*, ed. by Robert E. Baldwin (National Bureau of Economic Research Conference Report series (Chicago, IL and London: University of Chicago Press).

Lee, Jong-Wha. 1993. "International Trade, Distortions, and Long-Run Economic Growth," *IMF Staff Papers*, 40(June): 299–328.

Lucas, Robert E., Jr. 1988. "On the Mechanics of Economic Development," *Journal of Monetary Economics*, 22(July): 3–42.

Lundberg, Mattias and Lyn Squire. 2003. "The Simultaneous Evolution of Growth and Inequality," *The Economic Journal*, 113(487): 326.

Lustig, Nora. 2000. "Crises and the Poor: Socially Responsible Macroeconomics," Sustainable Development Department Technical Paper Series Pov-108 (Washington, DC: Inter-American Development Bank).

Luzio, Eduardo and Eduardo Greenstein. 1995. "Measuring the Performance of a Protected Infant Industry: The Case of Brazilian Microcomputers," *Review of Economics and Statistics*, 77(4)(November): 622–33.

Mankiw, N. Gregory, David Romer, and David N. Weil. 1992. "A Contribution to the Empirics of Economic Growth," *Quarterly Journal of Economics*, 107(May): 407–37.

Martin, Will. 2001. "Trade Policies, Developing Countries, and Globalization" (unpublished; Washington, DC: World Bank).

McCulloch, Neil, L. Alan Winters, Xavier Cirera, and Centre for Economic Policy Research. 2001. *Trade Liberalization and Poverty: A Handbook* (London: Centre for Economic Policy Research; Department for International Development).

Michaely, Michael. 1986. "The Timing and Sequencing of a Trade Liberalization Policy," in *Economic Liberalization in Developing Countries*, ed. by Armeane M. Choksi and Demetris Papageorgiou (New York: Blackwell).

Milesi-Ferretti, Gian Maria, and Assaf Razin. 1998. "Current Account Reversals and Currency Crises: Empirical Regularities," IMF Working Paper 98/89 (Washington, DC: International Monetary Fund).

Ng, Francis and Alexander Yeats. 1996. "Open Economies Work Better!," Policy Research Working Paper 1636 (Washington, DC: World Bank).

O'Rourke, Kevin H. 2001. "Globalization and Inequality: Historical Trends," NBER Working Paper 8339 (Cambridge, MA: National Bureau of Economic Research).

Orsmond, David W.H. 1992. "How Well Does the Black Market Premium Proxy the Restrictiveness of a Trade Regime?" PhD dissertation, Duke University.

Parente, Stephen L., and Edward C. Prescott. 2000. *Barriers to Riches* (Cambridge, MA and London: MIT Press).

Poulton, Colin, Jonathan Kydd, and Sharon Harvey. 1999. "Agricultural Trade and Marketing Liberalisation in Sub-Saharan Africa and Latin America: The Impact on Growth and Poverty," *Quarterly Journal of International Agriculture*, 38: 315–39.

Pritchett, Lant. 1996. "Measuring Outward Orientation in Ldcs: Can It Be Done?," *Journal of Development Economics*, 49(May): 307–35.

—— 2000. "Understanding Patterns of Economic Growth: Searching for Hills among Plateaus, Mountains, and Plains," *World Bank Economic Review*, 14(May): 221–50.

—— and Geeta Sethi. 1994. "Tariff Rates, Tariff Revenue, and Tariff Reform: Some New Facts," *World Bank Economic Review*, 8(January): 1–16.

Quah, Danny T. 2002. "One Third of the World's Growth and Inequality," CEPR Discussion Paper No. 3316 (London: Centre for Economic Policy Research).

Ravallion, Martin. 2001. "Growth, Inequality and Poverty: Looking Beyond Averages," *World Development*, 29(November): 1803–15.

—— and Gaurav Datt. 2001. "Why Has Economic Growth Been More Pro-Poor in Some States of India Than Others?," Available on the Internet at http://www.worldbank.org/research/growth/pdfiles/Ravallion%20joint.pdf

Roberts, Mark J. and James R. Tybout. 1997. "The Decision to Export in Colombia: An Empirical Model of Entry with Sunk Costs," *American Economic Review*, 87(September): 545–64.

Rodriguez, Francisco and Dani Rodrik. 1999. "Trade Policy and Economic Growth: A Skeptic's Guide to the Cross-National Evidence," NBER Working Paper 7081 (Cambridge: National Bureau of Economic Research).

Rodrik, Dani. 2000. "Comments on Dollar and Kraay" (unpublished).

—— 2001. "Trading in Illusions", *Foreign Policy*, March–April 2001.

——, Arvind Subramanian, and Francesco Trebbi. 2004. "Institutions Rule: The Primacy of Institutions over Geography and Integration in Economic Development," *Journal of Economic Growth*, 9(2): [131]–65.

Roemer, Michael and Mary Kay Gugerty. 1997. "Does Economic Growth Reduce Poverty?," CAER Discussion Papers (Cambridge, MA: Harvard Institute for International Development).

Sachs, Jeffrey D. and Andrew M. Warner. 1995. "Economic Reform and the Process of Global Integration," *Brookings Papers on Economic Activity: 1*, Brookings Institution, pp. 1–95.

Sala-i-Martin, Xavier. 1997. "I Just Ran Two Million Regressions," *American Economic Review*, 87(May): 178–83.

—— 2002. "The Disturbing 'Rise' of Global Income Inequality," NBER Working Paper No. 8904 (Cambridge: National Bureau of Economic Research).

Sharer, Robert L., Piritta Sorsa, and International Monetary Fund. 1998. *Trade Liberalization in IMF-Supported Programs*, World Economic and Financial Surveys (Washington, DC: International Monetary Fund).

Slaughter, Matthew J. 2001. "Trade Liberalization and Per Capita Income Convergence: A Difference-in-Differences Analysis," *Journal of International Economics*, 55(October): 203–28.

Solow, Robert M. 1956. "A Contribution to the Theory of Economic Growth," *Quaterly Journal of Economics*, 70(1): 65–94.

Spilimbergo, Antonio, Juan Luis Londono, and Miguel Szekely. 1999. "Income Distribution, Factor Endowments, and Trade Openness," *Journal of Development Economics*, 59(June): 77–101.

Srinivasan, T.N. 2001. *Trade, Development, and Growth*, Princeton Studies in International Economics, No. 225 (Princeton, NJ: Princeton University Press).

Ventura, Jaume. 1997. "Growth and Interdependence," *Quarterly Journal of Economics*, 112: 57–84.

Wacziarg, Romain. 1997. "Trade, Competition, and Market Size" (unpublished; Cambridge, MA: Harvard University).

Wang, Qing. 2001. "Import-Reducing Effect of Trade Barriers: A Cross-Country Investigation," IMF Working Paper 01/216 (Washington, DC: International Monetary Fund).

Warner, Andrew. 2003. "Once More into the Breach: Economic Growth and Global Integration," unpublished manuscript, (Washington: Center for Global Development) [in other words, updated but still unpublished].

Wei, Shang-Jin. 2000. "Natural Openness and Good Government," NBER Working Paper 7765 (Cambridge, MA: National Bureau of Economic Research).

Wolf, Holger. 1994. "Trade Orientation Measurement and Consequences," Working Paper EC-94-01 (New York: Stern School of Business).

World Bank. 2001. *Global Economic Prospects and the Developing Countries* (Washington, DC: World Bank).

Young, Alwyn. 1991. "Learning by Doing and the Dynamic Effects of International Trade," *Quarterly Journal of Economics*, 106(May): 369–405.

—— 1995. "The Tyranny of Numbers: Confronting the Statistical Realities of the East Asian Growth Experience," *Quarterly Journal of Economics*, 110(August): 641–80.

Part II
Public finances

4   Odious debt

Seema Jayachandran and Michael Kremer*

Many developing countries are carrying debt that was incurred by rulers who borrowed without the people's consent and used the funds either to repress the people or for personal gain. This chapter lays out a mechanism to limit the ability of dictators to run up debts, loot their countries, and pass on their debts to the population. Limiting dictators' ability to borrow can be considered a new form of economic sanction that has several attractive features relative to traditional trade sanctions. Many argue that trade sanctions are ineffective because they generate incentives for evasion. Others object to them as hurting the population of the target country as much as its leaders. We argue that loan sanctions would reduce creditors' incentive to extend loans to sanctioned regimes and thus, unlike trade sanctions, would be self-enforcing. Also, the population benefits when it is protected from being saddled with "odious debt." However, decisions on whether existing debt is odious might be subject to bias if the deciding body asymmetrically valued the welfare of debtor countries and their creditors. Restricting such decisions to cover only *future* lending would help avoid this time-consistency problem.

The campaign for sovereign debt relief is based on two ideas. First, certain countries are too poor to repay their loans. Second, some debts were illegitimate in the first place and thus the country should not be responsible for repaying them. The first rationale for debt relief has been examined extensively by economists.[1] Several countries have been granted debt relief under the Heavily Indebted Poor Countries (HIPC) initiative, which considers the level of debt and the income of the country as the criteria for debt relief, but not the circumstances under which the debt was incurred. Thus, countries that are not as impoverished but have a plausible claim that their debts are illegitimate are not on the current list of debt relief candidates.

The second rationale, which has received much less attention, is our focus. We lay out a mechanism that limits the ability of dictators to borrow internationally, loot the borrowed funds, or use them to finance the repression of their people, and then saddle the people with the debt. Our starting point is the belief that debt incurred by a dictator for personal and nefarious purposes should be considered illegitimate and that the country's citizens should not be considered responsible for repaying this debt. Individuals do not have to repay money that others fraudulently borrow in their name, in the same way that a corporation is not liable for contracts that the chief executive officer or another agent enters without the authority to bind the firm. If there were an analogous norm regarding fraudulent sovereign debt, banks would not issue loans to repressive or looting governments in the first place.

The United States argued along these lines during the 1898 peace negotiations after the Spanish–American War, contending that neither the United States nor Cuba should be responsible for debt that the colonial rulers had incurred without the consent of the Cubans and not for the Cubans' benefit. Spain never accepted the validity of this argument, but the United States implicitly prevailed, and Spain took responsibility for the Cuban debt under the Paris peace treaty. This episode inspired legal scholars to elaborate a legal doctrine of "odious debt" (Sack, 1927; Feilchenfeld, 1931). They argued that sovereign debt is odious and should not be transferable to a successor government if it (1) was incurred without the consent of the people and (2) did not benefit the people. Because both conditions must hold for debt to be considered odious under this definition, debts of a regime that loots but rules democratically or of a non-democratic regime that spends in the interests of the people would not be considered odious. Some scholars also added the requirement that creditors be aware of these conditions in advance (Sack, 1927).

However, this doctrine has gained little momentum within the international law community, and countries are held responsible for repaying illegitimate debt under the international system's current norm. South Africa is a case in point. The apartheid regime in South Africa borrowed from private banks through the 1980s, while a large percentage of its budget went to finance the military and police and otherwise repress the African majority. The South African people now bear the debts of their repressors. While the Archbishop of Cape Town has campaigned for apartheid-era debt to "be declared odious and written off," and South Africa's Truth and Reconciliation Commission has voiced a similar opinion, the post-apartheid government has deferred to the current international norm and accepted responsibility for the debt. South Africa seems to fear that defaulting would hurt its chances of attracting foreign investment and wants to be seen as playing by the rules of capitalism. Its top ministers recently denounced a lawsuit seeking reparations from banks that loaned to the apartheid regime because, "we are talking to those very same companies named in the lawsuits about investing in post-apartheid South Africa."[2]

Similarly, although Anastasio Somoza was reported to have looted $100–500 million from Nicaragua by the time he was overthrown in 1979, and the Sandinista leader Daniel Ortega told the United Nations General Assembly that his government would repudiate Somoza's debt, the Sandinistas reconsidered when their allies in Cuba advised them that repudiating the debt would unwisely alienate them from Western capitalist countries.[3]

There are a number of other cases in which dictators have borrowed from abroad, expropriated the funds for personal use, and left the debts to the population they ruled. For example, under Mobutu Sese Seko, the former Zaire accumulated over $12 billion in sovereign debt, while Mobutu diverted public funds to his personal accounts (his assets reached $4 billion in the mid-1980s) and used them in his efforts to retain power (e.g. payments to cronies, military expenses).[4] Similarly, when Ferdinand Marcos lost power in 1986, the Philippines owed $28 billion to foreign creditors, and Marcos' personal wealth was estimated at $10 billion.[5,6]

4.1   Policies to curtail odious debt

We argue for empowering an independent institution to assess whether regimes are legitimate and declare any sovereign debt subsequently incurred by illegitimate regimes as odious and thus not the obligation of successor governments. This could restrict dictators' ability to loot, limit the debt burden of poor countries, reduce risk for banks, and hence lower interest rates for legitimate governments that borrow. This policy can be viewed as a form of economic sanction, and, accordingly, the United Nations Security Council, which sometimes imposes trade sanctions, is one possible institution that could assess regimes. Later in this chapter, we discuss other possibilities.

Currently, countries repay debt even if it is odious because if they failed to do so, their assets might be seized abroad and their reputations would be tarnished, making it more difficult for them to borrow again or attract foreign investment.[7] However, if there were an institution that assessed whether regimes are odious and announced its findings, this could create a new equilibrium in which countries' reputations would not be hurt by refusal to repay illegitimate debts, just as individuals' credit ratings are not hurt by their refusal to pay debts that others fraudulently incur in their name. In this equilibrium, creditors would curtail loans to regimes that have been identified as odious, since they would know that successor governments would have little incentive to repay them. This argument draws upon the well-known result in game theory that repeated games have many possible equilibria, and simply making some information publicly known can create a new – and, in this case, arguably better – equilibrium. Clarity about which regimes are odious can engender a new international norm that a country is not responsible for the debt incurred by a dictatorial regime and its reputation will not be tarnished if it repudiates this type of debt.

While a public announcement that a regime is odious might curtail lending to such regimes, there is no guarantee that everyone would coordinate on this new equilibrium without some means of enforcement. Two enforcement mechanisms could ensure that lending to odious regimes is eliminated. First, laws in creditor countries could be changed to disallow seizure of a country's assets for non-repayment of odious debt. That is, odious debt contracts could be made legally unenforceable. Second, foreign aid to successor regimes could be made contingent on non-repayment of odious debt. For example, the International Monetary Fund (IMF) and World Bank could adopt a policy of not providing assistance to governments who are repaying creditors for illegitimate loans. If the foreign aid were valuable enough, successor governments would have incentives to repudiate odious loans, so banks would refrain from originating such loans. (Interestingly, the same reasoning suggests a potential way to solve the moral hazard problem associated with foreign aid (see Appendix).)

4.2   Advantages over traditional trade sanctions

When the international community wants to put pressure on a government that suppresses democracy and human rights, a common approach is to impose economic sanctions. Limiting an odious regime's ability to borrow can be considered a new form of economic sanction that has several attractive features relative to traditional trade sanctions. Like other sanctions that the international community uses to pressure governments without resorting to war, the threat of limits on borrowing could create incentives for regimes to reform. Governments might loot less to retain the ability to borrow. Would-be dictators might even be discouraged from seeking power if sovereign borrowing were not one of the spoils of office.

Traditional sanctions, however, are often criticized as either ineffective or inhumane. Limiting borrowing avoids these two shortcomings. First, when trade sanctions are deployed, smugglers and even some national governments will likely flout them, enticed by profit opportunities that are enlarged by the sanction itself. Curtailing odious debt, in contrast, is a self-enforcing sanction. The key difference is that banks cannot break this sanction unilaterally since they rely on others to enforce the reputational punishment. Whereas trade sanctions are eviscerated by one or a few defectors even if there are a large number of abiders, with the "loan embargo," a few creditors and investors who are willing to lend to and invest in a country that has repudiated odious debt would eliminate any incentive for the country to repay the debt. A private bank would think twice before lending to a regime if the world's leading powers, international organizations, and financial institutions had declared the regime odious and announced that they would consider successor governments justified in repudiating any new loans that the odious regime incurs. For example, when the United Nations imposed trade sanctions against the apartheid government of South Africa in 1985, it also could have declared that it would not consider debt incurred by the apartheid government as a legitimate obligation of the successor government. If banks doubted that successor regimes would repay loans issued after the announcement, they most likely would have been unwilling to make such loans.

Second, when trade sanctions are not evaded, they are thought to impoverish the people they were intended to help because of the loss of national income. For example, if firms in the country are prevented from selling their products abroad, the loss of revenue might cause them to fire workers or decrease wages. In contrast, curtailing dictators' ability to borrow, loot, and saddle the people with large debts would hurt illegitimate regimes but help their populations. The burden of repaying the debts would almost certainly outweigh any short-run benefit the population would obtain from proceeds of the loan that trickled down to them. (If a regime loots only a small amount and most of the proceeds flow to the people, the regime probably should not be considered odious.)

More countries engage in foreign trade than in sovereign borrowing, so limits on borrowing could only be applied as a sanction in certain cases. Nonetheless, it could have a significant impact in these cases. For example, Franjo Tudjman of

Croatia was arguably an odious ruler, having instigated violence against political opponents and looted public funds. In 1997, the IMF cut off aid that was earmarked for Croatia at the behest of the United States, Germany, and Britain, who were concerned about the "unsatisfactory state of democracy in Croatia." Despite this, commercial banks lent an additional $2 billion to the Croatian government between the IMF decision and Tudjman's death in December 1999.[8] If the proposed institution existed, creditors might not have granted Tudjman the subsequent $2 billion in loans, and the Croatian people would not bear the debt today. Such potential applications suggest that limits on borrowing should be part of the toolkit of policies available to the international community.

4.3   Incentives for truthfulness

There is clearly room for discretion in assessing whether loans to a particular regime are odious. Governments lie on a continuum in the extent to which they do or do not have the consent of the people and do or do not spend for their benefit. Someone could argue that the Mexican debt incurred during the era of PRI domination, or debts incurred in the United States before the passage of the Voting Rights Act of 1965, qualify as odious debt.

For a limit on borrowing to improve upon the status quo, it is necessary to provide incentives for the institution assessing the legitimacy of debt to do so truthfully. An institution that cares about the welfare of the people of developing countries more than that of banks and other creditors might be tempted to declare legitimate debt odious as a way to redistribute resources from creditors to the debtor country. However, if creditors anticipate being unable to collect on even legitimate loans, they will be wary of lending at all, and the availability of capital to borrowers will diminish. This danger is one of the main reasons why the doctrine of odious debt has gained little support within the legal community. An institution with the opposite bias of favoring banks over debtor nations might also make false rulings; in this case it might fail to designate debt as odious in order to help the creditors.

To overcome these risks, the institution could be empowered only to rule on future loans to a government and not on existing debt. Then creditors would not face the uncertainty that loans they issue will be declared odious later. Moreover, the institution will have stronger incentives to be truthful. Even if the institution is more concerned with the welfare of debtors than of creditors, it would have incentives to judge a regime honestly because honesty benefits the population. If the institution falsely calls a legitimate government odious, it deprives a country of profitable investments financed by loans. If it falsely calls an odious government legitimate, the government can borrow and loot the country.

Requiring an institution to judge the legitimacy of loans before they are incurred also limits the potential for favoritism toward creditors. An institution that favors creditors and rules on existing debt might fail to declare some debts odious. However, if it rules only on future loans, even a small degree of concern for truthfulness or for the welfare of people in borrowing countries should be sufficient to prevent an institution from calling an odious government legitimate.

This is because before a loan is issued, the expected profits of a loan are very small for banks, as they have many alternative uses for their capital. In contrast, outstanding debt is a "zero-sum game" between creditors and debtors, so a biased institution can help whichever party it favors. Because false rulings about future debt hurt the population of borrowing countries and cannot substantially help creditors, an institution empowered only to block future lending is unlikely to make biased judgments in order to help debtors or creditors.

There remains a possibility that an institution that rules on future debt may be biased for or against certain governments. If the major powers regard a country as an important trade partner or strategic ally, the institution might fail to brand the government odious regardless of potential misdeeds. For instance, it is unlikely that an institution would brand either China or Saudi Arabia as odious. Since such regimes with powerful friends can borrow presently, biased decisions in their favor would simply maintain the status quo. If instead the institution disfavors a government for foreign policy reasons, even though the government has the consent of the people or spends for their benefit, the institution might falsely term it odious, thus cutting it off from lending. For example, the United States might wish to block loans to the current government of Iran, independent of whether the regime satisfies the definition of odiousness. If this happened, citizens of the country would be worse off than under the status quo. The institution could be designed under a "do no harm" principle. Requiring unanimity or a two-thirds vote to declare a regime odious could safeguard against the possibility that a country would falsely be branded odious due to the biases of a few members of the institution, as the decisive voter would be less biased against the government than under a simple majority rule. Some illegitimate, self-serving regimes would continue to receive loans under this rule, but it would be an improvement on the status quo if even one such regime were denied loans.

4.4 Iraq as an example

Present-day Iraq illustrates both the burden that ill-spent loans can impose on a poor country, and also some of the potential difficulties of assessing the legitimacy of debt after the fact.

Under Saddam Hussein's rule Iraq amassed about $120 billion in debt. This figure remains an estimate, as the full details of Iraq's economic status have not been made public. What is known is that repaying the debt would be burdensome for Iraq. It faces $200 billion in Gulf War compensation claims in addition to the debt. Meanwhile, its gross domestic product is estimated at only $30 billion.

The people of Iraq can make a fairly strong case that Saddam Hussein borrowed in the 1970s without the consent of the Iraqi people and then spent much of the money to finance violence and repression. Hence, the new Iraqi government might argue, Saddam Hussein was not legitimately borrowing on behalf of the Iraqi people.

The United States, currently overseeing the administration of Iraq's transition to a post-Saddam Hussein regime, has intensely lobbied creditor nations for relief of Iraqi debt. Many US officials made public statements that the illegitimacy and misuse of the loans justified its write-off, but the United States mainly has argued that the debt relief is a necessary first step in the process of rebuilding Iraq's economy. Many of the creditor nations belong to the Paris Club – a group of creditor nations that have procedures in place to reschedule or write off some of the debt of developing countries on the rationale that repaying the debt would further impoverish the country. Much progress has been made with these nations: agreements have come from Germany, France, Japan, and Russia to forgive most or all of their respective debts. The size of these debts vary with Germany owed an estimated $2.5 billion, France $3 billion, Japan $7 billion, and Russia $8 billion. The Paris Club, however, accounts for only an estimated $40 billion of the $120 billion total in loans.

The reasons for the US position and the international support it has received may not be entirely straightforward. For the United States, an Iraq burdened with debt would be more dependent on American aid. In addition, concessions on debt by Russia, France, and Germany were a way for these countries to raise their chances of receiving contracts for US-financed reconstruction projects in Iraq. Meanwhile, much of the debt burden remains, including some owed to corporations such as Hyundai and Samsung who have stated they will not waive the debt. Whether it is a good idea to erase Iraq's debt is open to debate. What is clear is that the world needs a better system to determine which loans should be considered legitimate. Moreover, there are advantages of making clear *in advance* which loans will be considered odious instead of nullifying them after the fact. Would the international community in the 1970s have declared that future borrowing by Saddam Hussein was odious? The answer most likely depends on who the adjudicating body would have been. An international court might have. On the other hand, the United States was still supportive of the regime at that point. But a debate then within the international community about the odiousness of Saddam Hussein's regime might have shifted the US position – and, in any case, would have drawn attention to how the regime was governing and spending money. Similarly, the attention drawn to these issues by Iraq's situation today might spur the creation of a system that prevents lending to repressive rulers.

4.5 Other issues

4.5.1 Inherited debt

It also is important to consider how the new policy would affect an odious regime that inherits legitimate debt from the previous government. Even under the status quo, an odious regime likely would prefer not to repay its creditors and instead keep the repayment money for itself. It would be difficult to extract these resources from the regime; the best it may be possible to do is to prevent it from procuring more resources. To reduce the probability of the regime defaulting on its obligations, the international community might consider providing specific exemptions for the rollover of existing loans.

4.5.2   *Long-lasting dictators*

If a dictator stays in power for longer, banks might issue short-term loans as long as they believed that the dictator would be in power long enough to repay the loans. Even in this case, the dictator is worse off with the policy than without, since the risk that the odious regime will lose power before he can repay even a short-term loan will increase the interest rate he faces. Also, since the interest rate will be set so that, in expectation, the dictator repays the value of the loan, the dictator can loot only the surplus from borrowing and the population is not saddled with the debt.

4.5.3   *Good regimes can turn bad and bad regimes can reform*

It also may be the case that a government is non-odious at first but becomes odious. For example, Mobutu in Zaire became more corrupt over time. In practice, regimes could be monitored repeatedly or continuously perhaps in response to complaints, and a regime might be judged non-odious to begin with but odious at a later time. Only loans made after the revised judgment would be considered odious.

4.6   How should these policies be implemented?

An obviously important question in implementing the doctrine of odious debt is which institution would judge odiousness. The United Nations Security Council already imposes sanctions against governments, so it is a natural candidate. The United States and the other permanent members (China, France, Russia, and the United Kingdom) might prefer this option since they would have veto power. Another option is an international judicial body that hears cases brought against particular regimes and is composed of professional jurists representing several countries, similar to the International Court of Justice or the newly established International Criminal Court in the Hague.

It is also conceivable that the United States carries sufficient weight in the international system to implement such a system on its own. For example, US law could be amended to define odious debt and to disallow seizure of a foreign government's assets when the government repudiates odious debt; and the United States could announce that it would not provide foreign aid to countries that were repaying odious debt and would not support IMF or World Bank aid to such countries. Then banks even outside the United States would likely be reluctant to lend to that regime, fearing that successor governments would not repay, and creditors' recourse to that country's assets would be impaired.

It might also be possible for civil society to begin putting pressure on banks not to lend to illegitimate governments. If a well-respected nongovernmental organization identified odious regimes and promulgated a list of them, creditors might be reluctant to lend to governments on the list.

The most likely way that the institutional structure would take shape is that the international community, led by a few influential countries, would apply the loan embargo for a specific case and then the precedent would evolve into a general policy. The policy need not be adopted wholesale and in the abstract. For example, the United States recently pressured the ratings agency Moody's to withdraw its favorable credit rating of Iran. Iran planned to issue sovereign bonds, with European banks as the target bondholders, and the United States wished to limit Iran's ability to borrow as part of its economic sanctions program.[9] However, eliminating the Moody's rating is unlikely to compel European banks to fall in line with the US position. Suppose, though, that the hardliners in the Iranian government launched a coup and there was an international consensus that the Iranian government was neither representative of the people nor intending to spend in the people's interests. The United Nations Security Council could issue a declaration that Iran was odious and its bonds were unenforceable. The permanent members could vow to back foreign aid to a successor Iranian government that repudiated the bonds. Would-be bondholders would almost certainly fall in line with this sanction.

Or the case that triggers the new policy might involve the nullification of outstanding debt. There has been much debate recently about whether the estimated $100 billion in debt incurred by Saddam Hussein should be the responsibility of the Iraqi people now. Iraq can make a fairly strong case that Saddam Hussein borrowed without the consent of the Iraqi people and then spent much of the money to finance violence and repression. The argument that Iraq should not be expected to repay the debt has gained momentum partly because Iraq is unlikely to be *able* to repay it. Its debt burden far exceeds its gross domestic product. The United States, for example, might welcome an Iraqi decision to repudiate its debt since an Iraq burdened with debt would be more dependent on American aid. If the Iraqi government decides to renounce Saddam Hussein's debt, this might spur the creation of a system that discourages lending to repressive rulers like Saddam Hussein in the first place. We would have taken our first step toward creating a new norm under which a country is not responsible for odious debt.

This new policy could help legitimate debtors and their creditors. Creditors would benefit from knowing the rules of the game in advance. Currently, it is hard for creditors to anticipate which loans will be considered odious in the future. If odiousness were declared in advance, banks would avoid lending to odious regimes in the first place and no longer face the risk of large losses if a successful campaign nullifies their outstanding loans. Accordingly, with greater certainty, interest rates could fall for legitimate governments. Most important, dictators would no longer be able to borrow, loot the proceeds – or use them to finance repression – and then saddle their citizens with the debts.

4A.1   Appendix

4A.1.1   *When debt is not odious: an approach to bailouts*

In cases where legitimate governments borrow to finance economically disastrous policies, an approach similar to the one we propose for odious debt might be useful. If the population of a country chooses such a government, some would argue that it is their prerogative, and it would be a breach of international sovereignty to block the government's ability to borrow. However, many contend that the international financial institutions (IFIs), such as the World Bank and the IMF, subsidize wasteful spending in the form of international aid packages to countries whose economies have collapsed. This is the familiar moral hazard argument: the expectation of bailouts from IFIs encourages commercial banks and bondholders to make loans that governments could not reasonably repay on their own.

The IFIs could discourage this type of opportunistic lending by private creditors in the following way: the IFIs could, after assessing the creditworthiness of a government, announce that the government's policies are likely to make it unable to fulfill its debt obligations.[10] The IFIs could also announce that they will be willing to provide aid to the country once it resumes pursuing sound policies, but not to help repay debt issued after the announcement. In particular, a condition of future IFI assistance would be that countries do not simultaneously repay any loans made after the IFI announcement. In this way, the IFIs would avoid encouraging private lending to the country motivated by anticipation of a bailout. Unlike in the odious debt case, loans would not be considered illegitimate and unenforceable. If creditors thought the country could repay without an IFI bailout, they would continue to lend.

With this approach, the IFIs would be able to continue to give aid packages to countries that followed good policies but suffered bad luck. However, they would not bail out creditors who had opportunistically lent to countries that were following risky policies.

Notes

* Jayachandran: Department of Economics, Harvard University, 200 Littauer Center, Cambridge, MA 02138. Email: jayachan@fas.harvard.edu. Kremer: Department of Economics, Harvard University, 200 Littauer Center, Cambridge, MA 02138; The Brookings Institution; Center for Global Development; and National Bureau of Economic Research. Email: mkremer@fas.harvard.edu. This chapter is based on Kremer and Jayachandran (2003).

1 On the first rationale, Krugman (1989) and Sachs (1989) describe a debt overhang problem caused by negative shocks. On the second rationale, Adams (1991) and Hanlon (2002) argue the case that much developing-country debt is illegitimate, and Ashfaq *et al.* (2002) discuss related legal issues. The philosopher Pogge (2001) proposes that a panel assess the democratic status of governments in order to deter lending to autocratic regimes. We differ from earlier work in discussing the multiple equilibria of the debt market – which are what make assessments potentially efficacious – and the tradeoffs between *ex-ante* and *ex-post* assessments.

2 "S. Africa Shuns Apartheid Lawsuits" (*Guardian*, November 27, 2002).

3 "Somoza Legacy: Plundered Economy" (*Washington Post*, November 30, 1979); "Cuba's Debt Mistakes: A Lesson for Nicaragua" (*Washington Post*, October 5, 1980). Debt figures from World Bank (2003). All figures are in current dollars.

4 The *Financial Times* reports the $4 billion figure as the estimate of the United States Treasury and International Monetary Fund. An *FT* investigation found that Mobutu's wealth peaked at this value ("Mobutu built a fortune of $4 billion from looted aid," December 5, 1997). Others report his 1997 wealth as $9 billion ("Superstar eclipsed by greed," *Times* (London), May 5, 1997).

5 Adams, 1991; World Bank, 2003.
6 Other examples: Sani Abacha was reported to have $2 billion in Swiss bank accounts in 1999 after five years as Nigeria's ruler. ("Going after 'Big Fish', new Nigerian President trawls for corruption," *International Herald Tribune*, November 25, 1999.) Jean–Claude Duvalier's successors in Haiti claim he took $900 million with him when he left power in 1986. Haiti's debt was $700 million at the time ("Haiti in life and debt struggle," *Guardian*, June 17, 2000). Debt figures from Hanlon (1998).
7 In the few cases where a government has repudiated the debts of previous regimes as illegitimate, such as after the Russian revolution, the new government presumably had few plans to deal with foreigners and had few assets overseas subject to creditor countries' legal systems, so it had little to lose by defaulting.
8 "UK warns Croatia it risks losing aid," *Financial Times*, July 31, 1997; "Croats find Treasury plundered; state says former regime stole or misused billions," *Washington Post*, June 13, 2000. World Bank, 2003.
9 "Moody's, Citing US Concern, Cancels Ratings on Iran Debt" (*New York Times*, June 4, 2002).
10 Note that while the charters of the IFIs proscribe their judging governments on political grounds when making funding decisions – and hence they could not be the judges of odiousness – in this case their judgments would be on economic grounds, and no independent panel would be needed.

References

Adams, Patricia. 1991. *Odious Debts*. London: Earthscan.
Ashfaq, Khalfan, Jeff King, and Bryan Thomas. 2002. "Advancing the Odious Debt Doctrine," Working Paper, Center for International Sustainable Development Law, McGill University.
Feilchenfeld, Ernst. 1931. *Public Debts and State Succession*. New York: MacMillan.
Hanlon, Joseph. 1998. "Dictators and Debt," Jubilee 2000 Report, London. Available at http://www.jubilee2000.org
—— 2002. *Defining Illegitimate Debt and Linking Its Cancellation to Economic Justice*. Mimeo, Norwegian Church Aid.
Kremer, Michael and Seema Jayachandran. 2003. *Odious Debt*. Mimeo, Harvard University.
Krugman, Paul R. 1989. "Market-based Debt-reduction Schemes." In Jacob A. Frenkel, Michael P. Dooley, and Peter Wickham, eds, *Analytical Issues in Debt*. Washington, DC: International Monetary Fund.
Pogge, Thomas W. 2001. "Achieving Democracy," *Ethics and International Affairs*, 15: 3–23.
Sachs, Jeffrey D. 1989. "The Debt Overhang of Developing Countries." In Guillermo Calvo, Ronald Findlay, Pentti Kouri, and Jorge Braga de Macedo, eds, *Debt Stabilization and Development: Essays in Memory of Carlos Diaz-Alejandro*. Oxford, UK: Basil Blackwell.
Sack, Alexander N. 1927. *Les Effets de Transformations des États sur Leur Dettes Publiques et Autres Obligations Financières*. Paris: Recueil Sirey.
World Bank. 2003. Debtor Reporting System and Joint BIS-IMF-OECD-World Bank Statistics on External Debt. http://www.worldbank.org/data

5 Aid and fiscal management

Aleš Bulíř and Timothy Lane

This chapter focuses on the macroeconomic aspects of fiscal management in aid-receiving countries. Despite the declining share of aid in budgets of donor countries, aid continues to play an important role in many developing countries. The chapter first discusses the implications of aid in the economy as a whole and highlights the possibility of Dutch-disease effects of aid. Second, it discusses the implications of aid for short-term fiscal policy management – in particular, how actual or anticipated changes in aid receipts should be reflected in government spending.

5.1 Introduction

Foreign aid has dwindled in the budgets of many donor countries during the past several years, but it continues to loom very large for many of the recipients.[1] In many developing countries, foreign aid receipts are an important source of revenue and thus a key element in fiscal policy. Where domestic resources are very limited, aid may be an indispensable source of financing, in particular, for expenditures in areas such as health, education, and public investment that are essential to raise the living standards of poor people in developing countries.

In discussing the fiscal implications of aid, a basic question is whether aid receipts are any different from any other source of revenue. The literature has focused on two elements. First, in the long run, aid – unlike, for instance, tax revenues – tends to taper off as the economy develops (and, in some cases, much sooner); this should be taken into consideration in determining the appropriate intertemporal fiscal policy. Second, while all revenues are subject to uncertainty, the nature of the uncertainty is different for aid than for domestic tax revenues, as the former stems from the spending processes of donor countries and the design of conditionality. Thus, an important empirical question is how the uncertainty of aid compares with that of tax revenues. To the extent that aid receipts are relatively uncertain, the issue from the donors' standpoint is how to reduce this uncertainty and, from the recipients' standpoint, how to take it into account in designing fiscal policy.[2]

The remainder of the chapter is structured as follows. Section 5.2 discusses the macroeconomic implications of aid, focusing first on the allocative effects and then the implications for growth. Section 5.3 discusses short-term fiscal policy management. Section 5.4 presents some concluding remarks.

5.2 Macroeconomic implications of aid

Aid generally expands the recipient country's opportunities by expanding consumption and investment beyond the level of domestically generated income and saving, respectively. Aid has been sizable in many countries and reasonably stable during the 1990s (Table 5.1). The sheer magnitude of aid in a number of countries suggests that it may have important macroeconomic effects.[3] These can be considered at two levels: the allocative effects on the structure of production, consumption, and relative prices; and the effects on economic growth.

5.2.1 Allocative effects

5.2.1.1 Theory

The allocative effects of aid-financed spending can be illustrated first of all in a simple two-sector general equilibrium model with tradables and nontradables (Michaely, 1981). The economy produces and consumes tradable and nontradable goods, constrained by the production possibility frontier (PQ). The initial equilibrium relative price (RS) – which also gives the economy's consumption possibilities – determines the optimum at point A. We also draw an Engel curve, EC(1) as shown in Figure 5.1, with the income elasticity of demand for nontraded goods being greater than 1, an assumption fairly common in the literature (White, 1992).[4]

In this framework, aid can be represented as transfer in the form of traded goods (AB), expanding the country's consumption possibility frontier to R′S′. Assuming that the aid is provided as an in-kind transfer of tradables to residents, the new consumption equilibrium at unchanged domestic relative prices would be at point B. However, this would imply excess supply of traded goods, lowering their price relative to that of nontraded goods. The equilibrium relative price would be TU (or T′U′), corresponding to the new Engel curve EC(2), and equilibrium consumption would be at point D. Production remains on the production possibility frontier at point C, but its composition is shifted toward nontradables, reflecting their higher relative price.

Table 5.1 Selected countries: aid and foreign direct investment (FDI) in aid-dependent countries, 1989–99[a]

	In percent of GNI, unless stated otherwise					
	1990–99 average	*1990*	*1999*	*Compared to 1989, aid in 1999 was*	*FDI*[b]	*GDP*[c]
Bhutan	22.6	17.6	16.1	Lower	0.1	656
Cape Verde	27.2	31.7	23.7	Lower	1.9	1,461
Djibouti	21.3	n.a.	14.2	Lower	0.0	742
Guinea-Bissau	51.5	55.1	25.7	Lower	0.7	183
Kiribati	25.5	36.0	25.6	Lower	0.0	600
Malawi	26.7	28.6	25.1	Lower	1.3	156
Mauritania	23.7	22.0	23.6	Higher	0.5	483
Micronesia, Fed. States of	34.5	n.a.	48.9	Higher	0.0	1,707
Mongolia	23.6	n.a.	25.4	Higher	1.8	457
Mozambique	45.0	42.4	23.2	Lower	2.7	198
Nicaragua	40.7	33.6	33.0	Lower	4.4	472
Rwanda	29.8	11.3	19.2	Higher	0.2	235
Samoa	25.2	31.5	12.9	Lower	2.7	1,011
Sao Tome and Principe	112.7	104.2	65.1	Lower	0.0	337
Vanuatu	20.5	30.6	16.3	Lower	11.7	1,347
Zambia	26.5	16.0	20.8	Higher	3.5	389

Source: World Development Indicators (2002); authors' calculations.

Notes
GNI denotes gross national income.
a Countries where the 1990–99 average aid-to-GNI ratio was higher than 0.2.
b FDI; in percent of GDP.
c In constant 1995 US dollars; per capita terms.

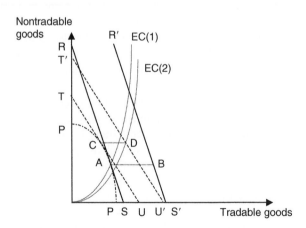

Figure 5.1 The effect of aid on the RS of traded and nontraded goods.

What is overall impact? Consumers are obviously better off: they consume more of both tradable and nontradable goods, while the change in relative shares of tradable and nontradable goods depends on the elasticity assumptions. Depending on the relative price change, the structure of the economy and factor rewards also change. If labor and capital are free to move between sectors, the factor used intensively in the nontradable sector gains and the other factor loses; on the usual assumption that nontradables are more labor-intensive than tradables, economy-wide real wages rise and real returns to capital fall.[5] Suppliers of any factor of production that is specialized in nontradables – for example, workers with specialized skills – tend to gain at the expense of specialized factors used in the tradables sector.

Donors provide aid mostly with a view of easing the domestic saving constraint and, hence, contributing to investment. It is relatively easy to adjust the model to reflect this effect by relaxing the assumption that aid is provided as a direct consumption transfer. First, there is the possibility that donors may insist that aid is consumed as tradables, say by financing projects that use only imported materials. In such a case, the impact on the relative price and composition of traded-to-nontraded goods will depend on fungibility of aid. If aid merely frees domestic resources that would have been used to finance these projects irrespective of aid – that is, if aid is fully fungible – the effect of aid would be identical to that described earlier.

A second possibility is that aid is used for investment in productive capacity that would not have been implemented in the absence of aid. In this case, the production possibility frontier would shift outward, with the nature of this shift depending on whether the investment is allocated to the production of tradables or nontradables. The effect on the structure of demand also depends on the extent to which aid-financed investment involves tradable versus nontradable goods as inputs.

This model illustrates the possibility that aid-financed spending could lead to "Dutch disease" – that is, a reduction in the recipient country's production of tradable goods.[6] But in this model, there is nothing wrong with the shift in production away from tradables; it is merely an efficient adaptation of the economy to the receipt of a transfer, which is unambiguously welfare-improving for the recipient country. For the effects of aid to be a problem, some other elements would need to be taken into consideration.[7] First, the shift away from tradables production can generate distortions, such as the possibility of a loss of positive externalities associated with "learning by doing." In that case, however, the distortion ought to be tackled directly as opposed to discouraging aid inflows.[8] Second, aid may be temporary, in which case the intertemporal use of aid is at issue: it would not be desirable for the structure of production and consumption to adapt fully to aid received during this period if it will not continue next period. Finally, large aid inflows may lead to a relaxation of tax discipline, effectively keeping the resource constraint at the pre-aid level, but with a less sustainable fiscal position.

5.2.1.2   *Empirical evidence*

The simple model just presented illustrates that aid-financed spending may increase the relative price of nontradables and reduce the production of tradables, that is, cause "Dutch disease." But it is an empirical question whether this hypothetical effect of aid outweighs the positive effect on productive capacity of aid-financed investment and welfare effect of aid-financed consumption.

As a starting point, we may consider the behavior of aid flows and real exchange rates in a number of aid-receiving countries. Figure 5.2 shows a diverse sample of aid-receiving countries, illustrating that aid inflows and appreciation of real exchange rates have often gone hand in hand.

This impression is borne out by a substantial body of more systematic empirical evidence.[9] Traces of aid-induced real exchange rate appreciation were found by van Wijnbergen (1986) and Elbadawi (1999) in two samples of African countries and these early results were subsequently confirmed by Younger (1992), Vos (1998), and Atingi-Ego and Sebudde (2000) for Ghana, Pakistan, and Uganda, respectively. However, Nyoni (1998) found aid inflows to depreciate the real exchange rate in Tanzania and Dijkstra and van Donge (2001) found no impact in Uganda.[10]

Of course, real appreciation may not necessarily depress exports; moreover, other developments, such as the terms of trade, the overall fiscal balance, or country's openness, can mitigate or even offset the change in relative prices. There are several channels which can negate the impact of appreciation on exports.[11] First, the aid-induced inflow of foreign commodities may have a deflationary impact by increasing the supply of commodities or by easing supply bottlenecks in the economy (see Hjertholm *et al.*, 1998). Second, real appreciation can be beneficial. As long as imports are used toward "productive" investments in a broad sense, say, physical, capital, health, or education products, appreciated currency will accommodate more of those imports, ultimately contributing to future growth.[12] Third, some shift of resources out of tradable goods may be desirable providing the increase in aid is permanent (Adam *et al.*, 1994). Falck (2000) claims to have found evidence of the latter effect in Mozambique. Finally, aid may lower transaction costs of doing business in low-income countries (Collier, 2000). But it is unclear to what extent such effects may mitigate, or dominate, the effects of real appreciation on production of tradables.[13]

Empirical evidence on the exchange rate–exports nexus of Dutch disease has not been convincing, a result which is to be expected given the circumstance in most aid-dependent countries. Exports in countries such as Ghana, Uganda, or Tanzania before the surge in aid in the 1980s and 1990s were falling both because the official exchange rate made those exports uncompetitive and because of high transaction cost owing to dilapidating infrastructure, bad macroeconomic policies, and high export taxes. Consequently, many of these economies have been able to increase their overall exports at appreciated real exchange rates simply on the account of policies lowering barriers to trade.

It has been argued recently that Dutch disease may affect the structure of exports rather than their overall level. In these models, aid supports employment in the low-skill nontradables sector and the correspondingly high wages then crowd out employment in the traded goods sector. There seems to be some

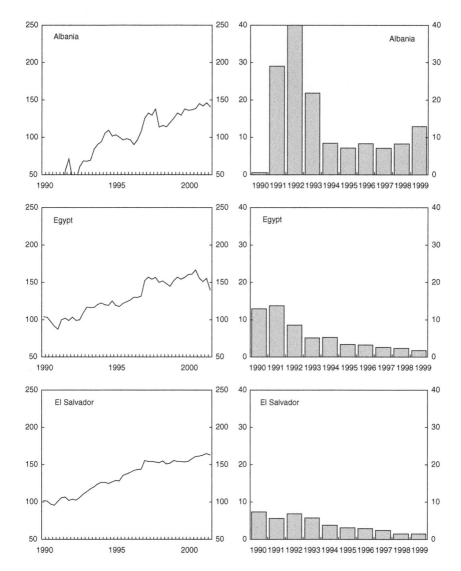

Figure 5.2 Selected countries: real effective exchange rate and aid (1990 = 100 and in percent of GNI).

Source: INS and WDI.

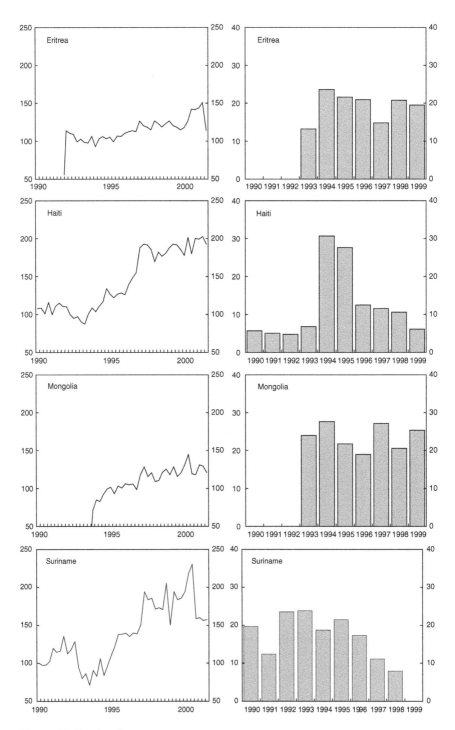

Figure 5.2 Continued.

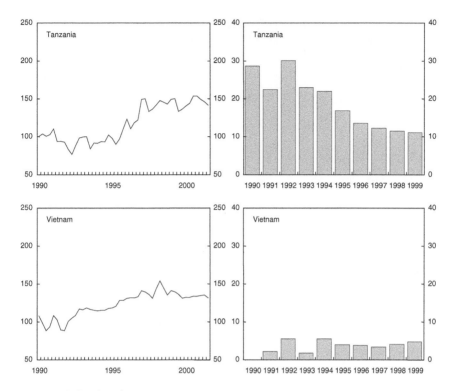

Figure 5.2 Continued.

evidence to support this hypothesis: manufacturing good exports in many of the less developed countries are substantially below what is predicted on the basis of their labor and capital endowments, and the rate of growth of exports is slower than predicted. These results have been documented in single-country studies for Ghana, Cameroon, and some South Pacific States by Teal (1999), Söderling (2000), and Laplagne *et al.* (2001), respectively, and in a large panel-data study of African countries by Sekkat and Varoudakis (2000).

We find that the tradable sector has shrunk dramatically in most aid-dependent countries between 1985 and 1999 (Figure 5.3).[14] The average decline in constant prices was more than 8 percentage points of GDP, while the decline increased to more than 10 percentage points of GDP when measured in current prices. Historically, the share of nontraded goods on GDP has been growing in all countries, especially in those that reached a certain level of development. In contrast, output in per capita terms either declined or stagnated in all but three countries (Bhutan, Burkina Faso, and Uganda) of our sample. In other words, these results imply an absolute decline in tradable output per capita as opposed to a relative decline in developed countries.

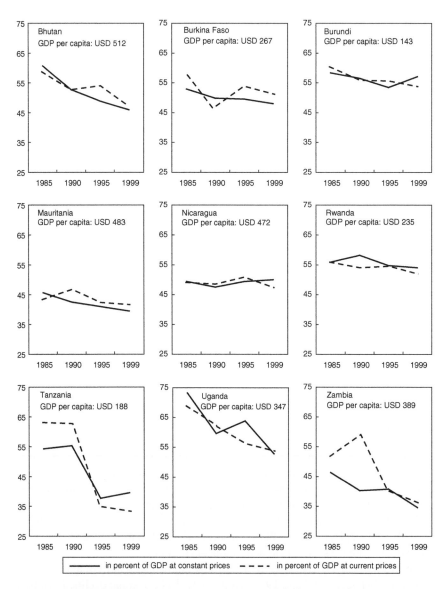

Figure 5.3 Selected countries: developments in traded goods sector, 1985–99[a,b] (in percent of GDP).

Source: IMF, Recent Economic Development and Statistical Appendix, various countries and issues.

Notes
a The traded goods sector is approximated by agriculture, mining, and manufacturing.
b Data for Uganda are for the following fiscal years: 1984–85, 1989–90, 1994–95, 1998–99; and the 1986 data are used for Mauritania and Nicaragua.

5.2.2 Aid and growth

5.2.2.1 Conceptual issues

There are different ways of modeling the linkage between aid and growth. From one perspective, aid fosters growth by enabling the country to finance more rapid accumulation of capital, supplementing private savings. This perspective is represented by the Harrod–Domar model, in which the effectiveness of aid in contributing to growth depends on the productivity of capital, as represented by the incremental capital output ratio (ICOR). This assumes that there is no scarcity of complementary factors of production such as labor. According to this model, a sustainable growth path may generate a financing gap which can be filled through aid or other sources of financing.

The Harrod–Domar model was supplanted in the academic literature about forty years ago by the Solow growth model, which allows for the possibility of substitution between capital and labor. It implies that the economy approaches a steady state in which the economy's savings are balanced by the need for investment to maintain a constant capital–labor ratio given labor force growth and productivity increases. In this model, the steady-state growth rate is equal to the rate of population growth plus the rate of technical change. A flow of aid thus does not affect the economy's growth rate once it reaches the steady state, but it does imply that this growth rate is reached at a higher level of GDP – itself a desirable outcome – and moreover, implies a higher growth rate during the transition.

Endogenous growth models emerged during the 1980s, motivated by concerns that the Harrod–Domar and Solow models did not explain some of the key facts about development in an international perspective – notably, the persistence of international differences in per capita incomes and in growth rates (Lucas, 1988). Endogenous growth models explain growth on the basis of some form of increasing returns to scale, often linked to human capital accumulation and positive externalities associated with "learning-by-doing." Because endogenous growth models leave open the possibility that the equilibrium growth rate is path-dependent (i.e. it depends on the previous history of production in the country) they open the way to empirical work on various factors that influence growth. In particular, in an endogenous growth model, aid may influence growth to the extent that it is used to add to human capital. This has focused attention in particular on the role of health and education spending in development. A related literature has focused on the role of institutions in influencing total factor productivity (Ensminger, 1997).

5.2.2.2 Empirical evidence

The literature showed rather convincingly that aid inflows are associated with higher rates of growth (Hansen and Tarp, 2001a). It has also been shown, however, that too much aid can be detrimental to economic growth, even though the estimates are rather imprecise as to what is the exact amount of aid necessary to bring about negative returns of aid (Durbarry *et al.*, 1998; Elbadawi, 1999; Lensink and White, 2001). It is troubling, however, that in none of the major development success stories, such as in Taiwan, China, Botswana, Korea, or Chile, does aid seem to have played an important role. In these cases either aid was small through the whole period or the country was weaned off aid early.

The empirical literature offers little agreement on what actually explains the growth performance of less-developed countries and what has been the role of aid during the last three decades. Nevertheless, the results can be summarized relatively easily. First, most studies found that aid increases total savings, albeit by less than the amount of aid inflows. In the underlying Harrod–Domar model, aid relaxes the saving constraint on investment and, hence, should contribute positively to economic growth. Second, the results from reduced form regression imply that the aid–investment link is positive and whenever aid increases saving, it also increases investment and growth. Aid does not, however, generate any multiplier effect: although the estimated coefficients are positive, they are generally smaller than 1. Third, whether "good economic policies" are necessary for aid to be effective is debated. Although countries with "good policies" obviously grow faster than those with "poor policies," it is not clear that aid given to the latter countries is simply wasted or that "good-policies" countries with sufficient aid can be assured of success in their economic development.[15] Finally, there is an apparent paradox in the aid-effectiveness literature: on the one hand, numerous microeconomic studies have shown that most development projects yield respectable rates of return; on the other hand, US dollar per capita GDP barely moved in the poorest countries that are major aid recipients.

The empirical findings on the aid–growth nexus provide limited insights on the quality of economic growth in aid-recipient countries. One of the key results from endogenous growth models is that an economy's ability to make use of new technologies is an important determinant of its growth. In this regard, many poor, aid-dependent countries fail and the level of FDI remains well below the level necessary to achieve sustainable growth (Table 5.1).[16] Although many alternative explanations have been suggested to account for this failure, the aid-driven expansion of the nontradable sector and a lack of support for the high-skill, traded goods sector is clearly one of them.[17] Indeed, the causality may run in the opposite direction: FDI tends to flow into countries with vibrant tradable good sectors, which tend to deteriorate with large aid inflows (Figure 5.3). Effectively, aid has left nontradables-driven growth vulnerable to its fluctuations.[18]

5.2.2.3   Policy implications

The models used to examine the impact of aid and the accompanying empirical results have implications for the appropriate time profile of aid. The Harrod–Domar and Solow models both imply that the bulk of aid should be provided when the country is poorest, as this will be the time when additional capital financed through aid will be most productive. Consequently, that analysis suggests that aid should taper out as the economy develops. Endogenous growth models, on the other hand, suggest that the productivity of capital may instead increase as the economy develops, suggesting that aid may do more good at a later stage. Empirical studies suggesting that aid is more effective in promoting growth in good policy environments also indicate that aid should "taper in" rather than "taper out." This path also implies that, during the early years of development, the aid ought to be used to support a higher level of government spending and/or to lower the burden of distortionary taxes on the country.

As a general principle, the argument for aid that "tapers in" seems rather compelling: it would provide support for infrastructure and human capital development while enabling the country to maintain a minimum level of consumption, especially for the poor. But applying this approach poses a number of challenges. First, one would need to project an appropriate path for development and financing, to identify the points at which aid should be increased, and at which it should taper out. For example, the recipient country authorities and donors could specify a comprehensive, long-term development plan with clear progress toward the goal of a sustainable path.[19] Second, donors would need to commit themselves to financing such a path, giving substance to the promise to deliver more aid – in a predictable manner – sometime in the future. The latter aspect is particularly important in view of the poor track record of aid commitments in predicting actual disbursements (see following paragraphs).

The view that the contribution of aid to growth depends very much on the policies in place focuses greater attention on the policy conditionality associated with aid. It can be used to justify a significant level of conditionality regarding economic governance, particularly the management of budgetary resources. In other words, conditionality would be attached to measures to build better institutions. At the same time, the argument that aid should be back-loaded (i.e. "tapering in") goes hand in hand with a shift toward outcomes-based conditionality – in contrast to traditional conditionality based on policy actions taken by the authorities. Outcomes-based conditionality is intended to ensure that aid is disbursed in the most productive environment while also giving recipient countries more freedom in selecting their policies. Its drawback from the standpoint of the recipient country is that it exposes it to greater uncertainty regarding future disbursements, as aid would continue to flow only if outcomes meet donor expectations (International Monetary Fund, 2002).[20]

Regardless of the form of conditionality, the issue remains whether the conditions attached to aid can in fact ensure that it is disbursed in a supportive policy environment. On the one hand, the evidence suggests that the number of conditions typically attached to aid has increased but, on the other hand, countries with higher aid-to-GNI ratios have tended to meet fewer of those conditions (Figure 5.4 upper panel).[21] More generally, it is increasingly believed that economic reforms are likely to be implemented only to the extent that they are strongly supported within the country itself (Khan and Sharma, 2001).

5.3 Aid and short-term fiscal management

Large aid inflows, sustained or temporary, have a powerful impact on the short-term conduct of fiscal and monetary policies. If aid is volatile, then some of the

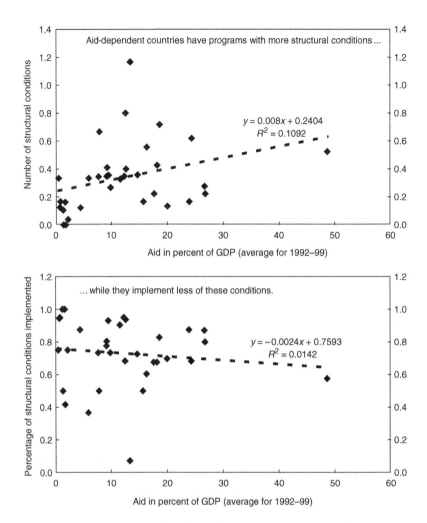

Figure 5.4 Selected countries: aid dependency and program ownership (sample of 33 countries with IMF-supported programs during the 1990s).

Source: Data from Bulíř and Moon (2004).

Note
The number of structural conditions is normalized by the length of the program.

potential positive effects of aid may not materialize: volatility is welfare-reducing and more so in developing countries that have limited domestic financial instruments to offset external shocks. Aid-heavy budgets may take the overall fiscal stance outside of the control of the recipient country, owing to limited predictability of aid disbursements. Also, to the extent that donors place conditions on spending, such budgets may lack flexibility on the expenditure side.

5.3.1 Volatility of aid

Most empirical studies that have examined the volatility of aid have found aid to be significantly more volatile than domestic fiscal revenue (Gemmell and McGillivray, 1998; Pallage and Robe, 2001; Bulíř and Hamann, 2003).[22] Of course, some volatility of aid is to be expected and may indeed have a stabilizing impact: certain forms of aid, such as food aid or balance of payment support, are disbursed only if the country is hit with an exogenous shock (say, a drought or a sudden drop in terms of trade). To confirm this hypothesis, one would require aid disbursements to be negatively correlated with those shocks. In fact, however, most researchers have reported that aid is positively correlated with economic activity, that is, aid is weakly procyclical (Gemmell and McGillivray, 1998; Bulíř and Hamann, 2003).[23] Highly volatile and procyclical aid is obviously less beneficial to recipient countries than a similar mean level of aid delivered in a less volatile form (Pallage and Robe, 2003); aid volatility is also likely to substantially attenuate the growth effects of aid (Lensink and Morrissey, 2000).

The results presented here, drawn from Bulíř and Hamann (2003), show that aid – measured by the OECD as the total development assistance (ODA) – has been much more volatile than domestic fiscal revenue, up to seven times in the case of heavily aid-dependent countries (Table 5.2). The volatility of aid increases with the aid dependency: when the sample is narrowed down to countries with aid-to-revenue ratio of 50 percent or more, the relative volatility increases by an

Table 5.2 Which is more volatile – aid or revenue?[a]

	The ratio of variances of aid and revenue	
	Countries with the aid-to-revenue ratio of 10% or more	*Countries with the aid-to-revenue ratio of 50% or more*
Aid and revenue in percent of GDP		
Average	4.96**	7.42**
Median	2.19**	4.91**
Correlation coefficient (average)	0.08	00.05
Number of countries	57	33
Aid and revenue in US dollars per capita		
Average	1.73*	3.00**
Median	0.80	2.25
Correlation coefficient (average)	0.09*	0.11
Number of countries	55	29

Source: Data from Bulíř and Hamann (2003). The data set covers the period from 1975 to 1997 and excludes countries with end-period population of less than 400,000.

Note

a The statistical significance of the average and median estimates is measured by the *F*-test and "runs test," respectively. The significance at the 95 and 99 percent levels is indicated by * and **, respectively.

additional 50–75 percent as compared to sample countries with aid-to-revenue ratio of 10 percent or more. The volatility of aid depends on whether aid is measured in US dollar terms or in percent of domestic GDP, each measure having some limitations. The former metric would be relevant if aid and tax revenues were spent entirely on tradables with prices fixed in US dollars; the latter would be relevant if the government wanted to use aid and tax revenues to finance spending equivalent to a given slice of GDP. In addition, there is not much evidence of a counter cyclical character of aid. While in a few countries the correlation coefficient between aid and revenue was negative, on average aid appears to be modestly procyclical, although this result is not statistically significant in most samples.[24]

These results suggest that aid is quite volatile in relation to other sources of revenues, and this may pose challenges for short-term fiscal management.[25] Of course, there is little reason to assume that aid volatility and procyclicality must be taken as given, indeed, there is significant room for both aid-recipients and donors to improve the pattern of aid disbursements.

One major source of aid variability is conditionality – not only the conditions attached by bilateral donors, but frequently the requirement by donors that aid recipients have the seal of approval of an on-track, IMF-supported program. There are two sides to this issue. From the country's point of view, it means that complying with conditionality is important not only because of the merits of the policies to which conditions are attached but because it reduces volatility in aid inflows. But from the perspective of the donors and the international financial institutions, there is an obvious tension between the need to ensure that "good policies" are being implemented versus the negative impact of disruptions in aid disbursements. This gives a particular point to recent efforts to ensure that conditionality is appropriately focused on those elements that are genuinely needed – a key element in the IMF's recent review of conditionality (International Monetary Fund, 2001a,b).

However, there are also factors that lead to disruptions in aid disbursements over which the recipient country has less control: the tendency for aid commitments to be scaled down through the domestic budget-making processes in the donor countries. This will be discussed in Section 5.3.2.

5.3.2   Predictability of aid

There has long been a perception that aid commitments err on the optimistic side of what is likely to be deliverable, even when the country's economic policy program remains on track. To the extent that this occurs, it implies that such commitments are a weak basis on which to base spending plans, particularly when aid is a large component of the budget. In turn, projected fiscal deficits including committed aid will tend to overstate the strength of the fiscal position.

Bulíř and Hamann (2003) examine aid commitments as a predictor of disbursements and find that aid commitments explain only a negligible part of the actual disbursement in a simple time series model and that short-term predictions – even those unrelated to commitments – have been excessively optimistic. These findings are robust to the type of aid: project aid versus program aid or loans versus grants.[26] Moreover, conditionality does not seem to be a factor here: the poor record of predicting aid has been found also for countries with "on-track" programs.

Total aid disbursements in countries with IMF-supported programs were on average some 20 percent less than what was projected at the beginning of the period (Table 5.3).[27] Contrary to intuition, these results change only little when the sample is divided into countries with and without interruptions in their programs (Table 5.4).[28] We find, however, that the prediction error differs markedly for project and program aid. Average project aid disbursements were about 10 percent below predictions, although the median estimate was again around 20 percent. We also find that project aid disbursements are independent of the status of their IMF-supported programs: countries with program interruptions received on average more project aid than was predicted, whereas countries with program interruptions received some 10 percent less. In contrast, average program aid disbursements were some 32 and 25 percent smaller than commitments in all countries and in countries without program interruptions, respectively. The penalty for program interruption was sizeable: aid in those countries fell by more than 80 percent below the committed level.

Aid cannot be predicted reliably on the basis of donors' commitments, as there seems to be a tendency for all parties involved (donors, the local authorities, and the IMF itself) to systematically overestimate aid disbursements.[29] The prediction errors are not symmetric – more countries experience unexpected shortfalls in aid than unexpected increases in aid.

Table 5.3 How good are short-term predictions of aid? (in percent of GDP; sample averages)

	Aid projections		Aid disbursements	
	Average	*Median*	*Average*	*Median*
Total aid	9.2	7.6	7.4	5.9
All countries of which:				
No program interruptions	9.3	7.4	7.7	5.8
Program interruption	8.5	7.8	5.8	7.5
Project aid	5.2	5.1	4.8	4.1
All countries of which:				
No program interruptions	5.3	4.8	4.7	3.9
Program interruption	4.6	5.8	5.2	7.5
Program aid	4.7	3.6	3.2	1.9
All countries of which:				
No program interruptions	5.0	3.6	3.7	2.2
Program interruption	3.4	3.6	0.6	0.7

Source: Data from Bulíř and Hamann (2003), a survey based on responses from 37 IMF desk economists. The period covered is 1998 for most countries. Aid projections correspond to projections in IMF-supported programs.

Table 5.4 List of countries used in the survey

Country	Period	Type of fund arrangement
Albania	January 1998–December 1998	ESAF
Algeria	July 1998–June 1999	EFF
Azerbaijan	January 1998–December 1998	ESAF
Bolivia	January 1998–December 1998	ESAF
Burkina Faso	January 1998–December 1998	ESAF
Cambodia	January 1998–December 1998	ESAF
Cameroon	July 1998–June 1999	ESAF
Cape Verde	January 1998–December 1998	Stand-by
Central African Republic*	January 1998–December 1998	ESAF
Côte d'Ivoire	January 1998–December 1998	ESAF
Djibouti	January 1998–December 1998	ESAF
Dominican Republic	January 1998–December 1998	None
Ecuador	January 1998–December 1998	None
Egypt	June 1998–June 1999	Stand-by
El Salvador	December 1997–December 1998	Stand-by
FYR Macedonia	January 1998–December 1998	ESAF
Gabon	January 1998–December 1998	EFF
Ghana	January 1998–December 1998	ESAF
Guyana	January 1998–December 1998	ESAF
Indonesia	April 1998–March 1999	Stand-by/EFF
Jordan	January 1998–December 1998	EFF
Kyrgyz Republic	January 1998–December 1998	ESAF
Lao PDR	October 1997–September 1998	None
Madagascar	January 1998–December 1998	ESAF
Mauritania	January 1998–December 1998	ESAF
Mongolia	January 1998–December 1999	ESAF
Mozambique	December 1997–December 1998	ESAF
Nepal	July 16, 1998–July 15, 1999	None
Nigeria	January 1998–December 1998	None
Panama	January 1998–December 1998	EFF
Papua New Guinea*	January 1998–December 1998	None
Republic of Congo*	December 1997–December 1998	ESAF
Sierra Leone	January 1998–December 1998	ESAF
Tajikistan	July 1998–June 1999	ESAF
Yemen	January 1998–December 1998	ESAF
Zambia*	January 1998–December 1998	ESAF
Zimbabwe*	January 1998–December 1998	Stand-by

Note
Countries denoted with an asterisk had an interruption in the IMF-supported program.

5.3.3   *What are the policy alternatives for aid recipients?*

If aid is volatile or unpredictable, or both, the recipient countries have two basic options: they could devise a flexible fiscal framework in which tax and spending plans can be adjusted in response to aid receipts; or they could try to smooth out fluctuations in aid disbursements by running down international reserves. A third option is to rely on domestic nonmonetary financing to handle variations in aid. Each of these options will be discussed in turn.

From a fiscal perspective, aid can be used to increase expenditure, lower taxes, reduce debt, or a combination of all three. The actual composition should reflect expectations of the nature of aid: for example, temporary aid increases should not be used for permanent tax reductions or for an increase in mandatory expenditures (entitlements), but should mainly be saved. In contrast, expected "permanent" increases could be channeled into higher spending or lower taxes with little consequences for fiscal stability.

The empirical evidence suggests that countries tend to treat all aid inflows as permanent in the long run, but as a financing item in the short run (see Heller, 1975; White, 1992). First, the available studies noted that past temporary increases were mostly consumed, leading to a permanently higher level of expenditure: a ratchet effect of aid-induced expenditure (McGillivray and Morrissey, 2001a). Second, strongest short-term interactions were found between aid and government borrowing, implying that aid windfalls or shortfalls tend to be mirrored in adjustments in deficits (see Gemmell and McGillivray, 1998). McGillivray and Morrissey (2001b) report similar findings from a sample of fiscal response studies. In other words, there is little evidence that aid recipients try to make the distinction between permanent and temporary aid flows.

Budgets can be designed to accommodate aid disbursements in excess of the conservative fiscal baseline, providing that established budgetary procedures are made more flexible. For example, domestic-currency funds could be released to the line ministries only after the equivalent foreign-currency denominated aid has been deposited at the central bank. But the flexibility of fiscal frameworks to make up for variations in aid receipts is limited. Fiscal flexibility is an idea that harks back to the heyday of Keynesian fiscal activism, when it was thought that taxes and spending plans could be shut on and off in response to new information on macroeconomic conditions.

In industrial countries, enthusiasm for the concept of fiscal flexibility was dampened by further analysis and experience. On the revenue side, variations in tax rates to compensate for temporary fiscal shortfalls shifts uncertainty onto the taxpayers and, through their effects on expectations, may result in changes in behavior that vitiate these intended effects (time inconsistency problem). On the expenditure side, it is generally disruptive to turn expenditures on and off at short notice, unless these expenditures are not serving an important purpose in the first place. Moreover, expenditures that are turned off for short-term reasons are often difficult to turn on again. For this reason, industrial countries have relied increasingly on "built-in fiscal flexibility" stemming from the income sensitivity of tax and spending items, rather than hoping to fine-tune activist policies. It is hard to believe that low-income countries can succeed where industrial countries failed.

The second option, allowing foreign exchange reserves to ride out fluctuations in aid receipts, poses different, but equally daunting problems. It implies that if aid falls short of projected levels, reserves are allowed to decline below the levels envisaged and domestic credit expanded to finance a larger-than-projected fiscal deficit. This approach requires that the country plan to follow conservative fiscal and monetary policies in order to build a cushion of reserves that can be drawn down to cover aid shortfalls;[30] this cushion represents resources that could be put to better use in the country if aid were delivered more reliably. Moreover, to the extent that aid shortfalls are chronic, as discussed earlier, this approach introduces an element of artificiality into fiscal plans, making fiscal targets look more conservative than probable outturns.

The third option mentioned, using domestic bond financing to maintain spending plans in the face of aid shortfalls, can also be used, subject to quantitative limitations. A necessary condition for this approach is to have functioning domestic financial markets. But even if those markets exist, there is a limit to the amount the government can finance domestically: for example, the evidence suggests that sub-Saharan countries cannot issue more domestic debt than equivalent to 15 percent of GDP without a recourse to printing money. Moreover, given the shallowness of domestic financial markets in most aid-dependent countries, heavy use of these markets by the government may to a significant degree crowd out private borrowing. Finally, the cost of domestic financing is generally higher than that of concessional external financing, even when the impact of devaluation is taken into account (Beaugrand *et al.*, 2002).

Thus, any of these ways of adapting to short-term variations in aid – fiscal flexibility, using a cushion of reserves, or domestic borrowing – has limitations.[31] As long as uncertainties on aid receipts remain substantial, it is likely that some combination of the three will need to be used, depending on the extent to which variations in aid are expected to be permanent or transitory. But these considerations also point to the need for aid recipients to formulate their fiscal plans on the basis of more realistic projections of the aid that is likely to materialize, and for donors to make stronger efforts to keep their promises.

5.4   Conclusions

Despite the declining share of aid in budgets of donor countries, aid continues to play an important role in many developing countries. While the impact of aid is typically divided between supplementing domestic saving and contributing to consumption, there is less agreement on the potential effects of aid on growth. The impact of large aid inflows on the relative price of traded and nontraded goods is well known, and several recent papers confirmed the importance of real exchange rate appreciation for the decline of the traded goods sector in developing countries. But in a dynamic context, the effects of aid depend on how aid-financed spending affects the productive capacity of the economy. While several empirical studies suggest that aid tends to enhance growth, they also suggest that the linkage is neither direct nor automatic, but depends very much on the environment that influences the use of aid.

The positive impact of aid has been undermined in some cases by the volatility and unpredictability of aid. Aid is significantly more volatile than domestic fiscal revenue, and volatility increases with aid dependency. In addition, aid is procyclical *vis-à-vis* domestic fiscal revenue – rather than smoothing out cyclical shocks, it tends to exacerbate them. Moreover, aid is not well predicted even in countries with "on-track" programs and the prediction error is asymmetric: aid commitments are more likely to overestimate disbursements than vice versa.

This chapter has highlighted a number of issues that aid poses for fiscal management. None of these findings alter the view that donors should be more generous with aid. However, it is important to take those issues into account to ensure that aid has its intended effect of boosting growth and alleviating poverty.

Notes

1 The first fact – that industrial countries presently devote only about one-quarter of 1 percent, significantly less than the goal of 0.7 percent, of GNP to foreign aid – has received more attention than the second fact that aid has hardly declined in importance to the countries that continue to receive it. In recent years, donors seem to have become more selective *vis-à-vis* economic policies pursued by recipient countries, and an increasing share of aid is being distributed based on economic and social considerations (World Bank, 2002) as opposed to geopolitical and historical considerations (Alesina and Dollar, 2000). Easterly (2002) challenged, however, the World Bank's findings and claimed that up to 1999 no link between economic performance and aid disbursements can be observed.

2 Discussions of the role of aid in fiscal policy have, at times, been overshadowed by the question of how to measure the fiscal deficit: with or without grants? There is a strong case for using the definition that includes grants, provided that grants are measured accurately (and projected realistically), since grants by definition do not generate an obligation to repay. A second issue is whether the grant element of concessional borrowing should be included as revenues. To avoid double counting, this would need to be offset on the expenditure side by imputing the costs of servicing outstanding concessional debt at market rates. But imputing the entire net present value of interest subsidy when the loan is received while spreading the interest costs paid with the subsidy over the life of the loan would seem to reduce, rather than enhance, the clarity of the accounts. Moreover, the imputation of the implicit grant element would depend heavily on assumptions regarding future exchange rates and interest rates.

3 Some economists have argued that aid is an inefficient instrument for spurring development in low-income countries and that it played a significantly negative role in those countries by encouraging waste and corruption (Bauer, 1979).

4 Given that the bulk of nontradables comprises services and construction, they both can be seen as "luxuries." In any case, changing the elasticity to 1 or even to less than 1 does not affect the results substantially.

5 This is, of course, a result of the Stolper–Samuelson theorem: a change in relative prices benefits the factor used intensively in the industry that expands (Stolper and Samuelson, 1941).

6 In practice, the upward pressure on the real exchange rate will be greater (i) the greater is the marginal propensity to spend on nontradable goods, (ii) the lower is their supply responsiveness, (iii) the higher the demand responsiveness to price changes, and (iv) the lower the policy coordination to sterilize aid inflows.

7 Another class of models dealing with the impact of aid looks at the political economy impact of aid flows and these models are mostly skeptical about any positive aid effects. The most prominent are: (i) "the war of attrition" models (Bulow and Klemperer, 1999), where aid results in bad policies, because individual factions in the recipient country cannot agree on how aid should be allocated and spent and (ii) "the voracity effect" models (Tornell and Lane, 1999), where weak institutional structure combined with fractionalization of the governing elite produce wasteful spending of

aid inflows. Empirical support for these models was provided by Casella and Eichengreen (1996) and Alesina and Weder (2002), respectively.

8 This argument goes back to Romer (1986). See also Lucas (1988) and Barro and Sala-i-Martin (1995).

9 Dutch disease models – see Edwards and van Wijnbergen (1989) for a model and White (1992) for a review – were originally formulated for countries with sudden discoveries of natural resources, but were eventually extended to the effects of aid inflows in developing countries.

10 From a technical point of view, the single-country studies are vulnerable to sample changes and regime switching: most of these countries have had alternating periods of very low and very high periods of aid inflows, casting doubts on the stability of the estimated parameters. Moreover, those models invariably use short time series only.

11 These channels also seem to imply that the traditional thinking about private investment crowding out through higher real interest rates is less relevant in developing economies.

12 This may not be an easy assumption to make. Even in relatively well-run countries, diversion of public funds may reach staggering proportions. For example, Reinikka and Svensson (2002) report that in Uganda "... on average, during the period 1991–95, schools received only 13 percent of what the central government contributed to the schools' nonwage expenditures. The bulk of the allocated spending was either used by public officials for purposes unrelated to education or captured for private gain."

13 Elbadawi (1998) estimated the relative role of endowment, transaction costs, and exchange rates for manufacturing exports in a sample of African countries. He found that high transaction costs and exchange rates misalignment explain the bulk of Africa's export underperformance *vis-à-vis* East Asia.

14 We approximate the share of traded goods by the share of agriculture (including fishing), mining, and manufacturing. We show results for those countries from Table 5.1 where the appropriate data were available. Our results are similar to those reported by Laplagne (1997), who reported the share of tradable goods for a sample of small South Pacific economies.

15 See Hadjimichael *et al.* (1995), Burnside and Dollar (2000), and Collier and Dehn (2001) for the good policies–aid–growth nexus and the critique by Lensink and White (2000), Guillaumont and Chauvet (2001), Dalgaard and Hansen (2001), Hansen and Tarp (2001b), and Easterly (2002). In contrast, Easterly (2001) argues that neither good policies nor exogenous shocks can explain much of the poor growth performance in developing countries and finds a strong link to the rate of growth in OECD countries in the context of a leader–follower model.

16 See, for example, Ajayi (2001) or Basu and Srinivasan (2002).

17 The most frequently cited reason for low FDI are negative investors' perceptions about poor countries economic and political stability, inadequate infrastructure, and a weak legal framework, particularly for the enforcement of contracts.

18 See Guillaumont and Chauvet (2001) for a similar argument in the context of the Dollar–Burnside regression: once "structural vulnerability" is taken into account, the aid–policy interactive term becomes insignificant.

19 Past attempts at formulating such long-term paths, such as the 25-year, UNDP-funded Vision 2020 that were formulated for a number of developing countries in the mid-1990s, failed to garner support both from the authorities and key donors.

20 It is not difficult to imagine situation when the domestic authorities bargain with the donor agencies about interpretation of outcomes in the same way they presently bargain about the thrust of future policies.

21 For example, IMF-supported programs during 1993–96 contained somewhat more structural measures in aid-dependent countries than in those where the role of aid has been negligible. The estimated parameter in regression of the number of structural conditions on aid in percent of GDP is statistically significant at the 90 percent level.

22 One widely cited and influential paper reports the opposite result (Collier, 1999), but this is mainly a reflection of some particular features of the empirical methodology used, including the failure to de-trend the data and the exclusive focus on US dollar measures of aid and tax revenues (discussed later). For a discussion of empirical issues in estimating the volatility of aid, see Bulíř and Hamann (2003).

23 Collier (1999) reported that aid was negatively correlated with revenue in a sample of African countries; however, his estimated covariance term incorporates the same empirical features as in the previous note, and moreover it is not significantly different from zero.

24 Aid was found to be countercyclical mostly in countries with large, short-lived shocks and post-conflict countries. From the donor perspective, French-speaking countries were more likely to receive aid in a countercyclical pattern, but as before, the results do not seem to be robust. See also Bulíř and Moon (2004), who found positive aid-to-revenue correlation in a model of medium-term fiscal developments.

25 These results do not necessarily mean that aid-financed budgets are more variable than budgets financed by the same level of tax revenues. This is because the variance of total revenues equals the sum of the variances of aid and non-aid revenues plus their covariance – an effect analogous to portfolio diversification. But this will be true in most cases, given that aid is several times as volatile as tax revenues and the covariance term is either zero or positive in most countries.

26 Project ("tied") aid constitutes payments for investment projects agreed between the donor and recipient and its fungibility depends on whether the authorities intended to finance these projects themselves, prior to the aid commitment (White, 1992). In contrast, program aid (also called balance of payment support or "untied" aid) generally comes in a "cash" form and is perfectly fungible – the authorities have complete control over the use of these resources.

27 See Table 5.4 for the list of countries.

28 Program interruption occurs if either (i) the last scheduled program review was not completed or (ii) all scheduled reviews were completed but the subsequent annual arrangement was not approved in multiyear arrangements.

29 To some extent, this may reflect the strategic behavior by the IMF, given its role in giving a "seal of approval" as the basis for other external assistance.

30 The majority of IMF-supported programs include adjusters to ensure that quarterly spending plans can continue even if aid falls short of projected levels. See International Monetary Fund (2002), Annex I for a discussion.

31 As a related issue, empirical evidence on a direct impact of aid in the monetary area is rather scanty and outdated (see White (1992) for a review). Recently, Fanizza (2001) illustrated, in the case of Malawi, inflationary pressures resulting from the government's inability to sell sufficient amount of foreign exchange, owing to the country's small and isolated foreign exchange market.

References

Adam, Chris, Arne Bigsten, Paul Collier, Eva Julin, and Steve O'Connell. 1994. "Evaluation of Swedish Development Co-operation with Tanzania: A Report for the Secretariat for Analysis of Swedish Development Assistance" (Stockholm: Secretariat for Analysis of Swedish Development Assistance, Ministry for Foreign Affairs).

Ajayi, S. Ibi. 2001. "What Africa Needs to Do to Benefit from Globalization," *Finance and Development*, 38 (December): 6–8.

Alesina, Alberto and David Dollar. 2000. "Who Gives Foreign Aid to Whom and Why?" *Journal of Economic Growth*, 5 (March): 33–63.

Alesina, Alberto and Beatrice Weder. 2002. "Do Corrupt Governments Receive Less Foreign Aid?" *American Economic Review*, 92(4) (September): 1126–37.

Atingi-Ego, Michael and Rachel Kaggwa Sebudde. 2000. "Uganda's Equilibrium Real Exchange Rate and its Implications for Non-Traditional Export Performance," *Bank of Uganda Staff Papers*, 2(1): 1–43.

Barro, Robert J. and Xavier Sala-i-Martin. 1995. *Economic Growth* (Cambridge, MA: MIT Press).

Basu, Anupam and Krishna Srinivasan. 2002. "Foreign Direct Investment in Africa – Some Case Studies," IMF Working Paper 02/61 (Washington, DC: International Monetary Fund).

Bauer, Peter T. 1979. "Foreign Aid Viewed Differently," *Aussenwirtschaft*, 34 (September): 225–39.

Beaugrand, Philippe, Boileau Loko, and Montfort Mlachila. 2002. "The Choice Between External and Domestic Debt in Financing Budget Deficits: The Case of Central and West African Countries," IMF Working Paper 02/79 (Washington, DC: International Monetary Fund).

Bulíř, Aleš and A. Javier Hamann. 2003. "Aid Volatility: An Empirical Assessment," *IMF Staff Papers*, 50(1): 64–89.

—— and Soojin Moon. 2004. "Is Fiscal Adjustment More Durable When the IMF is Involved?" *Comparative Economic Studies*, 46: 373–99.

Bulow, Jeremy and Paul Klemperer. 1999. "The Generalized War of Attrition," *American Economic Review*, 89(1): 175–89.

Burnside, Craig and David Dollar. 2000. "Aid, Policies, and Growth," *American Economic Review*, 90(4): 847–68.

Casella, Alessandra and Barry Eichengreen. 1996. "Can Foreign Aid Accelerate Stabilisation?" *Economic Journal*, 106 (May): 605–19.

Collier, Paul. 1999. "Aid 'Dependency': A Critique," *Journal of African Economies*, 8(4): 528–45.

—— 2000. "Africa's Comparative Advantage," in *Industrial Development and Policy in Africa*, H. Jalilian, M. Tribe, and J. Weiss, eds (Cheltenham: Edward Elgar).

—— and Jan Dehn. 2001. "Aid, Shocks, and Growth," *Policy Research Working Paper*, No. 2688 (Washington, DC: World Bank).

Dalgaard, Carl-Johan and Hendrik Hansen. 2001. "On Aid, Growth, and Good Policies," *Journal of Development Studies*, 37(August): 17–41.

Dijkstra, A. Geske and Jan Kees van Donge. 2001. "What Does the 'Show Case' Show? Evidence of and Lessons from Adjustment in Uganda," *World Development*, 29(5): 841–63.

Durbarry, Ramesh, Norman Gemmell, and David Greenaway. 1998. "New Evidence on the Impact of Foreign Aid on Economic Growth," CREDIT Research Paper 98/8, (University of Nottingham: Centre for Research in Economic Development and International Trade).

Easterly, William. 2001. "The Lost Decades: Developing Countries' Stagnation in Spite of Policy Reform 1980–1998," *Journal of Economic Growth*, 6 (June): 135–57.

—— 2002. "The Cartel of Good Intentions: The Problem of Bureaucracy in Foreign Aid," *Journal of Policy Reform*, 5(4): 223–50.

Edwards, Sebastian and Sweder van Wijnbergen. 1989. "Disequilibrium and Structural Adjustment," in *Handbook of Development Economics*, Vol. II, H. Chenery and T.N. Srinivasan eds (Amsterdam: Elsevier Science Publishers).

Elbadawi, Ibrahim A. 1998. "Can Africa Export Manufactures? The Role of Endowment, Exchange Rates, and Transaction Costs," a paper presented at the AERC/OECD/IMF workshop on "Policies for Competitiveness in Manufacturing in Sub-Saharan Africa," Johannesburg, South Africa (November 6–7, 1998).

—— 1999. "External Aid: Help or Hindrance to Export Orientation in Africa?" *Journal of African Economies*, 8(4): 578–616.

Ensminger, Jean. 1997. "Changing Property Rights: Reconciling Formal and Informal Rights to Land in Africa," in *The Frontiers of the New Institutional Economics*, J.N. Drobak and J.V.C. Nye, eds (San Diego, CA: Academic Press).

Falck, Hans. 2000. "Dutch Disease in Mozambique?" SIDA Country Report 2000: 1 (Sweden: Swedish Agency for International Development Cooperation) http://ww.sida.se/content/1/c6/02/84/11/Cer2000-1.pdf (accessed on September 26, 2005).

Fanizza, Domenico. 2001. "Foreign Aid, Macroeconomic Stabilization, and Growth in Malawi," in *Malawi – Selected Issues and Statistical Appendix*, Jon Shields, ed., Country Report No. 01/32 (Washington, DC: International Monetary Fund), pp. 11–30. http://www.imf.org/external/pubs/cat/longres.cfm?sk=3949.0 (accessed on August 3, 2000).

Franco-Rodriguez, Susana, McGillivray, Mark, and Morrissey, Oliver. 1998. "Aid and the Public Sector in Pakistan: Evidence with Endogenous Aid," *World Development*, 26(7): 1241–50.

Gemmell, Norman and Mark McGillivray. 1998. "Aid and Tax Instability and the Government Budget Constraints in Developing Countries," CREDIT Working Paper No. 98/1 (University of Nottingham Centre for Research in Economic Development and International Trade).

Guillaumont, Patrick and Lisa Chauvet. 2001. "Aid and Performance: A Reassessment," *Journal of Development Studies*, 37 (August): 66–92.

Hadjimichael, Michael T., Dhaneshwar Ghura, Martin Mühleisen, Roger Nord, and E. Murat Uçer. 1995. "Sub-Saharan Africa: Growth, Savings, and Investment, 1986–93," *Occasional Paper*, No. 118 (Washington, DC: International Monetary Fund).

Hansen, Henrik and Finn, Tarp. 2001a. "Aid and Growth Regressions," *Journal of Development Economics*, 64: 547–70.

—— 2001b. "Aid Effectiveness Disputed," *Journal of International Development*, 12: 375–98.

Heller, Peter S. 1975. "A Model of Public Fiscal Behavior in Developing Countries: Aid, Investment, and Taxation," *American Economic Review*, 65(3): 429–45.

Hjertholm, Peter, Jytte Laursen, and Howard White, 1998, "Macroeconomic Issues in Foreign Aid," revised paper presented at the conference on *Foreign Aid and Development: Lessons of Experience and Directions for the Future* (October 9–10, 1998, Copenhagen).

International Monetary Fund. 2001a. "Conditionality in IMF-Supported Program – Policy Issues," (Washington, DC: International Monetary Fund). http://www.imf.org/external/np/pdr/cond/2001/eng/policy/021601.pdf (accessed on July 10, 2001).

—— 2001b. "Streamlining Structural Conditionality: Review of Initial Experience," (Washington, DC: International Monetary Fund). http://www.imf.org/external/np/pdr/cond/2001/eng/collab/review.htm (accessed on July 10, 2001).

—— 2002. "The Modalities of Conditionality – Further Considerations" (Washington, DC: International Monetary Fund). http://www.imf.org/External/np/pdr/cond/2002/eng/modal/010802.htm

Khan, Mohsin S. and Sunil Sharma. 2001. "IMF Conditionality and Country Ownership of Programs," IMF Working Paper 01/142 (Washington, DC: International Monetary Fund).

Laplagne, Patrick. 1997. "Dutch Disease in the South Pacific: Evidence from the 1980s and Beyond," *Pacific Economic Bulletin*, 12 (June) (1): 84–96.

——, Malcolm Treadgold, and Jonathan Baldry. 2001. "A Model of Aid Impact in Some South Pacific Microstates," *World Development*, 29(2): 365–83.

Lensink, Robert and Oliver Morrissey. 2000. "Aid Instability as a Measure of Uncertainty and the Positive Impact of Aid on Growth," *Journal of Development Studies*, 36 (February): 31–49.

—— and Howard White. 2001. "Are There Negative Returns to Aid?" *Journal of Development Studies*, 37 (August): 42–65.

—— 2000. "Assessing Aid: A Manifesto for Aid in the 21st Century?" *Oxford Development Studies*, 28(1): 6–17.

Lucas, Robert. 1988. "On the Mechanics of Economic Development," *Journal of Monetary Economics*, 22 (July): 3–42.

McGillivray, Mark and Oliver Morrissey. 2001a. "Aid Illusion and Public Sector Fiscal Behaviour," *Journal of Development Studies*, 37 (August): 118–36.

—— 2001b. "A Review of Evidence on the Fiscal Effects of Aid," CREDIT Research Paper 01/13 (University of Nottingham: Centre for Research in Economic Development and International Trade).

Michaely, Michael. 1981. "Foreign Aid, Economic Structure, and Dependence," *Journal of Development Economics*, 9 (December): 313–30.

Nyoni, Timothy S. 1998. "Foreign Aid and Economic Performance in Tanzania," *World Development*, 26(7): 1235–40.

Pallage, Stéphane and Michel A. Robe. 2001. "Foreign Aid and the Business Cycle," *Review of International Economics*, 9(4): 636–67.

—— 2003. "On the Welfare Cost of Economic Fluctuations in Developing Countries," *International Economic Review*, 44(2): 677–98.

Reinikka, Ritva and Jakob Svensson. 2002. "Explaining Leakage of Public Funds," CEPR Discussion Paper Series 3227 (London: Centre for Economic Policy Research).

Romer, Paul M. 1986. "Increasing Returns and Long-Run Growth," *Journal of Political Economy*, 94 (October): 1002–37.

Sekkat, Khalid and Aristomene Varoudakis. 2000. "Exchange Rate Management and Manufactured Exports in Sub-Saharan Africa," *Journal of Development Economics*, 61: 237–53.

Söderling, Ludvig. 2000. "Dynamics of Export Performance, Productivity and Real Effective Exchange Rate in Manufacturing: The Case of Cameroon," *Journal of African Economies*, 9(4): 411–29.

Stolper, Wolfgang F. and Paul A. Samuelson. 1941. "Protection and Real Wages," *Review of Economic Studies*, 9 (November): 58–73.

Teal, Francis. 1999. *Why Can Mauritius Export Manufactures and Ghana Not?* WPS/99-10 (Oxford: Centre for the Study of African Economies).

Tornell, Aaron and Philip R. Lane. 1999. "The Voracity Effect," *American Economic Review*, 89(1): 22–46.

van Wijnbergen, Sweder. 1986. "Macroeconomic Aspects of the Effectiveness of Foreign Aid: On the Two-Gap Model, Home Goods Disequilibrium and Real Exchange Rate Misalignment," *Journal of International Economics*, 21(1–2): 123–36.

Vos, Rob. 1998. "Aid Flows and 'Dutch Disease' in a General Equilibrium Framework for Pakistan," *Journal of Policy Modeling*, 20(1): 77–109.

White, Howard. 1992. "The Macroeconomic Impact of Development Aid: A Critical Survey," *Journal of Development Studies*, 28(2): 163–240.

World Bank. 2002. *Global Development Finance* (Washington, DC: World Bank). http://siteresources.worldbank.org/INTGDF 2002/Resources/FullText-Volume1.pdf

Younger, Stephen D. 1992. "Aid and the Dutch Disease: Macroeconomic Management When Everybody Loves You," *World Development*, 20(11): 1587–97.

6 Who is protected?

On the incidence of fiscal adjustment

Martin Ravallion[*]

Standard policy advice at times of fiscal adjustment is to protect public spending on the poor. However, there is remarkably little theory or evidence to draw on in assessing the case for such policies. To help fill this gap, the chapter begins with a theoretical model of the incidence of fiscal expansions and contractions, identifying conditions under which the poor will be exposed to cuts without a policy change. The chapter then studies various social programs in Argentina, Bangladesh, and India, focusing on how targeting performance varied with aggregate outlays. The results suggest that it tends to be program spending on the non-poor that is protected from budget cuts. Drawing on these results, recommendations are made for reforming safety nets in developing countries.

6.1 Introduction

With heightened sensitivity to impacts on the poor, macroeconomic adjustment programs often call for a pro-poor shift in the composition of public spending, in combination with overall fiscal contraction. Donors have been particularly keen to support new public programs and "social funds" that aim to target extra assistance to the poor at times of aggregate fiscal austerity.

To assess the impact of such programs we need to know the counter-factual incidence of a fiscal contraction. In the absence of intervention, do cuts tend to fall more heavily on the poor? Do add-on programs really help the poor? What happens when such programs are also cut? What are the implications for assessing the impact of add-on social programs during adjustment periods?

In principle at least, it has long been recognized that political economy plays an important role in determining the incidence of budget cuts required to assure macroeconomic stability. For example, in an early discussion of the distributional impact of stabilization programs, Johnson and Salop (1980) argued that the distribution of political power was key to determining how the burden of adjustment was shared across income groups. It has also been recognized in the literature that finer targeting of public spending can be a mixed blessing for the poor. The main argument is that finer targeting undermines political support for the required taxation.[1]

In settings in which the majority of voters are not poor, it is often asserted that the poor will be obliged to bear a disproportionate share of a budget cut on the grounds that they are the least powerful. However, there are some problems with this argument:

- If the poor have little or no power, and power is all that matters to the allocation of public spending, then presumably the poor gained little from public spending before the cuts – in which case they can have little to lose from cuts.
- The non-poor may value spending on the currently poor. This might be due to altruism, negative externalities of poverty, or other spillover effects, such as arising from the public good nature of some types of public spending including social spending which offers insurance in risky environments. But then the non-poor will want to protect spending on the poor and will do so without further intervention.
- It has been argued that the non-poor can substitute easily between publicly provided goods and market goods and so protect their welfare, while the poor are more reliant on publicly provided goods and services.[2] Then marginal social gains from protecting spending on the poor will be larger than for the non-poor. To the extent that the political equilibrium respects such differences, spending on the poor will automatically be protected without further intervention.
- The aggregate fiscal contraction may come with a change in the balance of power. Depending on how an aggregate income shock is distributed, the resulting fiscal contraction may come with higher or lower relative power of the poor, with corresponding shifts in the composition of spending.

This chapter studies how the performance of social programs in reaching the poor varies with aggregate outlays. The theoretical model in the following section suggests that the outcome is unclear on a priori grounds even when the poor are a powerless minority. So it is an empirical question. One possible approach is to examine data on the composition of public spending, and to see how composition is affected by aggregate contractions. For example, Ravallion (2002) uses a time series of public spending data for Argentina to show that "social spending" in Argentina has not been protected in the past from aggregate cuts. Indeed, during the large fiscal contractions that were required to restore macroeconomic stability in the 1980s, social spending took more than a proportionate hit. This can be seen in Figure 6.1, which plots the proportionate changes in social spending on proportionate changes in total spending (both measured by first differences in logs).[3]

While this type of evidence provides important clues, "social spending" in Argentina (as elsewhere) is a heterogeneous category, and certainly cannot be equated with "spending on the poor." It includes types of spending such as pensions, formal unemployment insurance, and higher education that tend to favor the non-poor, as well as (probably) more pro-poor spending on basic education and health, and certain social assistance, and active labor market programs.[4]

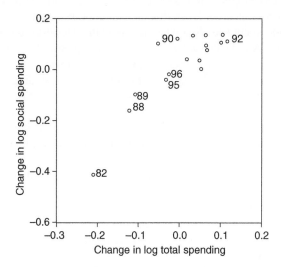

Figure 6.1 Has social spending in Argentina been protected from aggregate fiscal contractions?

Source: Government of Argentina (1999).

Notes
Annual data 1980–97; 1997 prices; selected years indicated. "Social spending" comprises "social insurance" (pensions, public health insurance, unemployment insurance) and "social services" (education, health, water and sewerage, housing and urban development, social assistance, and labor programs).

And even within the latter categories, there are likely to be both poor and non-poor beneficiaries. Breaking down social spending can be revealing; for example, using the same data source as Figure 6.1, there is no sign that the categories of social spending in Argentina that are thought to matter more to the poor were more protected (Ravallion, 2002). However, a deeper understanding of the incidence of fiscal contractions calls for a more micro-based approach in which there is a clearer mapping of spending to beneficiaries.

This chapter draws instead on micro-based empirical studies of various social programs in India, Bangladesh, and Argentina. The first two studies discussed later use cross-sectional comparisons of how incidence varies with aggregate spending, while the third case study uses longitudinal data. The final section tries to draw some lessons for institutional reforms that should be able to offer more reliable protection for the poor.

6.2 Are budget cuts simply passed onto the "powerless poor"?

Consider the following model. Public spending on a transfer payment or excludable good is allocated between equal numbers of poor (who receive G^p) and the non-poor (G^n). A natural assumption in this context is that the non-poor finance the spending out of their own income, Y^n, so that the non-poor have all the incentive from the revenue side to cut spending when income falls. However, one can readily allow some of the tax to be borne by the poor, by interpreting G^p (>0) as spending on the poor net of any taxes or user charges levied on them.

In this model, there are two possible reasons why some public spending goes to the poor. First, the non-poor may gain from spending on the poor. Non-poor people might view G^p as insurance, to the extent that they face a positive probability of becoming poor. Or G^p may yield an external benefit to the non-poor, such as when they gain as employers from having a healthier and better-schooled workforce.

The second possible reason why there is spending on the poor is that they have political power, meaning that the allocation gives positive weight to the welfare of the poor. This can be interpreted in various ways. One possibility is to assume that (however it is achieved in practice) the outcome of public decision making is Pareto-efficient, in that it maximizes some positively weighted sum of all utilities. Or one might interpret the weights are "capture coefficients" in a model of electoral competition in which there are differences between the poor and non-poor in voter information and ability to lobby (Grossman and Helpman, 1996; Bardhan and Mookherjee, 2000). An alternative interpretation is that the poor may revolt unless some reservation utility is assured. Maintaining political stability is sometimes identified as a justification for protecting the poor at times of macroeconomic adjustment.

Not much will hinge on these differences in the reasons why some of the spending goes to the poor prior to the cuts. The model will have a parameter that reflects the weight given to the welfare of the poor in the allocation of public spending. While I write the model as if there is no utility gain to the non-poor from spending on the poor, it becomes a matter of interpretation.

A natural assumption in this context is that both poor and non-poor prefer lower inter-temporal variability in spending at a given mean. This is virtually equivalent to assuming declining marginal utility of public spending for each group. For the non-poor, this can simply arise from the income effect of the taxation required to finance the spending; the non-poor may or may not have positive and declining marginal utility from public spending at given income net of taxes.

Utility of the non-poor is U^n ($Y^n - G$, G^n) where $G = G^n + G^p$. The function U^n is taken to be additively separable, though I will note implications of relaxing this assumption. The function is strictly increasing and concave in after-tax income, $Y^n - G$, and (at given $Y^n - G$) it is weakly increasing and at least weakly concave in G^n (i.e. $U_Y^n > 0$, $U_{YY}^n < 0$, $U_G^n \geq 0$, and $U_{GG}^n \leq 0$ in obvious notation). The non-poor will then prefer less variable G^n, allowing for effects on net income. (Notice that this holds even if $U_{GG}^n = 0$, given that $U_{YY}^n < 0$.) Utility of the poor is U^p (Y^p, G^p), which is increasing and strictly concave in both arguments and also additive separable.

One interpretation of these utility functions is as follows. For each group, imagine that there are two possible states of nature, with known probabilities.

The non-poor are taxed in the high-income state, which then yields utility $V(Y^n - G)$, while the non-poor rely on government transfers in the low-income state, giving utility $V^n(G^n)$ (subsuming income in the low-income state in the function V^n). For the poor, utility in their high-income state is $V(Y^p)$ while in their low-income state it is $V^p(G^p)$. The utility functions U^n and U^p can then be interpreted as the expected utility of each group embedding the two probability distributions across the states of nature:

$$U^n (Y^n - G, G^n) = (1-\pi^n)V(Y^n - G) + \pi^n V^n (G^n) \tag{6.1}$$
$$U^p (Y^p, G^p) = (1 - \pi^p)V(Y^p) + \pi^p V^p (G^p) \tag{6.2}$$

where π^n and π^p are the probabilities of the non-poor and poor falling into their low-income states. (Different probability distributions entail that the derived utility functions vary, even if the underlying "primal" utility functions do not vary.) I will return to this interpretation.

The allocation of spending maximizes:

$$U^n (Y^n - G, G^n) + \lambda(Y^n, Y^p)U^p(Y^p, G^p) \tag{6.3}$$

where $\lambda(Y^n, Y^p)$ is a non-negative number giving the relative power of the poor over public spending. (Alternatively, in an insurance model, λ would be interpreted as the odds ratio of the non-poor becoming poor; or λ might measure the external gain to the non-poor from spending on the poor.) The relative power of the poor is allowed to depend on the distribution of income, though I consider the special case in which λ is fixed. On a priori grounds, as seemingly plausible assumption is that higher inequality means that the poor have less power over fiscal decision making.[5] However, that is not the only possibility.

We can write the solutions to this problem in the generic forms:

$$G^n = G^n [Y^n, \lambda(Y^n, Y^p)] \tag{6.4}$$
$$G^p = G^p [Y^n, \lambda(Y^n, Y^p)] \tag{6.5}$$

(Without separability, the solutions also depend on the income of the poor, at given λ.) Aggregate spending is:

$$G = G^n + G^p = G[Y^n, \lambda(Y^n, Y^p)] \tag{6.6}$$

Now imagine that the non-poor receive a negative income shock which calls for a cut in G to restore equilibrium. In analyzing the implications, it is convenient to use (6.6) to eliminate Y^n from (6.4) and (6.5), and so write the following equations for how the spending allocation will vary with total spending in equilibrium (allowing for effects through λ and subsuming Y^p):

$$G^n = \Pi^n (G) \tag{6.7}$$
$$G^p = \Pi^p (G) \tag{6.8}$$

with slopes:[6]

$$\Pi_G^n = \frac{\lambda U_{GG}^p + \lambda_G U_G^p}{U_{GG}^n + \lambda U_{GG}^p} \qquad (6.9)$$

$$\Pi_G^p = \frac{U_{GG}^n - \lambda_G U_G^p}{U_{GG}^n + \lambda U_{GG}^p} \qquad (6.10)$$

where $\lambda_G \equiv \lambda_n / G_Y$ (in obvious notation). Equations (6.9) and (6.10) tell us the incidence of the change in aggregate spending.

Do the poor bear more of an aggregate cut than the non-poor? A natural measure of targeting performance is the "targeting differential" (*T*), given by the difference in per capita allocations to the poor and non-poor, that is, $T(G) \equiv \Pi^p$ $(G) - \Pi^n (G)$.[7] From (6.9) and (6.10) we have:

$$T_G = \frac{U_{GG}^n}{U_{GG}^n + \lambda U_{GG}^p} - \frac{(2\lambda_G U_G^p + \lambda U_{GG}^p)}{U_{GG}^n + \lambda U_{GG}^p} \qquad (6.11)$$

This can be either positive or negative. The first term on the RHS of (6.11) can be called the "utility effect" since it arises from declining marginal utility of spending for the non-poor. This effect tends to make targeting performance deteriorate during an aggregate fiscal contraction. With contraction, the marginal utility of spending rises for the non-poor, and so the equilibrium switches in their favor, at the expense of the poor. The second term on the RHS of (6.11) – the "power effect" – works in the opposite direction if the power of the poor is positive and is enhanced by the contraction.

Some special cases are instructive. First consider the case in which $\lambda = 0$ implying that $G^n (Y^n, 0) = G$ and $G^p(Y^n, 0) = 0$. Nothing will be spent on the poor, and so they will lose nothing from a fiscal contraction, which will be borne entirely by the non-poor. (In the expected utility interpretation, this will also be the case if the poor are fully protected from the low-income state ($\pi^p = 0$), for then there will be no reason to spend anything on the poor.) Suppose instead that λ is a positive constant, that is, the fiscal contraction has no effect on the relative power of the poor ($\lambda_G = 0$). It is then evident from (6.10) that the poor will be fully protected from a fiscal contraction as long as the non-poor do not have diminishing marginal utility of spending, that is, $U_{GG}^n = 0$. In this case, no further action to protect the poor during adjustment periods is needed. By the same token, the poor will not gain anything from "trickle down," here interpretable as higher public spending stemming from an income gain to the non-poor. By contrast, if U^p is nearly linear in G^p (i.e. U_{GG}^p close to zero) then the poor will bear virtually all of a retrenchment, and all of an increment to spending will go to the poor.

Now consider the case in which the relative power of the poor depends negatively on income inequality; $\lambda_G < 0$. Then we have the possibility that the poor gain from the fiscal contraction, through its effect on their relative power over spending allocations. This is sure to be the case if the non-poor do not experience diminishing marginal utility of spending, for then $\Pi^p_G = -\lambda_G U^p_G/(\lambda U^p_{GG})^{-1} < 0$. The upshot of the given observations is that the incidence of a fiscal contraction is ambiguous even in this simple model. The need for specific actions to protect the poor cannot be pre-judged and must be deemed an empirical question. In the cases studies we will see whether the "utility effect" dominates the "power effect."

6.3   Primary schooling and anti-poverty programs in India

One source of evidence on the incidence of changes in aggregate outlays is by examining the differences in incidence between geographic areas with different levels of total spending. This section will review evidence for various social programs in India.

For this purpose, let us define the *marginal odds of participation* (MOP) as the increment to the program participation rate of a given expenditure quintile (say) associated with a change in aggregate participation in that program. With appropriate survey data one can readily calculate the average participation rate for a given program for each quintile and each geographic area ("region" hereafter) identified in the survey (subject to sample design). One can then see how the participation rate for a given quintile varies across regions according to the level of public spending on the program in the political jurisdiction ("state") to which each region belongs. To estimate the MOP by program and expenditure quintile one can regress the quintile-specific participation rates across regions on the average state participation rates (all quintiles) for each program.[8]

The following analysis was based on India's National Sample Survey (NSS) for 1993–94. This survey includes standard data on consumption expenditures, demographics, and education attainments, including school enrollments. This particular NSS round also asked about participation in various anti-poverty programs. Participation in three key programs can be identified from the survey: public works schemes, a means-tested credit scheme called the "Integrated Rural Development Programme" (IRDP), and a food rationing scheme, the "Public Distribution System" (PDS).[9] The data on participation in these programs can be collated with data on total consumption expenditure per person at the household level.

Sampled households in the NSS were ranked by total consumption expenditure (including imputed values of consumption from own production) per person normalized by state-specific poverty lines. Quintiles were then defined over the entire rural population, with equal numbers of people in each. So the poorest quintile refers to the poorest 20 percent of the national rural population in terms of consumption per capita.

The analysis was done at the level of the NSS region, of which there are sixty-two in India, spanning nineteen states and with each NSS region belonging to only one state.[10] So, for any given combination of quintile and program, the participation rates across the sixty-two NSS regions were regressed on the average participation by state (irrespective of quintile).

Table 6.1 Average and marginal odds of primary school enrollment in rural India

Quintile	Boys		Girls		Total	
	Average odds	Marginal odds	Average odds	Marginal odds	Average odds	Marginal odds
Poorest	0.75	1.09 (6.90)	0.66	1.08 (9.65)	0.71	1.10 (8.99)
2nd	0.93	0.91 (6.05)	0.91	0.91 (6.99)	0.90	0.97 (7.92)
3rd	1.07	0.92 (5.85)	1.06	0.84 (6.54)	1.08	0.87 (7.65)
4th	1.16	0.66 (4.10)	1.26	0.66 (4.28)	1.21	0.67 (4.77)
5th	1.23	0.53 (4.08)	1.38	0.70 (5.53)	1.31	0.67 (5.69)

Notes
The average odds are based on the average primary school enrollment rates as a percentage of children aged 5–9, and the odds of enrollment, defined as the ratio of the quintile-specific enrollment rate to the mean rate. The marginal odds are estimated by an instrumental variables regression of the quintile-specific primary school enrollment rates across regions on the average rate by state for that program. The leave-out mean state enrollment rate is the instrument for the actual mean. The numbers in parentheses are *t*-ratios. Households were ranked by total expenditure per person in forming the quintiles.

Let us first consider primary schooling. Table 6.1 gives the average and marginal odds of enrollment amongst children 5–9 from the 1993–94 NSS data. Enrollment rates rise with household expenditure per capita and they tend to be higher for boys than girls.

The average odds of enrollment suggest that subsidies to primary schooling favor the non-poor.[11] However, that is not the case once we look at the estimated marginal odds of being enrolled, which are also given in Table 6.1. The MOP can be interpreted as the gain in subsidy incidence per capita for each quintile from a 1 Rupee increase in aggregate spending on each program. For example, an extra 100 Rupees per capita spent on primary schools will increase the public expenditure per capita going to the poorest quintile by 110 Rupees. The average odds indicate that the share of the total subsidy going to the poorest quintile is only 14 percent (0.71 times 0.2). However, the marginal odds imply that the poorest quintile would obtain about 22 percent of an increase in the total subsidy going to primary education. The MOP estimates suggest that an aggregate contraction in primary schooling would be borne heavily by the poor.

There are also gender differences. Average enrollment rates tend to be higher for boys than girls (Table 6.1). However, the marginal odds are almost identical for boys and girls from the poorest quintile (1.09 versus 1.08). And the marginal odds are higher for girls than boys in families from the richest quintile (0.70 versus 0.53). The boys are clearly favored first, by both rich and poor parents. For the poor, the gender gap does not change as the overall primary enrollment rate increases. Amongst the richest quintile, by contrast, the girls catch up as the program expands.

Table 6.2 gives the corresponding results for each of the anti-poverty programs. For both public works programs and IRDP, participation rates fall as expenditure per person increases. However, the rate of decline is not large; the odds of the

Table 6.2 Average and marginal odds of participation for India's anti-poverty programs

Quintile	Public works programs		Integrated rural development program		Public distribution system	
	Average odds	Marginal odds	Average odds	Marginal odds	Average odds	Marginal odds
Poorest	1.23	1.16 (3.27)	1.03	1.11 (15.49)	0.92	1.06 (8.14)
2nd	1.13	0.93 (3.64)	1.13	1.28 (17.73)	1.01	0.99 (7.26)
3rd	1.04	0.80 (2.98)	1.03	1.21 (23.52)	1.03	0.91 (6.88)
4th	0.86	0.92 (4.32)	0.96	0.96 (19.09)	1.00	0.86 (7.16)
5th	0.83	0.55 (3.29)	0.89	0.39 (8.06)	1.00	0.81 (6.27)

Note
See Table 6.1.

poorest quintile participating in public works programs is 1.23 versus 0.83 for the richest quintile; the rate of decline is even lower for IRDP. Participation rates amongst the richest 20 percent in terms of consumption per person are high even for public works programs. For PDS, the participation rate is actually lowest for the poorest quintile, with highest participation amongst the middle expenditure quintile.

Table 6.2 also gives the estimated marginal odds of participation. These fall far more rapidly than the average odds as expenditure rises. The MOP for the poorest quintile is highest for public works programs, while IRDP dominates for the three middle quintiles; the PDS has the highest MOP for the richest quintile. The MOP coefficients broadly confirm the conclusion from the average odds of participation that the public works programs perform best at reaching the poorest, while IRDP is more effective in reaching the middle quintiles, including those living at India's poverty line (at roughly the 40th percentile).

The difference between the MOP numbers for any two programs gives the estimated gain from switching 1 Rupee between the two programs. For example, switching 100 Rupees per capita from PDS to public works programs would increase public spending per capita on the poorest quintile by 10 Rupees (116 − 106 = 10, using the basic model).

For both the public works programs and IRDP, it is notable that the marginal odds of participation tend to fall more steeply as one moves from the poorest to the richest quintiles than do the average odds (Table 6.2). Thus the average odds underestimate how much the poor would lose from a cut in total spending on each of these programs. This bias is particularly large for IRDP, for which the average odds of participation are only slightly higher for the poorest quintile than the richest (1.03 versus 0.89), while there is a large difference in the MOP (1.11 versus 0.39), though with less difference amongst the first four quintiles. As compared to the average odds of participation, the share of the total IRDP spending imputed to the poorest 40 percent of the population is 11 percent higher, while that imputed to the richest 20 percent is 56 percent lower. For PDS, however, there is less difference between the average and marginal odds.

For the purpose of the present discussion, what is most striking from these results is that for all these social programs in India, higher aggregate outlays (as reflected in higher aggregate participation rates) tend to be associated with more pro-poor incidence of benefits. By the same token, aggregate cuts tend to be associated with worse targeting. Similar methods are used by Lanjouw *et al.* (2001) on data for primary health and education spending in Indonesia. They too find evidence of early capture by the non-poor in that the marginal odds of participation by the poor tend to exceed the average odds, with the reverse for upper quintiles.

6.4   Bangladesh's Food-for-Education Program

The second piece of evidence comes from a study of Bangladesh's Food-for-Education (FFE) Program. This was one of the earliest of many school-enrollment subsidy programs now found in both developing and developed countries. The official aim was to keep the children of poor rural families in school. On paper, the program distributes fixed food rations to selected households conditional on their school-aged children attending at least 85 percent of classes. Over two million children participated in 1995–96 (13 percent of total primary school enrollment). There is evidence of significant gains in terms of school attendance with only modest forgone income through displaced child labor (Ravallion and Wodon, 2000). There were two stages of targeting. First, economically backward areas were chosen by the center. Second, community groups – exploiting idiosyncratic local information – select participants within those areas.

Similarly to the method in the previous section, we will examine how incidence varies geographically with aggregate program outlays, but this time the analysis will be done at village level. Galasso and Ravallion (2005) estimate measures of the performance of villages in reaching the poor through FFE, using survey data from Bangladesh's Household Budget Survey for 1995–96 to assess program incidence within villages. I will draw on these results to see how incidence varies with aggregate outlays.

Targeting performance is measured by the targeting differential defined earlier, namely the difference between the per capita allocation to the poor and that to the non-poor. Two poverty lines are considered, one at the median and the other at the quantile of the 25th percentile from the bottom. It can be shown that this is exactly decomposable between "within-village" and "between-village" components (Ravallion, 2000). The targeting differential is also interpretable as a measure of association for the 2×2 contingency table formed by comparing who is poor or not and who gets the program (Galasso and Ravallion, 2005).

Table 6.3 summarizes the results on overall targeting performance. The aggregate targeting differential is positive and significantly different from zero.[12] Amongst all villages, 12 percent of the poor receive the program, as compared to 8 percent of the non-poor (in participating villages, the proportions are 46 and 32 percent). Virtually all of the aggregate targeting differential is accounted for by the intra-village component.

Performance differed greatly across villages; indeed, the targeting differential was negative in 24 percent of the villages. Table 6.4 (column 1) summarizes the results of a regression of targeting performance against the budget allocation to the village and the village poverty rate (proportion of village population living in poor households, by the above definition). The participation rates of both the poor and non-poor rise with the overall participation rate in the program (which closely approximates the aggregate budget allocation to the village, given that all participants received roughly the same amount). However, the rate of increase is higher for the poor, so that targeting performance tends to improve as the aggregate outlay on the program expands (Table 6.4).

To allow for heterogeneity in village characteristics, Table 6.4 (column 2) also gives the results when controls are added for program eligibility criteria, structural characteristics of villages (education, cropping, modernization in agriculture), and institutional characteristics (land inequality and indicators of local social capital). With these controls, it remains the case that targeting performance

Table 6.3 Targeting performance of Bangladesh's FFE Program

Poverty line	Participation rate of the poor	Participation rate of the non-poor	Targeting differential	Intra-village	Inter-village	ϕ	Prob. value
50 percent	0.118	0.079	0.039	0.036	0.003	0.004	0.000
25 percent	0.136	0.086	0.050	0.037	0.013	0.005	0.000

Table 6.4 Intra-village targeting performance of Bangladesh's FFE Program

	(1) Without controls for village characteristics			(2) With controls for other village characteristics		
	Targeting performance	Participation rate for the poor	Participation rate for the non-poor	Targeting performance	Participation rate for the poor	Participation rate for the non-poor
Budget allocation to village	0.324[b] (2.30)	1.177[b] (16.30)	0.853[b] (9.63)	0.156 (0.71)	1.013[b] (8.04)	0.857[b] (6.03)
Poverty rate in the village	0.081 (0.43)	−0.145 (0.99)	−0.226[b] (2.51)	0.314[a] (1.92)	0.055 (0.49)	−0.258[b] (2.32)
R^2	0.07	0.73	0.66	0.57	0.87	0.81
N	62	62	62	52	52	52

Notes
Robust *t*-statistics in parentheses.
a Denotes significant at 10 percent level.
b At 5 percent level.

rises with aggregate outlays. However, the effect is no longer statistically significant at a reasonable level.

Again there are concerns about assuming that the aggregate allocation (in this case across villages) is exogenous, even in the model with controls. Galasso and Ravallion exploit seemingly plausible assumptions about the information structure to test exogeneity of allocations across villages, and are unable to reject the null of exogeneity (though they do find signs that information provided by local authorities to the center is manipulated endogenously). Their identifying assumption is that a village's relative position in terms of the eligibility criteria influences the allocation across villages but does not influence outcomes conditional on that allocation.

The results for both India and Bangladesh point in a similar direction in suggesting that targeting performance deteriorates with program contraction. However, these tests cannot be considered conclusive. As I have emphasized, the main problem is the possibility that aggregate participation is endogenous; for example, local governments with a political preference in favor of the poor may simultaneously spend more and assure that the spending is more pro-poor. While both the India and Bangladesh case studies performed tests for this, and found that the results were reasonably robust, there are intrinsic limits to how far one can go in addressing this problem using cross-sectional data. By exploiting a panel-data structure, the next case study will be more robust to the possible endogeneity concerns.

6.5   A safety net program in Argentina

The Government of Argentina introduced the Trabajar Program in 1996, in the wake of a sharp rise in unemployment, and evidence that this was hurting the poor more than others. The program provides an interesting case study for the present purpose, both because of the unusually rich data available, and the fact that these data cover a period in which the program both expanded and contracted. We will examine how well the program performed in reaching the poor in a crisis, and see how its performance changed with both aggregate expansion and contraction.

The program's aim was to reduce poverty by providing work at a relatively low wage rate on community projects in poor areas. The central government pays for the wage cost, and local or provincial governments cover the non-wage costs. Within provincial budget allocations, proposals for sub-projects compete for central funding according to a points system. Three versions of the program have been tried, Trabajar I, II, and III. There were substantial design changes between TI and TII. The inter-provincial allocation of spending was reformed, moving away from a largely political process to an explicit formula based on the estimated number of poor unemployed workers in each province. TII also put greater emphasis on creating assets of value to poor communities. Poverty measures were included in the center's budget allocation rules and in the selection criteria for sub-projects. The poverty focus was also made clearer to provincial administrators.

TIII was very similar to its predecessor. The main difference was that greater emphasis was placed on the quality of sub-projects, to assure that the assets created were of value to the communities.[13]

From the point of view of this chapter, an important difference between the three versions of the program is in the level of funding. In TI, disbursements by the center (covering wages for participating workers) averaged $77 million per annum; for TII this rose to $160 million per annum, and it then fell to $98 million per annum under TIII. As we will see, there were also differences in levels of funding between sub-periods.

Survey-based impact evaluation methods have been used to assess the gains to participating workers and their families from TII and TIII (Jalan and Ravallion, 2003). The results have indicated that Trabajar jobs are well targeted to the poor; for example, 76 percent of people living in the households of participating workers had a household income per capita that placed them amongst the poorest 20 percent of Argentineans nationally. The program's targeting also appears to be better than any other targeted programs in Argentina (Ravallion, 2002).

While non-poor people are unlikely to find the Trabajar wage attractive, they would no doubt like to have the scheme producing things of value in their communities. (There is negligible cost recovery.) How well did the program perform in assuring that the work was provided in poor areas? How did this change when the program expanded and contracted?

One can monitor how well the program reached poor areas by tracking the geographic distribution of disbursements and comparing this to the poverty map of Argentina. By doing so within a period of budget expansion then contraction, and comparing the results across provinces, we will be able to test for budget effects on this aspect of the programs' poor-area targeting performance.

6.5.1 *Measuring targeting performance*

Each provincial government's optimal allocation to a household is unobserved, but it is assumed to depend on the household's level of welfare. That may in turn depend on where the household lives, but I assume that the poverty rate in the area where it lives within a given province does not matter to a household's allocation independently of its own level of welfare. In other words, there is no "poor-area bias" in that a poor person living in a poor local government area expects to get the same amount from the program as an equally poor person living in a rich area of the same province. (The allocations need not be identical, but only equal in expectation; random deviations are allowed.) The same holds for the non-poor. This assumption can be thought of as a form of horizontal equity within provinces (Ravallion, 2000).

Let us consider how to measure each province's performance, making this assumption of horizontal equity in expectation within the province. The central government allocates a total budget of G per capita across M provinces such that G_j per capita is received by province j. After that, each province decides how much should go to the poor versus the non-poor. The chosen allocation by province j is G_j^n per capita for the non-poor and G_j^p for the poor. Province j comprises M_j local government areas, called "departments." The per capita allocations to department i ($= 1, \ldots, M_j$) within province j can be written as:

$$G_{ij}^n = G_j^n + \varepsilon_{ij}^n \tag{6.12}$$

$$G_{ij}^p = G_j^p + \varepsilon_{ij}^p \tag{6.13}$$

where the ε's are departmental deviations from province means.

Total disbursements to the poor and non-poor must exhaust the budget. This creates an accounting identity linking total program expenditure per capita to the poverty rate in a department. Let G_{ij} denote program spending in the ith department of the jth province, and let the corresponding poverty rate be H_{ij} – the "headcount index," given by the proportion of the population that is poor (for which the overall poverty rate in the province is H_j). Then:

$$G_{ij} = H_{ij}G_{ij}^p + (1 - H_{ij})G_{ij}^n \tag{6.14}$$

Using equations (6.12) and (6.13) we can re-write (6.14) in the form of a simple linear regression across all departments in province j:

$$G_{ij} - G_j = T_j(H_{ij} - H_j) + v_{ij} \tag{6.15}$$

where

$$v_{ij} = \varepsilon_{ij}^n + (\varepsilon_{ij}^p - \varepsilon_{ij}^n)H_{ij} \tag{6.16}$$

and $T_j = G_j^p - G_j^n$ is the targeting differential already introduced, that is, the mean absolute difference between the allocations to the poor and that to the non-poor in province j.

How can the targeting differential be estimated? Under the horizontal equity assumption, the error term in (6.16) has zero mean for any given province and is uncorrelated with H_{ij} since the εs are zero-mean errors within any given province and are uncorrelated with H_{ij} (and its squared value) (Ravallion, 2000). Thus H_{ij} is exogenous in (6.15) and so one can estimate T_j from an OLS regression of G_{ij} on H_{ij} across all departments within a given province.[14] Provincial performance in reaching poor areas can thus be measured by the regression coefficient of spending per capita on the poverty rate, estimated across all departments in each province. The targeting differential for province j is then estimated by:

$$\hat{T}_j = \frac{\sum_{i=1}^{M_j}(G_{ij} - G_i)(H_{ij} - H_j)}{\sum_{i=1}^{M_j}(H_{ij} - H_j)^2} \tag{6.17}$$

One can similarly define a national inter-departmental targeting differential, by calculating (6.17) over all departments nationally (ignoring province boundaries). The targeting differential can be interpreted as a measure of absolute progressivity namely the difference between per capita spending on the poor and that on the non-poor. Poverty is measured by the most widely used measure in Argentina, given by the proportion of the population deemed to have unmet basic needs (UBN), based on the 1991 census.

6.5.2 Results

The overall targeting differentials across all 510 departments were $41, $110, and $76 per capita for TI, TII, and TIII respectively; all three are significant at the 1 percent level. To help interpret these numbers, compare the poorest department, namely Figueroa (in Santiago Del Estero province) where the incidence of UBN is 75.5 percent, with the least poor department namely Chacabuco (in Chaco province) where the poverty measure is 3.3 percent. The expected difference in spending between these two departments was $30 under TI, $79 under TII, and $55 under TIII. So the expansion to the program between TI and TII was associated with a more pro-poor allocation of funds geographically, while the contraction between TII and TIII came with a less pro-poor allocation. Next we will see if this aggregate correlation is borne out when we compare provinces over time.

With the extra degrees of freedom made possible by exploiting the changes in the inter-provincial allocation of spending, it is possible to test for statistically significant effects of fiscal expansion and contraction on the program's targeting performance. A better information system introduced for TII and TIII allows a breakdown of the aggregates into sub-periods by province. Intervals of five months were chosen.

To assess the effect of the cuts on targeting performance, one can regress the province and period-specific targeting differentials on program spending per capita across provinces, pooling all five-month periods and all provinces. The targeting differential will, however, vary across provinces according to other factors, such as the strength of provincial concern for the poor, how poor the province is as a whole (Ravallion, 1999a), the history of the provincial efforts at targeting the poor, and the capabilities of local managers. It is not implausible that some or all of these variables will also be correlated with program spending. So their omission will yield a biased estimate of the effect of cuts on targeting. However, this problem can be dealt with by treating these differences in provincial targeting performance as provincial fixed effects when estimating the impact of program spending. The fact that the resulting test is robust to latent geographic heterogeneity in targeting performance (as embodied in the province fixed effects) makes it more convincing than the earlier tests using cross-sectional data.

Given these considerations, the test for the effect of changes in program disbursements on targeting performance takes the form of a regression of the province and date-specific targeting differential on aggregate spending per capita in the province and a set of province-specific fixed effects. The regression is thus:

$$T_{jt} = \alpha + \beta G_{jt} + \eta_j + \mu_{jt} \quad (j = 1, ..., 22; t = 1, ..., 6) \tag{6.18}$$

where T_{jt} is the targeting differential for province j at date t, G_{jt} is spending by province j at date t, η_j is the province-specific effect and μ_{jt} is an innovation error, representing random, idiosyncratic, differences in targeting performance. As discussed earlier, the aggregate spending allocation G_{jt} is allowed to be endogenous in that it is correlated with the province effect η_j. It is assumed that $cov(G_{jt}, \mu_{jt}) = 0$. This would not hold if program spending was adjusted according to targeting performance. However, this would have been very difficult given the timing of data availability. In a meeting with the program's central manager and staff it was confirmed that program spending across provinces had not been adjusted according to indicators of performance in reaching poor areas within provinces.

Table 6.5 gives the results, both for the combined sample and split between TII and TIII. Targeting performance shows a significantly positive response to changes in aggregate outlays. Not only has targeting performance deteriorated in the change from TII to TIII, but the effect of changes in program spending on targeting performance has increased under TIII. I also tested whether the estimated value of β was different when spending increased versus decreased; there was no significant difference (the coefficient on the interaction effect between $G_{jt} - G_j$ and $I(G_{jt} - G_j)$, where I is the indicator function, had a t-ratio of -0.38). There is no difference in the absolute value of the effects of spending cuts versus increases.

Again we have found that targeting performance tends to worsen when aggregate spending on the program is cut, broadly consistent with the earlier evidence for India and Bangladesh. The results of all three studies are suggestive of an underlying tendency in the political economy to protect spending on the non-poor.

Table 6.5 Budget effects on poor-area targeting of Argentina's Trabajar Programs

	Full sample	Trabajar II	Trabajar III
Program spending (deviation from time mean TII + TIII)	3.13 (4.81)	3.55 (5.32)	10.39 (4.44)
R^2	0.778	0.813	0.903
N	132	66	66

Notes
Robust t-statistics in parentheses. The dependent variable is the targeting differential given by the regression coefficient of Trabajar spending per capita at department level for each province and time period on the incidence of unmet basic needs per capita. Each regression included province fixed effects. The observation period for each of TII and TIII was divided into 3 five-month intervals (1 six-month interval for TIII, converted into a five-month equivalent); a statistical addendum with details is available from the author.

6.6   Conclusions

Even when they have the power to do so, it is not obvious that it will be in the interests of the non-poor to shift the burden of fiscal adjustment to the poor. This depends on the preferences of the non-poor, notably the extent to which they gain directly from public spending on the poor, and (less obviously) how quickly the marginal utility of their spending on the poor declines relative to the marginal utility of spending on themselves. Nor is it clear that the poor will be powerless even when they are a minority. They may be able to form a small but influential special interest group, represented by non-governmental organizations, or they may be able to form a coalition with non-poor sub-groups who see it as in their interests to not have the burden of cuts fall on the poor.

As this chapter has demonstrated, the incidence of fiscal contraction, and hence the case for action to protect public spending on the poor at a time of overall fiscal austerity, is an empirical question. The chapter has tried to address that question drawing on case studies for various social programs in Argentina, Bangladesh, and India. The case studies have used a range of data and methods but share the common feature that they study the way in which the incidence of spending (notably how much goes to the poor relative to others) varies with the aggregate level of spending. While further work is needed in other settings before one can be confident in making generalizations, there are some common findings in these case studies that are at least suggestive.

The results reinforce the view that extra public action is warranted to protect public spending on the poor at times of aggregate fiscal contraction. In all the cases studied here, one finds signs of early program capture by the non-poor, but that targeting tends to improve as the program expands. In short, it appears from the evidence reviewed here that it is spending on the non-poor that are protected from aggregate outlays. In terms of the theoretical model, this suggests that the "utility effect" dominates the "power effect"; declining marginal utility of spending on the non-poor tends to mean that there is a switch in spending away from the poor during an aggregate contraction.

One implication of these findings concerns impact evaluations of add-on programs intended to compensate losers from fiscal adjustment. The results of this study suggest that evaluations which ignore the political economy of fiscal adjustment can greatly underestimate the impact on poverty of successful add-on programs, relative to the counter-factual of no intervention. Past performance in reaching the poor is clearly not a reliable guide to outcomes in the absence of the intervention. Restoring the pre-adjustment level of public spending on the poor is consistent with large gains relative to what would have happened without intervention. That is implied by this study's repeated finding that targeting performance tends to deteriorate when aggregate spending declines.

Another implication is that achieving a pro-poor shift in spending during an aggregate contraction will not be politically easy. While the given results strengthen the case for efforts to change the composition of spending at times of aggregate fiscal adjustment, they also point to the difficulty of doing so. If the empirical regularities found in the various data sets studied in this chapter prove to be general, then one is led to conclude that attempts to combine the short-term spending cuts required for macroeconomic adjustment with better targeting will meet opposition. As the case study for one such program in Argentina suggests, even successful add-on programs are not immune to the same underlying forces in the political economy that help protect spending on the non-poor from aggregate fiscal contractions. The Argentina program did help the families of poor unemployed workers at a time of need; given the pattern of past public spending, it appears unlikely that they would have received such help otherwise. But the local political economy tends to protect allocations to non-poor areas when the program contracts (and program expansions tend to favor poor areas). Deeper institutional and policy reforms may then be called for if the poor are to be more protected from fiscal adjustment.

This begs the question of whether it might be possible to design permanent policies that automatically protect the poor from short-term fiscal adjustments and other shocks. This is not so far fetched. With the better household survey data currently available (or feasible to generate) it is not difficult to identify *ex ante* the key line items of public spending on health, education, and social protection that will need to be protected. Investing in credible program impact assessments can create the information base needed to more effectively resist short-term political pressures during a time of fiscal adjustment.

There is also scope for establishing permanent programs that can respond endogenously to the income shocks facing the poor. Some promising clues can be found from developing country experience, notably in the success stories found in famine prevention and relief (Ravallion, 1997). Indeed, automatic protection is the essential idea of an important and long-standing class of anti-poverty programs, typified by the famous Employment Guarantee Scheme in the state of Maharashtra in India. This aims to assure income support in rural areas by providing unskilled manual labor at low wages to anyone who wants it. The scheme automatically contracts in good agricultural years and expands in poor years, and has provided effective protection when there is a threat of famine (Dréze and Sen, 1989). Design features are crucial, notably that the wage rate is not set too high; a high wage (relative to prevailing wages for unskilled work) can undermine the scheme.[15] The scheme is financed domestically, largely from taxes on the relatively well-off segments of Maharashtra's urban populations who perceive benefits from effective social protection such as in attenuating migration to cities in times of stress in rural areas (Ravallion, 1991).

This type of program may not be appropriate for fighting chronic poverty; the deadweight losses associated with the work requirement can entail that other schemes dominate in normal times (though this is an empirical question).[16] The big advantage of a well-designed workfare scheme is its ability to deal with transient poverty due to large negative shocks. This is essentially a public insurance scheme in which outlays are fully endogenous to the shocks to the economy. This means of course that funding must be secure, and that there is a permanent institutional capability for rapid disbursement when needed.

There are limits to social protection by this means alone. The work requirement means that not all those in need will be able to participate. A complementary set of transfers in cash or food will almost certainly be needed, targeted to specific groups who either cannot work, or should not be taken out of other activities (notably school) to join relief work. Their age or disability can fairly easily identify those who cannot be expected to work, though even then the administrative and political-economic difficulties in doing so should not be underrated. The judgment might also be made that certain groups should not work to obtain benefits even though they are able. Cash or FFE programs in poor areas (such as the Bangladesh program studied in this chapter) can help keep poor kids in school during times of macroeconomic contraction. These transfer schemes will need to be allocated by administrative means, and turned off and on according to indicators of crisis. The demand for relief work can provide a useful signal for this purpose. A rapid expansion of demand for low wage relief work is a good signal that other transfers also need to kick in.

While effective short-term social protection from aggregate shocks may well be the exception rather than the rule, some developing countries have demonstrated that it is possible to protect those who are poor or vulnerable at such times. The claims sometimes heard that this is beyond the means of developing countries are demonstrably wrong; the evidence found in this chapter that it is the non-poor who are protected belies the case that differential protection is unfeasible.

The real challenge ahead is to assure that an effective safety net is a permanent institution. The cost to the budget need not be higher than existing schemes, though in many settings current spending on social protection may well be too low. The budgetary outlay could well be highly variable over time, though possibly no more so than for poorly prepared and designed relief operations in which large sums of money have to be injected into an overdue response. To cover the variability in disbursements, a central safety-net fund can be established. There will no doubt be low probability events for which extra external help will be needed. However, the fund should be sufficient to cover a normal sequence of shocks as well as modest demand in normal years.

What is the role of donors and the International Financial Institutions in all this? Only coming into the picture in an *ad hoc* and delayed way during emergencies, and naively running against the local political economy, hardly constitute a credible external response. A potentially far more important role for external assistance is in assuring that an effective automatic safety net is in place with secure funding, as a crucial element of sound domestic policy making even in normal times. Setting up the capacity for effective social protection is arguably no less important to the ultimate welfare objectives of economic policy in risk-prone economies than is aiming to assure sustainable trajectories for macroeconomic aggregates. Neither goal should be compromised to placate short-term political interests.

Acknowledgment

For helpful comments the author is grateful to Michael Keen and Lant Pritchett, and seminar participants at Columbia University, the International Monetary Fund, and the World Bank.

Notes

* This chapter is a greatly expanded version of Ravallion (2004). These are the views of the author and should not be attributed to the World Bank or any affiliated organization.

1 On the political economy of targeting see the discussions in Besley and Kanbur (1993), Sen (1995), Gelbach and Pritchett (2000), and De Donder and Hindriks (1998).

2 This is consistent with cross-country evidence on the effects of differences in public spending on health care on aggregate health outcomes, allowing those effects to differ systematically between the poor and non-poor (Bidani and Ravallion, 1997).

3 The time series data for 1980–97 suggest that social spending in Argentina has responded elastically to cuts in total spending (with an elasticity of about 2) but that the elasticity of social spending to increases in total spending is not significantly different from zero (Ravallion, 2002).

4 Evidence consistent with these claims from survey-based incidence studies for Argentina in the 1990s can be found in Gasparini (1999) and World Bank (1999).

5 There is some (indirect) evidence to support that view in the finding of Galasso and Ravallion (2005) that the within-village performance of an anti-poverty program in Bangladesh in reaching the poor tended to deteriorate the more unequal the village.

6 A mathematical addendum is available from the author proving the given formulae.

7 For further discussion of the properties of this measure of targeting performance see Ravallion (2000). The case studies discussed later in this chapter will rely heavily on this measure.

8 However, Ordinary Least Squares regression will give a biased estimate of the MOP, since the region and quintile specific participation rate (on the left-hand side) is implicitly included when calculating the overall mean participation rate across all regions and quintiles (on the right-hand side). To deal with this problem Lanjouw and Ravallion (1999) use an Instrumental Variables Estimator in which the "leave-out mean" is used as the instrumental variable for the state average participation rate. (The leave-out mean is defined as the mean for the state excluding the region and quintile specific participation rate corresponding to each observation in the data.)

9 Participation in public works programs is based on whether any household member worked for at least 60 days on public works during the preceding 365 days. Participation in the IRDP program is defined as whether the household received any assistance during the last five years from IRDP. Participation in the PDS program is defined as whether the household purchased any commodity from a ration/fair price shop during the last 30 days.

10 The sample size (rural areas only) of the 1993–94 NSS was 61,464 households.

11 Notice that it is not possible to split public from private schooling in these data; public school enrollments may well be lower for the well off.

12 This is based on the standard chi-square test statistic for the test of independence in a contingency table.

13 All results quoted for TIII in this chapter relate to the first 16 months of its operation, up to November 1999.

14 Equation (6.16) indicates that the error term will not be homoskedastic. Standard errors of the targeting differential were corrected for heteroskedasticity.

15 Ravallion *et al.* (1993) provide evidence on how the EGS in India responds to aggregate shocks, and on how the ability of the scheme to insure the poor without rationing was jeopardized by a sharp increase in the wage rate.
16 See, for example, the cost effectiveness calculations for a national EGS for India in Murgai and Ravallion (2005). On how the cost effectiveness of workfare programs relative to uniform transfers depends on both design features and context see Ravallion (1999b).

References

Bardhan, Pranab, and Dilip Mookherjee. 2000. "Capture and Governance at Local and National Levels," *American Economic Review, Papers and Proceedings*, 90(2): 135–39.
Besley, Timothy and Ravi Kanbur. 1993. "Principles of Targeting," in Lipton, Michael and Jacques van der Gaag (eds) *Including the Poor*. Washington, DC: The World Bank.
Bidani, Benu and Martin Ravallion. 1997. "Decomposing Social Indicators Using Distributional Data," *Journal of Econometrics*, 77: 125–40.
De Donder, Philippe and Jean Hindriks. 1998. "The Political Economy of Targeting," *Public Choice*, 95: 177–200.
Dréze, Jean and Amartya Sen. 1989. *Hunger and Public Action*. Oxford: Oxford University Press.
Galasso, Emanuela and Martin Ravallion. 2005. "Decentralized Targeting of an Anti-Poverty Program," *Journal of Public Economics*, 85: 705–27.
Gasparini, Leonardo. 1999. "Incidencia Distributiva del Gasto Público," Fundacion de Investigaciones Economicas Latinoamericanas (FIEL), Buenos Aires, Argentina.
Gelbach, Jonah and Lant Pritchett. 2000. "Indicator Targeting in a Political Economy: Leakier can be Better," *Journal of Policy Reform*, 4: 113–45.
Government of Argentina. 1999. "Caracterización y Evolución del Gasto Público Social, Secretaria de Programacion Economia y Regional," Buenos Aires, Argentina.
Grossman, Gene and Elhanan Helpman. 1996. "Electoral Competition and Special Interest Politics," *Review of Economic Studies*, 63: 265–86.
Jalan, Jyotsna and Martin Ravallion. 2003. "Estimating the Benefit Incidence of an Anti-Poverty Program by Propensity Score Matching," *Journal of Business and Economic Statistics*, 21(1): 19–30.
Johnson, O. and J. Salop. 1980. "Distributional Aspects of Stabilization Programs in Developing Countries," *IMF Staff Papers*, 27: 1–23.
Lanjouw, Peter and Martin Ravallion. 1999. "Benefit Incidence and the Timing of Program Capture," *World Bank Economic Review*, 13(2): 257–74.
Lanjouw, Peter, Menno Pradhan, Fadia Saadah, Haneen Sayed, and Robert Sparrow. 2001. "Poverty, Education and Health in Indonesia: Who Benefits from Public Spending?," Policy Research Working Paper 2739, World Bank.
Murgai, Rinku and Martin Ravallion. 2005. "Is a Guaranteed Living Wage a Good Anti-Poverty Policy?" Policy Research Working paper 3640, World Bank.
Ravallion, Martin. 1991. "Reaching the Rural Poor through Public Employment: Arguments, Evidence, and Lessons from South Asia," *World Bank Research Observer*, 6: 153–76.
—— 1997. "Famines and Economics," *Journal of Economic Literature*, 35: 1205–42.
—— 1999a. "Are Poorer States Worse at Targeting their Poor?," *Economics Letters*, 65: 373–77.
—— 1999b. "Appraising Workfare," *World Bank Research Observer*, 14: 31–48.

Ravallion, Martin. 2000. "Monitoring Targeting Performance when Decentralized Allocations to the Poor are Unobserved," *World Bank Economic Review*, 14(2): 331–45.
—— 2002. "Are the Poor Protected from Budget cuts? Evidence for Argentina," *Journal of Applied Economics*, 5: 95–121.
——2004. "Who is Protected from Budget Cuts?" *Journal of Policy Reform*, 7(2): 109–22.
——and Quentin Wodon. 2000. "Does Child Labor Displace Schooling? Evidence on Behavioral Responses to an Enrolment Subsidy," *Economic Journal*, 110: C158–C176.
——, Gaurav Datt, and Shubhan Chaudhuri. 1993. "Does Maharashtra's Employment Guarantee Scheme Guarantee Employment? Effects of the 1988 Wage Increase," *Economic Development and Cultural Change*, 41: 251–75.
Sen, Amartya. 1995. "The Political Economy of Targeting," in D. van de Walle and K. Nead (eds), *Public Spending and the Poor: Theory and Evidence*, Baltimore, MD: Johns Hopkins University Press.
World Bank. 1999. *Poor People in a Rich Country: A Poverty Report for Argentina*, Washington, DC: World Bank.

7 Understanding the evolution of inequality during transition

The optimal income taxation framework

Ravi Kanbur and Matti Tuomala

What explains the spectacular increases in inequality of disposable income in transitional economies of Central and Eastern Europe? There are at least two possible explanations. First, the pre-tax distribution of income became more unequal because of the shift to a market economy. Second, the degree of progressivity of the income tax system declined. But each of these factors is in turn determined by other structural changes associated with transition – notably, the decrease in publicly provided goods, the decrease in non-income tax revenue sources such as profits from public production and perhaps a decline in society's inequality aversion. This chapter develops a framework in which these different forces on inequality can be assessed. Using a simple two-type and two-sector optimal income tax model with endogenous wages, we first of all show that a decrease in the public provision could indeed lead to increasing 'inherent' inequality, in other words inequality in market incomes. It then deploys the Mirrlees model of optimal non-linear taxation to assess the relative impacts of this increase in inherent inequality, the decreasing sources of non-income tax revenue, and possible declines in inequality aversion, to get a numerical feel for their possible impacts on inequality

7.1 Introduction

Tax/transfer system reform was central to the transition process from the centrally planned economy to a market-type economy in Central and Eastern Europe (CEE). In the old fiscal system a large share of tax revenue came directly or indirectly from state-owned firms. The new fiscal system is in turn designed to be compatible with future EU membership of CEE countries. A personal income tax, a value-added tax and entrepreneurial profits tax are all largely modelled on Western counterparts. The introduction of the new fiscal system, in concert with other structural feature of the transition, has had profound indirect and direct distributional effects. One common characteristic of the transition in CEE has been an increase in income inequality. Both market and disposable income inequality have risen in these countries during the 1990s. Driving this increase in inequality have been a variety of factors. In the pre-reform situation the requirement of government expenditure was largely met from non-tax revenue as the profits of public production, taxation of enterprise profits and commodity transactions. Privatisation of state-owned firms surely has had significant consequences for income inequality. Other factors such as trade liberalisation, changes to the level and composition of government spending including declines in the publicly provided private goods and changes in the wage setting process have all tended to raise inequality. At the same time, it can be argued that these societies have become less averse *per se* to inequality.[1]

This chapter develops a framework in which these different forces on inequality can be assessed. We start by surveying the salient empirical facts on income inequality and RD based on the Luxembourg Income Study (LIS) database in Section 7.2. In Section 7.3 we indicate the potentially important channels for changes in market income inequality, or 'inherent' inequality, using a simple two-type and two-sector optimal income tax model with endogenous wages. We argue that a reduction in public goods provision can indeed lead to an increase in inherent inequality in such models. Section 7.4 accepts an increase in inherent inequality but looks at optimal RD in the face of this increase, and also when sources of non-income tax revenue disappear as the structure changes, and as aversion to inequality falls – all forces that, it can be argued, have been present in the transition process. Section 7.5 concludes the chapter with a discussion of directions for further research.

7.2   The basic facts

This section sets the stage by reviewing empirical findings on income inequality and the extent of RD in the transition countries in CEE. Data on income distribution shown in Tables 7.1 and 7.2 are obtained from the LIS. The relatively high quality of this data source has been commented on elsewhere (see Atkinson and Brandolini, 2001). The income concepts employed are market income (MI) and disposable income (DI),[2] with household size being allowed for by deflating by the square root of the number of household members.

Table 7.1 provides estimates of the change in the DI distribution. In the period considered, the Gini coefficient of DI rose markedly, as did the various decile ratios. Table 7.2 shows that the inequality of market incomes also rose markedly, a factor confirmed by Table 7.3 which shows significant increases in the decile ratios of the gross earnings of employees. However, interestingly, Table 7.2 shows that the extent of RD, as measured by the percentage of decrease in inequality from MI inequality to DI inequality, actually increased in Hungary, Poland and Russia.[3] For example, between 1986 and 1995 in Poland the Gini coefficient for MI increased by over 20 percentage points. But the DI Gini only rose by around 10 points. Thus on one measure, the extent of RD increased by more than 10 percentage points.[4]

These facts set up our basic analytical questions. What explains the increase in market inequality? Given this increase, what explains the increased degree

Table 7.1 Income (disposable) inequality measures

Country	Year	Percentile ratio (90/10)	Percentile ratio (80/20)	Percentile ratio (90/50)
Czech-Republic	1992	2.54	1.83	1.60
	1996	3.04	2.11	1.85
Hungary	1991	3.67	2.34	1.91
	1994	4.21	2.47	2.21
Poland	1986	3.64	2.43	1.84
	1992	3.47	2.24	1.88
	1995	3.74	2.28	2.11
	1999	3.49	2.20	1.87
Russia	1992	7.25	3.88	2.58
	1995	11.36	4.12	2.96
Slovak-Republic	1992	2.25	1.68	1.49
	1996	2.88	1.93	1.62

Source: Own calculations based on LIS-data (02 October 2002).

Table 7.2 Gini (G) coefficients and RD in transition economies

Country	Year	G(MI)	G(DI)	RD %[a]
Czech-Republic	1992	50.3	21.8	56.6
	1996	50.9	26.2	50.9
Hungary	1991	56.4	30.6	45.6
	1994	64.8	33.4	52.9
Poland	1986	44.3	27.9	37.1
	1992	58.5	27.9	52.3
	1995	65.9	32.5	50.7
	1999	56.5	29.4	48.0
Russia	1992	61.5	46.6	24.3
	1995	66.7	47.7	28.5

Source: Own calculations based on LIS-data (02 October 2002).

Note
a RD = [G(MI)−G(DI)]/G(MI).

Table 7.3 Distribution of gross earnings of employees (P90/P10)

Country	1989	1990	1991	1992	1993	1994	1995	1996	1997
Czech-Republic	2.43		2.60	2.75	3.20	3.14	3.70	2.86	2.98
Hungary		3.40		3.56	3.70	3.75			4.17
Poland	2.43		2.85	2.91	3.01	3.40	3.35	3.48	3.53
Russia	3.33	3.36	4.28	8.17	15.55	9.41	9.96	9.60	10.40
Ukraine				3.12	5.51		5.74	5.74	

Source: Flemming and Micklewright (2000), Appendix B.

of RD especially if, as is often argued, the degree of inequality aversion also fell during the transition period? The next two sections take up these questions.

7.3   Public provision and market inequality

Consider the following model, a modified version of the model in Naito (1999).[5] There are two types of workers in the economy: workers of type 1 are less skilled and earn income w_1. The more skilled workers, type 2, earn a wage w_2 ($>w_1$). The number of workers of each type is 1. Workers supply labour, denoted by l, and consume two types of goods: a normal private good, x, and a publicly provided good, denoted by g. The latter good is provided by the state sector. Preferences are represented by a strictly monotone, strictly quasi-concave and twice differentiable utility function by $v(x_i,l_i,g)$. Workers maximise $v(x,l,g)$ with respect to his or her labour supply, subject to a given tax schedule, $T(y)$, and the budget constraint $x = y - T(y)$, where $y = wl$ denotes workers gross income.

   The good x is produced in the private sector according to an aggregate, constant returns to scale, production function $H(l_1^x,l_2^x)$, where l_1^x and l_2^x denote the labour inputs in the private sector. The good g in turn is produced according to the aggregate production function $G(l_1^g,l_2^g)$, where l_1^g and l_2^g are the labour inputs in the public sector. Note that the same technology is used to produce both goods. They have thus similar producer prices as well. For simplicity, the prices for both goods are normalised to unity. This specification captures two important features of the model. First, the wage rates are endogenous in a similar way as in Stern (1982) and Stiglitz (1982). In the following, $\Omega = w_1/w_2$ depicts the relative wage of the low-skilled type. Assuming a competitive labour market, Ω is a function of l_1/l_2, $w_1/w_2 = H_1(l_1,l_2)/H_2(l_1,l_2)$, where H_i ($i = 1,2$) denotes the partial derivatives of the production function with respect to the labour inputs l_i^x. It captures the idea that the relative wage rate of type 1, determined at the market, is a decreasing function of l_1/l_2. Labour is supposed to be completely mobile between the two sectors. This means that the public sector must pay the same wage that prevails in the private sector. The public sector may yet use different shadow prices when making the employment decisions of different types of labour. Public enterprises are assumed to minimise the costs of production with respect to the shadow wages, r_1 and r_2, set by the government. Thus the public sector minimises production costs by equating the marginal rate of transformation between unskilled and skilled workers to the ratio of equilibrium wage rates, that is, $r_1/r_2 = G_1(l_1,l_2)/G_2(l_1,l_2)$, where G_i ($i = 1, 2$) in turn denotes the partial derivatives of the public sector production function with respect to labour inputs l_i^g.

   Following the standard idea of Pareto-optimal taxation, the government maximises the utility of the low-skilled workers subject to the constraint that the skilled worker must stay at a given utility level. The government redistributes income by taxing income on a non-linear scale. It may also use a uniform public provision of g as a policy variable. We apply the information-based approach to tax policy by assuming that the government can observe the labour income y, but it does not observe the income earning abilities (the wage rates) of the workers.

Therefore, the government must select the tax schedule subject to the self-selection constraint that the skilled worker has an incentive to work $l_2 = y_2/w_2$, report income y_2 and consume x_2 instead of wishing to pretend to be the unskilled household, that is, mimic, working $y_1/w_2 = w_1 l_1/w_2 = \Omega l_1$, reporting income y_1, and consuming x_1. The government chooses the optimal tax schedule (or labour $-$ after-tax income) bundles to the two different worker types subject to the constraint that the skilled worker be at a given utility level, the self-selection constraint of the skilled worker, and the resource constraint of the economy $(l_1 = l_1^x + l_1^g, l_2 = l_2^x + l_2^g)$. We concentrate here on the 'normal' case where the redistribution occurs from the skilled workers to the unskilled ones. Thus the self-selection constraint of the skilled workers is binding. The Lagrangean of the government optimisation problem can be expressed in terms of the controls x_i, l_i, l_i^x, l_i^g $(i = 1, 2)$

$$
\begin{aligned}
L = {} & v(x_1, l_1, g) + \delta[v(x_2, l_2, g) - \bar{v}^2] \\
& + \mu[v(x_2, l_2, g) - v(x_1, \Omega l_1, g)] \\
& + \rho_x[H(l_1^x, l_2^x) - x_1 - x_2] \\
& + \rho_g[G(l_1^g, l_2^g) - 2g)] + \alpha_1[l_1 - l_1^x - l_1^g] + \alpha_2[l_2 - l_2^x - l_2^g] \qquad (7.1)
\end{aligned}
$$

The first-order conditions are the following:

$$
\begin{aligned}
& x_1 : v_x^1 - \mu \hat{v}_x^2 - \rho_x = 0 && (7.2) \\
& l_1 : v_l^1 - \mu \hat{v}_l^2 \Omega + \alpha_1 = 0 && (7.3) \\
& x_2 : (\delta + \mu) v_x^2 - \rho_x = 0 && (7.4) \\
& l_2 : (\delta + \mu) v_l^2 + \alpha_2 = 0 && (7.5) \\
& l_i^x : \rho_x H_i - \mu \hat{v}_l^2 \Omega_i l_1 - \alpha_i = 0 \quad i = 1, 2 && (7.6) \\
& l_i^g : \rho_g G_i - \alpha_i = 0 && (7.7)
\end{aligned}
$$

where the hat terms refer to the so-called mimickers, that is type 2 workers when mimicking the choice of type 1 and $\Omega_i = (\partial \Omega / \partial l_i^x)$, $i=1,2$.[6]

Suppose that the government has chosen to produce a certain amount of consumption, g. Given this, suppose further that the government's income tax and public employment policy is optimal. We will now show that the marginal rate of transformation between these two types of labour in public production is smaller than that one in the private sector, that is $(r_1/r_2) \le (w_1/w_2)$.

From the equation (7.6) we see that only in the case that the second term is zero the production efficiency holds, that is $G_1/G_2 = H_1/H_2$. But we also note that the term $-\mu \hat{v}_l^2 l_1$ is positive. Thus the Diamond–Mirrlees efficiency theorem does not hold in this model. Given our assumptions about the public production function (7.6) implies the following result: to produce a given amount of consumption the government should employ more unskilled workers and less skilled workers than is necessary to minimise cost at the prevailing gross wage rates. This means that if the supply of low-skilled workers becomes scarcer in the private sector, through hiring more of these workers into the public sector, this reduces the wage differentials of the workers. Thus, indirect RD through public sector employment will Pareto-improve welfare by mitigating the incentive problem of the non-linear income tax system. Or put it in terms of envelope arguments. If in the beginning the production efficiency holds, then the marginal change in hiring more low-skilled workers to the public sector has no first order welfare costs. It affects only relative wages of the low-skilled workers.

Given the optimal income tax and employment policy, we may also use the envelope argument to detect the change in the social welfare from an increase in the level of the publicly provided good as follows:

$$\frac{dL}{dg} = v_g^1 + (\delta + \mu)v_g^2 - \mu\hat{v}_g^2 - \mu\hat{v}_I^2\frac{d\Omega}{dg}l_1 - 2\rho_\gamma \tag{7.8}$$

Our focus is, however, more in the production side of the economy, and therefore we concentrate on the case with the weakly separable (between consumption and labour (or leisure)) utility function. Rewriting (7.8) by substituting for ρ_x from (7.2) and (7.4) yields

$$\frac{dL}{dg} = -\mu\hat{v}_I^2\frac{d\Omega}{dg}l_1 \tag{7.9}$$

What is interesting in (7.9) is the link between the publicly provided private good and the wage structure of the economy (the term $-\mu\hat{v}_I^2(d\Omega)/(dg)l_1$). If its provision leads to a relative increase in the wage rate for type 1 workers, then indirect RD through public provision will Pareto-improve welfare by mitigating the incentive problem of the non-linear income tax system.

Thus if wage rates are endogenous, RD devices that otherwise would not be applied become welfare improving. These theoretical results support the view that the privatisation and a decrease in public provision such as education, health care and social services may have been important factors in explaining increasing inherent inequality in transition economies during the 1990s.[7]

7.4   Optimal non-linear redistribution

An analytical framework for thinking through the relationship between inherent inequality and the extent of RD is put forward by James Mirrlees in his Nobel Prize-winning paper (Mirrlees, 1971). It captures the central features in thinking about the evolution of RD policy. Certain key elements of the Mirrlees model are useful for our purposes. First is the concept of inherent inequality reflecting among other things skilled/unskilled wage differentials, asset inequality and social norms. If there is no intervention by the government, the inherent inequality will be fully reflected in the disposable income. However, if the government wants to intervene – as seems to be the case in the transition countries – it will find the second component of the Mirrlees model, the egalitarian objectives of the government. And if the government tries to redistribute income from high-income people to low-income people, there will be incentive and disincentive effects. In other words, the RD policy is the product of circumstances and objectives. Finally, the Mirrlees model has a revenue requirement from the tax/transfer system to finance an exogenously given level of public goods. In this framework, we use numerical simulations to study questions such as how optimal RD might respond when inherent inequality increases, the government becomes less averse to inequality and the role of non-tax revenue decreases.[8]

It is useful to lay out the basic model, even though it is well known. There is a continuum of individuals, each having the same preference ordering which is represented by an additive utility function $u = U(x) - V(l)$ defined over consumption x and hours worked l, with $U_x > 0$ and $V_l < 0$ (subscripts indicating partial derivatives) and where $V(\cdot)$ is convex. Workers differ only in the pre-tax wage w they can earn. There is a distribution of w on the interval (s,h) represented by the density function $f(w)$. Gross income $y = wl$.

Suppose that the aim of policy can be expressed as maximising the following social welfare criterion

$$S = \int_s^h W(u(w))f(w)dw \tag{7.10}$$

where $W(.)$ is an increasing and concave function of utility. The government cannot observe individuals' productivities and thus is restricted to setting taxes and transfers as a function only of earnings, $T[y(w)]$. The government maximises S subject to the revenue constraint

$$\int_s^h (y(w) - x(w))f(w)dw = R \tag{7.11}$$

where in the Mirrlees tradition R is interpreted as the required revenue for essential public goods. The more non-tax revenue a government receives from external sources (as in the old fiscal system from state-owned firms), the lower is R. In addition to the revenue constraint, the government faces incentive compatibility constraints. These in turn state that each w-individual maximises utility by choice of hour. Totally differentiating utility with respect to w, and making use of workers utility maximisation condition, we obtain the incentive compatibility constraints,

$$\frac{du}{dw} = -\frac{lV_l^9}{w} \tag{7.12}$$

Since $T = wl - x$, we can think of government as choosing schedules $l(w)$ and $x(w)$. In fact, it is easier to think of it choosing a pair of functions, $u(w)$ and $l(w)$, which maximise welfare index (7.10) subject to the incentive compatibility condition (7.12) and the revenue requirement (7.11). Omitting details for an exposition (see Tuomala, 1990), the first-order conditions of this problem imply a pattern of marginal rates,[10] $t(y) = T'(y)$, satisfying

$$\frac{t}{1-t} = (E^{-1} + 1)U_x\mu(w)/\lambda wf(w) \tag{7.13}$$

where λ is the multiplier on the revenue constraint and

$$\mu(w) = \int_s^w ((W'U_x - \lambda)(1/U_x)f(p)dp) \tag{7.14}$$

is the multiplier on the incentive compatibility constraint. This latter satisfies the transversality conditions

$$\mu(s) = \mu(h) = 0 \tag{7.15}$$

Finally, as in Atkinson and Stiglitz (1980) $E = V'/lV''$. It is the elasticity of labour supply with respect to net wage, holding marginal utility of income constant, that is E is 'compensated' wage elasticity in a rather unusual sense.

Unfortunately, however, as is well recognised in the non-linear taxation literature, closed form analytical results are few and far between.[11] It should be clear from (7.13) that the variation of the optimal marginal tax rate (MTR) with the level of income is a complex matter, and that comparative statics of inequality and averages as parameters vary will not be available in closed form. This is a general feature on the optimal non-linear income taxation literature (see Tuomala, 1990) where, following the lead of Mirrlees (1971), numerical calculations have proved useful in generating useful results.[12] We follow this route here. With these techniques, we can compute post-tax income at each level of w, and thus calculate inequality of pre- and post-tax income as well as total income for different values of key parameters. Our focus is on identifying the combined effects of greater inherent inequality (the standard deviation of w), smaller inequality aversion and larger tax revenue requirement.

We assume w to be distributed lognormally with parameters m and σ (see Aitchison and Brown, 1957). This assumption is common in the literature, following Mirrlees (1971). For numerical simulations we choose $\sigma = 0.39, 0.5, 0.7$ and 1 and $m = -1$ (and -0.8).[13] The utility function $u(.)$ has the constant elasticity of substitution form

$$u(x,l) = [(1 - \phi)x^{-a} + \phi(1 - l)^{-a}]^{-1/a} \tag{7.16}$$

where the elasticity of substitution between consumption and leisure $\varepsilon = 1/(1 + a)$. Where $\varepsilon < 1$, the labour supply function is backward sloping. Stern (1976) pays special attention to the question of how to relate the assumptions about labour supply to econometric research on labour supply behaviour.[14]

He reports estimates of the labour supply (uncompensated) elasticity ranging from -0.07 to -0.30, with a central value of -0.15, and corresponding estimates of elasticity of substitution ε from 0.75 to 0.2, with preferred value of 0.4. Our calculations were carried out for the cases $\varepsilon = 0.4$ ($a = 1.5$), $\varepsilon = 0.5$ ($a = 1$), $\varepsilon = 0.66$ ($a = 0.5$) and $\varepsilon = 1$ (Cobb–Douglas case, $u = \ln x + \ln(1 - l)$). Hence as a by-product we also extend previous numerical simulations in the framework of non-linear income taxation. The social welfare function of the government is specified[15] $W(u) = -(1/\beta)e^{-\beta u}$ so that β measures the degree of inequality aversion in the social welfare function of the government (in the case of $\beta = 0$, we define $W = u$). $R = 1 - \int x(w) f(w)\, dw / \int y(w) f(w)\, dw$ is specified as a fraction of national income, and is assumed to vary between -0.1 and 0.1.

Tables 7.4–7.9 give net income (x), gross income (y), MTR and utility levels (u) at various percentiles of the ability distribution.[16] Tables 7.4 and 7.5 reflect 'the old fiscal system' ($\beta = 1$, $\varepsilon = 0.5$ or 1, $\sigma = 0.39$, $R = -0.1$, 0.0) and Tables 7.6a, 7.6b, 7.7, 7.8 and 7.9 in turn 'the new one' ($\beta = 0$, $\varepsilon = 0.5$ or 1, $\sigma = 0.5$, 0.7 and 1, $R = 0.0$, 0.1). Tables 7.4–7.9 also provide the decile ratio (P90/P10) for net income and gross income. Unlike the scalar inequality measures the use of fractile measures such as the decile ratio allows us to consider changes in inequality at various different points in the distribution. Since MTR may be a poor indication of the redistribution powers of an optimal tax structure we measure the extent of redistribution as the proportional reduction between the decile ratio for MI, y, and the decile ratio for DI, x.

Consider first the progressivity of the tax structure as a function of market inequality and revenue requirement. Tables 7.4–7.9 show that optimal tax/transfer systems become more progressive when inequality increases, $\sigma = 0.5$, $\sigma = 0.7$ and $\sigma = 1.0$, and when R becomes more negative (i.e. more non-tax revenue). To understand this, we can combine the results of two earlier studies. Kanbur and Tuomala (1994) show that with greater market income 'inherent' inequality optimal MTR increase with income over the majority of the population. On the other hand, we know from Immonen *et al.* (1998) that as the revenue requirement becomes negative so that, for example, non-tax revenue is available the minimum

Table 7.4 The old fiscal system ($\varepsilon = 0.5$)

$F(w)$	$R = -0.1$				$R = 0.0$			
	x	y	MTR%	u	x	y	MTR%	u
0.10	0.17	0.09	62	-7.63	0.16	0.10	65	-8.10
0.50	0.20	0.18	56	-6.85	0.19	0.19	59	-7.24
0.90	0.27	0.32	45	-5.78	0.26	0.33	47	-6.06
0.99	0.38	0.49	28	-4.78	0.36	0.50	29	-4.99
RD	0.55				0.51			
Decile ratio (P90/P10)	1.59	3.5			1.63	3.3		

Note
$\varepsilon = 0.5$, $\beta = 1$, $\sigma = 0.39$, $m = -1$.

Table 7.5 The old fiscal system ($\varepsilon = 1$)

F(w)	R = −0.1				R = 0.0			
	x	y	MTR%	u	x	y	MTR%	u
0.10	0.11	0.08	30	−2.68	0.10	0.07	33	−2.57
0.50	0.17	0.15	28	−2.39	0.15	0.15	30	−2.30
0.90	0.27	0.28	24	−2.00	0.25	0.28	25	−1.94
0.99	0.41	0.44	20	−1.64	0.38	0.45	18	−1.60
RD	0.31				0.37			
Decile ratio (P90/P10)	2.48	3.58			2.50	3.97		

Note
$\varepsilon = 1, \beta = 1, \sigma = 0.39, m = -1.$

Table 7.6a The new fiscal system ($\varepsilon = 0.5, \sigma = 0.5$)

F(w)	R = 0.0				R = 0.0, m = −0.8			
	x	y	MTR%	u	x	y	MTR%	u
0.10	0.15	0.10	51	−8.67	0.18	0.11	50	−7.44
0.50	0.20	0.20	50	−7.13	0.24	0.24	48	−6.17
0.90	0.29	0.37	45	−5.58	0.35	0.43	43	−4.94
0.99	0.49	0.59	38	−4.33	0.51	0.68	35	−3.85
RD	0.48				0.50			
Decile ratio (P90/P10)	1.93	3.7			1.90	3.83		

Note
$\varepsilon = 0.5, \sigma = 0.5, m = -1, \beta = 0.$

Table 7.6b The new fiscal system ($\varepsilon = 1, \sigma = 0.5$)

F(w)	R = 0.0			
	x	y	MTR%	u
0.10	0.09	0.06	30	−2.79
0.50	0.15	0.15	29	−2.59
0.90	0.24	0.32	26	−2.05
0.99	0.47	0.57	22	−1.41
RD	0.45			
Decile ratio (P90/P10)	2.9	5.3		

Note
$\varepsilon = 1, \beta = 0, \sigma = 0.5, m = -1.$

income requirement for the poor can be met without clawing back revenue with a high MTR. Thus we have low MTR on the poor. In other words, optimal progressivity, taking into account incentive effects, increases with higher inherent inequality and with non-tax revenue. Thus, while the increasing 'inherent'

Table 7.7 The new fiscal system ($\varepsilon = 0.5$, $\sigma = 0.7$)

F(w)	R = 0.0				R = 0.1			
	x	y	MTR%	u	x	y	MTR%	u
0.10	0.16	0.06	56	−7.89	0.14	0.06	60	−8.86
0.50	0.20	0.17	60	−6.89	0.19	0.18	63	−7.22
0.90	0.31	0.45	57	−4.95	0.30	0.47	60	−5.41
0.99	0.54	0.91	45	−3.79	0.55	0.96	37	−3.85
RD	0.74				0.73			
Decile ratio (P90/P10)	1.94	7.56			2.14	7.91		

Note
$\varepsilon = 0.5$, $\beta = 0$, $\sigma = 0.7$, $m = -1$.

Table 7.8 The new fiscal system ($\varepsilon = 0.5$, $\sigma = 1$)

F(w)	R = 0.0				R = 0.1			
	x	y	MTR%	u	x	y	MTR%	u
0.10	0.17	0.02	55	−7.69	0.16	0.02	59	−7.55
0.50	0.21	0.14	68	−6.35	0.20	0.15	71	−6.67
0.90	0.35	0.55	71	−4.65	0.33	0.61	72	−4.88
0.99	0.70	1.61	58	−3.21	0.67	1.65	59	−3.31
RD	0.92				0.93			
Decile ratio (P90/P10)	2.06	27.5			2.06	30.1		

Note
$\varepsilon = 0.5$, $\beta = 0$, $\sigma = 1$, $m = -1$.

Table 7.9 The new fiscal system ($\varepsilon = 0.66$, $\sigma = 0.4$)

F(w)	$\varepsilon = 0.66$, $\beta = 0$, $\sigma = 0.5$, $m = -1$				$\varepsilon = 0.4$, $\beta = 0$, $\sigma = 0.5$, $m = -1$			
	x	y	MTR%	u	x	y	MTR%	u
0.10	0.13	0.09	41	−4.11	0.17	0.10	58	−17.41
0.50	0.19	0.18	40	−3.69	0.21	0.20	58	−13.75
0.90	0.29	0.35	35	−3.26	0.29	0.38	52	−9.74
0.99	0.45	0.58	28	−2.89	0.42	0.61	39	−6.73
RD	0.45				0.54			
Decile ratio (P90/P10)	2.23	4.08			1.70	3.70		

inequality would have induced a partially correcting 'optimal' increase in progressivity of the tax/transfer system, the decrease in non-tax revenue (and hence increase in the revenue requirement from the tax system) that was also seen in the transition would have been a force for decreasing progressivity.

In Tables 7.4–7.9 we see what happens when the government becomes less averse to inequality, 'inherent' inequality increases and the revenue requirement also increases. Figure 7.1 shows the relationship between the extent of optimal, RD, and the wage dispersion, σ, in the case of ($\beta = 0$, $\varepsilon = 0.5$, $R = 0.0$). The effects of varying inequality aversion, β, from 0 to 1 and maximin ($\beta = \infty$) can be seen in Figure 7.2, plotted for a distribution $\sigma = 0.39$. The extent of optimal RD increases as a consequence of increasing the wage dispersion. This is just what we can see in those transition countries having at least two observations (see Table 7.2). An interesting question is when might an increase in 'inherent' inequality, an increase in the tax revenue requirement and a decrease in inequality aversion, be roughly offsetting? We see in Tables 7.5 and 7.6b ($\varepsilon = 1$) that in terms of MTR structure the effect of increasing the wage dispersion from $\sigma = 0.39$ to $\sigma = 0.5$ is the same as moving from $\beta = 1$ to $\beta = 0$. If the extent of

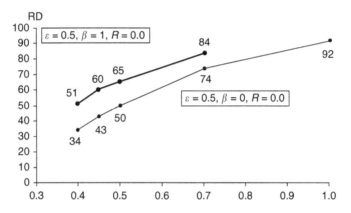

Figure 7.1 Graph showing how the extent of RD varies with the wage dispersion.

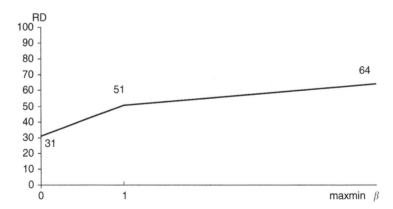

Figure 7.2 Graph showing how the extent of RD varies with inequality aversion. Other parameters are fixed as follows ($\varepsilon = 0.5$, $\sigma = 0.39$, $R = 0.0$).

Table 7.10 The extent of RD (%)

Cases	0.39	0.5	0.7
($\beta = 1$, $\varepsilon = 0.5$, $R = -0.1$)	55	67	84
($\beta = 1$, $\varepsilon = 0.5$, $R = 0.0$)	51	65	84
($\beta = 0$, $\varepsilon = 0.4$, $R = 0.0$)	39	54	75
($\beta = 0$, $\varepsilon = 0.5$, $R = 0.0$)	34	50	74
($\beta = 0$, $\varepsilon = 0.5$, $R = 0.1$)	31	48	73
($\beta = 0$, $\varepsilon = 0.66$, $R = 0.0$)	29	45	72

RD is used as the criterion, then the cases ($\varepsilon = 0.5$, $\beta = 1$, $\sigma = 0.39$, $R = 0.0$) (Table 7.4) and ($\varepsilon = 0.5$, $\beta = 0$, $\sigma = 0.5$, $m = -0.8$, $R = 0.0$) (Table 7.6a) are roughly speaking the same. Thus given this criterion the effect of increasing the 'inherent' inequality from $\sigma = 0.39$ to $\sigma = 0.5$ (and $m = -1$ to $m = -0.8$), is the same as moving from $\beta = 1$ to $\beta = 0$. In other words if market income inequality has risen as much as represented by this move, then it would need a considerable decrease in concern for equity to offset the case for the same extent of RD. If we in turn change the elasticity of substitution, ε, then the cases ($\varepsilon = 0.5$, $\beta = 1$, $\sigma = 0.39$, $R = 0.0$) and ($\varepsilon = 0.4$, $\beta = 0$, $\sigma = 0.5$, $R = 0.0$) yield the same extent of RD. The Table 7.10 summarises how the extent of RD varies with the wage dispersion in different cases.

7.5 Conclusions

In this chapter, we argue that an analysis of the evolution of pre- and post-tax income inequality in the transition economies of CEE can be structured and the different forces in play understood through the framework of optimal income taxation. Using the simple two-type and two-sector optimal income tax model we first of all show that the privatisation and a decrease in public provision of public goods may have been an important factor in explaining increasing pre-tax ('inherent') inequality in transition economies during the 1990s. We also ask, in the framework of non-linear optimal tax theory, how RD might respond when inherent inequality increases, the government becomes less averse to inequality and the role of non-tax revenue decreases, all of which happened during transition. We use numerical simulations to study these questions. We discuss when these forces are offsetting and when they reinforce each other as governments choose tax/transfer schedules optimally in response to them, in trying to understand the stylised facts of pre- and post-tax income inequality during transition. While the increase in 'inherent' inequality induces a response of greater progressivity, this is counteracted by the tendency of the other two forces to decrease progressivity. Overall 'optimal' progressivity thus increases, but not sufficiently to overcome the increase in 'inherent' inequality, which leads to an increasing post-tax inequality. And these are precisely the stylised facts of inequality and progressivity during transition that we set out to investigate.

Notes

1 According to Atkinson and Micklewright (1992) CEE countries were during the 1970s and 1980s very egalitarian in their disposable income distribution compared with comparable Western market economies.

2 LIS (http://lisweb.ceps.lu/techdoc.htm).

3 A new personal income tax was introduced in Hungary already in 1988 under the old system. In the beginning the MTR structure was very progressive with ten bands ranging from 20 to 60 per cent. In 1994 there were six bands rising from 0 to 44 per cent and in 1997 also six bands rising from 20 to 42 per cent. In Czech-Republic there were in 1994 six bands ranging from 15 to 44 per cent and in 1997 five bands rising from 15 to 40 per cent. The Polish income tax system in turn differs from those of Hungary and Czech-Republic in the sense that there are only three bands (20, 32, 44 in 1997). (See Table 7.1 in Piotrowska, 2000.)

4 According to Milanovic (1998) the average level of social cash transfers as a per cent of GDP over the period from the first year of the transition through 1997 was among the highest one in Poland, 17.7 per cent.

5 See also Gaube (2000) and Pirttilä and Tuomala (2002).

6 The function Ω is homogeneous of degree zero in (l_1^x, l_2^x). It implies $\Omega_1 < 0$ and $\Omega_2 > 0$.

7 As pointed out to us by Roger Gordon a publicly owned firm may acquire information about the hourly wages of its workers. Given this information RD towards to less skilled workers will be cheaper than when done outside public sector.

8 These questions were examined by Newbery (1997) in the framework of optimal linear taxation.

9 The first-order condition of individual's optimisation problem is only a necessary condition for the individual's choice to be optimal, but we assume here that it is sufficient as well. Assumptions that assure sufficiency are provided by Mirrlees (1976). Note also that while we here presume an internal solution for l, (7.12) remains valid even if individuals were bunched at $l = 0$ since, for them, $du/dw = 0$.

10 There are other works that have looked at alternative derivations and formulae for non-linear taxation, see Revesz (1989), Roberts (2000) and Saez (2001).

11 Equations (7.13–7.15) lead to the few qualitative conclusions available in this framework (see Tuomala, 1990). It can be shown that the MTR on income is non-negative. This is more striking than it at first looks. It may very well be optimal to have the average tax rate less than zero, but it is never optimal to subsidise earnings at margin. An intuition is that it is cheaper to get people to given indifference curve by reducing average rate rather than by exacerbating deadweight loss through distorting their labour supply decisions. It can also be shown that the MTR is less than 1. We also have the famous 'end point' results. If wage distribution is bounded above, then the MTR at the top is zero. If it is optimal for least able individual to work then the MTR on least able is zero. An intuition behind these endpoint results is that only reason to have an MTR differing from zero is to raise an average tax rate above that point and lower it below that is, equity considerations. But at the top is no one to take from and at the bottom there is no one to give to. So at the end points only efficiency considerations matter. Numerical solutions (Tuomala, 1984, 1990) have shown, however, that these results have very little practical relevance.

12 Tuomala (1990) gives details of the computational procedure.

13 As in Kanbur and Tuomala (1994) we also try to calibrate the lognormal distribution so that the income distribution inferred from the ability distribution matches the actual one. Of course, it would be important to solve MTR formula using the empirical earnings distribution. This is not possible to make directly because the earnings distribution is affected by the tax schedule itself. Saez (2001) makes an important innovation in this question. He calibrates the ability distribution so that given the utility function chosen and the actual tax schedule the resulting pre-tax distribution replicates the empirical earnings distribution.

14 Unfortunately we are not aware of any econometric labour supply study in transition countries.
15 For further discussion on the transformation of each individual's utility see Tuomala (1990)
16 With the utility function we use, there is 'bunching' – all those below a critical value of w choose not to work. Their pre-tax income is thus zero and their post-tax income is whatever the optimal tax and transfer regime gives them.

References

Aitchison, J. and J.A.C. Brown. 1957. *The Lognormal Distribution with Special Reference to its Uses in Economics* (Cambridge: Cambridge University Press).

Atkinson, A.B. and J.E. Stiglitz. 1980. *Lectures on Public Economics* (McGraw-Hill).

—— and J. Micklewright. 1992. *Economic Transformation in Eastern Europe and the Distribution of Income* (Cambridge: Cambridge University Press).

—— and A. Brandolini. 2001. 'Promise and Pitfalls in the Use of "Secondary" Data-Sets. Income Inequality in OECD Countries as a Case Study', *Journal of Economic Literature*, 39(3): 771–800.

Flemming, John S. and J. Micklewright. 2000. *Income Distribution, Economic Systems and Transition*, Handbook of Income Distribution, Vol. 1, A.B. Atkinson and F. Bourguignon (eds) (North Holland: Elsevier, Amsterdam).

Gaube, Thomas. 2005. 'Income Taxation, Endogenous Factor Prices and Production Efficiency', *The Scandinavian Journal of Economics*, 107(2): 335–52.

Immonen, R., R. Kanbur, M. Keen, and M. Tuomala. 1998. 'Tagging and Taxing: The Optimal Use of Categorical and Income Information in Designing Tax/Transfer Schemes', *Economica*, 65(258): 179–92.

Kanbur, R. and M. Tuomala. 1994. 'Inherent Inequality and the Optimal Graduation of Marginal Tax Rates', *Scandinavian Journal of Economics*, 96(2): 275–82.

Milanovic, B. 1998. 'Income, Inequality and Poverty during the Transition from Planned to Market Economy', World Bank Regional and Sectoral Studies (Washington, DC: World Bank).

Mirrlees, J.A. 1971. 'An Exploration in the Theory of Optimum Income Taxation', *Review of Economic Studies*, 38: 175–208.

—— 1976. 'Optimal Tax Theory: A Synthesis', *Journal of Public Economics*, 6: 327–58.

Naito, H. 1999. 'Re-examination of Uniform Commodity Taxes under a Non-Linear Income Tax System and its Implication for Production Efficiency', *Journal of Public Economics*, 71: 165–88.

Newbery, D. 1997. 'Optimal Tax Rates and Tax Design during Systemic Reform', *Journal of Public Economics*, 63: 177–206.

Piotrowska, M. 2000. *Taxes and Transfers as Instruments Influencing Income Inequality in Transition Countries* (Girona, Spain: ISQOLS-Conference).

Pirttilä, J. and M. Tuomala. 2002. 'Publicly Provided Private Goods and Redistribution; A General Equilibrium Analysis', *Scandinavian Journal of Economics*, 104(1): 173–88.

Revesz, J. 1989. 'The Optimal Taxation of Labour Income', *Public Finance*, 44: 453–75.

Roberts, K. 2000. 'A Reconsideration of Optimal Income Tax, in Incentives, Organization and Public Economics', papers in Honour of Sir James Mirrlees, P. Hammond and G. Myles (eds) (Oxford: Oxford University Press).

Saez, E. 2001. 'Using Elasticities to Derive Optimal Income Tax Rates', *Review of Economic Studies*, 68: 205–29.

Stern, N.H. 1976. 'On the Specification of Models of Optimum Income Taxation', *Journal of Public Economics*, 6: 123–62.
—— 1982. 'Optimal Taxation with Errors in Administration', *Journal of Public Economics*, 17: 181–211.
Stiglitz, J.E. 1982. 'Self-Selection and Pareto-Efficient Taxation', *Journal of Public Economics*, 17: 213–40.
Tuomala, M. 1984. 'On the Optimal Income Taxation: Some Further Numerical Results', *Journal of Public Economics*, 23: 351–66.
—— 1990. *Optimal Income Tax and Redistribution* (Oxford: Clarendon Press).

Part III
Finance and trade

8 Evaluation of financial liberalization

A general equilibrium model with constrained occupation choice

Xavier Giné and Robert M. Townsend

The objective of this chapter is to assess both the aggregate growth effects and the distributional consequences of financial liberalization as observed in Thailand from 1976 to 1996. A general equilibrium occupational choice model with two sectors, one without intermediation and the other with borrowing and lending, is taken to Thai data. Key parameters of the production technology and the distribution of entrepreneurial talent are estimated by maximizing the likelihood of transition into business given initial wealth as observed in two distinct datasets. Other parameters of the model are calibrated to try to match the two decades of growth as well as observed changes in inequality, labor share, savings, and the number of entrepreneurs. Without an expansion in the size of the intermediated sector, Thailand would have evolved very differently, namely, with a drastically lower growth rate, high residual subsistence sector, non-increasing wages but lower inequality. The financial liberalization brings welfare gains and losses to different subsets of the population. Primary winners are talented would-be entrepreneurs who lack credit and cannot otherwise go into business (or invest little capital). Mean gains for these winners range from 17 to 34 percent of observed, overall average household income. But liberalization also induces greater demand by entrepreneurs for workers resulting in increases in the wage and lower profits of relatively rich entrepreneurs, of the same order of magnitude as the observed overall average income of firm owners. Foreign capital has no significant impact on growth or the distribution of observed income.

8.1 Introduction

The objective of the chapter is to assess the aggregate, growth effects, and the distributional consequences of financial liberalization and globalization. There has been some debate in the literature about the benefits and potential costs of financial sector reforms. The micro credit movement has pushed for tiered lending, or linkages from formal financial intermediaries to small joint liability or community groups. But a major concern with general structural reforms is the idea that benefits will not trickle down, that the poor will be neglected, and that inequality will increase. Similarly, globalization and capital inflows are often claimed to be associated with growth although the effect of growth on poverty is still a much debated topic.[1]

Needless to say, we do not study here all possible forms of liberalization. Rather, we focus on reforms that increase outreach on the extensive domestic margin, for example, less restricted licensing requirements for financial institutions (both foreign and domestic), the reduction of excess capitalization requirements, and enhanced ability to open new branches. We capture these reforms, albeit crudely in the model, thinking of them as domestic reforms that allow deposit mobilization and access to credit at market clearing interest rates for a segment of the population that otherwise would have neither formal sector savings nor credit.

We take this methodology to Thailand from 1976 to 1996.[2] Thailand is a good country to study for a number of reasons. First, Thailand is often portrayed as an example of an emerging market with high income growth and increasing inequality. The GDP growth from 1981 to 1995 was 8 percent per year and the Gini measure of inequality increased from 0.42 in 1976 to 0.50 in 1996. Second, Jeong (1999) documents in his study of the sources of growth in Thailand, 1976–96, that access to intermediation narrowly defined accounts for 20 percent of the growth in per capita income while occupation shifts alone account for 21 percent. While the fraction of non-farm entrepreneurs does not grow much, the income differential of non-farm entrepreneurs to wage earners is large and thus small shifts in the population create relatively large income changes. In fact, the occupational shift may have been financed by credit. Also related, Jeong finds that 32 percent of changes in inequality between 1976 and 1996 are due to changes in income differentials across occupations. There is evidence that Thailand had a relatively restrictive credit system, but also liberalized during this period. Officially, interest rates ceilings and lending restrictions were progressively removed starting in 1989.[3] The data do seem to suggest a rather substantial increase in the number of households with access to formal intermediaries although this expansion (which we call a liberalization) begins two years earlier, in 1987. Finally, Thailand experienced a relatively large increase in capital inflows from the late 1980s to the mid-1990s.

Our starting point is a relatively simple but general equilibrium model with credit constraints. Specifically, we pick from the literature and extend the Lloyd-Ellis and Bernhardt (2000) model (LEB for short) that features wealth-constrained entry into business and wealth-constrained investment for entrepreneurs. For our purposes, this model has several advantages. It allows for *ex ante* variation in ability. It allows for a variety of occupational structures, that is, firms of various sizes, for example, with and without labor, and at various levels of capitalization. It has a general (approximated) production technology, one which allows labor share to vary. In addition, the household occupational choice has a closed form solution that can easily be estimated. Finally, it features a dual economy development model which has antecedents going back to Lewis (1954) and Fei and Ranis (1964), and thus it captures several widely observed aspects of the development process such as the following – industrialization with persistent income differentials, a slow decline in the subsistence sector, and an eventual increase in wages, all contributing to growth with changing inequality.

Our extension of the LEB model has two sectors, one without intermediation and the other allowing borrowing and lending at a market clearing interest rate. The intermediated sector is allowed to expand exogenously at the observed rate in the Thai data, given initial participation and the initial observed distribution of wealth. Of course, in other contexts and for many questions one would like financial deepening to be endogenous.[4] But here the exogeneity of financial deepening has a peculiar, distinct advantage because we can vary it as we like, either to mimic the Thai data with its accelerated upturns in the late 1980s and early 1990s, or keep it flat providing a counterfactual experiment. We can thus gauge the consequences of these various experiments and compare among them. In short, we can do general equilibrium policy analysis following the seminal work of Heckman *et al.* (1998), despite endogenous prices and an evolving endogenous distribution of wealth in a model where preferences do not aggregate.

We use the explicit structure of the model as given in the occupation choice and investment decision of households to estimate certain parameters of the model. Key parameters of the production technology used by firms and the distribution of entrepreneurial talent in the population are chosen to maximize the likelihood as predicted by the model of the transition into business, given initial wealth. This is done with two distinct microeconomic datasets, one a series of nationally representative household surveys – Socioeconomic Survey (SES) and the other gathered under a project directed by one of the authors, with more reliable estimates of wealth, the timing of occupation transitions, and the use of formal and informal credit. Not all parameters of the model can be estimated via maximum likelihood. The savings rate, the differential in the cost of living, and the exogenous technical progress in the subsistence sector are calibrated to try to match the two decades of Thai growth and observed changes in inequality, labor share, savings, and the number of entrepreneurs.

As mentioned earlier, this structural, estimated version of the Thai economy can then be compared to what would have happened if there had been no expansion in the size of the intermediated sector. Without liberation, at estimated parameter values from both datasets, the model predicts a dramatically lower growth rate, high residual subsistence sector, non-increasing wages, – granted, lower, and decreasing inequality. Thus financial liberalization appears to be the engine of growth it is sometimes claimed to be, at least in the context of Thailand.

However, growth and liberalization do have uneven consequences, as the critics insist. The distribution of welfare gains and losses in these experiments is not at all uniform, as there are various effects depending on wealth and talent – with liberalization, savings earn interest, although this tends to benefit the most wealthy. On the other hand, credit is available to facilitate occupation shifts and to finance setup costs and investment. Quantitatively, there is a striking conclusion. The primary winners from financial liberalization are talented but low wealth would-be entrepreneurs who without credit cannot go into business at all or entrepreneurs with very little capital. Mean gains from the winners range from 60,000 to 80,000 baht, and the modal gains from 6,000 to 25,000 baht, depending on the dataset used and the calendar year. To normalize and give more meaning to these numbers, the modal gains ranges from 17 to 34 percent of the observed, overall average of Thai household income.

But there are also losers. Liberalization induces an increase in wages in latter years, and while this benefits workers, *ceteris paribus*, it hurts entrepreneurs as they face a higher wage bill. The estimated welfare loss in both datasets is approximately 115,000 baht. This is a large number, roughly the same order of magnitude as the observed average income of firm owners overall. This fact suggests a plausible political economy rational for (observed) financial sector repressions.

Finally, we use the estimated structure of the model to conduct two robustness checks. First, we open up the economy to the observed foreign capital inflows. These contribute to increasing growth, increasing inequality, and an increasing number of entrepreneurs, but only slightly, since otherwise the macro and distributional consequences are quite similar to those of the closed economy with liberalization. Indeed, if we change the expansion to grow linearly rather than as observed in the data, the model cannot replicate the high Thai growth rates in the late 1980s and early 1990s, despite apparently large capital inflows at that time. Second, we allow informal credit in the sector without formal intermediation to see if our characterization of the dual economy with its no-credit sector is too extreme. We find that at the estimated parameters it is not. Changes attributed to access to informal credit are negligible.

The rest of the chapter is organized as follows. In Section 8.2 we describe the LEB model in greater detail. In Section 8.3 we describe the core of the model as given in an occupational choice map. In Section 8.4 we discuss the possibility of introducing a credit liberalization. In Section 8.5 we turn to the maximum likelihood estimation (MLE) of seven of the ten parameters of the model from micro data, whereas Section 8.6 focuses on the calibration exercise used to pin down the last three parameters, matching, as explained, more macro, aggregate data. Section 8.7 reports the simulations at the estimated and calibrated values for each dataset. Section 8.8 performs a sensitivity analysis of the model around the estimated and the calibrated parameters. Section 8.9 delivers various measures of the welfare gains and losses associated with the liberalization. Section 8.10 introduces international capital inflows and informal credit to the model. Finally, Section 8.11 concludes.

8.2   Environment

The LEB model begins with a standard production function mapping a capital input k and a labor input l at the beginning of the period into output q at the end of the period. In the original[5] LEB model, and in the numerical simulations presented here, this function is taken to be quadratic. In particular, it takes the form:

$$q = f(k,l) = \alpha k - \tfrac{1}{2}\beta k^2 + \sigma kl + \xi l - \tfrac{1}{2}\rho l^2 \qquad (8.1)$$

This quadratic function can be viewed as an approximation to virtually any production function and has been used in applied work.[6] This function also facilitates the derivation of closed form solutions and allows labor share to vary over time.

Each firm also has a beginning-of-period setup or fixed cost x, and this setup cost is drawn at random from a known cumulative distribution $H(x, m)$ with $0 \leq x \leq 1$. This distribution is parameterized by the number m:

$$H(x, m) = mx^2 + (1 - m)x, \quad m \in [-1, 1] \tag{8.2}$$

If $m = 0$, the distribution is uniform; if $m > 0$ the distribution is skewed toward low-skilled or, alternatively, high x people, and the converse arises when $m < 0$. We do suppose this setup cost varies inversely with talent, that is, it takes both talent and an initial investment to start a business but they are negatively correlated. More generally, the cumulative distribution $H(x, m)$ is a crude way to capture and allow estimation of the distribution of talent in the population and is not an unusual specification in the industrial organization literature,[7] for example, Das *et al.* (1998), Veracierto (1998). Setup cost x is expressed in the same units as wealth. Every agent is born with an inheritance or initial wealth b. The distribution of inheritances in the population at date t is given by $G_t(b) : \mathbb{B}_t \rightarrow [0, 1]$ where $\mathbb{B}_t \subset \mathbb{R}_+$ is the changing support of the distribution at date t. The time argument t makes explicit the evolution of $\mathbb{B}_t$ and G_t over time. The beginning-of-period wealth b and the setup cost x are the only sources of heterogeneity among the population. These are modeled as independent of one another in the specification used here, and this gives us the existence of a *unique* steady state. If correlation between wealth and ability were allowed, we could have poverty traps, as in Banerjee and Newman (1993). We do recognize that in practice wealth and ability may be correlated. In related work, Paulson and Townsend (2001) estimate with the same data as here a version of the Evans and Jovanovic (1989) model allowing the mean of unobserved ability to be a linear function of wealth and education. They find the magnitude of both coefficients to be small.[8]

All units of labor can be hired at a common wage w, to be determined in equilibrium (there is no variation in skills for wage work). The only other technology is a storage technology which carries goods from the beginning to the end of the period at a return of unity. This would put a lower bound on the gross interest rate in the corresponding economy with credit and in any event limits the input k firms wish to utilize in the production of output q, even in the economy without credit. Firms operate in cities and the associated entrepreneurs and workers incur a common cost of living measured by the parameter v.

The choice problem of the entrepreneur is presented first:

$$\pi(b, x, w) = \max_{k, l} \quad f(k, l) - wl - k$$
$$\text{s. t.} \quad k \in [0, b - x], \quad l \geq 0 \tag{8.3}$$

where $\pi(b, x, w)$ denotes the profits of the firm with initial wealth b, without subtracting the setup cost x, given wage w. Since credit markets have not yet been introduced, capital input k cannot exceed the initial wealth b less the setup cost x as in (8.3). This is the key finance constraint of the model. It may or may not be binding depending on x, b, and w. More generally, some firms may produce, but if wealth b is low relative to setup cost x, they may be constrained in capital input use k, that is, for constrained firms, wealth b limits input k. Otherwise unconstrained firms are all alike and have identical incomes before netting out the setup cost x. The capital input k can be zero but not negative.

Even though all agents are born with an inherited nonnegative initial wealth b, not everyone need be a firm. There is also a subsistence agricultural technology with fixed return γ. In the original LEB model everyone is in this subsistence sector initially, at a degenerate steady-state distribution of wealth. For various subsequent periods, labor can be hired from this subsistence sector, at subsistence plus cost of living, thus $w = \gamma + \nu$. When everyone has left this sector, as either a laborer or an entrepreneur, the equilibrium wage will rise. In the simulations we impose an initial distribution of wealth as estimated in the data and allow the parameter γ to increase at an exogenous imposed rate of γ_{gr}, thus also increasing the wage.

For a household with a given initial wealth–cost pair (b, x) and wage w, the choice of occupation reduces to an essentially static problem of maximizing end-of-period wealth $W(b, x, w)$ given in equation (8.4):

$$W(b, x, w) = \begin{cases} \gamma + b & \text{if a subsistence worker} \\ w - \nu + b & \text{if a wage earner} \\ \pi(b, x, w) - x - \nu + b & \text{if a firm} \end{cases} \tag{8.4}$$

At the end of the period all agents take this wealth as given and decide how much to consume C and how much to bequest B to their heirs, that is

$$\max_{C, B} U(C, B)$$
$$\text{s.t.} \quad C + B = W \tag{8.5}$$

In the original LEB model and in simulations here the utility function is Cobb–Douglas, that is

$$U(C, B) = C^{1-\omega}B^\omega \tag{8.6}$$

This functional form yields consumption and bequest decision rules given by constant fractions $1 - \omega$ and ω of the end-of-period wealth, and indirect utility would be linear in wealth. Parameter ω denotes the bequest motive. More general monotonic transformations of the utility function $U(C, B)$ are feasible, allowing utility to be monotonically increasing but concave in wealth. In any event, the overall utility maximization problem is converted into a simple end-of-period wealth maximization problem. If we do not wish to take this short-lived generational overlap too seriously, we can interpret the model as having an exogenously imposed myopic savings rate ω which below we calibrate against the data. We can then focus our attention on the nontrivial endogenous evolution of the wealth distribution.

The key to both static and dynamic features of the model is a partition of the equilibrium occupation choice in (b, x) space into three regions: unconstrained firms, constrained firms, and workers or subsisters. These regions are determined by the equilibrium wage w. One can represent these regions as (b, x) combinations yielding the occupation choices of agents of the model, using the exogenous distribution of costs $H(x, m)$ at each period along with the endogenous and evolving distribution $G_t(b)$ of wealth b. The population of the economy is normalized so that the fractions of constrained firms, unconstrained firms, workers, and subsisters add to unity. This implies that $G_t(b)$ is a cumulative distribution function.

An equilibrium at any date t given the beginning-of-period wealth distribution $G_t(b)$ is a wage w_t, such that given w_t, every agent with wealth–cost pair (b, x) chooses occupation and savings to maximize (8.4) and (8.5), respectively, and the wage w_t clears the labor market in the sense that the number of workers, subsisters, and firms adds to unity. As will be made clear below, existence and uniqueness are assured. Because of the myopic nature of the bequest motive, we can often drop explicit reference to date t.

8.3 The occupation partition

For an individual with beginning-of-period wealth b facing an equilibrium wage w, there are two critical skill levels $x^e(b, w)$ and $x^u(b, w)$ as shown in Figure 8.1. If this individual's skill level x is higher than $x^e(b, w)$, she becomes a worker, whereas if it is lower, she becomes an entrepreneur. Finally, if x is lower than $x^u(b, w)$ she becomes an unconstrained entrepreneur.

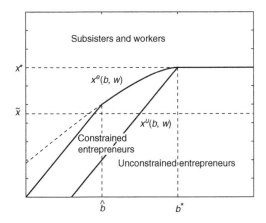

Figure 8.1 Occupational choice map.

We proceed to obtain the curves $x^e(b, w)$ and $x^u(b, w)$. Naturally, these are related to optimal input choice and profitability. Recall that gross profits from setting up a firm are equal to $\pi(b, x, w)$. The optimal choice of labor l given capital $k(b, x, w)$ is given by[9]

$$l(b, x, w) = \frac{\sigma k (b, x, w) + (\xi - w)}{\rho} \tag{8.7}$$

Suppressing the arguments (b, x), we can express profits and labor as a function of capital k given the wage w, namely,

$$\pi(k, w) = f(k, l(k, w))) - wl(k, w)) - k$$

$$= k\left[\alpha - 1 + \frac{\sigma}{\rho}(\xi - w)\right] + \frac{k^2}{2}\left[\frac{\sigma^2}{\rho} - \beta\right] + \frac{(\xi - w)^2}{2\rho} \tag{8.8}$$

which yields a quadratic expression in k.

We define x^* as the maximum fixed cost, such that for any $x > x^*$, the agent will *never* be an entrepreneur. More formally, and suppressing the dependence of profits on the wage w, x^* is such that

$$x^* = \pi^u - w, \quad \text{where } \pi^u = \max_k \pi(k, w) \tag{8.9}$$

that is, if $x > x^*$, the maximum income as an entrepreneur will always be less than w and therefore the agent is always better off becoming a worker.

Denote by b^* the wealth level of an entrepreneur with cost x^* such that she is *just* unconstrained. That is,

$$b^* = x^* + k^u, \quad \text{where } k^u = \arg\max_k \pi(k, w) \tag{8.10}$$

By construction b^* is the wealth level such that for any wealth $b > b^*$ and $x < x^*$, the household would be both a firm and be unconstrained. Therefore by the definition of $x^e(b, w)$ as defining the firm-worker occupation choice indifference point, $x^e(b, w) = x^*$ for $b \geq b^*$. In addition, since $x^u(b, w)$ is the curve separating constrained and unconstrained entrepreneurs, $x^u(b, w) = x^*$ for $b \geq b^*$ also and thus the two curves coincide. Again, see Figure 8.1. Notice that for $b \geq b^*$ and $x \leq x^*$, a firm is fully capitalized at the (implicit) rate of return in the backyard storage technology. In this sense they are neoclassical unconstrained firms.

Now we proceed to define the occupational choice and constrained/unconstrained cutoffs for $b < b^*$. We begin by noting that for $b < b^*$, the agent will always be constrained as a firm at the point of occupational indifference $x^e(b, w)$ between the choice of becoming a worker or an entrepreneur.[10] This fact implies that we can use the constrained capital input $k^c = b - x$ to determine $x^e(b, w)$ with the additional restriction that $x^e(b, w) \leq b$, because the entrepreneur must have enough wealth to afford at least the setup cost.

We define the occupation indifference cost point $x^e(b, w)$ by setting profits in (8.8) less the setup cost equal to the wage. In obvious notation,

$$w = \pi (k^c, w) - x, \quad k^c = b - x \qquad (8.11)$$

This is a quadratic expression in x which, given $b < b^*$ yields the level of x that would make an agent indifferent between becoming an entrepreneur and worker, again, denoted $x^e(b, w)$.[11] It is the only nonlinear segment in Figure 8.1.

The given equation, however, does not restrict x to be lower than b. Define $\hat{b}$, such that $x^e(\hat{b}, w) = \hat{b}$. For $b < \hat{b}$ in Figure 8.1, $x^e(b, w)$ would exceed b. Households will not have the wealth to finance the setup cost x, and are forced to become workers. They are constrained on the extensive margin.[12] Henceforth, we restrict $x^e(b, w)$ to equal to b in this region, $b < \hat{b}$. Note as well that agents with $b = x^e(b, w)$ will start businesses employing only labor as they used up all their wealth financing the setup cost. This captures in an extreme way the idea that small family owned firms use little capital.

8.4   Introducing an intermediated sector

A major feature of the baseline model is the credit constraint in (8.3) associated with the absence of a capital market. For example, a talented person (low fixed cost) may not be able to be an entrepreneur because that person cannot raise the necessary funds to buy capital. Likewise, some firms cannot capitalize at the level they would choose if they could borrow at the implicit backyard rate of return. Thus the most obvious variation to the baseline model is to introduce credit market and allow the fraction of population to this market to increase over time. This is what we mean by a financial liberalization.[13]

We consider an economy with two sectors of a given size at date t, one open to borrowing and lending. Agents born in this sector can deposit their beginning-of-period wealth in the financial intermediary and earn gross interest R on it. If they decide to become entrepreneurs, they can borrow at the interest rate R to finance their fixed cost and capital investment. We suppose that the borrowing and lending rate is the same for all those in the financial, intermediated sector. Again, we do not take liberalization to mean a reduction in the interest rate spread but rather an expansion of access on the extensive margin.

Labor (unlike capital) is assumed to be mobile, so that there is a unique wage rate w for the entire economy, common to both sectors.

Notice that in the intermediated sector, gross profits neither depend on wealth nor setup costs. Since all entrepreneurs operate the same technology and face the same factor prices w and R, they will all operate at the same scale and demand the same (unconstrained) amount of capital and labor, regardless of their setup cost or wealth.

The decision to become an entrepreneur or a worker or subsister is dictated by the value of the fixed cost. Indeed, given factor prices w and R there is a value of $\tilde{x}(w, R)$ at which an agent would be indifferent between the two options. Anybody who has a setup cost greater than $\tilde{x}(w, R)$ will be a worker and vice versa. Figure 8.1 also displays in a thick dotted line the threshold fixed cost $\tilde{x}(w, R)$.

Figure 8.1 is thus the overlap of the occupational map relevant in each sector: thick solid curves for the non-intermediated sector and a thick dotted line for the intermediated one. It thus partitions the (b, x) space into different regions that, as explained in Section 8.9, will experience a differentiated welfare impact from a financial sector liberalization.

As in a standard two-sector neoclassical model, the factor prices R and w can be found solving the credit and labor market clearing conditions. Existence and uniqueness of the equilibrium is again assured.[14] We do suppose a uniform wage, as if all workers were relatively unskilled. We do not distinguish the borrowing and lending rate although typically they differ to cover actual intermediation costs.

8.5   Estimation from micro data

Although the original LEB model without intermediation is designed to explain growth and inequality in transition to a steady state, there are recurrent or repetitive features. Specifically, the decision problem of every household at every date depends only on the individual beginning-of-period wealth b and setup cost x and on the economy-wide wage w. Further, if the initial wealth b and the wage w are observable, while x is not, then the likelihood that an individual will be an entrepreneur can be determined entirely as in the occupation partition diagram from the curve $x^e(b, w)$ and the exogenous distribution of talent $H(x, m)$. That is, the probability that an individual household with initial wealth b will be an entrepreneur is given by $H(x^e(b, w), m)$, and the likelihood that setup cost x is less than or equal to $x^e(b, w)$. The residual probability $1 - H(x^e(b, w), m)$ dictates the likelihood that the individual household will be a wage earner.

The fixed cost x takes on values in the unit interval and yet *enters additively* into the entrepreneur's problem defined at wealth b. Thus setup costs can be large or small relative to wealth depending on how we convert from 1997 Thai baht into LEB units.[15] We therefore search over different scaling factors s in order to map wealth data into the model units. Related to that, we pin down the subsistence level γ in the model by using the estimated scale s to convert to LEB model units, the counterpart of subsistence measured in Thai baht in the data, corresponding to the earnings of those in subsistence agriculture.

Now let θ denote the vector of parameters of the model related to the production function and scaling factor, that is $\theta = (\beta, \alpha, \rho, \sigma, \zeta, s)$. Suppose that we had a sample of n households, and let y_i be a zero–one indicator variable for the observed entrepreneurship choice of household i. Then with the notation $x^e(b_i|\theta, w)$ for the point on the $x^e(b, w)$ curve for household i with wealth b_i, at parameter vector θ with wage w, we can write the explicit log likelihood of the entrepreneurship choice for the n households as

$$L_n(\theta, m) = \frac{1}{n}\sum_{i=1}^{n} y_i \ln H[x^e(b_i|\theta, w), m] + (1 - y_i) \ln \{1 - H[x^e(b_i|\theta, w), m]\}$$

$$(8.12)$$

The parameters over which to search are again the production parameters $(\beta, \alpha, \rho, \sigma, \zeta)$, the scaling factor s and the skewness m of $H(\cdot, m)$.

Intuitively, however, the production parameters in vector θ cannot be identified from a pure cross-section of data at a point in time. For if we return to the decision problem of an entrepreneur facing wage w, we recall that the labor hire decision given by equation (8.7) is a linear function of capital k. Then substituting $l(k, w)$ back into the production function as in equation (8.8), we obtain a relationship between output and capital with a constant term, a linear term in k, and a quadratic term in k. Essentially, then, only three parameters are determined, not five.

If data on capital and labor demand at the firm level were available, we could solve the identification problem by directly estimating the additional linear relation $l(k)$ given in equation (8.7). This would give us two more parameters thus obtaining full identification. Unfortunately, these data are not available. However, equation (8.8) suggests that we can fully identify the production parameters by exploiting the variation in the wages over time observed in the data. The Appendix shows in detail the coefficients estimated and how the production parameters are recovered.

The derivatives of the likelihood in equation (8.12) can be determined analytically, and then with the given observations of a database, standard maximization routines can be used to search for the maximum numerically.[16] The standard errors of the estimated parameters can be computed by bootstrap methods using 100 draws of the original sample with replacement.

It is worthwhile mentioning that for some initial predetermined guesses, the routine converged to different local maxima. However, all estimates using initial guesses around a neighborhood of any such estimate converged to the same estimate. The multiplicity of local maxima may be due to the computational methods available rather than the non-concavity of the objective function in certain regions. See also the experience of Paulson and Townsend[17] (2001) with LEB and other structural models.

We run this maximum likelihood algorithm with two different databases. The first and primary database is the widely used and highly regarded SES[18] conducted by the National Statistical Office in Thailand. The sample is nationally representative, and it includes eight repeated cross-sections collected between 1976 and 1996. The sample size in each cross section: 11,362 in 1976, 11,882 in 1981, 10,897 in 1986, 11,046 in 1988, 13,177 in 1990, 13,459 in 1992, 25,208 in 1994, and 25,110 in 1996. Unfortunately, the data do not constitute a panel, but when stratified by age of the household head, one is left with a substantial sample. As in the complementary work of Jeong and Townsend (2000), we restrict attention to relatively young households, aged 20–29, whose current assets might be regarded somewhat exogenous to their recent choice of occupation. We also restrict attention to households who had no recorded transaction with a financial institution in the month prior to the interview, a crude estimate of lack of financial access, as assumed in the LEB model. However, the SES does not record directly measures of wealth. From the ownership of various household assets, the value of the house, and other rental assets, Jeong (1999) estimates a measure of wealth based on Principal Components Analysis which essentially estimates a latent variable that can best explain the overall variation in the ownership of the house and other household assets.[19]

We use the observations for the first available years, 1976 and 1981, to obtain full identification as the wage varied over these two periods. The sample consists of a total of 24,433 observations with 9,028 observations from 1976 and 15,405 from 1981.

The second dataset is a specialized but substantial cross-sectional survey conducted in Thailand in May 1997 of 2,880 households.[20] The sample is special in that it was restricted to two provinces in the relatively poor semi arid northeast and two provinces in the more industrialized central corridor around Bangkok. Within each province, 48 villages were selected in a stratified clustered random sample. Thus the sample excludes urban households. Within each village 15 households were selected at random. The advantage of this survey is that the household questionnaire elicits an enumeration of all potential assets (household, agricultural, and business), finds out what is currently owned, and if so when it was acquired. In this way, as in Paulson and Townsend (2001), we create an estimate of past wealth, specifically wealth of the household six years prior to the 1997 interview, in 1991. The survey also asks about current and previous occupations of the head, and in this way it creates estimates of occupation transitions, that is, which of the households were not operating their own business before 1992, five years prior to the 1997 interview, and started a business in the following five years. Approximately 21 percent of the households made this transition in the last 5 years and 7 percent between 5 and 10 years ago. A business owner in the Townsend–Thai data is a store owner, shrimp farmer, trader, or mechanic.[21] Among other variables, the survey also records the current education level of household members; the history of use of the various possible financial institutions: formal (commercial banks, Bank for Agricultural cooperatives (BAAC), and village funds) and informal (friends and relatives, landowners, shopkeepers, and moneylenders); and whether households claimed to be currently constrained in the operation of their business.[22,23]

Since the LEB model is designed to explain the behavior of those agents without access to credit, we restrict our sample to those households that reported having no relationship with any formal or informal credit institution, another strength of the survey.[24] A disadvantage of the second dataset is that as a single cross-section, there is no temporal variation in wages. Thus, we identify the production parameters by dividing the observations into two subsamples containing the households in the northeast and central regions, exploiting regional variation in the wages.[25] The final sample consists of a total of 1,272 households with 707 households from the northeast region and 565 households from the central region.

Figure 8.2 displays the occupational map generated using the estimated parameters. For the SES dataset, observations in 1981 seem to be less constrained than those in 1976, naturally as the country was growing and wealth was higher. For the Townsend–Thai dataset, the central region appears to be less credit constrained than the northeast, reflecting perhaps the fact that the central region is more prosperous.

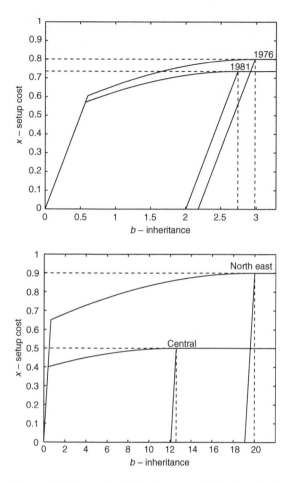

Figure 8.2 Occupational choice map: SES data (top) and Townsend–Thai data (bottom).

Table 8.1 reports the estimated parameters as well as the standard errors.[26] The parameter γ for both datasets was found by multiplying an estimate of the sub-sistence level from the data by the scaling factor estimated. For the SES data, we used the mean income of farmers in 1976 which amounted to 19,274 baht. Analogously, we used the average income of workers in the northeast region without access to credit as reported in the Townsend–Thai data, or 10,727 baht. The wage for the two time periods in the model units at the estimated scaling factor s were $w_{76} = 0.048$ and $w_{81} = 0.053$ for the SES dataset and $w_{NE} = 0.016$ and $w_C = 0.037$ for the two regions in the Townsend–Thai dataset. The maximized value of the likelihood function obtained using the SES data was $-8,233.92$ whereas the Townsend–Thai dataset yielded a value of -616.92.

Table 8.1 MLE results

	SES		Townsend–Thai	
	Coefficient	*S.E.*	*Coefficient*	*S.E.*
Scaling factor s^a	1.4236	0.00881	1.4338	0.03978
Subsistence level γ	0.02744	0.00119	0.01538	0.00408
Fixed cost distribution m	−0.5933	0.05801	0.00559	0.17056
Technology				
α	0.54561	0.06711	0.97545	0.00191
β	0.39064	0.09028	0.0033	0.00013
ρ	0.03384	0.00364	0.00966	0.00692
σ	0.1021	0.02484	0.00432	0.00157
ξ	0.2582	0.03523	0.12905	0.04146
Number of observations	24,433		1,272	
Log-likelihood	−8,233.92		−616.92	

Note
a The parameter value and standard error reported are multiplied by a factor of 10^6.

From the standard errors one can construct confidence intervals. Indeed, they reflect the curvature of the likelihood function at the point estimates and hence they also reveal the potential for errors in the convergence to a global maximum. The magnitude of the standard errors, however, tell us little about how sensitive the dynamics of the model are to the parameters. In Section 8.8 we address this issue by performing a sensitivity analysis. It is also interesting that both estimates of m fall within the permitted boundaries. Related to this, the SES data estimate of the parameter m implies a distribution of talent more skewed toward low cost agents.

8.6   Calibration

We still need to pin down the cost of living ν and the "dynamic" parameters namely the savings rate ω and the subsistence income growth rate γ_{gr}. One way to determine these parameters is using calibration: look for the best ν, ω, and γ_{gr} combination according to some metric relating the dynamic data to be matched with the simulated data.

In this section, we first discuss the Thai macro dynamic data that will be used to calibrate the model and then discuss some issues concerning the calibration itself.

8.6.1   Data

The Thai economy from 1976 to 1996 displayed nontrivial growth with increasing (and then decreasing) inequality. LEB and related models are put forward in the literature as candidate qualitative explanations for this growth experience. Here we naturally go one step further and ask whether the LEB model at some parameter values can match quantitatively the actual Thai economy, focusing in particular on the time series of growth, labor shares, savings rates, fraction of entrepreneurs, and the Gini measure of income inequality. The actual Thai data are summarized in Table 8A.1 in the Appendix.

The data show an initially high net growth rate of roughly 8 percent in the first three years. This then fell to a more modest 4 percent up through 1986. The period 1986–94 displayed a relatively high and sustained average growth of 8.43 percent, and within that from 1987 to 1989 the net growth rate was 8.83 percent. During this same period, the Thai economy GDP growth rate was the highest in the world at 10.3 percent. These high growth periods have attracted much attention. Labor share is relatively stable at 0.40 and rising, after 1990, to 0.45 by 1995. A trend from the 1990–95 data was used to extrapolate labor share for 1996. Savings as a percent of national income was roughly 22 percent from the initial period to 1985. Savings then increased after 1986 to 33 percent in the higher growth period. These numbers, though typical of Asia, are relatively high. The fraction of entrepreneurs is remarkably steady, though slightly increasing, from 14 to 18 percent. The Gini coefficient stood at 0.42 in the 1976 SES survey and increased more or less steadily to 0.53 in 1992. Inequality decreased slightly in both the 1994 and 1996 rounds to 0.50. This downward trend mirrors the rise in the labor share during the same period, and both may be explained by the increase in the wage rate. This level of inequality is relatively high, especially for Asia, and rivals many countries in Latin America (though dominated as usual by Brazil). Other measures of inequality, for example, Lorenz, display similar orders of magnitude within Thailand over time and relative to other countries.[27]

The fraction of population with access to credit in 1976 was estimated at 6 percent and increased by 1996 to 26 percent. The data also reveal that as measure of financial deepening, it grew slowly in the beginning and from 1986 grew more sharply. We recognize that at best this measure of intermediation is a limited measure of what we would like to have ideally, and it seems likely we are off in levels.

8.6.2 Issues in the calibration method

8.6.2.1 Financial liberalization

We begin with the standard, benchmark LEB model, shutting down credit altogether. We then consider an alternative intermediated economy with two sectors, one open to credit and saving. Only labor is mobile, hence a unique wage rate, whereas capital cannot move to the other sector. In other words, a worker residing in the non-intermediated sector may find a job in the credit sector, even though she will not be able to deposit her wealth in the financial intermediary. The relative size[28] of each sector is taken to be exogenous and changing over time given by the fraction of people with access to credit reported in Table 8A.1 in the Appendix. As mentioned, this is our key measure of liberalization.

8.6.2.2   *Initial wealth distribution*

Relevant for dynamic simulations is the initial 1976 economy-wide distribution of wealth.[29] As mentioned before, Jeong (1999) constructs a measure of wealth from the SES data using observations on household assets and the value of owner occupied housing units.

8.6.2.3   *The metric*

Any calibration exercise requires a metric to assess how well the model matches the data. As an example, the business cycles literature has focused on models that are able to generate plausible co-movements of certain aggregate variables with output. Almost by definition, the metric requires that the economy displayed by these models be in a steady state. Even though the economy we consider here eventually reaches a steady state, we are interested in the (deterministic) transition to it, thus the metric put forth as our objective function suffers from being somewhat *ad hoc*. In particular, we consider the normalized sum of the period by period squared deviations of the predictions of the model from the actual Thai data for the five time series[30] displayed in Table 8A.1 in the Appendix. We normalize the deviations in the five variables by dividing them by their corresponding means from the Thai data. More formally,

$$C = \sum_{s=1}^{5} \sum_{t=1976}^{1996} w_{st} \left[\frac{z_{st}^{sim} - z_{st}^{ec}}{\mu_{z_s}} \right]^2 \tag{8.13}$$

where z_s denotes the variable s, t denotes time, and w_{st} is the weight given to the variable s in year t. In order to focus on a particular period, more weight may be given to those years. Analogously, all the weight may be set to one variable to assess how well the model is able to replicate it alone. All weights are renormalized so that they add up to unity. Finally, sim and ec denote respectively "simulated" and "Thai economy," and μ_{z_s} denotes the variable z_s mean from the Thai data.

We search over the cost of living ν, subsistence level growth rate γ_{gr}, and the bequest motive parameter ω using a grid of 20^3 points or combinations of parameters.[31]

All the statistics except the savings rate have natural counterparts in the model. We consider "savings" the fraction of end-of-period wealth bequested to the next generation. The savings rate then is computed by dividing this measure of savings by net income.[32]

8.7   Results

In this section we present the simulation results using the calibrated and estimated parameters from both datasets.

8.7.1 Simulations using SES data parameters

The original LEB model without liberalization fails to explain the levels and changes in roughly all variables.[33] In the simulation, the growth rate of income is flat at roughly 2 percent. Growth is driven mainly by the exogenous growth of the subsistence level γ_{gr}. Overall, the economy shrinks in the early periods, and then by 1983 it grows at the exogenous rate of growth of the subsistence level.

If we had tried to match the growth rate alone, we do somewhat better on that dimension. In fact, we are able to replicate the low growth–high growth phases seen in the data. However, the improvement in the growth rate comes at the expense of increasing the model's savings rate above one from 1985 onwards, far above the actual one. Labor share increases sharply in the model, but not in the data. The income Gini coefficient and the fraction of entrepreneurs are very poorly matched as both drop to zero. The reason for such drastic macroeconomic aggregates is the choice of model parameters which try to match the growth rate of income. The subsistence sector is so profitable relative to setting up a business that by 1988 all entrepreneurial activity disappears and everyone in the subsistence sector earns the same amount. It is clear that focusing on the growth rate alone has perverse effects on the rest of the statistics.

We now modify the benchmark model to mimic what is apparently a key part of the Thai reality, allowing an exogenous increase in the intermediated sector from 6 to 26 percent from 1976 to 1996 as described in Table 8A.1 in the Appendix. We weigh each year and all the variables equally and search again for the parameters ν, ω, and γ_{gr}, allowing the best fit of the five variables. The parameters are $\nu = 0.026$, $\omega = 0.321$, and $\gamma_{gr} = 0$. The corresponding graphs are presented in Figure 8.3.

The intermediated model's explanation of events differs sharply from that of the benchmark without an intermediated sector. Now the model is able to generate simulated time series which track the Thai economy more accurately. In the model, the growth rate of income is again lower than that of the Thai economy. The model still starts with negative growth until 1984. The initial phase of negative growth comes from an initial overly high aggregate wealth in the economy. But growth jumps to 5.4 percent by 1987. This high growth phase comes from the rapid expansion of the intermediated sector during those years. Finally, the growth rate declines after 1987 monotonically, driven by the imposed diminishing returns in the production function. The model matches remarkably well the labor share levels and changes, especially after 1990 where they both show a steady rise. The savings rate is only closely matched for the period 1987–96. The model also predicts a slightly decreasing fraction of entrepreneurs until 1985 and then a steady increase from 8.7 percent in 1985 to 16.1 percent in 1995, resembling more the actual levels. Finally, the Gini coefficient follows a slightly decreasing, then slightly increasing, and finally sharply decreasing trend, starting at 0.481 in 1976, then 0.377 by 1985, increasing to

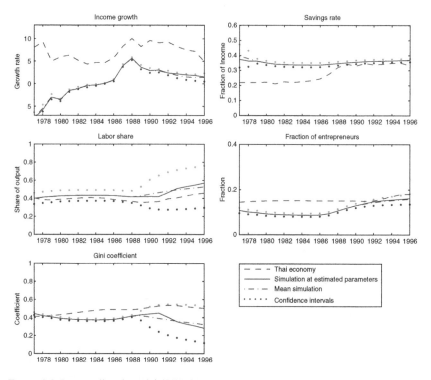

Figure 8.3 Intermediated model (SES data).

0.451 by 1991, and declining again to 0.284 by 1996. Beneath these macro aggregates lie the model's underpinnings. Growth after 1985 is driven by a steady decline out of the subsistence sector, with income from earned wages and from profits steadily increasing to 1990. Profits per entrepreneur are particularly high. Then, with the subsistence sector depleted entirely, the wage increases faster and profits begin to decrease. Thus labor share picks up and inequality falls.

To isolate the role of credit, we can consider the same economy, at the same parameter values, but without the intermediated sector.[34] This experiment will be useful to assess the welfare gains from the liberalization, explained later. In such a no-credit benchmark economy, roughly 80 percent of the labor force are still subsisters by 1996. In fact, this benchmark model is only capable of replicating the savings rate. It under-predicts labor share, the Gini coefficient, and the fraction of entrepreneurs. Income growth is very badly matched, starting low initially and converging from negative to zero growth rate by 1996. We conclude then that the financial liberalization is responsible for the growth experience that the intermediated model displays.

8.7.2   Simulations with parameters from the Townsend–Thai data

The simulation generated from the economy with no access to intermediation at the Townsend–Thai parameters displays similar characteristics to the one using the SES data parameters and hence is not reported.

We now turn attention to the intermediated economy at these parameter values. If we weigh each year and all the variables equally, the calibrated parameters[35] are $\nu = 0.004$, $\omega = 0.267$, and $\gamma_{gr} = 0.006$. The corresponding graphs are presented in Figure 8.4.

The model here also does well at explaining the levels and changes in all variables, even better than the earlier one with the SES data. Striking in particular is the growth rate of income, which although somewhat low in levels, tracks the Thai growth experience well. The model also does remarkably well in matching labor share and the Gini measure of inequality. It under-predicts, however, the fraction of entrepreneurs, although it is able to replicate a positive trend. As usual, the model features a flatter savings rate although it matches well the last subperiod, 1988–96. Economy-wide growth is driven primarily by growth in the intermediated sector.

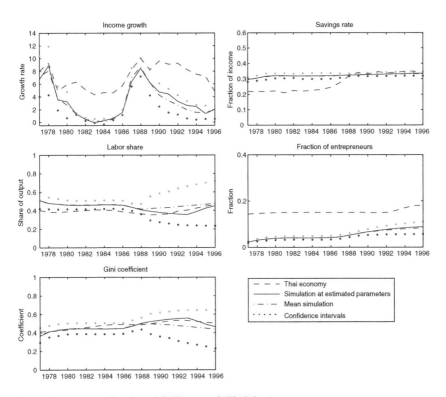

Figure 8.4 Intermediated model (Townsend–Thai data).

That is where the bulk of the economy's entrepreneurs lie and a relatively high number of workers from both the intermediated and non-intermediated sector.

8.8   Sensitivity analysis of MLE parameters

We address the robustness of the model in two ways. First, we change one parameter at a time and check whether the new simulation differs significantly from the benchmark one. Alternatively, we could see how sensitive the model is to changes in *all* the estimated parameters at the same time. We now explain each approach in detail.

From the estimated parameters and their standard errors, confidence intervals can be constructed.[36] One can then set one parameter at a time to its confidence interval lower or upper bound while fixing the rest of the parameters at their original values. Keeping the calibrated parameters also fixed, one can then simulate the economy. When we do this, it becomes clear that the simulations are more sensitive to some parameters than others. The reason is that some parameters are close to the value that would make the constraints described in note 9. When we perturb these parameters by changing them to their confidence interval bounds, we approach the constraints, so the model delivers very different dynamics. This is especially true for the parameters ρ and ξ. In fact, the lower bound of the confidence interval for ρ obtained from the Townsend–Thai dataset violates some of the restrictions that the model must satisfy to be well behaved. Indeed, the unconstrained labor demand is zero, in which case no agent will ever want to become an entrepreneur regardless of his setup cost x.

When we change the setup distribution parameter m beyond its confidence interval to its extreme values of $[-1, 1]$, and still fix the rest of the parameters, we obtain somewhat more distorted pictures than if m were contained in the confidence interval. However, we do not obtain the cycles discussed by Lloyd-Ellis and Bernhardt.

From the confidence intervals of the estimated parameters, we draw at random 5,000 different sets of parameter values. It turns out, by chance, that none violated the conditions in note 9. Notice that since we also vary the scale parameter s, we are examining sensitivity to the initial wealth distribution when we use the SES dataset. Fixing the calibrated parameters at their original level, we run 5,000 simulations for each, the SES and the Townsend–Thai dataset. We then compute the mean and standard deviation at each date over these 5,000 simulations of each of the five variables. Figures 8.3 and 8.4 also display (in dots) the 95 percent confidence intervals around the mean.

Figure 8.3 shows that income growth, the savings rate, and the fraction of entrepreneurs are quite insensitive to changes in the parameters within the 95 percent confidence intervals. Labor share and the Gini coefficient can potentially display different dynamics judging by the wider bands, especially after 1989 at the peak of the credit expansion. The reason for this diversity of paths depends on whether or not the subsistence sector was completely depleted by 1996. If such was the case, then demand for workers would drive up wages, increasing the labor share and reducing inequality. If, on the contrary, such depletion did not occur, labor share would remain fairly stable and inequality could increase.[37]

Similar to the SES data results, the confidence intervals in Figure 8.4 show that the savings rate and the fraction of entrepreneurs are robust to changes in the parameters. Income growth is more sensitive than its SES analogue, especially in the earlier years, 1976–80, and after 1990. However, the bands shrink during the period of high growth. This indicates that all parameter combinations delivered this high growth phase. Finally labor share and the Gini coefficient were very similar to their SES counterparts.

We thus conclude that with the exceptions enumerated earlier, the model is robust to changes in the estimated parameters within their confidence intervals. We are yet more confident that the upturn of the Thai economy in the late 1980s could be attributed to the expansion of the financial sector.

8.9 Welfare comparisons

We seek a measure of the welfare impact of the observed financial sector liberalization. As there can be general equilibrium effects in the model from this liberalization, we need to be clear about the appropriate welfare comparison. We shall compare the economy with the exogenously expanding intermediated sector to the corresponding economy without an intermediated sector at the same parameter values. The criterion will be end-of-period wealth – that is what households in the model seek to maximize. For a given period, then, we shall characterize a household by its wealth b and beginning-of-period cost x and ask how much end-of-period wealth would increase (or decrease) if that household were in the intermediated sector in the liberalized economy, as compared with the same household in the economy without intermediation, a restricted economy.[38]

If in fact the wage is the same in the liberalized and restricted economies, then this is also the obvious, traditional partial equilibrium experiment – a simple comparison of matched pairs, each person with the same (b, x) combination but residing in two different sectors of a given economy, one receiving treatment in the intermediated sector and one without it. The wage is the same with and without intermediation in both SES and Townsend–Thai simulations before 1990, when the subsistence sector is not depleted.

If the wage is different across the two economies, this latter comparison does not measure the net welfare impact of the liberalization. Rather it measures end-of-period welfare differences across sectors of a given economy that has experienced price changes due to liberalization. To be more specific, those in the non-intermediated sector of the liberalized economy will experience the impact of the liberalization through wage changes – workers in the non-intermediated sector may benefit from wage increases while entrepreneurs in the non-intermediated sector suffer losses, since they face a higher wage. And of course there is a similar price impact for those in the intermediated sector, but there is a credit effect there as well. There are such wage effects using the parameters estimated from both datasets after 1990.

More to the point, differences in differences estimates for a given economy provide an inaccurate assessment of welfare changes if liberalization influences the wage. In this case, the differences in differences estimator of income of laborers would only pick up changes in income from savings since both sectors face a common wage. Analogously, losses due to wage changes would not be captured in a comparison of entrepreneurial profits across both sectors.[39]

Implicit in this discussion is another problem which has no obvious remedy here, given the model. Although households in the model maximize end-of-period wealth, they pass on a fraction of that wealth to their heirs. Thus the end-of-period wealth effects of the liberalization are passed onto subsequent generations. The problem is that there is no obvious summary device – households do not maximize discounted expected utility, as in Greenwood and Jovanovic (1990) and the analysis of Townsend and Ueda (2001), for example. Here then we do not attempt to circumvent the problem but rather present the more static welfare analysis for various separate periods. A related issue is the difficulty of weighing welfare changes by the endogenous and evolving distributions of wealth in the two economies – see later for more specifics on that.

We take a look first at the liberalized economy in 1979, three years after the 1976 initial start up, using the overall best fit Townsend–Thai data economy with liberalization. As noted earlier, the wage has not yet increased as a result of the liberalization. Its value is 0.0198 in the liberalized and restricted benchmark economies. The interest rate in the intermediated sector of the liberalized economy is very high, at 93 percent. This reflects the high marginal product of capital in an economy with a relatively low distribution of wealth.

Figure 8.5b displays the corresponding occupation partition, but now denoting for given beginning-of-period (b, x) combinations the corresponding occupation of a household in the no-credit economy and in the credit sector of the intermediated economy. The darker shades of Figure 8.5b denote households with (b, x) combinations that do not change their occupation as a result of the liberalization, that is, they are entrepreneurs (E) in the no-credit (NC) economy and in the intermediated sector of the liberalized (C) economy, or workers (W) in both instances. The light shades denote households that switch: low wealth but low cost agents who were workers become entrepreneurs and high wealth, high cost agents who were entrepreneurs become workers. As explained before, the picture is the overlap of the occupational maps in both sectors. For the credit sector, the key parameter is $\bar{x}$, whereas for the no-credit sector, it is the curve $x^e (b, w)$.

Figure 8.5a displays the corresponding end-of-period wealth percentage changes in the same (b, x) space. Since the wage is the same in both sectors, agents will only benefit from being in the credit sector, not only because they can freely borrow at the prevailing rate if they decide to become entrepreneurs, but also because they can deposit their wealth and earn interest on it. The wealth gain due to interest rate earnings can be best seen by fixing x and moving along the b axis, noting the rise.

If on the other hand we look at the highest wealth, $b = 0.5$ edge, we can track the wealth changes that correspond to changing setup costs x. Going from the rear

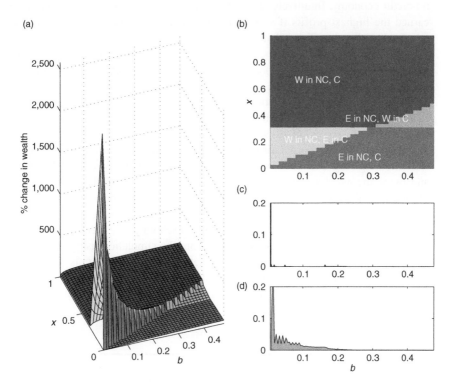

Figure 8.5 Welfare comparison in 1979: Townsend–Thai data. (a) Percent change in wealth in 1979; (b) $w_{NC} = 0.02$, $w_C = 0.02$, $r = 1.93$; (c) and (d) Wealth distribution: Ncr and C.

of the diagram, at high x, we see that the wealth increment is constant, but these households were workers in both economies, so setup costs x are never incurred. Then the wealth increment drops – these households were entrepreneurs in the no-credit economy and were investing some of their wealth in the setup costs x – those with high x gain the most, quitting that investment and becoming workers in the intermediated sector. Thus the percentage wealth increment drops as x decreases. One reaches a trough, however, when the household decides to remain an entrepreneur. Yet lower setup costs benefit entrepreneurs in the intermediated sector more than in the corresponding no-credit economy, because the residual funds can be invested at interest. Hence, the back edge rises up as x decreases further.

The most dramatic welfare gains, however, are experienced by those agents who are compelled to be workers in the no-credit economy but become entrepreneurs in the intermediated sector. Although their setup cost was relatively low, their wealth was not enough to finance it. They were constrained on the extensive margin. When credit barriers are removed, they benefit the most. The sharp vertical rise corresponds to those on the margin of becoming an entrepreneur in the no-credit economy. Intuitively, this is because with their low x, they would have earned the highest profits if they could have been entrepreneurs. Credit in the intermediated sector allows that.

A problem with this analysis, however, is that we may be computing welfare gains for household with (b, x) combinations that do not actually exist in either the liberalized economy or the no-credit economy, that is have zero probability under the endogenous distribution of wealth. To remedy this, Figures 8.5c and 8.5d display the wealth distributions of the no-credit economy and credit economy (over both sectors) in 1979.

The upper part of Table 8.2 displays the welfare gains from liberalization in 1979 for both weighting distributions. The mean gain correspond to roughly 1.5 times and twice the average household yearly 1979 income[40] using the intermediated economy wealth distribution and the non-intermediated economy wealth distribution, respectively, as weighting functions. The modal gains are significantly lower, roughly 17 or 19 percent of the 1979 average household yearly income.

We now turn to the welfare comparison from the simulation using the best fit estimated MLE parameters using the SES data in 1996. The wage is 0.05 in the non-intermediated economy and 0.08 in the intermediated one. Thus, agents that remain workers in the credit sector are better off because they earn a higher

Table 8.2 Welfare gains and losses

	Intermediated economy wealth distribution			Non-intermediated economy wealth distribution		
	1997 Baht	*Dollar*	*% of income*	*1997 Baht*	*Dollar*	*% of income*
Townsend–Thai data, 1979						
Welfare gains						
Mean	82,376	3,295	200.93	61,582	2,463	150.21
Median	22,839	914	55.71	3,676	147	8.97
Mode	7,779	311	18.97	6,961	278	16.98
Percent of population		100			100	
SES data, 1996						
Welfare gains						
Mean	76,840	3,074	100.54	83,444	3,338	109.18
Median	25,408	1,016	33.24	20,645	826	27.01
Mode	25,655	1,026	33.57	18,591	744	24.32
Percent of population		86			95	
Welfare losses						
Mean	117,051	4,682	107.59	115,861	4,634	106.50
Median	113,705	4,548	104.51	112,097	4,484	103.04
Mode	117,486	4,699	107.99	118,119	4,725	108.57
Percent of population		14			5	

wage, and those that remain entrepreneurs in both sectors end up losing somewhat because they face higher labor costs. The interest rate in the intermediated sector has fallen to 9 percent. The occupation partition diagram has no agents who were entrepreneurs becoming workers. In contrast, the relative number of those who were workers and become entrepreneurs is higher. The three-dimensional diagram in Figure 8.6a of wealth changes is still somewhat tilted upward toward high wealth, owing to the interest rate effect. On the back edge, at the highest wealth shown, wealth increments are positive and constant for those who stay as workers, both due to higher wages and interest rate earnings, but those who were workers and become entrepreneurs have high wealth gains which increases as x falls, since net profits of entrepreneurs increases as setup costs fall and funds can be put into the money market. However, one reaches a point where they would have been entrepreneurs in both economies, incurring x in both economies, and then the wealth gains though increasing as x decreases are relatively small or negative. Note that, on the one hand, entrepreneurs in the intermediated sector face higher wages, obtaining lower profits. On the other, they are able to collect interest on their wealth. These opposing wealth effects will translate into net gains or losses depending on their relative magnitude.

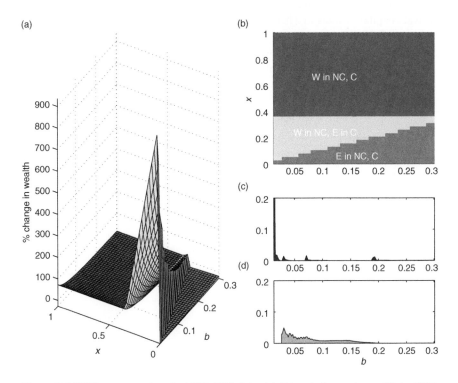

Figure 8.6 Welfare comparison in 1996: SES data. (a) Percent change in wealth in 1996; (b) $w_{NC} = 0.05$, $w_C = 0.08$, $r = 1.09$; (c) and (d) Wealth distribution: Ncr and C.

These welfare gains and losses are reported in the lower part of Table 8.2. Using the intermediated economy wealth distribution as weighting function, the model predicts that 85 percent of the population benefits from the financial liberalization, and an even higher 95 percent if we use the non-intermediated wealth distribution. The modal welfare gains of those who gain correspond to roughly 34 and 24 percent of 1996 average household yearly income. The mean losses, for those worse off amount to 1.08 or 1.06 times the average household yearly income for the sample of entrepreneurs. Thus, it seems that there is a fraction of the population that loses much from the liberalization.

8.10   Extensions: international capital inflows and alternative credit regimes

In this section, we explore two important extensions to the model. These may be viewed as robustness checks to the results presented in the previous sections. The first concerns the liberalization of the capital account that Thailand experienced, especially after 1988. The second relaxes the assumption of restricted credit to allow for some external financing. We now take each one in turn.

Figure 8.7 displays the capital inflows as a fraction of GDP. The data come from the Bank of Thailand as reported in Alba *et al.* (1999). From 1976 to 1986, private capital inflows to Thailand remained relatively low at an average of 1.05 percent of GDP. From 1986 to 1988, however, they increased rapidly to 10 percent of GDP, remaining at that average level until 1996.

This enhanced capital availability was funneled through the financial sector and thus it is modeled here as additional capital for those households that have access to the financial market (i.e. residing in the credit sector). We run this

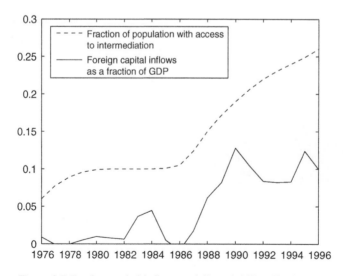

Figure 8.7 Foreign capital inflows and financial liberalization.

extended (open) version of the model at the estimated and calibrated parameters and compare it to the previous closed credit economy model at the same estimated and calibrated parameter values from the two datasets.[41] Although not shown, capital inflows contribute to a larger number of entrepreneurs and larger firm size, in particular, in the late 1980s and early 1990s. Since the marginal product of labor increases with capital utilization, more labor is demanded and thus the fraction of subsisters is depleted earlier. Thus labor share rises and inequality decreases, both relative to the actual path and relative to the earlier simulation. The interest rate tends to be lower with capital inflows. Nevertheless, the welfare changes are small, indeed, almost negligible.

Because the surge in capital inflows coincides with the phase of high growth of per capita GDP, it has often been portrayed as an important factor contributing to that high growth. In order to disentangle the extent to which the phase of high growth was due to increased participation in the credit market versus additional capital availability due to capital account liberalization, we simulate the economy at the estimated and calibrated parameter values allowing for international capital inflows but using a linearized credit participation from 6 to 26 percent, that is, a 1 percent increase per year for each of the 20 years. As displayed in Figure 8.8, this version of the model fails to match the upturn in GDP growth as compared to the benchmark credit economy. Thus, it seems from the model that capital inflows *per se* were not the cause of the high growth that Thailand experienced in the late 1980s.

The assumption of restricted credit may artificially deliver quantitatively large welfare gains from liberalization if those assumed to have no access were in fact able to receive some credit, perhaps from informal sources. Indeed, in the model so far, we have not allowed any form of lending (formal or informal) for those households residing in the no-credit sector. We now relax that assumption and explore whether the welfare gains from liberalization would differ significantly from those reported in the previous section.

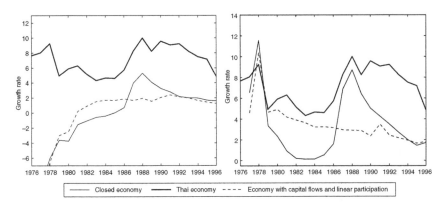

Figure 8.8 Access to capital and foreign capital inflows: SES (left) and Townsend–Thai (right).

We follow Lloyd-Ellis and Bernhardt (2000) and introduce intermediation which is limited by a moral hazard problem.[42] In particular, given an interest rate of r, possibly different from that in the formal sector, entrepreneurs borrow L and put up their wealth b as collateral. After production they can abscond losing rb but escaping the repayment obligation rL. Absconders are apprehended with probability p and if so they can hide their income but receive a punishment corresponding to an additive disutility of d. Borrowers will renege on the loan contract if $rb + pd < rL$, so lenders only make loans that satisfy $L \leq b + \Delta$, where $\Delta = pd/r$. Thinking again about help from friends and relatives, we set $r = 1$ so that the objective function for households that now can "borrow" from the informal sector is the same as before. However, the constraint in (8.3) is now modified to

$$k + x \leq b + \Delta$$

In effect, parameter Δ is treated as a lump sum addition to wealth but only for those who borrow from the informal sector and choose to start firms. This would allow more talented households to alleviate credit constraints.[43]

As shown in the Appendix, parameter Δ would be identified in cross-sectional MLE. However, to give parameter Δ a greater opportunity to influence the dynamic paths relative to the earlier simulation, we calibrate the parameter Δ against the dynamic aggregate data for each dataset using the previously estimated and calibrated parameter values for the other parameters. The calibrated values of parameter Δ are $\Delta = 0.0163$ for the Townsend–Thai dataset and $\Delta = 0.0082$ for the SES dataset. These correspond to 1.1 times and 30 percent of the subsistence income in 1976 for each dataset respectively.

Similar to the open economy version, the increased informal finance speeds up the creation of firms resulting in an earlier depletion of the fraction of subsisters. Again, labor share begins to increase along with a decline in the Gini coefficient, both at an earlier date.

Although the parameter Δ could in principle have a large welfare impact, at the calibrated parameter Δ that best fits the Thai economy, these welfare gains and losses remain much as before. In particular, the counterparts of Figures 8.5a–8.6a still feature the tent-shaped gains for relatively talented but poor people. Recall that in the intermediated sector, only the most talented individuals will start a firm, irrespective of their wealth. However, even when we relax the constraint in the no-credit sector by allowing informal finance, wealth still matters in determining who becomes an entrepreneur, and thus the tent-shaped welfare gains still appear. In addition, the increased wage in the latter periods does benefit workers in the liberalized economy. In the no-credit economy which now has informal credit, some households become richer but the additional capital from informal sources is insufficient to trigger an increase in the equilibrium wage rate. Thus, in the welfare experiment comparing the intermediated to the no-formal-credit economies, wage earners benefit more from the liberalization, but not much. In contrast, firms lose from the relative increase in the wage, but not much.

A prediction of the model that could seemingly be checked in the data concerns rates of return to capital. One might suppose that with limited credit the rate of return to capital would be high. This is true for some firms in the simulations. However, for other firms without access to intermediation, wealth cannot be lent at interest and is thus invested internally at low rates of return. Thus the implication of the model is unclear about the mean, average rate of return to capital and only asserts that the dispersion of rates of return is higher for firms without access relative to those who can borrow and lend.

8.11   Conclusions

From the welfare numbers presented, there seems to be a lot at stake in credit liberalizations. Even by our most conservative estimates there is a group of low wealth talented households that have much to gain, period by period, in income and wealth. On the other hand, the estimates reveal a group of entrepreneurs who have much to lose, period by period, in income and wealth, particularly if one takes into account the growth in wages. We do not push here any particular number as the most compelling, because the numbers do vary and do depend on the dataset used. Indeed, the larger point is that welfare gains and losses are sensitive to the presumed, estimated micro underpinnings of the economy. If there were more substantial intermediation, then variations associated with further liberalization would matter less. Indeed, if there were more substantial intermediation, then the impact on dynamics of (endogenous) changes in the wealth distribution would matter less, as in Krusell and Smith (1998). But the micro data reject such presumed underpinnings, making welfare gains, potential losses, and the dynamic aspect of liberalization more substantial.

Still, the surprisingly large order of magnitude of these gains and losses suggests the need for further refinements along a number of dimensions, to see if the magnitude survives somewhat more realistic specifications.

One refinement has to do with labor and the labor market. The labor of the model here is uniform with respect to productivity, that is, every laborer earns the same wage. This flies in the face of much empirical work mapping wage differentials to skills differentials and acquired human capital. More generally, earnings inequality contributes to overall inequality, and this might be salient, as in the work of Paes de Barros *et al.* (1995) in Brazil, for example. Jeong and Townsend (2000) document the success and failure of the LEB model in explaining inequality movements in Thailand, comparing it to an extended version of Greenwood and Jovanovic (1990). Though the LEB model at the maximum likelihood parameter estimates does surprisingly well, it is clear that wage differentiation is needed in models and in model-based empirical work. In the model of occupation choice of Evans and Jovanovic (1989), for example, unobserved heterogeneous skills influence both wage earnings and the profits from entrepreneurship. This might suggest that entrepreneurs worry less about increased wages as they potentially exit to become part of a skilled work force.

Second, one could endogenize access to credit as in the Greenwood and Jovanovic (1990) model with transactions costs. This would slow down the growth of financial infrastructure and would rationalize some of the limited participation that we see but there would be no Pareto-improving policy intervention. However, Townsend and Ueda (2001) in an extended version of the Greenwood and Jovanovic model draw the conclusion that restrictive financial sector policies may have nevertheless slowed down entry into the financial sector below the endogenous rate. Thus financial sector liberalization, allowing intermediation at its otherwise endogenous value, is also associated with welfare gains, as in this chapter. Although occupation choice models should allow more endogenous financial sector participation, they illustrate well as they stand the fact that there may be welfare losses for some sectors of the population, and not just gains to liberalization. This offers a political economy rational for the apparently restrictive policies that we observed in Thailand.

Third, the imagined industrial organization of the Thai economy is relatively simple. In the model here, fixed setup costs are allowed to vary across potential entrepreneurs, as if drawn from a quadratic cumulative distribution, but the quadratic production function mapping labor and capital into output is uniform across potential entrepreneurs. This delivers the occupation partition diagram and variation over time in the size distribution of firms, a function of the wage and the endogenous distribution of wealth. Indeed, an industrial organization literature starting with Lucas (1978) begins the same way, at least in spirit. He postulates an underlying distribution of personal managerial talent and then studies the division of persons into managers and employees and the allocation of productive inputs across managers. This has implications for secular changes in average firm size. This point is revisited by Gollin (1999).

Here the distribution of size and profits among firms is driven by self-financing, an endogenous and evolving distribution of wealth, and differential access to credit. That is, high setup costs and limited credit can limit the use of real physical capital in the standard part of the production function or can impede entry entirely. Likewise, some portion of end-of-period profits is passed on to subsequent time periods if not subsequent generations. This could be an explanation for some of the serial correlation in size, profits, and employment that is seen in actual data, even when shocks in the form of setup costs are independent and identically distributed over time and households. There would be implications for the cross-sectional dispersion in growth rates. Indeed, it seems that in Thailand larger firms, those with financial access, may have grown faster than smaller ones as the credit market expanded in the late 1980s. Recent theoretical work is beginning to readdress earlier the supposed facts of firm growth and survival in the context of endogenous limited financial contracts. See Albuquerque and Hopenhayn (2004), and Cooley *et al.* (2004).

More generally both the industrial organization and credit market literature need to be brought together. Existing empirical work has documented relationships between investment and the balance sheet, for example, but much of this work is somewhat atheoretic, documenting that the world is not neoclassical but leaving us wondering what the impediments to trade really are. The general equilibrium models of Banerjee and Newman (1993), Piketty (1997), and Aghion and Bolton (1997) take different stands on those underpinnings but collectively make the point that growth and inequality can be related to imperfect credit markets. That of course was our starting point here.

Indeed, in related work Paulson and Townsend (2001) use the Townsend–Thai data to estimate via maximum likelihood methods not only the LEB model featured here, but also collateral-based lending as in model of Evans and Jovanovic (1989) (EJ for short), for example, and also incentive-based lending as in the mechanism design literature of Aghion and Bolton (1997) and Lehnert (1998) (ABL for short). Observed relationships of entrepreneurship, investment, and access to credit as functions of wealth and talent suggest that the ABL model fits the micro Thai data best, but the EJ model fits well for those with relatively low levels of wealth and those in the northeast, while LEB, the model here, is a close contender. This suggests that a calculation of the welfare gains and losses to financial intermediation based on these other models would be worthwhile, though the average and modal estimates here should not be rejected out of hand. It does seem plausible, however, that the dramatic gains near the wealth equal setup costs or 45° line would be vulnerable to alternative specifications.

The growth and inequality literature relying on each of these underpinnings presupposes, as in the LEB model here, either an overlapping generations model with a bequest motive or a simplistic, myopic solution to the household savings problem. More needs to be done to make the models dynamic. Coupling households with firms and modeling the firms' inter-temporal decision problems will require more work, but again, given the preliminary results here, that work would appear to be warranted.

8A.1 Appendix

8A.1.1 Data

Data on the growth rate of GDP is taken from the computations of Tinakorn and Sussangkarn (1998) of the Thailand Development Research Institute (TDRI). They use data from the the National Economic Social Development Board (NESDB) in Thailand. Data for the missing years 1976–80 were taken directly from the NESDB "Gross Regional Product and Gross Provincial Product" national income accounts and for 1996 as reported by the Bank of Thailand. The real GDP growth series in Table 8A.1 is constructed by subtracting a three-year moving average of the reported Total Factor Productivity (TFP) growth in Tinakorn and Sussangkarn (1998) from the observed GDP growth rate. TFP growth was extrapolated for the missing years. We subtract TFP growth because we are only interested in growth due to factor accumulation, as the model allows no technological progress.[44] The data on labor share come also from the calculations of Tinakorn and Sussangkarn (1998). The savings rate can also be estimated from national income accounts. Here we use the numbers provided by the Bank of Thailand from 1980 to 1996 and extrapolate the missing years. Data on the number of entrepreneurs as a fraction of the Thai population come from successive rounds of the national level income and expenditures SES mentioned earlier, administered by the National Statistics

Table 8A.1 Thai data

Year	GDP growth	Savings rate	Labor share	Fraction of entrepreneur	Income Gini	Financial liberalization
1976	7.656	0.219	0.402	0.140	0.418	0.060
1977	8.048	0.219	0.402	0.143	0.412	0.078
1978	9.255	0.219	0.382	0.146	0.413	0.089
1979	4.944	0.219	0.380	0.148	0.420	0.096
1980	5.911	0.222	0.388	0.149	0.430	0.099
1981	6.309	0.210	0.395	0.150	0.443	0.100
1982	5.149	0.224	0.401	0.150	0.457	0.100
1983	4.328	0.220	0.407	0.151	0.469	0.100
1984	4.662	0.225	0.405	0.150	0.480	0.100
1985	4.607	0.231	0.401	0.150	0.487	0.101
1986	5.737	0.244	0.385	0.150	0.489	0.105
1987	8.262	0.275	0.373	0.150	0.486	0.124
1988	10.008	0.320	0.365	0.150	0.486	0.150
1989	8.231	0.341	0.351	0.150	0.496	0.172
1990	9.580	0.330	0.357	0.150	0.512	0.190
1991	9.078	0.347	0.362	0.148	0.527	0.206
1992	9.237	0.338	0.393	0.150	0.535	0.220
1993	8.237	0.341	0.404	0.158	0.532	0.231
1994	7.515	0.348	0.425	0.170	0.521	0.240
1995	7.181	0.349	0.447	0.179	0.509	0.249
1996	4.850	0.332	0.458	0.180	0.503	0.260

Office. Here we use the occupation of the head of the household unit. There are four broad categories for occupation: wage worker, farmer, non-farm entrepreneur, and inactive. We define entrepreneur as the head of household listed as non-farm entrepreneur. We approximate the missing years using cubic spline interpolation. The same SES surveys were used to compute the widely used Gini index as a measure of inequality. Finally, we again use the SES data and the calculations of Jeong (1999) to determine the fraction of the population which has access to intermediated, credit, and savings markets, that is, that reside in the credit sector.[45]

8A.1.2   ML estimation

In this appendix we first derive the parameters that are estimated and then show how we recover the five technology parameters from the ML estimates. We then explain in full detail the constraints on the parameter space imposed by the theory.

8A.1.2.1   Deriving the estimated parameters

The occupation indifference point x^e (b, w) given in Equation (8.11) in the main text can be written as

$$w = k\left[\alpha + \frac{\sigma}{\rho}(\xi - w)\right] + \frac{k^2}{2}\left(\frac{\sigma^2}{\rho} - \beta\right) + \frac{(\xi - w)^2}{2\rho} - k - x \qquad (8A.1.2.1)$$

Define the following constants

$$K_1 = \frac{\sigma^2}{\rho} - \beta, \quad K_2 = \alpha + \frac{\sigma}{\rho}(\xi - w) \quad \text{and} \quad K_3 = \frac{(\xi - w)^2}{\rho} \qquad (8A.1.2.2)$$

We can then write equation (8A.1.2.1) as

$$w = \frac{(b-x)^2}{2}K_1 + (b-x)K_2 + \frac{K_3}{2} - b \qquad (8A.1.2.3)$$

where we made explicit again that $k^c = b - x$.

Solving the given quadratic equation for x and taking the root which ensures[46] that $dk/dx > 0$ in (8A.1.2.1), we obtain

$$x^e(b, w) = b + \frac{K_2 - \sqrt{K_2^2 - K_1[K_3 - 2(w + b)]}}{K_1} \qquad (8A.1.2.4)$$

The constants which can be estimated are K_1, $K_2(w)$, and $K_3(w)$ defined earlier in equation (8A.1.2.2) where now the dependence on the wage w is made explicit in the notation. It can be shown with some tedious algebra that numbers like $k^u(w)$, $\hat{b}(w)$, and $b^*(w)$ in Figure 8.1 are entirely determined by these constants. In addition, with a non-linear transformation into constants

$$C_1(w) = -\frac{K_2(w)}{K_1}, \quad C_2(w) = \frac{2w - K_3(w)}{K_1}, \quad \text{and} \quad C_3 = -\frac{2}{K_1} \qquad (8A.1.2.5)$$

we can rewrite all the key parameters of the occupation partition as follows:

$$\hat{b}(w) = \frac{C_2(w)}{C_3}, \quad b^*(w) = \frac{C_1(w)^2 + C_2(w)}{C_3} - \frac{C_3}{4},$$

$$x^*(w) = \frac{C_3}{4} + \frac{C_1(w)^2 + C_2(w)}{C_3} - C_1(w) \qquad (8A.1.2.6)$$

and finally, as in equation (8A.1.2.4),

$$x^e(b, w) = b - C_1(w) + \sqrt{C_1(w)^2 + C_2(w)} - C_3 b \qquad (8A.1.2.7)$$

In the estimation, we make use of the constants defined in (8A.1.2.5) rather than those in (8A.1.2.2) because as equation (8A.1.2.7) shows, the unknown parameters enter additively or with low power on exponents rather than the more complicated case of (8A.1.2.4).

As explained in Section 8.5, only three parameters are identified in a simple cross-section and not five. However, if we exploit the variation in the wages observed in the data we can fully identify all the production parameters. In particular, if we are able to partition the original sample into two subsamples[47] facing different underlying wages $w_j, j = 1, 2$, then we obtain estimates of C_{11}, C_{12}, C_{21}, C_{22}, C_3, and m, where $C_{ij} = C_i(w_j)$. More specifically, if we group the parameters m, C_{11}, C_{21}, C_3 for Subsample 1 and m, C_{12}, C_{22}, C_3 for Subsample 2, with m and C_3 common across subsamples, then the likelihood of the sample in the two regions is determined. In other words, the MLE algorithm searches over the parameters C_{ij}, C_3, m, and s in such a way as to make the observed sample most likely. Then, the five production parameters can be recovered from the four C_{ij}, C_3, and an estimate of the average wage[48] in each subsample converted to LEB units. Therefore, full identification is achieved.

Finally, Equation (8A.1.2.7) can be modified to allow for the limited intermediation introduced in Section 8.10:

$$x^e(b, w, \Delta) = b + \Delta - C_1(w) + \sqrt{C_1(w)^2 + \tilde{C}_2(w)} - C_3 b$$

where

$$\tilde{C}_2(w) = \frac{2(w + \Delta) - K_3(w)}{K_1} \tag{8A.1.2.8}$$

It is clear from the expression above that Δ enters as a separate parameter and would be identified in cross-sectional MLE.

8A.1.2.2   Recovering the technology parameters

Given the estimates of C_{11}, C_{12}, C_{21}, C_{22}, and C_3 we first recover the constants K_1 and K_{21}, K_{22}, K_{31}, K_{32} where $K_{ij} = K_i(w_j)$ as before. From the definition of the Cs given in (8A.1.2.5), we can write

$$K_1 = -\frac{2}{C_3}, \quad K_2(w) = \frac{2C_1(w)}{C_3} \quad \text{and} \quad K_3(w) = 2\left(w + \frac{C_2(w)}{C_3}\right) \tag{8A.1.2.9}$$

We now use the definition of the K's given in equation (8A.1.2.2) to recover the five production parameters. We first find ξ by dividing K_{31} by K_{32}. After some algebra we obtain

$$\xi = \frac{w_2\sqrt{K_{31}} - w_1\sqrt{K_{32}}}{\sqrt{K_{31}} - \sqrt{K_{32}}} \tag{8A.1.2.10}$$

Using the definition of either K_{31} or K_{32} and using the expression for ξ derived above we obtain a similar expression for ρ:

$$\rho = \left(\frac{w_2 - w_1}{\sqrt{K_{31}} - \sqrt{K_{32}}}\right)^2 \tag{8A.1.2.11}$$

Now subtracting K_{22} from K_{21} and using the expression for ρ we can solve for the parameter σ yielding

$$\sigma = \frac{(w_2 - w_1)(K_{21} - K_{22})}{(\sqrt{K_{31}} - \sqrt{K_{32}})^2} \tag{8A.1.2.12}$$

We obtain α by using the expressions for σ and ρ just derived and either combination of K_{21}, w_1 or K_{22}, w_2 into its definition. After some algebra, we obtain

$$\alpha = \frac{K_{22}\sqrt{K_{31}} - K_{21}\sqrt{K_{32}}}{\sqrt{K_{31}} - \sqrt{K_{32}}} \tag{8A.1.2.13}$$

Finally, we recover β from its definition using the expressions from σ^2 and ρ. This yields

$$\beta = \left(\frac{K_{21} - K_{22}}{\sqrt{K_{31}} - \sqrt{K_{32}}}\right)^2 - K_1 \tag{8A.1.2.14}$$

8A.1.2.3 Constraints on the parameter space

The nature of the constraints that the model suggests should be imposed on the parameter space guided by the choice of the MATLAB maximization routine fmincon. It allows for bounds, and for linear and non-linear constraints. In what follows, we explain each in turn. The parameters that the algorithm searches over are m, C_{11}, C_{12}, C_{21}, C_{22}, C_3, and s. First, the specification of the talent distribution restricts the support of $m \in [-1, 1]$. In addition, the expression for profits given in (8.8), written as a quadratic expression in k, is well-behaved as long as the constant K_2 defined in (8A.1.2.2) is negative. This implies that C_3 needs to be positive. Finally, the scaling factor s must be positive.

In addition to these bounds on the parameters, the critical value of $\hat{b}$ must satisfy

$$0 \le \hat{b}(w_i) \le 1 \quad \text{for } i = 1, 2 \tag{8A.1.2.15}$$

If the cutoff value $\hat{b}$ is larger than 1, then the parameters governing the cutoff level x^i given in (8A.1.2.7) will not be identified. However, since the probability of being a worker and having wealth in LEB units $b > 1$ is zero, the log-likelihood of this zero probability event is minus infinity and so we do not need to impose the restriction.

In addition, since the cutoff level x^i is increasing in b and concave, it must be the case that

$$\hat{b}(w_i) \le x^*(w_i) \quad \text{and} \tag{8A.1.2.16}$$

$$x^*(w_i) \le b^*(w_i) \quad \text{for } i = 1, 2 \tag{8A.1.2.17}$$

It turns out that both expressions are satisfied if $k_i'' > 0$ for $i = 1, 2$ or in terms of the estimates, if we impose the linear constraints

$$C_{1i} > \frac{C_3}{2} \quad \text{for } i = 1, 2 \tag{8A.1.2.18}$$

Finally, note 9 imposes additional constraints on the parameters. In particular, $\xi > w_i$ for $i = 1, 2$ and $\sigma > 0$. Assume without loss of generality that $w_2 > w_1$.

226   *Xavier Giné and Robert M. Townsend*

From the expression for ξ in equation (8A.1.2.10), $\xi > w_2$ as long as $K_{31} > K_{32}$. Some algebra yields that this is equivalent to

$$\hat{b}_1 - \hat{b}_2 > w_2 - w_1$$

or in terms of the estimated parameters,

$$C_{21} > C_{22} + C_3(w_2 - w_1) \tag{8A.1.2.19}$$

Likewise, from the expression for σ in equation (8A.1.2.12), $\sigma > 0$ as long as $K_{21} > K_{22}$. We can rewrite this as

$$k_1^u > k_2^u \quad \text{or simply} \quad C_{11} > C_{12} \tag{8A.1.2.20}$$

However, in the actual estimation rather than imposing the constraints given in (8A.1.2.19) and (8A.1.2.20) *ex ante*, we learned from experience that the numerical algorithm performed better without imposing them, then checking and eliminating the estimates that did not satisfy them after convergence had been achieved.

Acknowledgment

We would like to thank Guillermo Moloche and Ankur Vora for excellent research assistance and the referees for their both detailed and expository comments. Giné gratefully acknowledges financial support from the Bank of Spain. Townsend would like to thank NSF and NIH for their financial support. We are especially indebted to Sombat Sakuntasathien for collaboration and for making possible the data collection in Thailand. Comments from Abhijit Banerjee, Ricardo Caballero, Bengt Holmström, and participants at the MIT macro lunch group are gratefully acknowledged. We are responsible for all the errors.

Notes

1 See for example Gallup *et al.* (1998) and Dollar and Kraay (2002) for evidence that growth helps reduce poverty and the concerns of Ravallion (2001, 2002) about their approach.
2 We focus on this 20-year transition period, not on the financial crisis of 1997. Our own view is that we need to understand the growth that preceded the crisis before we can analyze the crisis itself.
3 Okuda and Mieno (1999) recount from one perspective the history of financial liberalization in Thailand, that is, with an emphasize on interest rates, foreign exchange liberalization, and scope of operations. They argue that in general there was deregulation and an increase in overall competition, especially from the standpoint of commercial banks. It seems that commercial bank time deposit rates were partially deregulated by June 1989 and on-lending rates by 1993, hence with a lag. They also provide evidence that suggests that the spread between commercial bank deposit rates and on-lending

prime rates narrowed from 1986 to 1990, though it increased somewhat thereafter, to June 1995. Likewise there was apparently greater competition from finance companies, and the gap between deposit and share rates narrowed across these two types of institutions, as did on-lending rates. Thai domestic rates in general approached from above international, London Interbank Offered Rate (LIBOR) rates. Most of the regulations concerning scope of operations, including new licenses, the holding of equity, and the opening of off-shore international bank facilities are dated March 1992 at the earliest. See also Klinhowhan (1999) for further details.

4 See Greenwood and Jovanovic (1990) or Townsend and Ueda (2001).

5 We use the functional forms contained in the 1993 working paper, although the published version contains slight modifications (Lloyd-Ellis and Bernhardt (1993)).

6 See Griffin *et al.* (1987) and references therein.

7 In extended models this would be the analog to the distribution of human capital, although obviously the education investment decision is not modeled here.

8 We also estimate the LEB model for various stratifications of wealth, for example, above and below the median, to see how parameter m varies with wealth. This way, wealth and talent are allowed to be correlated. Even though the point estimates of m vary significantly, simulations with the different estimates of m are roughly similar.

9 For certain combinations of σ, ξ, and ρ, labor demand could actually be *negative*. Lloyd-Ellis and Bernhard did not consider these possibilities by assuming that $\xi > w$, and $\sigma > 0$, $\rho > 0$. However, one could envision situations where $\xi < w$ and $\sigma > 0$ in which case, for low values of capital k it may not pay to use labor. Still at the same parameters, if the capital employed were large, then the expression in (8.7) may be positive. The intuition is that although labor is rather unproductive, it is complementary to capital. In this chapter, however, we follow Lloyd-Ellis and Bernhard and assume that such cases of negative labor do not arise. Therefore, capital and labor demands will always be non-negative.

10 Intuitively, if the agent were not constrained, it can be shown that he would strictly prefer to be an entrepreneur than a worker, contradicting the claim. Assume that $b < b*$ and suppose the agent is not constrained. Then, $x + k^u < b$ or $x < b* - k^u = x*$. Given that $\pi^u - x* = w$ (from equation (8.9)), it follows that $\pi^u - x > w$, hence the agent is not indifferent.

11 See Appendix B for the explicit solution.

12 According to the model we need to restrict the values of x^u and x^e to the range of their imposed domain, namely [0, 1]. Note for example that if the previously defined $x^e(b, w)$ were negative at some wealth b, everyone with that wealth b would become a worker. Alternatively, if $x^e(b, w)$ crossed 1 then everyone with that wealth b would be an entrepreneur. We therefore restrict x^e and x^u to lie within these boundaries, by letting them coincide with the boundaries {0, 1} otherwise.

13 The model is at best a first step in making the distinction between agents with and without access to credit. Here we assume that intermediation is perfect for a fraction of the population and nonexistent for the other. We do not model selection of customers by banks, informational asymmetries, nor variation in the underlying technologies.

14 Note in particular that *Net* aggregate deposits in the financial intermediary can be expressed as total wealth deposited in the intermediated sector less credit demanded for capital and fixed costs. For low levels of aggregate wealth, the amount of deposits will constrain credit and the net will be zero. However, note that net aggregate deposits can be strictly positive if there is enough capital accumulation, in which case the savings and the storage technology are equally productive, both yielding a gross return of $R = 1$.

15 The relative magnitude of the fixed costs will drop as wealth evolves over time.

16 In particular, we used the MATLAB routine fmincon starting from a variety of predetermined guesses.

17 See their technical appendix for more information about the estimation technique and its drawbacks.

18 See Jeong(1999) for details or its use in Deaton and Paxson (2000) or Schultz (1997).

19 See Jeong (1999) and Jeong and Townsend (2000) for details.

20 Robert M. Townsend is the principal investigator for this survey. See Townsend *et al.* (1997).

21 Reassuringly, table 1C in Paulson and Townsend (2001) shows that the initial investment necessary to open a business is the roughly same in both regions among the most common types of businesses.

22 The percentage of households in non-farm businesses is 13 and 28 percent in the central versus northeast regions. The fraction of the population with access to formal credit (from commercial banks or BAAC) is 34 and 55 percent for non-business versus business, respectively, in the northeast region, and 48 and 73 percent, respectively, for the central region.

23 Paulson and Townsend (2001) provide a much more extensive discussion of the original data, the derivation of variables to match those of the LEB model, additional ML estimates of the LEB model, and the relationship of LEB estimates to those of various other models of occupation choice. However, the maximum likelihood procedure in Paulson and Townsend (2001) is different to the one discussed here in that no attempt is made to recover the underlying production parameters.

24 These households, however, could have borrowed from friends and relatives, although the bulk of the borrowing through this source consists of consumption loans rather than business investments.

25 Unfortunately, estimating a model that features a unique wage by exploiting the geographical variation in the wage observed in the data is a contradiction. Of course costly migration could be introduced but we do not take that explicit approach here. We draw some confidence from the fact that these are secondary data and we are comparing its estimates to those from the SES dataset, with its temporal variation in wages consistent with the estimated model.

26 Note that $\xi > w_{76}$, $\xi > w_{81}$ and $\xi > w_{NE}$, $\xi > w_C$ and $\rho > 0$, $\sigma > 0$ for both datasets as required in note 9.

27 The interested reader will find a more detailed explanation in Jeong (1999).

28 We assume that the intermediated sector, with its distribution of wealth, is scaled up period by period according to the exogenous credit expansion. Alternatively, we could have sampled from the no-credit sector distribution of wealth and selected the corresponding fraction to the exogenous expansion, but the increase is small and his would have made little difference in the numerical computations.

29 Since this estimated measure of wealth is likely to differ in scale and units to the wealth reported in the Townsend–Thai data, we allow for a different scaling factor to convert SES wealth into the model units. In other words, we use *two* scaling factors when we calibrate the model using the parameters estimated with the Townsend–Thai data. One is estimated with ML techniques and converts wealth and incomes reported in the data, whereas the other is calibrated and converts the SES wealth measure used to generate the economy-wide initial distribution.

30 Note that in computing the growth rate we lose one observation, so the time index in the formula given in (8.13) runs from 1977 to 1996 for the growth rate statistic.

31 As mention earlier, when we use the Townsend–Thai data, we also search over a grid of 20 scaling factors for the initial distribution of wealth.

32 More formally we can express the savings rate (in an economy without credit) as

$$\text{Savings rate} = \frac{\omega \int_{\mathbb{B}} \int_0^1 W(b,\ x,\ w)\, dH(x,m)\, dG(b)}{\int_{\mathbb{B}} \int_0^1 Y(b,\ x,\ w)\, dH(x,m)\, dG(b)} \tag{8.14}$$

where income $Y (b, x, w)$ is given by $W (b, x, w) = Y (b, x, w) + b$ as expressed in equation (8.4). Note that for some parameters, the savings rate may be larger than 1.

33 See the working paper version for graphs of this simulation (Giné and Townsend (2003)).

34 A more natural benchmark would be an intermediated economy where the intermediated sector is fixed at 6 percent, the level estimated at the beginning of the sample in 1976. As will become clear in Section 8.9, the welfare comparison is however complicated because we now have two sectors in both economies, the one which is fixed at 6 percent throughout and the one with further deepening. We have run the appropriate simulations and found that the welfare impact comparing those in the credit sector in the liberalized economy with those in the non-intermediated sector of the constant intermediated economy are virtually the same as assuming no intermediation at all.

35 The scaling factor chosen for the initial distribution is 15 percent of the one used to convert wealth using in the MLE.

36 We construct standard asymptotic 95 percent confidence intervals using the normal distribution.

37 This dichotomous feature of the model could be improved by imposing diminishing returns in the subsistence sector.

38 If we had conducted the comparison with an intermediated economy where the intermediated sector is fixed at 6 percent, then when we compare agents living in the credit sectors of both economies, welfare gains and losses arise due to interest rate levels, being larger in the economy that did not experience liberalization. Therefore, there may be wealthier but less talented agents that would be workers in the benchmark economy who will be better off without liberalization because they earn a higher interest rate income.

39 A cross-country comparison would be more accurate if we could control for the underlying environment but country-wide aggregates would conceal the underlying gains and losses in the population.

40 The 1979 average household yearly income is estimated from the SES data. Since we do not have actual SES data in 1979, we interpolate it using the average annual growth rate between 1976 and 1981.

41 In addition, we re-calibrated the cost of living ν, subsistence level growth rate γ_{gr} and the bequest motive parameter ω for this open economy version and found even fewer differences compared to the closed economy model. In particular, the calibrated bequest motive parameter ω is lower for both datasets in the open economy version, so that the depletion of subsisters happens at a slower rate.

42 We also tried modifying the constraint in (8.3) to $k \in \kappa[0, b - x]$, where the parameter κ measures the severity of the financing constraints. Thus, if some of the assets that make up wealth are illiquid, we would expect $\kappa < 1$. Unfortunately, this specification is not useful because the parameter κ cannot be identified.

43 We are implicitly assuming a partial equilibrium, unlimited supply of funds by setting $r = 1$. However, the magnitude of the calibrated parameter Δ as reported later is comparable to the average amount of informal borrowing found in the Townsend–Thai dataset by those households who borrow informally.

44 Our version of the LEB model allows exogenous technological progress in the subsistence sector γ_{gr} but when we calibrate the intermediated economy in Section 8.6 in the text, the parameter γ_{gr} is virtually zero.

45 The SES survey records whether any member of the household transacted during the previous month with any of the formal financial institutions, such as commercial banks, savings banks, BAAC, government housing banks, financial companies, or credit financiers. A household is categorized as having access to credit if it transacted with any formal financial institution.

46 The intuition for choosing the positive root is that if the setup cost x is larger, more capital k is required for the agent to be indifferent between both occupations.

47 In principle and depending on the data, we could use more than two subsamples, thus obtaining different estimates for the production parameters. We could then use Minimum Classical Distance methods to obtain the estimates for the whole sample.
48 We take the wage to be the labor income for those individuals who reported having no business.

References

Aghion, P. and Bolton, P. 1997. "A Trickle-down Theory of Growth and Development with Debt Overhang." *Review of Economic Studies*, 64(2): 151–72.
Alba, P., Hernandez, L., and Klingebiel, D. 1999. Financial Liberalization and the Capital Account: Thailand 1988–1997. Manuscript, Worldbank.
Albuquerque, R. and Hopenhayn, H. 2004. "Optimal Lending Contracts and Firm Dynamics." *Review of Economic Studies*, 71: 285–315.
Banerjee, A. and Newman, A. 1993. "Occupational Choice and the Process of Development." *Journal of Political Economy*, 101(2): 274–98.
Cooley, T., Marimon, R., and Quadrini, V. 2004. "Aggregate Consequences of Limited Contract Enforceability." *Journal of Poltical Economy*, 112(4): 817–47.
Das, M., Roberts, M., and Tybout, J. 1998. Experience, Expectations and Export Dynamics. NBER Working Paper 862.
Deaton, A. and Paxson, C. 2000. "Growth and Saving among Individuals and Households." *Review of Economics and Statistics*, 82(2): 212–25.
Dollar, D. and Kraay, A. 2002. "Growth is Good for the Poor." *Journal of Economic Growth*, 7(3): 195–225.
Evans, D. and Jovanovic, B. 1989. "An Estimated Model of Entrepreneurial Choice under Liquidity Constraints." *Journal of Political Economy*, 97: 808–27.
Fei, J.C.H. and Ranis, G. 1964. *Development of the Labor Surplus Economy: Theory and Policy*. Richard D. Irwin, Inc.
Gallup, J.L., Radelet, S., and Warner, A. 1998. Economic Growth and the Income of the Poor. Mimeo, Harvard Institute for International Development.
Giné, X. and Townsend, R. 2003. Evaluation of Financial Liberalization: A General Eequilibrium Model with Constrained Occupation Choice. World Bank Policy Paper.
Gollin, D. 1999. Nobody's Business but My Own: Self Employment and Small Entreprise in Economic Development. Mimeo, Williams College.
Greenwood, J. and Jovanovic, B. 1990. "Financial Development, Growth, and the Distribution of Income." *Journal of Political Economy*, 98: 1076–107.
Griffin, R., Montgomery, J., and Rister, M. 1987. "Selecting Functional Form in Production Function Analysis." *Western Journal of Agricultural Economics*, 12(2): 216–27.
Heckman, J., Lochner, L., and Taber, C. 1998. "Explaining Rising Wage Inequality: Explorations with a Dynamic General Equilibrium Model of Labor Earnings with Heterogeneous Agents." *Review of Economic Dynamics*, 1: 1–58.
Jeong, H. 1999. *Education and Credit: Sources of Growth with Increasing Inequality in Thailand*. PhD thesis, University of Chicago, Chicago, IL.
—— and Townsend, R. 2000. An Evaluation of Models of Growth and Inequality. Mimeo, University of Chicago.
Klinhowhan, U. 1999. Monetary transmission mechanism in Thailand. Master's thesis, Thammasat University, Bangkok.
Krusell, P. and Smith, A. 1998. "Income and Wealth Heterogeneity in the Macroeconomy." *Journal of Political Economy*, 106: 867–96.

Lehnert, A. 1998. Asset Pooling, Credit Rationing and Growth. Working Paper 1998-52, Federal Reserve Board: Finance and Economics Discussion Series.

Lewis, A. 1954. "Economic Development with Unlimited Supplies of Labor." *Manchester School of Economics and Social Studies*, 28: 139–91.

Lloyd-Ellis, H. and Bernhardt, D. 1993. Enterprise, Inequality, and Economic Development. Mimeo, Queen's University.

—— 2000. "Enterprise, Inequality, and Economic Development." *Review of Economic Studies*, 67(1): 147–68.

Lucas, R.E. 1978. "On the size Distribution of Business Firms." *Bell Journal of Economics*, 9(2): 508–23.

Okuda, H. and Mieno, F. 1999. "What Happened to Thai Commercial Banks in Pre-Asian Crisis Period: Microeconomic Analysis of Thai Banking Industry." *Hitotshubashi Journal of Economics*, 40(2): 97–121.

Paes, R. de Barros and R. Mendonça. 1995. The Evolution of Welfare, Poverty and Inequality in Brazil over the Last 3 Decades: 1960/90. *Pesquisa e Planejamiento Econômico*, 25(1).

Paulson, A. and Townsend, R. 2001. The Nature of Financial Constraints: Distinguishing the Micro Underpinnings of Macro Models. Mimeo.

Piketty, T. 1997. "The Dynamics of the Wealth Distribution and the Interest Rate with Credit Rationing." *Review of Economic Studies*, 64: 173–89.

Ravallion, M. 2001. "Growth, Inequality and Poverty: Looking Beyond Averages." *World Development*, 29(11): 1803–15.

—— 2002. "The Debate on Globalization, Poverty and Inequality: Why Measurement Matters." Mimeo, The World Bank.

Schultz Paul, T. 1997. Diminishing Returns to Scale in Family Planning Expenditures: Thailand, 1976–81. Mimeo, Yale University.

Tinakorn, P. and Sussangkarn, C. 1998. Total Factor Productivity Growth in Thailand: 1980–1995. Mimeo, Macroeconomic Policy Program, TDRI.

Townsend, R. and Ueda, K. 2001. Transitional Growth with Increasing Inequality and Financial Deepening, Mimeo, University of Chicago.

Townsend, R. principal investigator with Paulson, A., Sakuntasathien, S., Lee, T.J., and Binford, M. 1997. Questionnaire design and data collection for NICHD grant "Risk, Insurance and the Family," and NSF grants. Mimeo.

Veracierto, M. 1998. Plant Level Irreversible Investment and Equilibrium Business Cycles. Mimeo.

9 Trade reforms and wage inequality in Colombia

Orazio Attanasio, Pinelopi K. Goldberg, and Nina Pavcnik

We investigate the effects of the drastic tariff reductions of the 1980s and 1990s in Colombia on the wage distribution. We identify three main channels through which the wage distribution was affected: increasing returns to college education, changes in industry wages that hurt sectors with initially lower wages and a higher fraction of unskilled workers, and shifts of the labor force toward the informal sector that typically pays lower wages and offers no benefits. Our results suggest that trade policy played a role in each of these cases. The increase in the skill premium was primarily driven by skill-biased technological change; however, our evidence suggests, that this change may have been in part motivated by the tariff reductions and the increased foreign competition to which the trade reform exposed domestic producers. With respect to industry wages, we find that wage premiums decreased more in sectors that experienced larger tariff cuts. Finally, we find some evidence that the increase in the size of the informal sector is related to increased foreign competition – sectors with larger tariff cuts and more trade exposure, as measured by the size of their imports, experience a greater increase in informality, though this effect is concentrated in the years prior to the labor market reform. Nevertheless, increasing returns to education, changes in industry premiums, and informality alone cannot fully explain the increase in wage inequality we observe over this period. This suggests that overall the effect of the trade reforms on the wage distribution may have been small.

9.1 Introduction

Starting in 1985, Colombia experienced gradual trade liberalization that culminated in the drastic tariff reductions of 1990–91. The trade reform was accompanied by major modifications of the labor regime in order to reduce labor rigidities and reforms in the financial sector for the purpose of enhancing resource mobility. The purpose of the trade reforms was to expose domestic producers to international competition, increase efficiency, accelerate growth, and reduce at the same time the prices faced by consumers. While the empirical evidence to date suggests that the reforms have indeed been associated with increased efficiency and growth, there have also been concerns that trade liberalization may have contributed to an increase in income inequality. These concerns are partly rooted in the experience of Mexico which experienced a substantial rise in the skill premium and overall income inequality following the trade reform of the mid-1980s. While a causal link between the Mexican trade liberalization and inequality was never established beyond dispute, the chronological coincidence of the increase in wage dispersion with the trade reforms was nevertheless a disappointment to those who hoped that globalization would benefit the poor in developing countries.

The purpose of our work is to provide an empirical investigation of the relationship between wage inequality and trade liberalization in Colombia using detailed micro-level data from 1984 to 1998. In particular, we exploit detailed data on workers' earnings, characteristics, and industry affiliation from the Colombian National Household Survey (NHS) and link this information to industry-level tariff changes and trade exposure. The main advantage of focusing on Colombia is that Colombia, like other developing countries, had not participated in the tariff reducing rounds of the GATT, so that tariff levels were high priority to the reforms. Trade reform consisted primarily of drastic tariff reductions.[1] Tariffs are both well measured and unlike non-tarrif barriers (NTBs) comparable across time. In addition, the period 1985–94 includes multiple tariff reduction episodes that affected not only the *average* tariff, but also the *structure* of protection across industries. Changes in the structure of protection reflected the country's commitment to economy-wide reforms that reduced tariff dispersion, and set tariff rates to levels comparable to those in developed countries. These rates were negotiated with the WTO. Policy makers had accordingly less room to cater to special lobby interests; from an individual industry's perspective, the final tariff rates were exogenously predetermined.

We conduct our analysis in several steps. We start by documenting the basic facts concerning wage inequality in Colombia over 1984–98. We find that while inequality gradually increased over this period, the increase was by no means as pronounced as in Mexico. Next, we decompose inequality into a component that reflects changes in the returns to education, and a component that captures inequality within educational groups. While consistent with the experience in other Latin American economies, the return to college education increases over our sample period, this increase is modest compared to Mexico. At the same time, we document an increase in inequality within educational groups, suggesting that the skill premium alone cannot explain the rise in wage inequality.

Next, we use regression analysis to identify, for each year, the effects that several factors such as industry affiliation, education, and various individual and job characteristics (e.g. informality) have on individual wages. Having many years of data, we can examine how the coefficients on the given variables change over time. We show that individuals with the same characteristics and skills receive different compensation depending on the industry sector in which they work, the occupation they have, and whether their job is formal or informal. Moreover, we show that industry premiums, and returns to education, occupation, and informality change over time.

This descriptive analysis motivates our focus on the skill premium, industry premiums, occupations, and informality in the rest of the chapter. For each of the given factors, we discuss through which channels trade reform is expected to have had an effect, and then examine whether our expectations are confirmed by relating the observed changes to changes in tariffs. As our sample is representative of the urban workforce, we also analyze how its composition changes in terms of skills, and how these changes differ across sectors. We again relate these changes to the changes in tariffs and interpret our results in the light of different theoretical models.

Our main findings can be summarized as follows: first, we find that changes in skill premiums are roughly the same across industries and cannot be related to changes in tariffs across sectors. At the same time, we find no evidence of labor reallocation across sectors. We argue that this piece of evidence is inconsistent with the hypothesis that the skill premium increase was driven by the adjustment mechanism indicated by the workhorse model of international trade, the Heckscher–Ohlin model. This mechanism would suggest labor reallocation from sectors that experienced larger tariff reductions (and hence a reduction in the price of their output) toward sectors that were affected less by trade liberalization. However, the industry employment shares remain stable over our sample period, and the small changes we observe cannot be related to trade policy.

Second, we find that the proportion of skilled workers rose in every industry, consistent with the hypothesis of skill-biased technological change. At the same time, we find that skill-biased technological change was larger in sectors that experienced larger tariff reductions, suggesting that skill-biased technological change itself was partly an endogenous response to increased foreign competition.

Third, we find that the trade reforms impacted industry wage premiums. Wage premiums represent the portion of industry wages that cannot be explained through worker or firm characteristics. They can be interpreted as either industry rents, or returns to industry-specific skills that are not transferable in the short run, and are particularly relevant in the presence of imperfect competition, and/or in cases in which labor mobility is constrained. We find that sectors that were associated with proportionately larger decreases in protection experienced a decrease in their wage premiums relative to the economy-wide average. This suggests an additional channel through which the wage distribution in Colombia was affected. Our empirical evidence suggests that trade liberalization was concentrated in labor-intensive sectors employing a high percentage of low-skill labor. If these sectors experienced a decrease in their wage premiums, then less-skilled workers were "hit" by the reforms twice: first, they saw the average return to their skill decrease and, second, they saw the industry-specific return in the sectors they were employed go down. Moreover, the sectors that had the highest protection before the reform were typically characterized by the smallest wage premiums. Our finding of a trade reform induced reduction in wage premiums, therefore, explains, at least in part, the observed increase in inequality.

Finally, we find some evidence that the trade reforms contributed to an increase in the size of the informal sector. Critics of trade liberalization have expressed the fear that intensified foreign competition may induce large and medium-sized firms to cut worker benefits in order to reduce costs. To this end, such firms may replace permanent by temporary workers, or outsource activities to small, informal firms, including home-based, and self-employed microentrepreneurs. This view finds some support in our results which indicate that sectors that experienced larger tariff reductions and an increase in imports saw a rise in informal employment, though this effect is concentrated in the years prior to the labor market reform. Because the informal sector does not provide benefits and is believed to offer lower job quality, this trend would contribute to an increase in inequality.

Overall, we conclude that the trade reforms in Colombia did affect the wage distribution (via their impact on skill-biased technological change, industry wage premiums, and informality), but the overall effect was modest compared to other countries, especially Mexico.

9.2 Data

9.2.1 Data on trade reforms

Colombia's trade policy underwent significant changes during the past three decades. Although Colombia considerably liberalized its trading environment during the late 1970s, the government increased protection during the early 1980s, in an attempt to combat the impact of the exchange rate appreciation and intensified foreign competition.[2] As a result, the average tariff level increased to 27 percent in 1984. The level of protection varied widely across industries. Manufacturing industries enjoyed especially high levels of protection with an average tariff of 50 percent. Imports from the two most protected sectors textiles and apparel, and wood and wood product manufacturing faced tariffs of over 90 and 60 percent respectively. This suggests that Colombia protected relatively unskilled, labor-intensive sectors, which conforms to findings by Hanson and Harrison (1999) for Mexico. From 1985 to 1994, Colombia gradually liberalized its trading regime by reducing the tariff levels and virtually eliminating the NTBs to trade.

Table 9.1a provides the average tariff across all industries, and across manufacturing from 1984 to 1998, the period of our study.[3] The average tariff declined from 27 to about 10 percent from 1984 to 1998. The average tariff level in manufacturing dropped from 50 to 13 percent during the same period. The bottom part of Table 9.1a summarizes the average NTBs in 1986, 1988, and 1992.[4] In 1986, the average coverage ratio was 72.2 percent. As is the case with tariffs, NTB protection varies widely across industries, with textiles and apparel industry, and the manufacturing of wood and wood products enjoying the highest level of protection. Between 1990 and 1992, the average NTB dropped to 1.1 percent.

What is remarkable about the Colombian trade reforms is that they did not just reduce the *average* level of tariffs and NTBs, they more importantly changed the *structure* of protection. As a result, the correlation between the tariffs before and after the reforms is very low (e.g. the year-to-year correlation between tariffs in 1984, the year preceding the reforms, and 1992, the year following the major reforms, is 0.54). The same is true for NTBs; the correlation of NTBs between

Table 9.1a Trade policy summary

Year	N	Mean	SD	Min.	Max.
Tariffs					
All industries					
1984	21	27.4	24.8	0.0	91.0
1985	21	22.2	16.7	0.0	50.1
1988	21	20.7	16.0	0.0	48.7
1990	21	17.5	14.0	0.0	38.7
1992	21	10.6	4.1	5.0	17.7
1994	21	9.7	4.8	0.0	17.8
1996	21	9.8	5.1	0.0	17.9
1998	21	9.9	5.1	0.0	17.9
Manufacturing					
1984	9	49.8	19.0	29.2	91.0
1985	9	36.6	9.5	22.5	50.1
1988	9	33.5	11.1	17.1	48.7
1990	9	29.1	9.1	15.2	38.7
1992	9	12.9	3.4	8.4	17.7
1994	9	12.9	3.6	8.0	17.8
1996	9	13.0	3.9	7.5	17.9
1998	9	13.1	3.8	7.8	17.9
NTBs					
All industries					
1986	17	72.4	15.3	38.5	89.5
1988	17	72.9	16.1	37.7	93.7
1992	17	1.1	1.2	0.0	4.5

Note
N stands for number of two-digit ISIC industries with available data. Authors' calculations based on tariff and NTB data provided by DNP and the UN.

1986 and 1992 is not significantly different from zero (0.10 with a *p*-value of 0.69). In our empirical work we exploit this cross-sectional variation in protection changes to identify the differential impact of the reforms on earnings in each sector, and examine whether these changes contributed to the increase in inequality.

9.2.2   National Household Survey

We relate the trade policy measures to household survey data from the 1984, 1986, 1988, 1990, 1992, 1994, 1996, and 1998 June waves of the Colombian NHS administered and provided by the Colombian National Statistical Agency (DANE). The data is a repeated cross-section and covers urban areas. The data provide information on earnings, number of hours worked in a week, demographic characteristics (age, gender, marital status, family background, educational attainment, literacy, occupation, job type), sector of employment, and region. The survey includes information on about 18,000–36,000 workers in a year.[5] The industry of employment is reported at the two-digit ISIC level, which gives us thirty-three industries per year.

We use the household survey to create several variables. We construct an hourly wage based on the reported earnings and the number of hours worked normally in a week. Using the information on the highest completed grade, we define four education indicators: no completed education, completed primary school, completed secondary school, completed college (university degree). We distinguish between seven occupation categories: professional/technical, management, personnel, sales, service workers and servants, blue-collar workers in agriculture/ forest, blue-collar industry workers. In addition, we control for whether an individual works for a private company, government, a private household, or whether a worker is an employer or is self-employed. Descriptive statistics for each year of the data are provided in Table 9.1b.[6]

Of particular interest in this table are the percentages of workers belonging to the various education groups. First, note the low proportion of individuals with completed college education. Second, the table indicates that while the proportion of individuals with college education and high school degrees increases during our sample period, Colombia, like other countries in Latin America, lags behind the economies of South East Asia in terms of human capital accumulation. Moreover, there are no signs that the gap is closing. This is consistent with the evidence presented in other papers. Attanasio and Szekely (2000) show that in the cohort of individuals born between 1955 and 1959, the proportion of individuals with at least secondary education is about 40 percent in Mexico and Perú, while Nuñez and Sanchez (2001) report that for the same Colombian cohort, the number is between 30 and 40 percent. In contrast, this proportion is almost twice as high in Taiwan. The aggregate numbers presented in Table 9.1b hide sizeable cohort effects in the proportion of college educated and high school graduates. These are well documented in Nuñez and Sanchez (2001) for Colombia, and in Attanasio and Szekely (2000) for Mexico, Perú, Taiwan, and Thailand.

Our data also provide detailed information on informality and workplace characteristics unavailable in many other labor force surveys. First, the survey asks each worker whether a worker's employer pays social security taxes.[7] The employer's compliance with social security tax (and thus labor market) legislation provides a good indicator that a worker is employed in the formal sector. Given that between 50 and 60 percent of Colombian workers work in the informal sector, the inclusion of information on informality seems crucial. Moreover, Colombia implemented large labor market reforms in 1990 that increased the flexibility of the labor market by decreasing the cost of hiring and firing a worker (see Kugler, 1999 for details). These reforms most likely affected the incentives of firms to comply with labor legislation and their hiring and firing decisions, as well as the worker's choice between formal and informal employment. Descriptive statistics suggest that about 57 percent of workers worked in informal sector prior to 1992. This is also the share of informal workers in 1992, however the share fluctuates significantly thereafter from 0.51 in 1994 to about 0.6 in 1996 and 1997. Furthermore, the survey provides several workplace characteristics. We create four indicator variables to capture whether a worker works alone, whether the worker works in an establishment with 2–5 people, 6–10 people, or 11 or

Table 9.1b NHS Summary statistics

	1984	1986	1988	1990	1992	1994	1996	1998
Hourly wage (current pesos)	115.4	168.7	259.1	430.5	686.9	1,337.6	1,850.6	2,725.0
Log hourly wage	4.4	4.8	5.2	5.7	6.1	6.7	7.0	7.4
Weekly wage (current pesos)	5,109.0	7,158.4	11,396.0	18,787.2	30,000.1	59,260.2	79,884.4	112,281.7
Log weekly wage	8.2	8.5	9.0	9.5	9.9	10.5	10.8	11.2
Male	0.622	0.619	0.601	0.606	0.587	0.591	0.589	0.553
Age	33.7	33.8	33.9	34.3	34.3	34.7	35.2	35.6
Married	0.427	0.413	0.385	0.411	0.392	0.357	0.358	0.356
Head of the household	0.471	0.468	0.453	0.474	0.459	0.462	0.464	0.457
Literate	0.970	0.973	0.978	0.980	0.978	0.985	0.982	0.981
No complete schooling	0.218	0.197	0.178	0.155	0.144	0.121	0.118	0.119
Elementary school complete	0.489	0.479	0.480	0.479	0.473	0.465	0.434	0.393
Secondary school complete	0.218	0.238	0.250	0.264	0.282	0.304	0.326	0.350
University complete	0.076	0.087	0.092	0.102	0.101	0.109	0.121	0.137
Lives in Bogota	0.434	0.435	0.424	0.429	0.402	0.524	0.439	0.386
Occupation indicators								
Professional/technical	0.103	0.103	0.107	0.109	0.113	0.111	0.121	0.135
Management	0.012	0.013	0.013	0.018	0.020	0.020	0.016	0.021
Personnel	0.138	0.133	0.128	0.126	0.124	0.137	0.130	0.132
Sales	0.180	0.186	0.195	0.192	0.190	0.191	0.201	0.196
Servant	0.194	0.196	0.188	0.185	0.191	0.172	0.174	0.194
Agricultural/forest	0.013	0.013	0.015	0.016	0.013	0.009	0.010	0.010
Manual manufacturing	0.360	0.356	0.354	0.353	0.348	0.360	0.347	0.312

Job type indicators								
Private employee	0.530	0.550	0.551	0.546	0.564	0.585	0.569	0.523
Government employee	0.118	0.116	0.107	0.108	0.099	0.080	0.085	0.089
Private household employee	0.064	0.067	0.058	0.054	0.050	0.035	0.032	0.047
Self-employed	0.242	0.220	0.227	0.227	0.224	0.234	0.261	0.282
Employer	0.046	0.047	0.056	0.065	0.064	0.066	0.053	0.059
Place of work characteristics								
Single-person establishment		0.250	0.244	0.253	0.247	0.252	0.263	0.311
2–5 person establishment		0.218	0.223	0.192	0.215	0.193	0.205	0.196
6–10 person establishment		0.080	0.093	0.063	0.083	0.085	0.078	0.073
11 or more person establishment		0.451	0.440	0.492	0.455	0.470	0.454	0.420
Work in a building		0.597	0.600	0.674	0.608	0.615	0.616	0.597
Informal sector		0.577	0.568	0.574	0.564	0.516	0.609	0.590
Number of observations	36,717	28,481	31,006	25,950	27,521	18,070	27,365	30,092

Notes

The reported means are weighted using survey weights.

a We define complete university if a person completes five or more years of post-secondary education.

more people. We also use an indicator for whether a worker works in a permanent establishment in a building (as opposed to outdoors, kiosk, home, etc.). These workplace characteristics potentially control for differences in the quality of the workplace across industries.

9.3 Measuring inequality over 1984–98

9.3.1 Basic trends

We start by asking the basic question of whether inequality has increased over our sample period. We use two measures of inequality. The first one is the standard deviation of the log wages. The second one is the difference between the 90th and 10th percentile of the log wage distribution. The aggregate trends are documented in Table 9.2a.

Both the standard deviation of the log wages and the difference between the 90th and the 10th percentile suggest a modest increase in inequality between 1990 and 1996, and a substantially larger increase between 1996 and 1998. In interpreting these trends, it is important to remember that our sample is confined to the urban sector in Colombia, which accounts for approximately 85 percent of the Colombian labor force. Accordingly, our inequality measures do not adequately capture changes in the wage distribution that may result from changes in the relative incomes of rural workers; as Johnston (1996) has shown, this may result in underestimating the overall change in inequality. A further trend that is visible from Table 9.2a is that the increase in the 90–10 differential over 1990–96 is less pronounced than the increase in the standard deviation. This indicates that most of the change in the standard deviation of the log wages is accounted for by changes in the wages of the top 10 percent of the population. Given that these top 10 percent are comprised primarily of college educated workers (the percentage of college educated individuals in our data ranges between 7 and 14 percent), it is likely that the increase in the wage dispersion can be partially accounted for by an increase in the returns to college education. The experience in other developing countries, especially Mexico, that experienced a large increase in the college premium in the aftermath of trade reforms,

Table 9.2a Aggregate wage inequality

Year	Standard log wage	90–10 percentile
1984	0.809	1.881
1986	0.816	1.938
1988	0.793	1.841
1990	0.773	1.833
1992	0.812	1.938
1994	0.816	1.857
1996	0.820	1.897
1998	0.893	2.164

reinforces this interpretation. We investigate the relevance of this explanation more rigorously later in the chapter.

To get a preliminary idea of whether changing returns to education are responsible for the increase in inequality, we compute how inequality has changed within well-defined educational groups. In particular, we distinguish between three groups: workers with completed primary, or less than primary education; workers with completed secondary education (and maybe some college); and workers with completed college education. For each group we compute the standard deviation of the log wages within the group, and the difference between the 90th and 10th percentiles. The results are displayed in Table 9.2b.

The basic conclusion that we draw from these results is that within group inequality increased over 1990–96 for all three groups, with the college-educated group exhibiting the largest increase. Though the increase in the inequality measures for the college-educated group may be exaggerated by changes in the top coding procedures in the NHS in the early 1990s, the message that the results in Table 9.2b send is clear: the college premium alone cannot explain the increase in wage dispersion. Other factors, such as industry effects or changing returns to occupations are potentially important.

9.3.2 Factor returns

To investigate the contribution of alternative explanations in explaining wage dispersion in Colombia over this period, we regressed log wages in each year against a series of demographic controls, educational, occupational, and industry dummies, and workplace characteristics. Under certain assumptions, the coefficients in these Mincer-type regressions can be interpreted as the prices of different factors at different points in time. The results from these regressions are displayed in Table 9.3.[8]

The results in Table 9.3 can be used to inform the investigation of inequality in two ways. First, the increase in the R^2 of the regression as we successively include more controls gives some indication as to which factors contribute most to

Table 9.2b Wage inequality within education categories

Year	Standard of log wage			90–10 percentile		
	No school/ elementary	Secondary	University	No school/ elementary	Secondary	University
1984	0.722	0.652	0.673	1.650	1.519	1.611
1986	0.742	0.670	0.706	1.695	1.504	1.747
1988	0.696	0.690	0.734	1.609	1.455	1.792
1990	0.675	0.656	0.702	1.540	1.447	1.828
1992	0.717	0.687	0.695	1.649	1.553	1.757
1994	0.680	0.718	0.845	1.482	1.571	1.920
1996	0.694	0.699	0.789	1.584	1.558	1.879
1998	0.754	0.742	0.798	1.735	1.658	1.897

Table 9.3 Estimate of earnings equation

	1986	1988	1990	1992	1994	1996	1998
Age	0.033	0.030	0.028	0.032	0.022	0.026	0.030
	[0.002]	[0.002]	[0.002]	[0.002]	[0.002]	[0.002]	[0.002]
Age squared	−0.0003	−0.0003	−0.0003	−0.0003	−0.0002	−0.0002	−0.0003
	[0.0000]	[0.0000]	[0.0000]	[0.0000]	[0.0000]	[0.0000]	[0.0000]
Male	0.119	0.142	0.107	0.124	0.059	0.077	0.085
	[0.010]	[0.009]	[0.010]	[0.010]	[0.013]	[0.010]	[0.010]
Married	0.102	0.098	0.076	0.076	0.078	0.083	0.092
	[0.009]	[0.008]	[0.009]	[0.009]	[0.011]	[0.009]	[0.009]
Head of the household	0.065	0.076	0.081	0.068	0.098	0.095	0.082
	[0.010]	[0.009]	[0.010]	[0.010]	[0.012]	[0.010]	[0.010]
Elementary school	0.225	0.194	0.165	0.219	0.210	0.191	0.189
	[0.011]	[0.010]	[0.011]	[0.012]	[0.016]	[0.013]	[0.013]
Secondary school	0.512	0.456	0.428	0.483	0.490	0.448	0.474
	[0.014]	[0.013]	[0.014]	[0.015]	[0.019]	[0.015]	[0.015]
University degree	0.878	0.849	0.784	0.877	0.955	0.921	0.984
	[0.023]	[0.020]	[0.021]	[0.022]	[0.027]	[0.022]	[0.022]
Literate	0.190	0.229	0.183	0.186	0.115	0.152	0.157
	[0.023]	[0.023]	[0.026]	[0.026]	[0.038]	[0.029]	[0.028]
Lives in Bogota	0.128	0.112	0.130	0.087	0.071	0.177	0.241
	[0.009]	[0.008]	[0.009]	[0.009]	[0.010]	[0.010]	[0.013]
Professional	0.397	0.457	0.476	0.479	0.477	0.480	0.459
	[0.022]	[0.020]	[0.020]	[0.020]	[0.027]	[0.021]	[0.021]
Management	0.600	0.742	0.836	0.935	0.701	0.671	0.613
	[0.040]	[0.038]	[0.035]	[0.035]	[0.040]	[0.036]	[0.037]
Personnel	0.127	0.120	0.111	0.143	0.141	0.144	0.097
	[0.018]	[0.016]	[0.017]	[0.017]	[0.022]	[0.017]	[0.018]
Sales	0.155	0.156	0.147	0.191	0.218	0.198	0.149
	[0.019]	[0.018]	[0.018]	[0.018]	[0.023]	[0.018]	[0.019]

	(1)	(2)	(3)	(4)	(5)	(6)	(7)
Blue-collar worker agriculture	0.117	0.210	0.156	0.153	0.257	0.116	0.143
	[0.050]	[0.046]	[0.049]	[0.049]	[0.065]	[0.056]	[0.051]
Blue-collar worker manufacturing	0.075	0.092	0.071	0.104	0.100	0.110	0.032
	[0.016]	[0.015]	[0.015]	[0.015]	[0.020]	[0.016]	[0.016]
Private firm employee	−0.468	−0.499	−0.478	−0.433	−0.525	−0.433	−0.425
	[0.020]	[0.017]	[0.018]	[0.018]	[0.023]	[0.019]	[0.019]
Government employee	−0.379	−0.401	−0.356	−0.327	−0.368	−0.312	−0.264
	[0.027]	[0.025]	[0.025]	[0.026]	[0.035]	[0.028]	[0.028]
Private HH employee	−0.298	−0.223	−0.341	−0.224	−0.317	−0.084	−0.213
	[0.032]	[0.029]	[0.032]	[0.031]	[0.044]	[0.034]	[0.032]
Self-employed	−0.527	−0.496	−0.394	−0.402	−0.459	−0.336	−0.498
	[0.024]	[0.021]	[0.024]	[0.024]	[0.031]	[0.024]	[0.023]
Born in urban area	0.053	0.051	0.079	0.070	0.043	0.058	0.076
	[0.020]	[0.019]	[0.020]	[0.022]	[0.028]	[0.022]	[0.025]
Time in residence	0.000	−0.001	−0.001	−0.002	−0.002	−0.003	−0.001
	[0.001]	[0.001]	[0.001]	[0.001]	[0.001]	[0.001]	[0.001]
Urban birth*time in residence	0.001	0.002	0.001	0.002	0.002	0.002	0.000
	[0.001]	[0.001]	[0.001]	[0.001]	[0.001]	[0.001]	[0.001]
Informal sector	−0.045	−0.056	−0.058	−0.036	−0.017	−0.131	−0.116
	[0.011]	[0.010]	[0.009]	[0.010]	[0.013]	[0.010]	[0.011]
Establishment with 2–5 people	−0.015	−0.016	0.011	0.025	−0.035	0.070	0.016
	[0.017]	[0.015]	[0.015]	[0.019]	[0.026]	[0.018]	[0.017]
Establishment with 6–10 people	0.044	0.096	0.128	0.124	0.043	0.139	0.088
	[0.022]	[0.020]	[0.025]	[0.023]	[0.031]	[0.023]	[0.022]
Establishment with 11 or more people	0.117	0.129	0.169	0.190	0.088	0.181	0.130
	[0.020]	[0.019]	[0.022]	[0.022]	[0.028]	[0.020]	[0.019]
Works in a building	0.150	0.176	0.134	0.117	0.156	0.138	0.113
	[0.011]	[0.010]	[0.011]	[0.011]	[0.014]	[0.011]	[0.011]
Number of observations	28,481	31,006	25,950	27,521	18,070	27,365	30,092
R^2	0.37	0.40	0.41	0.40	0.37	0.39	0.41
Industry indicators	Yes	Yes	Yes	Yes	Yes	Yes	Yes

explaining the variance of log wages. The problem of course with this inference is that the covariates tend to be highly correlated with each other, so that the contribution to the increase in the R^2 will depend on the order in which we add controls. Nevertheless, one can obtain a rough idea as to whether there is a set of controls (e.g. occupational dummies or industry dummies) that seems to have particularly high explanatory power. Our experimentation with various specifications in the given regressions failed to isolate such a set of variables. In terms of our inequality discussion this implies that there is not a single factor that we can attribute the increase in inequality to, but that the increase in inequality is the result of several forces working in the same direction.

Second, by examining the change in the coefficients across years, we can get a preliminary idea as to which returns to which worker characteristics seem to have changed most over this period. Given the experience in other developing countries and the theoretical literature on the effects of trade policy, there are four sets of variables that seem a priori likely to have been affected by the reforms:

(1) Returns to education   Between 1986 and 1998, the return to college education increases by *c.*11 percent relative to the return to the lowest educational category (less than primary school); for the period 1990–98, the effect is even larger (20 percent). The returns to secondary and primary education remain relatively stable in comparison.

(2) Industry wage premiums   These are captured through industry dummies in each year. While these dummies are not displayed in the tables for expositional reasons, the low correlation of their estimates across years suggests that industry premiums have changed substantially during this period, possibly because of the reforms.

(3) Returns to Occupations   In their study of the Mexican trade liberalization, Cragg and Epelbaum (1996) report significant changes in the returns to specific occupations, in particular professionals and managers. In fact, changing returns to occupations explain in Mexico a large fraction of the changing return to the college premium. However, this does not seem to be the case in the Colombian data. The returns to various occupations remain relatively stable over the 1986–94 period; the stability of the returns to professionals in particular is in sharp contrast with the pattern reported for Mexico. Only in 1992 there is a substantial increase in the return to managers. This is intuitive and consistent with the interpretation given by Cragg and Epelbaum for a similar finding for Mexico: During periods of substantial economic reforms managerial talent is in high demand. Since the Colombian reforms were concentrated in the 1991–93 period, the increase in the managerial premium in 1992 is consistent with an increase in demand for managerial skill. Nevertheless, this increase gets reversed in later years, and it is not by itself sufficient to explain the overall increase in wage dispersion.

(4) Informality   The negative coefficients on the informality dummies imply that workers employed in the informal sector earn less than workers with similar characteristics in the formal sector throughout our sample period. However, the

informality "discount" varies substantially across years. From 1986 to 1994, the difference between the compensation of formal and informal workers gradually declines; from 1994, however, the informality discount starts increasing, and it reaches unprecedented magnitudes in 1996 and 1998. At the same time, the informal sector seems to expand in the later years of our sample (the share of informal employment rises from 56–57 to 59–60 percent). These trends contribute to the rise in inequality since the informal sector employs a higher fraction of low-wage workers.

Given these patterns we focus our discussion in the rest of the chapter on three sets of variables: the skill premium, the industry premiums, and the informality discount. In each case, we start our discussion by indicating what the predictions of trade theory are regarding the effects of trade liberalization on each of these variables. Next, we contrast these predictions with the data. We do not devote further attention to returns to occupations, both because (with the exception of the return to managers in 1992) these do not seem to substantially change over this period, and because it is unclear how trade reforms would affect particular occupations through channels other than industry affiliation or changing returns to education.

9.4   The skill premium

The discussion of the evolution of the returns to education in the previous section suggests that the returns to secondary and elementary education remain stable over this period, while the return to college education increases by 21 percent between 1990 and 1998. The increase in the college premium could be driven by changes in the rents of specific industries that employ a higher proportion of educated workers, or by changes in the returns to particular occupations that are highly correlated with education. To examine, to which extent the increase in the average skill premium can be accounted for by changes in occupational or industry returns, we compute in Table 9.4 the average returns to education based on a series of regressions, each of which controls for a different set of characteristics. The table includes two measures of educational returns: the secondary school premium relative to elementary education and the university premium relative to elementary. If the rise in the skill premium were driven by changes in occupational returns and/or industry rents, we would expect the increase in the college premium to go down once we control for occupation and/or industry affiliation. However, this expectation is not confirmed in Table 9.4. In a regression without any industry or occupational controls, the change in the university degree–elementary premium is 16.7 percent between 1986 and 1998 (top panel). Controlling for both industry and occupational effects (bottom panel) reduces this increase to 14.2 percent. This suggests that only a very small fraction of the skill premium increase can be accounted for by changes in industry premiums and occupational returns.

To put these numbers in context, it is instructive to compare them to the ones obtained by Cragg and Epelbaum (1996) who conducted a similar exercise for

Table 9.4 Returns to education relative to elementary school

	1986	1988	1990	1992	1994	1996	1998	Change 1998–86
No industry or occupation indicators								
Secondary school–elementary	0.370	0.345	0.350	0.343	0.352	0.322	0.346	−0.024
University degree–elementary	0.942	0.961	0.963	1.007	1.070	1.038	1.109	0.167
Industry indicators								
Secondary school–elementary	0.342	0.316	0.327	0.321	0.333	0.301	0.322	−0.020
University degree–elementary	0.887	0.899	0.905	0.956	1.025	0.988	1.049	0.162
Industry indicators*(secondary or college education) interaction*								
Secondary school–elementary	0.399	0.348	0.335	0.338	0.408	0.311	0.368	−0.031
University degree–elementary	0.927	0.917	0.892	0.956	1.088	0.985	1.083	0.156
Occupation indicators								
Secondary school–elementary	0.302	0.275	0.274	0.272	0.290	0.268	0.295	−0.007
University degree–elementary	0.680	0.680	0.650	0.681	0.776	0.755	0.818	0.138
Industry and occupation indicators								
Secondary school–elementary	0.287	0.262	0.263	0.264	0.280	0.257	0.285	−0.002
University degree–elementary	0.653	0.655	0.619	0.658	0.745	0.730	0.795	0.142

Notes
Entries are the differences between estimated education returns for secondary school and elementary school (university degree and elementary school) based on education coefficients from regressions that always include the following regressors: age, age squared, male, married, head of the HH, literate, lives in Bogota, job type indicators (private firm employee, government employee, private HH employee, self-employed), informal, establishment with 2–5 people, establishment with 6–10 people, establishment with 11 or more people, works in a building.

Mexico. The increase in the skill premium in Mexico over 1987–93 is substantially larger than our estimate for Colombia: the return to post-secondary education relative to secondary education is reported to rise by 60 percent between the two years. However, a large portion of this increase is accounted for by changes in the returns to occupations, the rising returns to managers and professionals in particular. Controlling for occupation alone reduces the increase in the Mexican skill premium to 40 percent. In contrast, the skill premium increase in Colombia is more modest and cannot be accounted for by occupational returns.

A further exercise we conducted to investigate whether the increase in the skill premium was tied to particular sectors was to interact educational dummies with industry dummies. Most industry–college dummy interactions were insignificant. More of the interactions of industry dummies with dummies for either college or secondary education were statistically significant, but their inclusion did not affect the estimate of the average skill premium increase. Despite the fact that these interactions were individually insignificant, F-tests reject the hypothesis that they were jointly insignificant (the p-values were always 0.01 or smaller). To investigate whether there is a relationship between trade policy and changes in sector-specific skill premiums, we regressed the sector-specific skill premiums in each year (the college–industry dummy interactions) against tariffs, sector-fixed effects, and time indicators. If the increase in the skill premium was the consequence of trade liberalization, and if labor mobility was constrained in the short run, we would expect sectors with smaller tariff reductions to be associated with a larger increase in the (sector-specific) skill premium. All regressions, however, produced statistically insignificant coefficients. This could be interpreted as evidence that trade policy was not the primary reason for the skill premium increase. Alternatively, our results are consisted with a scenario where labor was mobile across sectors, so that the returns to education were equalized across sectors. In this latter case, trade policy might have led to an increase in the economy-wide skill premium, but it would not have impacted sectors with larger tariff reductions differentially. We investigate this possibility in the following section.

To summarize, the results from this section lead us to conclude that the increase in the skill premium we document in Table 9.3 represents an increase in the economy-wide return to college education that cannot be accounted for by sector-specific or occupation-specific effects. We now turn to the question of whether trade liberalization could be responsible for this change in the economy-wide skill premium.

9.4.1 Was the increase in the economy-wide skill premium due to the trade reforms?

The link between trade liberalization and changes in the economy-wide skill premium is provided by the workhorse model of international trade, the Heckscher–Ohlin model, and its companion theorem, Stolper–Samuelson. The Heckscher–Ohlin model predicts that countries will export goods that use intensively the factors of production that are relatively abundant and import goods that use intensively the relatively scarce factors of the country. The Stolper–Samuelson theorem links factor prices to product prices. According to this theorem, trade affects wages only through changes in product prices. In its simple 2×2 version, the theorem states that a decrease in the price of a good will reduce the return to the factor that is used intensively in the production of this good and increase the return to the other factor. Because trade policies change product prices, the Stolper–Samuelson theorem can be used to infer how factor prices (e.g. wages) will respond to a change in the trade regime.

While the sharp predictions of the 2×2 version of the model are typically lost in its multifactor versions, it is the logic of the Stolper–Samuelson theorem that led to the hope that trade liberalization would benefit the poor in developing countries, and thus contribute to a decrease in inequality. To illustrate the argument, consider a stylized view of the world in which there are two countries, a developed and a developing one, and two factors of production, skilled and unskilled labor. The developed country is relatively skilled-labor abundant, while the developing country is relatively unskilled-labor abundant. According to Heckscher–Ohlin, the developing country will export unskilled-labor intensive products, let's say apparel, and import skilled-labor intensive commodities, let's say manufactures. Now consider the effect of a trade barrier reduction in the developing country. The decrease in protection will lead to a drop in the price of the import sector and a price increase in the export sector. According to Stolper–Samuelson, the price decrease in the import sector will hurt the factor that is used intensively in this sector (skilled labor) and benefit the factor that is used intensively in the export sector (unskilled labor). Note that the price changes affect only economy-wide and not sector-specific returns. This is because the factors of production are assumed to be mobile across uses within the country, so that their returns are equalized across sectors; the relative price increase in the export sector leads to an increase in the demand for the factor that is used intensively in this sector (unskilled labor) and hence an increase in its economy-wide return. Labor mobility (along with perfect competition and given technology) is thus an essential ingredient of this argument.

Against this theoretical background, the experience in many developing countries that witnessed an increase in the skill premium and overall inequality in the aftermath of trade liberalization has been both a disappointment and a puzzle. How can unskilled-labor abundant countries experience an *increase* in the skill premium when trade barriers are reduced? This pattern seems at first in sharp contrast with the prediction of the Stolper–Samuelson theorem.

We argue that the increase in the skill premium in Colombia is not only "not puzzling," but also perfectly consistent with the Stolper–Samuelson theorem. The reason is simply that the sectors that experienced the largest tariff reductions (and hence the largest reductions in the price of their output) were precisely the sectors that employed a higher fraction of unskilled workers. This is shown clearly in Figure 9.1 that plots the tariff decline between 1984 and 1998 for each industry against the share of unskilled workers in 1984 (unskilled is defined as having at most complete primary education). The graph shows a positive correlation

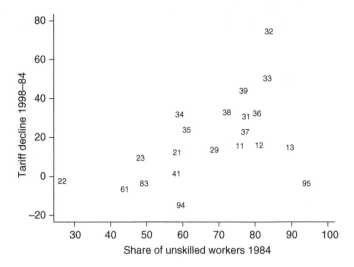

Figure 9.1 Tariff reductions and share of unskilled workers.

between the size of tariff reductions and the share of unskilled workers. A regression of the annual change in tariffs against the share of unskilled workers in 1984 yields a coefficient of -0.092 for the share of unskilled workers (t-statistic $= -2.4$), and an R^2 of 0.18 (unlike in Figure 9.1, tariff cut is a negative number in this regression). It is interesting to note that Hanson and Harrison (1999) report a similar pattern for Mexico. Given this evidence, the increase in the skill premium is exactly what Stolper–Samuelson would predict: since trade liberalization was concentrated in unskilled-labor intensive sectors, the economy-wide return to unskilled labor should decrease.[9,10]

While the argument demonstrates that the rise in the skill premium documented in the previous section could *in principle* be attributed to the trade reforms, it does not of course constitute proof that it was the trade reforms that led to this rise. In search for Stolper–Samuelson effects on wages we take an indirect route. We check whether there is evidence that the general equilibrium adjustment mechanism suggested by the Heckscher–Ohlin model is at work. The mechanism at the heart of the Heckscher–Ohlin model implies a contraction of the sectors that experience a (trade-barrier reduction induced) decline in their output price, and an expansion of the sectors that experience a relative price increase. Accordingly, we would expect to see labor reallocation from the sectors with the largest tariff reductions to the sectors with the smaller tariff reductions. The left panel of Table 9.5 shows the industry shares in total employment in 1984 and in 1998. These shares remain remarkably stable. There is certainly no evidence of labor real-location across sectors. Regressing industry employment shares on industry tariffs, industry, and time indicators confirm this following conclusion: the tariff coefficient is small in magnitude (0.01) and statistically insignificant. In sum, the employment

Table 9.5 Industry employment

ISIC Code	Industry share in overall employment		Share of skilled workers in industry	
	1984	1998	1984	1998
11	0.0130	0.0091	0.247	0.289
12	0.0001	0.0001	0.194	0.272
13	0.0003	0.0006	0.110	0.481
21	0.0015	0.0005	0.421	0.537
22	0.0015	0.0017	0.738	0.899
23	0.0002	0.0001	0.522	0.371
29	0.0005	0.0005	0.317	0.380
31	0.0358	0.0343	0.230	0.498
32	0.0908	0.0763	0.167	0.336
33	0.0194	0.0166	0.171	0.321
34	0.0158	0.0120	0.414	0.603
35	0.0241	0.0211	0.394	0.621
36	0.0107	0.0097	0.200	0.490
37	0.0034	0.0031	0.232	0.389
38	0.0348	0.0280	0.283	0.471
39	0.0063	0.0053	0.237	0.505
41	0.0049	0.0047	0.422	0.665
42	0.0028	0.0016	0.295	0.701
50	0.0691	0.0570	0.141	0.267
61	0.0108	0.0155	0.565	0.625
62	0.1932	0.1955	0.249	0.456
63	0.0354	0.0406	0.133	0.278
71	0.0560	0.0624	0.233	0.416
72	0.0054	0.0109	0.502	0.830
81	0.0219	0.0202	0.776	0.947
82	0.0058	0.0057	0.752	0.918
83	0.0436	0.0564	0.512	0.685
91	0.0425	0.0369	0.545	0.851
92	0.0017	0.0015	0.328	0.502
93	0.0883	0.1078	0.705	0.857
94	0.0132	0.0175	0.410	0.626
95	0.1469	0.1461	0.063	0.194
96	0.0003	0.0005	0.555	0.953

Note
Skilled workers are workers with complete secondary or university education.

patterns over 1984–98 are not consistent with an explanation that would attribute the rise in the skill premium to changes in trade policy operating through Stolper–Samuelson effects. Even though more general versions of the model fail to deliver the sharp predictions of the 2 × 2 version, it is remarkable that in the face of large and differential tariffs reductions we see virtually no change in employment shares across sectors.

We should note that the stability of the employment patterns is consistent with the evidence from Mexico; Revenga (1997), Hanson and Harrison (1999), and

Feliciano (2001) all report that the adjustment of the Mexican labor market to trade liberalization occurred through relative wage adjustments and not through labor reallocation across sectors. This adjustment process contrasts with the evidence from the United States, where Grossman (1986) and Revenga (1992) find greater employment than wage sensitivity to trade shocks. The differences in the adjustment mechanisms of Colombia and Mexico on one side, and the United States on the other, are suggestive of greater labor mobility in the United States compared to the other two countries. This is consistent with the view that labor market rigidities in developing countries *might* obstruct labor reallocation in response to economic reforms.

Finally, if Stolper–Samuelson forces were at work, firms would substitute away from skilled labor with the rising skill premium, and we would expect to see the share of skilled labor in industry employment decline. The right panel of Table 9.5 reports the share of skilled workers in each industry and shows that this share has increased substantially in every industry between 1984 and 1998. This evidence is hard to reconcile with Stolper–Samuelson effects as the primary mechanism leading to the rise in the skill premium. Instead, Table 9.5 seems more consistent with skilled-biased technological change.[11] Evidence from several countries seems to suggest that the latter has had important effects on the wage distribution in the last two decades (see Berman *et al.*, 1998; Pavcnik, 2003). However, the evidence in favor of skill-biased technological change does not imply that trade policy did not have an indirect effect on changes in the wage distribution. To the extent that technological change was an endogenous response to intensified competition from abroad (see Acemoglu, 2003[12]), one could argue that the trade reforms were indirectly responsible for the increase in the skill premium.

To investigate this claim, we regress in Table 9.6 the share of skilled workers in each industry against industry tariffs, industry and time indicators. Table 9.6 reports the least square (LS) results and 2SLS to account for the potential endogeneity of trade policy (e.g. in setting tariffs, policy makers could be taking into

Table 9.6 Share of skilled workers and trade policy

	(1)	(2)	(3)	(4)	(5)	(6)
Nominal tariff	−0.172** [0.076]	−0.156** [0.072]	−0.232** [0.104]	−0.046 [0.069]	−0.0798 [0.0945]	−0.2110** [0.0906]
Instruments	None	Exchange rate* tariffs 83	Coffee price* tariffs 83	None	Tariffs 83, exchange rate* tariffs 83	Tariffs 83, coffee price* tariffs 83
First differences	No	No	No	Yes	Yes	Yes
Year indicators	Yes	Yes	Yes	Yes	Yes	Yes
Industry indicators	Yes	Yes	Yes	No	No	No

Notes
** and * indicate 5 and 10 percent significance, respectively. Reported standard errors are robust and clustered on industry. Columns 1–3 are estimated with industry-fixed effects. Columns 4–6 are estimated in first differences. N is 168 in columns 1–3 and 147 in columns 4–6.

account industry characteristics, such as the share of skilled or unskilled workers, wages, etc.). To find appropriate instruments for tariffs we rely on the history of protection in Colombia and the institutional details of the reforms. Anecdotal evidence and World Bank reports suggest that the Colombian government initiated liberalization in response to exchange rate fluctuations and the trade balance. The trade balance in Colombia has in turn always been heavily influenced by world coffee prices (see Roberts and Tybout, 1997), since coffee is a major export of this country. This indicates that at the macroeconomic level, exchange rates and world coffee prices are some of the factors responsible for the trade policy changes. However, exchange rates or coffee prices alone cannot explain why some sectors experienced larger tariff reductions than others. In explaining the latter, two facts seem to be of importance. First, before the onset of trade liberalization, there was substantial tariff dispersion across sectors. As discussed earlier, in examining the cross-sectional pattern of protection we find that the single most important determinant of tariff levels was the share of unskilled workers: sectors with a high share of unskilled workers (where unskilled is defined as having at most primary education) had higher tariffs. Second, the Gaviria government was committed to economy-wide liberalization and aimed at reducing tariffs to the levels negotiated within the WTO. As a result, the final tariff rate was almost uniform implying that there was little (if any at all) room for industry lobbying[13]; from an individual industry's point of view, the tariff rate at the end of the trade liberalization period was exogenously predetermined. This policy translated to proportionately larger tariff reductions in sectors that had historically higher tariff levels. The close link between the magnitude of tariff reductions and the initial level of protection in 1983 (a year prior to our sample) is evident in a regression that relates the 1998–84 tariff reductions to the 1983 tariff levels: it yields a coefficient on the 1983 tariff of 1.06 (with a *t*-statistic of 26.3) and an R^2 of 0.97. This discussion suggests that the 1983 industry tariff levels and their interaction with exchange rates (or coffee prices) are highly correlated with the industry tariff reductions and may provide good instruments for the tariff changes.[14]

The results in columns 1–3 of Table 9.6 indicate that the share of skilled workers in each industry is inversely related to protection; industries with larger tariff reductions experienced more rapid skill-biased technological change, as measured by the proportion of skilled workers.[15] We also estimate the relationship between the share of skilled workers and tariffs in first differences and those results are reported in columns 4–6. These results confirm the negative association between skill-biased technological change and tariff changes (but are at time imprecisely estimated). Overall, the evidence in Table 9.6 is consistent with what Adrian Wood has labeled "defensive innovation"; firms in sectors facing intensified import competition (and these, in Colombia, are the sectors employing more unskilled workers) look for new methods of production that economize on unskilled labor.

In summary, our results suggest that the increase in the skill premium cannot be linked to developments in particular sectors of the economy – it was an economy-wide phenomenon. While this, in principle, opens the door for Stolper–Samuelson effects, we find no evidence of the labor reallocation mechanism across sectors that should accompany such effects. However, we do find evidence in favor of skill-biased technological change, which was more rapid in sectors that experienced larger tariff reductions. To the extent that skill-biased technological change was induced, at least partially, by changes in the trade regime, we conclude that trade liberalization may have had an indirect effect on the rise of the skill premium.

9.5 Effects of trade reforms on industry wage premiums

9.5.1 Theoretical background and methodology

As noted in Section 9.3, changes in the economy-wide returns to education can only partially explain the increase in inequality, since wage dispersion also increases within each educational group. To explain the rise in the within group inequality, we now turn to the role of other factors such as changing industry wage premiums. Our focus on industry premiums is motivated by two considerations.

First, our empirical results suggest that industry premiums (captured through industry dummies in the regressions of Table 9.3) change substantially over this period. Year-to-year correlations of industry premiums are as low as 0.14. This contrasts sharply with the evidence on wage premiums in the United States, where wage premiums have been shown to be stable across years (year-to-year correlations are always estimated to be above 0.9).[16] This raises the possibility that the trade reforms changed the structure of industry wages.

Second, there are good theoretical reasons to believe that trade reforms that changed the structure of protection would affect relative, and not only economy-wide, wages. The focus on economy-wide returns that underlies our discussion of the skill premium is premised on the assumption that labor is mobile across sectors. Yet, this is an assumption that is unlikely to hold, especially in the short- and medium run, and in developing countries like Colombia where labor markets are characterized by significant labor rigidities. Indeed, our results on employment shares in Table 9.5 suggest limited labor mobility across sectors. In addition, there is substantial evidence that wages for observationally equivalent tasks differ across industries; this inter-industry variation is hard to reconcile with the assumption of perfect factor mobility.

The perhaps most natural point of departure for thinking about the effects of trade on relative wages is the specific factors model. This model is short run by nature as it considers factors of production immobile across sectors. It predicts that sectors that experienced relatively large tariff cuts will see a decline in their wages relative to the economy-wide average, while sectors with proportionately smaller trade barrier reductions will benefit in relative terms. The medium-run (Ricardo–Viner) model yields similar predictions. Note that these implications of models with constrained factor mobility differ from the ones of the Heckscher–Ohlin model which predicts that trade reform should affect only economy-wide returns to the factors of production, but not industry specific returns, since all factors of productions are mobile across uses.

It is important to note that the above trade models assume perfectly competitive product and factor markets. The existence of industry wage premiums is hence perfectly consistent with perfect competition in the presence of industry-specific skills. Introducing imperfect competition opens up additional channels through which trade policy may impact wages. In the presence of unionization, it is possible that unions extract the rents associated with protection in the form of employment guarantees rather than wages (an idea developed in Grossman (1984)). Liberalization induced productivity changes may further impact relative wages. There is by now a voluminous literature on the effects of trade reform on firm productivity. While in theory the effects of liberalization on productivity are ambiguous (see Rodrik, 1991; Roberts and Tybout, 1991, 1996 for a discussion), most empirical work to date has established a positive link between liberalization and productivity (Harrison (1994) for Côte d' Ivoire; Krishna and Mitra (1998) for India; Kim (2000) for Korea; Pavcnik (2002) for Chile). For Colombia specifically, Fernandes (2001) estimates that the trade reforms up to 1992 had a significant impact on plant-level productivity. To the extent that productivity enhancements are passed through onto industry wages, we would expect wages to increase in the industries with the highest productivity gains. If these occur in the industries with the highest trade barrier reductions, industry wages would be positively correlated with trade liberalization.

The discussion so far suggests that, based on theoretical considerations alone, it is not possible to sign the effect of trade liberalization on industry wages unambiguously. To investigate this effect empirically, we employ a two-stage estimation framework familiar from the labor literature on industry wages. In the first stage we regress the log of worker i's wages ($\ln(w_{ijt})$) on a vector of worker characteristics H_{ijt} (age, age squared, gender, marital status, head of the household indicator, education indicators, literacy, location indicator, occupational indicators, job type indicators, born in urban area indicator, time in residence, urban birth*time in residence), and a set of industry indicators (I_{ijt}) reflecting worker i's industry affiliation (the regressions reported in Table 9.3 correspond to this stage of the estimation):[17]

$$\ln(w_{ijt}) = H_{ijt}\beta_{Ht}thn + I_{ijt}*wp_{jt} + \varepsilon_{ijt} \qquad (9.1)$$

The coefficient on the industry dummy, the wage premium, captures the part of the variation in wages that cannot be explained by worker characteristics, but can be explained by the workers' industry affiliation. Following Krueger and Summers (1988), we normalize the omitted industry wage premium to zero and express the estimated wage premiums as deviations from the employment-weighted average wage premium.[18] This normalized wage premium can be interpreted as the proportional difference in wages for a worker in a given industry relative to an average worker in all industries with the same observable characteristics. The normalized wage differentials and their exact standard errors are calculated using the Haisken-DeNew and Schmidt (1997) two-step restricted LSs procedure provided to us by John P. Haisken-DeNew and Christoph M. Schmidt.[19]

The first-stage regressions are estimated separately for each year in our sample as the subscript t in equation (9.1) indicates. In the second stage, we pool the industry wage premiums wp_j over time and regress them on a vector of trade related industry characteristics T_{jt}, and a vector of industry-fixed effects, and time indicators D_{jt}:

$$wp_{jt} = T_{jt}\beta_T + D_{jt}\beta_D + u_{jt} \tag{9.2}$$

We also estimate the second-stage regression in first-differences.[20] Since the dependent variable in the second stage is estimated, we estimate (9.2) with weighted least squares (WLS), using the inverse of the variance of the wage premium estimates from the first stage as weights. This procedure puts more weight on industries with smaller variance in industry premiums. We account for general forms of heteroskedasticity and serial correlation in the error term in (9.2) by computing robust (Huber–White) standard errors clustered by industry.

9.5.2 Second-stage results and their implications for wage inequality

Table 9.7 reports results from relating the wage premiums to tariffs. The industry-fixed-effects results are presented in columns 1–2. First-differences results are presented in columns 3–4. Because the two specifications yield similar findings, we focus our discussion on the first-differences results. The coefficient on tariff in column 3 is negative and significant. This implies that increasing protection in a particular sector raises wages in that sector. The magnitude of the effect is also significant and suggests that a 50 percentage point reduction in tariffs (0.5) translates to a 6 percent (0.1191 × 0.5) decrease in the wage premium in this sector. For the most protected sectors (91 percent tariff) this effect increases to 10.8 percent (0.1191 × 10.91).

Note that because we condition our industry wage premium estimates on worker characteristics in the first stage, our estimates of the relationship between tariffs and wages are not driven by observable differences in worker composition across industries that also affect industry ability to obtain protection. Moreover, to the extent that political economy factors and sorting based on unobserved worker attributes are time-invariant, we control for them through industry-fixed effects or through first differencing. Assuming that political economy determinants of protection do not vary much over relatively short time periods seems a reasonable identification assumption in many cases. However, given that the structure of protection changes over our sample period, time-variant political economy considerations are expected to be important. For example, if protection responds to exchange rate pressures and exchange rates also have a direct effect on wages, one would expect the tariff coefficient to be biased. Albeit the year effects included in (9.2) already control for the *aggregate* effects of exchange rates (and other economy-wide shocks), unobserved industry-specific time-varying shocks could still bias our estimates. We address this concern in two ways.

Table 9.7 Industry wage premiums and trade policy

	(1)	(2)	(3)	(4)	(5)	(6)	(7)	(8)
Nominal tariff	0.0660** [0.0125]	0.0682** [0.0161]	0.1191** [0.0257]	0.1356** [0.0251]	0.0444** [0.0120]	0.0416 [0.0244]	0.0496* [0.0241]	0.0401** [0.0158]
Lagged imports		-0.00008** [0.00002]		0.00002 [0.00005]				0.00002 [0.00003]
Lagged exports		0.00004 [0.00011]		0.00007 [0.00017]				-0.00002 [0.00013]
Lagged imports* exchange rate		0.0000003 [0.0000004]		0.0000001 [0.0000005]				0.0000001 [0.0000004]
Lagged exports* exchange rate		0.0000005* [0.0000002]		0.0000015* [0.0000008]				0.0000008 [0.0000006]
Instruments	None	None	None	None	Exchange rate* tariffs 83	Tariffs 83, exchange rate* tariffs 83	Tariffs 83, coffee prices* tariffs 83	Tariffs 83, coffee prices* tariffs 83
First-differences	No	No	Yes	Yes	Yes	Yes	Yes	Yes
Year indicators	Yes	Yes	Yes	Yes	Yes	Yes	Yes	Yes
Industry indicators	Yes	Yes	No	No	No	No	No	No

Notes
** and * indicate 5 and 10 percent significance, respectively. Reported standard errors are robust and clustered by industry. Columns 1–2 are estimated with industry-fixed effects. Columns 3–8 are estimated in first-differences. N is 168 in columns 1–2 and 147 in columns 3–8.

First, we control for variables such as lagged imports and exports, and their interactions with the exchange rate. Because trade flows are arguably endogenous (they depend on factor costs), we include the first lags of import and export measures in the estimation rather than their current values.[21] We interact the exchange rate with lagged trade flows because a priori we would expect the effects of currency fluctuations to vary depending on the trade exposure of the sector. The first-differences results are reported in column 4 of Table 9.7. The inclusion of these additional controls hardly changes the coefficient on tariffs.

Second, we account for the potential endogeneity of trade policy *changes* by instrumenting for tariff *changes* in the first-differences specification with the pre-sample protection measures (1983 industry tariff levels), and their interaction with exchange rates (and world coffee prices).[22] Columns 5–8 of Table 9.7 contain the 2SLS results. Although the magnitude of the tariff coefficient changes, the positive (and statistically significant) relationship between tariff reductions and declines in industry wage premiums is robust. The estimated effect of liberalization on wages drops however from 0.119 in column 1 to 0.05 in column 7. The coefficient of 0.05 implies that a 50 percentage point tariff reduction would lead to a 2.5 percent decline in wage premiums. Moreover, while the year indicators already control for the direct aggregate effect of the exchange rate on wages, direct industry-specific exchange rate affect could still *potentially* bias our 2SLS estimates (especially those that use exchange rate interacted with 1983 tariffs as an instrument). This omitted bias is however unlikely important because the coefficient on tariffs hardly changes in columns 2 and 4 (relative to columns 1 and 2) after we control for the interactions of the exchange rate with lagged exports and imports. Nevertheless, column 8 reports the 2SLS specification that includes lagged imports and exports and their interactions with the exchange rate as controls and uses world coffee prices interacted with 1993 tariffs and 1993 tariffs as instruments. We continue to find that tariff declines are associated with declines in wage premiums.

These results suggest that trade policy had a significant effect on relative wages. Workers employed in industries with larger tariff reductions experienced a decline of their wages relative to the economy-wide average. This by itself does not imply an increase in inequality. If the industries with the larger tariff reductions had been the industries with the initially highest wage premiums, then trade policy would have reduced wage dispersion. However, our findings suggest exactly the opposite pattern. The sectors that experienced the largest tariff reductions were in fact the sectors with the highest shares of unskilled workers and lowest wages (see Section 4.1 and Figure 9.1). In the manufacturing sector in particular, where most of the trade liberalization was concentrated, the lowest wage premiums are estimated in textiles and apparel, food processing, and wood and wood processing, all sectors that were heavily protected prior to the reforms and experienced the largest tariff cuts. In particular, textiles and apparel had tariff cuts around 73 percentage points between 1984 and 1998, while the tariff reductions in food processing and wood and wood processing were 29 and 49 percentage points respectively. These tariff reductions are to be contrasted with the ones in

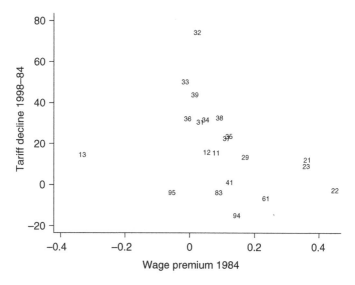

Figure 9.2 Tariff reductions and initial (1984) wage premiums.

the high wage premium sectors of coal mining (tariff cut: 11 percentage points) and crude petroleum (tariff went actually up by 4 percentage points).

The negative relationship between tariff reductions and pre-reform wage premiums is also illustrated in Figure 9.2 that plots tariff reductions between 1984 and 1998 against the wage premiums in the first year of our sample, 1984. A regression of annual tariff reductions against wage premiums in 1984 confirms the impression conveyed by Figure 9.2: the wage premium coefficient is negative and statistically significant (coefficient: -0.064; p-value: 0.069) indicating that the larger the wage premium the smaller the tariff cut (note tariff cuts are positive numbers in this regression). The trade reform induced changes in the wage premiums could thus only increase inequality.

9.6   Effects of trade reforms on informality

As noted in Section 9.3, trade reforms could lead to an increase in inequality by expanding the size of the informal sector. In Colombia, the informal sector employs 50–60 percent of the labor force and has been expanding during the 1990s.[23] The presence of a large informal sector provides an additional margin through which labor markets can adjust to external shocks in developing economies. An emerging concern in many Latin American countries is that trade liberalization has contributed to the rise in the number of informal workers (Stallings and Peres, 2000). In particular, opponents of globalization have argued that firms exposed to increased international competition may try to reduce costs by cutting worker benefits. To do this, large and medium-sized firms or multinationals may outsource activities to small, informal firms, including home-based and self-employed microentrepreneurs. Alternatively, they may replace permanent, full-time workers, with temporary and/or part-time labor. Currie and Harrison (1997), for instance, indeed find that after the trade liberalization in Morocco firms started hiring more temporary workers. Consistent with this view, Goldberg and Pavcnik (2003) present a theoretical model that formally shows that permanent trade liberalization can result in an increase in the informal employment.

Because the informal sector does not provide benefits and it is believed to provide lower job quality, a trade reform induced rise in informality may then contribute to the rise in inequality, where inequality is broadly defined as the gap between those who have well paid jobs with benefits and high job quality and those who face lower wages, no benefits, and worse workplace conditions. This claim is controversial. There is a large literature that claims that employment in the informal sector is voluntary and should not therefore be considered an inferior option. However, a special module in the 1994 NHS contains questions about work conditions and job satisfaction that allow us to assess the validity of the claim that informality is associated with lower job quality. We find that working in the informal sector is indeed negatively correlated with job satisfaction, good workplace conditions, good employee relations, and job training. The negative correlation between informality and various measures of job quality suggests that it is potentially important to account for the informal sector in a study of inequality.

While the concerns about informality have received a lot of attention recently, there is no sound empirical evidence linking the trade reforms to the increase in informal employment and addressing the possible effects that increased informality may have on wage inequality. Our dataset with its detailed information on the informal sector is ideal for filling in this gap. As described in Section 9.2.2, the main criterion we use to assign firms to the informal sector is compliance with labor market regulation. The NHS June waves ask workers whether their employer contributes to social security. This information is an excellent proxy for formality, as it indicates whether or not the employer complies with labor legislation. Furthermore, this definition has an obvious appeal to trade economists as it relates to the debate on how labor standards/legislation affect prices of tradable goods and trade flows.

We examine the claim that trade liberalization leads to an increase in informality by employing a two-stage empirical framework similar to the one in Section 9.5, but with an indicator for whether a worker is employed in the informal establishment as the dependent variable. In the first stage, the informality indicator is regressed against the same regressors as in equation (9.1). The coefficient on the industry indicator captures the variation in the probability of informal employment that cannot be explained by worker characteristics, but can be explained by workers' industry affiliation. We call these coefficients industry informality differentials. We then express the informality differentials as deviation from the employment-weighted average informality differential. This normalized informality differential can be interpreted as the percentage point difference in probability of informal employment for a worker in a given industry relative to the average worker in all industries with the same observable characteristics. Equation (9.1) is estimated separately for each year of our sample. In the second stage, we pool these industry informality differentials across years and relate it to trade policy as in equation (9.2). If the likelihood of employment in the informal sector increases with the magnitude of the tariff reductions, trade liberalization will have contributed to the increase in informality.

We should note that it is crucial to exploit both the cross-industry and time variation in the trade policy changes to look at how informality relates to trade reforms. During the early 1990s Colombia implemented labor reforms that are thought to have significantly reduced the rigidities in the formal labor markets and to have contributed to a shift from the informal to the formal sector (Kugler, 1999). The use of the cross-sectional and time variation in the trade policy changes enables us to separate the effects of industry-specific trade policy changes from the effects of economy-wide labor reforms. All our specifications include year indicators which capture the effect of economy-wide labor reforms, exchange rates, and other macro shocks. In addition, as is the case in the analysis of wage premiums, because we condition our industry informality differential estimates on worker characteristics in the first stage, our estimates of the relationship between tariffs and informality are not driven by observable differences in worker composition across industries that also affect industry ability to obtain protection. Finally, industry-fixed effects (or first-differencing) control for the unobserved time-invariant industry (or worker) characteristics that might independently affect informality and tariffs.

Table 9.8 presents the findings. Columns 1–3 report the results from the industry-fixed-effects regressions. In all specifications the effect of tariffs on informality is negative and significant. To interpret the size of the tariff coefficients, consider an industry from the manufacturing sector with an average level of tariffs in 1998 (13 percent). Suppose that we conducted the conceptual experiment of reducing tariffs to zero in this industry. Then the estimated coefficient in column 1 suggests that the probability of this worker having an informal job would rise by 1.1 percentage points (0.13×0.087). The corresponding effect in 1984, when the average tariff was 50 percent, would be 4.4 percentage points (0.5×0.087).[24]

Increased exposure to foreign markets could affect the probability of informal employment through channels other than tariff reductions such as import competition. Column 2 of Table 9.8 reports the results from regression specifications that include the first lags of imports and exports. The results contain two noteworthy findings. First, the tariff coefficient seems robust to the inclusion of the additional trade controls. Second, the positive sign on the coefficient on imports suggests that the probability of informal employment increases when an industry faces higher import penetration. This supports the view that increased foreign competition forces domestic firms to become more competitive and reduce cost by either subcontracting in the informal sector or by firing workers that in turn seek employment in the informal sector. In column 3 of Table 9.8, we allow the impact of imports and exports on informality to vary with exchange rate

Table 9.8 Probability of informal employment and trade policy

	(1)	(2)	(3)	(4)	(5)	(6)
Nominal tariff	−0.087**	−0.096*	−0.0930	0.0180	−0.0110	−0.0040
	[0.038]	[0.053]	[0.059]	[0.012]	[0.033]	[0.033]
Lagged imports		0.00025**	0.00044**		0.00009*	0.00035**
		[0.00006]	[0.00009]		[0.00004]	[0.00008]
Lagged exports		−0.00033*	−0.00031		−0.00022**	−0.00008
		[0.00017]	[0.00027]		[0.00010]	[0.00009]
Lagged imports* exchange rate			−0.0000026**			−0.000002**
			[0.0000007]			[0.000001]
Lagged exports* exchange rate			−0.0000002			−0.000002*
			[0.0000012]			[0.000001]
First-differences	No	No	No	Yes	Yes	Yes
Year indicators	Yes	Yes	Yes	Yes	Yes	Yes
Industry indicators	Yes	Yes	Yes	No	No	No

Notes
* and ** indicate 5 and 10 percent significance, respectively. Reported standard errors are robust and clustered on industry. N is 147 in columns 1–3 and 126 in columns 4–6. Columns 1–3 are estimated with industry-fixed effects. Columns 4–6 are estimated in first-differences.

fluctuations. We control for exchange rate fluctuations by interacting the exchange rate with lagged values of imports and exports. While the inclusion of exchange rate hardly changes the magnitude of the coefficients on tariff, the coefficients become statistically insignificant. Moreover, our results continue to suggest that probability of informal employment increases when an industry faces higher import competition.

We also estimate the relationship between informality and trade policy in first-differences form and those results are reported in columns 4–6. Interestingly, while the positive association between import competition and informality continues to hold, first-differences results suggest no relationship between industry informality differentials and tariffs. In Goldberg and Pavcnik (2003) we investigate the discrepancy between the industry-fixed-effects results and first-differences results further. We find that the labor market reform in 1990 that reduced the costs of firing and hiring a worker and increased labor market turnover (see Kugler, 1999; Heckman and Pages, 2000) plays an important role. In particular, we allow the relationship between informality and trade policy to differ before and after the Colombian labor market reform. Those specifications yield interesting findings: tariff reductions are associated with increases in informality before labor market reform in both the industry-fixed effects and first-differences specifications. However, we find no statistically significant (or a small positive association) between informality and tariff changes after the labor market reform. These differences in the results indicate that labor market institutions play a potentially important role in how trade reform affects informal employment. In sum, we find that tariff declines are associated with an increase in informal employment, but only in period before the labor market reforms.

Given that the "discount" of informality increases in the later years of our sample, we also examined if this increase was driven by changes in the return to informality in specific sectors of the economy that were affected more by trade policy. To this end, we allowed in the framework described earlier interactions between industry premiums and informality and related these interactions to industry tariffs. The tariff coefficients in these specifications were, however, not statistically significant, indicating that the effect of trade policy on industry wages did not vary across the formal and informal sectors. Put differently, the falling wages in the informal sector cannot be attributed to decreasing wages in the informal sectors of industries that experienced larger tariff reductions.

In summary, our results provide some suggestive evidence that trade liberalization contributed to an increase in the size of the informal sector in Colombia in the period before the labor market reform. Because jobs in the informal sector do not provide benefits and are associated with lower job satisfaction and quality of work, the rise in informality contributes to the increase in inequality.

9.7   On the role of labor market institutions

Our analysis so far has abstracted from the contributions of labor market institutions, such as minimum wages and unions, to wage inequality. Changes in the minimum wage could potentially affect the skill premium by compressing the lower end of the wage distribution. However, while evidence suggests that the minimum wages are binding in Colombia (see Bell, 1997), *changes* in minimum wages are of secondary importance during our sample period in Colombia. The most significant increases in the minimum wage took place in the late 1970s and early 1980s (see Bell, 1997: table 9.2). The changes in the late 1980s and 1990s were in comparison small. Moreover, the minimum wage is set in Colombia at the national level, so that minimum wages do not vary by industry. As a result, changes in the minimum wage cannot explain the relationship between tariffs changes and changes in wage premium (or changes in informality) in our study. Note that any effects minimum wage changes may have had on industry wages (or probability of informal employment) through compositional channels, for example, because some industries employ more unskilled workers than others, are already controlled for in our approach in Sections 9.5 and 9.6, since the first-stage regressions control for industry composition in each year and allow the returns to various educational and professional categories to change from year to year.

Regarding unionization, our individual level data do not provide information on the union membership of each worker. Unfortunately, detailed industry-level information on union membership is also not available. As a result, the economy-wide increases in skill premium over time documented in this chapter could potentially reflect changes in union power (e.g. increases in skill premium could be attributed to unions if unions usually increase the relative wages of the unskilled workers and the union power has declined over time). While in the absence of industry-level union data we cannot formally address this issue, we believe that changes in unionization are unlikely to be of concern during this period (especially in the analysis that related industry-specific tariff changes to various labor market outcomes). Anecdotal evidence suggests that unions do not have significant power in most

Colombian industries (public sector and the petroleum industry are the exception). In his book on Colombian reforms, Edwards (2001) confirms these anecdotal reports. More importantly, there is no evidence (or even a claim) in the literature that union strength changed during the period of trade liberalization. We therefore believe that changes in unionization are unlikely to be driving our results.

Finally, our discussion is premised on the existence of labor market rigidities in Colombia. While we do not attempt a formal investigation of the role of such rigidities, their existence seems a priori relevant in Colombia, a country characterized by one of the most restrictive labor market regimes in Latin America. Indicatively, Heckman and Pages (2000) report that the cost of dismissing a worker in Colombia is approximately six times the monthly wage at the end of the 1980s and 3.5 times the monthly wage at the end of the 1990s (after the labor market reform). Kugler (1999) reports similar findings on the costs of firing workers in Colombia. In addition, several of our results seem consistent with the view that labor markets in Colombia are rigid, and labor market regulation is to some extent binding. For example, we fail to find big labor reallocations in the aftermath of a major trade reform, from sectors that experienced large protection declines to sectors that were less affected by liberalization: regressions of changes in sectoral employment shares on tariff changes fail to detect any relationship between trade liberalization and sectoral employment. This stability of industry employment shares seems consistent with constrained labor mobility. Still, the lack of labor reallocation seems rather surprising given the existence of a large informal sector in Colombia that does not comply with labor market regulation. One possible explanation is that labor is more mobile across the formal and informal sectors, than across industries. Indeed, in a related paper (Goldberg and Pavcnik, 2003), we find that while the share of informal workers increased in Colombia in the aftermath of the trade reforms, the entire increase is accounted for by within-industry changes from the formal to the informal sector rather than by between-industry shifts of informal workers.

9.8   Unemployment

Upto this point, we have abstracted from the relationship between trade policy and transition into unemployment. Table 9.9 reports the unemployment rate in urban Colombia during our sample based on June waves of NHS Montenegro and Peña (2000) report similar trends in overall unemployment based on the Department of National Planning data. Because unemployment may be an important component of the adjustment mechanism to trade shocks, at least in the short run, the natural question arises whether trade policy contributed to these unemployment changes. Table 9.9 suggests that the urban unemployment rate declined from about 14 percent in 1984 to 9.7 percent in 1994. Until the very end of our sample period unemployment rates were remarkably stable and particularly so during the years around the tariff cuts. Only in 1998, at the beginning of the worst recession in Colombian recent history and with no changes in tariffs did unemployment increase to 16 percent.

Table 9.9 Aggregate unemployment

Year	Unemployment
1984	0.1369
1986	0.1459
1988	0.1193
1990	0.1097
1992	0.1113
1994	0.0974
1996	0.1175
1998	0.1584

Note
Share of unemployed in total labor force
based on June waves of NHS.

Although the aggregate statistics seem to suggest that tariff reductions are unlikely to be the main cause of the unemployment surge during the late 1990s, inferences based on macroeconomic trends can be misleading. The link between trade policy and unemployment could be better identified by relating detailed industry tariff changes to changes in industry unemployment in an analysis parallel to the study of the relationship between informality and tariffs in Section 9.6. Unfortunately, the lack of detailed data on industry affiliation of the unemployed in the NHS precludes such an analysis. In particular, the unemployed workers that were previously employed report the last industry of employment at the one-digit ISIC level. Similarly, the unemployed individuals who were not previously employed report the industry in which they are seeking employment at the one-digit ISIC level. This leads to 9 industry observations per year and only 6 out of 9 of these industries have available tariffs. Most importantly, most of the time-variation in tariffs occurred within the manufacturing industries which are now treated as a single sector. As a result, we cannot pursue such an approach.

To get a rough idea whether trade policy changes could be associated with increases in unemployment, we instead check whether the increase in the probability of being unemployed was greater for workers employed in traded-good sectors (such as manufacturing) than for workers with the same observable characteristics in non-traded-good sectors (such as wholesale and retail trade, restaurants, hotels, construction, etc.). We perform this analysis for two years at a time, using a year before and after the major trade reforms in 1990–91. In particular, we regress an indicator for whether an individual is unemployed on one-digit ISIC industry indicators (wholesale and retail trade, restaurants/hotels (ISIC 6) is the omitted category), an indicator for a year following the trade reform, the interaction of industry indicators with the year indicator, and a set of worker characteristics (age, age squared, male, married, head of the household, education indicators, literate, lives in Bogota, born in urban area, time in residence, urban birth*time in residence). If the probability of being unemployed increased relatively more over time in manufacturing relative to a sector such as wholesale and retail trade and restaurants and hotels (i.e. the coefficient on the interaction of the manufacturing indicator with year indicator is positive and significant), this could provide some indirect (and suggestive) evidence that trade reforms were associated with increases in the probability of unemployment.

Table 9.10 presents the results. Column 1 focuses on the changes in probability of unemployment between the first and last year of our sample, 1984 and 1998 respectively. Two findings emerge. First, as expected, the coefficient on the post trade reform year is positive and significant, which reflects the aggregate increase in unemployment in Colombia during the 1990s. Second, the coefficient on the interaction of manufacturing indicator and the post trade reform indicator is negative and insignificant. This suggests that conditional on worker characteristics, the probability of unemployment did not change in a statistically different way in manufacturing sector relative to the non-traded-reference sector. In fact, with the exception of the transportation sector, we find no statistical differences in changes of the probability of unemployment across industries between 1984 and 1998. This analysis seems to support the view that the probability of unemployment did not change significantly in the manufacturing sector relative to most non-traded sectors over the long run, even though the manufacturing sector experienced drastic tariff declines. However, the given analysis might potentially miss short-term adjustments to trade reform that occur during times closer to trade reform. As a result, in column 2 we consider the unemployment adjustment in periods right before and after the major tariff declines by focusing on changes in unemployment between 1988 and 1992. While the coefficient on the interaction of the manufacturing indicator with the post trade reform year continues to be negative, its magnitude increases in absolute value and is now statistically significant (this could be potentially due to exchange rate depreciation in 1990 that lowered the demand for non-traded goods relative to traded goods).

In sum, albeit we cannot directly identify the effects of tariff declines on the probability of employment, our data suggest that increases in the probability of unemployment before and after tariff reductions were not larger in traded sectors (such as manufacturing) than in non-traded sectors (such as wholesale and retail trade). If anything, the short-term changes in unemployment suggest the opposite.

9.9 Conclusions

In this chapter, we investigated the effects of the drastic tariff reductions of the 1980s and 1990s in Colombia on the wage distribution. We identified three main channels through which the wage distribution could have been affected: increasing returns to college education, changes in industry wages that hurt sectors with initially lower wages and a higher fraction of unskilled workers, and shifts of the labor force toward the informal sector that typically pays lower wages and offers no benefits. Our results suggest that trade policy played a role in each of the above cases. The increase in the skill premium was primarily driven by skill-biased technological change. However, as the sectors with the largest reductions in tariffs were those with the sharpest increase in the share of skilled workers, we

Table 9.10 Probablility of unemployment

	(1)	(2)
Agriculture, hunting, forestry (ISIC 1)	0.059**	0.026**
	[0.012]	[0.011]
Mining/quarrying (ISIC 2)	0.087**	0.026
	[0.028]	[0.022]
Manufacturing (ISIC 3)	−0.006	−0.009*
	[0.004]	[0.004]
Electricity/gas/water (ISIC 4)	0.029*	−0.005
	[0.017]	[0.016]
Construction (ISIC 5)	0.097**	0.046**
	[0.007]	[0.008]
Transportation/communication (ISIC 7)	0.016**	0.008
	[0.006]	[0.006]
Financing/insurance/business services (ISIC 8)	0.036**	0.046**
	[0.007]	[0.008]
Community/Social/Personal Services (ISIC 9)	−0.044**	−0.031**
	[0.004]	[0.004]
ISIC_1* post trade reform year	−0.014	−0.003
	[0.019]	[0.017]
ISIC_2* post trade reform year	−0.041	0.047
	[0.041]	[0.037]
ISIC_3* post trade reform year	−0.008	−0.018**
	[0.007]	[0.006]
ISIC_4* post trade reform year	−0.035	0.014
	[0.025]	[0.023]
ISIC_5* post trade reform year	−0.016	−0.001
	[0.011]	[0.011]
ISIC_7* post trade reform year	−0.033**	−0.010
	[0.009]	[0.009]
ISIC_8* post trade reform year	−0.010	−0.028**
	[0.010]	[0.011]
ISIC_9* post trade reform year	0.005	−0.006
	[0.006]	[0.006]
post trade reform year	0.026**	0.005
	[0.004]	[0.004]
Age	−0.015**	−0.012**
	[0.000]	[0.000]
Age squared	0.000**	0.000**
	[0.000]	[0.000]
Male	−0.042**	−0.043**
	[0.003]	[0.003]
Married	−0.032**	−0.017**
	[0.002]	[0.002]
Head of the HH	−0.075**	−0.064**
	[0.003]	[0.003]
Elementary school	0.015**	0.009**
	[0.003]	[0.003]
Secondary school	0.009**	0.005
	[0.004]	[0.004]
University degree	−0.035**	−0.037**
	[0.004]	[0.004]

Table 9.10 Continued

	(1)	(2)
Literate	0.011*	0.016**
	[0.007]	[0.006]
Lives in Bogota	−0.022**	−0.023**
	[0.003]	[0.003]
Born in urban area	0.027**	0.023**
	[0.006]	[0.006]
Time in residence	0.001**	0.001**
	[0.000]	[0.000]
Urban birth*time in residence	−0.001**	−0.001**
	[0.000]	[0.000]
Years used	1984, 1998	1988, 1992
Post trade reform year	1998	1992
Number of observations	91,393	79,807

Notes
** and * indicate 5 and 10 percent significance, respectively. ISIC 6 (wholesale and retail trade and restaurants and hotels) is the excluded one-digit ISIC industry.

argue that this change may have been in part motivated by the tariff reductions and the increased foreign competition to which the trade reform exposed domestic producers.

With respect to industry wages, we find that wage premiums decreased by more in sectors that experienced larger tariff cuts. As these were the sectors with the lowest premiums, this shift increased inequality. Finally, we find some evidence that the increase in the size of the informal sector is related to increased foreign competition – sectors with larger tariff cuts and more trade exposure, as measured by the size of their imports, saw a greater increase in informality, but only in the period prior to the labor market reform. Nevertheless, increasing returns to education and changes in industry premiums and informality alone cannot fully explain the increase in wage inequality we observe over this period. This suggests that overall the effect of the trade reforms on the wage distribution may have been small.

Much work remains to be done. The two items that should be at the top of the research agenda in this area are the study of the flows into unemployment (as this is bound to be an important component of the adjustment mechanism, at least in the short run), and the effect that unemployment – to the extent that it is not randomly distributed – may have on measured wage inequality. Unfortunately, our current data is not well suited for answering this question. In addition, the difference between the Colombian and Mexican experience is interesting and worth further exploring, as it provides a fruitful ground for studying the conditions under which policies aimed at promoting growth and efficiency have no (or relatively small) adverse effects on the wage distribution. One potential explanation for the larger effect of the reforms on wage inequality in Mexico hinges on the role of foreign direct investment which was large in Mexico (see Cragg and

Epelbaum, 1996; Feenstra and Hanson, 1997). We do not attempt to resolve these issues in this chapter, but we leave them as a topic for further research. Finally, the effect that competitive pressures may have on technology adoption and therefore on the demand for skills is, in our opinion, a particularly important question deserving further investigation.

Notes

Prepared for the 2002 IMF Conference on Macroeconomic Policies and Poverty Reduction, Washington, DC, March 14–15, 2002.

1 Trade liberalization in Colombia also reduced NTBs to trade.

2 High world prices of coffee, significant foreign borrowing by Colombia, and illegal exports all contributed to the large appreciation of the peso during the late 1970s and early 1980s (Roberts and Tybout, 1997).

3 The source of tariff information is the Colombian National Planning Department (DNP). Overall, they are available for 21 two-digit ISIC industries. See Goldberg and Pavcnik (2005) for details.

4 The source of NTB information is the United Nation's publication Directory of Import Regimes. NTBs are measured as coverage ratios. They are available for 17 two-digit ISIC sectors.

5 We have excluded all workers for which one or more variables were not reported.

6 One potential shortcoming of the data on worker's characteristics is the lack of information on the union status. Edwards (2001) suggests that unions are ineffective in most industries. See also the discussion in Section 9.7.

7 This information is not available in 1984.

8 Because workplace variables and informality were not available for 1984, Table 9.3 omits 1984. We have also estimated Table 9.3 for all years without workplace characteristics. Without such controls, our estimates of the college premium increase. This is intuitive since college educated workers work primarily in the formal sector, and wages in the formal sector are higher. The college premium then also captures the premium of working in the formal sector. Moreover, we have also repeated the analysis only for males in an effort to eliminate the impact of selection effects that are potentially important in female labor supply. The main difference between the full and the male-only samples seems to be the magnitude of the estimated return to college education, which is higher for males only. Nevertheless, the trends across years remain robust across the different samples.

9 What is perhaps more surprising (and inconsistent in some sense with the simple 2×2 version of the Heckscher–Ohlin model) is the fact that it was the unskilled-labor intensive sectors that were heavily protected prior to the reforms. These sectors (especially textiles and apparel, and wood and wood products) are characterized by low imports. This pattern of protection could be explained within a political economy model of protection such as Grossman and Helpman (1994), or alternatively, by an extension of Heckscher–Ohlin to a three-factor (natural resources, unskilled, and skilled labor) version (see Wood, 1999; Leamer *et al.*, 2002).

10 Given that the most protected sectors are unskilled-labor intensive, these sectors are potentially net exporters producing differentiated products. Lower tariffs are likely to lead to lower wages even in the presence of product differentiation and intra-industry trade, as long as lower tariffs are not counterbalanced by higher export prices in this sector. Because Colombia is a small country and it experienced a drastic unilateral liberalization during our study, it is unlikely that trade liberalization was accompanied by a rise in export prices.

11 Leamer has made the argument in several papers that it is sector bias, and not factor bias that is relevant for the income distribution. Skilled-biased technological change that is

concentrated in unskilled-intensive sectors would benefit unskilled workers in the general equilibrium, while skill-biased technological change concentrated in skilled-intensive industries would benefit skilled workers. Motivated by this argument we regressed the annual change in the share of skilled workers in each industry on the initial skill intensity of the industry in 1984. A positive coefficient would suggest bias that would favor skilled workers (skill-biased technological change would be more pronounced in sectors that are initially skill intensive). However, this regression did not produce a statistically significant coefficient. If anything, the negative sign of the "initial skill-intensity" coefficient would suggest the presence of skill-biased technological change that is concentrated in low-skill sectors. Note, however, that Leamer's argument rests on the assumption of fixed product prices which is unlikely to hold during trade liberalization.

12 This argument is also related to Wood (1995) and to the more recent paper by Thoenig and Verdier (2002). See also the survey by Acemoglu (2002).

13 In reality, some dispersion in tariff rates remained even after the trade reforms, but this dispersion is substantially smaller than the pre-reform tariff rate dispersion. See standard deviations in Table 9.1a.

14 The exchange rate we use is the nominal effective rate (source: IMF) that is computed taking into account Colombia's major trade partners. IMF is also the source of coffee prices.

15 Note that we cannot include the 1983 tariffs as an instrument in industry-fixed effects 2SLS regressions because the variable is time-invariant. As a result, we only use the interaction of the 1983 tariffs with the exchange rate (coffee prices) as an instrument.

16 See Dickens and Katz (1986), Krueger and Summers (1987, 1988), Katz and Summers (1989), Gaston and Trefler (1994).

17 We have also experimented with several other specifications (see Goldberg and Pavcnik, 2005). The overall conclusions are similar to those reported in this chapter. Moreover, these specifications were estimated using both the log of the weekly earnings and the log of hourly earnings as dependent variables. The wage premiums based on these two definitions were highly correlated. We therefore focus our discussion on hourly wage premiums.

18 The sum of the employment weighted normalized wage premiums is zero.

19 Haisken-DeNew and Schmidt (1997) adjust the variance covariance matrix of the normalized industry indicators to yield an exact standard error for the normalized coefficients.

20 Alternatively, we could combine the regressors in (9.1) and (9.2) and estimate the relationship between wages and tariffs directly in one stage. In fact, we have implemented this one-stage approach, and the coefficient on tariff was 0.081 and highly significant. However, because our individual-level data are a repeated cross-section, we cannot estimate the one-stage regression in first-differenced form. The main reason that we focus on the two-stage approach is that it allows us to difference the industry-level data (our preferred specification).

21 Of course, to the extent that imports and exports are serially correlated, this approach does not completely eliminate simultaneity bias. While we fail to reject that there is no serial correlation for exports, we reject the test of no serial correlation in the case of imports (rho is 0.27 with p-value of 0.001). However, the specification that includes imports as a control variable is merely a robustness check and the coefficient on tariffs is not sensitive to the inclusion of imports.

22 See the discussion in Section 9.4.1 that motivates the choice of instruments.

23 An interesting feature of the Colombian data is that informality is present in *all* industries. This contrasts with the widely held view that informality is a feature of specific sectors, such as wholesale and retail trade. While these sectors do have the highest shares of informal workers in our sample (76 and 67 percent respectively), the share of informal employment in manufacturing is 48 percent. Moreover, this share has increased over time in manufacturing, peaking in 1996 and 1998.

24 As in the case of wage premiums, we have also estimated the relationship between informality and tariffs in one-step approach. This yielded similar conclusions as the two-stage industry fixed-effects regressions. The coefficient on tariff was -0.126 and highly significant.

References

Acemoglu, D. 2002. "Technical Change, Inequality, and the Labor Market," *Journal of Economic Literature*, 40: 7–72.

—— 2003. "Patterns of Skill Premia," *Review of Economic Studies*, 70: 199–230.

Attanasio, O. and M. Szekely. 2000. "Household Saving in East Asia and Latin America: Inequality Demographics and All That," ed. by B. Pleskovic and N. Stern, *Annual World Bank Conference on Development Economics* (Washington, DC: World Bank).

Bell, L. 1997. "The Impact of Minimum Wages in Mexico and Colombia," *Journal of Labor Economics*, 15: S103–135.

Berman, E., S. Machin, and J. Bound. 1998. "Implications of Skill-Biased Technological Changes: International Evidence," *Quarterly Journal of Economics*, 113: 1245–79.

Cragg, M.I. and M. Epelbaum. 1996. "Why has Wage Dispersion Grown in Mexico? Is it the Incidence of Reforms or the Growing Demand for Skills?" *Journal of Development Economics*, 51: 99–116.

Currie, J. and A. Harrison. 1997. "Trade Reform and Labor Market Adjustment in Morocco," *Journal of Labor Economics*, 15: S44–71.

Dickens, W.T. and L.F. Katz. 1986. "Interindustry Wage Differences and Industry Characteristics," NBER Working Paper No. 2014 (Cambridge, MA: National Bureau of Economic Research).

Echavarria, J., C. Gamboa, and R. Guerrero. "Escenarios de Reforma a la Estructura Arancelaria de la Comunidad Andina," Fedesarrollo, manuscript (n.p.).

Edwards, S. 2001. "The Economics and Politics of Transition to an Open Market Economy: Colombia" (OECD: Paris and Washington, DC).

Feenstra, R. and G. Hanson. 1997. "Foreign Direct Investment and Relative Wages: Evidence From Mexico's Maquiladoras," *Journal of International Economics*, 42(3–4): 371–93.

Feliciano, Z. 2001. "Workers and Trade Liberalization: The Impact of Trade Reforms in Mexico on Wages and Employment," *Industrial and Labor Relations Review*, 55(1): 95–115.

Fernandes, A.M. "Trade Policy, Trade Volumes and Plant-Level Productivity in Colombian Manufacturing Industries," Yale University, manuscript (n.p.).

Gaston, N. and D. Trefler. 1994. "Protection, Trade and Wages: Evidence from U.S. Manufacturing," *Industrial and Labor Relations Review*, 47(4): 574–93.

—— 2003. "The Response of the Informal Sector to Trade Liberalization," *Journal of Development Economics*, 72: 463–96.

Goldberg, P. and N. Pavcnik. 2005. "Trade Protection and Wages: Evidence from the Colombian Trade Reforms," *Journal of International Economics*, 66: 75–105.

Grossman, G. 1984. "International Competition and the Unionized Sector," *Canadian Journal of Economics*, 17(3): 541–56.

—— 1986. "Imports as a Cause of Injury: The Case of the U.S. Steel Industry," *Journal of International Economics*, 20(3–4): 201–23.

—— and E. Helpman. 1994. "Protection for Sale," *American Economic Review*, 84(4): 833–50.

Haisken-DeNew, J.P. and C.M. Schmidt. 1997. "Inter-Industry and Inter-Region Wage Differentials: Mechanics and Interpretation," *Review of Economics and Statistics*, 79(3): 516–21.

Hanson, G. and A. Harrison, 1999. "Who Gains from Trade Reform? Some Remaining Puzzles," *Journal of Development Economics*, 59: 125–54.

Harrison, A. 1994. "Productivity, Imperfect Competition and Trade Reform: Theory and Evidence," *Journal of International Economics*, 36 (1–2): 53–73.

—— and E. Leamer. 1997. "Labor Markets in Developing Countries: An Agenda for Research," *Journal of Labor Economics*, 15: S1–19.

Heckman J. and C. Pages. 2000. "The Cost of Job Security Regulation: Evidence from Latin American Labor Market," NBER Working Paper 7773 (Cambridge, MA: National Bureau of Economic Research).

Johnston, L.N. 1996. "Trade Liberalization and Income Distribution: Insight from the Colombian Reform," Chapter 1 of Ph.D thesis: "Returns to Education, Human Capital and Income Inequality in Colombia" (Cambridge, MA: Harvard University).

Katz, L.F. and L.H. Summers. 1989. "Industry Rents: Evidence and Implications," *Brookings Papers on Economic Activity, Microeconomics*, pp. 209–75.

Kim, E. 2000. "Trade Liberalization and Productivity Growth in Korean Manufacturing Industries: Price Protection, Market Power and Scale Efficiency," *Journal of Development Economics*, 62(1): 55–83.

Krishna, P. and D. Mitra. 1998. "Trade Liberalization, Market Discipline and Productivity Growth; New Evidence from India," *Journal of Development Economics*, 56(2): 447–62.

Krueger, A.B. and L.H. Summers. 1987. "Reflections on the Inter-Industry Wage Structure," ed. by K. Lang and S. Leonard, *Unemployment and the Structure of Labor Markets*, 17–47 (Oxford: Basil Blackwell).

—— 1988. "Efficiency Wages and the Inter-Industry Wage Structure," *Econometrica*, 56: 259–93.

Kugler, A. 1999. "The Impact of Firing Costs on Turnover and Unemployment: Evidence from The Colombian Labour Market Reform," *International Tax and Public Finance Journal*, 6(3): 389–410.

Leamer, E. 1994. "Trade, Wages and the Revolving Door Ideas," NBER Working Paper, No. 4716 (Cambridge, MA: National Bureau of Economic Research).

—— 1996. "What's the Use of Factor Contents?" NBER Working Paper No. 5448, (Cambridge, MA: National Bureau of Economic Research).

—— 1998. "In Search of Stolper-Samuelson Effects on U.S. Wages," ed. by S. Collins, *Exports, Imports and the American economy* (Washington, DC: Brookings Institution).

——, H. Maul, S. Rodriguez, and P. Schott. 2002. "Does Natural Resource Abundance Cause Latin American Inequality?" *Journal of Development Economics*, 59(1): 3–42.

Montenegro, S. and X. Peña. "Labor Reforms, Macroeconomic Imbalances, and Unemployment in Colombia," Los Andes University: manuscript (n.p.).

Nuñez Mendez, J. and F. Sanchez Torres. "A Dynamic Analysis of Household Decision Making in Urban Colombia, 1976–1998," Bogota, Colombia: manuscript (n.p.).

Pavcnik, N. 2002. "Trade Liberalization, Exit and Productivity Improvements: Evidence from Chilean Plants," *Review of Economic Studies*, Vol. 69 (January): 245–76.

—— 2003. "What Explains Skill Upgrading in Less Developed Countries?," *Journal of Development Economics*, 71: 311–28.

Revenga, A. 1992. "Exporting Jobs? The Impact of Import Competition on Employment and Wages in U.S. Manufacturing," *Quarterly Journal of Economics*, 107(1): 255–84.

Revenga, A. 1997. "Employment and Wage Effects of Trade Liberalization: The Case of Mexican Manufacturing," *Journal of Labor Economics*, 15: S20–43.

Robbins, D. 1996. "Evidence on Trade and Wages in the Developing World," OECD Technical Paper No. 119 (Paris: Organization for Economic Cooperation and Development).

Roberts, M. and J. Tybout. 1991. "Size Rationalization and Trade Exposure in Developing Countries," ed. by R. Baldwin, *Empirical Studies of Commercial Policy* (Chicago, IL: University of Chicago Press).

—— (eds). 1996. *Industrial Evolution in Developing Countries: Micro Patterns of Turnover, Productivity and Market Structure* (New York: Oxford University Press).

—— 1997. "The Decision to Export in Colombia: An Empirical Model of Entry with Sunk Costs," *American Economic Review*, 87: 545–564.

Robertson, R. (n.d.). "Inter-Industry Wage Differentials Across Time, Borders, and Trade Regimes: Evidence from the U.S. and Mexico," Macalester College: manuscript (n.p.).

Rodrik, D. 1991. "Closing the Productivity Gap: Does Trade Liberalization Really Help?," ed. by G. Helleiner, *Trade Policy, Industrialization and Development* (Oxford: Clarendon Press).

Stallings, B. and W. Peres. 2000. *"Growth, Employment and Equity. The Impact of the Economic Reforms in Latin American and Caribbean,"* Economic Commission for Latin American and Caribbean (Washington, DC: Brookings Institution Press).

Thoenig, M. and T. Verdier. 2003. "A Theory of Defensive Skill-Based Innovation and Globalization," *American Economic Review*, 93: 709–28.

United Nations. 1994. *Directory of Import Regimes Part I: Monitoring Import Regimes*, (Geneva: United Nations).

Wood, A. 1995. "How Trade Hurt Unskilled Workers," *Journal of Economic Perspectives*, 9(3): 57–80.

—— 1999. "Openness and Wage Inequality in Developing Countries: The Latin American Challenge to East Asian Conventional Wisdom," ed. by R. Baldwin, D. Cohen, A. Venables and A. Sapir, in *Market Integration, Regionalism and the Global Economy*, 153–81 (Cambridge: Cambridge University Press).

Part IV
Crises and shocks

10 Financial crises, poverty, and income distribution

*Emanuele Baldacci, Luiz de Mello, and
Gabriela Inchauste*

Developing and transition economies are prone to financial crises including
balance of payments and banking crises. These crises affect poverty and the
distribution of income through a variety of channels – slowdowns in economic
activity, relative price changes, and fiscal retrenchment, among others. This chapter
deals with the impact of financial crises on the incidence of poverty and income
distribution, and discusses policy options that can be considered by governments
in the aftermath of crises. Empirical evidence based on both macro and
microlevel data shows that financial crises are associated with an increase in
poverty and, in some cases, income inequality. The provison of targeted safety
nets and the protection of specific social programs from fiscal retrenchment
remain the main short-term pro-poor policy responses to financial crises.

10.1 Introduction

Developing and transition economies are prone to financial crises including balance
of payments and banking crises. These crises affect poverty and income distribution
through a variety of channels (Box 10.1). Financial crises typically lead to slowdowns in economic activity and consequently rises in formal unemployment and/or
falls in real wages. A contractionary policy mix is conventionally implemented in
response to a financial crisis including fiscal retrenchment and a tightening of the
monetary stance. Fiscal retrenchment, in turn, often leads to cuts in public outlays on
social programs, transfers to households, and wages and salaries among others
(World Bank, 2000). Exchange rate realignments result in changes in relative prices
likely to affect some social groups more adversely than others and consequently
result in changes in poverty and income distribution indicators. Conventional
wisdom is that the poor suffer disproportionately to the non-poor in periods of crisis.

The question this chapter addresses is how the poor are affected by financial
crises.[1] Important policy questions are whether income distribution, not only the
incidence of poverty, is affected by financial crises and whether the impact of
crises on poverty and on income distribution is stronger in countries where the
distribution of income is more skewed. Easterly (2001) shows that the poor are
hurt less by falling standards of living in countries where the distribution of

Box 10.1 Financial crises, poverty, and income distribution

The main channels through which financial crises affect poverty and income distribution are:

- *A slowdown in economic activity*   A financial crisis may lead to a fall in earnings of both formal- and informal-sector workers due to job losses in the formal sector and reduced demand for services in the informal sector. Reduced working hours and real wage cuts also adversely affect the earnings of the poor. Entry of unemployed formal-sector workers into the informal sector puts additional pressure on the informal labor market (Bourguignon and Morrisson, 1992; Morley, 1995; Lustig and Walton, 1998; Walton and Manuelyan, 1998).
- *Relative price changes*   After a currency depreciation, the price of tradables rises relative to nontradables leading to a fall in earnings of those employed in the nontrade sector. At the same time, there may be an increase in the demand for exports and consequently employment and earnings in the sectors producing exportables, thereby offsetting some of the losses due to the decline in GDP. The exchange rate change may affect the price of imported food, increasing domestic food prices; this increase in turn hurts poor individuals and households that are net consumers of food (Sahn *et al.*, 1997).
- *Fiscal retrenchment*   Spending cuts affect the volume of publicly provided critical social services including social assistance outlays, and limit the access of the poor to these services at a time when their incomes are declining (Lanjouw and Ravallion, 1999).
- *Changes in assets*   Wealth effects or changes in the value of assets have a significant impact on income distribution (Bléjer and Guerrero, 1990; Datt and Ravallion, 1998). Changes in interest rates, as well as in asset and real estate prices, affect the wealth of the better off.[a]

Note

a Trade liberalization, the removal of price subsidies, and privatization are likely to affect social groups asymmetrically over the medium term. Easterly (2001) shows that IMF or World Bank adjustment programs tend to reduce the impact of recessions on the poor. The poor also benefit less from expansions in the presence of an adjustment program.

income is more unequal because the poor have a lower share of income to begin with. In the wake of financial crises, emphasis on poverty headcounts, without reference to changes in income distribution, may lead to inadequate policy recommendations. This is because the impact of financial crises on the incidence of poverty is often estimated under the assumption that the distribution of income remains unchanged in the short term.

The objectives of this chapter are (1) to estimate the impact of financial crises on the incidence of poverty and on the distribution of income; and (2) to evaluate the policy options considered by governments in the aftermath of crises to mitigate their adverse impact on the poor.[2] The postcrisis impact on the poor is yet to be assessed through a systematic analysis, both from the cross-country perspective and at the microlevel. Macrolevel data allow for the estimation of the empirical relationship between financial crisis and poverty from a cross-country perspective. Microlevel data allow for a more in-depth analysis of the individual and household characteristics that are correlated with poverty, including demographics and earnings by occupation. We also assess whether the cross-country evidence presented here is consistent with that based on microlevel data. In this study, we use microlevel data for Mexico.

With regard to *policy implications*, the empirical analysis will shed light on (1) the main channels through which financial crises are likely to have an impact on poverty as well as the magnitude of the impact; (2) the short-run policy instruments that can be used to shelter the poor before, during, and after financial crises; and (3) the characteristics of poverty and inequality that should be taken into account in the policy responses to crises.

10.2   The methodology

10.2.1   The cross-country analysis

The cross-country analysis will be carried out by analogy with the differences-in-differences methodology used conventionally in microdata analysis. The empirical literature on currency crises and leading indicators (summarized in Box 10.2) also uses methodologies conventionally applied to the analysis of microeconomic phenomena such as the event analysis borrowed from the micro-finance literature. In a nutshell, the methodology consists of examining outcomes such as the impact of a financial crisis on poverty, using observations in a treatment group (i.e. the crisis-stricken countries) relative to a control group (i.e. countries unaffected by the crisis) that are not randomly assigned. In other words, the methodology (1) assesses precrisis and postcrisis average changes in poverty and income distribution indicators in countries affected by financial crises and (2) compares these changes in poverty and income distribution indicators relative to a sample of control countries that have not been affected by financial crises.[3] All relevant variables are defined as differences between the crisis-affected countries under examination and the control group.[4]

The estimating equation can be defined as

$$\Delta P_i(t) - \Delta P_j(t) = a_0 + a_1 \Delta[F_i(t) - F_j(t)] + a_2 \Delta[X_i(t) - X_j(t)] + u_i(t)$$

$$(10.1)$$

where $\Delta P_i(t) = \ln P_i(t) - \ln P_i(t-s)$ denotes the change in a poverty/income distribution indicator (for instance, poverty headcount ratios, Gini coefficient, and income shares, among others) of a crisis-stricken country i between a postcrisis period t and a precrisis period $t - s$; $\Delta P_j(t) = \ln P_j(t) - \ln P_j(t-s)$ denotes the

Box 10.2 The financial crisis literature: an overview

There have been important developments in the literature on currency and banking crises (e.g. Eichengreen *et al.*, 1995; Milesi-Ferretti and Razin, 1996, 1998; Flood and Marion, 1997; Kaminsky *et al.*, 1997). Financial crises are attributed to rapid reversals in international capital flows and prompted chiefly by changes in international investment conditions. Flow reversals are likely to trigger sudden current account adjustments, and subsequently currency and banking crises (e.g. Frankel and Rose, 1996; Eichengreen and Rose, 1998).

A first generation of currency crisis models – pioneered by Krugman (1979) – explained the collapse of exchange rate regimes on the grounds that weak fundamentals lead foreign investors to pull resources out of the country, and as a result the depletion of foreign reserves needed to sustain the currency leads to the collapse of the exchange rate regime. A second generation of models suggests that currency crises may also occur despite sound fundamentals as in the case of self-fulfilling expectations (Obstfeld, 1996), speculative attacks, and changes in market sentiment (Frankel and Rose, 1996; Flood and Marion, 1997).

Identifying crises

The currency/banking crisis literature favors the event analysis methodology for identifying crises. Frankle and Rose (1996) define a currency crash "as a nominal depreciation of the currency of at least 25 percent that is also a 10 percent increase in the rate of depreciation" (p. 3). A three-year window is also considered between crisis episodes to avoid counting the same crisis twice. Eichengreen *et al.* (1995) define a currency crisis not only in terms of large nominal depreciations but also in terms of speculative attacks that are successfully warded off. Noncrisis observations are defined as "tranquil" observations. The methodology allows for the analysis of the chronology of crisis episodes and their characteristics. It also allows for multivariate analysis of the crisis episodes and other macroeconomic variables. Kaminsky *et al.* (1997) also use event analysis and construct an index of currency market turbulence defined as a weighted average of exchange rate changes and reserve changes.

change in the poverty indicator in a control country j (or control sample) over the time periods defined as precrisis and postcrisis for the crisis-affected country i; $\Delta F_i(t) = \ln F_i(t) - \ln F_i(t-s)$ denotes the change between a postcrisis period t and the precrisis period $t-s$ in the explanatory variables capturing the channels through which financial/economic crises are expected to affect poverty in country i (the same variable is defined for the control country j); $\Delta X_i(t) = \ln X_i(t) - \ln X_i(t-s)$ denotes the change in a set of variables controlling for noncrisis poverty determinants between precrisis and postcrisis periods in the crisis-affected country i (the same variable is defined for the control country j); and $u_i(t)$ is an error term.

10.2.2 The microlevel analysis

The cross-country approach described earlier is complemented with *microlevel analysis* to assess the effect of financial crises on poverty. In particular, cross-sectional Mexican household survey data are used to estimate the probability of being poor before and in the wake of the 1994–95 financial crisis.[5] A two-step strategy is followed for the microlevel empirical analysis: first, the factors affecting the probability of being poor in each year (i.e. before and after the crisis) are estimated using a logit model; then a logit regression is estimated using the pooled dataset, in order to assess the impact over time of the financial crisis on the stability of the relevant parameter estimates. Exogenous variables are chosen among the set of structural factors that are deemed to affect poverty (i.e. household socioeconomic characteristics and demographics, among other factors) and those that are more likely to proxy the impact of financial crises on the living conditions of the population.

The underlying model can be specified in terms of an unobservable latent variable λ_i^* measuring deprivation, lack of welfare, or poverty in its multidimensional form.[6] The probability of being poor can be specified and estimated as

$$P(d_i = 1) = P(\lambda_i^* \geq 0) = P(\varepsilon_i < E(\lambda_i^*, x_i)) = F(x_i' \beta) \tag{10.2}$$

where d_i is a binary variable equal to 1 if household i lies below the poverty line at time t ($t = 1992, 1994, 1996$) and zero otherwise.[7] The vector of independent variables x_i includes individual control variables, as well as variables proxying for the fiscal and macroeconomic policy stance (i.e. public transfers, unemployment, level of wages and salaries, among others).

We first compare the parameter vector β estimated before and after the crisis to assess the impact of the crisis on the logistic regression coefficients. This effect is measured by changes in the odds ratios Ω.[8] We then use the pooled dataset of the two years to estimate the following logit model:

$$P_{i,t} = P(d_{i,t} = 1) = F(x_{i,t}' \beta + z_{i,t}' x_{i,t} \gamma) \tag{10.3}$$

where $d_{i,t}$ is the probability of being poor in period t ($t = 1992$ and 1996, or alternatively 1994 and 1996) for household i. This probability can be defined as a function of the set of independent variables used in the previous step and of a dummy variable $Z_{i,t}$ that assumes a unit value for the postcrisis year and zero otherwise. Hypothesis testing on the significance of vector γ of parameter estimates allows for the assessment of the impact of the financial crisis on the link between poverty and its causal factors.

Some caution is needed in the interpretation of the results of equation (10.3). The estimate of γ does not account solely for the effects of financial crisis. In fact, this parameter measures the change in the factors underlying the probability of being poor in the period of analysis. Other factors could be responsible for a change in the structure of the poverty risk between 1994 and 1996. During this period there were major reforms that affected agriculture and the rural areas, large changes in commodity prices, and North America Free Trade Agreement (NAFTA) came into effect (Lustig, 1998). However, given the relatively short period of time, it is very unlikely that profound modifications of the structure of poverty would have taken place in the absence of the crisis and, therefore, we refer to the estimate of γ as a first approximation for the impact of the 1994–95 financial crisis on the probability of being poor in Mexico.

10.3   The cross-country regressions

10.3.1   *Identifying a financial crisis and selecting a control group*

Financial crises are conventionally characterized by currency crashes. Recent studies have attempted to define financial crises by focusing on event analysis and leading indicators (i.e. Kaminsky *et al.*, 1997). In line with this body of literature, we have used Frankel and Rose's (1996) definition of a currency crash "as a nominal depreciation of the currency of at least 25 percent that is also a 10 percent increase in the rate of depreciation" (p. 3). The Frankel–Rose methodology has been used for a number of reasons. First, it focuses on currency crises rather than balance of payments and banking crises and therefore country-specific information which is hard to come by and/or quantify is not required. Second, low-frequency (annual) data are used, given the availability of poverty indicators. Third, information is not needed on changes in nominal interest rates which are not market determined in most countries in the sample and on foreign exchange reserves.[9]

We have also examined an alternative definition of financial crisis that takes account of the association between currency crashes and income losses. However, most definitions of financial crises, summarized in Box 10.2, are based exclusively on currency crashes or indicators of exchange rate pressure.[10] The alternative definition considered in the sensitivity analysis that follows focuses on those currency crash episodes in which the rate of growth of GDP per capita was negative between the crisis year and the precrisis year. Motivation for this alternative definition is that depreciations may be expansionary, particularly if the economy has been in a recession due to, for example, high interest rates to defend a currency peg; in this case, a currency crash may not necessarily lead to a fall in average income. Also, as discussed later, the economy may recover from the exchange rate depreciation during the year in which the crisis episode takes place leading therefore to no average income losses in the crisis year relative to the precrisis year.

Several options were entertained but we have opted for treating the sample of OECD countries that did not experience a financial crisis in the period under examination as the control group. This is due to two main reasons. First, unlike for most developing countries, information on the relevant indicators is available for most OECD countries on a yearly basis. Crisis episodes have been identified for different time periods, thereby requiring information on these indicators for the control group for all the years in which a crisis episode was identified in the treatment group. Second, the quality of the data for these OECD countries is typically higher than for most developing countries.[11] Despite the data constraints, we are aware that the choice of the OECD group as the control group has some pitfalls. Although OECD and non-OECD countries are inherently different, the methodology analyzes the difference in changes between the control and crisis countries, rather than at the differences in levels. The methodology would be invalidated if these two groups differed significantly in their responses to crises. In other words, the question is whether the impact on poverty and income distribution would be significantly different in the OECD countries if they experienced the same crisis episodes as the treatment group.

Problems would arise if the channels through which crises affect poverty and income distribution were significantly different in the OECD group (before and after the crisis episodes) and in the treatment group before the crisis.

To address this issue, we performed a simple specification test consisting of rewriting equation (10.1) as:

$$\Delta P_i(t) = \beta_0 + \beta_1 \Delta P_j(t) + \beta_2 \Delta F_i(t) + \beta_3 \Delta F_j(t) + \beta_4 \Delta X_i(t) \\ + \beta_5 \Delta X_j(t) + v_i(t) \tag{10.4}$$

and testing the following hypothesis:

$$H_0: \quad \beta_1 = 1, \beta_2 - \beta_3 = 0 \quad \text{and} \quad \beta_4 - \beta_5 = 0 \tag{10.5}$$

Acceptance of this hypothesis, based on standard F-tests (reported later), allows for the definition of the main variables as differences relative to the control group. If this is the case, the control group provides a valid representation of the behavior of the crisis-stricken countries in the absence of the crisis.

10.3.2   *The macrolevel data*

Data on bilateral exchange rates are available from the IMF's International Financial Statistics (IFS). Annual data have been collected for developing and industrial countries since the late 1960s. The poverty incidence data are available from the World Bank (Chen and Ravallion, 2000). Information based on household expenditure/income surveys is available on mean household income, poverty headcount ratios, and poverty gaps for a sample of developing countries starting with the early 1980s.[12] The income distribution data used are available from the Deininger and Squire (1998) database. Information is available on the Gini coefficient and the distribution of income per quintile for developing and industrial countries starting with the early 1980s. The caveats in using these cross-country data are well documented (Deininger and Squire, 1998; Chen and Ravallion, 2000; Ravallion, 2000).

After identifying the crisis episodes using the given methodology and matching these episodes with the available data on poverty incidence and income distribution, we are left with at the most 65 observations in the sample. The construction of the database is described in detail in Appendix I. Our sample contains a cross-section of crisis episodes covering a variety of countries mainly in the developing world. Data on the relevant macroeconomic indicators are available for most crisis-stricken countries. Nevertheless, information is not always available for the poverty and income distribution indicators for all the countries identified as having had a crisis episode. Collection of internationally comparable time series for poverty/inequality indicators is a relatively recent endeavor, and information for the 1970s and 1980s is not readily available. The sample is much smaller for the poverty incidence indicators than for the income inequality indicators. As a result, caution is recommended in interpreting the parameter estimates reported later.

10.3.3   *Financial crises and poverty: preliminary findings*

In the sample under examination, financial crises – defined as currency crashes – are associated with sizeable changes in the macroeconomic indicators used to capture the main channels through which crises are expected to affect poverty and income distribution (Table 10.1). For example, consumer price inflation increases in the crisis year by nearly 62 percent relative to the precrisis year. Formal unemployment rises by 1.1 percent in crisis years relative to precrisis years. GDP per capita rises by nearly 1 percent relative to precrisis years. Government spending on education and health care also declines slightly.[13]

Financial crises are also associated with a deterioration in poverty indicators. On average, poverty headcount ratios increase during financial crises. Notwithstanding the increase in the incidence of poverty, the poor in the lowest income quintile do not suffer the greatest income losses during crises (Table 10.1). The main losers in terms of changes in income shares are not the poorest (lowest income quintile) but those in the second (lowest) income quintile. The income share of the highest income quintile also falls in crisis years relative to precrisis years.[14] It can be argued that the very poor may find income in informal-sector activities, thereby protecting themselves from income losses due to financial crises.[15] The poor also tend to recover their income losses faster than the wealthy in the recovery periods following financial crises.

The association between crises and poverty/distribution indicators is stronger if financial crises are followed by average income losses. Based on the alternative definition of financial crisis which focuses on currency crashes that are also associated with average income losses, GDP per capita contracts by 1.4 percent on average in the crisis year relative to the precrisis year. Inflation increases by nearly 92 percent and unemployment increases by nearly 1.6 percent relative to the precrisis year. Based on the Gini coefficient, inequality also increases by 0.63 percent relative to the precrisis year. The fall in the income share of the highest quintile is lower (-0.03 percent) and the increase in the income share of the

Table 10.1 Financial crisis episodes: summary statistics (all variables are defined as rates of change (in percent) in the crisis year relative to precrisis year)

	Mean minimum	Standard deviation	Minimum	Maximum	Sample size
Macroeconomic variables					
GDP per capita	1.02	4.56	−14.61	13.73	64
Inflation (CPI)	62.16	189.90	−65.57	1322.05	59
Unemployment rate	1.11	2.37	−2.00	9.40	23
Government spending on					
Education	−0.13	0.74	−4.06	0.90	45
Health care	−0.05	0.45	−1.61	1.20	45
Social security	0.07	1.58	−6.52	3.93	41
Total	0.51	3.81	−7.55	14.73	53
Poverty incidence					
Mean income	5.48	17.33	−29.86	40.46	25
Poverty headcount	14.76	143.77	−93.17	629.03	21
Poverty gap	93.48	508.56	−97.36	2308.33	21
Poverty gap squared	328.40	1575.00	−98.53	7200.00	21
Income distribution					
Gini coefficient	0.22	12.39	−43.89	34.11	65
Q1 income share	3.32	18.04	−23.68	60.57	38
Q2 income share	−1.61	9.34	−20.75	20.75	38
Q3 income share	0.56	7.92	−11.85	22.32	38
Q4 income share	1.72	10.09	−10.59	41.68	38
Q5 income share	−0.16	6.81	−20.93	15.82	38

Sources: World Bank and IMF data sets; and IMF staff calculations, various years, see Appendix 10A.1.

fourth quintile (nearly 2 percent) is higher, relative to the financial crisis episodes defined as currency crashes alone.

10.3.4   The cross-country evidence

Because of the limited sample size, the association between each channel and poverty/income distribution indicator is estimated separately.[16] Parameter estimates are reported in Tables 10.2 and 10.3 for a variety of variables capturing the channels through which financial crises affect poverty:

- A fall in GDP per capita in the wake of financial crisis is associated with an increase in the incidence of poverty and a deterioration in income distribution measured by the Gini coefficient (Table 10.2).[17] A fall in per capita income is associated with falling mean household income, as expected, and an increase in income inequality measured by the Gini coefficient.[18] Declining per capita income explains about 15–30 percent of the observed change in the poverty and inequality indicators. Because the Gini coefficient is a summary statistic that is too sensitive to changes in the middle of the income distribution, we also focused on income shares.[19] The deterioration in

Table 10.2 Income, inflation, unemployment, and poverty[a]

	GDP per capita			Inflation			Unemployment		
	Coefficient	R-squared	No. of observations	Coefficient	R-squared	No. of observations	Coefficient	R-squared	No. of observations
Mean household income	0.9** (2.244)	0.15	25	0.01 (0.788)	0.09	23	-0.11 (-0.266)	0.09	9
Poverty headcount	-8.73 (-1.187)	0.18	21	0.65 (1.127)	0.19	20	1.92 (1.078)	0.25	7
Poverty gap	-27.89 (-1.044)	0.13	21	2.31 (1.084)	0.15	20	5.13 (0.663)	0.23	7
Poverty gap squared	-84.51 (-1.018)	0.13	21	7.09 (1.071)	0.15	20	13.46 (0.515)	0.23	7
Gini coefficient	-0.36* (-1.634)	0.02	62	-0.005 (-0.495)	0.03	56	-0.001 (-0.010)	0.05	23
Income shares									
Q1	1.98* (7.167)	0.32	37	0.02 (0.899)	0.28	33	-0.31 (-1.731)	0.74	11
Specification test	9.694***			2.950**			1.054		
Q2	0.98*** (4.298)	0.22	37	0.01 (0.820)	0.29	33	-0.09 (-1.179)	0.71	11
Specification test	13.465***			7.972***			0.700		
Q3	0.52** (2.484)	0.15	37	0.01* (1.859)	0.16	33	-0.03 (-0.385)	0.13	11
Specification test	3.475**			4.487***			0.228		
Q4	0.12 (0.592)	0.01	37	0.004 (0.857)	0.03	33	0.01 (0.115)	0.01	11
Specification test	4.654**			6.387***			0.196		
Q5	-0.67*** (-4.533)	0.23	37	-0.01* (-1.694)	0.24	33	-0.005 (-0.069)	0.53	11
Specification test	11.060***			7.032***			0.225		

Notes
***, **, and * denote significance at the 1 percent, 5 percent, and 10 percent levels, respectively. The specification test is an F-test. Significant values of the F-test reject the specification restrictions.
a All models are estimated by OLS and include an intercept. The rate of change in per capita GDP is used as a control variable in all models, except when it is the main transmission mechanism under examination (first column). In this case, inflation is used as the control variable. Heteroskedasticity-consistent t-ratios in parentheses.

Table 10.3 Public spending and poverty[a]

	Education			Health care			Social security		
	Coefficient	R-squared	No. of observations	Coefficient	R-squared	No. of observations	Coefficient	R-squared	No. of observations
Mean household income	-0.02* (-1.815)	0.38	17	-0.22*** (-3.446)	0.50	17	-0.02 (-1.532)	0.35	15
Poverty headcount	0.01 (0.439)	0.00	14	0.36* (1.771)	0.10	14	0.01 (0.261)	0.05	12
Poverty gap	0.02 (0.734)	0.00	14	0.45* (1.945)	0.09	14	0.02 (0.488)	0.05	12
Poverty gap squared	0.03 (1.085)	0.00	14	0.54* (1.864)	0.05	14	0.03 (0.907)	0.06	12
Gini coefficient	-0.007** (-2.072)	0.04	0	-0.05 (-1.191)	0.05	44	-0.006 (-1.017)	0.04	40
Income shares									
Q1	0.02* (1.937)	0.41	25	0.26** (2.086)	0.42	25	0.04** (2.197)	0.35	22
Specification test	1.060			0.960			0.734		
Q2	0.15** (2.146)	0.49	25	0.16** (2.057)	0.48	25	0.02* (1.984)	0.42	22
Specification test	5.939***			6.680***			6.622***		
Q3	0.002 (0.534)	0.27	25	0.02 (0.450)	0.26	25	0.001 (0.082)	0.11	22
Specification test	1.036			1.003			1.182		
Q4	-0.01 (-0.891)	0.03	25	-0.09 (-0.973)	0.04	25	-0.02 (1.172)	0.11	22
Specification test	3.499**			3.450**			4.634***		
Q5	-0.005 (-1.086)	0.37	25	-0.05 (-1.007)	0.37	25	-0.004 (-0.583)	0.22	22
Specification test	2.033			2.323*			1.921		

Notes
*** **, and * denote significance at the 1, 5, and 10 percent levels, respectively. The specification test is an F-test. Significant values of F-test reject the specification restrictions.
a All models are estimated by OLS and include an intercept. The rate of change in per capita GDP is used as a control variable in all models. Heteroskedasticity-consistent t-ratios in parentheses.

income distribution as a result of crisis-induced average income losses is due to a more-than-proportional fall in the income share of the lowest income quintiles and an increase in the income share of the highest quintile.

- A rise in inflation is associated with an increase in the income share of the middle-income quintile. In the aftermath of a financial crisis, rising inflation is associated with a fall in the income share of the highest quintile and an increase in the income share of the middle-income quintile. The correlation between changes in inflation and in poverty indicators is not statistically significant at classical levels.

- The analysis for formal unemployment is inconclusive. The association between changes in formal unemployment and in indicators of poverty and income distribution is not statistically significant at classical levels. The lower number of observations would also compromise the statistical validity of the results.

- Fiscal retrenchment in the aftermath of crises is associated with a deterioration in the distribution of income.[20] An increase in government spending on education, health care, and social security programs is associated with a rise in the income share of the lowest quintiles. The elasticities are small in magnitude, reflecting, at least in part, the fact that outlays on social programs are often poorly targeted. Higher spending on health care programs is also associated with a reduction in the incidence of poverty.[21,22] This provides evidence in support of preserving social spending programs from cuts in the aftermath of financial crises. Incidentally, Dollar and Kraay (2000) show that a rise in inflation and a fall in government spending have an adverse impact on the income of the poor controlling for changes in mean income.

10.3.5 Robustness analysis

A variety of robustness checks have been carried out and can be summarized as follows:

- The parameter estimates reported earlier do not account for the impact on poverty of differences in initial levels of inequality within countries. This may affect the impact of changes of income on the incidence of poverty. Typically, the higher the level of inequality in a country, the lower the elasticity of poverty incidence to economic growth. The equations were reestimated for the sample of low-inequality countries defined as those with a Gini coefficient less than 0.45. Parameter estimates are typically higher for the low-inequality sample, as expected. Significance levels are comparable to those reported for the full sample.

- The baseline results are robust to alternative definitions of financial crisis. In this case, the crisis episodes in which per capita GDP rises, rather than falls, in the aftermath of crises are eliminated from the sample. The elasticities are slightly higher when currency crashes are associated with average income losses, as expected.

10.3.6 The caveats

The cross-country analysis provides preliminary, but by no means conclusive, evidence that financial crises are correlated with poverty and changes in income distribution, and the empirical results should be interpreted with caution. The cross-country analysis suffers from well-known *caveats*:

- The use of low-frequency data does not allow for a detailed analysis of when crises peak and bottom out during the year in which they are identified. As discussed earlier, economic recovery during, as opposed to after, the crisis year affects indicators constructed on an annual basis.
- Data on income distribution is hard to come by for a large sample of countries. Therefore, in certain cases, it was not possible to match the years when crises occurred and those for which data were available. This may cause some discrepancies in the empirical association between financial crises and poverty.
- Data on income distribution by quintile do not allow for the analysis of intraquintile income distribution. As shown in the case of the Mexican crisis described later, the association between crises and poverty is likely to be affected by changes in income distribution within the lowest quintiles, particularly in countries where the poor are clustered below that income threshold.

10.4 The Mexican experience

10.4.1 The 1994–95 Mexican crisis

Mexico was hit particularly hard by the financial crisis of 1994–95. Following the nominal depreciation of the peso by nearly 47 percent between 1994 and 1995, consumer price inflation soared to 52 percent at the end of 1995, and real GDP fell by more than 6 percent, recovering to the precrisis level in 1997 (Table 10.4).

Table 10.4 Mexico: selected indicators (percent changes)

	1994	1995	1996	1997
Real GDP	4.4	−6.2	5.2	7.0
Consumer prices (end of period)	7.0	52.0	27.7	15.7
Consumer prices (average)	7.1	35.0	34.4	20.6
Real effective exchange rate (average, depreciation −)	−3.8	−33.2	13.0	17.3
Nominal exchange rate (average, depreciation −)	−7.7	−47.4	−15.6	4.0
	(In percent of GDP)			
Total expenditures and net lending[a]	23.3	23.0	22.8	23.7
Education	3.9	3.7	3.7	3.7
Health	3.6	3.5	3.3	3.7

Source: Mexican authorities; and IMF staff estimates.

Note
a Nonfinancial public sector.

Concomitantly, fiscal policy was tightened, including some cuts in health and education expenditures. The labor market was affected by the slowdown in economic activity: open unemployment doubled to 7.4 percent in 1995. By the end of 1996, the economy had started to recover and the rate of open unemployment fell back to 4.7 percent.

10.4.2   The 1994–95 crisis: the microlevel data

A number of studies have found that the impact of the Mexican crisis on poverty and income distribution was mixed.[23] Our results confirm these findings, but go beyond previous studies in that we use a survey that is representative of households both in urban and in rural areas, where poverty is concentrated. Moreover, the use of expenditure data to calculate poverty lines, as opposed to income data, is preferable because it serves as a better proxy for permanent income.

Based on the microlevel data, available from the 1992, 1994, and 1996 National Income and Expenditure Surveys conducted by the Mexican Statistical Institute,[24] average monthly household income in constant 1994 prices fell by 31 percent between 1994 and 1996, while household consumption experienced a decline of 25 percent during the same period (Table 10.5).[25] The number of households with unemployed, self-employed, or pensioner household heads rose between 1992 and 1996 in line with worsening conditions in the labor market.

Mexican microdata show an increase in the incidence of poverty[26] and in the poverty gap[27] relative to the precrisis period. Higher poverty incidence in the aftermath of the 1994–95 financial crisis resulted from two separate factors: (1) the increase in the number of households that were lying slightly above the poverty line before the crisis and did not benefit from effective social safety nets preventing them from falling into poverty; (2) the worsening of the living conditions of those households that were already classified as poor in 1992 and in 1994. Relevant results of the analysis can be summarized as follows (Table 10.6):

- The poverty headcount ratio defining the incidence of poverty rose to nearly 17 percent of the population in 1996 from 10.6 percent in 1994 reversing the gains made between 1992 and 1994.[28] However, the characteristics of poor households did not change significantly relative to the precrisis period. Poverty rates are higher among households headed by farmers or self-employed persons; less-educated individuals; those living in rural areas, the southern states, and the Yucatán peninsula, and households with numerous family members.

- The poverty gap, defining the income shortfall of the poor, increased in the 1994–96 period, although this increase was insufficient to reverse the gains made in reducing the depth of poverty between 1992 and 1994. This result was determined by the increase in poverty depth for those household groups that had experienced the largest reduction in the poverty gap in the 1992–94 period. Thus, in the aftermath of the 1994–95 crisis, some of the poor households that had climbed closer to the poverty line in the 1992–94 period may

Table 10.5 Mexico: descriptive statistics (percentage values, unless otherwise specified)

	1992	1994	1996
Household consumption[a]	2,348	2,349	1,762
Share of durables	6.4	4.9	4.5
Share of nondurables	93.6	95.1	95.5
Share of food	35.9	35.7	36.2
Household income[a]	2,661	2,772	1,914
Share of wages and salaries	46.9	45.7	46.6
Share of profits	19.5	17.6	17.9
Share of property incomes	0.9	0.8	0.8
Share of cooperative incomes	0.1	0.1	0.1
Share of transfers	7.5	7.5	9.6
Share of self-employed income	11.2	11.8	11.0
Share of other incomes	4.0	3.9	4.1
Household typology			
Single	8.7	9.9	9.2
Single parents	9.1	9.6	10.8
Couples without children	8.7	8.4	8.3
Couples with children	58.6	56.6	56.6
Other	15.0	15.5	15.1
Household size			
1 member	5.0	6.2	5.9
2 members	11.6	11.1	11.9
3 members	15.0	15.6	16.5
4 members	19.2	20.7	20.4
5 or more members	49.3	46.5	45.4
Area of residence			
Urban	62.5	61.0	62.6
North	26.4	26.4	26.7
Centre	54.3	54.6	54.6
South	10.3	10.7	10.1
Yucatán	9.0	8.4	8.5
Household head characteristics			
Share of males	86.0	85.2	83.8
Share of illiterate	14.6	15.6	14.7
Share with technical education	7.9	9.27	11.1
Share with house's ownership	76.7	76.2	76.2
Employee	51.8	48.8	51.0
Self-employed[b]	21.0	24.4	23.3
Farmer	10.4	10.0	8.9
Pensioner	4.1	4.2	4.4
Unemployed	1.1	1.5	1.3
Other	11.6	11.1	11.1
No school	18.3	19.5	16.2
Elementary school	48.5	45.7	45.8
Middle school	15.6	16.5	17.5
High school	7.4	7.5	9.3
College or higher	10.4	10.8	11.2
Less than 40 years of age	45.7	44.0	43.5
40–59 years	36.7	36.6	37.8
60–74 years	14.0	15.7	15.0
75 years and older	3.7	3.7	3.7
Number of household	10,530	12,814	14,037

Source: IMF staff estimates based on 1992, 1994, and 1996 ENIGH.

Notes
a Local currency at constant 1994 prices.
b Other than farmers.

Table 10.6 Poverty incidence and poverty gap[a] (in percent, unless otherwise specified)

	Poverty head count			Change 1994–96	Poverty gap			Change 1994–96
	1992	1994	1996		1992	1994	1996	
Moderate poverty	38.2	36.3	48.0	32	36.3	33.4	37.6	13
Extreme poverty	12.7	10.6	16.9	60	30.3	25.8	28.8	12
Household typology								
Single	4.1	3.2	4.8	49	31.0	15.9	30.0	89
Single parents	8.3	5.1	11.3	119	22.7	29.8	27.9	−6
Couples without children	6.6	4.4	7.3	67	30.7	26.2	24.9	−5
Couples with children	13.6	12.4	18.4	48	30.6	26.0	28.3	9
Other	20.5	15.1	27.7	83	31.3	25.7	30.9	20
Household size								
1 member	1.6	1.4	3.1	127	31.2	15.3	31.3	105
2 members	4.4	3.1	5.2	69	25.9	25.3	24.2	−4
3 members	5.6	4.8	5.7	18	30.4	21.0	21.4	2
4 members	6.6	4.8	10.1	110	29.8	20.6	23.6	14
5 or more members	20.3	18.0	28.8	60	30.6	27.0	30.4	13
Area of residence								
Urban	6.0	4.6	11.4	148	22.8	21.3	24.6	15
Rural	23.9	19.8	26.0	31	33.4	27.5	32.0	16
North	7.2	6.3	11.6	84	28.7	26.8	23.3	−13
Centre	11.0	9.9	14.8	50	27.6	24.3	28.7	18
South	28.3	18.8	28.3	50	32.6	29.4	31.6	8
Yucatán	21.9	17.9	33.1	85	36.6	25.3	32.6	29
Household head characteristics								
Males	13.7	11.3	17.8	57	30.7	25.8	28.8	12
Females	6.8	6.0	12.1	101	25.8	26.4	29.0	10
Home owner	13.9	11.0	17.8	62	30.9	25.7	29.5	15
Does not own house	8.9	9.2	14.0	52	27.1	26.2	26.4	0
Employee	6.3	5.2	10.8	110	22.3	21.6	22.9	6
Self-employed[b]	21.9	14.4	25.5	78	33.0	27.3	31.8	16
Farmer	34.5	31.6	36.2	15	34.8	29.0	33.4	15
Pensioner	1.6	2.4	5.3	121	6.4	19.4	20.3	5
Unemployed	5.6	19.5	20.5	5	16.9	25.4	28.5	12
Other	9.8	8.8	15.4	75	30.1	21.5	30.4	41
No school	25.5	21.3	29.1	37	35.4	27.4	33.3	22
Elementary school	15.2	12.6	22.3	77	28.1	25.4	28.2	11
Middle school	3.9	3.1	8.6	181	18.1	18.0	21.3	18
High school	1.4	0.8	3.8	394	24.5	17.1	19.5	15
College or higher	0.0	0.7	0.8	12	7.6	31.3	26.7	−15
Less than 40 years of age	12.5	11.1	17.3	56	30.5	26.4	29.3	11
40–59 years of age	14.3	10.2	17.6	73	29.4	26.8	28.5	6
60–74 years of age	9.9	9.9	14.0	42	31.1	23.4	27.4	17
75 years and older	10.0	11.1	16.4	48	37.5	19.4	32.9	70
Number of households	10,530	12,814	14,037					

Source: IMF staff estimates based on 1992, 1994, and 1996 ENIGH.

Notes
a Poverty is measured as consumption relative to a basic basket as defined by INEGI in 1992.
b Other than farmers.

have experienced a sharp reduction in their living conditions. In addition, those households that became poor as a result of the crisis could have experienced a large drop in their consumption levels, which brought them far below the poverty line. The poverty gap remained highest after the crisis for households headed by farmers, self-employed, elderly, and less educated heads; for those living in rural areas, the Yucatán peninsula and the southern states, and for larger households.

- The households that were already poor before the crisis were not necessarily the hardest hit by the crisis. The increase in poverty rates was worst for single-parent households and those headed by individuals with middle school or high school educations, by pensioners, by the self-employed, and by employees. Note that the gains in poverty reduction for the self-employed between 1992 and 1994 were reversed by 1996, while the large increase in poverty among the unemployed observed in 1994 persisted after the crisis. In the wake of the crisis, the poverty gap increased relatively more for single-parent and single-person households, and those headed by individuals with no schooling, elderly and above 75 years of age, and for those living in the Yucatán peninsula. For these households, the depth of poverty increased, implying that they were especially hard hit by the crisis and therefore fell deeper into poverty.

All the estimates of income inequality presented in Table 10.7 point to a significant reduction in the differences between the upper and the lower tail of the income distribution in the 1992–96 period.[29] This is unlike the cross-country evidence reported earlier, and the evidence of some Latin American countries hit by recession in the late 1980s and in the early 1990s (Lustig, 2000).[30] In Mexico, the income and expenditure shares of the lowest quintile increased relative to the precrisis period by over 10 precent, while the income and expenditure shares of

Table 10.7 Mexico: inequality measures (percentage values)

	1992	1994	1996
Household consumption			
Gini coefficient	52.7	51.6	50.2
Theil index	55.4	51.1	50.9
Atkinson index ($\varepsilon = 0.5$)[a]	22.9	21.7	20.9
Atkinson index ($\varepsilon = 1.0$)[a]	37.9	37.1	35.4
Atkinson index ($\varepsilon = 2.0$)[a]	59.3	56.5	54.2
Household income			
Gini coefficient	54.1	54.2	51.6
Theil index	61.6	59.0	53.2
Atkinson index ($\varepsilon = 0.5$)[a]	24.5	24.3	22.0
Atkinson index ($\varepsilon = 1.0$)[a]	40.7	40.8	37.5
Atkinson index ($\varepsilon = 2.0$)[a]	61.3	62.0	58.3

Source: IMF staff estimates based on 1992, 1994, and 1996 ENIGH.

Note

a Inequality avertion parameter.

the highest quintile decreased by over 2 percent between 1994 and 1996 (Figure 10.1). This confirms the results presented in Cunningham *et al.* (2001).[31] It is also important to note that monthly average expenditures of the poorest 20 percent of the population, despite its growing share in total income, fell in absolute terms from M$433 in 1994 to M$386 in 1996 measured in 1994 Mexican pesos. Given their margin of survival, this may be extremely significant and should continue to merit the attention of public policy. When looking at the subsample of poor households, one notes that the average expenditures loss between 1994 and 1996 was 1.6 percent, but the poorest 10 percent of the poor

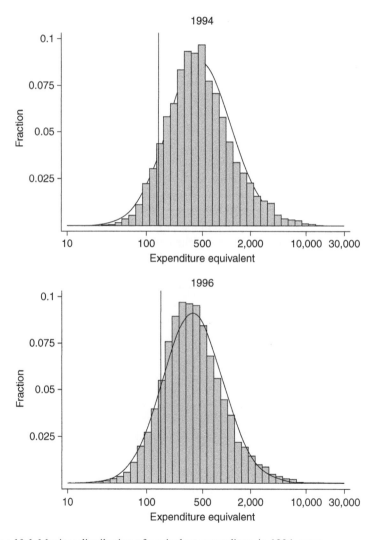

Figure 10.1 Mexico: distribution of equivalent expenditure in 1994 pesos.

experienced an expenditure loss of 12 percent. This confirms the fact that the depth of poverty increased despite an improvement in income distribution (Table 10.8).

Changes in income distribution can be attributed, at least in part, to a disproportionate fall in the income of the richest deciles relative to the precrisis period. In particular, as shown in Table 10.9, average wages for the richest decile fell by nearly 41 percent relative to an average drop in wages of 34 percent.[32] The decrease in profits was 25 percent on average with the greatest decrease among the richest 50 percent of the population suggesting a possible channel for the fall in the relative income of the wealthy.[33] Average transfers fell by 13 percent for the poorest decile, compared to a drop by 37 percent for the richest decile between 1994 and 1996.

To assess the impact of transfers on poverty, a simulation was performed by excluding all transfers from household income and then comparing the resulting poverty headcount with that calculated with after-transfer income. The results imply that transfers kept only a slightly higher share of the population

Table 10.8 Mexico: changes in average income and expenditure by decile subsample of poor households

	Average total expenditures	Average total income	Average wage	Average transfer	Average profit	Average other income
Relative growth per decile 1992–94						
1	46.9	17.1	13.4	31.1	−11.2	50.2
2	17.1	1.1	43.6	−35.9	−32.2	8.6
3	9.9	−1.2	−3.7	31.2	−21.3	26.7
4	1.6	−5.2	15.7	21.3	−17.0	8.5
5	7.5	−9.9	−25.5	21.1	−20.2	19.6
6	6.9	9.0	28.2	0.6	−30.4	22.2
7	−2.5	−5.2	10.1	−8.3	−10.3	−0.1
8	−5.7	−4.0	24.8	85.4	−41.2	0.1
9	0.9	0.1	13.2	−33.4	−20.9	19.6
10	−3.3	−9.0	−9.8	−0.8	18.5	31.5
Total	3.0	−3.1	1.7	8.2	−18.3	16.9
Relative growth per decile 1994–96						
1	−11.9	−21.6	−24.0	−20.7	−14.9	−15.8
2	−5.2	−5.3	−27.3	124.4	7.7	−3.6
3	−4.7	−10.5	−17.6	−12.6	2.6	−21.3
4	−1.1	1.1	−13.3	−21.5	43.0	−19.8
5	4.1	1.0	2.1	57.7	16.3	−7.4
6	0.5	−8.3	−4.8	21.4	18.3	−28.1
7	2.2	−7.2	−12.1	4.5	10.3	−13.6
8	1.7	−7.0	−23.8	−34.9	31.5	−16.8
9	4.1	0.3	−7.7	19.4	3.7	−18.4
10	−8.9	−14.4	−18.0	−14.5	−19.3	−34.2
Total	−1.6	−7.0	−12.1	0.0	6.8	−19.6

Source: IMF staff estimates based on 1992, 1994, and 1996 ENIGH.

Table 10.9 Mexico: changes in average income and expenditure by expenditure decile

	Average total expenditures	Average total income	Average wage	Average transfer	Average profit	Average other income
Relative growth per decile 1992–94						
1	15.5	5.7	13.5	28.7	−16.5	21.2
2	0.2	−3.4	11.5	16.7	−25.2	14.0
3	4.2	1.6	9.0	20.7	−20.2	16.9
4	7.6	8.3	18.7	13.9	−19.2	33.0
5	4.9	3.7	1.0	43.7	−6.3	17.6
6	−0.6	2.3	−2.2	−10.5	0.5	19.5
7	1.6	3.2	5.4	−32.6	−3.3	15.4
8	3.3	13.3	11.3	35.5	24.1	16.3
9	0.3	1.6	2.8	−26.0	−10.1	11.4
10	−2.3	5.1	30.7	30.5	−36.0	9.9
Total	0.0	4.2	14.9	11.4	−21.2	12.9
Relative growth per decile 1992–94						
1	−13.0	−17.2	−24.5	−12.6	−0.3	−19.3
2	−13.1	−17.5	−23.6	1.5	−19.4	−28.8
3	−18.9	−26.0	−30.5	−16.1	−25.7	−32.7
4	−21.6	−29.0	−34.2	−18.7	−33.4	−32.1
5	−22.8	−28.1	−26.7	−25.7	−34.2	−35.6
6	−20.7	−25.1	−24.2	0.8	−31.8	−35.4
7	−22.7	−28.3	−31.6	4.9	−25.3	−36.2
8	−23.0	−27.2	−25.7	−22.4	−23.0	−43.1
9	−25.3	−28.3	−28.2	14.2	−20.6	−40.5
10	−28.0	−36.2	−40.5	−36.8	−25.0	−38.1
Total	−25.0	−31.0	−33.8	−23.0	−25.2	−37.8

Source: IMF staff estimates based on 1992, 1994, and 1996 ENIGH.

out of poverty in 1996 than in 1994. In 1994, 4.5 percent of the population was kept out of poverty because of transfers, against 6.1 percent of the population in 1996. This points to the fact that the targeting of transfers did not improve substantially after the crisis, nor did transfers prevent many people from becoming poor given the large increase in the number of poor.[34] This is also confirmed by the fact that the shares of transfers in total income remained highest in the top deciles.[35]

10.4.3   *The determinants of poverty: the empirical findings*

The results of the logit estimations allow for comparisons of the probability of being poor for the precrisis and postcrisis periods as follows:

• In 1992, 1994, and 1996, the probability of being poor was found to be higher for larger households; for those living in rural regions, in the southern states and in the Yucatán peninsula; and for households headed by less-educated individuals, by the self-employed, or by farmers (Table 10.10). The risk of being poor is significantly lower for those households headed by pensioners and more-educated individuals, and for household heads in the 60–74-year-old range. A higher share of nondurable and food consumption in total household expenditures is generally associated with a higher risk of poverty.

- The 1994–95 crisis changed slightly the profile of poverty risk by household characteristics. When comparing the logit results for 1994 and 1996, we find that the probability of being poor increased for households headed by employees and pensioners.[36] Households that were disproportionately hit by the crisis include those headed by individuals having a middle-school or high-school education, by those aged between 40 and 59 years, and by those living in the south and the Yucatán peninsula. Urban households were affected more adversely by the crisis than rural households. The probability of being poor fell for households headed by farmers, by adults aged 60 and older, and by those with elementary school education. Residents in the central states and those with three or four household members also experienced a moderate decline in their relative risk of poverty. Gender of the household head was found to have no significant impact on the risk of poverty, once all other determinants are held constant.
- Home ownership further became a protection against poverty after the crisis. Because other sources of income, including labor income, typically fall during crises, owning a home can protect the household from the risk of falling into poverty as homeowners do not need to spend their income on rent.[37] The relative risk of poverty was also reduced for individuals living in households headed by farmers, or with more than three family members. In these cases, consumption of self-production and pooling of household resources across family members could have helped to protect from declining household welfare.
- The regression analysis using the pooled data for both 1994 and 1996 confirms the previous results and sheds some light on the gap in poverty incidence between urban and rural areas (Table 10.11). The pooled regression analysis shows that the risk of becoming poor in the aftermath of the crisis increased disproportionately for those resident in urban areas, for the households in the Yucatán, and for those that are headed by either very young or very old individuals. Despite the long-term trend toward widening inequality between rural and urban areas, as documented in other empirical studies (Bouillon *et al.*, 1998), rural households were better protected than urban households from the risk of poverty during the 1994–95 financial crisis, once all the other determinants of the probability of being poor are held constant. A possible explanation for this result is that higher unemployment and soaring inflation had a stronger impact on the living conditions of the urban poor, particularly those households slightly above the poverty line. At the same time, the incidence of poverty remained much higher in rural areas than in urban areas: the relative risk of poverty for households living in rural areas was more than twice that of urban households.

Table 10.10 Results of the estimates of the logit model – dependent variable: probability of being poor (percent values, unless otherwise speficied, consumption-based definition of poverty)

	1992			1994			1996		
	β	Wald	Ω	β	Wald	Ω	β	Wald	Ω
Household consumption									
Share of nondurables	6.94***	119.77	1,034.65	10.24***	105.55	8,000.78	10.94***	165.27	6,288.22
Share of food	−0.63**	6.52	0.54	1.32***	23.79	3.74	0.88***	14.67	2.40
Household income									
Share of wages and salaries	0.30	1.87	1.35	−0.31	2.61	0.73	−0.09	0.22	0.92
Share of profits	−0.04	0.02	0.96	−1.37***	18.75	0.26	−0.26	1.24	0.77
Share of property incomes	1.44**	4.33	4.21	−2.38*	3.76	0.09	−1.10	1.77	0.33
Share of cooperative incomes	−31.10	0.20	0.00	−5.31	0.94	0.00	−11.36	0.34	0.00
Share of transfers	0.20	0.46	1.22	−0.44	2.50	0.65	−0.53**	6.09	0.59
Share of self-employed income	0.19	0.41	1.20	1.09***	9.64	2.96	0.31	1.37	1.36
Share of other incomes	−8.87***	74.51	0.00	−9.10***	47.50	0.00	−7.32***	88.80	0.00
Household size									
2 members	−0.29**	4.04	0.75	−0.62***	15.48	0.54	−0.47***	17.45	0.62
3 members	0.06	0.25	1.06	0.21*	2.84	1.23	−0.29***	8.94	0.74
4 members	0.31**	6.84	1.36	0.47***	15.68	1.60	0.43***	26.13	1.53
5 or more members	1.38***	203.58	3.96	1.62***	291.77	5.06	1.55***	497.74	4.69
Area of residence									
Urban	−0.53***	41.02	0.59	−0.68***	60.01	0.51	−0.11*	2.74	0.89
Centre	−0.19***	12.08	0.83	−0.16***	8.41	0.85	−0.38***	72.28	0.68
South	0.41***	34.94	1.51	0.18**	5.43	1.19	0.29***	19.51	1.33
Yucatán	0.25***	10.00	1.28	0.29***	11.72	1.34	0.45***	43.89	1.57

Household head characteristics

Males	−0.13	0.97	0.88	−0.10	0.67	0.90	−0.05	0.31	0.95
Literate	−1.30***	48.37	0.27	−0.20	1.42	0.82	−0.79***	36.82	0.45
Home owner	−0.07	0.59	0.93	−0.19**	4.06	0.83	−0.23***	9.39	0.79
Technical education 1	−5.76	0.67	0.00	0.37	0.56	1.45	−0.31	1.17	0.73
Technical education 2	−3.62***	8.97	0.03	−1.90***	9.56	0.15	−0.39**	4.71	0.67
Employee	−0.18	2.05	0.84	−0.36***	11.46	0.70	−0.29***	12.67	0.75
Self-employed[a]	0.74***	24.21	2.09	0.15	1.46	1.17	0.30***	7.89	1.34
Farmer	1.02***	61.92	2.77	0.81***	58.58	2.25	0.54***	32.71	1.71
Pensioner	−1.29***	13.71	0.28	−0.87***	10.04	0.42	−0.65***	12.49	0.52
Other	−0.17	1.45	0.84	−0.39***	10.00	0.68	−0.31***	10.31	0.73
Elementary school	1.64***	17.76	5.14	0.77***	41.36	2.17	1.00***	146.77	2.72
Middle school	0.79**	3.92	2.21	−0.24	2.27	0.79	0.13	1.71	1.14
High school	0.04	0.01	1.05	−1.00***	9.30	0.37	−0.50***	11.28	0.61
College or higher	−3.79**	6.26	0.02	−0.80***	7.74	0.45	−1.59***	41.24	0.20
40–59 years of age	0.03	0.17	1.03	−0.46***	40.13	0.63	−0.22***	14.51	0.80
60–74 years of age	−0.40***	19.11	0.67	−0.24***	7.71	0.79	−0.45***	38.92	0.63
75 years and older	0.02	0.01	1.02	0.48***	10.49	1.62	0.40***	10.82	1.50
Constant	−9.40***	148.88		−13.06***	165.71		−12.75***	222.18	
Chi square	2,422			2,339			180		
Goodness of fit test	8.4			18.4			5.5		
Percent of correct classified cases	88.6			90.5			85.6		
Number of household	10,530			12,814			14,037		

Source: Data provided by the 1992, 1994, and 1996 Mexican income and expenditure surveys (ENIGH), and IMF staff estimations.

Notes
*, **, and *** denote statistical significanceat the 10, 5, and 1 percent levels, respectively.
a Denote other than farmers.

Table 10.11 Results of the estimates of the pooled logit model – dependent variable: probability of being poor (percent values, unless otherwise specified; consumption-based definition of poverty)

	1992/96			1994/96		
	β	Wald	Ω	β	Wald	Ω
Household consumption						
Share of nondurables	8.42***	259.17	4,518.84	10.6***	295.1	42,639.38
Share of food	0.09	0.29	1.10	1.02***	36.69	2.76
Household income						
Share of wages and salaries	0.10	0.51	1.11	−0.20	2.57	0.82
Share of profits	−0.16	0.71	0.86	−0.66***	13.83	0.51
Share of property incomes	0.28	0.28	1.33	−1.59**	5.79	0.20
Share of cooperative incomes	−15.12	0.80	0.00	−6.49	1.96	0.00
Share of transfers	−0.26	2.10	0.77	−0.52***	10.29	0.60
Share of self-employed income	0.27	1.81	1.31	0.53***	7.18	1.71
Share of other incomes	−8.11***	156.36	0.00	−7.87***	146.52	0.00
Household size						
2 members	−0.27**	3.51	0.77	−0.62**	17.42	0.54
3 members	0.08	0.43	1.08	0.21	3.38	1.24
4 members	0.29**	6.18	1.33	0.46***	17.86	1.59
5 or more members	1.37***	214.78	3.92	1.58***	330.9	4.85
Area of residence						
Center	−0.19***	12.19	0.83	−0.15***	8.81	0.78
South	0.40***	33.48	1.49	0.20***	8.15	1.07
Yucatán	0.21***	7.09	1.23	0.26***	11.00	1.11
Household head characteristics						
Males	−0.08	1.00	0.92	−0.04	0.34	0.96
Literate	−0.98***	78.57	0.37	−0.55***	30.67	0.96
Homeowner	−0.12	1.55	0.89	−0.27***	9.29	0.77
Urban residence	−0.56***	47.23	0.57	−0.73***	80.82	0.48
Technical education 1	−0.14	0.46	0.87	0.09	0.31	1.10
Technical education 2	−0.33**	4.53	0.72	−0.36***	7.17	0.70
Employee	−0.19	2.59	0.83	−0.35***	14.67	0.71
Self-employed	0.62***	22.52	1.86	0.15	2.18	1.16
Farmer	1.00***	64.64	2.73	0.76***	64.08	2.14
Pensioner	−1.27***	13.60	0.28	−0.78***	9.54	0.46
Other	−0.07	0.28	0.93	−0.42***	14.42	0.66
Elementary school	1.10***	192.77	3.02	0.92***	212.49	2.51
Middle school	0.20**	4.58	1.23	−0.04	0.23	0.96
High school	−0.45***	10.24	0.64	−0.69***	28.66	0.50
College or higher	−1.84***	51.57	0.16	−1.28***	51.75	0.28
40–59 years of age	0.06	0.94	1.06	−0.26***	21.61	0.77
60–74 years of age	−0.31***	24.09	0.74	−0.25***	20.22	0.78
75 years and older	0.00	0.00	1.00	0.42***	13.47	1.52
Interactions with dummy (1996 = 1)						
Employee	−0.13	0.84	0.88	0.05	0.20	1.05
Self-employed[a]	−0.26*	3.54	0.77	0.18*	2.93	1.20
Farmer	−0.49*	9.94	0.62	−0.22*	2.96	0.81
Pensioner	0.58	2.19	1.79	0.11	0.13	1.11
Other	−0.31*	3.62	0.73	0.09	0.40	1.09

Table 10.11 Continued

| | 1992/96 | | | 1994/96 | | |
	β	Wald	Ω	β	Wald	Ω
2 members	−0.23	1.52	0.79	0.13	0.47	1.14
3 members	−0.44***	7.29	0.64	−0.57***	14.07	0.57
4 members	0.13	0.75	1.13	−0.04	0.10	0.96
5 or more members	0.25**	4.39	1.28	0.04	0.17	1.05
Center	−0.18***	6.68	0.83	−0.22***	11.11	0.80
South	−0.12	1.14	0.89	0.09	0.87	1.09
Yucatàn	0.28***	7.07	1.32	0.18*	3.13	1.20
Homeowner	−0.03	0.05	0.97	0.11	0.99	1.12
Urban residence	0.48***	20.58	1.62	0.65***	41.24	1.92
Age	−0.11***	54.00	0.90	−0.07***	25.37	0.93
Age squared	0.00***	45.88	1.00	0.00***	16.94	1.00
Constant	−11.15***	395.74	0.00	−13.42***	441.10	0.00
Chi square	5,224			6,182		
Goodness of fit test	10.55			8.34		
Percent of correct classified cases	87.2				88.0	
Number of household	24,567			26,851		

Source: Data provided by the 1992 and 1996 Mexican income and expenditure surveys (ENIGH), and IMF staff estimations.

Notes
*, **, and *** denote statistical significance at the 10, 5, and 1 percent levels, respectively.
a Denote other than farmers.

10.4.4 Data quality and robustness of estimates

Previous studies using Mexican data have noted the discrepancies between national accounts data and household survey data. In particular, aggregate private consumption data available from the national accounts statistics include purchases by nonprofit institutions providing services to households such as religious organizations which household surveys do not include. In addition, in contrast to household surveys, national accounts data incorporate purchases by nonresidents and exclude purchases by resident household members in the foreign market. These differences have led to an underestimation of private expenditures in household surveys.[38] As noted by Lustig and Székely (1997), these discrepancies are problematic to the extent that the directions of changes in private consumption differ over time between household survey and national accounts data, as the authors find for the period between 1984 and 1989.

To address these discrepancies, several adjustments to household survey data have been suggested.[39] We adjusted the 1994 and 1996 household data to maintain the ratio to national accounts private consumption at the estimated 41 percent in 1992 and found that this leads to a poverty headcount ratio of 13 percent in 1996, rather than 17 percent reported earlier in the unadjusted sample. However, the estimation results using the adjusted 1994 and 1996 samples are not significantly different.[40] This is expected, as the adjustment leads to a change in the level of consumption for all households, and therefore the relative impact across household types remains unchanged.

10.5   Conclusions and policy recommendations

Both macro- and microlevel data show an increase in poverty due to a financial crisis. The macrolevel analysis presents stronger results for changes in income distribution than in the incidence of poverty, unless the income share of the lowest quintile is interpreted as an indicator of poverty. The four transmission mechanisms of the effects of financial crises on poverty and inequality identified in this chapter namely inflation, unemployment, growth, and government spending explain approximately 60–70 percent of the total observed change in the dependent variable. The decline in per capita GDP alone only explains up to one-third of the change in the poverty indicator during a financial crisis. It is nevertheless deceptive to conclude, based on cross-country data, that crises have a limited impact on poverty. The poverty rate may change little over time but the number of people falling into poverty and escaping poverty over the same period may be large and the depth of poverty could widen. Aggregate statistics only show the average balance of gains and losses. Macrolevel data on poverty and income distribution are fraught with deficiencies; this calls for caution in interpreting cross-country evidence of an association between financial crises and poverty, and income distribution.

The incidence of poverty was found to increase relative to the precrisis period based on Mexican data. Poverty rates soared with a disproportionate increase in the probability of being poor for households in urban areas and in the Yucatán region, and those headed by either very young or very old individuals. This latter result is related to the increase in formal unemployment, notably in urban areas, and the insufficient adjustment of the level of social benefits in the wake of rising inflation. Along with the increase in the incidence of poverty, the poverty gap widened leading to an increase in the depth of poverty. As the overall income distribution shifted to the left, owing to the decline in average real consumption resulting from the crisis, the poorest 10 percent of the poor became poorer. In addition, those households that were marginally above the poverty line before the crisis are likely to have fallen into poverty in the aftermath of the crisis pointing to the absence of an adequate social safety net to prevent them from falling into poverty. The poverty gap increased relatively more for single parents, single-person households, households headed by individuals with no education and by elderly, and those in the Yucatán region.

In contrast to the macrolevel results, income and expenditure inequality did not rise in the aftermath of the crisis. Inequality fell between 1994 and 1996, in line with the trend observed between 1992 and 1994. Differences between the upper and the lower tail of the income/consumption distribution fell in the aftermath of the financial crisis, despite the overall increase in the incidence of poverty. This confirms previous results in the literature based on selected subsamples of the population and can be explained by a disproportionate decline in the consumption/income of the wealthiest quintiles relative to the precrisis period. In fact, the microlevel analysis shows that households that were already poor before the crisis were not necessarily the hardest hit. This result points to the evidence that the poorest segment of the vulnerable groups in the population is more likely to be engaged in informal-sector activities, thereby being more protected from revenue losses during a financial crisis.

Adequate social safety nets, through small, well-targeted income transfers, would have prevented many households from falling into poverty as a result of the crisis. The simulations reported earlier show that transfers to individuals/households did little to prevent them from falling into poverty and the targeting of the existing transfer schemes did not improve substantially after the crisis. At the same time, some households that were already poor before the crisis suffered disproportionately to the averge poor, as a consequence of the absence of an adequate social safety net. In particular, the existing public sector programs did not prevent declining consumption for households headed by single parents, less-educated individuals, and individuals aged 75 years or more. This decline contributed to an increase in the depth of poverty for groups of the population that were already among the most vulnerable in the precrisis period.

The empirical findings given here support some specific policy recommendations. The results reported earlier suggest that policy should focus on avoiding an acceleration of inflation while keeping unemployment rates low in the wake of the crisis. Increasing inflation is particularly bad for the poor as it affects negatively their real disposable income. The poor are also less likely to protect themeselves against a decline in real consumption by dissaving, as they do not have sufficient financial assets. Sound macroeconomic policies (e.g. those leading to balanced economic growth and low inflation) reduce the risk of crisis and allow for the return to macroeconomic stability in the aftermath of financial crisis. The main challenge in the aftermath of financial crises is the choice of a policy mix that restores macroeconomic equilibrium while at the same time it reduces the social costs of the crisis. In doing this, the negative effect of unemployment on the poor documented in this chapter has to be addressed by adequate labor policies. This chapter, however, does not allow to reach specific conclusions on the possible trade-off between unemployment and inflation. According to the empirical results, both factors are channels through which financial crises can affect the poor with a similar strength.

The provision of safety nets and the protection from cuts of specific social programs remain the main short-term pro-poor policy response to financial crisis. The key goal of safety nets is to insure the poor against the risk of income losses.

- Pro-poor spending should be protected in the wake of a financial crisis. Adequate mechanisms must be put in place so that pro-poor spending is protected during times of austerity. The protection of social spending from cuts ensures continuity of development policies but often does not ensure short-term social protection, particularly when spending under these programs is poorly targeted.

- A social safety net system should be in place prior to a crisis. The aim should be to have safety nets as permanent institutions to be deployed as needed. Medium-term planning is crucial in this respect. Setting up safety nets takes time and requires the ability of the government to react at short notice. Social safety nets should be flexible, so that they can be adjusted to changes in the size and the characteristics of the poor when the economy is hit by a shock such as a financial crisis. As shown in the case of Mexico, had such a social safety net been in place before the crisis, it would have prevented many households from falling into poverty. In particular, the Mexican experience highlighted the absence of safety nets targeted at the urban poor.
- The design of a safety net should take account of the poverty risks of different population groups with effective targeting to the most vulnerable groups. As the poorest of the poor are often engaged in informal-sector activities, policies targeted at this group should be designed differently from those programs aimed at helping the vulnerable groups of workers in the formal sector. The Mexican case highlights the vulnerability of the urban poor. PRO-GRESA – a targeted human development program implemented in 1997, hence after the period under study – provides cash transfers to rural households, school supplies, and nutrition supplements conditional on children's school attendance, and regular preventive health care visits.

Geographical targeting could also be used in the design of safety nets for Mexico. As noted earlier, the incidence of poverty increased disproportionately for residents living in certain parts of the country during the financial crisis. Moreover, the differences among the north, south, and Yucátan regions need to be addressed in the effort to reduce poverty and inequality. Finally, the results have shown that the effect of the crisis have not been gender-specific but exhibit a marked age-related profile, with the households headed by the youngest, and the oldest individuals suffering from the largest increase in the depth of poverty. This points to the need to promote employment of young people in the aftermath of crisis (e.g. through self-selecting public work schemes) and to revise the current system of social protection for the elderly, guarding the level of lower social benefits against price increases.

10A.1   Appendix: data and methods

10A.1.1   *The cross-country methodology*

The control group comprises the OECD countries that did not experience a crisis episode between 1960 and 1998. The following countries were excluded: Finland, France, Greece, Iceland, Italy, New Zealand, Portugal, Spain, Sweden, and the United Kingdom. Most of these countries experienced a currency crisis in the early 1990s related to the Exchange Rate Mechanism realignment in 1992.

Mexico, the Republic of Korea, and Turkey were not included in the OECD sample.

Information on income distribution and poverty is scarcer than on macroeconomic indicators of financial crises. Therefore, some adjustments were needed. In particular:

- Data on poverty and income distribution are not available for some countries that have experienced a crisis episode. Sometimes, data are available but not for the years near the crisis episodes (e.g. Sudan). The following countries were dropped from the sample; they include the Islamic State of Afghanistan, Benin, Bhutan, Burundi, Cambodia, Cape Verde, Chad, the Comoros, the Democratic Republic of Congo, the Republic of Congo, Côte d'Ivoire, Egypt, Equatorial Guinea, Fiji, The Gambia, Iceland, the Lao People's Democratic Republic, Lebanon, the former Yugoslav Republic of Macedonia, Maldives, Mongolia, Morocco, Mozambique, Namibia, Nepal, Niger, Papua New Guinea, Paraguay, Rwanda, Samoa, São Tomé and Príncipe, Sierra Leone, the Solomon Islands, Sudan, Suriname, Swaziland, Togo, Ukraine, Uruguay, and Vietnam.

- Data on income distribution and poverty are available for one time period only for some countries that have experienced a crisis episode. The following countries were also excluded from the sample; these include (with the time period in parenthesis) Algeria (1988), Argentina (1961), Botswana (1986), Burkina Faso (1995), Cameroon (1983), the Central African Republic (1992), Guinea-Bissau (1991), Guyana (1993), Lesotho (1987), Madagascar (1993), Malawi (1993), Mali (1994), Nicaragua (1993), Senegal (1991), Uganda (1989), and Zimbabwe (1990).

- Certain crisis episodes, rather than countries, were eliminated due to lack of information on income/poverty for the relevant years. These episodes were in Bolivia, Brazil, Chile, Colombia, Ecuador, Gabon, Ghana, Israel, Kenya, South Africa, Tanzania, Turkey, and Zambia.

- The period for which data are available for the income and poverty indicators do not necessarily coincide with the crisis episodes. In this case, the income/poverty data used are the ones nearest in time to the crisis episode. These adjustments include (with the data points of the income/poverty data in parentheses): Bolivia (1968 and 1990), Botswana (1986), Brazil (1960 and 1970, 1972, 1996), Burkina Faso (1991), Cameroon (1983), the Central African Republic (1992), Chile (1971 and 1980), China (1988 and 1995), Colombia (1978), Costa Rica (1971 and 1969, 1979, 1986, and 1989), the Dominican Republic (1984, 1989), Ecuador (1968, 1993, and 1994), France (1979), Gabon (1975 and 1977), Ghana (1988 and 1989), Greece (1981 and 1988), Guatemala (1987), Honduras (1992 and 1994), Indonesia (1980 and 1981, 1987, and 1990), Israel (1979, 1986, and 1992), Italy (1993), the Republic of Korea (1985 and 1988), the Kyrgyz Republic (1988 and 1990), Mauritius (1986 and 1991), Mexico (1977 and 1984, 1989), New Zealand

Table 10A.1 Distribution by average equivalent expenditure deciles of selected indicators

Deciles	Age	Education	Size	Wage share	Transfer share	Self-employed share	Business share	Property share	Average expenditure	Average income	Average wage	Average transfer	Average profit	Average other income	Poverty
1992															
1	43.4	3.1	6.6	34.3	5.9	22.2	32.0	0.3	469	616	409	230	260	148	100.0
2	44.1	3.9	6.3	41.0	6.8	16.6	27.5	0.6	815	1,014	640	324	517	218	49.3
3	43.8	4.4	5.7	48.5	6.9	14.7	22.1	0.4	990	1,238	852	422	614	252	7.2
4	42.3	5.0	5.2	49.4	6.5	14.1	21.9	0.2	1,173	1,416	972	461	844	279	0.0
5	43.7	5.5	4.8	51.1	7.7	10.8	16.8	0.6	1,365	1,611	1,153	415	829	365	0.0
6	43.7	6.0	4.8	52.0	8.3	8.8	15.5	0.5	1,673	1,880	1,353	627	933	442	0.0
7	45.6	6.7	4.4	49.6	7.9	9.3	16.6	1.3	1,934	2,230	1,542	866	1,115	546	0.0
8	43.8	6.9	3.9	48.3	8.6	8.0	14.0	1.1	2,292	2,477	1,698	651	1,158	696	0.0
9	43.7	8.5	3.7	49.1	7.9	9.1	15.1	1.2	3,147	3,586	2,452	1,234	1,891	947	0.0
10	44.9	11.2	3.3	43.4	7.6	5.1	19.2	2.0	7,183	7,912	4,435	1,773	7,376	2,054	0.0
d10/d1	1.0	3.7	0.5	0.1	1.3	0.2	0.6	6.5	15.3	12.9	10.8	7.7	28.4	13.9	0.0
Total	44.0	6.4	4.7	46.9	7.5	11.2	19.5	0.9	2,348	2,661	1,714	805	1,514	666	12.7
1994															
1	44.2	3.3	6.5	40.6	6.1	16.0	21.0	0.2	541	651	464	296	217	179	100.0
2	45.8	3.7	6.0	43.0	7.3	15.7	20.3	0.7	817	979	714	378	387	249	29.7
3	44.9	4.4	5.5	47.9	7.1	13.2	18.2	0.5	1,032	1,257	928	510	490	294	1.8
4	45.3	4.6	5.3	47.5	7.8	11.9	18.4	0.3	1,262	1,534	1,154	525	682	372	0.0
5	43.4	5.5	4.8	47.4	7.7	12.5	18.6	0.2	1,432	1,670	1,165	596	777	429	0.0
6	44.5	6.0	4.5	44.2	7.3	12.0	17.9	0.5	1,663	1,924	1,322	561	938	528	0.0
7	44.2	6.7	4.3	45.7	6.3	13.0	18.6	0.5	1,965	2,301	1,625	583	1,079	630	0.0
8	44.6	7.7	3.9	45.5	8.1	11.1	16.5	1.0	2,368	2,807	1,860	882	1,438	809	0.0
9	44.0	8.6	3.5	48.2	7.8	8.3	13.9	1.6	3,155	3,645	2,521	914	1,701	1,056	0.0
10	46.7	11.3	3.1	46.0	8.9	7.5	15.3	1.8	7,017	8,317	5,798	2,314	4,724	2,258	0.0
d10/d1	1.1	3.5	0.5	1.1	1.4	0.5	0.7	10.3	13.0	12.8	12.5	7.8	21.8	12.6	0.0
Total	44.8	6.5	4.6	45.7	7.5	11.8	17.6	0.8	2349.4	2771.8	1969.0	896.7	1193.5	752.2	10.6

1996

1	44.1	3.7	6.8	35.8	7.7	18.5	25.7	0.2	471	539	350	259	216	145	100.0
2	44.5	4.4	6.0	43.0	10.4	16.7	22.0	0.3	709	807	546	383	312	177	72.3
3	44.7	4.9	5.3	47.7	10.3	12.7	18.5	0.5	837	930	645	428	364	198	28.9
4	43.9	5.4	5.1	47.7	8.6	13.0	18.3	0.3	989	1,089	760	427	455	252	0.0
5	44.5	6.0	4.6	50.8	8.1	11.5	17.3	0.7	1,105	1,202	853	443	511	276	0.0
6	43.6	6.6	4.5	48.1	10.0	9.9	17.0	0.5	1,318	1,441	1,002	566	639	341	0.0
7	45.0	7.0	4.1	47.6	10.0	9.8	16.5	0.6	1,520	1,650	1,111	612	806	401	0.0
8	45.2	7.6	3.8	48.6	10.8	8.4	15.2	0.7	1,822	2,043	1,404	685	1,108	460	0.0
9	44.7	9.1	3.4	47.8	10.7	8.1	15.5	1.3	2,356	2,613	1,809	1,044	1,351	629	0.0
10	45.5	11.4	3.0	46.6	9.1	5.7	15.9	1.8	5,056	5,309	3,452	1,463	3,545	1,398	0.0
d10/dl	1.0	3.1	0.4	1.3	1.2	0.3	0.6	8.7	10.7	9.9	9.8	5.7	16.4	9.7	0.0
Total	44.6	6.9	4.5	46.6	9.6	11.0	17.9	0.8	1762.3	1913.7	1304.0	690.1	892.3	467.7	16.9

Source: IMF staff estimates based on 1992, 1994, and 1996 ENIGH.

Table 10A.2 Distribution by average equivalent expenditure deciles – subsample of poor households

Deciles	Age	Education	Size	Wage share	Transfer share	Self-employed share	Business share	Property share	Average expenditure	Average income	Average wage	Average transfer	Average profit	Average other income	Poverty
1992															
1	43.3	2.6	6.7	26.3	4.1	31.1	41.3	0.0	249	396	255	149	185	97	100
2	44.6	1.9	7.0	28.9	8.5	21.3	33.7	0.6	392	540	305	236	254	134	100
3	42.4	3.2	6.8	38.2	3.9	20.7	29.5	0.4	455	613	416	225	277	147	100
4	43.2	3.6	6.7	39.7	4.8	16.1	25.6	0.8	517	620	402	188	222	167	100
5	43.5	3.3	6.1	35.7	5.5	22.8	35.1	0.0	536	744	579	170	334	154	100
6	42.3	3.2	6.1	33.2	7.6	24.0	30.1	0.0	586	678	392	261	312	180	100
7	45.9	3.8	6.5	41.4	6.6	19.1	27.8	0.0	671	863	492	386	329	188	100
8	43.9	3.7	6.8	39.4	5.9	16.6	26.9	0.2	750	926	587	314	417	212	100
9	44.7	4.2	6.4	45.6	8.0	20.8	26.1	0.0	778	941	674	424	518	198	100
10	40.5	5.3	6.4	60.1	6.6	8.0	12.5	2.5	944	1,193	915	342	465	221	100
d10/d1	0.9	2.0	1.0	2.3	1.6	0.3	0.3		3.8	3.0	3.6	2.3	2.5	2.3	1.0
Total	43.3	3.6	6.5	39.8	6.1	19.5	28.1	0.6	601	768	546	277	316	171	100
1994															
1	43.5	2.3	7.7	30.4	5.1	24.4	29.0	0.0	365	463	289	196	164	145	100
2	45.5	3.2	7.0	43.6	4.4	15.8	21.7	0.0	459	546	438	152	172	145	100
3	42.7	3.5	6.5	36.9	6.5	16.3	19.6	0.4	500	606	401	295	218	186	100
4	43.8	3.0	6.1	33.6	7.7	13.3	18.1	0.0	525	587	465	228	184	182	100
5	42.4	3.0	6.2	40.7	3.6	22.2	26.4	0.1	576	670	431	206	267	184	100
6	44.9	3.3	6.2	47.9	4.3	10.2	16.3	0.8	626	739	502	262	217	220	100
7	45.0	3.4	6.1	46.4	7.7	12.1	18.9	0.0	654	818	542	354	295	188	100
8	47.9	4.8	6.3	48.4	9.5	11.9	16.4	0.7	707	889	732	583	245	213	100
9	46.9	3.1	6.5	41.4	5.5	17.5	21.6	0.0	785	942	763	282	409	237	100
10	42.9	4.9	6.1	54.9	5.8	11.8	14.6	0.1	912	1,086	826	339	551	290	100
d10/d1	1.0	2.2	0.8	1.8	1.1	0.5	0.5		2.5	2.3	2.9	1.7	3.4	2.0	1.0
Total	44.5	3.5	6.4	42.6	6.0	15.5	20.1	0.2	619	744	556	300	258	200	100

1996

1	44.8	3.0	7.9	24.8	5.8	21.6	30.6	0.0	322	363	220	155	140	122	100
2	43.4	3.4	7.0	33.3	10.3	19.3	25.3	0.1	435	517	319	340	185	140	100
3	45.9	3.3	6.4	37.9	8.0	15.3	24.8	0.1	477	542	330	258	224	146	100
4	42.0	4.6	6.1	42.9	5.8	19.0	24.4	0.1	520	594	404	179	263	146	100
5	44.3	4.3	6.4	39.6	8.3	17.7	24.1	0.6	600	677	440	325	310	170	100
6	43.4	4.5	6.2	45.0	9.5	13.3	19.9	0.5	629	677	478	318	256	158	100
7	44.5	4.1	6.1	45.0	7.7	17.6	24.3	0.2	669	759	477	370	326	163	100
8	45.0	4.4	6.2	45.2	10.7	16.1	21.1	0.4	720	826	558	379	323	177	100
9	42.6	5.4	6.2	53.6	7.9	15.0	19.5	0.1	818	945	704	337	425	193	100
10	43.2	6.1	5.4	56.5	5.4	11.7	17.1	0.6	831	930	678	290	445	191	100
d10/dl	1.0	2.0	0.7	2.3	0.9	0.5	0.6		2.6	2.6	3.1	1.9	3.2	1.6	1.0
Total	43.9	4.4	6.4	42.8	7.9	16.6	23.0	0.3	609	692	489	300	275	161	100

Source: IMF staff estimates based on 1992, 1994, and 1996 ENIGH.

(1973, 1985), Nigeria (1982 and 1986), Peru (1981, 1986), the Philippines (1985, 1988, 1994), Portugal (1973 and 1980, 1990, and 1991), the Russian Federation (1995 and 1996), South Africa (1995 and 1996), Spain (1980 and 1985), Sri Lanka (1973 and 1979), Tanzania (1977 and 1991), Thailand (1992 and 1996), Turkey (1987), Venezuela (1981 and 1987, 1989, and 1990), and Zambia (1993 and 1996).

- Sometimes data are available for the relevant years but more information is available on different income/poverty indicators for a year that is close enough. In this case, the close enough information is used (e.g. Sweden).

With the adjustments given, a sample of 65 crisis episodes is available. Further adjustments were made to take into account the differences in the income/poverty data. These include the following:

- To maximize the degrees of freedom, different Gini coefficients were conflated. Information on the Gini coefficient is most readily available for gross income (40 episodes), followed by net income (19 episodes). When information was available for the same crisis episode for more than one Gini coefficient, preference was given to the indicators constructed for gross income, followed by net income. Because Gini coefficients are typically higher for income than expenditures, conflating these indicators for the same crisis episode was avoided.
- Information on the distribution of income per quintile is harder to come by than on the Gini coefficient. Data are available for income distribution based on gross income (28 episodes), followed by net income (10 episodes). After conflating the available information, a sample of 38 episodes was obtained. Again, the data were not conflated for income distribution based on expenditure and income.

Additional variables used in the cross-country analysis are the following:

- Social spending variables are defined in percent of GDP to construct the differences between crisis and precrisis values.
- Annual inflation is defined in percent.
- GDP per capita is defined in constant 1995 US dollars to construct percent rates of change in crisis years relative to precrisis years.

10A.1.2   The microlevel methodology

The data used in the analysis are drawn from the annual household budget surveys conducted by the Mexican Statistics Bureau. The sample includes 10,508 households for 1992, 12,814 for 1994, and 14,020 for 1996 after the elimination of those households that did not report income or consumption levels. The original data were converted into 1994 prices to insure intertemporal comparability.

In the microlevel analysis, poverty is defined as the inability to attain a minimum standard of living as measured by the poverty line. Due to the multi-dimensional nature of poverty, both income-and expenditure-based poverty measures were used.[41] The expenditure-based poverty line, presented in the text, was calculated on the basis of a minimum consumption basket based on a daily caloric intake by the Mexican Statistical Institute.[42] The main advantage of this poverty line is that it may better proxy for the permanent income losses of the crisis. In order to check the robustness of the results to alternative definitions of poverty, an income-based poverty line was set equal to 50 percent of the sample average per capita income in 1992 and then adjusted in line with price changes.[43] Results using this definition confirmed the findings presented in the text.

Two different measures of poverty are used: (1) the headcount ratio, measuring the share of poor households in the sample, and (2) the poverty gap, measuring the difference in household consumption/income to the poverty line as a percent of the poverty line.[44] Consumption/income is defined in per equivalent person terms according to the following formula:

$$y_i^{eq} = \frac{y_i}{(N_i)^{\varepsilon}}$$

where y is household consumption/income, ε is an elasticity parameter equal to $\partial y^{eq}/\partial N$, and N is the household size.[45]

Acknowledgment

The authors wish to thank Sanjeev Gupta, Ben Clements, Robert Gillingham, Ravi Kanbur, Nora Lustig, Philip Young, Kevin Fletcher, and the participants of the Poverty Workshop held during April 12–13, 2001, in Washington, DC for useful comments and suggestions on earlier versions of this chapter.

Notes

1 Recent research on poverty and income inequality has focused on how the income of the poor is affected by an increase in average income in periods of economic growth (Ravallion and Chen, 1997; Dollar and Kraay, 2000; Ravallion, 2000; Foster and Székely, 2001). Underlying this line of research is the question of whether the relationship between changes in average income and in income distribution and/or the incidence of poverty are symmetrical in the sense that the poor lose in periods of economic downturn as much income as they gain in periods of acceleration, and whether these effects on the poor are temporary or permanent (Ravallion, 2001).

2 The IMF's Fiscal Affairs Department has analyzed the immediate impact of the financial crises in Asia and Brazil. See, for instance, Chu and Gupta (eds) (1998), for more information on social safety nets; Gupta *et al.* (SM/99/180), for an analysis of the Brazilian experience in the aftermath of the currency devaluation in January 1999.

3 The literature offers analogous examples of the use of this methodology. For instance, Simon (1966) examines liquor sales before and after state price increases, using as a control group states that did not have law or price changes.

4 This methodology is standard in the empirical study of a broad class of microeconomic issues including tax incidence, migration, and consumption behavior, among other issues. See Meyer (1994), for more information on quasi-experiments in economics. The main advantage of the differences-in-differences methodology is that it allows the study of the effects of exogenous variations in a given explanatory variable that, in other situations, may be endogenously related to the outcome of interest. In the case of financial crises and poverty, it is difficult to distinguish the effect of fiscal retrenchment on poverty in response to a financial crisis from the effects of poverty on the structure of government spending, and hence the programs affected by fiscal retrenchment in the wake of financial crises. Note that this methodology differs from that of Dollar and Kraay (2000) who estimate the correlation between poverty and growth by regressing mean income on the income of the poor (in first differences).

5 Other studies have used household survey data to estimate changes in poverty and inequality during crises. For instance, for the case of Mexico, see Cunningham *et al.* (2001), and for Peru, see Glewwe and Hall (1994, 1998).

6 Since the multiple dimensions of poverty are difficult to measure, household deprivation can be proxied by the difference between the poverty line (y^p) and the level of welfare of the household (y_i^*) as $\lambda_i^* = y^p - y_i^*$, which can be parameterized as $\lambda_i^* = x_i'\beta + \varepsilon_i$ where x_i is a vector of explanatory variables. Although the latent variable is not observable, an index function can be constructed using a dummy variable which indicates whether the household is above the poverty line: $d_i = 1$, if $\lambda_i^* \geq 0$, and $d_i = 0$, otherwise. For a description of latent variable models and this type of formalization, see Maddala (1986).

7 We recognize the caveats of specifying poverty as a discrete variable. In doing so, the multiple dimensions of poverty are ignored and emphasis is placed on the level, rather than the depth, of poverty. See Sen (1976), Wiegand (2000), and Foster and Székely (2001), for a discussion of these problems. However, we use the standard measure of poverty, the headcount ratio, because it is a conventional eligibility criterion for most targeted social programs, thus leading to readily usable policy implications.

8 The odds ratio measures the relative risk of being poor versus the probability of lying above the poverty line for a household with given specific characteristics relative to a given reference category.

9 Note that the definition of financial crisis based on currency crashes excludes episodes of financial distress, such as banking crises, which are not associated with drastic exchange rate movements. A case in point is banking crises in industrial countries, such as the S&L crisis in the United States.

10 Alternative definitions of crisis are less common in the literature. For instance, Ferreira *et al.* (1999) define a crisis episode as a decline in gross national product following a financial crisis, or an increase in the country's monthly rate of inflation to above 40 percent per year within the 12-month period, or both.

11 We also tried to define the control group as the noncrisis periods for all countries that experienced financial crises. Unfortunately, for a number of crisis countries, information on poverty indicators is scarce and typically not available for a sufficiently large number of years.

12 The poverty headcount data are based on the internationally comparable poverty line of US$1 per day expressed in Purchasing Power Parity (PPP) terms. The choice of a poverty line is always difficult and arbitrary. Although international low-income standards marginalize poverty in rich countries, the use of country-specific poverty lines in cross-country studies introduces idiosyncratic elements in the definition of poverty. However, in country-specific studies, the use of the national, rather than the international, poverty line is preferred. The poverty gap is defined as the income shortfall of

the poor, or the average difference between the income of those below the poverty line and the income level that defines the poverty line.

13 Social spending tends to be procyclical in many crisis-prone countries, thereby making a poor social safety net during recessions. See Ravallion (2000), for more information on the Argentine experience.

14 Recent cross-country evidence reported by Dollar and Kraay (2000) confirms these results by suggesting that the income of the poor does not fall disproportionately to that of the rich during crises. This is also in line with the evidence presented below based on microlevel data.

15 There is some Mexican evidence that informal-sector workers do not suffer disproportionately higher income losses during crises (Cunningham *et al.*, 2001).

16 The raw bivariate correlations between the proxies for the transmission mechanisms (not reported but available upon request) are in general low, varying between 0.2 and 0.5 in absolute terms. The argument for including the proxies together in the estimating equation, rather than one at a time, is therefore less compelling. In any case, the results remain broadly unchanged, in most models, if all the relevant proxies are included together in the equation. Another argument is in favor of using one regressor at a time in the estimation of the model, is that this allows one to assess the contribution of each transmission mechanism to the change observed in the dependent variable.

17 Changes in income cannot be interpreted as changes in consumption, unless individuals have no ability to smooth out consumption variations in the presence of income shocks. This issue is discussed in greater detail in the given microlevel analysis. Chen and Ravallion (2000) construct a time series of cross-country consumption-based poverty indicators by multiplying income by 1 minus the saving rate.

18 Changes in income, measured in the national accounts, may differ from average household living standards as measured in household surveys. Because of differences in the definition of income and measurement errors, average household income based on national accounts data may not fully reflect changes in income based on household surveys. For instance, short-term changes in national income may involve the nonhousehold sector predominantly.

19 An alternative option would be to assess the effects of the transmission mechanisms on the average income of the poorest quintile. The average income of the poorest quintile is not readily available in our data set. A simple way to estimate it is to multiply the income shares by per capita GDP and divide it by 0.2 (Deininger and Squire, 1998). While this measure would combine income and inequality effects in one indicator, in practice it would be highly collinear to the change in per capita growth, which is also a trasmission channel for the effects of financial crises on poverty and inequality.

20 It can be argued that cuts in public spending on social programs may force the poor to pay for similar services provided by the private sector, thereby putting more pressure on their budget at times when earning opportunities are reduced. Lower public spending on health care may also affect poverty because sickness reduces the ability of the poor to earn a living. Collection of informal charges in the provision of public social services may also affect poverty when public spending is reduced in the aftermath of a crisis. Crisis-induced cuts in allocations for social assistance and insurance programs are also likely to affect the poor adversely.

21 We cannot reject the specification restrictions at classical levels of significance for the income share equations when the unemployment transmission mechanisms are under examination and, for most income share equations, when the fiscal retrenchment mechanisms are being estimated. See equation (10.5) for the definition of the specification restrictions.

22 Other studies have suggested that the composition of social spending matters. When it is targeted toward primary education and preventive health care social spending is more likely to improve social indicators and reduce poverty. See Gupta *et al.* (1999).

23 See Cunningham *et al.* (2001), Lopez-Acevedo and Salinas (2000), and Lustig (2000).

24 The 1992 survey covers 10,530 households, the 1994 survey covers 12,814 house-holds, and the 1996 survey covers 14,042 households. The sample presented here excludes households with no information on income or expenditures. Information pro-vided includes income by source and socio-demographic characteristics for each household member, the characteristics of the head of the household, and detailed expenditures by consumption items. Household income and expenditures include an imputed value of owner-occupied housing, as well as the monetary value of gifts, self-production, and in-kind payments.

25 See the robustness check for comparisons with National Accounts data.

26 The poverty line is defined by a minimum consumption basket for rural and urban households by the Mexican Statistical Institute defined as the "extreme poverty line" (INEGI, 1993). Expenditure is defined as per equivalent person expenditure to take into account differences in household size. See Appendix I for a description of the methodology and definitions of the measures of poverty used. An alternative poverty line was defined as 50 percent of mean income in 1992, and then corrected for infla-tion in 1994 and 1996. Parameter estimates based on this alternative definition of poverty are fully consistent with the estimates based on the definition of poverty adopted in the text. The results based on the alternative poverty line definition are not presented here due to space constraints, but are available upon request.

27 The poverty gap is calculated as the difference between household equivalent expenditures and the poverty line as a percentage of the poverty line. We also calcu-lated the income gap, or cost of bringing everyone up to at least the poverty line, at 0.08 percent of GDP in 1992, 0.06 percent of GDP in 1994, and 0.12 percent of GDP in 1996.

28 Lustig and Székely (1997) find an income poverty headcount ratio of 16.1 percent for 1992 and 15.5 percent for 1994 using the same poverty line and same dataset, which is consistently higher than the 12.7 and 10.6 percent presented here for 1992 and 1994 respectively. Data for 1996 was not available at the time of their study.

29 Inequality fell both in the rural and in the urban areas in the same period.

30 This result is, however, consistent with previous findings for the case of Brazil (1992), Costa Rica (1984), Uraguay (1983), and Venezuela (1991). The Gini coefficient for 1992 presented in Table 10A.1 is consistent with Lustig and Székely (1998) who find a Gini of 0.53 for income in 1992 using the same 1992 Mexican data.

31 Cunningham *et al.* (2001) find that the lowest quintile did better than the highest quintile in terms of changes in income during the 1995 crisis. The authors conclude that the poor recovered their income losses faster than the wealthy during upturns after crises.

32 The share of income derived from wages is lower among low-income households, thus confirming the previous findings by Lopez-Acevedo and Salinas (2000). Self-employed income represents 18.5 percent of total income of poorer households as compared to only 6 percent for those in the highest deciles.

33 Lopez-Acevedo and Salinas (2000) show that the higher income loss of the highest income decile is due to loss not only in capital income, as expected, but also in labor income, given that the rich tend to work in the nontrade sector. This result is consistent with our findings.

34 Note that the transfers measured here do not include the more recent PROGRESA transfer scheme initiated in 1997.

35 The share of transfers in total income varies across expenditure deciles, with a peak of around 9 percent in the richest decile in 1994. In 1996, transfers peak at around 10.8 percent in the eighth and ninth deciles. See Table 10A.1.

36 This suggests that pensions may be an ineffective social safety net for the elderly. However, pensioners continued to have a lower risk of poverty among the different occupational categories in 1996.

37 According to the definitions of consumption and income used in this study, consistent with international practice, household income and consumption include imputed rents from owner-occupied housing. Therefore, home losses could increase the risk of becoming poor.

38 Lustig (1981) finds that household survey consumption accounts for only 80 percent of the private consumption estimates in the national accounts in 1968 and 64 percent in 1977. Castro-Leal Talamás (1995) reports this ratio at 45 percent in 1984 and 54 percent in 1989. Calculations in this study suggest that this ratio fell to 41 percent in 1992, 41 percent in 1994, and 37 percent in 1996.

39 See Lustig and Székely (1997).

40 Results of the logit and pooled logit estimations using the adjusted 1994 and 1996 sample are not presented here due to space constraints, but are available upon request.

41 Both income and expenditures are defined as the sum of all monetary and nonmonetary components (in-kind payments, gifts, and self-production) and the imputed values of the home owner's property. Results based on the income definition of poverty are available upon request.

42 The poverty lines used here refer to the 1992 "extreme" and "moderate" poverty lines defined by INEGI. The extreme poverty line is M$167,955 for urban households and M$124,751 for rural households. The moderate poverty line is M$335,910 for urban households and M$218,314 for rural households in current Mexican pesos per month.

43 This poverty line lies between the extreme and the intermediate poverty lines calculated by UN/ECLAC and INEGI (1993) for the 1992 ENIGH taking into account the cost of the minimum consumption basket (Table 10A.2).

44 Both headcount and poverty gap ratios are insensitive to the extent of inequality among the poor.

45 In the estimates presented in the chapter, ε is set equal to 0.8.

References

Bléjer, Mario I., and Isabel Guerrero. 1990. "The Impact of Macroeconomic Policies on Income Distribution: An Empirical Study of the Philippines," *The Review of Economics and Statistics*, 72(August): 414–23.

Bouillon, César P., Arianna Legovini, and Nora Claudia Lustig. 1998. "Rising Inequality in Mexico: Returns to Household Characteristics and the 'Chiapas' Effect" (Washington, DC: Inter-American Development Bank; World Bank). Available via the Internet: http://ssrn.com/abstract=182178 (accessed on April 19, 1999).

Bourguignon, François and Christian Morrisson. 1992. *Adjustment and Equity in Developing Countries: A New Approach* (Paris: Organization of Economic Cooperation and Development).

Castro-Leal Talamás and Florencia Teresa. 1995. "Economic Inequality, Poverty and Growth: Mexico, 1984–89" (PhD dissertation; Austin, TX: University of Texas).

Chen, Shaohua and Martin Ravallion. 2000. "How Did the World's Poorest Fare in the 1990s?" Policy Research Working Paper No. 2409 (Washington, DC: World Bank).

Chu, Ke-young and Sanjeev Gupta (eds). 1998. *Social Safety Nets: Issues and Recent Experiences* (Washington, DC: International Monetary Fund).

Cunningham, Wendy, William F. Maloney, and Mariano Bosch. 2001. "Who Suffers Income Falls During Crises? An Application of Quantile Analysis to Mexico: 1992–95," background paper for De Ferranti *et al.* "Securing Our Future" (Washington, DC: World Bank).

Datt, G. and M. Ravallion. 1998. "Why Have Some Indian States Done Better than Others at Reducing Rural Poverty?" *Economica*, 65(February): 17–38.

Deininger, Klaus and Lyn Squire. 1998. "New Ways of Looking at Old Issues: Inequality and Growth," *Journal of Development Economics*, 57(December): 259–87.

Dollar, David and Aart Kraay. 2000. "Growth is Good for the Poor," International Monetary Fund Seminar Series No. 2000–35 (Washington, DC: International Monetary Fund).

Easterly, William Russell. 2001. "The Effect of International Monetary Fund and World Bank Programs on Poverty," Policy Research Working Paper No. 2517 (Washington, DC: World Bank). Available via the Internet: http://ssrn.com/abstract=256883 (accessed on December 2000).

Eichengreen, Barry and Andrew K. Rose. 1998. "Staying Afloat When the Wind Shifts: External Factors and Emerging-Market Banking Crises," NBER Working Paper No. 6370 (Cambridge, MA: National Bureau of Economic Research).

Eichengreen, Barry, Andrew K. Rose, and Charles Wyplosz. 1995. "Exchange Market Mayhem: The Antecedents and Aftermath of Speculative Attacks," *Economic Policy*, 21(October): 249–312.

Ferreira, Francisco H. G., Giovanna Prennushi, and Martin Ravallion. 1999. "Protecting the Poor from Macroeconomic Shocks," World Bank Policy Research Working Paper No. 2160 (Washington, DC: World Bank).

Flood, Robert P. and Nancy P. Marion. 1997. "Policy Implications of 'Second-Generation' Crisis Models," *Staff Papers*, International Monetary Fund, 44(September): 383–90.

Foster, James E. and Miguel Székely. 2001. "Is Economic Growth Good for the Poor? Tracking Low Incomes Using General Means," paper presented at the Asia and Pacific Forum on Poverty, Manila, February.

Frankel, Jeffrey A. and Andrew K. Rose. 1996. "Currency Crashes in Emerging Markets: Empirical Indicators," CEPR Discussion Paper No. 1349 (London: Centre for Economic Policy Research).

Glewwe, P. and G. Hall. 1994. "Poverty, Inequality, and Living Standards During Unorthodox Adjustment: The Case of Peru, 1985–1990," *Economic Development and Cultural Change*, 42(4): 689–717.

—— 1998. "Are Some Groups More Vulnerable to Macroeconomic Shocks Than Others? Hypothesis Tests Based on Panel Data from Peru," *Journal of Development Economics*, 56(1): 181–206.

Gupta, Sanjeev, Luiz de Mello, and Robert Gillingham. 1999. "Strengthening Social Policy Instruments," in *Brazil – Selected Issues and Statistical Appendix*, IMF Staff Country Report No. 99/97 (Washington, DC: International Monetary Fund). Available via the Internet: http://www.imf.org/external/pubs/cat/longres.cfm?sk=3206.0

Gupta, Sanjeev, Calvin McDonald, Verhoeven Schiller, Marijn Christian, and Zara Bogetic. 1999. *Mitigating the Social Costs of the Economic Crisis and the Reform Programs in Asia*, IMF Economic Review, No. 1 (Washington, DC: International Monetary Fund).

Institute Nacional de Estadística, Geografía e Informática (INEGI). 1993. *Magnitud y Evolución de la Pobreza en México: 1984–1992, Informe Metodológico* (México: Instituto Nacional de Estadística, Geografía e Informática).

Kaminsky, Graciela, Saul Lizondo, and Carmen M. Reinhart. 1997. "Leading Indicators of Currency Crises," IMF Working Paper 97/79 (Washington, DC: International Monetary Fund).

Krugman, Paul. 1979. "A Model of Balance-of-Payments Crises," *Journal of Money, Credit, and Banking*, 11(August): 311–25.

Lanjouw, Peter and Martin Ravallion. 1999. "Benefit Incidence, Public Spending Reforms, and the Timing of Program Capture," *World Bank Economic Review*, 13(May): 257–73.

Lopez-Acevedo, Gladys and Angel Salinas. 2000. "How Mexico's Financial Crisis Affected Income Distribution," World Bank Policy Research Working Paper No. 2406 (Washington, DC: World Bank).

Lustig, Nora. 1981. *Income Distribution and Growth in Mexico*. El Colegio de Mexico. Mexico D.F.

—— 1998. *Mexico: The Remaking of an Economy* (Washington, DC: Brookings Institution Press).

—— 2000. "Crises and the Poor: Socially Responsible Macroeconomics," Technical Papers Series (Washington, DC: Inter-American Development Bank). Available via the Internet: http://www.iadb.org/sds/publication/publication_1566_e.htm

—— and Michael Walton, 1998, "Crises and the Poor: A Template for Action" (unpublished; Washington, DC: World Bank and Inter-American Development Bank). Available via the Internet: http://www.iadb.org/sds/doc/854eng.pdf

Maddala, G.S., 1986, *Limited-Dependent and Qualitative Variables in Econometrics*, Econometric Society Monographs Series (Cambridge, England: Cambridge University Press).

Meyer, Bruce D. 1994. "Natural and Quasi-Experiments in Economics," NBER Working Paper No. T0170 (Cambridge, MA: National Bureau of Economic Research).

Milesi-Ferretti, Gian Maria and Assaf Razin. 1996. "Current Account Sustainability: Selected East Asian and Latin American Experiences," NBER Working Paper No. 5791 (Cambridge, MA: National Bureau of Economic Research).

—— 1998. "Sharp Reductions in Current Account Deficits: An Empirical Analysis," *European Economic Review*, 42(May): 897–908.

Morley, Samuel A. 1995. *Poverty and Inequality in Latin America: The Impact of Adjustment and Recovery in the 1980s* (Baltimore, MD: The Johns Hopkins University Press).

Obstfeld, M. 1996. "Models of Currency Crises with Self-Fulfilling Features,"*European Economic Review*, 40(April): 1037–47.

Ravallion, Martin. 2000. "Are the poor protected from, Budget Cuts? Theory and Evidence for Argentina," World Bank Policy Research Working Paper No. 2391 (Washington, DC: World Bank).

—— 2001. "Growth, Inequality and poverty: Looking Beyond Averages," World Bank Policy Research Working paper No. 2558 (Washington, DC: World Bank).

—— and S. Chen. 1997. "What Can New Survey Data Tell Us About Recent changes in Distribution and Poverty?" *World Bank Economic Review*, 11(2): 357–82.

Sahn, E. David, Paul A. Dorosh, and Stephen D. Younger. 1997. *Structural Adjustment Reconsidered: Economic Policy and Poverty in Africa* (Cambridge, United Kingdom; New York: Cambridge University Press).

Sen, Amartya K. 1976. "Poverty: An Ordinal Approach to Measurement," *Econometrica*, 44(March): 219–31.

Simon, Julian L. 1966. "The Price Elasticity of Liquor in the U.S. and a Simple Method of Determination," *Econometrica*, 34(January): 193–205.

Walton, Michael and Tamar Manuelyan. 1998. "Social Consequences of the East Asian Financial Crisis," in Richard Newfarmer (ed.), *East Asia: The Road to Recovery* (Washington, DC: World Bank). Available via the Internet: http://www.worldbank.org/eapsocial/library/socconsq/

Wiegand, J. 2000. "A Model for the Conditional Evaluation of Poverty Risks, With an Application to Prime-Age Germans, 1991–95," paper presented at a World Bank Thematic Group on Inequality, Poverty, and Socio-Economic Performance Seminar, Washington, November.

World Bank. 2000. *World Development Report 2000/2001: Attacking Poverty* (Washington, DC: World Bank).

11   Growth and shocks

Evidence from rural Ethiopia

Stefan Dercon

Using panel data from rural Ethiopia, the chapter discusses the determinants of consumption growth (1989–97), based on a microgrowth model, controlling for heterogeneity. Consumption grew substantially, but with diverse experiences across villages and individuals. Rainfall shocks have a substantial impact on consumption growth which persists for many years. There also is a persistent growth impact from the large-scale famine in the 1980s as well as substantial externalities from road infrastructure. The persistent effects of rainfall shocks and the famine crisis imply that welfare losses due to the lack of insurance and protection measures are well beyond the welfare cost of short-term consumption fluctuations.

11.1   Introduction

The study of poor people's impediments to escape poverty remains at the core of development economics. This chapter discusses the determinants of growth in living standards in a number of rural communities in Ethiopia between 1989 and 1997. The focus is on the role of shocks, such as drought and famine, on poverty persistence as well as on identifying the correlates of welfare improvements.

Inspired by the standard growth literature, the chapter uses household panel data covering 1989–97 and six villages across the country to study rural consumption growth in this period using a linearised empirical growth model. The focus is on the impact of shocks, and more specifically on persistent effects of rainfall shocks on growth. The results suggest that idiosyncratic and common shocks had substantial contemporaneous impact. Especially better rainfall contributed to the observed growth. I also test for persistence of the effects of past shocks. I find that there is evidence of some persistence – lagged rainfall shocks matter for current growth. Furthermore, indicators of the severity of the famine in 1984–85 are significant to explain growth in the 1990s, further suggesting persistence. Finally, road infrastructure is a source of divergence in growth experience across households and communities.

The study of growth in developing countries using micro-level household data is not common, largely because suitable panel data sets are missing to embark on such work. Deininger and Okidi (2003) and Gunning *et al.* (2000) look into the determinants of growth in Ugandan and Zimbabwean panel data. As part of a number of papers using data from rural China, Ravallion and Jalan (1996) use a framework inspired by both the Solow model and the endogenous growth literature to investigate sources of divergence and convergence between regions. In further work using the household level data from their panel (e.g. Jalan and Ravallion (1997, 1998, 2002), divergence due to spatial factors is explicitly tested for and discovered, suggesting spatial poverty traps. This chapter draws inspiration from their approach by explicitly disentangling community and individual effects. It goes beyond their approach by focusing explicitly on the impact of uninsured risk on household outcomes.

It is well documented that households and individuals in developing countries use different strategies to cope with risk including self-insurance via savings, informal insurance mechanisms or income portfolio adjustments towards lower overall risk in their activities. Literature surveys suggest that these mechanisms typically only succeed in partial insurance (Morduch, 1995; Townsend, 1995). Given that households are generally 'fluctuation averse', the resulting fluctuations in consumption and other welfare outcomes imply a loss of welfare due to uninsured risk. However, beyond this transient impact on welfare, there may also be a 'chronic' impact from uninsured risk, that is, persistent or even permanent effects on levels and growth rates of income linked to uninsured risk. In particular, one can distinguish two effects. First, an *ex ante* or behavioural impact: uninsured risk implies that it is optimal to avoid profitable but risky opportunities. Households may diversify, enter into low risk but low return activities or invest in low risk assets, all at the expense of mean returns. Second, an *ex post* impact, after a 'bad' state has materialised: the lack of insurance against such a shock implies that human, physical or social capital may be lost reducing access to profitable opportunities. In short, uninsured risk may be a cause of poverty. Several theoretical models of poverty traps and persistence have been developed whereby temporary events affect long-term outcomes (Banerjee and Newman, 1993; Acemoglu and Zilibotti, 1997). A number of empirical studies (e.g. Rosenzweig and Binswanger, 1993; Rosenzweig and Wolpin, 1993; Morduch, 1995) find evidence consistent with permanent effects linked to risk. There is also evidence from studies focusing on health and educational outcomes consistent with permanent impacts of shocks such as drought (Alderman *et al.*, 2001; Hoddinott and Kinsey, 2001). A few recent studies investigate the impact of risk on growth using household data. Jalan and Ravallion (2004) and Lokshin and Ravallion (2001) test the idea of a shock-induced poverty trap by testing for whether the transition dynamics after a shock are convex; they do not find evidence of a transition to a low-outcome equilibrium but the recovery after a shock in income is nevertheless slow. Elbers *et al.* (2003), using data from Zimbabwe, calibrate and simulate a household optimal growth model accounting for both *ex ante* and *ex post* responses to risk, allowing them to quantify the losses linked to uninsured risk which proved substantial in their data set.

This chapter uses a reduced-form econometric approach to test for the impact of uninsured risk. Measured recent and past shocks are directly introduced in the regressions, and their cumulative impact is quantified. This is similar to the study of persistence in macroeconomic series. Campbell and Mankiw (1987) investigate persistence in the log of Gross National Product (GNP), that is, whether shocks continue to have an effect 'for a long time into the future'. Formally, they estimate the growth in GNP as stationary autoregressive moving average process. Their persistence measure is based on cumulative impact of past shocks on the level of GNP. This is not the same as testing for the existence of a 'poverty trap' in the sense of the investigation of the threshold, below which there is a tendency to be trapped in permanently low income, from which no escape is possible except for by large positive shocks. Persistence within the time period of the data does not exclude permanent effects but does not imply them either.

Ethiopia is an obvious setting to study the impact of uninsured risk. About 85 per cent of the population lives in rural areas and virtually all rural households are dependent on rain-fed agriculture as the basis for their livelihoods. Droughts are recurrent events, while high incidence of pests, as well as animal and human disease affect their livelihoods as well. Insurance and asset markets function relatively poorly, while safety nets, even though present and widespread, are not able to credibly guarantee support when needed (Jayne *et al.*, 2002; Dercon and Krishnan, 2003). The data set used is relatively small – only 342 households with complete information are used for the core parts of the analysis. It implies that some care will have to be taken to interpret the findings; the chapter may however give insights and suggestions on how to study these issues in other contexts and on larger data sets. Furthermore, the information available is relatively comprehensive: there are data on events, shocks and experiences over the survey period as well as data collected using longer-term recall – including on experiences during the (by far largest recent) famine in the mid-1980s.

The sample is not a random sample of rural communities in Ethiopia, but they were initially selected since they had suffered from the drought in the mid-1980s which had developed into a large-scale famine due to the civil war and other political factors. During the 1990s, growth rates in GDP picked up considerably, with GDP per capita growing by about 14 per cent between 1990 and 1997 (the study period). While the economic reform taking place in this period is likely to have been a necessary condition for this growth experience, it begs the question whether these growth rates should not be largely viewed as recoveries from earlier shocks. Indeed, it took until about 1996 for GDP per capita to surpass levels reached in the early 1980s, before the war, famine and repressive politics plunged Ethiopia into the crisis of the late 1980s. Furthermore, growth rates fluctuated considerably as well in the 1990s. In the survey villages, the issue of recovery and weather-induced growth may even be more important. Consumption growth was well beyond national levels in the 1990s, implying impressive poverty reductions (Dercon and Krishnan, 2002). However, since the villages were chosen because the famine had strong effects, the question of recovery and differential effects across households and villages during this recovery becomes crucial to understanding of the long-term impact of this type of crisis.

In the next section, I present the theoretical and empirical framework used. It is based on the standard 'informal' empirical growth model, drawing inspiration from both Mankiw *et al.* (1992) and endogenous growth theory, for example, Romer (1986), and introduce into this framework an approach to the study of persistence. A number of testable hypotheses are derived. In Section 11.3, the context and data are presented. In Section 11.4, the econometric specifications are discussed and the estimates are presented in Section 11.5. Section 11.6 concludes.

11.2 Theoretical and empirical framework

The framework used is a standard empirical growth model, allowing for transitional dynamics, inspired by Mankiw *et al.* (1992). In this model, growth rates are negatively related to initial levels of income as well as related to a number of variables determining initial efficiency and the steady state, including investment rates in human and physical capital. In the context of panel data on per worker incomes of N households i ($i = 1,\dots N$) across periods t, y_{it}, this empirical model can be written as (see e.g. Islam, 1995):

$$\ln y_{it} - \ln y_{it-1} = \alpha + \beta \ln y_{it-1} + \delta Z_{it} + \gamma X_i + u_{it} \tag{11.1}$$

in which Z_{it} are time-varying and X_i fixed characteristics of the household, for example, determining savings rates or investment in human capital, while α is a common source of growth across households and u_{it} is a transitory error term with mean zero. There are numerous reasons why one should be careful in applying this framework to any context, given the theoretical and empirical assumptions implied by this model (e.g. see the reviews by Temple, 1999; or Durlauf and Quah, 1998). Still, one could use this framework as a starting point. A standard question is whether there is conditional convergence in the household data: a negative estimate for β would suggest convergence, allowing for underlying differences in the steady state. A relevant question in this respect is at which level this convergence is occurring: within or between villages. Equation (11.1) can be rewritten as:

$$\ln y_{it} - \ln y_{it-1} = \alpha + \beta(\ln y_{it-1} - \ln \bar{y}_{it-1}) + \beta_1 \ln \bar{y}_{it-1} + \delta Z_{it} + \gamma X_i + u_{it} \tag{11.2}$$

in which $\bar{y}_{it-1}$ is the average per worker income in a community. A rejection of the null hypothesis of $\beta_1 = \beta$ would suggest that convergence within and across villages is occurring at different speeds. Of course, the growth theoretical literature is far richer than implied by this discussion. In different endogenous growth models, convergence may not exist. For example, models such as Romer (1986) imply that overall, inputs exhibit increasing returns to scale, so that capital levels (and by implication, output levels) may be positively related to growth levels. Ravallion and Jalan (1996) exploit this in the context of a convergence test, by distinguishing regional versus household initial levels of capital. A positive estimate for β_1, for example, would suggest divergence related to external effects from community wealth levels. Unpacking these effects further allows a more careful discussion of the role of different types of initial conditions in this respect. For example, let us define k_i as (a vector of) household level capital per worker and h_v village level capital such as infrastructure or mean levels of household capital per worker. Let us write the relationship as in (11.2), but now in terms of capital goods as:[1]

$$\ln y_{it} - \ln y_{it-1} = \alpha + \zeta \ln k_{it-1} + \eta \ln h_{vt-1} + \delta Z_{it} + \gamma X_i + u_{it} \qquad (11.3)$$

Although in the Solow model growth rates will be decreasing in the level of each production factor, the specification in (11.3) allows growth rates to be increasing functions of the endowment of some factors and decreasing of some other factors, as in some endogenous growth models.

Shocks have no explicit role to play in this formulation, even though it is generally acknowledged that shocks, for example, due to climate, could be an appropriate justification to introduce a stationary error term. One way of interpreting this effect is that initial efficiency (the technological coefficient in the underlying production function) may be influenced by period-specific conditions (Temple, 1999). An important shortcoming of such approach is that it is assumed that there is no persistence in the impact of shocks. An alternative route would be to introduce information about shocks directly in (11.1)–(11.3). To do so, and again referring back to the Cobb–Douglas technology assumptions as in the Solow model, let us assume that there is multiplicative risk, affecting the technological coefficient. Let us call the value of this source of risk at tS_{it}, which could be thought of as the level rainfall or a measure of health status in this particular period. This risk could be idiosyncratic or common. It is then possible to introduce risk into equations (11.1)–(11.3), both as controls for shocks in growth rates, as well as to investigate whether there is any tendency of persistence in relation to shocks. No further distributional assumptions about these shocks need to be imposed. A positive impact from positive current shocks (changes in the log of S) would be expected.

It is possible to assess whether there is any persistence in shocks: do shocks in the period preceding the one for which growth has been measured still affect current growth? The notion of persistence used is similar to the presence of a distributed lag on shock terms (e.g. Campbell and Mankiw, 1987). If these past shocks matter, then persistence has been identified. Finally, adding indicators of serious shocks substantial time before the measurement of the growth rates would allow us to identify a further form of persistence. They are captured by $F_{it-\tau}$, measures of serious events that have occurred at $t - \tau$. In particular, I will introduce indicators of the impact of the famine of the mid-1980s on the household, which occurred several years before the beginning of the data period. If these shocks still affect *growth* a decade later, this would be a further sign of persistence. Persistence of shocks on growth and levels of income is not the same as identifying whether there is ever any recovery from these shocks in terms of outcome levels. Still, if these shocks have persistent effects on growth, the least that can be concluded is that these households would actually take a long time to recover from them, after first diverging. The presence of permanent shocks cannot be tested using this linear model, that is, whether the steady state is permanently affected (see e.g. Jalan and Ravallion, 2002). A general model to investigate determinants of growth in reduced form regression could then be written as:

$$\ln y_{it} - \ln y_{it-1} = \alpha + \zeta \ln k_{it-1} + \eta \ln h_{vt-1} + \theta(\ln S_{it} - \ln S_{it-1})$$
$$+ \lambda(\ln S_{it-1} - \ln S_{it-2}) + \delta Z_{it} + \gamma X_i + \varphi F_{it-\tau} + u_{it}$$

$$(11.4)$$

In this formulation it is assumed that all cross-sectional variation in growth rates is captured by initial capital and by shocks, but specifically allowing for some other sources of heterogeneity across households. The econometric model later will take this up again.

11.3   Data

The data used in this chapter is from six communities in rural Ethiopia. In each village, a random sample was selected yielding information on about 350 house-holds (the attrition rate between 1989 and 1994 was about 3 per cent, between 1994 and 1997 only about 2 per cent).[2] The villages are located in the central and southern part of the country. In 1989, the war made it impossible to survey any northern villages. Nevertheless, the villages combine a variety of characteristics, common to rural Ethiopia. Four of the villages are cereal growing villages, one is in a coffee/enset area and one grows mainly sorghum but has been experiencing the rapid expansion of chat (a valuable, aphetamine-like drug). All but one are not too far from towns, but only half have an all-weather road. The villages were initially selected to study the crisis and recovery from drought and famine in the mid-1980s (Webb *et al.*, 1992). Details on the survey are in Dercon and Krishnan (1998) and in Dercon (2002).

The households in the survey are virtually all involved in agriculture. Almost all have access to land, although with important differences in quality and across villages. On average, about half their income is derived from crops, the rest from livestock and off-farm activities. Most of the off-farm activities (such as selling home-made drinks or dung cakes) are closely linked to the agricultural activities. Alternatives are collecting firewood, making charcoal and weaving.

In this chapter, I use data from 1989 and from the revisits during four rounds in 1994–97. Growth is measured using the growth rates in food consumption. Non-food consumption data were not collected in 1989 in all communities, so the analysis had to limit itself largely to food consumption – its implication for the analysis will be discussed later. Calorie intake data and a smaller data set on total consumption (using only four villages) are used to test the robustness of the results. Data are reported in per adult equivalent and in real terms, in prices of 1994. The food price deflator and any other price data used in this study are based on separate price surveys conducted by the survey team and by the Central Statistical Authority. The procedures used are discussed in Dercon and Krishnan (1998).

Nutritional equivalence scales specific for East-Africa were used to control for household size and composition. Since food consumption is unlikely to be characterised by economies of scale, no further scaling is used (Deaton, 1997).

The underlying questionnaire was based on a one-week recall of food consumption, from own sources, purchased or from gifts. Seasonal analysis using the panel revealed rather large seasonal fluctuations in consumption seemingly linked to price and labour demand fluctuations (Dercon and Krishnan, 2000a,b). Therefore, the data used for the analysis in this chapter for food consumption in 1994/95 are for food consumption levels in the same season as when the data had been collected in 1989. Consequently, only one observation of the three possible data points collected during the 1994/95 rounds are used. The data for 1997 are matched to those of 1994/95 in a similar way. The result was three observations on food consumption (1989, 1994/95 and 1997) and two growth rates for each households.

Table 11.1 reports average real food consumption per adult for each village. The table suggests substantial growth in mean per adult food consumption in this period: the average household level growth rate in the sample (i.e the average of household level growth rates) is equivalent to more than 12 per cent per year. There are nevertheless substantial differences between villages. In all but one village, growth was above national growth rates. In another paper, we studied poverty, and the data revealed substantial poverty declines as well, but again with substantial differences between villages (Dercon and Krishnan, 2002). In that paper, it is also shown that the choice of the data sources for the deflators matter for the exact magnitude of the results, but not for the overall and relative patterns involved.

These poverty declines are surprisingly high and they definitely do not square with the overall impressions of rural Ethiopia in this period. In general, an improvement in living standards could be expected but not at this scale. Nationally representative data for rural Ethiopia are only available for 1995 and 2000; estimates on these data suggest some marginal declines in poverty in rural Ethiopia and definitely not at this scale. However, the findings on other welfare indicators in the national Welfare Monitoring Survey would not necessarily

Table 11.1 Food consumption per adult equivalent (in 1994 prices) ($n = 346$) (6 birr = US$1)

	Dinki	Debre Berhan	Adele Kele	Koro Degaga	Gara Godo	Doma'a	Whole sample
1989	42.2	45.6	52.2	31.0	21.0	22.4	35.0
1994/95	68.2	84.4	86.7	43.9	17.0	76.2	60.2
1997	61.8	163.2	122.6	64.5	74.3	49.2	87.4
Growth (% p.a.)	0.7	13.6	12.2	16.9	23.4	3.4	12.4

Note
Growth rates are average annual village level and sample annual growth rates calculated as the average of annual household level growth rates between 1989 and 1997.

Table 11.2 Yearly growth rates of alternative welfare and wealth indicators, per adult
(*n* = 346) (6 birr = US$1)

	Dinki	Debre Berhan	Adele Kele	Koro Degaga	Gara Godo	Doma'a	Whole sample
Food consumption	0.7	13.6	12.2	16.9	23.4	3.4	12.4
Total consumption	−0.1	12.0	9.0	—	19.0	—	10.0
Calories	2.4	11.5	4.2	14.0	21.5	−5.2	9.1
Livestock values	1.0	0.8	1.5	3.7	1.0	2.3	1.9
Livestock units	4.4	−0.4	14.4	29.7	12.1	29.1	16.1

Notes
Growth rates are average annual village level and total annual growth rates calculated as the average
of annual household level growth rates between 1989 and 1997. Calorie conversion using World
Health Organisation conversion tables. Total consumption based on complete data for four villages
only. Livestock Units are standard tropical units of different types of livestock, calculated on the basis
of oxen = 1, cows = 0.70, bulls = 0.75, horse = 0.50, goat = 0.10, sheep = 0.100 and other similar
values.

contradict some substantial improvement. Primary school enrolment, for example,
doubled in both gross and net terms between 1994 and 1998. But this only
brought net primary enrolment to about 19 per cent. For these and other welfare
measures, only by 1997 were the levels reached again equivalent to those from
before the 1985 famine. In short, the increases in consumption in the sample may
be an overestimate, but other indicators suggest substantial upward movement in
some rural areas. But much of this movement may well be the recovery from the
lower levels in the late 1980s.

One may be concerned that these observed poverty declines are a consequence
of the use of food consumption as an indicator of welfare. Table 11.2 gives a
number of alternative measures calculated from data in this sample. Using the
complete data from four villages, it can be seen that the increase in total consumption is slightly lower than those of food consumption in each village, but the
differences are relatively small. Calorie intake data show a very similar pattern.
Overall, this suggests that the evolution of relative food versus non-food prices,
or in general, problems with the valuation and deflators of consumption are
unlikely to be at the heart of the observed large changes. A look at the evolution
of livestock confirms large positive improvements in this period. As in many
of the poorest countries in the world, livestock is by far the most important
marketable asset and typically is accounting for more than 90 per cent of the value
of assets. In all but one village, livestock values increased considerably during the
survey period. In value terms, the yearly growth has been low, but this is largely
due to a decline in livestock prices relative to consumer prices. In terms of
standardised units, the overall increase is again very substantial, even though the
pattern across villages is not identical to the consumption evolution.[3] Still, across
the sample, livestock changes are positively correlated with changes in food
consumption (the correlation coefficient is significant at 10 per cent).

Both the high consumption and livestock levels may well have been helped by
the overall rainfall pattern in this period. Table 11.3 gives details of the recent

Table 11.3 Rainfall between 1989 and 1997 (rainfall in particular period relative to the long term mean, reported as a percentage deviation)

	Dinki	Debre Berhan	Adele Kele	Koro Degaga	Gara Godo	Doma'a	Whole sample
1988–89	−13	+6	−7	+2	+5	−13	+2
1993–94	+16	+7	+13	−19	−8	+16	+4
1996–97	−23	+4	+52	+32	+7	−23	+10
1985–89	+5	−1	+5	+16	+7	−6	+4
1990–94	−6	−2	+17	+21	−7	+6	+4
1994–97	+6	−15	+18	+48	+9	−2	+8

Notes

Rainfall in the nearest rainfall station, based on data from the National Meteorological Office, Addis Ababa. The reported data are the rainfall in a particular period relative to the 'long-term' mean, expressed as a percentage deviation, that is $(rainfall/mean) - 1$ Yearly rainfall is the rainfall in the 12 months preceding the survey. Long-term rainfall data are the percentage deviation of average rainfall in a particular five-year period, relative to the long-term average. The long-term average is based on all available observations of the relevant rainfall station before the first interview in 1989, typically covering about 15–20 years. So, for example, in the whole sample, the rainfall in 1994–97 was 8 per cent better than the long-term average.

rainfall experience in these villages. The indicator used is the rainfall level in the village in the 12 months preceding the consumption data collection. In all villages included in the analysis, there is one main rainy season and a relatively less important short rainy season. The consumption data were collected outside the rainy season, so that the use of a 12 months recall period would be appropriate. Other indicators, those using the relevant 'main' rainy season, did not make much difference for the analysis. The data were collected from the nearest rainfall station from the community, with means calculated using all available historical data from before the first interview. For most of these villages, data have only been collected for less than 20 years.

Rainfall was on average better in more recent rounds, so it could plausibly account for some of the large increases in consumption and asset levels. This will be addressed in the econometric analysis. Note also the large fluctuations in rainfall in some of the villages in this period, and that mean levels in the 1990s have been above 'long-term' levels – which are strongly influenced by the disastrous levels in the early 1980s in these communities.

As mentioned earlier, these villages were initially selected because they had been affected relatively seriously by the famine crisis of the early 1980s. One of the questions is whether there are any persistent effects of this crisis period: do households that suffered substantially during this period have different growth in the 1990s? During the 1994 data collection round, the households' experience during the famine period was investigated further. It is not straightforward to find good individual level indicators of the severity of the famine. Table 11.4 gives details on the extent that households were affected by the famine, largely using indicators of the coping strategies households had to use to cope with the crisis. First, it reports whether households experienced a serious loss of wealth directly

Table 11.4 Responses and actions during famine in mid-1980s

	Dinki	Debre Berhan	Adele Kele	Koro Degaga	Gara Godo	Doma'a	Whole sample
Harvest failure?[a]	0.98	0.19	0.44	0.91	0.40	0.71	0.63
Meals consumed (no.)	1.04	2.85	1.71	1.98	1.51	2.43	1.94
Cut food quantities?[a]	1.00	0.49	0.90	0.92	0.91	0.90	0.85
Ate wild foods?[a]	0.88	0.05	0.78	0.63	1.00	0.73	0.66
Sold valuables?[a]	0.27	0.14	0.56	0.26	0.81	0.49	0.39
% of livestock sold?	0.21	0.08	0.12	0.21	0.55	0.62	0.29
Food aid in crisis?[a]	0.96	0.00	0.49	0.13	0.79	0.59	0.44
% suffering in village?[b]	0.74	0.51	0.66	0.66	0.69	0.65	0.65
Anyone to feeding camp?[a]	0.00	0.02	0.13	0.01	0.36	0.21	0.11
Any distress migration ?[a]	0.04	0.00	0.07	0.19	0.04	0.04	0.07

Notes
a Percentage of households responding in particular way.
b Is the village level average estimate, based on household estimates on percentages suffering in the village during crisis.

triggered by harvest failure in this period. Two-thirds of the sampled households reported such a crisis. Household harvest failure is of course not a sufficient indicator of the severity of the crisis, as famine analysis has shown in general and in this particular case (Sen, 1981; Webb *et al.*, 1992). Information on coping with strategies provides some suggestive evidence of the extent households were affected. The table reports the number of meals households had during the famine (with a local norm of three meals a day) and whether they cut meal sizes. Fewer meals were taken and most households report to have cut back on quantities consumed. Two-thirds also report the consumption of unusual wild foods, and more than one-third sold some of their most valued possessions in the worst year. The data also allowed an estimate (based on recall data) of the percentage of the value of their livestock households had to sell or that died during this period. Households reported substantial sales and losses of livestock, so that by 1989 only about half the households owned any significant levels, compared to about 75 per cent before the famine. In some communities, food aid was distributed to many during the crisis period, and about 11 per cent even left for a feeding camp, and another 7 per cent migrated during the crisis out of the region of their communities. An average assessment by households of the percentage of households that suffered during the crisis in each community suggested that about two-thirds suffered on average, with less suffering in Debre Berhan and most in Dinki. The other indicators seem to be consistent with this overall picture.

11.4   Econometric model

In this section, the framework and equations developed in Section 11.2 will be specified in more detail as an econometric model to take to the data. The left-hand-side variable used is the annualised growth rate in real food consumption per adult between 1989 and 1994, and between 1994 and 1997, with data carefully matched so that the data 1989 and 1997 (for which only one observation is available) are from the same period in the year as the respective data used from the 1994–95 survey rounds, in order to avoid seasonality driving the results. The use of food consumption as the left-hand-side variable is potentially problematic. It is conceivable that growth in food consumption occurs leaving total consumption unchanged, purely due to relative price changes (food versus non-food). Indeed, local or national rainfall shocks may be responsible for these changes, so that the current analysis linking shocks to food consumption may simply identify the impact of relative price changes. Urban non-food prices decreased relative to food prices between 1989 and 1994, while they increased relative to food prices between 1994 and 1997, so they cannot account for the average increase in food consumption taking into consideration both periods. Rural patterns could have been different, but unfortunately, local non-food prices are not available. Still, to test the robustness of the results to these relative price effects, the impact of shocks was also investigated using the sub-sample of households for whom total consumption data is available. Further robustness to the specific deflators used is tested by using growth of total calorie consumption per adult as the left-hand-side variable.

The basic specification is based on (11.2), but augmented for a number of specific shock variables $(\ln S_{it} - \ln S_{it-1})$. In line with the discussion before, rainfall *shocks* are defined as the change in the logarithm of rainfall at t relative to $t - 1$.[4] The data set also includes information on idiosyncratic shocks: an index of reported crop damage due to a number of reasons, including frost, animal trampling, weed and plant disease. 'No problems' is equal to the value 0, while problems reduce the index, with -1 the lowest value. An index of the extent to which livestock suffered due to lack of water or fodder is also included (the value 0 is best, -1 is worst). The average number of adults suffering serious illness, affecting the ability to work in between rounds, is included as well (zero is no illness). More details on these measures can be found in Dercon and Krishnan (2000b). Changes in demographics, in particular variables giving changes in male and female adults and children, are included as well (Z_{it}) to control for lifecycle and other demographic effects over this relatively long period.

$$\ln y_{it} - \ln y_{it-1} = \alpha + \beta(\ln y_{it-1} - \ln \bar{y}_{it-1}) + \beta_1 \ln \bar{y}_{it-1}$$
$$+ \theta(\ln S_{it} - \ln S_{it-1}) + \delta Z_{it} + u_{it} \qquad (11.5)$$

This basic specification was then augmented to investigate the persistence of rainfall shocks. Two approaches were used. First, between each round of data used in the regression, about four years have lapsed. It is then possible to distinguish differences in rainfall in the year just before each survey round, and differences in average rainfall in the preceding years. For example, it could be that only the most recent rainfall failures affect consumption, but recovery is swift. Second, rainfall *shocks* in the period preceding $t - 1$ that is $(\ln S_{it-1} - \ln S_{it-2})$, were included as well. Significant impact of past shocks would be evidence of persistence.

This first set of regressions includes lagged consumption as a regressor. This may present econometric problems related to the endogeneity of lagged consumption in a consumption growth regression. All equations involved were also estimated using instrumental variables, including household and locational characteristics related to land, labour, human capital and infrastructure at $t - 1$ as instruments, and Hausman endogeneity tests were implemented and reported. A more general problem typically bedevilling growth regressions is related to individual heterogeneity. The growth evolution observed in the data may simply be individual specific – for example, related to different time preferences, implying different savings behaviour. Although more general forms of heterogeneity will be explored later, the basic specifications will assume that $u_{it} = \omega_i + \varepsilon_{it}$, with ε_{it} assumed to i.i.d. with zero mean and ω_i is a household-specific effect.

Next, the hypothesis of persistent effects from the deepest crisis in recent history, the famine in 1984–85, was explored further. In particular, a number of indicators from Table 11.4 were included that suggest the extremes households had to go to cope with its impact, such as cutting back on meals, reducing quantities consumed, selling their most valuable possession, relying on unusual wild foods, moving to feeding camps or migrating outside the region in search of food. Basic correlation analysis between these variables showed that they were all correlated, which may well lead to multicollinearity problems. Preliminary analysis using these variables highlighted these problems so a simple index was constructed providing an average of these six indicators.[5]

Finally, the lagged household and village level consumption variables were unpacked further, as in (11.3) and (11.4). In line with standard empirical growth model approaches, variables measuring capital goods suitable for accumulation and the underlying technology are relevant. The data set contains three variables that could be most relevant in this context: livestock, the standard asset for accumulation in this rural economy, which, in per capita terms, may or may not be liable to decreasing returns; education levels (average years of education of adults in the household), providing scope for increasing returns, for example, linked to the ability to innovate and a geographical variable capturing whether there was a road connecting the village, relevant given the general poor road infrastructure in Ethiopia. Work in China using micro-growth models has found evidence in favour of positive externalities from roads as well as positive growth effects from household level education (Jalan and Ravallion, 2002), but De Vreyer *et al.* (2002) did not find a significant effect for either in Peru. Deininger and Okidi (2003) find evidence of the impact of community level infrastructure and of household level education on growth in their data, but only in a model without any control for heterogeneity. Limitations in the data from 1989 do not allow us to test the impact of other geographical variables. For example, both the Peru and the China study find evidence on the impact of health-related variables (prevalence of particular diseases and the presence of health centres in the case of Peru, and the presence of medical personnel in the case of China), but this could not be tested in the Ethiopia data. Other variables are less relevant for the period under consideration. For example, Jalan and Ravallion (2002) find evidence of the impact of farm assets and of initial fertiliser use at the community level positively affecting growth, while Gunning *et al.* (2000) identify productivity increases linked to modern input use and extension as the most important source of growth in their Zimbabwe panel. In Ethiopia, the use of modern inputs was hardly relevant in the communities studied by 1989, even though during the second half of the 1990s they become again more important.[6]

The variables related to the 1984 famine and, since no new roads were built in this period, road infrastructure are time-invariant in this model. A standard fixed effects estimator would wipe out these effects, even though they are of interest. Assuming that all time-invariant and time-varying variables are all uncorrelated with the fixed effect would allow the estimation by random effects, but this is an extreme assumption unlikely to be met in this data set. The econometric analysis explores three alternative ways of allowing a fixed effect, correlated with variables of interest, to be present, but still identifying time-invariant variables. The first method involves estimating a model using the fixed effects (within) estimator, but with initial levels of consumption unpacked using time-variant variables (levels at $t-1$ of the average years of education per adult and the level of livestock holdings per adult), and fixed effects. The fixed effects were then regressed on a series of time-invariant variables, providing suggestive evidence of the impact of roads and of the famine on growth in the 1990s. Second, the Hausman–Taylor model (Hausman and Taylor, 1981) is used. This involves partitioning the time-invariant and time-varying vector of variables in two groups each, of which one group of variables is assumed to be uncorrelated with the fixed effect. The orthogonality assumptions provide then enough restrictions for a method of moments procedure. The partitioning assumptions are strong, but in the approach below all demographic variables and the illness shocks were included as endogenous time-varying variables, and the extent to which drastic coping strategies had to be used and (in the relevant version of the econometric model) the presence of a road were treated as endogenous time-invariant variables. Furthermore, depending on the version of the model, lagged consumption at the village and household level, or initial levels of livestock and education, and the presence of a road, are also treated as endogenous. All agricultural and rainfall shocks are treated as exogenous, while whether there was a harvest failure in 1984, the estimate of the proportion of the community that suffered substantially and the pre-famine levels of livestock were used as further instruments for the extent drastic household-level coping strategies had to be used. As a third alternative, the Jalan–Ravallion (Jalan and Ravallion, 2002) estimator that allows for some time-varying heterogeneity was used to check the robustness of the results (see also Holtz-Eakin *et al.*, 1988). This estimator relies on a decomposition of the error term as $u_{it} = \rho_t \omega_i + \varepsilon_{it}$, with ε_{it} assumed to i.i.d. with zero mean, ω_i is a household-specific effect and ρ_t are exogenous shocks, whose impact on the household is modified by ω_i. Quasi-differencing techniques can then be used to obtain estimates of parameters of interest, except for the household specific effect. To illustrate the procedure, consider a simplified version of (11.3), but with the error term allowing for a fixed effect multiplied by a time-varying shifter.

$$\Delta \ln y_{it} = \alpha + \gamma_0 \ln k_{it-1} + \delta Z_{it} + \gamma X_i + \rho_t \omega_i + \varepsilon_{it} \qquad (11.6)$$

Defining $r_t = \rho_t / \rho_{t-1}$, then lagging and premultiplying (11.6) with r_t, and subtracting it from (11.5) gives a quasi-differenced equation in which the fixed effects ω_i have been removed, but in which δ can be identified provided $r_t \neq 1$.

$$\Delta \ln y_{it} = \alpha(1 - r_t) + r_t \Delta \ln y_{it-1} + \gamma_0 \ln k_{it-1} - r_t \gamma_0 \ln k_{it-2} \\ + \delta Z_{it} - r_t \delta Z_{it-1} + \gamma(1 - r_t)X_i + \varepsilon_{it} - r_t \varepsilon_{it-1} \tag{11.7}$$

which can be estimated by imposing the relevant restrictions on the following equation:

$$\Delta \ln y_{it} = a_t + b_t \Delta \ln y_{it-1} + c \ln k_{it-1} + d_t \ln k_{it-2} \\ + e Z_{it} + f_t Z_{it-1} + g_t X_i + v_{it} \tag{11.8}$$

All the parameters can be recovered from this equation (except for the level of the household-specific effect ω_i) since r_t is the only cause of time-varying coefficients in this model. With three rounds of data (i.e. two growth rates), as in the available data set, the procedure can just be implemented. The model was estimated using restricted maximum likelihood estimation, imposing the cross-equations restrictions. In principle, the General Method Moments (GMM) procedure as in Jalan and Ravallion (2002) or in De Vreyer *et al.* (2002) would be most efficient, but the current procedure gives consistent estimators.

It is not self-evident to test whether the restriction that the fixed effects are time-invariant after all ($\theta_t = 0$). Standard chi-squared asymptotic tests are not appropriate, since under the null $r_t = 1$, the parameters associated with the constant and the time-invariant variables are not identified. Jalan and Ravallion (2002) proceed by using a test suggested by Godfrey (1988), but, as they note as well, the power of this test will be weak in small samples such as the one used in this chapter. As a consequence, the different procedures are not tested against each other, but just presented as cumulative evidence using different assumptions regarding the role of heterogeneity in explaining the present results.

11.5   Estimation results

Tables 11.5 and 11.6 present the results from testing the hypotheses against the data. Table 11.5 first focuses on the basic specification, presenting a fixed effects estimator of the growth in food consumption on initial levels of household and village consumption, and a set of common and idiosyncratic shock variables. Note that the regressions control for changes in demographic variables. The first column points to higher growth rates in richer villages, but lower growth rates for richer individual households. Overall, the coefficients point to a process of convergence within villages, but for a given initial consumption level, households experience a higher growth rate in richer than in poorer villages (i.e. village with a higher initial mean level of consumption).[7] Rainfall *shocks* clearly matter and a 10 per cent decline in rainfall reduces food consumption by about 5 per cent. There is some evidence of non-rainfall *shocks* also mattering. The impact of

Table 11.5 Econometric results: basis specification

	Δln food cons (1)		Δln total cons (2)		Δln cal cons (3)		Δln food cons (4)		Δln food cons (5)	
	Coefficient	p-value	Coefficient	p-value	Coefficient	p-value	Coefficient	p-value	Coefficient	p-value
ln food cons$_{t-1}$	−0.319	0.000					−0.318	0.000	−0.316	0.000
Village mean ln food cons$_{t-1}$	0.213	0.000					0.216	0.000	0.075	0.000
ln total cons$_{t-1}$			−0.294	0.000						
Village mean ln cons$_{t-1}$			0.461	0.000						
ln calories$_{t-1}$					−0.284	0.000				
Village mean calories$_{t-1}$					0.194	0.000				
Rainfall shocks$_t$	0.514	0.000	0.278	0.023	0.608	0.000				
Rainfall shocks$_t$ (last year only)							0.211	0.000	0.139	0.000
Rainfall shocks$_t$ (preceding years)							0.299	0.000	0.355	0.000
Rainfall shocks$_{t-1}$									0.160	0.001
Adult serious illness	−0.019	0.421	−0.029	0.383	−0.072	0.037	−0.016	0.495	−0.029	0.383
Crop shock (−1 is worst)	0.109	0.075	0.037	0.633	0.195	0.029	0.075	0.213	0.037	0.633
Livestock shock (−1 is worst)	0.015	0.757	−0.008	0.894	−0.052	0.453	0.011	0.811	−0.008	0.894
Constant	0.501	0.000	−0.569	0.070	0.440	0.013	0.481	0.000	1.011	0.000
Number of observations	682		402		674		682		682	
Number of groups	342		201		342		342		342	
Overall r^2	0.42		0.30		0.29		0.44		0.40	
Hausman-test p-value chi^2(10)	0.986		0.992		0.998					

Notes

Real consumption growth between $t-1$ and t. Dependent variable: change in ln consumption per adult between survey waves (1989–94 and 1994–97). Fixed effects estimator.

Regressions control for demographic changes, Δln(male adults+1), Δln(female adults+1), Δln(male children+1), Δln(female children+1). Adult serious illness = whether adults had a serious illness in the period between survey rounds. Livestock shocks: index of self-reported extent of problems related to fodder and water, 0 is best (no problems) and −1 is worst possible outcome. Non-crop shocks: index of self-reported extent of problems on plots, beyond rain, 0 is best and −1 is worst. Rainfall shocks at t are defined as the difference in the logarithms of rainfall levels at t and $t-1$. Rainfall shocks at $t-1$ are defined as the difference in logarithms of rainfall levels at $t-1$ and $t-2$. Rainfall shocks at t (last year only) only consider the rainfall in the 12 months preceding t and $t-1$. Rainfall shocks at t (preceding years) only consider the average rainfall in the relevant period for t and $t-1$, but excluding the rainfall in the 12 months preceding t and $t-1$. Sample and group size differ only due to missing observations for particular variables.

shocks is robust to the use of other welfare outcome measures. Using the four communities with complete total consumption data, the impact of a rainfall *shock* is smaller at about 3 per cent for a 10 per cent decline in rainfall.[8] This may suggest that some but not all impact of the rainfall shock is in fact the consequence of relative price changes: at higher rainfall levels, possibly locally declining food prices relative to non-food prices, increases food relative to non-food consumption and vice versa. But the fact that total consumption in real terms responds to rainfall *shocks* suggests also that the results are not explained by just a relative price effect. Finally, column (3), using calorie intake data, suggests also that the sensitivity to rain and other effects are not driven by the choice of deflators – the effects are similar to using the growth in the value of food consumption in real terms.

All these specifications were estimated using instruments for lagged consumption (i.e. assets and infrastructure at $t - 1$). A Hausman test for endogeneity could never reject the assumption of exogeneity. Similarly, using lagged characteristics (at $t - 2$) and using twice lagged consumption as instruments similarly showed that exogeneity of lagged consumption could not be rejected.[9] As a consequence, I only report the uninstrumented regressions – in any case, the estimated coefficients were qualitatively very similar (which is of course what the Hausman test systematically investigated, by comparing the actual estimated coefficients using Two Stage Least Squares (TSLS) and Ordinary Least Squares (OLS)).

To investigate persistence, the specification in column (1) has been expanded in column (4), disentangling rainfall in the 12 months relevant for the particular level of consumption, and the preceding years within the period during which growth has been observed. For example, to explain growth between 1994 and 1997, the shock based on rainfall in the 12 months before these years has been entered separately from average rainfall *shock*, based on the period 1994–96 compared to 1989–92. As column (4) shows, there is some sign of persistence: rainfall *shocks* in the beginning of the period of observation have a significant impact on outcome changes, controlling for the effect from *shocks* as reflected in the most recent rainfall levels. A 10 per cent decrease in rainfall several years ago still has an impact of about 3 per cent on food consumption. There is also evidence of persistence over longer periods. To test this, lagged rainfall was introduced, for example, rainfall *shocks* in the years before 1994 was used to explain growth between 1994 and 1997. Column (5) shows that a 10 per cent decline in lagged rainfall reduces food consumption by 1.6 per cent: rainfall shocks have a persistent effect, lasting many years.

Table 11.6 explores the impact of unpacking village and household level effects using specific community and household level variables, in particular livestock and education, as well as the presence of road infrastructure. Furthermore, the impact of the severity of the famine in the mid-1980s on growth in the 1990s is explored using the index of dependence on 'extreme' coping mechanisms in this period, based on six indicators as described before. Since the severity of the famine index and the presence of road infrastructure are time-invariant variables, simple fixed effects estimation cannot illuminate matters. As discussed before, three different approaches have been used. The findings are broadly consistent,

Table 11.6 Econometric results: testing for persistence and unpacking initial conditions

	Δln food cons (6) (FE)		FE from (5) (6a)		Δln food cons (7) (HT)		Δln food cons (8) (HT)		Δln food cons (9) (JR)		Δln food cons (10) (JR)	
	Coefficient	p-value	Coefficient	p-value	Coefficient	p-value	Coefficient	p-value	Coefficient	p-value	Coefficient	p-value
ln food cons$_{t-1}$					−0.318	0.000			−0.204	0.000		
Village mean ln food cons$_{t-1}$					0.211	0.000			0.135	0.004		
Rainfall shocks$_t$	0.700	0.000			0.622	0.000	0.723	0.000	0.614	0.002	0.086	0.675
Rainfall shocks$_{t-1}$	0.097	0.025			0.069	0.016	0.106	0.017	0.195	0.013	0.048	0.605
Adult serious illness	−0.066	0.039			−0.043	0.076	−0.078	0.018	−0.053	0.064	0.001	0.983
Crop shock (−1 is worst)	−0.091	0.298			−0.014	0.757	−0.119	0.099	−0.217	0.041	0.011	0.870
Livestock shock (−1 is worst)	0.029	0.667			−0.018	0.704	0.014	0.773	−0.009	0.910	0.035	0.507
Severity of famine impact			−0.083	0.089	−0.116	0.079	−0.591	0.021	−0.397	0.068	0.039	0.445
Any road?			0.150	0.000			0.121	0.011			0.156	0.000
ln livestock per adult$_{t-1}$	−0.019	0.023					−0.015	0.066			−0.005	0.368
ln education per adult$_{t-1}$	−0.007	0.833					0.002	0.946			0.014	0.303
Constant	0.215	0.000	0.551	0.000	0.519	0.000	0.281	0.006	0.920	0.071	0.016	0.697
r									0.516	0.000	−1.085	0.000
Number of observations	682		338		636		636		319		319	
Number of groups	342				319		319					
Wald χ² joint significance	0.000				0.000		0.000		0.000		0.000	
R-squared	0.095		0.064									

Notes

Real consumption growth between $t-1$ and t. Dependent variable: change in ln food consumption per adult between survey waves (1989–94 and 1994–97). Fixed effects, Hausman–Taylor and Jalan–Ravallion estimators.

For variable definitions, see under table Regressions (7) and (8) use the Hausman–Taylor model, and assume rainfall shocks, livestock shocks and crop shocks as time-varying, exogenous variables, and demographic changes, illness shocks and (if applicable) lagged consumption at household and village level as time-varying endogenous variables. The index of the severity of the crisis experienced (coping index) was treated as time-invariant exogenous, as was (if applicable) whether there was a road available. As time-invariant exogenous variables and instruments, the presence of harvest failure during the famine period, the estimated percentage of households suffering in each village and the ln of live-stock before the famine were used. They were each and jointly insignificant when introduced in equations (11.7) and (11.8). A first stage regression predicting the coping index using these time-invariant variables found each and jointly significant, with pre-famine livestock negatively correlated with the coping index, and the estimated percentage suffering and the presence of harvest failure positively predicting the coping index. Sample and group size differ only due to missing observations for particular variables.

despite the small sample. First, the fixed effects were retrieved from estimating a specification in which initial levels of livestock and years of education were introduced. It can be seen that in this equation, livestock has a significant negative impact, suggesting decreasing returns per adult to livestock. This may be a reflection of increasing land pressure, resulting in more land brought into cultivation and less land available for grazing, which usually took place on common land. In this (and other) specifications, there is no detectable effect from education. A possible explanation may lie in the limited diversification of the Ethiopian rural economy in non-farm activities, limiting returns to education. It should also be emphasised that the levels of education per adult by 1989 were very low (on average less than three years of education per adult and many households with no formal educated adults at all). Column (6a) gives the results of a simple regression of the fixed effects on the severity of famine impact index and the presence of a road. Controls for household composition were included as well (not reported). It can be seen that there appears to be a high impact of both: the presence of a road increases growth by about 15 per cent (about one-third of the sample do not have access to a road in or near the village), while households with a less severe impact compared to those with a much higher impact of the famine (comparing the index at its 25th and 75th percentile) would have experienced about 3 per cent lower growth in the 1990s (significant at 9 per cent). Similar results can be found when using the Hausman–Taylor model.[10] Column (7) gives a version with lagged food consumption, rather than the specific assets. All results are similar to earlier reported results, including the impact of the severity of the impact of the famine, significant at 8 per cent. Column (8), using initial levels of education and livestock, and the presence of a road also gives comparable results, even though the impact of the famine is substantially higher and significant at a higher percentage. The results from applying the Jalan–Ravallion estimator are reported in columns (9) and (10), based on specifications with lagged food consumption and unpacked in terms of initial assets.[11] Recall that to estimate this model, three rounds are minimally required. The results in column (9) are closely in line with earlier results, with evidence of convergence within villages, but higher growth in richer villages, a substantial and persistent effect from rainfall *shocks*, a (significant) negative impact from serious illness shocks and a persistent effect from the impact of the famine. The size of the effect related to the severity of the famine is again larger than the results implied by column (6a) or (7), and significant at 7 per cent: comparing the 25th and 75 percentile of households in terms of the severity of suffering, the latter had about 16 percentage points lower growth in the 1990s. The final specification, in which initial levels of consumption were unpacked in terms of assets and infrastructure using the Jalan–Ravallion estimator, provides generally unstable and imprecise estimates and showed convergence problems. For example, note the different sign of the ratio of exogenous shifters of the fixed effects in column (10) compared to (9). In (10), virtually all coefficients are now insignificant. Slightly different specifications provided substantially different, but equally insignificant point estimates, except for very different and significant estimates of r. In short, with only three rounds, the model can in theory be estimated, but for the data set available, it proved difficult. Still, it is striking that the only strongly significant effect – and robust across different specifications – is the effect of the presence of roads, with a point estimate very close to other estimates using alternative models discussed before, with roads adding more than 15 percentage points to growth.

11.6 Conclusions

In this chapter, I have analysed the growth experience in a number of villages in rural Ethiopia using a household panel data set covering 1989–97. The focus was on the persistent impact of shocks and the famine of the 1980s on growth rates in the 1990s. Using a concept of persistence as used in macroeconomic analysis, the evidence suggests that rainfall shocks are not just strongly affecting food consumption in the current period, but its impact lingers on for many years: the evidence suggests that a 10 per cent lower rainfall about 4–5 years earlier had an impact of 1 percentage point on current growth rates. Furthermore, there is evidence linking the household-level severity of the crisis in the 1980s to the growth experience in the 1990s. Although it is difficult to disentangle the impact, estimates controlling for heterogeneity suggest a substantial impact of about 16 percentage lower growth in the 1990s, when comparing groups that suffered substantially compared to those only moderately affected. There appears to be evidence of some diminishing returns to livestock per adult, which may well help in explaining some of the convergence within villages observed in the data. No discernible effect from education could be detected, but for significant externalities from road infrastructure resulting in divergence across villages.

A word of caution is in order regarding the results from this chapter. First, the sample is small, with only 6 villages and about 342 households available for (most of) the analysis, limiting power of the estimates. Second, the villages had been selected because of their suffering during the famine period, and the high observed growth rates are bound to be at least partly a recovery from earlier low levels, given that growth rates in the sample were well above national growth rates. It may well mean that the findings, including the responsiveness of growth to particular assets and shocks, should be treated with caution and may not be easily generalisable. Still, the fact that the observed high growth may be partly a recovery is interesting as well, since it lasted about ten years for households to recover from the famine crisis – in line with a long persistence of the consequences of shocks.

This analysis does not allow us to fully understand the actual processes involved. Evidence in Dercon and Krishnan (1996), looking at income portfolios in 1989 in this data set, found evidence of households sorting themselves into groups in which basic farming is combined with either low return, low risk or low entry cost activities on the one hand (weaving, firewood collection, dung cakes and charcoal production), and farming combined with more lucrative off-farm activities or livestock products related activities. Both risk considerations as well as entry constraints (the need to have skills or capital) appear to explain this sorting behaviour. Those entering into the low return activities are typically located in the more remote areas, or had extremely low livestock and other asset levels by 1989, partly linked to asset losses during the famine period. The evidence in the current chapter is consistent with this process, since it would have resulted in lower returns to some groups compared to others, affecting growth subsequently. More work on the actual activity and asset portfolio behaviour, for example, in line with Rosenzweig and Binswanger (1993), could shed more light on whether this is indeed the process involved.

If anything, this chapter shows that risk and shocks may well be an important cause of poverty persistence. The evidence presented here suggests that more protection, in the form of *ex ante* insurance and post-shock safety nets would have substantial returns, not just in terms of the short-run welfare gains, but also in terms of subsequent growth.

Acknowledgements

Paper prepared for the Conference on Macroeconomic Policies and Poverty Reduction, Washington, DC, 14–15 March 2002, organised by the International Monetary Fund. I am grateful for encouragement and useful comments from Jan Willem Gunning, Martin Ravallion, Cathy Pattillo and seminar participants at Oxford, Bristol, WIDER/UNU and the World Bank, as well as from two anonymous referees of this journal. All errors are mine.

Notes

1 Given Cobb–Douglas production technology defined over capital, labour and human capital, and constant returns to scale, as in the original Solow model, then (11.3) follows directly, from (11.2), and γ and η can be derived from the parameters of the production function and β.
2 It is worthwhile to comment on the definition of the household used in these eight years. The household was considered the same if the head of the household was unchanged, while if the head had died or left the household, the household was considered the same if the current household head acknowledged that the household (in the local meaning of the term) was the same as in the previous round.
3 The patterns are better understood once taking into account circumstances in a number of the villages. Average livestock values and units were in Debre Berhan by 1989 already more than three times the levels in any other of the villages in the sample. Its location close to a zonal capital may well have made alternative off-farm investments more relevant, while in Doma'a levels were close to zero, linked to the fact that these households had only been resettled from other areas as part of a relief scheme in 1987, and still had to start building up livestock herds.
4 This way of measuring rainfall *shocks* is consistent with the discussion in Section 11.2, and the data presented in Table 11.3. Rainfall levels are measured by S. In preparing Table 11.3 these levels were scaled by local long-term means, that is, $S/\bar{S}$, to allow comparison across areas. Growth between t and $t-1$ is then linked to *shocks*, which following from the definition used in Table 11.3 could be defined as $\ln(S_{it}/\bar{S}) - \ln(S_{it-1}/\bar{S})$, equivalent to the definition used in the rest of the chapter.
5 In this index, all 'yes/no' variables were simply given 1 if the strategy was used, and 0 if not. If the household reduced meals from 3 to 1, 1 was added, while if it reduced to

2 meals, 0.5 was added. The simple average of these six values was then used as an index of the severity of the crisis.
6 The work on Zimbabwe also highlighted the relevance of land holdings for growth, but given that in Ethiopia all land is state owned and in the period considered was liable to repeated redistribution, the scope for investing in larger farm size was non-existent, justifying the use of livestock as the key asset for understanding accumulation.
7 Referring to equation (11.2) the estimates here suggest $\beta = -0.319$ and $\beta_1 = -0.106$, and β_1 is significantly different from zero at less than 1 per cent, that is there is a significantly different effect across than within villages.
8 The total consumption regression suggests divergence between communities. However, with only a small number of communities included in this regression, the power of the estimates related to community level variables is obviously small, and overall, the issue of divergence and convergence between communities has to be interpreted with caution.
9 Note that when using two lags, the regressions were reduced to a cross-section estimate of growth rates between 1994 and 1997, using values in 1989 as instruments, so that no fixed effects could be used.
10 In this model, lagged consumption, illness shocks, household demographics, the severity index, lagged livestock and education levels and the presence of a road are all treated as endogenous, using community perceptions of the crisis in the mid-1980s, harvest failure shocks and pre-famine levels of livestock as additional instruments. The results are only marginally affected when using different partitioning and/or different additional instruments. Note that in principle, the partitioning of the time-variant and time-invariant matrices of variables provides enough restrictions to identify the endogenous variables.
11 These estimates treat the initial level of consumption and the lagged changes in consumption as endogenous, using pre-famine assets, community level crisis perceptions and harvest failure in the mid-1980s as identifying instruments.

References

Acemoglu D. and F. Zilibotti. 1997. 'Was Prometheus Unbound by Chance? Risk, Diversification and Growth', *Journal of Political Economy*, 105: 709–51.

Alderman, H., J. Behrman, V. Lavy and R. Menon. 2001. 'Child Health and School Enrollment: A Longitudinal Analysis', *Journal of Human Resources*, 36: 185–205.

Banerjee, A. and A. Newman. 1993. 'Occupational Choice and the Process of Development', *Journal of Political Economy*, 101(2): 274–98.

Campbell, J.Y. and G.N. Mankiw. 1987. 'Are Output Fluctuations Transitory', *Quarterly Journal of Economics*, 102(4): 857–80.

Deaton, A. 1997. *The Analysis of Household Surveys: A Microeconometric Approach to Development Policy*, Washington, DC and Baltimore, MD: The World Bank and Johns Hopkins University Press.

Deininger, K. and K. Okidi. 2003. 'Growth and Poverty Reduction in Uganda, 1992–2000: Panel Data Evidence', *Development Policy Review*, 21(4): 481–509.

Dercon, S. 2002. *The Impact of Economic Reforms on Rural Households in Ethiopia: A Study From 1989 to 1995*, Washington, DC: The World Bank.

—— and P. Krishnan. 1996. 'Income Portfolios in Rural Ethiopia and Tanzania: Choices and Constraints', *Journal of Development Studies*, 32(6): 850–75.

—— 1998. 'Changes in Poverty in Rural Ethiopia 1989–1995: Measurement, Robustness Tests and Decomposition', CSAE Working Paper Series WPS 98.7, Centre for the Study of African Economies, Oxford.

—— 2000a. 'Vulnerability, Seasonality and Poverty in Ethiopia', *Journal of Development Studies*, 36(6): 25–53.

Dercon, S. and P. Krishnan. 2000b. 'In Sickness and in Health: Risk-Sharing in Rural Ethiopia', *Journal of Political Economy*, 108(4): 688–727.

—— 2002. 'Changes in Poverty in Villages in Rural Ethiopia: 1989–95', in A. Booth and P. Mosley (eds), *The New Poverty Strategies*, Palgrave MacMillan: Basingstoke.

—— 2003. 'Risk-Sharing and Public Transfers', *Economic Journal*, 113, 486 (March): C86–C94.

De Vreyer, P., J. Herrera and S. Mesplé-Somps. 2002. 'Consumption Growth and Spatial Poverty Traps: An Analysis of the Effects of Social Services and Infrastructures on Living Standards in Rural Peru', document de travail DIAL, no. 2002–17.

Durlauf, S. and Quah, D. 1998. *The New Empirics of Economic Growth*. CEP discussion paper no. 384, Prepared for the Handbook of Macroeconomics, London.

Elbers, C., J.W. Gunning and B. Kinsey. 2003. 'Growth and Risk: Methodology and Micro Evidence', Free University Amsterdam, Mimeo.

Godfrey, L.G. 1988. *Misspecification Tests in Econometrics*, Cambridge: Cambridge University Press.

Gunning, J.W., J. Hoddinott, B. Kinsey and T. Owens. 2000. 'Revisiting Forever Gained: Income Dynamics in the Resettlement Areas of Zimbabwe, 1983–1997', *Journal of Development Studies*, 36: 131–54.

Hausman, J.A., and W.E. Taylor. 1981. 'Panel Data and Unobservable Individual Effects', *Econometrica*, 49(6): 1377–398.

Hoddinott, J. and B. Kinsey. 2001. 'Child Health in the Time of Drought', *Oxford Bulletin of Economics and Statistics*, 63: 409–36.

Holtz-Eakin, D., W. Newey and H. Rosen. 1988. 'Estimating Vector Autoregressions with Panel Data', *Econometrica*, 56: 1371–395.

Islam, N. 1995. 'Growth Empirics: A Panel Data Approach', *Quarterly Journal of Economics*, 110(4): 1127–170.

Jalan, J. and M. Ravallion. 1997. 'Spatial Poverty Traps?', Policy Research Working Paper Series, 1862, December.

—— 1998. 'Are There Dynamic Gains from a Poor-Area Development Program?', *Journal of Public Economics*, 67(1): 65–86.

—— 2002. 'Geographic Poverty Traps? A Micro Model of Consumption Growth in Rural China', *Journal of Applied Econometrics*, 17: 329–46.

—— 2004. 'Household Income Dynamics in Rural China', in S. Dercon (ed.), *Insurance against Poverty*, Oxford: Oxford University Press.

Jayne, T.S., J. Strauss, T. Yamano and D. Molla. 2002. 'Targeting of Food Aid in Rural Ethiopia: Chronic Need or Inertia?', *Journal of Development Economics*, 68: 247–88.

Lokshin, M. and M. Ravallion, M. 2001. 'Short-Lived Shocks with Long-Lived Impacts? Household Income Dynamics in a Transition Economy', Papers 2459, World Bank – Country Economics Department.

Mankiw, N.G., D. Romer and D.N. Weil. 1992. 'A Contribution to the Empirics of Economic Growth', *Quarterly Journal of Economics*, 107: 409–37.

Morduch, J. 1995. 'Income Smoothing and Consumption Smoothing', *Journal of Economic Perspectives*, 9(3): 103–14

Ravallion, M. and J. Jalan. 1996. 'Growth Divergence due to Spatial Externalities', *Economics Letters*, 53(2): 227–32

Romer, P. 1986. 'Increasing Returns and Long-run Growth', *Journal of Political Economy*, 94: 1002–37.

Rosenzweig, M. and H. Binswanger, 1993. 'Wealth, Weather Risk and the Composition and Profitability of Agricultural Investments', *Economic Journal*, 103: 56–78.

—— and K. Wolpin. 1993. 'Credit Market Constraints, Consumption Smoothing and the Accumulation of Durable Production Assets in Low-income Countries: Investments in Bullocks in India', *Journal of Political Economy*, 101(2): 223–44.

Sen, A. 1981. *Poverty and Famine*, Oxford: Oxford University Press.

Temple, J. 1999. 'The New Growth Evidence', *Journal of Economic Literature*, 37(1), March: 112–56.

Townsend, R. 1995. 'Consumption Insurance: An Evaluation of Risk-bearing Systems in Low Income Economies', *Journal of Economic Perspectives*, 2(Summer): 83–102.

Webb, P., J. von Braun and Y. Yohannes. 1992. 'Famine in Ethiopia: Policy Implication of Coping Failure at National and Household Levels', Research Report no.92, International Food Policy Research Institute, Washington, DC.

12 Economic shocks, wealth, and welfare

Elizabeth Frankenberg, James P. Smith, and Duncan Thomas

The immediate effects of the Asian crisis on the well-being of Indonesians are examined using the Indonesia Family Life Survey (IFLS), an on-going longitudinal household survey. There is tremendous diversity in the effect of the shock: for some households, it was devastating; for others it brought new opportunities. A wide array of mechanisms was adopted in response to the crisis. Households combined to more fully exploit benefits of scale economies in consumption. Labor supply increased even as real wages collapsed. Households reduced spending on semi-durables while maintaining expenditures on foods. Rural households used wealth, particularly gold, to smooth consumption.

12.1 Introduction

Indonesia is in the midst of a major financial, economic, and political crisis. In late 1997, credit markets tightened and the Indonesian rupiah began to weaken. In early 1998, the currency collapsed falling from Rp 4,000 per US$ to Rp 16,000 per US$ in just three days. The rupiah gained ground in the following months but has remained extremely volatile. The decline in the exchange rate in conjunction with substantial reductions of subsidies on food and energy contributed to spiraling prices. The consumer price index is estimated to have increased by around 80 percent in 1998, while food prices doubled and the price of rice increased by around 120 percent.

The crisis has not been limited to prices or to the financial sector. Real GDP fell by around 15 percent in 1998 and real wages declined by some 40 percent in the formal wage sector. Moreover, a drought associated with El Nino had depressed agricultural output in many parts of the country. The effects of these "shocks" have probably been compounded by the political upheavals in Indonesia during this period.

The magnitude and unexpected nature of the crisis are particularly stunning when contrasted with the country's recent economic success. During the three decades prior to the crisis, Indonesia enjoyed sustained economic growth, accompanied by an impressive reduction in poverty, significant improvements in the health and human capital of the population, and a shift in the structure of production away from agriculture toward higher paying manufacturing and service sector jobs.

Because the crisis was to a large extent unanticipated, it provides an excellent laboratory for yielding insights into how large negative economic shocks affect individuals and households and how they respond to those shocks. The mechanisms that the households may employ to smooth out the impacts of such shocks are likely to take many forms. There is a prominent literature on the role played by spending down accumulated household wealth. (See Deaton, 1992, for an insightful review.) However, there are many other mechanisms that individuals and households might employ to smooth fluctuations in the marginal utility of consumption. Households may seek to reallocate resources across time by, for example, borrowing on formal or informal markets (Rosenzweig and Wolpin, 1993; Udry, 1994; Fafchamps *et al.*, 1998); sharing risk among people within a community (Platteau, 1991; Townsend, 1994); or across communities through public or private transfers (Rosenzweig and Stark, 1989; Cox and Jimenez, 1998). Households may also change the allocation of resources in any period. This might involve the reallocation of the total consumption bundle away from more durable and deferrable expenditure items (Browning and Crossley, 1997); changes in work effort and type of work undertaken by household members (Murruggarra, 1996); the entry and exit of household members (Alamgir, 1980); or changes in location of residence of some or all household members (Rosenzweig, 1988, 1996).

Using panel data that were specially collected to assess the effect of the crisis on the lives of Indonesians, this chapter provides new empirical evidence on how households smooth out the effects of unanticipated shocks. We consider several potential mechanisms, placing emphasis on the role of wealth. The study is part of a larger project, the ultimate goal of which is to provide insights into the strategies adopted by households in Indonesia, in response to the economic crisis and to evaluate the immediate and medium-term consequences of those strategies for a broad array of welfare indicators.

The next section of this chapter provides a background on the Indonesian setting we are investigating. It is followed by a description of our main data source, the IFLSs. We focus on the immediate consequences of the crisis for changes in household consumption levels. There is no question that the crisis was large: on average, household *per capita* expenditure (PCE) declined by around 20 percent in one year. There is also a tremendous diversity in the impact of the crisis with some households becoming better off while many others are much worse off. Section 12.4 discusses possible smoothing mechanisms that households may employ in order to mitigate the impacts of the crisis. Our main findings are presented in Section 12.5 that highlights some of the key smoothing mechanisms that appear to have been adopted by Indonesian households. Changes in household size and composition as well as changes in the allocation of time to work are an important part of the picture. Special attention is paid to the role that wealth plays in smoothing household PCE. We find that both the level of wealth and the form in which wealth is held matter: households that held more wealth in the form of gold were better able to smooth consumption than other similar households at the onset of the crisis. The chapter ends with conclusions.

12.2   The Indonesian context

Thirty years ago Indonesia was one of the poorest countries in the world. Until the recent financial crisis, it enjoyed high economic growth rates (4.5 percent per annum from the mid-1960s until 1998) and by the late 1990s was on the verge of joining the middle-income countries. Not surprisingly, employment in the formal wage sector expanded, rising from a quarter to a third of all jobs during the same years while agricultural employment fell (from 55 percent of total employment in 1986 to 41 percent by 1997). Economic changes, however, have not been uniform across the country and, if anything, economic heterogeneity has increased over time.

Optimism about Indonesia's future was suddenly challenged by the economic crisis and the ensuing changes in the political landscape of the country. As indicated in Figure 12.1a, the rupiah came under pressure in the last half of 1997 when the exchange rate began showing signs of weakness. After falling by half from around 2,400 per US$ to about 4,800 per US$ by December 1997, the rupiah collapsed in January 1998 when, over the course of just a few days, the exchange rate fell by a factor of four. Although it soon recovered ground, by the middle of 1998 the rupiah had slumped back to the lows of January 1998. Since then, the rupiah has continued to oscillate, albeit at a lower amplitude and frequency. The extremely volatile exchange rate has contributed to considerable uncertainty in financial markets. This uncertainty is reflected in interest rates which quadrupled in August 1997 and were subsequently very volatile. The banking sector fell into disarray and several major banks have been taken over by the Indonesian Bank Restructuring Agency. Turmoil in the financial sector has created havoc with both the confidence of investors and with the availability of credit.

Prices of many commodities spiraled upward during the first three quarters of 1998, as shown in Figure 12.1b. The rise was particularly sharp for food prices during the first half of the year. In comparison, non-food prices rose less rapidly. Annual inflation is estimated by the *Badan Pusat Statistik* (BPS), the central statistical bureau, to be about 80 percent for 1998. In part, this reflects the removal of subsidies for several goods – most notably rice, oil, and some fuels. A substantial part of the increase in the CPI reflects the fact that rice accounts for a substantial fraction of the average Indonesian's budget and that its price was more than doubled. Since the share spent on rice is greatest for the poorest, inflation more likely had a bigger impact on the purchasing power of the poorest. Offsetting that effect, however, is the fact that some of the poorest are rice producers and as the price of food rose, (net) food producers have benefited from the improvement in their terms of trade.[1]

That the Indonesian crisis particularly its severity and the speed with which it took hold were unanticipated is pointed out in remarks by leaders within and outside of Indonesia. In January 1998, the IMF described Indonesia's economic

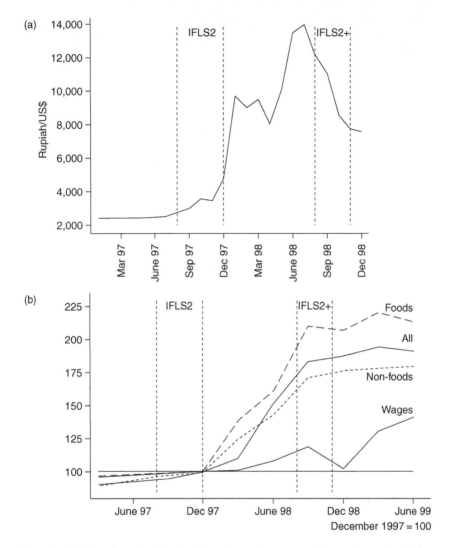

Figure 12.1 (a) Timing of IFLS and Indonesian exchange rate; (b) rate of growth of prices and wages.

situation as a "worrisome" (IMF, 1999) and President Soeharto announced measures that he expected to improve economic performance, but nevertheless predicted zero economic growth and inflation of 20 percent for 1998. In fact, economic growth in 1998 declined by 15 percent and inflation hit 80 percent. In July 1998, James Wolfensohn, president of the World Bank, remarked "we were caught up in the enthusiasm of Indonesia. I am not alone in thinking that 12 months ago, Indonesia was on a very good path." Nor did one's concern about the crisis seem to much affect the Indonesian public until January 1998. During January concern about rising food prices touched off buying sprees that resulted in brief shortages of staple goods, and some workers returning to the cities after the *Idul Fitri* holiday in early February found that their jobs had disappeared.

Ultimately, the crisis has left few Indonesians untouched. For some, the impacts may have been devastating, but for others the crisis has likely brought new opportunities. Exporters, export producers, and food producers fared far better than those engaged in the production of services and non-tradables or those on fixed incomes. Indeed, among the community leaders who answered the IFLS Community Survey (described later), some of those in rural areas told us that life in their community improved between 1997 and 1998 as a result of rising rice prices and increased business opportunities. Many others told us that life was much worse, for a variety of reasons. In both urban and rural areas, individuals likely vary in the degree to which they have identified and embraced new opportunities or were able to offset the effects of the economic shocks that they have faced.

Given the complexity and multi-faceted nature of the crisis, it is only with detailed broad-purpose panel data on individuals and households that it is possible to fully explore the nature and extent of the behavioral responses by individuals and families to the crisis and, thereby, provide sound micro-level evidence about the combined impacts of the various facets of the crisis and how they have varied across socioeconomic and geographic strata. Moreover, the massive upheavals in the Indonesian economy – and the diversity of their impact – provides an unparalleled opportunity to better understand the dynamics of urban and rural factor and product markets in low income settings as well as mechanisms used by families to smooth out the effects of large, unanticipated shocks.

12.3   Data: Indonesia Family Life Surveys

The IFLS is an on-going longitudinal survey of individuals, households, families, and communities. The first wave, IFLS1, took place in 1993, when 7,224 households were interviewed. This baseline survey, which was conducted in 321 communities drawn from 13 of Indonesia's 27 provinces, was representative of 83 percent of the Indonesian population.[2] The second wave, IFLS2, was fielded four years later (between August 1997 and February 1998).[3] Excluding households in which everyone had died (mostly single-person households), over 94 percent of the IFLS1 households were re-interviewed and 93 percent of target individuals were re-interviewed (more than 33,000 individuals were interviewed in total). There are 7,600 households in IFLS2. The increase in the number of households surveyed relative to IFLS1 arises because respondents were followed when they split off from their 1993 household and set up their own households.

The IFLS household data are accompanied by an extensive survey of the 321 communities in which the respondents live and of the markets, health facilities, and schools to which they have access. These contextual data provide information on the availability, quality, and prices associated with various institutions and types of infrastructure, as well as on the prices of food and other goods.

Fieldwork for IFLS2 was drawing to a close when the Indonesian rupiah collapsed in early 1998. The survey was uniquely well positioned to serve as a baseline for follow-ups that will trace out the impact of the crisis on the lives of Indonesians. Since there is very little solid empirical evidence regarding the immediate consequences of a major shock on the well-being and behaviors of individuals and households, we decided to conduct a re-survey a year after IFLS2: IFLS2+ was fielded in late 1998.

Given the turnaround time, it was impossible to re-field the entire IFLS. Instead, we conducted interviews in 25 percent of the enumeration areas which were chosen to span the full socioeconomic spectrum represented by IFLS. About 2,000 households are included in IFLS2+ and interviews were conducted with over 10,000 respondents. With the social, political, and economic turmoil in Indonesia in 1998, the issue of attrition warranted special concern. Re-interviews were completed with 98.5 percent of those households that were in the target sample and interviewed in 1997; the recontact rate among individuals was over 95 percent.[4]

In all waves of IFLS, respondents provide detailed information on a broad array of demographic, social, and economic topics. These include household structure, household consumption, individual earnings and labor supply, assets, and wealth. All of these modules will be used extensively in this chapter.

At the beginning of each follow-up interview, basic socio-demographic characteristics of each household member is collected using a pre-printed roster that lists all household members from prior waves. The current location of respondents who have moved away is noted and new entrants are added to the roster.

Household expenditure in the IFLS is collected in a "short form" type of consumption module that takes about 30–40 minutes to administer. Questions are asked about a series of commodity categories; for each item, the respondent is asked first about money expenditures and then about the imputed value of consumption out of own production or provided in kind. The reference period for the recall varies depending on the goods. Expenditures are reported for the previous week for thirty-seven food items/groups of items (such as rice, cassava, tapioca, dried cassava, tofu, tempe, etc.). For those people who produce their own food, the respondent is asked to value the amount consumed in the previous week. There are nineteen non-food items. A reference period of the previous month is used for some (electricity, water, fuel, recurrent transport expenses, domestic services), while for others the reference period is a year (clothing, medical costs, education). It is difficult to obtain good measures of housing expenses in these sorts of surveys. We record rental costs (for those who are renting) and ask the respondent for an estimated rental equivalent (for those who are owner-occupiers/live rent free). Because expenditure items are aggregates, quantities are not asked; instead the respondent is asked for the price paid the last time when a set of specific items were purchased.

Wealth may play an important role in determining how successfully households are able to smooth consumption. IFLS contains information on the value of assets that are associated with family businesses and, in a separate module, the value of all non-business assets owned by the household. These are divided into ten categories which include property: savings, stocks and loans, jewelry, household semi-durables, and household durables. An unusual aspect of the wealth data in the IFLS is that individuals are asked about the value of each asset group owned by the household, the fraction the respondent owns, and the fraction his or her spouse owns. It is, therefore, possible to measure wealth at the individual level.

To gauge the severity of the economic crisis and the various mechanisms households have used to smooth its most severe impacts, this chapter will focus on those individuals and households that were interviewed in 1997 and re-interviewed in 1998 as part of IFLS2/2+. Prior to presenting the empirical results, Section 12.4 describes some of the mechanisms that may be important in the Indonesian context.

12.4   Consumption smoothing mechanisms

Households in Indonesia were confronted with an arguably unanticipated price shock that resulted in a large shock to real income. This chapter highlights some of the mechanisms that households adopted to mitigate the immediate effect of the shock on well-being. Emphasis is placed on the role that accumulated savings plays in reducing fluctuations in PCE. We also consider other mechanisms for smoothing well-being including reallocating the time and consumption budget and shifts in living arrangements.

The literature on motives for wealth accumulation and savings is immense and has not reached a consensus.[5] The starting point for much of this literature is the *life cycle model* (or "life cycle hypothesis") which emphasizes the role that savings (and dis-savings) play in dealing with timing issues surrounding non-coincidence in income and consumption. According to this theory, individuals or households seek to "smooth" consumption in order to keep the marginal utility of consumption constant across periods, which implies they will tend to save when income is high and dis-save when income is low.

Declining marginal utility of consumption within any period also implies that households will want to smooth out the impact of an economic shock, so that the associated consumption decline is not concentrated in a single or relatively few time periods. Their ability to do so, however, may be constrained by circumstances of the household or the markets with which they interact. Additional resources are required to finance current consumption at levels above the now "shock" depleted levels of current income.

In the absence of liquidity constraints, households will presumably borrow resources when times are bad and pay back these loans when times improve. During the crisis in Indonesia, liquidity constraints were probably binding. The crisis was exacerbated by the weakness of financial and political institutions. There was a spectacular collapse of the banking system with many of the largest banks becoming insolvent and being taken over by the public sector. Evidence in IFLS indicates the formal credit market substantially shrank: relative to 1997, fewer households borrowed from the formal sector and the amounts borrowed were substantially smaller in 1998.[6] Households did turn to informal credit markets although the amounts borrowed tended to be relatively small. The IFLS2 and IFLS2+ data are not well suited to a detailed exploration of credit markets and the crisis and so we will ignore those markets in this chapter.

There are, however, several less formal mechanisms through which resources can be transferred across time including borrowing from family, friends, or through a network at the village or community level. These kinds of networks have been the focus of much of the consumption smoothing literature in development (see, for example, Townsend, 1994; Platteau, 1991).[7] We put community-level smoothing to one side in this chapter and draw attention, instead, to the role that household-specific smoothing strategies have played in responding to the crisis in Indonesia.

Four such mechanisms are considered in detail: spending down accumulated savings (wealth); reallocation of time to work or leisure; shifts in living arrangements; and reallocation of the budget away from goods like semi-durables. We discuss each in turn.

12.4.1 Spending down wealth

Given that the crisis was largely unanticipated in terms of its timing, magnitude, and longevity, the life cycle model suggests that households should use their accumulated savings, or wealth, to help finance their current consumption at the onset of the crisis. Ownership of assets should, therefore, serve to smooth fluctuations in PCE.

In addition to ownership, there are several dimensions in which assets can be usefully differentiated. Not all assets are equally liquid. Holding more assets that are relatively liquid should facilitate consumption smoothing. Many households in Indonesia own assets that are associated with a business activity; land is the most common such asset and is used for farming. These assets are typically not liquid and, as the economy collapsed, their prices fell dramatically. The income generated by some of these productive assets, such as land or livestock, became more important as the crisis unfolded. The sale of such assets has powerful implications for future consumption and choices regarding the acquisition and disposal of these assets will depend critically on expectations about future prices and preferences regarding inter-temporal substitution. Of course, not all business assets provided protection from the effect of the crisis through income generation: some business activities were all but wiped out by the crisis (construction, low-skill services, for example).

Among non-business assets, housing, land, and durables are the least liquid; like business assets, their prices tended to fall at the onset of the crisis. Financial assets, including cash and stocks, lie at the other end of the liquidity spectrum. As the crisis unfolded and inflation spiraled, the values of these assets also declined substantially. Real interest rates on savings accounts turned negative and by mid-1998, the Jakarta Stock Exchange had lost 75 percent of its precrisis value.

Many Indonesian households store some of their wealth in the form of gold (usually as jewelry). There is a very active market in gold, with at least one trader operating in virtually every community across the archipelago. Gold is bought and sold according to its weight, with the price set at the prevailing world price. As the rupiah collapsed, the price of gold rocketed and so, in contrast with financial assets and illiquid assets, wealth held in the form of gold increased in value at the onset of the crisis. Given that the market for gold is very active, it is reasonable to think of jewelry as being a relatively liquid asset which in combination with its capital appreciation suggests it should be an important tool for smoothing consumption during the crisis. The empirical analyses given here will explore the effect of wealth, taken as a whole, on fluctuations in PCE and also examine the role that different assets have played in mitigating the impact of the crisis.

12.4.2   Reallocation of leisure across time

Consumption smoothing models are typically expressed in a single aggregate per period. However, households and individuals may have preferences over many dimensions of the total consumption bundle. Leisure is one such dimension. Since real wages declined at the onset of the crisis, one would expect substitution away from time at work so leisure would increase and work hours fall. While there will presumably be a countervailing income effect which would encourage additional work effort, there is no reason to expect that the income effects would offset substitution effects in this context.

Leisure and expenditure consumption differ in another important dimension. If borrowing against the future is difficult, credit-constrained households may have to absorb a tremendous decline in consumption in this period. Households may borrow future leisure hours from themselves and actually choose to increase current work hours at the onset of the crisis in order to lessen the impact of reduced earnings on consumption expenditures.

More generally, labor market activity of family members may play a similar role especially given that the self-employed have considerable flexibility in choosing hours of work and are better able to exploit new opportunities. Even if jobs in the formal wage sector are difficult to find because of the crisis, opportunities may exist for expanded work effort in family businesses and farms. The extent to which family labor supply responded to the crisis will be explored.

12.4.3   Changes in household living arrangements

A related aspect of household choice that is typically neglected in consumption smoothing models involves the number of members in the household. In an extended family context such as Indonesia, the optimal number of households per extended family, presumably, involves a tradeoff between taking advantage of economies of scale in consumption and the utility derived from individual or sub-family privacy. The crisis may have disturbed the prevailing equilibrium if inter-temporal smoothing across these two dimensions is not equivalent. We hypothesize that privacy may be more substitutable over time and that households attempt to minimize the impacts on consumption compared to privacy. If so, households should tend to recombine and become larger during the crisis.

Indeed, one important mechanism through which non co-resident kin may spread the impact of the crisis is through reallocation of different types of members of extended families across different households. For example, those family members who are net consumers may relocate to relatives living in places where consumption costs are low while those who are earners may move to help out in the family businesses.

12.4.4   *Reallocation of spending on semi-durables across time*

Time allocation and location choice are not the only components of the consumption bundle that might be responsive to income shocks. Some parts of the consumption bundle (such as food) may be poorly substitutable over time while others such as durables, semi-durable purchases, and household investments are likely to be more readily substituted over time and hence postponeable. For example, postponement of expenditures on semi-durables such as clothing is not likely to have as large an effect on life-time utility as postponing spending on staples. For some items, it is not obvious that there will be any longer-run effect on utility, at least for the majority of the population; delaying preventive health care investments is a good example. For many, such delay will be of little consequence; for some, however, the costs may be very large.

All consumption smoothing models rely on an implicit or explicit assumption about household expectations. We believe that the nature and magnitude of the Indonesian crisis, as described earlier, makes it plausible that this crisis was largely unanticipated. A more difficult question involves household expectations in the midst of the crisis in 1998. For example, household behavior would be quite different if they expected the crisis to worsen considerably in the future. In that case, households may desire to save even in 1998 to lessen the impact in the future. As further waves of IFLS are added to the database, these dynamic issues will be addressed.

12.5   Results

This section summarizes our principal research findings about the ability of Indonesian households to mitigate the impact of the crisis on their welfare during the first year of the economic crisis. The section is organized as follows: we begin with a discussion of the measurement of household welfare and note that household consumption and household welfare are not one and the same thing. In line with the vast majority of the literature, we then lay out the basic facts in terms of PCE and discuss the magnitude and distribution of the crisis by this metric.

The following sub-section develops measures of the community-specific "shock" that households faced which are later used to provide insights into the mechanisms households have used to smooth welfare during this shock. We focus on two mechanisms that appear to have played a role in the Indonesian crisis. We first describe changes in household size and composition between the 1997 and 1998 interviews; these reflect changes in living arrangements and migration of individual household members. Second, we present evidence on changes in labor supply – including sector of work and hours of work – of household members.

This study emphasizes the role played by wealth, which is discussed in the rest of the section. We begin with a description of wealth ownership and note that the crisis is associated with declines in the values of some assets but *increases* in the values of others. We proceed to examine how the level of wealth and its distribution among asset groups is related to reduced fluctuations in PCE. We also assess whether other household characteristics – particularly household structure and levels of human capital – are associated with greater smoothing of consumption.

12.5.1   *Changes in household consumption*

How large were the changes in household welfare that accompanied the economic crisis in Indonesia during 1998? Which types of households experienced the largest declines? Because IFLS2 was fielded almost entirely before prices spiraled upwards in the early 1998 (Figure 12.1b), and IFLS2+ was fielded about a year later; these data are uniquely well-suited to provide insights into the immediate impact of the crisis and the extent to which households have mitigated the effects on the well-being of their members.

It is standard in this literature to equate household PCE with the welfare of individuals within the household. Mean levels of PCE in 1997 and 1998 are reported in the first row of Table 12.1 along with the mean percentage change in PCE at the household level. The average household reduced real PCE by almost 25 percent in one year.[8] This is a stunning decline that is of the same magnitude as the crisis in Russia, in the 1980s, and the first year of the Great Depression. (Throughout the chapter, all values are converted to 1997 rupiah.)[9]

Two strong assumptions underlie the interpretation of PCE as indicative of the well-being of households with different size and composition. First, economies of scale are ignored. Second, children and adults are treated as equals in the household budget. While there are many proposals of weights that might be attributed to different demographic groups, there is no consensus in the literature (Deaton and Muellbauer, 1980; Lazear and Michael, 1988). To confirm, our results are not driven by the assumption that a child and adult are equivalent, the second row of Table 10.2 reports per adult equivalent household consumption in 1997 and 1998, where we have assumed each child costs half an adult. The percentage change in per adult equivalent consumption is identical to the change in PCE.[10] We conclude that the change in PCE does a good job of reflecting the changes in real resources available to individuals; it will serve as our main consumption-based indicator of well-being. The role of changes in household size and composition will be taken up again later.

Table 12.1 Household consumption

1997 Rp000s	1997	1998	% change
Per capita household consumption	176	117	−23
	[12]	[9]	[2]
Per adult equivalent household	206	133	−24
consumption	[14]	[9]	[2]
Total household consumption	629	491	−16
	[48]	[42]	[1]
Household size	4.33	4.53	7
	[0.05]	[0.04]	[0.8]
Composition of per capita household consumption			
Food	79.7	68.9	−9
	[4.9]	[7.4]	[2]
Non-foods	95.2	48.4	−34
	[10.2]	[2.2]	[2]
Deferrable items	9.1	6.4	−35
(Clothing, furniture, and ceremonies)	[0.4]	[0.4]	[3]
Human capital investments	9.0	5.7	−37
(Health and education)	[0.6]	[0.3]	[3]

Notes
Consumption measured in thousands of 1997 Rupiah. Percent change is $\ln X_{1998}-\ln X_{1997}$ for each indicator. Per adult equivalent household consumption assigns a weight of 0.5 to a child, 1.0 to an adult. 1,971 households interviewed in 1997 and 1998 included in sample.
Means and [standard errors].

The distribution of the decline in PCE is reported in Figure 12.2a which presents non-parametric estimates of the percentage change in real household PCE between 1997 and 1998 across the distribution of prior PCE. To avoid biases due to correlated measurement error that will arise from regressing $\ln PCE_{1998}-\ln PCE_{1997}$ on $\ln PCE_{1997}$, we use, on the x-axis, 1993 levels of $\ln PCE$ (measured in IFLS1) to rank households by their baseline levels of consumption.[11]

The striking fact that emerges from the figure is the diversity of changes in PCE across households with the initially better off household reducing their PCE by much larger percentage amounts. For example, taking all households, the fall in consumption was 30 percent or more in the upper quartile of 1993 lnPCE but approximately 15 percent or less in the bottom quartile.

Figure 12.2b separates households by whether they live in urban or rural areas (in 1997). This distinction turns out to be critical in understanding the impact of the crisis. Two salient patterns are produced by this distinction. First, for households within the bottom and top quartile of the 1993 PCE distribution, percentage changes in PCE run between 5 and 15 percentage points more negative in urban areas compared to households living in rural locations.[12] Second, among rural households within the lower and upper quartiles of the PCE distribution, proportionate consumption declines are largely independent of baseline levels of PCE. In the urban sector, in contrast, we find a more uniform pattern of a larger consumption decline among households with higher PCE at baseline.

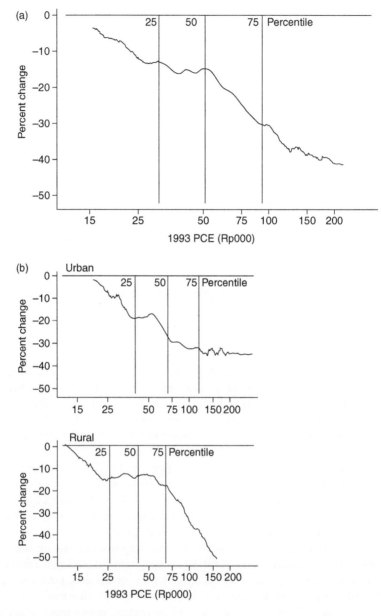

Figure 12.2 Relationship between change in HH PCE (1988–97) and HH PCE in 1993: (a) all Indonesia; (b) by sector.

To be sure, for many households, the crisis in Indonesia was devastating. However, for some, it surely brought new opportunities. For example, net food producers (particularly rice producers) benefited from the increase in the relative price of food; similarly, those who produced for the export sector saw substantial increases in the relative price of their output when the rupiah collapsed. In fact, about one-third of households report higher levels of PCE in 1998, relative to 1997. While at least some of these apparent increases in PCE likely reflect measurement error in expenditure (or random fluctuations in consumption), there are at least three reasons why we think the evidence suggests that some households were better off in 1998 than in 1997.

First, a regression of change in lnPCE on household and community characteristics indicates that households in food-producing communities tended to fare better during the crisis as did households with more members who entered the labor market between 1997 and 1998 (see Thomas *et al.*, 2000). Second, in 1998, all adult respondents were asked whether their lives had improved or worsened during the previous twelve months (using a 5-point scale). One in six reported their lives had improved whereas about 40 percent said they were worse off in 1998. Third, we have aggregated these individual responses to the household level and estimated an ordered probit relating reported change in well-being (using the same 5-point scale) to levels of PCE, household size, and location. Holding PCE in 1993 and 1997 constant, higher levels of PCE in 1998 are associated with a significantly higher probability the household is reported as being better off in 1998; *ceteris paribus*, higher PCE in 1997 is associated with lower levels of household welfare in 1998. Thus, at the household level, changes in PCE between 1997 and 1998 are significant predictors of changes in the perceptions of household well-being, with all of these measures being collected independently of each other. Holding constant household size in 1993 and 1997, an increase in the number of household members in 1998 is associated with an increase in the probability a household reports itself as being better off. This may be because the addition of members to a household is viewed as welfare-improving or because households that absorbed additional members were better able to respond to the crisis by, for example, exploiting new opportunities.

Returning to Table 12.1, in the third row, we see that total household consumption declined by considerably less than per capita consumption, particularly in rural areas. This suggests that individuals and households have responded to the crisis by shifting living arrangements between 1997 and 1998. This is reflected in changes in household size which, as shown in row 4, increased by 7 percent during this time. Changes in household size are discussed in more detail later. For now, it is sufficient to note that studies which focus exclusively on PCE are ignoring a potentially important smoothing mechanism.

PCE is separated into components in the next four rows. On average, *per capita* food consumption was reduced by 9 percent whereas expenditures on non-foods took a much bigger cut and were reduced by about a third. Part of this difference can be explained by the fact that food prices rose more rapidly than other prices although that is probably not the full story. It is likely that households smooth welfare by reallocating the budget away from spending on goods that can be deferred at little immediate cost to welfare; semi-durables such as clothing and household furniture are natural candidates since delay of expenditure on these items is unlikely to affect utility as much as, say, reducing spending on basic foods. Of course, as the period over which spending is delayed lengthens, the welfare costs of deferring expenditure rise and so the extent to which this smoothing mechanism is adopted likely depends on expectations about future income (see Browning and Crossley, 1997; Thomas *et al.*, 2001). In Indonesia, households substantially reduced *per capita* spending on "deferrable" items, including clothing, furniture, and spending on ceremonies which declined by over one-third. They also reduced investments in human capital (i.e. health and education spending) by around 40 percent, which may have rather different implications for longer-run welfare. The evidence in Indonesia suggests that households do smooth welfare through reallocating the budget, which means that the link between changes in PCE and welfare of households is not direct; this is important to keep in mind when interpreting the evidence on household smoothing behavior in the following sections.

12.5.2   *Measurement of economic shocks*

Prior to assessing the extent to which Indonesian households were able to smooth the effects of the economic shocks associated with the crisis, it is useful to construct a measure of the size of the shock faced by different households which is independent of their own smoothing behavior. Using household level data alone, it would not be possible to distinguish between a household that faced no economic disruption during the crisis and one that was able to completely smooth the impact of the shock that they did confront.

We have explored several approaches to measuring the magnitude of the shock. The first issue to address concerns the level of geographic aggregation. This calls for balancing at least two competing concerns: on the one hand, the geographic unit should be small enough so that the estimated shock reflects the nature of the local economy; on the other hand, the greater the number of estimates of the shock within a local economy, the smaller the measurement error. If labor markets clear immediately, then all shocks would be national as migration of labor would smooth out spatial variation in relative demand. Given its geography (an archipelago of 13,000 islands) and its level of development and infrastructure, it seems unlikely that the Indonesian labor market is perfect. We will present some evidence on this score given here. With this in mind, we have chosen to measure economic shocks at the level of *kecamatan* (which, roughly speaking, is analogous to a county in the United States). The analyses are based on data from 85 *kecamatans*, 49 of which are in urban areas.[13]

The next question involves how to best characterize shocks at the local economy level. There are several alternatives that we have explored, each with some advantages and disadvantages. A natural starting point is the real change in the local wage. Whereas inflation in 1998 was around 80 percent, nominal wages in the market sector increased by around 40 percent. Evidence based on IFLS demonstrates that inferences about the impact of the crisis based on market sector wages alone misses an important part of the picture. Specifically, there was a dramatic downward shift in real wages in the market sector of some 40 percent in both the rural and the urban sectors and a similar decline in real hourly earnings from self-employment in the urban sector. However, hourly earnings of the rural self-employed declined by much less – 15–20 percent – which is likely to reflect the increased returns to food production during the crisis (Smith *et al.*, 2002). Our estimates of shocks will, therefore, be based on hourly earnings of market workers and the self-employed taken in combination.

This raises serious issues regarding measurement since estimation of hourly earnings from self-employment is fraught with difficulties.[14] Compared with market sector earnings, self-employment income is often very volatile; disentangling profits from returns to capital is very difficult; it is not clear how to allocate earnings to individuals in family business with multiple members working in the activity. Moreover, even if one can estimate earnings, the estimation of hours of work in self-employed activities is well known to be very hard. Given these difficulties and the fact that self-employment activities increased in importance between 1997 and 1998 (which implies that measurement error is not likely to be differenced out), we expect estimates of the shock based on hourly earnings to be contaminated by substantial measurement error. In addition, our tests of smoothing revolved around changes in PCE which is measured at the household level and it is not obvious how to aggregate individual hourly earnings so that they are comparable without incorporating a model of family labor supply.

This suggests the first of two alternative measures: the community-specific mean change in the logarithm of *per capita* income (PCY). Our second alternative is the average change in lnPCE. In contrast with hourly earnings of individuals, these measures have the advantage that they are measured at the same level of aggregation as the outcome in the analyses – household PCE. Relative to PCE, PCY has two shortcomings. First, it is more likely to be measured with error and subject to contamination due to outliers. Second, it reflects labor supply responses to the crisis.

Figure 12.3a and 12.3b displays the three measures of community "shock." In an effort to provide insights into the distributional impact of the crisis, we have attributed to each household the shock they faced between 1997 and 1998 and then related those shocks to household PCE (measured in 1993).[15] In the urban sector, the "wage shock" is around −40 percent whereas the shock measured by PCY and PCE is close to −20 percent. This gap reflects both the effect of aggregation of individual earnings to the household level and also the existence of substantial increases in labor supply. In the rural areas, the shock is much smaller as is the difference among the three measures of the shock. Whereas the wage shock ranges from −12 percent to −30 percent, the shock measured by PCE and PCY lies between −12 percent and −20 percent.

Apart from an intercept difference in the urban sector, our estimates of the shocks based on PCE and PCY are remarkably similar and yield the same inferences about the distribution of the shock. Specifically, in both the rural and urban

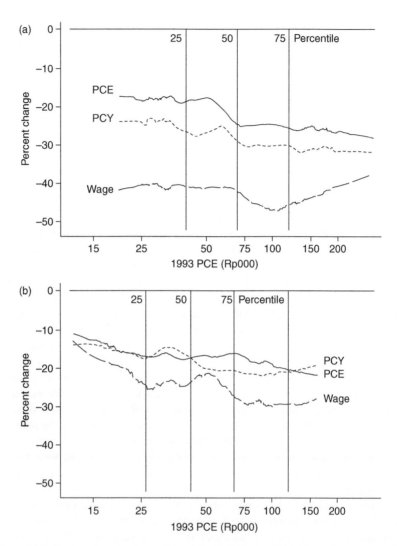

Figure 12.3 Community shocks and household PCE in 1993: (a) urban households; (b) rural households.

sectors, the shock is largest for those who were best off in 1993. Among urban households, there is a tendency for the magnitude of the *kecamatan*-level shock to increase as 1993 household PCE increases. In rural areas, the middle 50 percent of households faced essentially the same shock, while those in the bottom quartile of PCE faced a slightly smaller shock.

    We will use the community-mean change in lnPCE as our measure of the local economy shock. Its main disadvantage is that it may be affected by joint consumption smoothing for the community as a whole in which case we will under-estimate the magnitude of the shock. Since our focus is on the link between household wealth and smoothing, as long as household-specific wealth holdings and community-specific smoothing behaviors are not related, our results should not be contaminated. Given the complexities associated with measurement of the shock we will, in addition, take a less parametric and arguably more robust approach and allow the community shock – as well as all community-specific smoothing behaviors – be captured in a community fixed effect.

12.5.3   Smoothing mechanisms: household size and composition

There are many dimensions over which households may "smooth" consumption in order to mitigate the welfare reducing consequences of a severe economic shock. One often ignored a dimension that involves changes in household size and composition. In order to share fixed living expenses such as housing and food preparation, households may try to combine into larger units, forgoing at least temporarily the luxury of some privacy. Similarly, those households hit more severely may send some members to live with other households less severely affected by the crisis or to places where the cost of consumption may be lower. Consumption costs may not be the only reason for reshuffling of household members. Spatial variation in the size of economic disruptions may lead some household members to relocate to places where the prospects for generating income are better.

The upper panel of Figure 12.4 plots the change in household size between 1997 and 1998 in the urban and rural sectors.[16] The figures indicate that, on average, IFLS households became somewhat larger during the economic crisis, an increase that was greater for households with higher levels of 1993 PCE. More revealing, however, is the separation of these household size trends by rural and urban residence. In the urban sector, the bottom quarter of households as ranked by their 1993 PCE actually lost household members during the crisis while urban households above median 1993 PCE gained new members. In contrast, across the entire distribution of 1993 PCE, household size was expanding in the rural sector. This expansion was small for the poorest rural households, but reached about half an additional member for the most well-off rural households.

To see why the direction of household size changes may have differed between the urban and the rural sector, we have examined changes in relative hourly earnings (or wages for shorthand) in the two sectors. We have calculated the wage at each percentile in the urban wage distribution in 1997 and again in 1998; we treat the difference as the change in wage for a person at that percentile in the skill distribution in the urban sector in 1997. The same exercise was repeated for rural workers. In order to directly compare urban and rural workers, we have located the sector-specific percentiles in the distribution for the whole country. For example, an urban male at the 10th percentile of the urban wage distribution earns the same real wage as a rural male at the 45th percentile of the rural wage

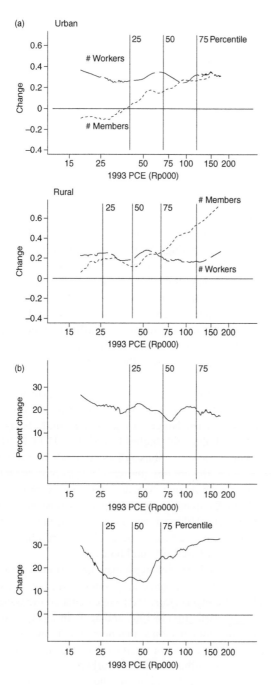

Figure 12.4 (a) Changes in number of household members and number of workers; (b) percent change in hours worked per worker.

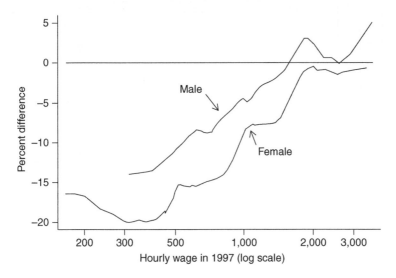

Figure 12.5 Urban–rural differential in percent wage decline between 1997 and 1998.

distribution. Intuitively, we assume those two workers have the same level of skill and we compare the change in wages they experienced between 1997 and 1998. The percent difference in the decline in urban wages relative to the decline in rural wages is displayed in Figure 12.5. It presents our (smoothed) estimates of the urban–rural differential in the decline in hourly earnings during the year of the shock across the 1997 wage distribution. The estimates are reported separately for males and females.

The patterns are remarkably systematic. Among the least skilled men, there was about a 15 percent decrease in urban wages relative to the drop in rural wages. This greater relative wage deterioration in urban markets mono-tonically declines as we move up the wage (skill) distribution until there is a roughly equal reduction of male urban and rural wages at the highest wage (skill) levels.

These between sector relative wage changes map neatly into the household size changes documented in the upper panel of Figure 12.4. The Indonesian economic crisis hit unskilled labor markets harder in urban areas than in rural settings. Some low-skill workers in poor urban households exited the urban sector to find work in the rural sector. While doing so, many of them apparently joined middle income or higher income households in rural areas.

Additional insight can be obtained on how changes in household membership are operating by examining the characteristics of those who enter or leave the household. To do so, we separated household members by gender and into four age groups: 0–14, 14–25, 25–54, and 55+. These changes in household size and composition are subdivided by quartiles of PCE in Table 12.2.

Table 12.2 Household size and composition by quartile of HH PCE

Characteristic	Percentile of 1993 PCE											
	0–25 percentile			26–50 percentile			51–75 percentile			76–100 percentile		
	1997	1998	Change	1997	1998	Change	1997	1998	Change	1997	1998	Change
Rural												
Percent no change in HH size	58.0			58.1			58.4			54.5		
HH size	4.74	4.79	0.05	4.22	4.40	0.18	4.13	4.36	0.23	3.34	3.80	0.46
(std error)	(0.12)	(0.12)	(0.08)	(0.11)	(0.12)	(0.07)	(0.11)	(0.11)	(0.07)	(0.11)	(0.10)	(0.08)
# males age												
0–14	1.01	1.00	−0.01	0.82	0.80	−0.02	0.71	0.70	−0.01	0.50	0.58	0.08
15–24	0.38	0.37	−0.01	0.33	0.41	0.08	0.38	0.45	0.07	0.23	0.32	0.08
25–54	0.71	0.72	0.01	0.67	0.68	0.01	0.64	0.69	0.05	0.56	0.65	0.08
> = 55	0.29	0.29	0.00	0.26	0.29	0.03	0.29	0.32	0.03	0.23	0.25	0.01
# females age												
0–14	0.87	0.89	0.02	0.75	0.75	0.00	0.70	0.70	0.00	0.56	0.63	0.06
15–24	0.37	0.38	0.00	0.32	0.34	0.02	0.36	0.42	0.05	0.32	0.36	0.05
25–54	0.81	0.80	−0.01	0.78	0.78	−0.01	0.79	0.79	0.00	0.66	0.72	0.06
> = 55	0.29	0.33	0.04	0.29	0.36	0.07	0.26	0.30	0.03	0.27	0.31	0.04
Urban												
Percent no change in HH size	55.8			57.8			57.8			51.3		
HH size	5.03	4.92	−0.11	4.84	5.01	0.17	4.53	4.76	0.22	4.03	4.37	0.35
(std error)	(0.15)	(0.14)	(0.10)	(0.14)	(0.14)	(0.09)	(0.15)	(0.13)	(0.10)	(0.14)	(0.13)	(0.10)
# males age												
0–14	0.77	0.75	−0.02	0.79	0.80	0.01	0.72	0.76	0.04	0.50	0.53	0.03
15–24	0.48	0.44	−0.04	0.52	0.57	0.05	0.51	0.57	0.06	0.48	0.54	0.06
25–54	0.79	0.77	−0.02	0.77	0.85	0.08	0.90	0.93	0.03	0.82	0.91	0.09
> = 55	0.26	0.30	0.04	0.20	0.19	0.00	0.19	0.18	−0.01	0.22	0.26	0.05
# females age												
0–14	0.86	0.79	−0.08	0.83	0.79	−0.04	0.59	0.60	0.01	0.48	0.50	0.02
15–24	0.55	0.58	0.03	0.48	0.53	0.05	0.42	0.44	0.02	0.43	0.47	0.04
25–54	0.97	0.92	−0.05	0.89	0.92	0.03	0.93	1.00	0.07	0.83	0.89	0.07
> = 55	0.35	0.38	0.03	0.35	0.36	0.00	0.27	0.26	0.00	0.28	0.29	0.01

Note
Size and composition in 1997, 1998, and change between those years; HH PCE measured in 1993.

Relative to changes in the urban sector, increases in household size are larger in the rural sector particularly in the bottom and top quartiles of PCE. The rural–urban differential is sharpest among older rural women. In the bottom quartile of 1993 PCE urban households, the most striking pattern is that male and female children under age 14 apparently left their original household. These young children may have been accompanied by their mothers since there was also a decrease in women ages 25–54. No similar trends exist among rural households in the bottom quartile of PCE. In the top quartile of PCE in both the rural and urban sectors, there was a large increase in the number of men in the prime age worker category (ages 15–54) and a slightly smaller increase in the number of women in this age range.

The evidence indicates that dependents tended to have exited urban households that were poorest (measured by PCE in 1993) and moved to lower-cost rural areas. At the same time, households that were better off in 1993 have been net recipients of working age adults which likely reflects the fact that these households were better able to exploit new opportunities to generate income as the crisis unfolded, possibly because the households had land or other forms of capital.

12.5.4   Smoothing mechanisms: labor supply and number of workers

In addition to the exit or entry of additional people into the household, a household may attempt to adjust to the crisis by altering the labor supply decisions of its members. On the demand side, some workers especially in the formal wage sector may have lost their jobs and are no longer working. Other family members may have increased their work effort by helping out in family businesses.

There are several aspects of total family labor supply that we examine in this chapter – the number of workers in the family and the hours of work. Table 12.3 lists changes between 1997 and 1998 in the number of workers in each household in the rural and urban sector. While there was a greater increase in household membership among rural households, there was actually a greater increase in number of workers in urban areas. This indicates that the increase in number of workers in urban households was not simply at the extensive margin – that is, adding new members – but also resulted from additional work by members already present there. The increase in numbers of workers was concentrated in the wage sector in urban areas and in the family business in rural areas.

The last three rows of Table 12.3 focus on hours of work. The total number of hours worked by all household members increased substantially in both the rural and the urban areas: the average household spent an additional 25 hours at work per week after the onset of the crisis. The per worker increase in hours worked was about 10 hours per week. It turns out that these additional hours represent the combination of a reduction in the extent of part time work and, for some full-time workers, a large increase in hours spent working, particularly among the self employed.

Table 12.3 Household labor supply

Characteristic	Rural			Urban		
	1997	1998	Change	1997	1998	Change
# workers in HH	1.77	1.98	0.21	1.69	1.99	0.30
	(0.031)	(0.032)	(0.030)	(0.039)	(0.042)	(0.036)
# market sector workers in HH	0.48	0.54	0.06	0.97	1.23	0.26
	(0.021)	(0.023)	(0.021)	(0.032)	(0.037)	(0.031)
# self-employed workers in HH	0.89	0.96	0.07	0.62	0.72	0.10
	(0.022)	(0.021)	(0.021)	(0.026)	(0.026)	(0.024)
# family workers in HH	0.40	0.67	0.27	0.10	0.20	0.10
	(0.020)	(0.025)	(0.024)	(0.011)	(0.018)	(0.017)
# hrs worked per week (HH total)	60.18	86.20	26.02	70.49	98.93	28.44
	(1.438)	(1.618)	(1.670)	(2.069)	(2.313)	(2.142)
# hrs worked per worker	35.10	45.11	10.01	41.84	50.93	9.09
	(0.634)	(0.781)	(0.949)	(0.734)	(0.770)	(0.937)
# hrs worked per HH member	16.60	21.38	4.78	17.08	22.16	5.08
	(0.463)	(0.404)	(0.489)	(0.570)	(0.603)	(0.565)

Notes
1997, 1998, and changes for rural and urban HHs.
Means and (standard errors).

Table 12.3 indicates that one important adjustment mechanism to the economic crisis was a sharp increase in hours worked. The lower panel of Figure 12.4 presents more detail about the nature of that adjustment by relating the percent change in total household hours worked by each household with 1993 lnPCE. There was a very large increase of over 20 percent in total household hours worked in the rural sector. These increases were roughly independent of 1993 PCE in urban areas, but were roughly U shaped in rural areas. The large increase in work effort in response to the crisis is one reason why changes in PnPCY are higher than *percent* changes in wages in Figure 12.3.

The data presented in this section highlights two important adjustments that the households made in the face of this crisis. First, households consolidated and became larger, presumably to economize on fixed consumption costs. The composition of households also changed, especially in urban areas, so that members who were primarily consumers (such as young children and their mothers) left while earners moved in. The second adjustment was a significant increase in total work effort by the household.

12.5.5   Smoothing mechanisms: wealth

For those households that own assets prior to an economic shock, their wealth may serve as a buffer to soften the potential blow to their consumption. As central as the total value of assets is likely to be, portfolio composition may also be important since the more liquid an asset, the more readily it may be converted to resources to finance consumption. Many economic and financial crises, including the Indonesian case, have been accompanied by substantial swings in the relative prices of assets. The associated capital gains and losses are also likely to result in consumption and savings adjustments by households. We explore each of these mechanisms in the following sections.

12.5.5.1 *Distribution of ownership of wealth*

IFLS pays considerable attention to the collection of information on wealth. The rates of ownership in 1997 and 1998 are reported in Table 12.4. Values of wealth in 1997 and 1998 are reported in Table 12.5 in thousands of 1997 Rp. Because the distribution is extremely right skewed, the value at the median, bottom and top quartile, and bottom and top decile are reported in the table.

Essentially all Indonesian households owned some wealth in both 1997 and 1998. The total value of business and non-business wealth of the median urban household is about Rp 10 million and the median rural household owns about Rp 6 million in such assets. (This is equivalent to about a year and a half of consumption for the median household.) In both sectors, the median for total assets has remained remarkably stable through the crisis. In fact, in the rural sector, the distribution of wealth has remained reasonably constant below the median but has stretched out substantially above the median. The reverse is true in urban areas, where the right-hand tail of the wealth distribution has been substantially curtailed and the left-hand tail has expanded.

These differences are primarily a reflection of the fact that business wealth has tended to increase (or at least fall less than non-business wealth) between 1997 and 1998. In the rural sector, four out of five households own wealth that is associated with a business (typically farming) whereas two out of three urban households own a business that involves some assets. As noted earlier, self-employment activities – particularly those revolving around the production of food – became relatively more attractive as the price of rice and other crops spiraled up. Households apparently responded by building up their family businesses. Excluding business wealth, household wealth has declined throughout

Table 12.4 Household wealth: ownership rates

Percent of HHs that own	*Rural*		*Urban*	
	1997	*1998*	*1997*	*1998*
Any business or non-business wealth	99.6	99.9	99.8	99.6
Business wealth	82.9	87.8	62.5	68.9
Non-business wealth	99.5	99.8	99.6	99.4
Housing wealth	91.7	92.1	71.7	74.8
Land wealth	74.5	79.9	70.6	74.1
Financial wealth	21.8	24.4	41.6	37.2
Jewelry	50.9	34.5	63.5	50.8
Other wealth	96.3	98.7	97.7	98.5

Table 12.5 Distribution of household wealth: 1997 and 1998 (in 1997 Rp000s)

		Percentile of wealth distribution				
		10	25	50	75	90
Rural						
Net household +	1997	797	2,395	6,048	13,091	25,410
business wealth	1998	626	2,349	6,296	15,008	30,630
Business wealth	1997	−40	0	715	4,004	10,025
	1998	−25	10	1,900	7,093	19,035
Housing wealth	1997	8	500	2,000	5,000	10,000
	1998	4	508	1,473	3,657	8,439
Land wealth	1997	0	0	120	1,660	5,500
	1998	0	11	105	1,071	3,681
Financial wealth	1997	0	0	0	0	200
	1998	0	0	0	0	277
Jewelry	1997	0	0	8	150	464
	1998	0	0	0	49	326
Urban						
Net household +	1997	427	2,655	10,104	31,800	94,564
business wealth	1998	717	3,104	10,039	29,204	72,691
Business wealth	1997	−625	0	0	650	7,000
	1998	−608	0	0	1,085	11,180
Housing wealth	1997	0	0	3,000	15,000	50,000
	1998	0	0	3,590	13,331	34,479
Land wealth	1997	0	0	150	5,000	25,000
	1998	0	0	171	4,316	17,233
Financial wealth	1997	0	0	0	200	2,000
	1998	0	0	0	107	1,752
Jewelry	1997	0	0	90	500	1,000
	1998	0	0	4	283	1,066

the distribution among rural households and it has declined for all households above the median in the urban sector.

Excluding business wealth, the dominant assets owned by households are their home and land. Over 90 percent of rural and 70 percent of urban households own their own home with almost no change in ownership during the crisis. The value of houses declined between 1997 and 1998. Commercial property values, particularly in the largest urban centers, plummeted as construction contracts were canceled and many developers went out of business. The collapse of the banking system – and lack of credit – took its toll on the home property market. Arable land, on the other hand, presumably became more valuable although the absence of credit likely muted activity in this market. Turning to more liquid assets, about one-quarter of rural households and 40 percent of urban households keep some of their wealth in the form of cash, bonds, or stocks. A higher fraction of households store wealth in the form of gold (as jewelry), particularly in rural areas. This reflects the fact that financial services are much less accessible in rural areas, relative to urban areas, whereas there is an active market in gold throughout

Indonesia. Moreover, whereas aggregate ownership rates for all other assets have remained remarkably stable, ownership of jewelry has declined dramatically between 1997 and 1998 – falling by more than 30 percent in rural areas and slightly less than that in urban areas. In fact, not only is jewelry more common than financial assets among rural households, but these households store a larger fraction of their wealth in the form of gold rather than in financial instruments. The same is true of most urban households.

The distribution of changes in wealth between 1997 and 1998 is reported in Table 12.6 (in thousands of 1997 Rps). The table reflects the combined effects of changes in prices of assets and changes in asset holdings. The first main point that emerges from the table is the tremendous amount of change in asset values between 1997 and 1998. For some assets, real values declined because of the crisis. Housing prices, for example, did not keep up with the 80 percent inflation rate of 1998. Financial wealth collapsed as real interest rates became negative in early 1998, as the stock market collapsed and as a large number of banks – including several of the largest in the country – closed their doors because they could not meet their obligation while their customers were clamoring outside for their savings. In contrast, the value of certain types of businesses possibly increased – and certainly the returns to food production increased – with arable land presumably also increasing in value. The starkest contrast, however, lies in jewelry. The price of gold is set in world terms and so the four-fold decline in the value of the rupiah resulted in a four- to five-fold increase in the value of gold – far outstripping the inflation rate. Those households in Indonesia that had stored their wealth in gold fared far better than those who had entrusted banks with their savings.

Table 12.6 Distribution of change in household wealth: 1998–97 (in 1997 Rp000s)

	Percentile of change in wealth distribution				
	10	25	50	75	90
Rural					
Net household + business wealth	−8,933	−2,568	57	3,776	14,016
Business wealth	−3,025	−320	150	3,425	12,719
Housing wealth	−4,336	−1,478	−187	543	2,614
Land wealth	−3,478	−746	0	128	1,218
Financial wealth	−98	0	0	0	111
Jewelry	−251	−73	0	0	119
Urban					
Net household + business wealth	−35,623	−7,917	−316	5,016	21,272
Business wealth	−3,300	−297	0	872	7,513
Housing wealth	−21,451	−4,379	0	973	8,875
Land wealth	−9,681	−1,344	0	373	5,746
Financial wealth	−962	−40	0	0	565
Jewelry	−600	−200	0	58	566

As noted earlier, increases in the value of wealth are primarily a reflection of the increase in the value of business wealth, particularly in the rural sector. The decline in housing prices in the urban sector took an especially large toll although there does appear to be a fairly active market in both the housing and land markets as some households report increases in values of these assets. Financial losses are substantial with a small number of household increasing their holding of financial instruments (presumably because of sales of other assets). Since the price of jewelry increased substantially, the declines in their value reflect sales of the asset which appear to have also been substantial. Note that these numbers are likely to understate the value of sales. Consider, for example, the decline in jewelry wealth at the 25 percentile which is Rp 73,000 (among rural households) and around Rp 200,000 (among urban households). Assume, for simplicity, that a household reported jewelry worth Rp 73,000 in 1997 in the rural sector (and Rp 200,000 in the urban sector) and sold all the jewelry in the second quarter of 1998. The household reported no jewelry in 1998. The difference is recorded in Table 12.6. However, by the time the jewelry was sold, the rupiah had collapsed and so the gold price had increased some four-fold. The value of jewelry reported in 1997 would have been some four times its reported value (Rp 292,000 in the rural sector and Rp 800,000 in the urban sector) and so the value of the sale is understated. While we do not know when the jewelry was sold, given the speed with which the crisis hit Indonesia, it is reasonable to suppose that the majority of sales were after the collapse of the rupiah in early 1998. (To put the change in the value of jewelry into some perspective, it is equivalent to about 4 months of food consumption in the average rural household and 9 months in the average urban household.)

12.5.5.2   Asset markets

The given evidence presents a picture of wealth ownership that is far more equitable in Indonesia than in any developed country. Home ownership is very high, businesses are common and the majority of households own some form of liquid wealth. Since the banking system all but collapsed in Indonesia in early 1998, if this wealth is going to serve to smooth consumption, there must also be an active market for the assets. We do not know details about sales and purchases of assets in IFLS. However, Table 12.7 presents evidence that speaks to this issue. For each asset group, the table records the percentage of households that owned the asset in both years, that sold all their assets, new owners, and the percentage that did not own in either year. These percentages are recorded for households in each quartile of the PCE distribution (measured in 1997).

There is some evidence that business assets were sold, particularly in the urban sector, and that a substantial fraction of households started new businesses between 1997 and 1998. Of households that did not own any business assets in 1997, about 60 percent of rural and 40 percent of urban households had acquired some business assets by 1998. There also appears to be a very active land market with the poorest households most likely to enter that market, presumably by buying low price tracts of land. It is likely that most of these acquisitions were intended for the production of food although it is worth noting that households were not entering both the land and business asset market at the same time. For example, of those who entered the land market, only 15 percent also entered the business asset market. A similar fraction of the new business asset owners were new land owners. Relative to these markets, the housing market is comparatively thin.

Whereas households at the top of the PCE distribution are more likely to own financial assets, jewelry ownership is only modestly linked to PCE although (median) values are positively associated with PCE in both cases. A very large fraction of households that owned financial assets in 1997 had exited the market by 1998 and a roughly equal fraction entered the market. (There was a slight increase in ownership of financial assets in the rural sector and net decline in the urban sector.)

There is clear evidence of an active jewelry market with a substantial fraction of households selling their gold, possibly to finance consumption. Specifically, over half the households in the rural sector and close to one-third of urban households who owned jewelry in 1997 had sold all their holdings by 1998. There are considerably fewer households who entered the jewelry market during this time, which should not be surprising given it had become relatively expensive. The fraction of households who sold their holdings is approximately constant across the distribution of PCE, as is the fraction of new entrants indicating that gold transactions involved households at all levels of consumption.

It is not only the IFLS household data that clearly points to an active jewelry market in both the rural and urban Indonesia and a more limited role of financial services in rural Indonesia. The importance of gold as a savings method is confirmed in the anthropological literature on family economics. The acquisition of gold, usually in the form of jewelry, is seen as an investment and has long been an important way to save money in Indonesia. Women, in particular, buy gold earrings, rings, and bracelets with savings from their household budget, their wages, or from *arisan* winnings (Papanek and Schwede, 1988; Gondowarsito, 1990; Wolf, 1991; Adioetomo *et al.*, 1997). Such gold jewelry, typically 18 or 22 carat, is priced by weight, and can be quickly resold for cash in times when the household needs money (Wolf, 1991). Stores that buy and sell gold are common, as are more informal traders and brokers, many of whom are women (Papanek and Schwede, 1988; Sullivan, 1994).

Further confirmation is provided in the IFLS community surveys which asked community leaders to identify the ways that community residents save money. Gold was mentioned as a form of savings in both rural and urban areas, while financial instruments such as CDs and stocks were much more commonly identified by urban informants. In rural areas, opportunities to buy and sell gold are more available than opportunities to save money through formal credit institutions. The IFLS community survey queried community leaders in each IFLS community

Table 12.7 Changes in ownership of wealth and median value of wealth owned (by quartile of PCE in 1997)

Percentile of PCE	Rural				Urban			
	0–25	26–50	51–75	76–100	0–25	26–50	51–75	76–100
Business wealth								
% HHs own in both years	80	79	79	73	54	53	52	46
Sell all	6	4	5	7	12	8	13	11
New owners	8	9	11	13	16	16	18	19
Not own either year	6	8	5	7	19	22	16	23
Value in Rp000								
1997	1,128	1,881	1,709	1,923	52	81	550	460
1998	2,085	3,045	2,675	3,250	45	140	293	1,290
Non business wealth								
% HHs own in both years	100	99	99	100	99	100	100	98
Sell all	0	1	0	0	1	0	0	0
New owners	0	1	1	0	0	0	0	1
Not own either year	0	0	0	0	0	0	0	0
Value in Rp000								
1997	2,034	2,978	4,100	7,170	3,727	8,254	14,165	24,500
1998	1,528	2,387	2,938	5,359	4,117	6,799	12,451	19,968
Housing								
% HHs own in both years	92	91	89	84	76	68	64	62
Sell all	2	2	4	2	4	4	3	6
New owners	2	3	3	3	6	8	8	9
Not own either year	4	4	4	10	14	20	26	23
Value in Rp000								
1997	1,000	2,000	2,000	4,000	3,000	8,000	15,000	20,000
1998	1,011	1,473	1,777	2,810	3,343	5,969	9,113	18,520

Land								
% HHs own in both years	54	59	67	70	56	59	65	65
Sell all	13	13	12	8	8	9	10	11
New owners	23	19	13	14	16	13	15	9
Not own either year	9	9	8	8	20	19	10	16
Value in Rp000								
1997	290	518	550	1,530	150	1,530	3,000	6,900
1998	163	259	253	826	162	533	2,765	7,082
Financial								
% HHs own in both years	5	6	11	22	11	18	31	40
Sell all	10	8	11	15	11	21	15	19
New owners	10	13	13	17	12	11	14	11
Not own either year	74	73	65	47	65	49	40	31
Value in Rp000								
1997	47	100	148	375	125	200	400	1,000
1998	52	63	174	396	119	327	603	593
Jewelry								
% HHs own in both years	17	20	27	38	33	41	40	47
Sell all	23	26	28	26	22	20	28	23
New owners	9	10	9	9	11	10	11	9
Not own either year	51	45	36	27	34	29	21	20
Value in Rp000								
1997	81	125	150	220	150	283	400	500
1998	74	109	135	261	148	191	373	500

Note
Value is median value conditional on owning wealth in that year in 1997 Rp000s.

about whether they could identify a private bank or any of six government credit institutions. Those who could were asked to estimate the distance to the credit institution from the community center. The median distance to a government credit institution was 6 kilometers in rural areas, but only 1 kilometer in urban areas. The difference is much more stark for private banks. While 75 percent of urban informants could identify a private bank used by community members, only 40 percent of rural informants could do so. In those communities where a bank could be identified, the banks were an average of 2.5 kilometers from urban communities, but 13.4 kilometers from rural communities.

12.5.6   Regression models of characteristics associated with smoothing PCE

In this section, we summarize regression results which seek to identify the characteristics of Indonesian households associated with greater smoothing of PCE. The dependent variable in each case is the change in lnPCE between 1997 and 1998, ΔlnPCE, measured at the household level in IFLS2 and IFLS2+ and converted to 1997 Rupiah. The economic shock in the local (*kecamatan*) economy is measured by ΔlnPCE averaged over all households who lived in the *kecamatan* in both 1997 and 1998.[17] Tests of smoothing behavior are based on the interaction between our measure of the local economy shock and household characteristics that are likely to be associated with reducing fluctuations in lnPCE. In each case, if the characteristic is associated with greater smoothing of PCE, the interaction will be negative.[18]

Regressions are reported separately for rural and urban households. Two models are presented for each regression. The first includes all households. The second excludes those households that have changed household size in order to check that our results are not driven by changes in household size and composition. Similarity of results in each pair will indicate that the array of demographic controls included in each regression does a good job of capturing the differences in smoothing behaviors across these groups of households. In all models that include interactions with the local economy shock, we present estimates with and without *kecamatan* fixed effects. The fixed effects estimates sweep out the main effects of spatial variation in the magnitude of the shock as well as all other changes in the local economy including changes in prices. The table reports only the coefficients of main interest.

As a starting point, the specifications in Panel A provide an estimate of the magnitude of the effect of the community shock on household PCE. In both the rural and the urban sector, we cannot reject the hypothesis that this effect is unity. This may be interpreted as indicating that our measure of the local economy shock has the same impact on all households; it is also consistent with the measure reflecting the local shock after all community-level smoothing has taken place.

The rest of Table 12.8 focuses on the extent to which household-specific smoothing is associated with three sets of characteristics: household wealth, household size, and the level of human capital, all of which are measured in 1997. In general, since wealth and human capital are positively correlated, the inclusion of both characteristics in the regressions provides an opportunity to isolate a wealth effect from an information or background effect.

We begin with levels of human capital, measured by the education of the household head. A better educated person may be more able to exploit new opportunities that arise in times of upheaval – as in Indonesia in the late 1990s – and the better educated may be better able to make ends meet in bad times.

The better educated do appear to be more able to smooth fluctuations in PCE. The effects are large and significant in the rural sector; they are smaller and only marginally significant in urban areas. Relative to households whose head has no education, those with heads who have more than primary schooling (in the urban sector), and those with any education (in the rural sector) have smaller fluctuations in lnPCE for any given local economy shock. When *kecamatan* effects are included in the model, the coefficient estimates are smaller but the standard errors are considerably larger and so the effects are no longer statistically significant. A significant amount of variation in education is across *kecamatan*s limiting our statistical ability to draw strong conclusions about schooling effects when the models include local economy fixed effects. There is also a suggestion that part of the additional smoothing observed for higher human capital households may take place through changes in household size. When we restrict attention to households with no change in size, the effect of the household head's education is slightly greater.

The second set of smoothing mechanisms we investigate highlights the role of household size. We noted earlier that there have been significant changes in household size and composition between 1997 and 1998 and those changes may serve as a cushion to smooth consumption. Empirical support for that hypothesis is limited to the urban sector, where the interaction between household size and the local economy shock is negative and significant.

We have also explored whether there are important household composition effects. The analyses yielded one consistent pattern: urban households with more older women appear to be especially able to smooth PCE. This effect is considerably muted in magnitude among those households that do not change household size (for they would need to swap an older woman for someone else). There are no significant benefits associated with having more household members in rural areas.[19]

We turn next to the effects of wealth (as of 1997). We interpret the direct effects of wealth (in column 2) as indicative of the distributional impact of the crisis, controlling household, and community characteristics. There are no direct wealth effects in urban areas, but negative direct effects in rural places. This indicates that, within rural communities, households with more wealth in 1997 experienced larger changes in their consumption levels.

Our results on the link between consumption smoothing and wealth are based on the interaction between wealth and the local economy shock (reported in

Table 12.8 Changes in HH lnPCE, community shocks, and consumption smoothing mechanisms – urban and rural sectors

Estimator	Sample	Community shock (1)	Wealth (2)	Shock* wealth (3)	Shock*(1) education of HH head		Shock*#HH members excluding older women (6)	Shock* # older women (7)
					primary (4)	>primary (5)		
Urban sector								
Panel A								
OLS	All HHs	0.783 (5.65)						
OLS	|No Δ HHsize	0.722 (4.28)						
Panel B								
OLS	All HHs	1.782 (5.01)	0.000 (0.07)	0.002 (0.62)	−0.322 (1.56)	−0.372 (1.79)	−0.125 (2.23)	−0.501 (3.20)
OLS	|No Δ HHsize	1.914 (4.96)	−0.001 (1.25)	−0.003 (0.92)	−0.232 (0.86)	−0.565 (1.96)	−0.143 (2.59)	−0.218 (1.38)
FE	All HHs		0.000 (0.77)	0.003 (1.39)	−0.134 (0.35)	−0.144 (0.32)	−0.130 (2.42)	−0.452 (2.11)
FE	|No Δ HHsize		−0.001 (0.99)	−0.002 (0.73)	−0.178 (0.37)	−0.489 (0.93)	−0.146 (2.15)	−0.309 (1.20)

Rural sector

Panel A								
OLS	All HHs	1.073						
		(7.63)						
OLS	|No Δ HHsize	1.191						
		(7.05)						
Panel B								
OLS	All HHs	1.794	−0.003	−0.007	−0.328	−0.843	−0.080	−0.328
		(6.52)	(3.30)	(1.50)	(2.06)	(2.50)	(1.17)	(1.16)
OLS	|No Δ HHsize	1.975	−0.002	−0.003	−0.443	−0.856	−0.097	−0.428
		(5.08)	(2.01)	(0.60)	(2.37)	(1.78)	(0.92)	(1.21)
FE	All HHs		−0.004	−0.009	−0.251	−0.626	−0.082	−0.328
			(2.58)	(1.55)	(1.09)	(1.67)	(1.53)	(1.45)
FE	|No Δ HHsize		−0.004	−0.007	−0.251	−0.516	−0.091	−0.336
			(2.05)	(0.99)	(0.84)	(1.00)	(1.11)	(1.11)

Notes

Community shock is measured by mean ΔlnPCE of all sampled households living in the vicinity of an IFLS enumeration area in 1997 and 1998 (excluding index household). "Shock" is then applied to all households living in that *kecamatan* in 1997. Households living in a *kecamatan* that does not include an IFLS enumeration area are given the sector-specific province-level shock. Models include controls for education of HH head (indicators for each level), spline for age of HH head, indicator variable for whether head was male (all measured in 1997), household composition in 1997 (number of people, by gender, in each of four age groups (0–14, 15–24, 25–54, and ≥55), change in number of people in each of those groups between 1997, and 1998, month of interview in 1997 and in 1998, province of residence in 1997, whether the HH was living in same *kecamatan* in 1993, 1997, and 1998 (and thus used in calculation of shock). *t* statistics in parentheses are robust to heteroskedasticity and intra-*kecamatan* correlations. FE include *kecamatan* fixed effects. 864 urban households (503 with no change in HH size) and 1107 rural households (658 with no change in HH size) included in regressions.

column 3). There are likely to be two competing effects. On the one hand, assets may be depleted and those resources used to smooth consumption, on the other hand, there may be capital gains (or losses) which will also affect savings and consumption choices. In general, wealth appears to play no role at all in smoothing lnPCE in urban households. This is true in aggregate and also when we distinguish components of wealth. In the rural sector, there is a suggestion that as the magnitude of the local economy shock increased, households with more wealth in 1997 were better able to smooth their consumption.

Recall from the discussion earlier that the impact of the crisis on wealth differed dramatically across assets groups. For some, such as jewelry, the depletion and capital gains effects are reinforcing and we would expect those assets to play a role in smoothing consumption (in which case the interaction between wealth and the local economy shock should be negative). For other assets, such as financial assets and housing, the capital gains and depletion effect operate in different directions yielding no predictions on their role in smoothing consumption. With this in mind, we have re-estimated the models in Table 12.8 with the same set of covariates and interactions but explicitly distinguish the major asset classes. The results are reported in Table 12.9.

Mirroring our result on total household wealth, there is no evidence that any components of wealth have a significant impact on consumption smoothing among urban households. Results for those households are not reported. The results for education and household size are unaffected by the separation of wealth into components and so those results are not repeated. Table 12.9 reports, for rural households, the direct effects of components of wealth along with their interactions with the local economy shock. We have separated business wealth, housing, other wealth, and financial wealth, land, and jewelry.

There is no evidence that rural households with more business wealth in 1997 were better able to smooth fluctuations in PCE at the onset of the crisis. The same inference emerges for those with greater wealth in housing, financial assets, or other wealth. Two dimensions of wealth do appear to be associated with smoothing consumption: land and jewelry.

Among households that did not change household size, more land is associated with greater smoothing and it is significant at 10 percent. Roughly two-thirds of Indonesian households are landowners and there is an active market for land. The link between land ownership and consumption smoothing is not likely to be a reflection of greater income from a family business in agriculture, since we have distinguished business wealth in the regressions and we see no evidence that business wealth (most of which is land and agricultural equipment) is associated with greater smoothing. The fact that land is used to smooth consumption among those households that do not change in size suggests there are complex interactions between changes in wealth and changes in family structure.

The clearest evidence that wealth is associated with consumption smoothing emerges for jewelry. The interaction term is much larger in magnitude than that of land and it is significant at a 5 percent size of test in three of the models.

Table 12.9 Changes in HH lnPCE, community shocks, and composition of wealth rural sector

Estimator shock	Sample	Community shock	Direct effect of wealth				Wealth*shock interaction			
		Business (1)	House etc. (2)	Land (3)	Jewelry (4)	Business (5)	House etc. (6)	Land (7)	Jewelry (8)	Business (9)
OLS	All HHs	1.873 (6.11)	−0.001 (0.44)	−0.001 (0.30)	−0.008 (2.32)	−0.100 (1.77)	−0.004 (0.51)	0.016 (0.71)	−0.012 (1.34)	−0.653 (2.58)
OLS	|No Δ HHsize	2.086 (4.95)	0.002 (0.58)	−0.003 (0.47)	−0.009 (2.26)	−0.137 (2.18)	0.011 (0.58)	−0.001 (0.03)	−0.015 (1.60)	−0.642 (2.00)
FE	All HHs		−0.002 (0.71)	−0.001 (0.20)	−0.009 (1.96)	−0.112 (1.41)	−0.009 (0.91)	0.018 (0.77)	−0.012 (0.99)	−0.723 (2.17)
FE	|No Δ HHsize		0.002 (0.59)	−0.006 (0.86)	−0.013 (2.40)	−0.163 (1.52)	0.009 (0.64)	−0.016 (0.48)	−0.022 (1.63)	−0.675 (1.53)

Note
See Table 12.8.

The magnitude of the estimated effect is slightly larger in models that include *kecamatan* fixed effects but the standard errors increase and the effect is not significant among households that did not change size. (We suspect this primarily reflects lack of power.)

That gold should serve as a mechanism for smoothing consumption is not surprising. First, we have noted that its value more than quadrupled at the onset of the crisis. Second, we noted earlier, that gold is owned by households throughout the income distribution. Third, there is an active market in gold across the Indonesian archipelago. Fourth, there is evidence in IFLS that many households sold gold during the hiatus between the two survey rounds.

A tantalizing fact revolves around the distribution of jewelry within households. The IFLS wealth module asks about the share of each asset group owned by the respondent and the share owned by the respondent's spouse. In IFLS2, among those households that own jewelry, 20 percent report that it is owned jointly with the spouse. In 75 percent of the households, the woman owns all the jewelry and males own the jewelry in only 5 percent of households. Moreover, 85 percent of the value of jewelry is attributed to women and only 15 percent to men – facts that are consistent with the anthropological evidence discussed earlier. In the context of a collective model of household decision-making, the (exogenous) increase in the price of gold associated with the crisis increased the value of assets owned by a woman and improved her "bargaining" position relative to her husband. Evidence in IFLS2/2+ suggests that jewelry sold between 1997 and 1998 was more often under the control of women since the fraction of households in which men and women jointly own jewelry increased by 25 percent (from 20 percent to 25 percent). This suggests that preferences for consumption smoothing may not be the same among all household members and, therefore, that within household dynamics in decision-making may be extremely complex. These issues will be explored in detail in future work.

12.6   Conclusions

The year 1998 marked a dramatic and unexpected reversal of economic fortunes in Indonesia. After thirty years of sustained growth, the economy shrank by about 15 percent in one year. Using data that were specially collected to measure the immediate effects of the economic and financial crisis, we have shown that there is considerable diversity in the magnitude of the economic shock, as measured by changes in household PCE. For some, the crisis has been devastating; for others it has brought new opportunities.

Rural and urban households in Indonesia have adopted a wide array of mechanisms to mitigate the deleterious impact of the shock – and to exploit the new opportunities that have emerged since the onset of the crisis. Households and families have reorganized living arrangements with dependents tending to move to lower-cost locations and working age family members joining households that are able to absorb additional workers. There is also evidence that in spite of the collapse of hourly earnings, labor supply has increased. On net, individuals have entered the labor force and many of those who were working prior to the crisis have increased their hours of work. Changes in the allocations of time of household members have been accompanied by rerrangement of other dimensions of the budget. There is evidence that households have cut back spending on "deferrable" items (such as clothing, household furniture, and similar semi-durables) while maintaining real expenditures on foods.

The role of wealth in strategies adopted to smooth consumption has played a central role in this chapter. In contrast with developed countries, the vast majority of Indonesian households store some wealth in the form of assets. As the rupiah collapsed and inflation spiraled, the value of most assets declined very substantially in value. This capital loss should dampen the impact of wealth on consumption smoothing. Gold stands out as being different. Since the price of gold is set in world terms, its value increased four-fold in early 1998, when the rupiah collapsed. Moreover, a good deal of evidence indicates there is a very active market in gold throughout the Indonesian archipelago. We see clear evidence that rural households used gold to smooth their consumption. There is more limited evidence that rural households with more land were better able to smooth their consumption.

The picture that emerges from the empirical evidence in the IFLS is one of tremendous diversity and great complexity in the response of households to the massive economic and financial crisis in Indonesia. Households appear to adopt multiple strategies to smooth out the impact of the crisis on their current and future welfare.

Over and above these substantive contributions, the chapter illustrates the value of designing longitudinal research surveys that measure a broad array of social, economic, and demographic circumstances of individuals, households, and their communities. The chapter also highlights the tremendous value of on-going longitudinal surveys which can be put into the field very rapidly and provide basic scientific evidence that help us understand the effects of major innovations on well-being and behaviors in society.

Notes

1 The hypothesis that net food producers may have been partially protected from the effects of the crisis needs to be tempered since a severe drought immediately preceded the financial crisis and it affected agriculture in many parts of the country – particularly in the east. Country-wide, rice production fell by 4 percent in 1997 with rice and soybeans being imported. Moreover, unusually severe forest fires raged in parts of Sumatra, Kalimantan, and Sulawesi affecting many aspects of economic life including agriculture and tourism.

2 The sample includes four provinces on Sumatra (North Sumatra, West Sumatra, South Sumatra, and Lampung), all five of the Javanese provinces (DKI Jakarta, West Java, Central Java, DI Yogyakarta, and East Java), and four provinces covering the remaining major island groups (Bali, West Nusa Tenggara, South Kalimantan, and South Sulawesi). The IFLS1 sampling scheme balanced the costs of surveying the more remote and sparsely populated regions of Indonesia against the benefits of capturing the ethnic and socioeconomic diversity of the country.

3 Most of the interviews were completed by December 1997; the first two months of 1998 were spent tracking down movers who had not already been found. (Frankenberg and Thomas, 2000, describe the survey.)

4 See Thomas *et al.* (2001) for a discussion of attrition and Frankenberg *et al.* (1999) for a fuller description of IFLS2+.

5 For an excellent survey, see Browning and Lusardi (1996).

6 For example, nearly 1 in 10 households reported borrowing from the formal credit sector during the 12 months prior to the 1997 interview but fewer than 1 in 20 did so in the 1998 interview. Amounts borrowed also declined. Among those who did borrow, the median amount was 45 percent lower in 1998, relative to 1997. One in four loans were for more than Rp 4 million in 1997 but loans of this magnitude accounted for only 1 in 20 in 1998.

7 Many of the informal networks in developing countries extend across community boundaries. Transfers across (possibly related) households living in different communities experiencing different magnitude of shocks is an often cited dimension of smoothing behavior. IFLS contains information on transfers among non-resident kin. Preliminary explorations suggest they were not a principal smoothing mechanism used during this crisis. While the incidence of loans from friends and families during the prior 12 months increased from 24 percent of households in 1997 to 32 percent in 1998, the magnitude of these transfers fell by 40 percent. These kinds of transfers are not discussed further in this chapter; see Frankenberg and Thomas (2000). Similarly, government's programs might also serve to smooth the effects of fluctuations in income. The majority of social safety net programs in Indonesia was instituted around or after the fielding of IFLS2+ and so are not reflected in the data used here.

8 In this chapter, consumption includes market expenditures and the imputed value of own production on foods and non-foods. Expenditures on durables are excluded.

9 Calculation of price indices is far from straightforward. See, for example, Levinsohn *et al.* (1999) and Thomas *et al.* (2000) for a discussion in the context of the Indonesian crisis and Deaton and Tarozzi (2000) who examine the general issue in the Indian context. All 1993 values are inflated to 1997 prices using the price series for each province published by the *BPS*, the Indonesian central bureau of statistics. Those prices are collected in the capital city of each province and the prices reported for the province capital are attributed to all households living in that province (see Ravallion and Bidani, 1993). Price deflators for 1998 values are based on data collected in the IFLS community surveys which are conducted in each of the EAs included in the original frame. These community surveys collect information on 10 prices of standardized commodities from up to 3 local stores and markets in each community; in addition, prices for 39 items are asked of the *Ibu PKK* (leader of the local women's group) and knowledgeable informants upto 3 *posyandus* (health posts) in each community. Using those prices, in combination with the household-level expenditure data, we have calculated EA-specific (Laspeyres) price indices for the IFLS communities for 1997 and 1998. That price series is used to deflate all 1998 values in this chapter. An alternative approach would be to use the price series for capital cities of each province provided by BPS. Our series has two key advantages. First, in our data, there is evidence for considerable price heterogeneity within provinces and that rural prices have increased slightly more than urban prices during this period. Second, as shown in Figure 12.1, relative prices have changed substantially during this time with food prices increasing faster than other prices. Food shares tend to be higher for poorer households and so there is an advantage in using a deflator that is sensitive to the fact that the poorest likely faced a bigger real shock by adopting a deflator that varies across the distribution of initial PCE. We go a long way to achieving that goal by using an EA-specific price series – over 50 percent of the variation in lnPCE in IFLS is across communities. Overall, province differences in the IFLS price series mimics the BPS series although estimates of the level of inflation are slightly higher in IFLS.

10 We have also experimented with more complicated equivalence scales. Assigning a weight of unity to prime males, 0.8 to prime age females and to older adults and a weight of 0.5 to children, the percentage change in per adult equivalent expenditure is 24 percent.

11 The non-parametric estimates presented in this chapter are based on locally weighted, smoothed scatterplots (LOWESS) using a tricube weighting function. These are nearest-neighbor type estimators (Cleveland, 1979; Cleveland *et al.*, 1988). The estimates in Figure 12.2 are calculated with 20 percent of the sample in each band.

12 The result that rural areas were not hit as hard by the crisis as urban areas is born out in the data from community leaders of each of the IFLS communities. In 1998 these leaders were asked how life for residents in their community has changed in the past 12 months. About half the respondents in both sectors responded that life was somewhat worse. Eighteen percent of urban leaders said that life was much worse but no rural leaders said that life was much worse. In fact, one quarter of rural leaders said that life was better.

13 There are three obvious alternatives. First, we could exploit the cluster-design of IFLS and use an EA to define the local economy. This is unsatisfactory for two reasons. First, EAs are very small (akin to a census block) and the local economy surely casts a wider net. Second, we would exclude a substantial fraction of our households who had moved within the vicinity of the EA between 1993 and 1998 but were no longer living with the EA. Systematically excluding these movers from the calculation of the local economy shock will result in biased estimates of the shock if movers and stayers are not drawn from the same underlying distribution of unobserved characteristics. Moreover, from a practical point of view, it is very difficult to determine whether a household is living within an EA. This issue can be side-stepped by defining the local economy in terms of the lowest level of administrative boundary defined in Indonesia: *desa* or *kelurahan* (village or neighborhood). (There are over 60,000 *desas* in Indonesia.) The costs of this approach are two-fold. As with EAs, we exclude households that have moved locally (but across a *desa* border). And second, several of the 90 EAs in IFLS2/2+ are located in close proximity to one another and likely shared common shocks (10 EAs are drawn from 4 *kecamatans*). The third potential level of geographic aggregation is the *kabupaten*, the level above the *kecamatan*. Inspection of the magnitudes of estimated shocks at the *kecamatan* level suggested that there is heterogeneity within *kabupatens* and so we prefer not to aggregate to this level. A key distinction is whether a community is rural or urban. We treat those *kecamatans* that contain both rural and urban areas as two separate markets. The calculation of shocks is based only on those households that lived in the same *kecamatan* in 1997 and 1998. (This includes people who had moved from their original EA between 1993 and 1997.)

14 It is well-known that collection of income from self-employment in a survey setting is extremely difficult – especially, perhaps, in a low-income and substantially agricultural setting like Indonesia. Difficulties arise because of the need to calculate costs and net those out to compute profit, because incomes tend to be volatile over time and often contain an important seasonality component. The panel feature of IFLS may provide some assistance. To the extent that the difficulties in measurement for a particular individual do not change between 1997 and 1998, these concerns will be somewhat mitigated; inferences based on changes in self-employment incomes over the period may not be as seriously contaminated as inferences about levels in incomes.

15 In this figure, PCE in 1993 is used as our metric of a household's original position in the economic hierarchy to mitigate any measurement error biases induced by having 1997 lnPCE on both the x and y-axes. Locally weighted smoothed scatterplots (LOWESS) estimates are reported using a 30 percent bandwidth for income and expenditure and a 35 percent bandwidth for wages.

16 It is possible that the estimates in the figure slightly overstate the increase in household size since larger households were somewhat easier to find and therefore less likely to attrit in IFLS2+. Given the very low attrition rate (<1.5 percent of households), we do not think this is a serious concern. LOWESS estimates are presented with a 35 percent bandwidth in each case.

17 Households that moved out of a *kecamatan* between 1997 and 1998 are assumed to have faced the shock in their 1997 location. Households that did not live in a kecamatan that included an IFLS EA were assigned the average shock for their province and sector of residence in 1997. The regressions include a control for these households, for whom the shock may be measured with greater error. Estimates of the local economy shock faced by a particular household do not include that household in the calculation.

18 The regression models control the number of males and the number of females in the household in 1997, stratified into four age groups (children, young adults, prime age adults, older adults) as well as controls for a change in the number of people in each of these eight groups between 1997 and 1998. These controls provide a flexible mechanism for incorporating equivalence scales into the analysis. The regressions also control age and education of the household head in 1997 (specified as a spline) and gender of the household head; month of interview in 1997 and in 1998 is included to control any time effects not captured by prices; province controls are also included in models that do not contain *kecamatan* fixed effects.

19 While we have attempted to explore the link between consumption smoothing and employment status (in 1997) of household members, we have failed to identify a simple pattern. We suspect that we will need to develop more complex structures that take into account both changes in household composition and the probability a particular type of household member will enter the labor force between 1997 and 1998. Those analyses are left for future work.

References

Adioetomo, Toersilaningsih, Asmanedi, Hendratno, Fitriwati, Egglestone, Hardee, and Hull. (1997). "Helping Husband, Maintaining Harmony," Demographic Institute, University of Indonesia.

Alamgir, M. (1980). *Famine in South Asia: Political Economy of Mass Starvation*, Cambridge, MA: Oelgeschlager, Gunn and Hain Publishers.

Browning, Martin and Thomas E. Crossley. (1997). "Consumption Smoothing and the Replacement of Durables During an Unemployment Spell," Mimeo.

Browning, Martin and Annamaria Lusardi. (1996). "Household Saving: Micro Theories and Micro Facts," *Journal of Economic Literature*, 34(4): 1797–1855.

Cleveland, William S. (1979). "Robust Locally Weighted Regression and Smoothing Scatterplots," *Journal of the American Statistical Association*, 74: 829–36.

——, Susan J. Devlin, and Eric Grosse. (1988). "Regression by Local Fitting: Methods, Properties and Computational Algorithms," *Journal of Econometrics*, 37: 87–114.

Cox, Donald and Emmanuel Jimenez. (1998). "Risk Sharing and Private Transfers: What About Urban Households?," *Economic Development and Cultural Change*, 46(3): 621–37.

Deaton, Angus. (1992). *Understanding Consumption*, Oxford: Clarendon Press.

—— and Alessandro Tarozzi. (2000). "Prices and Poverty," Mimeo.

—— and John Muellbauer. (1980). *Economics and Consumer Behavior*, New York: Cambridge University Press.

Fafchamps, Marcel, Christopher Udry, and Katherine Czukas. (1998). "Drought and Saving in West Africa: are Livestock a Buffer Stock?," *Journal of Development Economics*, 55(2): 273–305.

Frankenberg, Elizabeth and Duncan Thomas. (2000). "The Indonesia Family Life Survey (IFLS): Study Design and Results from Waves 1 and 2," DRU-2238-1/NIA/NICHD, Santa Monica, CA: RAND.

Frankenberg, Elizabeth, Duncan Thomas, and Kathleen Beegle. (1999). "The Real Costs of Indonesia's Economic Crisis: Preliminary Findings from the Indonesia Family Life Surveys," DRU-2064-NIA/NICHD, Santa Monica, CA: RAND.

Gondowarsito, R. (1990). "Transmigrasi Bedol Desa: Inter-island Village Resettlement from Wonogiri to Bengkulu," *Bulletin of Indonesian Economic Studies*, 26(1): 48–68.

IMF. (1999). "World Economic Outlook: International Financial Contagion," World Economic and Financial Surveys, IMF, Washington, DC.

Lazear, Edward P. and Robert T. Michael. (1988). *Allocation of Income within the Household*, Chicago, IL: University of Chicago Press.

Levinsohn, James, Steven Berry, and Jed Friedman. (1999). "Impacts of the Indonesian Economic Crisis: Price Changes and the Poor," NBER Working Paper 7194.

Murruggarra, Eduardo. (1996). "Economic Shocks, Agricultural Production and Family Composition," Mimeo, UCLA.

Papanek, Hanna and Laurie Schwede. (1988). "Women are Good with Money: Earning and Managing in an Indonesian City," in Daisy H. Dwyer and Judith O. Bruce (eds), *A Home Divided: Women and Income in the Third World*. Stanford, CA: Stanford University Press, pp. 71–98.

Platteau, Jean-Philippe. (1991). "Traditional Systems of Social Security and Hunger Insurance: Some Lessons from the Evidence Pertaining to Third World Countries," in Ehtisham Ahman, Jean Dreze, John Hills and Amartya K. Sen (eds) *Social Security in Developing Countries*, Oxford: Clarendon Press.

Ravallion, Martin and Benu Bidani. (1993). "A Regional Poverty Profile for Indonesia," *Bulletin of Indonesian Economic Studies*, 29(3): 37–68.

Rosenzweig, Mark R. (1988). "Risk, Implicit Contracts and the Family in Rural Areas of Low-Income Countries," *Economic Journal*, 98(393): 1148–70.

——(1996). "Labor Markets in Low Income Countries," in Hollis Chenery and T.N. Srinivasan (eds) *Handbook of Development Economics*, North Holland.

—— and Oded Stark. (1989). "Consumption Smoothing, Migration, and Marriage: Evidence from Rural India," *Journal of Political Economy*, 97(4): 905–26.

—— and Kenneth Wolpin. (1993). "Credit Market Constraints, Consumption Smoothing and the Accumulation of Durable Production Assets in Low Income Countries: Investments in Bullocks in India," *Journal of Political Economy*, 101(2): 223–44.

Smith, James P., Duncan Thomas, Kathleen Beegle, Elizabeth Frankenberg and Graciela Teruel. (2002). "Wages, Employment and Economic Shocks: Evidence from Indonesia," *Journal of Population Economics*, 15: 161–93.

Sullivan, Norma. (1994). *Masters and Managers: A Study of Gender Relations in Urban Java*, St Leonards, Australia: Allen and Ulwin.

Thomas, Duncan, Elizabeth Frankenberg, Kathleen Beegle, and Graciela Teruel. (2000). "Household Budgets, Household Composition and the Crisis in Indonesia: Evidence from Longitudinal Household Survey Data," Mimeo, Santa Monica, CA: RAND.

Thomas, Duncan, Elizabeth Frankenberg, and James P. Smith. (2001). "Lost but not Forgotten: Attrition and Follow-up in the Indonesia Family Life Survey," *Journal of Human Resources*, 36(3): 556–92.

Townsend, Robert. (1994). "Risk and Insurance in Village India," *Econometrica*, 62: 539–91.

Udry, Christopher. (1994). "Risk and Insurance in a Rural Credit Market – an Empirical Investigation," *Review of Economic Studies*, 61(3): 495–526.

Wolf, Diane L. (1991). "Female Autonomy, the Family, and Industrialization in Java," in R. Blumberg (ed.), *Gender, Family, and Economy: The Triple Overlap*, London: Sage Publications, pp. 128–48.

Index

Note: Page numbers in italic indicate illustrations.

For Product Safety Concerns and Information please contact
our EU representative GPSR@taylorandfrancis.com Taylor & Francis
Verlag GmbH, Kaufingerstraße 24, 80331 München, Germany

T - #0053 - 230425 - C0 - 234/156/21 - PB - 9780415649827 - Gloss Lamination